June 25–27, 2014
London, Ontario, Canada

I0038012

**Association for
Computing Machinery**

Advancing Computing as a Science & Profession

SACMAT'14

Proceedings of the 19th ACM Symposium on Access Control Models and Technologies

Sponsored by:
ACM SIGSAC

Supported by:
Western University & ASU

Association for
Computing Machinery

Advancing Computing as a Science & Profession

The Association for Computing Machinery
2 Penn Plaza, Suite 701
New York, New York 10121-0701

Notice to Past Authors of ACM-Published Articles

ISBN: 978-1-4503-2939-2 (Digital)

ISBN: 978-1-4503-3114-2 (Print)

Additional copies may be ordered prepaid from:

ACM Order Department
PO Box 30777
New York, NY 10087-0777, USA

Phone: 1-800-342-6626 (USA and Canada)
+1-212-626-0500 (Global)
Fax: +1-212-944-1318
E-mail: acmhelp@acm.org
Hours of Operation: 8:30 am – 4:30 pm ET

Printed in the USA

Foreword

It is our great pleasure to welcome you to the 19th ACM Symposium on Access Control Models and Technologies (SACMAT 2014). This year's symposium continues its tradition of being the premier forum for presentation of research results on leading edge issues of access control, including models, systems, applications, and theory, with an expanded scope to include cyber-physical systems, applications, systems, hardware, cloud computing, and usability

58 papers have been submitted from a variety of countries around the world. Submissions were anonymous; each paper has been reviewed by at least four reviewers who are experts in the field. Extensive online discussions took place to make the selections for the symposium. The program committee finally accepted 17 papers that cover a variety of topics, including Privacy & Compliance, Policy Management & Enforcement, Systems & Information Flow, Policy Analysis, and Applications. The program again contains two demo sessions with four demos covering topics such as risk aware role mining, privacy, attribute based access control, and integrity in Linux. In addition, the program includes a panel on the challenges of access control in new computing domains, such as mobile, cloud, and cyber-physical systems, and two keynote talks by Dr. Ari Juels and Dr. Andrew Clement. We hope that these proceedings will serve as a valuable reference for security researchers and developers.

Putting together SACMAT 2014 was a team effort. First of all, we would like to thank the authors for submitting to the symposium, the keynote speakers for graciously accepting our invitation, the demo presenters and panelists for contributing to the program. We are grateful to the program committee members and external reviewers for their efforts in reviewing the papers and their engagement in online discussions during the review process. Special thanks go to Florian Kerschbaum and Lujo Bauer (Panels Chairs), Adam J. Lee (Demonstrations Chair), Dongwan Shin (Webmaster), Anna Squicciarini and Dongwan Shin (Publicity Chairs) and Hongxin Hu (Proceedings Chair) for their help in organizing and publicizing the symposium. We also thank the members of the steering committee and especially its chair, Gail-Joon Ahn, for providing valuable advice and support. Many thanks also go to the local arrangements chair, Sylvia Osborn.

We would like to thank our sponsor, ACM SIGSAC, for their continued support of this symposium. We would also like to acknowledge University of Western Ontario for supporting the organization of the conference.

We hope that you will find this program interesting and that the symposium will provide you with a valuable opportunity to share ideas with other researchers and practitioners from institutions around the world.

Sylvia Osborn
SACMAT'14 General Chair
University of Western Ontario,
Canada

Mahesh V. Tripunitara
SACMAT'14 Program Chair
University of Waterloo,
Canada

Ian Molloy
SACMAT'14 Program Chair
IBM Research TJ Watson,
USA

Table of Contents

Panel

Session: Privacy and Confidentiality

Session: Risk, Redaction and RDF

Keynote II

Session: New Approaches

Author Index

2014 ACM Symposium on Access Control Models and Technologies

General Chair: Sylvia Osborn *(University of Western Ontario, Canada)*

Program Chairs: Mahesh V. Tripunitara *(University of Waterloo, Canada)*
Ian M. Molloy *(IBM Research, USA)*

Panels Chairs: Florian Kerschbaum *(SAP, Germany)*
Lujo Bauer *(CMU, USA)*

Demonstrations Chair: Adam J. Lee *(University of Pittsburgh, USA)*

Proceedings Chair: Hongxin Hu *(Clemson University, USA)*

Publicity Co-Chairs: Anna Squicciarini *(Pennsylvania State University, USA)*
Dongwan Shin *(New Mexico Tech, USA)*

Treasurer: Basit Shafiq *(LUMS, Pakistan)*

Webmaster: Dongwan Shin *(New Mexico Tech, USA)*

Steering Committee Chair: Gail-Joon Ahn *(Arizona State University, USA)*

Steering Committee: Axel Kern *(Beta Systems Software AG, Germany)*
Bhavani Thuraisingham *(University of Texas at Dallas, USA)*
Indrakshi Ray *(Colorado State University, USA)*
Ninghui Li *(Purdue University, USA)*
James Joshi *(University of Pittsburgh, USA)*

Program Committee: Gail-Joon Ahn *(Arizona State University, USA)*
Vijay Atluri *(Rutgers University, USA)*
Lujo Bauer *(Carnegie Mellon University, USA)*
Barbara Carminati *(University of Insubria, Italy)*
Sonia Chiasson *(Carleton University, Canada)*
Omar Chowdhury *(Carnegie Mellon University, USA)*
Mauro Conti *(University of Padua, Italy)*
Jason Crampton *(Royal Holloway, University of London, UK)*
Philip W. L. Fong *(University of Calgary, Canada)*
Mario Frank *(UC Berkeley, USA)*
Vinod Ganapathy *(Rutgers University, USA)*
Deepak Garg *(Max Planck Institute for Software Systems, Germany)*
William Harris *(University of Wisconsin at Madison, USA)*
Hongxin Hu *(Clemson University, USA)*
Karthick Jayaraman *(Microsoft, USA)*
James Joshi *(University of Pittsburgh, USA)*
Murat Kantarcioglu *(University of Texas at Dallas, USA)*

ACM SACMAT 2014 Sponsor & Supporters

Sponsor:

Supporters:

A Bodyguard of Lies:
The Use of Honey Objects in Information Security

Ari Juels
Cornell Tech
New York, NY, USA
juels@cornell.edu

ABSTRACT

Decoy objects, often labeled in computer security with the term *honey*, are a powerful tool for compromise detection and mitigation. There has been little exploration of overarching theories or set of principles or properties, however. This short paper (and accompanying keynote talk) briefly explore two properties of honey systems, *indistinguishability* and *secrecy*. The aim is to illuminate a broad design space that might encompass a wide array of areas in information security, including access control, the main topic of this symposium.

1. INTRODUCTION

From time immemorial, deception been a cornerstone of counterintelligence. In particular, the use of decoys, realistic but fake objects to divert or detect attacks, has proven a powerful technique. Like most clever ideas, decoys arose in the natural world before human beings stumbled upon them. For example, many insects and fish have false eyes known as "eye-spots." These prominent dark circles lure attackers away from more vulnerable body parts. Also like most clever ideas, decoys are the subject of a quip by Winston Churchill. He famously remarked, "In war-time, truth is so precious that she should always be attended by a bodyguard of lies."

In computer security, the term *honey* is often favored to denote decoys [2]. Honeypots, servers deployed to lure attackers for observation, are the best known example [6]. But there are many varieties of honey system, such as honeyfiles [10], honey documents [1], honeytokens [7], and honey encryption [3].

While honey objects are fairly widely used, there is little literature articulating overarching concepts in their use or design. This paper will briefly discuss two properties required for successful deployment of honey objects. While these properties are simple, intentional reflection on them can lead to better architectures and a richer design space for honey systems.

As a point of reference, let us consider a simple system in which $S = \{s_1, \ldots, s_n\}$ denotes a set of n objects of which one, $s^* = s_j$, for $j \in \{1, \ldots, n\}$ is the *true* object, while the other $n-1$ are *honey objects*. It's convenient to refer to the objects in S generically as *sweet* objects.

SACMAT'14, June 25–27, 2014, London, Ontario, Canada.
ACM 978-1-4503-2939-2/14/06.
http://dx.doi.org/10.1145/2613087.2613088 .

The two principles we'll explore then are:

1. *Indistinguishability:* To deceive and attacker, honey objects must be hard to distinguish from real objects. They should, in other words, be drawn from a probability distribution over possible objects similar to that from which a real object s^* was selected.

2. *Secrecy:* In a system with honey objects, j is a secret. Honey objects can, of course, only deceive an attacker that doesn't know j, so j cannot reside alongside S. Kerckhoffs's principle therefore comes into play: the security of the system must reside in the secret, i.e., the distinction between honey objects and real ones, not in the mere fact of using honey objects. The secret j may reside with either or both of two types of entity: An *actor* (generally a user) that selects objects from S and a *honeychecker*, a system that signals an attack when an object other than $s^* = s_j$ is selected and is distinct from the system that stores S.

This paper will illustrate these two concepts as they arise in a system called *honeywords* and how they influence the larger design space for honey systems. Then it will very briefly discuss how honey objects might be deployed in access-control systems.

2. AN EXAMPLE: HONEYWORDS

Honeywords are decoy passwords used to detect the breach of a password database [4].

A password database is an authentication system component that contains a set of passwords, one per account.[1] An attacker that breaches the system and obtains the database can impersonate a user by authenticating to the system using her password. A spate of recent such breaches has shown how pervasive this threat is.

In a honeywords system, for a given user, a *list* of n passwords $S = \{s_1, s_2, \ldots s_n\}$ is stored. In this list, $s^* = s_j$ is the user's real password, while s_i for $i \neq j$ is a honeyword, a fake password. The term "sweetwords" is applied to elements of S in general.

When a user tries authenticating to the system using a password s, it is checked against the list S. If it doesn't lie in the list, then the authentication attempt is rejected as in a normal password system. If $s = s_j$, then authentication proceeds normally.

If, however, s is a honeyword, meaning $s = s_i$ for some $i \neq j$, an alarm is triggered in the system. It is improbable that a user will accidentally submit a honeyword rather than her correct password when authenticating. So submission of a honeyword is good evidence (although not necessary proof positive) of a breach that disclosed S to an attacker.

---

[1] The passwords should be hashed and salted, but exactly how they are stored and checked isn't important for our purposes here.

The two principles of indistinguishability and secrecy are addressed in this system as follows:

1. *Indistinguishability:* Suppose that we model a true password $s^* = s_j$ as coming from a probability distribution U, and honeywords as selected from a distribution G. Suppose an attacker breaches the system and learns S, and that it knows U and G. It can be shown that the attacker that tries to impersonate a user by proffering a sweetword s_i as the user's password achieves the highest probability of success by guessing the sweetword $s_i \in S$ that maximizes $U(s_i)/G(s_i)$.

   Thus, indistinguishability in this setting means that the distributions U and G are close. There are a number of strategies for achieving this property and generating good honeywords. For example, in a large system, a given user might be assigned the passwords of other users as honeywords.

2. *Secrecy:* If j is stored alongside S, then an attacker that breaches the system can immediately identify $s^* = s_j$. The architecture of the honeywords system proposed in [4] is therefore distributed. A honeychecker is deployed as a system distinct from the computer system that stores S. This honeychecker stores the index j for every user. The computer system transmits to the honeychecker the index of any submitted sweetword, which the honeychecker verifies. Given its minimal functionality—it can be designed as a input-only device—the honeychecker may be harder for an attacker to breach than the computer system.

   The actor in this case is the user. The user stores $s^* = s_j$ and thus j in her head.

3. THE DESIGN SPACE

There are many other ways in which indistinguishability and secrecy can be enforced. A few other examples deserve mention to illustrate the breadth of the design space for honey systems.

3.1 Indistinguishability

There are some cases in which the true object s^* comes from a mathematically well defined distribution, e.g., credit card numbers, RSA private keys, and so forth. A number of such examples are given in [3]. In these cases, generation of good honey objects may be relatively straightforward. Alternatively, s^* might come from a distribution that can be well characterized using public sources of data, such as user-selected passwords. Generation of valid honey objects may nonetheless remain somewhat challenging [4].

When the true object s^* comes from a complicated distribution, constructing good honey objects may seem nearly impossible. Honey documents—e-mail messages, for example—could in principle require the generation of fake but semantically and contextually realistic natural language, an intractable problem today.

On the other hand, to be effective, honey objects need not necessarily bear up under intensive manual scrutiny by an attacker. If manual analysis of honey objects is costly, then it is sufficient for samples from the probability distributions U and G to be difficult to distinguish by means of machine classification. In [5], a project history is simulated for a piece of bogus software is produced by introducing obfuscated software variations. Similarly, in [9], the creation of documents in foreign languages is proposed to deceive attackers without the ability to apply translation tools on the fly.

A good design principle is to minimize the complexity of U by creating a honey system that presents a highly constrained distinguishability problem. For example, a decoy document system is proposed in [8] whose efficacy relies on attackers searching documents differently than legitimate users. The documents themselves need not look realistic, though, only their names and directory placement.

Measuring indistinguishability can be a serious challenge when U is complex—particularly when an attack may be manual. An additional challenge, when honey objects are visible to users, is ensuring that valid users can themselves distinguish effortlessly between true and honey objects, or otherwise do not trigger false positives by frequently touching honey objects. Legitimate users should preferably encounter honey objects only rarely.

3.2 Secrecy

A honeychecker can in principle be a simple, dedicated service, as in the honeywords system, and the secret j the index of a valid object. But a honeychecker can in fact assume a wide variety of forms, as can the secret.

In the Decoy Document Distributor (D^3) system [1], several types of honey and thus honeychecker are deployed. Documents contain watermarks in their associated binaries that can be detected upon document exfiltration from a network, code that beacons to a server upon opening of a document, and bogus credentials whose use signals document exfiltration to a relying party.

In [8], inside attackers are detected by merit of the fact that they click on documents that a well behaving user would not access. Thus there are cases in which the secret in a honey system is not an index j, but rather a behavioral profile that might be stored by a honeychecking service and reside in the mind of an actor, i.e., a user, as a pattern of behavior.

Honey encryption [3] operates in a rather different setting. It permits the construction of a ciphertext that decrypts under any key to a plausible looking plaintext. An attacker therefore cannot tell when the ciphertext has been correctly decrypted. For example, given a password vault encrypted under a master password using honey encryption, an attacker that tries to guess master passwords cannot determine when decryption has been successful. The attacker therefore does not know when passwords extracted from the vault are safe for use in impersonating the owner of the vault. There is no explicit honeychecker associated with a honey encryption system.

A service that consumes and verifies the correctness of the plaintext in a honey encryption system, however, may act in effect as a honeychecker. For example, if a password vault is encrypted using honey encryption, then any server that consumes a password in the vault effectively acts as a honeychecker.

4. HONEY IN ACCESS CONTROL

Honey objects can be used in an access-control system against a range of possible adversaries: rogue administrators, misbehaving users or other subjects, outside attackers, and so forth—as well as for audit. Similarly, access-control systems can conveniently support general honey systems. Here we give a couple of examples.

Consider the case of a user seeking to access resources illegitimately. One might imagine a role-based access control (RBAC) system in which roles include "honey permissions," that is, permissions that exceed the organic responsibilities associated with the role (e.g., access to financial spreadsheets for an IT administrator). Indistinguishability in this case means the inability of an attacker to determine whether a permission was assigned legitimately to a role or as bait. The secret is the set of honey permissions; a honeychecker might monitor for use of these permissions. In a real-world system, accommodation would need to be made for (inevitable) false positives, and a policy decision would have to be made as to whether resource-access granted by honey permissions would be allowed by the system or blocked upon alert by the honeychecker.

Access-control systems can be a convenient point at which to insert honeychecking capabilities for a honey system. In particular, a reference monitor may be used to store secrets for honey systems—watchlists of honey objects. Access-control systems can also support real-time response to suspected breaches. If permission is requested to touch a honey object, the reference monitor might alert an administrator, isolate critical systems by revoking permissions, etc.

There are no doubt many other opportunities to combine honey objects, with their rich design space, and access-control systems, with their widespread use in real-world system.

5. REFERENCES

[1] B.M. Bowen, S. Hershkop, A. D. Keromytis, and S. J. Stolfo. Baiting inside attackers using decoy documents. In *Security and Privacy in Communication Networks*, pages 51–70, 2009.

[2] F. Cohen. The use of deception techniques: Honeypots and decoys. In H. Bidgoli, editor, *Handbook of Information Security*, volume 3, pages 646–655. Wiley and Sons, 2006.

[3] A. Juels and T. Ristenpart. Honey encryption: Beyond the brute-force barrier. In *Eurocrypt*, 2014. To appear.

[4] A. Juels and R. Rivest. Honeywords: Making password-cracking detectable. In *ACM CCS*, pages 145–160, 2013.

[5] Y. Park and S. J. Stolfo. Software decoys for insider threat. In *ASIACCS*, pages 93–94, New York, NY, USA, 2012.

[6] L. Spitzner. *Honeypots: Tracking Hackers*. Addison-Wesley Longman Publishing Co., Inc., Boston, MA, USA, 2002.

[7] L. Spitzner. Honeytokens: The other honeypot. Symantec SecurityFocus, July 2003.

[8] M. B. Salem S. J. Stolfo. Modeling user search behavior for masquerade detection. In *RAID*, pages 181–200, 2011.

[9] J. Voris, N. Boggs, and S.J. Stolfo. Lost in translation: Improving decoy documents via automated translation. In *IEEE Symposium on Security and Privacy Workshops (SPW)*, pages 129–133, 2012.

[10] J. Yuill, M. Zappe, D. Denning, and F. Feer. Honeyfiles: deceptive files for intrusion detection. In *IAW*, pages 116–122, 2004.

Hardware-Enhanced Distributed Access Enforcement for Role-Based Access Control

Gedare Bloom
Dept. of Computer Science
George Washington University
gedare@gwu.edu

Rahul Simha
Dept. of Computer Science
George Washington University
simha@gwu.edu

ABSTRACT

The protection of information in enterprise and cloud platforms is growing more important and complex with increasing numbers of users who need to access resources with distinct permissions. Role-based access control (RBAC) eases administrative complexity for large-scale access control, while a client-server model can ease performance bottlenecks by distributing access enforcement across multiple servers that consult the centralized access decision policy server as needed. In this paper, we propose a new approach to access enforcement using an existing associative array hardware data structure (HWDS) to cache authorizations in a distributed system using RBAC. This HWDS approach uses hardware that has previous been demonstrated as useful for several application domains including access control, network packet routing, and generic comparison-based integer search algorithms. We reproduce experiments from prior work on distributed access enforcement for RBAC systems, and we design and conduct new experiments to evaluate HWDS-based access enforcement. Experimental data show the HWDS cuts session initiation time by about a third compared to existing solutions, while achieving similar performance to authorize access requests. These results suggest that distributed systems using RBAC could use HWDS-based access enforcement to increase session throughput or to decrease the number of access enforcement servers without losing performance.

Categories and Subject Descriptors

Security and privacy [**Security in hardware**]: Hardware security implementation

Keywords

access control, enforcement, hardware data structures

1. INTRODUCTION

Large enterprises have tens of thousands of employees who are distinct users that access tera- to peta-bytes of data composed of objects with tens to hundreds of thousands of distinct permissions [19]. Small businesses/enterprises have similar security needs as large

businesses, but at a smaller and more flexible scale from tens to hundreds of users and hundreds to thousands of permissions. For large or small enterprises, data security is big business as intellectual property theft costs an estimated and growing 250 billion US dollars per year [22]. Hardening enterprises from external attacks is not sufficient, as over 85% of federal cases involving theft of trade secrets were perpetrated by insiders (former employee or business partner) [3]. Thus, protection mechanisms must control access to proprietary data by users in such a way that the users can execute their job functions without compromising the security of corporate intellectual property. The prevalent solution for enterprise data security is to use role-based access control (RBAC) [11, 24] with a client/server model. RBAC decouples users from permissions via roles, which are the principals to whom authorization is granted to access objects. A typical RBAC system will have about 3–4% as many roles as users [25], so an enterprise with 100,000 employees might use about 4000 roles. Although RBAC simplifies administration by reducing the number of principals, the number of permissions can cause performance bottlenecks in the software data structures used during access enforcement. We propose to enhance access control data structures with fast, parallel hardware to accelerate permission checking for RBAC systems.

In this paper, we enhance client/server RBAC with a hardware data structure (HWDS) that supports access control enforcement. HWDSs exploit hardware parallelism to reduce the asymptotic complexity of data structure operations, which can yield substantial performance improvements compared with software implementations [6]. A problem with the scale of enterprise security is that centralized access control becomes a bottleneck for the performance and availability of networked services, but centralization is viewed as necessary to facilitate policy administration. Therefore, modern systems divide access control into stages consisting of centralized authentication and a mix of centralized and distributed authorization and audit. (Audit happens off the critical path of access requests.) Authorization is split further into access decision and enforcement; the former consults policy to construct an authorization token, e.g. an access control list or capability, and the latter will grant/deny access to protected resources based on the token presented during an access request. Enforcement in this setting needs efficient mechanisms that can process authorizations without going to the centralized decision server; the solutions in prior work on client/server RBAC, which we review in Section 5, focus on caching, prefetching, and predicting authorizations.

Importantly, RBAC models use the notion of a *session* to permit users to activate subsets of their permitted roles when requesting an authorization, which supports good security practices such as the principle of least privilege [23] while making RBAC a good fit for client-server models such as the Common Open Policy Ser-

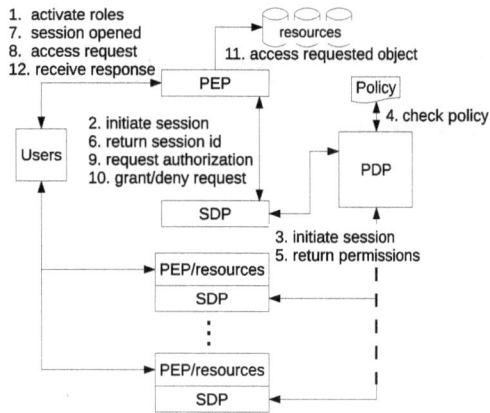

Figure 1: A client/server model based on the COPS standard extended with Secondary Decision Points.

vice (COPS) standard [14]. In typical client/server models, authorizations are created at the Policy Decision Point (PDP), which responds to Policy Enforcement Points (PEPs) that request whether or not to allow users to access protected resources. A common approach to improve PEP performance is to cache authorizations from the PDP so that repeated access requests may be enforced directly by the PEP without inducing communication and computation overhead to query the PDP. Crampton et al. [10] proposed adding a Secondary Decision Point (SDP) to cache and predict authorizations, which the authors called precise and approximate authorization recycling, respectively. Prediction (approximate recycling) infers authorizations for access requests that miss the cache. The architecture resulting from adding an SDP to the COPS model, shown in Figure 1, distributes authorization while maintaining a centralized policy. Wei et al. [28] show how to use the extended model with RBAC.

Good access enforcement performance requires an SDP with a high cache hit rate, no mis-predictions, and a low latency response time. In this paper, we demonstrate such an SDP using an associative array HWDS [5]. We implemented this HWDS-based SDP, which we call the HWDS BitSet SDP, using the gem5 [4] processor simulator and a Java library; we describe our implementation in Section 3. Our implementation enables performance evaluation of the HWDS BitSet SDP using the dist-rbac-eval benchmark [18, 2]. We improved the benchmark by adding skewed distributions of access requests and measurements of holistic SDP performance including session initiation and destruction times. The software library enables the SDP to use the pre-existing associative array HWDS without modification to the hardware, and the potential for commoditization together with good performance make the HWDS BitSet SDP well-suited to replace software SDPs in enterprise-scale RBAC deployments.

We evaluate the time efficiency of the HWDS BitSet SDP along with two SDPs—access matrix and CPOL—from prior work using the experiments described by Komlenovic et al. [18] to measure SDP access request time. The prior work evaluated SDPs using a series of experiments, which we reproduce to evaluate the new HWDS BitSet SDP. Furthermore, we describe and use new experiments to evaluate the effect on access request time due to the number and skewness in the distribution of access requests made during a session; see Section 4.

The experimental results show that the HWDS BitSet SDP typically is more efficient than the existing work for session initation and destruction, while remaining competitive for access request

time. For workloads with 2 to 15 sessions having 100 roles, 250 permissions, 4 active roles per session, and each role has about 10 permissions, the session initiation time of the HWDS SDP has a speedup between 0.8 to 4.7 compared to the access matrix, and speedup of 1.46 to 2.61 over CPOL. Session destruction time for the HWDS SDP has speedup between 1.09 and 2.01 for access matrix, and 5.11 to 6.06 for CPOL. Averaged across these workloads, the time to initiate a session with the HWDS was 210.4 microseconds (μs) with standard deviation of 36, whereas the CPOL and access matrix SDPs took about 351.3 μs and 319.8 μs with standard deviations of 6.65 and 131.38, respectively. The averaged per-session destruction time was 30.3 μs for the HWDS with standard deviation 1.9, with CPOL at 165 μs and standard deviation 2.1, and the access matrix at 40.2 μs and 9.9 standard deviation. Note that some costs of SDP destruction go to garbage collection, which was not included in any of the reported data. The mean access time of the HWDS was between 0.15–0.6 μs, with CPOL taking 0.19–1.47 μs and the access matrix 0.15–0.49 μs. The results also indicate that when data are more skewed the HWDS BitSet SDP's access time is even more competitive.

The HWDS SDP can open and close sessions at a greater throughput than the other SDPs without losing access request time performance. A greater session throughput can be used to increase the number of active sessions each SDP can handle, which permits scaling up the number of users or scaling down the number of SDP servers. The advantage of a HWDS approach is that a HWDS can be used generically across multiple application domains in much the same way as software uses libraries containing optimized data structure implementations. The same HWDS that we use has also been used in part to improve SELinux performance [12] and network packet routing [21]. By integrating the HWDS support with software libraries, existing applications such as web browsers and physics simulators could benefit simply by linking to the modified library [5]. The HWDS approach is appealing because it improves data structure performance without requiring application- or problem domain-specific custom hardware designs.

This work makes three contributions. First, we show how to use a HWDS for distributed RBAC access enforcement. Second, we reproduce some of the experiments presented by Komlenovic et al. [18] and discuss how our findings compare with the previous results. Third, we describe new experiments and present results related to session timing results, skewness in the probability of access requests, and duration of sessions in terms of number of access requests made. The experimental results indicate the HWDS approach is a promising alternative to the best-performing software implementations of distributed access enforcement.

2. HWDS FOR DISTRIBUTED RBAC

The basic requirement of an SDP is to check access requests to determine whether a given session has the authorization (permissions) to access the requested resource. Associated with a session lifetime, the SDP must initialize and destroy session-specific data, i.e. the portion of the data structure related to the session. An SDP also must support updating its data structures to reflect any administrative changes that are made in the PDP's policy. These requirements motivate an associative array HWDS that stores a map between session identifiers and permissions as an SDP. An associative array, or map, is a data structure that organizes data to support efficient searching, or finding the node with a specific key from a set of (key, value) nodes. The specified key is the *argument* to the search [17]. Usual operations on an associative array are:

- *insert*: adds/replaces a key-value node

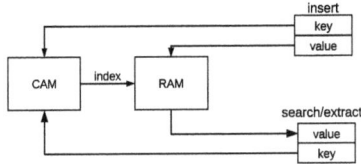

Figure 2: An associative array implemented in hardware. Keys are stored in the CAM, values are stored in the RAM.

- *extract*: removes a node
- *search*: finds a node using the given argument

An *exact* search returns the node with the same key as the argument if it exists. The *skewness* of a search is a measure of the asymmetry of the probability distribution of the argument. In this paper, we consider exact search with varying skewness.

The search operation supports access requests, and inserting a node with the same key as an existing node supports modifications to the permissions that a session can access in response to administrative changes. Thus, an associative array is a good candidate for an SDP implementation. An associative array can be implemented as a HWDS that supports numerical key-value pairs using a content-addressable memory (CAM) with a RAM of equal size, as shown in Figure 2. This HWDS has been used previously by others [21, 12, 5], which we discuss further in Section 5. CAMs are addressed by the stored data word instead of memory address, so given a data word, the CAM returns the memory address containing that word. To insert a key-value node, the map HWDS stores the key in the CAM and the value in the RAM at the same address in both memories. Extract and search operations use the argument to find the address of the value in the RAM and remove or return it respectively. The HWDS uses an extra 1 bit of RAM per data word as metadata to indicate whether that word is storing a value or garbage.

The advantages of a HWDS are parallelism and applicability to multiple application domains due to the generic hardware-software interface offered by data structure operations. Hardware can insert to a sorted structure faster than software because of the advantage of parallel comparisons. To insert a new node, a tree-based software data structure may need to traverse the depth of the tree, comparing the new node with the tree's node at each level. Hardware can compare the new node in parallel with all of the stored nodes. Similar performance improvements exist for other common data structure operations, such as deleting or searching for a node.

A HWDS reduces operation execution times to a small, fixed latency similar to a cache hit, but only for a data structure that has a maximum size less than HWDS capacity. Although software can request more storage for large data structures, a HWDS cannot request more capacity. The solution for a HWDS is to use runtime overflow management [5] so that arbitrary-sized data structures can utilize the HWDS resources. Overflow management consists of handling overflow and underflow conditions during HWDS operations. An overflow occurs when the HWDS has no more available space for an insertion. Underflow occurs when a HWDS operation misses in the hardware, for example an extract or search does not find the node in the HWDS.

2.1 HWDS BitSet SDP

We assume that a session identifier can be represented internally by an SDP as an opaque integer, and that a set of permissions map resources identified by integers between 0 and n inclusive to boolean values (true, false). The logical choice for a key-value pair

for an SDP is to use the session identifier as a key, and some representation of permissions as a value. Although the map HWDS can implement an SDP by storing a pointer to a permission set in main memory as the value, the overhead of managing the HWDS and accessing main memory nullifies the performance advantage of the hardware. Another approach for using the map HWDS is to store a permission set directly in the RAM as a bitset (a vector of bits that represent the permissions of a session). This approach is problematic when the number of permissions is large, unknown a priori, or cannot be represented as a dense bitset.

Our approach, which we call *HWDS BitSet SDP*, is to create a session identifier and permission bitset for each session. The bitset is split into parts equal to the size of the data word that can be stored in the HWDS RAM. Then each part becomes a value, and the key is a combination of the session identifier and the offset of the part in the bitset. The key must be split between the session identifier and an offset into the permission bit vector. We choose to split the key in half, which is an arbitrary choice that users of the HWDS BitSet SDP can change by allocating more bits to the session identifier or the offset. The example in Section 2.2 uses an 8-bit key and value, which allows up to 2^7 permission identifiers (2^4 offsets, and 8 permission bits per offset) and up to 2^4 session identifiers. Our implementation uses a 64-bit value and 32-bit keys, so there can be 2^{22} permission identifiers (2^{16} offsets and 64 permission bits) and 2^{16} session identifiers.

When a session is initiated, all of the permissions for the active roles of the session are converted to a bitset, and then the bitset is divided into values. Each value is inserted to the HWDS with a key equal to the concatenation of the session identifier and the offset of the value in the bitset, padded with leading zeroes so the session identifier can be located correctly. The cost to initiate a session depends on how many values are created from the permissions, and is at most the number of offsets times the cost of a HWDS insert. However, when permissions exhibit good spatial locality in the bitset, the cost can be much lower, for example just one insert can represent up to 64 active permissions.

For an access request, the SDP computes the offset of the requested permission identifier by dividing the identifier by the size of the stored values. An argument for a HWDS search is constructed by concatenating the session identifier with the computed offset. The permission identifier's bit position is calculated by masking off bits in the identifier that are in positions greater than the size of the stored values. The bit at the calculated bit position is then checked in the return value from the HWDS search to determine whether the requested permission is in the session's permission bitset.

A session is destroyed by iterating over all possible offsets and extracting the node with a key equal to the session identifier concatenated with each offset. The cost to destroy a session can be quite large if the session has a large set of active permissions, so to reduce this cost the SDP tracks the maximum offset used in a session. During session destruction the number of HWDS extracts is equal to the maximum offset.

Overflow can occur when the number of HWDS inserts exceeds the capacity of the HWDS. The cost of overflow affects session initiation time to handle the overflow, and may affect access request or session destruction time to deal with associated underflows. Our implementation can hold up to 128 nodes before inducing overflow. A node permits one offset of 64 permissions per session, so without overflow a 128-node HWDS can hold 128 sessions with permissions ranging from 0–63, or 1 session with permission identifiers spanning from 0–8191. Overflow handling allows more sessions or permissions, but at some cost to move data from the HWDS to the overflow data structure.

Our approach to overflow management is *interposition-based* [5] similar to how Chandra and Sinnen [9] handle overflow for their priority queue HWDS. With interposition-based overflow management, HWDS operations are checked by software. If an operation causes an overflow, underflow, or any other problem, the software invokes a handler that corrects the problem and either emulates or replays the operation.

Overflow can be governed by different policies about which nodes to move between the HWDS and overflow storage. The associative array HWDS we use supports three policies for spilling overflow nodes from the hardware: least-recently used (LRU), least-frequently used, and priority-ranked by integer comparison of keys. The HWDS BitSet SDP's overflow handler moves half of the nodes from the HWDS to a software implementation of an associative array using the LRU policy. For underflow, the handler passes through the operation to the software associative array: for a search, if the node is found in the software data structure, that node is removed and re-inserted to the HWDS. The policies governing overflow and underflow were chosen to exploit temporal locality.

Discussion.

We considered several alternatives before settling on the design of the HWDS BitSet SDP. The primary consideration for this design was to avoid introducing custom hardware modifications to the existing HWDS logic. We considered loading each permission separately into the HWDS, but sessions with a lot of permissions would put pressure on the HWDS capacity while inducing high session initiation and destruction costs. We also considered loading a single pointer reference to a permission bit-vector in the HWDS, but we found the overhead to fetch the bit-vector from memory and then compute the permission offset and mask led to poor performance in small or sparse sets of permissions. Loading the HWDS with chunks of the bit vector offers a good compromise between search speed and HWDS utilization. An alternative to interposition-based overflow management is exception-based, which relies on the hardware to check for error conditions and raise an exception in case of a problem. We found that the cost of passing an exception from hardware through the operating system into the JVM and finally to the Java application was prohibitive, so we used interposition exclusively.

2.2 RBAC Example

Figure 3 depicts an RBAC policy and an example of HWDS BitSet SDP operations. Although our implementation uses 64-bit values and 32-bits keys, this example uses 8-bit values and keys for clarity.

Suppose Alice wants to approve a time card and enter her time card. She will start by initiating a session activating the roles of Manager and Employee. The PEP will forward this request through the SDP to the PDP, which responds with a new session identifier, say 3, and the set of permissions for the role Manager, which is {12, 6, 10}. The HWDS BitSet SDP will use the returned session identifier and permissions as follows. First, the set of permissions is converted to a vector of bits with a set bit at each position of the allowed permissions: 0001 0100 0100 0000. This bit vector is then split into multiple values, 0001 0100 and 0100 0000 corresponding to the two 8-bit values that compose the bit vector. The offset of the values are 0 and 1, respectively, and recall that the session identifier is 4, so the keys are 1000 and 1001. Thus, the SDP inserts two nodes into the HWDS: insert(1000, 01000000) and insert(1001, 00010100). The SDP also returns the session identifier (4) to the PEP, which forwards the identifier to the user.

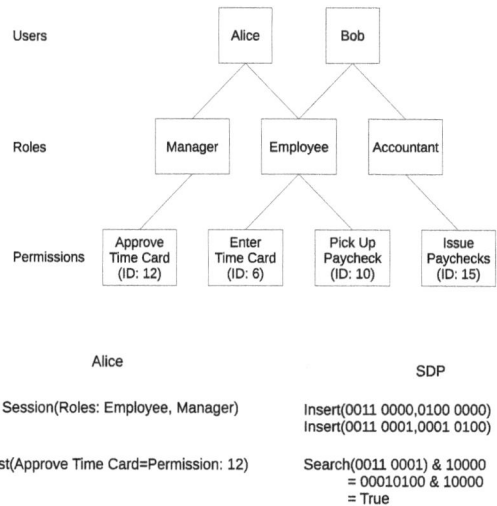

Figure 3: An example RBAC policy and a session initiation and access request using the HWDS BitSet SDP. Note that the session identifier is 3, and the key is split into 4 bits for the session identifier and 4 bits for the offset in the permission bit-vector.

Now that Alice has opened a session, she can approve a time card. She issues a request to the PEP to access the resource associated with approving time cards. The PEP translates her request into an access request to the SDP for session identifier 4 and permission 12. The SDP calculates the offset of the requested permission by dividing 12 / 8 and discarding the remainder, getting an offset of 1. The SDP then computes the argument by shifting the session identifier and merging it with the offset, that is the SDP executes search(1001) and gets back the 8-bit value (00010100) associated with offset 1. The SDP then computes the bit position of permission 12 in that value by masking off (12 & 7), obtaining 4. (If instead Alice had requested to enter her time card—permission 6—the offset would be 0 and the bit position of the permission in the returned value would be 6.) Finally, the SDP checks if the returned value has a set bit at position 4, which it does, so the SDP responds to the PEP that the access should be granted. The PEP allows Alice to approve time cards.

3. EXPERIMENTAL SETUP

We implemented the associative array HWDS in the gem5 simulator [4]. Our implementation introduces a new gem5op—a pseudo instruction that executes atomically and non-speculatively—that software executes to perform a HWDS operation. We wrote a software library that encapsulates HWDS operations in a Java class using the Java Native Interface to execute gem5ops. The library and the underlying HWDS use 32-bit keys and 64-bit values, and can model arbitrary-sized HWDSs; we use only a 128-node HWDS, i.e. 128 key-value pairs can be stored in the hardware at a time. The library accepts the size parameter in its class constructor, which programs the size into the HWDS during its initialization. Every HWDS operation returns a value in a register that the library checks for error codes that signal the library to handle the problems of overflow and underflow as described in Section 2.1. The library uses a Java Collections TreeMap as the software associative array for overflow.

3.1 Benchmark

We adapted the dist-rbac-eval benchmark for RBAC access enforcement described by Komlenovic et al. [18], which the authors made available online [2]. This benchmark evaluates the time-efficiency of SDP-based access enforcement for RBAC. An RBAC policy is encoded as a directed graph by the benchmark, which calls a specific instance of a policy an RBAC configuration. For each configuration, multiple session profiles can be created, each of which is a sequence of instructions comprising session initations, access requests, and session destructions. The benchmark executes the session profile over the RBAC configuration for an SDP implementation, six of which are provided from the prior work by Komlenovic et al. [18]: access matrix, Bloom filter, cascade Bloom, CPOL, directed graph, and authorization recycling.

3.2 Session Profile Modifications

We introduce a new parameter for session profiles that controls the access request distribution. The default behavior for the unmodified benchmark is to choose a session at random and generate sequentially-ordered access requests for permissions available to that session. Access requests are generated until the limit on the number of access checks is reached. If all of the permissions for a session have been requested, a new session is activated and access requests are issued until the limit is reached. We introduce a new parameter α to the class such that when $\alpha = 0$ the permissions used in access requests are chosen uniformly at random, and when $\alpha = 1.0$ the permissions follow Zipf's law [17].

Zipf's law, or Zipf's distribution, is a power law distribution that, applied to access requests, means the probability of the nth most common resource (permission) is requested with probability approximately equal to $1/n$. This distribution originated from observations made about the popularity of words in languages, and has been observed in web document popularity [8]. When using the new parameter, access requests are made at random according to the skewed distribution across all active sessions and permissions until the limit on access requests is reached. The reason to introduce the new parameter α is that some data structures optimize for skewed search patterns, for example the splay tree is a self-adjusting binary tree that moves frequently-accessed nodes closer to the root. Indeed, many cache-like structures will do best on data that are skewed. Thus, we aim to quantify whether some SDPs may do better when access requests are skewed.

3.3 Benchmark Modifications

We modified the benchmark to reduce its execution time so that we could simulate realistic workloads in a timely manner. Importantly, the benchmark was changed to instantiate only one PDP and to pre-compute the PDP's responses by running through one iteration of the benchmark's workload before beginning the iterations that time the SDP. These changes remove the overhead of PDP instantiation and policy evaluation from the benchmark's workload loop, which substantially reduced the benchmark runtime without sacrificing accurate timing of SDP access enforcement; we validate the timing is correct by reproducing experiments conducted in the prior work. We estimate these changes resulted in a speedup of about 7–10 in the time to run the benchmark. The time for one run of the benchmark in gem5 for the three SDPs we used was reduced from about a day to just over 3 hours, which allows running the benchmark multiple times with different configurations and session profiles as needed by the experiments we conducted. Modifications to the PDP required rewriting the initiation code for the SDPs. Since the access matrix and CPOL SDPs were the most time-efficient in the prior work, we chose to focus on those two SDPs along with our implementation of the HWDS BitSet SDP.

The focus in the literature on mean access time as a proxy for SDP performance is misleading in case an SDP has extremely poor session initiation and destruction times. Many data structures can optimize the search path at the expense of the insert/delete path, for example a balanced search tree does extra work to keep the tree height in balance during insertions and deletions so that searches achieve logarithmic asymptotic time complexity. The time it takes to start a session can negatively impact a user's experience especially if the delay is noticeable. Therefore, we aim to quantify the effect of the SDP on session initiation and destruction. To do so, we added timing measurements to the benchmark for session initiation and destruction that measure the time needed by the PDP to construct and destroy session authorizations for the SDP. By measuring the initiation and destruction costs for the SDP data structure, the benchmark now estimates the entire cost of a particular SDP implementation.

3.4 SDP Implementation

We implemented the HWDS BitSet SDP in the dist-rbac-eval benchmark using our gem5 implementation of the associative array HWDS. The HWDS BitSet SDP works as described in Section 2. A list of permissions associated with a session is converted into a Java BitSet by the PDP, which returns the BitSet and session identifier to the SDP. The SDP extracts and inserts each 64-bit chunk of the BitSet into the HWDS with a key constructed from the session identifier and offset of the chunk. An access request computes the offset for a requested permission and searches the HWDS using an argument constructed from the session identifier and offset. The return value is checked at the bit position of the requested permission and access is granted (denied) if the bit is set (clear). A session is destroyed by extracting keys for every offset for the session.

3.5 Methodology

The hardware platform is a simulated system using the gem5 simulator with the timing CPU, which is a simplified processor core that models the timing of memory accesses and cache, but it does not include detailed pipeline interactions or out-of-order execution. For the gem5 platform, we use the X86 full system simulation with 1 core and 512 MB of RAM, 64K data cache, 32K instruction cache, running at 500 MHz, with Linux 2.6.28.4, java version 1.7.0_51, and the OpenJDK VM. We set the VM memory heap size to 512 MB. We use this platform to evaluate the HWDS BitSet SDP.

Our methodology for executing the benchmark is similar to that of Komlenovic et al [18], but we did make some minor variations. This methodology is inspired by the work of Georges et al. [13], who present a detailed analysis of Java performance analysis and experimental design with Java. Most important, Java programs exhibit two primary phases with distinct performance characteristics, a startup phase and a steady-state phase. Experiments that measure performance in Java must take into consideration which phase to observe. We are interested in the steady-state performance of the SDP, therefore we use the four-step methodology proposed by Georges et al [13]. However, we do not run the VM multiple times because executing the benchmark on the same inputs and parameters gives the same timing results in the simulator, so there is no variance between VM invocations. Each invocation runs at most 25 iterations of the session profile for the benchmark. The first 16 iterations are ignored, and the benchmark terminates when 5 iterations in a row achieve a mean access time with a coefficient of variation (CoV) less than 0.02. (CoV is equal to the sample standard deviation divided by the sample mean.) If the CoV of 0.02 is not achieved within 25 iterations, the benchmark terminates and reports the 5 consecutive iterations with the smallest CoV. We record the access time along with the session initiation and destruction times for these 5 iterations for each VM invocation. The first 16 iterations are ignored because we found that the variation between iterations is small even in the startup phase, which causes a small CoV that terminates the benchmark before it reaches the steady-state.

In the experimental results, we report mean access time performance that was calculated as the mean of the recorded access times across the repeated VM invocations. We also compute and report the 95% confidence interval for each mean. For the initiation and destruction times, we calculate the average of the times reported across all VM invocation, and we discard any measurement that is outside of 1.5 times the interquartile range. The reason to discard these outliers is that the initiation and destruction times in the steady-state are still affected by Java-induced variations, especially garbage collection. Discarding the outliers gives a more accurate estimate for the performance of session initiation and destruction without garbage collection.

4. EXPERIMENTS AND RESULTS

We conducted a series of experiments using the experimental setup described in Section 3.

4.1 Reproduced Experiments

The first set of experiments aim to reproduce those presented by Komlenovic et al. [18] using the benchmark. We reproduce the prior work in order to validate the modifications we made to session profiles and the benchmark workload, and also to determine useful parameters for executing the benchmark on the gem5 platform. We chose the parameters used in these reproduced experiments to match the parameters of the prior work.

We attempted to recreate the RBAC configurations and session profiles for the inter- and intra-session experiments described in the prior work. An inter-session experiment consists of multiple benchmark executions with increasing numbers of sessions for each execution. For the inter-session experiment configurations, we set the number of users to 25, roles to 100, permissions to 250, roles per user to 4, and roles per permission to 3. The benchmark is agnostic to the number of users, since each user can generate multiple sessions in parallel by activating different sets of roles and permissions. 100 roles is reasonable for an organization with approximately 2500 users considering 4% ratio of users to roles.

An intra-session experiment executes the benchmark multiple times for the same number of sessions and fixed number of permissions with varying roles, and fixed number of roles with varying permissions. For the intra-session experiment configurations, we set the number of sessions to 15, users to 2, and varied the roles and permissions.

The inter-session experiments investigate SDP performance as parameters related to multiple sessions changes, whereas the intra-session experiments investigate SDP performance with fixed session parameters and varying other RBAC configuration and session parameters that can affect performance.

The results from running the reproduced experiments for the access matrix and CPOL SDPs are presented in the appendix. Using the same configurations and session profiles as in the reproduced experiments, we also measured session initiation and destruction times as described in Section 3.5. The results for session initiation and destruction times are in the appendix.

To evaluate the effect of skewness on SDP performance, we generated session profiles with the parameter α equal to 0, 0.25, 0.5, 0.75, and 1.0. We found no statistically significant difference in mean access time between the access matrix and CPOL SDPs with increasing access request skewness; that is, the mean confidence intervals overlap even for the extreme cases of $\alpha = 0.0$ and $\alpha = 1.0$.

We attribute this lack of difference to the benchmark's SDP being sufficiently small enough to fit into cache that the access pattern has no effect on performance since these two SDPs both prefetch the entire permissions data needed for authorizations.

4.2 HWDS BitSet SDP

To evaluate the effectiveness of the HWDS BitSet SDP, we conducted similar experiments to those described above. For these experiments, we focused on the inter-session behavior of the HWDS BitSet SDP, and the intra-session behavior for the increasing number of permissions.

As the number of sessions and permissions increase, the expectation is that the HWDS BitSet SDP performance will degrade due to overflow handling. In particular, the threshold for overflowing a HWDS is when the number of inserted nodes exceeds the number of sessions times the maximum permission identifier divided by 64. So with 250 permissions, overflow occurs when there are more than 32 sessions. We therefore varied the number of sessions up to 60 to observe the effect of overflow. 60 sessions requires approximately double the capacity of the HWDS. Each session generates 1000 access requests and we used α equal to 0.0 and 1.0.

We executed the benchmark using the inter-session profiles and access matrix, CPOL, and HWDS BitSet SDPs in the gem5 simulator. Each session generates 1000 access requests and we investigated both α equal to 0.0 and 1.0. Figure 4 shows the results for these benchmark executions. The total session initiation time averaged across the steady-state iterations used to compute the mean access time is presented in Figure 4a for $\alpha = 0.0$ and in Figure 4d for $\alpha = 1.0$. Figures 4.2 and 4.2 depict the mean access time for $\alpha = 0.0$ and $\alpha = 1.0$ respectively. and Figures 4c and 4f shows the session destruction time.

The mean access time and session destruction time for the HWDS BitSet SDP and the access matrix track closely, and they both outperform CPOL. Session initiation time with the HWDS BitSet SDP is about one-third less than with CPOL, and as the sessions increase the problems with access matrix session initiation are evidenced by the divergence between the HWDS BitSet and access matrix initiation times. With 15 sessions, the HWDS BitSet session initiation time is 28% less than the access matrix SDP's time, and the gap widens as the number of sessions increases. The per-session destruction time in the inter-session experiments was between 34.6–64.2 μs for the access matrix, 27–32.1 μs for the HWDS, and 163–170 μs for CPOL.

Even in the presence of HWDS overflow, the performance of the HWDS BitSet SDP is better than the software SDPs. Overflow occurs in the inter-session profiles when the number of sessions exceeds 32, and in the intra-session profiles when the number of permissions exceeds 546. When there is overflow, the HWDS BitSet SDP performs better with skewed access requests (Figure 4.2) than with uniform access requests (Figure 4.2), because the LRU overflow handling exploits temporal locality.

In the reproduced experiments, we found that the access matrix suffers heavy performance degradation for session initiation with the intra-session profiles, and it especially scales poorly with the increasing numbers of permissions. Thus, we executed the intra-session profiles using only the CPOL and HWDS BitSet SDPs in the gem5 simulator. Neither of these SDPs are affected by changing the number of roles, so the intra-session profiles use 100 roles and take the number of permissions from {100, 500, 700}. With 700 permissions, 15 sessions, and 128-node capacity, the HWDS BitSet SDP overflows 37 nodes.

Figure 5 shows the mean access time, average total session initiation time, and average total session destruction time as the number

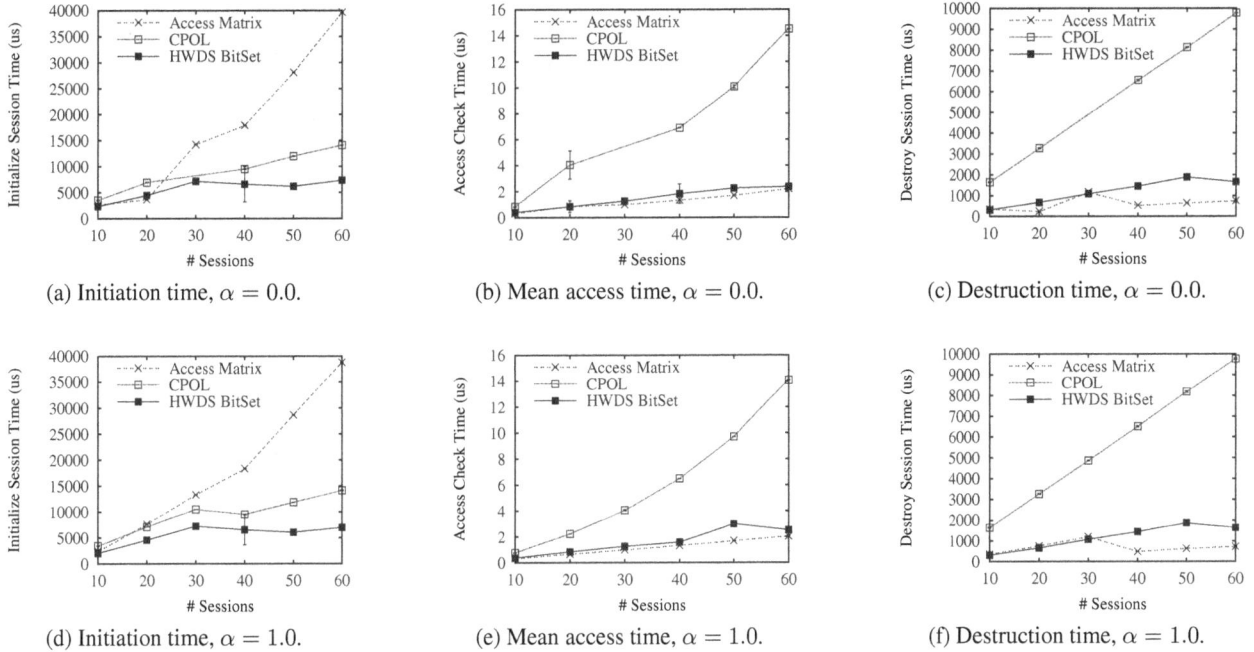

(a) Initiation time, $\alpha = 0.0$. (b) Mean access time, $\alpha = 0.0$. (c) Destruction time, $\alpha = 0.0$.

(d) Initiation time, $\alpha = 1.0$. (e) Mean access time, $\alpha = 1.0$. (f) Destruction time, $\alpha = 1.0$.

Figure 4: Inter-session results

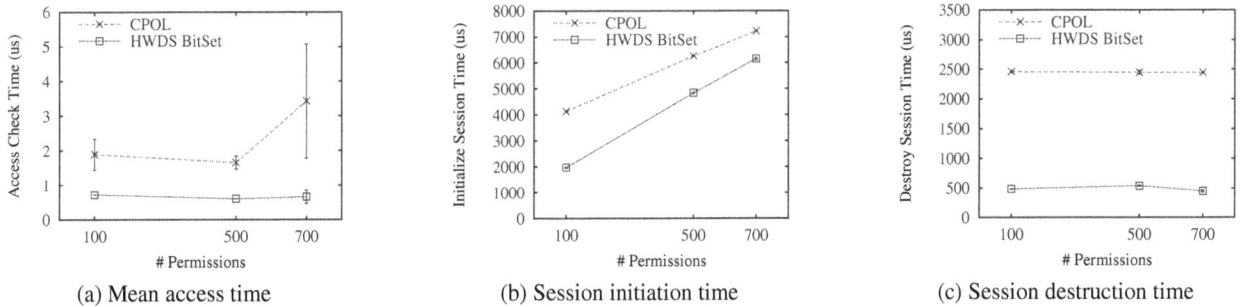

(a) Mean access time (b) Session initiation time (c) Session destruction time

Figure 5: Intra-session results for varying permissions using gem5.

of permissions changes. For these experiments, we used 1000 access requests per session and set α equal to 0.0. Figure 5a shows that the HWDS BitSet outperforms CPOL in terms of access check time. The mean access time for these data exhibit large variance for CPOL, none of which resulted with a CoV less than 0.02, though all of the HWDS BitSet measurements do. Such large variance indicates the experiment does not reach a stable steady-state when using the CPOL SDP. The session initiation time of the HWDS Bit-Set SDP scales worse as the number of permissions increases, since more permissions causes increased overflow while constructing the SDP data structure. Figure 5 shows how the HWDS BitSet SDP compares with the CPOL SDP for initiation time when scaling the number of permissions; the improvement is 52% at 100 permissions but only about 15% at 700 permissions.

The experimental results suggest that the HWDS BitSet SDP is a good choice for a high-performing SDP. We found that the HWDS BitSet performs comparably to the best SDP implementation for mean access time and session destruction, and the HWDS BitSet outperforms the prior work for session initiation time in all of the experiments, even those which induce overflow handling.

5. RELATED WORK

Access control solutions in commercial distributed systems—for example, IBM Tivoli [15], Oracle Entitlements Server [1], and CA SiteMinder Web Access Manager [16]—replicate policy to improve access enforcement performance when authorization is divided. Replication reduces the bottleneck of a centralized policy, but at the increased cost to keep the replicas consistent. Authorization still incurs computation time overhead to query the policy database, which others have argued can be the limiting factor in access request throughput [7]. Furthermore, communication overhead will degrade authorization performance unless each enforcement point has its own replica.

Policy replication is complementary to other approaches that improve the time efficiency of access enforcement in distributed systems, namely caching, predicting, and prefetching. Caching authorizations is a well-known and widely-deployed mechanism to improve the performance of access enforcement [26, 16, 1]. Authorization caching works well when access requests are repetitive and exhibit good temporal locality. In case access requests are not repeated exactly, Crampton et al. [10] proposed the secondary and approximate authorization model (SAAM) introducing approximate authorization recycling. Approximate recycling predicts an authorization without consulting the PDP during an access request. Wei et al. [28, 29] applied the SAAM to RBAC. Good performance for authorization recycling depends heavily on cache warmness, which can be a problem especially for short duration sessions or access requests with low temporal locality. To circumvent the problem of a cold cache, Tripunitara and Carbunar [27] proposed implementing an SDP using a *push* model that prefetches authorizations into the SDP. The authors proposed the novel cascade Bloom filter as a data structure for caching authorizations. Komlenovic et al. [18] proposed and implemented a Java benchmark to evaluate implementations of 6 SDPs for RBAC. The 6 SDPs included reproductions of the above SAAM authorization recycling and cascade Bloom filter, along with new implementations using a directed graph representation, access matrix encoding derived from the work of Liu et al [20], Bloom filter, and a re-implementation of CPOL [7]. Other than authorization recycling, these SDPs use the same push model as Tripunitara and Carbunar. The HWDS BitSet SDP adopts the push model to provide a prefetched authorization cache at the SDP.

The HWDS BitSet SDP also extends some of the prior work in the area of hardware support for access control and hardware support for data structures. Our implementation of the associative array HWDS is inspired by the map HWDS used by Bloom [5] for generic search and Fiorin et al [12]—see below. The Java interface and implementation of overflow handling we use is similar to that used by Chandra and Sinnen [9] for their priority queue HWDS. The novelty of our work, however, is not in the design of a HWDS or its overflow handling, but rather in applying and evaluating the HWDS to the domain of RBAC and interfacing the HWDS with the Java environment of the access enforcement benchmark.

Hardware support for access control is not new—indeed, most modern systems use CAM hardware with memory protection bits to implement the translation lookaside buffer, which does virtual to physical memory address translation. Even hardware support for RBAC has been proposed by Fiorin et al. for improving the performance of SELinux by replacing the access vector cache with a similar hardware design as the associative array HWDS [12]. Our work differs from the prior work on hardware-enhanced access control by using only the HWDS as the hardware component, and the rest of the access enforcement is implemented in software.

6. CONCLUSION

In this paper, we presented a novel SDP, the HWDS BitSet SDP, that uses an associative array HWDS to store permissions in bit vectors. We evaluated this SDP using an open-source benchmark for distributed access enforcement, and we found that the time-efficiency of the HWDS BitSet SDP is competitive with the best SDP implementations provided with the benchmark. By including the cost of session initiation time in the benchmark's measurements we also found that the HWDS SDP takes much less time—about one-third less—to instantiate the data structure for caching session authorizations. The experiments we conducted included reproductions of a prior study [18] using the benchmark, and new experiments we designed that investigate the effect on access request times due to skewed probability distributions in access request patterns and to duration of sessions in terms of numbers of access requests. The experimental results for the reproduced experiments are commensurate to those reported by the prior work. We found that skewness in access requests does not affect mean access time for the access matrix and CPOL SDPs. However, the number of access requests made in a session has a strong influence on SDP performance—especially of CPOL—with larger access times

observed for shorter sessions, which we attribute to not reaching the best steady-state phase fast enough. These experimental results suggest that the HWDS BitSet SDP is a promising approach to improve the performance of distributed access enforcement in a client-server RBAC system.

While this paper makes a step in enhancing access control with hardware support, future work can further investigate how the HWDS approach can be used to improve access enforcement. Some areas that remain open to explore include the hardware design space, new HWDS operations that can support more efficient access enforcement, and applying the HWDS approach to other access control domains such as in single-user systems. In terms of the hardware design, the CAM-based HWDS is power-hungry and does not scale well beyond the 128-entry size we modeled in this paper. Alternative HWDS designs could scale better to larger capacities without sacrificing the performance advantages of hardware parallelism. Furthermore, instructions could be added to the HWDS that would benefit its use for access enforcement: an operation that can extract all of the nodes with the same session by matching a subset, or mask, of the key would reduce the cost of session destruction to the time needed to execute a single HWDS operation; operations to audit the use of the HWDS would benefit practical deployments by making accountability part of using the hardware; and operations that divide an array into multiple key-value nodes automatically would reduce some of the costs associated with loading permission identifiers into the HWDS.

7. ACKNOWLEDGMENTS

The authors are supported in part by NSF CNS-0934725. The authors thank the reviewers and shepherd, Mahesh Tripunitara, for helping to improve the presentation of our work. The modified benchmark source code and experimental harness we used is available at https://github.com/gedare/dist-rbac-eval/tree/SACMAT14

8. REFERENCES

[1] Fine grained authorization: Technical insights for using oracle entitlements server. Technical report, Oracle, 2012.

[2] dist-rbac-eval - a platform for assessing approaches to distributed role-based access control (RBAC) enforcement https://code.google.com/p/dist-rbac-eval/, 2014.

[3] D. S. Almeling, D. W. Snyder, M. Sapoznikow, W. E. McCollum, and J. Weader. A statistical analysis of trade secret litigation in federal courts. *Gonzaga Law Review*, 45(2):291–334, 2010.

[4] N. Binkert, B. Beckmann, G. Black, S. K. Reinhardt, A. Saidi, A. Basu, J. Hestness, D. R. Hower, T. Krishna, S. Sardashti, R. Sen, K. Sewell, M. Shoaib, N. Vaish, M. D. Hill, and D. A. Wood. The gem5 simulator. *SIGARCH Comput. Archit. News*, 39(2):1–7, Aug. 2011.

[5] G. Bloom. *Operating System Support for Shared Hardware Data Structures*. PhD thesis, The George Washington University, Jan. 2013.

[6] G. Bloom, G. Parmer, B. Narahari, and R. Simha. Shared hardware data structures for hard real-time systems. In *Proceedings of the tenth ACM international conference on Embedded software*, EMSOFT '12, pages 133–142, Tampere, Finland, 2012. ACM.

[7] K. Borders, X. Zhao, and A. Prakash. CPOL: high-performance policy evaluation. In *Proceedings of the 12th ACM Conference on Computer and Communications Security*, CCS '05, pages 147–157, Alexandria, VA, 2005.

[8] L. Breslau, P. Cao, L. Fan, G. Phillips, and S. Shenker. Web caching and zipf-like distributions: evidence and implications. In *IEEE INFOCOM '99. Eighteenth Annual Joint Conference of the IEEE Computer and Communications Societies. Proceedings*, pages 126–134, New York, NY, Mar. 1999.

[9] R. Chandra and O. Sinnen. Improving application performance with hardware data structures. In *2010 IEEE International Symposium on Parallel Distributed Processing, Workshops and Phd Forum (IPDPSW)*, pages 1–4, Atlanta, GA, USA, Apr. 2010.

[10] J. Crampton, W. Leung, and K. Beznosov. The secondary and approximate authorization model and its application to bell-LaPadula policies. In *Proceedings of the Eleventh ACM Symposium on Access Control Models and Technologies*, SACMAT '06, pages 111–120, Lake Tahoe, CA, 2006.

[11] D. F. Ferraiolo and D. R. Kuhn. Role-based access controls. pages 554–563, Baltimore, MD, Oct. 1992.

[12] L. Fiorin, A. Ferrante, K. Padarnitsas, and F. Regazzoni. Security enhanced linux on embedded systems: A hardware-accelerated implementation. In *Design Automation Conference (ASP-DAC), 2012 17th Asia and South Pacific*, pages 29–34, Sydney, NSW, 2012.

[13] A. Georges, D. Buytaert, and L. Eeckhout. Statistically rigorous java performance evaluation. In *Proceedings of the 22Nd Annual ACM SIGPLAN Conference on Object-oriented Programming Systems and Applications*, OOPSLA '07, pages 57–76, Montreal, Quebec, Canada, 2007. ACM.

[14] Jim Boyle, Ron Cohen, David Durham, Raju Rajan, Shai Herzog, and Arun Sastry. The COPS (common open policy service) protocol. Technical Report 2748, IETF, Jan. 2000.

[15] G. Karjoth. Access control with IBM tivoli access manager. *ACM Trans. Inf. Syst. Secur.*, 6(2):232–257, May 2003.

[16] Kire Terzievski, Steven Turvey, and Matt Tett. CA WAM solution hundred million user test. Technical Report 080202, Enex TestLab, Jan. 2009.

[17] D. E. Knuth. *The art of computer programming, volume 3: (2nd ed.) sorting and searching*. Addison Wesley Longman Publishing Co., Inc., 1998.

[18] M. Komlenovic, M. Tripunitara, and T. Zitouni. An empirical assessment of approaches to distributed enforcement in role-based access control (RBAC). In *Proceedings of the first ACM conference on Data and application security and privacy*, CODASPY '11, pages 121–132, San Antonio, TX, USA, 2011. ACM.

[19] Laura DuBois and Natalya Yezhkova. Distinctions between SMB and enterprise requirements for protection, archiving, and recovery. Technical report, IDC, Framingham, MA, USA, Apr. 2009.

[20] Y. A. Liu, C. Wang, M. Gorbovitski, T. Rothamel, Y. Cheng, Y. Zhao, and J. Zhang. Core role-based access control: Efficient implementations by transformations. In *Proceedings of the 2006 ACM SIGPLAN Symposium on Partial Evaluation and Semantics-based Program Manipulation*, PEPM '06, pages 112–120, Charleston, South Carolina, USA, 2006. ACM.

[21] K. Pagiamtzis and A. Sheikholeslami. Content-addressable memory (CAM) circuits and architectures: a tutorial and survey. *IEEE Journal of Solid-State Circuits*, 41(3):712–727, Mar. 2006.

[22] Preeta M. Banerjee and Eric Openshaw. Democratizing technology: Crossing the "CASM" to serve small and medium businesses. *Deloitte Review*, (14), Jan. 2014.

[23] J. Saltzer and M. Schroeder. The protection of information in computer systems. *Proceedings of the IEEE*, 63(9):1278–1308, 1975.

[24] R. Sandhu, E. Coyne, H. Feinstein, and C. Youman. Role-based access control models. *Computer*, 29(2):38–47, 1996.

[25] A. Schaad, J. Moffett, and J. Jacob. The role-based access control system of a european bank: A case study and discussion. In *Proceedings of the Sixth ACM Symposium on Access Control Models and Technologies*, SACMAT '01, pages 3–9, Chantilly, Virginia, USA, 2001. ACM.

[26] R. Spencer, S. Smalley, P. Loscocco, M. Hibler, D. Andersen, and J. Lepreau. The flask security architecture: System support for diverse security policies. In *Proceedings of the 8th Conference on USENIX Security Symposium - Volume 8*, SSYM'99, pages 123–139, Washington, D.C., USA, 1999. USENIX Association.

[27] M. V. Tripunitara and B. Carbunar. Efficient access enforcement in distributed role-based access control (RBAC) deployments. In *Proceedings of the 14th ACM Symposium on Access Control Models and Technologies*, SACMAT '09, pages 155–164, Stresa, Italy, 2009. ACM.

[28] Q. Wei, J. Crampton, K. Beznosov, and M. Ripeanu. Authorization recycling in RBAC systems. In *Proceedings of the 13th ACM symposium on Access control models and technologies*, pages 63–72, Estes Park, CO, 2008. ACM.

[29] Q. Wei, J. Crampton, K. Beznosov, and M. Ripeanu. Authorization recycling in hierarchical RBAC systems. *ACM Trans. Inf. Syst. Secur.*, 14(1):3:1–3:29, June 2011.

APPENDIX

A. EXTENDED RESULTS

The experimental results presented here do not use the HWDS BitSet SDP, so the experiments are conducted using a typical user workstation. The hardware platform for these experiments was a 2.5GHz Intel Core2 Quad (Q9300) with 3 GB of main memory running CentOS 6 with Linux 2.6.32, java version 1.7.0_51, and the OpenJDK VM; we set the maximum memory usage for the VM to 1.5 GB. (Note: the benchmark is single-threaded, so only one core was used. The system was otherwise idle.) We use this platform to validate that the performance of the software-only SDPs are commensurate with the prior work, and to explore parameters for the new experiments measuring session initation and destruction times, and the effect of skewed access requests.

With this platform, we execute the VM 4 times, and ignore the first 8 iterations of the each invocation. If the CoV of a measured mean access time is larger than 0.02, then we discard that measurement for the Intel Core2 Quad platform. Discarded measurements reduce the number of samples and therefore the degrees of freedom in the Student's t-test used to compute the confidence interval. Otherwise, this platform is used the same as the gem5 simulator platform.

A.1 Reproduced Experiments

We generated configurations using the benchmark's RBAConfiguration Java class. For all the configurations, we set the parameters for the role, user, and permission connectivity to sequential (which the benchmark author's call uniform, and have as a parameter value of 1). We set the role hierarchy to 0 for all of the results we report in this paper, meaning no role hierarchy was used. We found that the role hierarchy has little effect on the performance of access enforcement for the SDPs we considered, because the SDP data structure does not traverse the role-permission map.

With the number of permissions at 250, we generated one configuration for the number of roles in {500, 700, 2000, 3000, 6000, 8000, 10000}. We set the number of roles per user to the number of roles, and the number of roles per permission to the number of roles divided by the number of permissions. With the number of roles set at 100, we generated one configuration for the number of permissions in {100, 500, 700, 2000, 3000, 6000}.

We generated session profiles for the above configurations using the modified SessionProfile Java class as described in Section 3.2. For each inter-session configuration, we generated thirty-nine session profiles: three session profiles with 5, 100, and 1000 access requests per session for each of the number of sessions between 2 and 15, All of these session profiles set the number of sessions per access check equal to the number of sessions, activated 3 roles per session, and only issued access requests to resources the user has permission to access with the activated roles. We generated three session profiles—with 5, 100, and 1000 access requests per session made to permitted resources—for each intra-session configuration, and with 15 sessions in each profile, 15 sessions per access check, and the number of roles per session equal to the total number of roles in the configuration. We attempted to match the configuration and session profile parameters to those reported in the prior work, but the number of access requests per session was not available, so it is introduced as a variable in our study.

We ran the benchmark using the above configurations and session profiles with the access matrix and CPOL SDPs on the Intel Core2 Quad. Figure 6 shows the mean access time using the methodology described in Section 3.5. The first row shows the inter-session experiments, with the second and third rows showing the intra-session experiments with varying roles and permissions, respectively. The first column is with 5 access requests per session, and the second and third are with 100 and 1000. All error bars show the 95% confidence interval.

Both SDPs perform best and with least variance when 1000 access requests are issued per session, which was the largest we tried. The long duration of the session enables the benchmark to reach the best steady-state performance sooner with respect to benchmark iterations. With only 5 access requests per session, the access matrix has fairly stable performance around $1.5\mu s$ per access request across the inter- and intra-session experiments. CPOL reaches an underperforming steady-state, and the benchmark terminates with a lower performance than that seen with longer sessions. The large confidence intervals for CPOL in the intra-session experiment with varying permissions is due to this failure to reach the steady-state.

In comparison to the prior work, our results show a smaller gap between the access matrix and CPOL access request times when the number of access requests per session is large. The performance of the access matrix is slightly higher than the previously reported numbers, possibly due to differences in the platform or modifications to the benchmark and methodology. CPOL however performed better than the previous work, which we attribute to sensitivity to the number of access requests per session.

A.2 Session Initiation and Destruction

Figures 6j, 6k, and 6l show the total initiation time averaged across all steady-state iterations and VM invocations for each of the experiments. Although these times will not be affected by the session duration, shorter sessions will suffer more due to larger initiation and destruction costs. For these particular measurements, we chose to use 1000 access requests per session. As more sessions are added, we expect a linear increase in the total session initiation time, as seen in Figure 6j. For the inter-session experiments, the average initiation time for a single session with CPOL is between about 60 and 100 μs, and the access matrix is between about 45 and 100 μs. As the number of roles increases, the session costs remain flat because these two SDPs do not operate on roles. Figure 6l shows the inititation time with increasing permissions, for which the access matrix SDP scales poorly. With 6000 permissions, the inititation time per session is over 45 milliseconds.

Figures 6m, 6n, and 6o shows the mean of the total destruction time for the inter- and intra-session experiments. The access matrix SDP seems to have a good destruction time, although the system-wide cost to destroy a session is not captured since garbage collection is not included in these times. For the inter-session experiments, the average time to destroy a single session with CPOL ranges between about 35 and 50 μs, and with the access matrix about 10 to 15 μs. The intra-session experiments have flat destruction times, indicating that the time needed to destroy a session with these SDPs is independent of the number of roles or permissions a session uses.

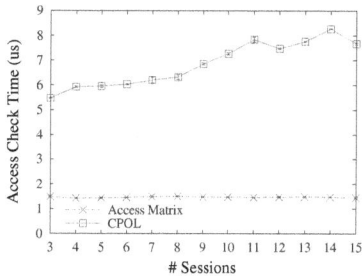

(a) 5 access requests/session (b) 100 access requests/session (c) 1000 access requests/session

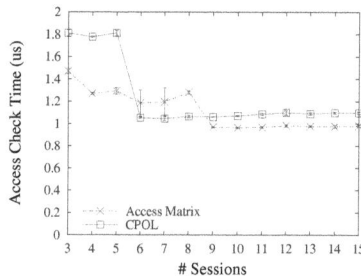

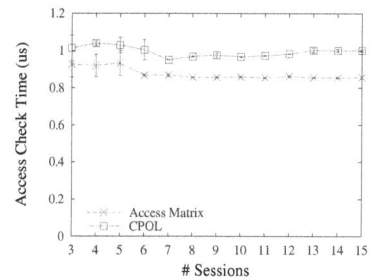

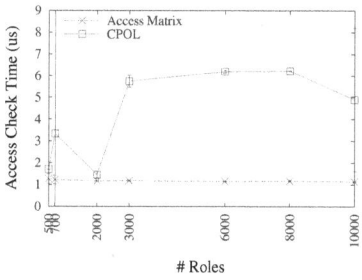

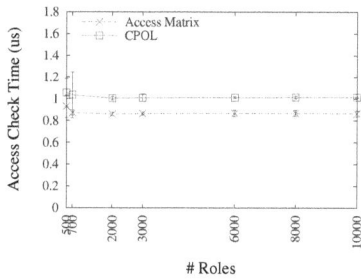

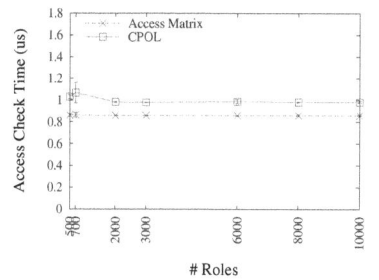

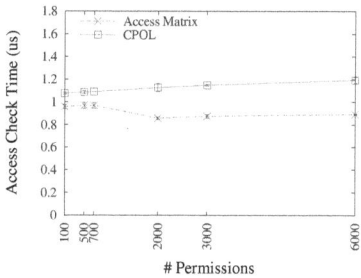

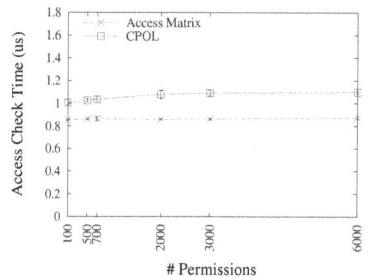

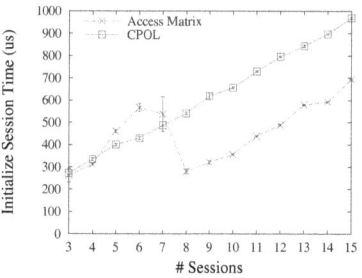

(d) 5 access requests/session (e) 100 access requests/session (f) 1000 access requests/session

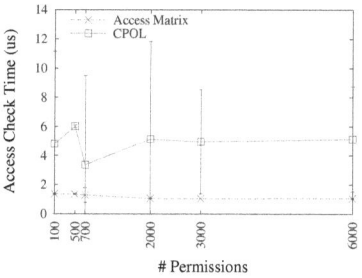

(g) 5 access requests/session (h) 100 access requests/session (i) 1000 access requests/session

(j) Inter-session initiation time. (k) Intra-session initiation time, varying roles (l) Intra-session initiation time, varying permissions

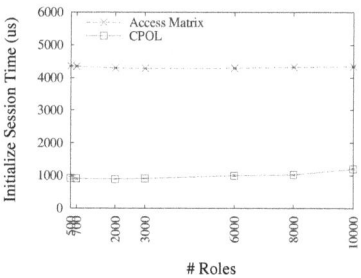

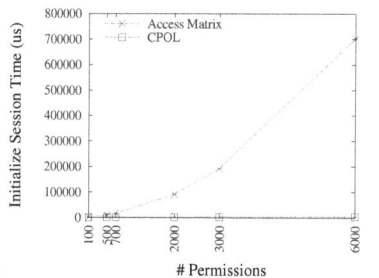

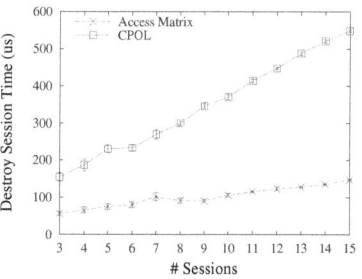

(m) Inter-session destruction time. (n) Intra-session destruction time, varying roles (o) Intra-session destruction time, varying permissions

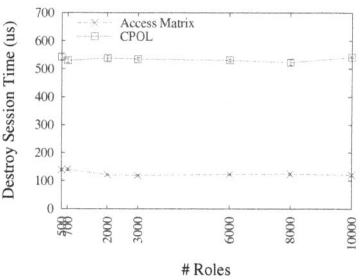

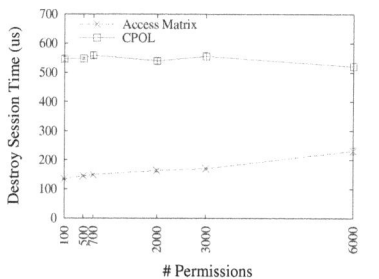

Figure 6: Experimental results with the modified benchmark

An Access Control Concept for Novel Automotive HMI Systems

Simon Gansel*   Stephan Schnitzer†   Ahmad Gilbeau-Hammoud†   Viktor Friesen*

Frank Dürr†   Kurt Rothermel†   Christian Maihöfer*

*System Architecture and Platforms Department
Mercedes-Benz Cars Division, Daimler AG
Sindelfingen, Germany
Email: firstname.lastname <at> daimler.com

†Institute of Parallel and Distributed Systems
University of Stuttgart
Stuttgart, Germany
Email: lastname <at> ipvs.uni-stuttgart.de

ABSTRACT

The relevance of graphical functions in vehicular applications has increased significantly during the few last years. Modern cars are equipped with multiple displays used by different applications such as speedometer or navigation system. However, so far applications are restricted to using dedicated displays. In order to increase flexibility, the requirement of sharing displays between applications has emerged. Sharing displays leads to safety and security concerns since safety-critical applications as the dashboard warning lights share the same displays with uncritical or untrusted applications like the navigation system or third-party applications. To guarantee the safe and secure sharing of displays, we present a formal model for defining and controlling the access to display areas in this paper. We prove the validity of this model, and present a proof-of-concept implementation to demonstrate the feasibility of our concept.

Categories and Subject Descriptors

D.4.6 [**Security and Protection**]: Access controls; H.5.2 [**User Interfaces**]: Windowing systems

Keywords

Access Control; State-based Model; Automotive; Windows

1. INTRODUCTION

Innovations in cars are mainly driven by electronics and software today [6]. In particular, graphical functions and applications enjoy growing popularity as shown by the increasing number of displays integrated into cars. For instance, the head unit (HU)—the main electronic control unit (ECU) of the infotainment system—uses the center console screen to display the navigation system, or displays integrated into the headrests of the front seats together with the center console screen to display multimedia content. Displays connected to the instrument cluster (IC) replace analog indicators displaying speed information or warnings. Additionally, head-up displays are used for displaying navigation instructions or assistance messages on the windshield.

Moreover, as demonstrated by advanced use cases already implemented in concept cars [1], there is a trend to *share* the different available displays *flexibly* by displaying content from different applications on dynamically defined display areas. For instance, while parking, applications can output information on any display including, in particular, the IC display. For example, this allows for playing full-screen videos on the IC display while the car is not moving. Moreover, the window size can be configured dynamically, for instance, to reduce the size of the speedometer in favor of a larger display area of the navigation software. Note that the flexible and dynamic usage of displays allows applications running on *different* ECUs to access all available displays. Even third-party applications downloaded from an app store [12, 3] and running in isolated execution environments—e.g., an Android partition within QNX [3] or on the mobile phone of the user [2]—can be granted access to these displays.

Although these use cases are very attractive for the user, they come with a great challenge: ensuring safety. Different standards and guidelines consider the safety aspect of displaying information in vehicles. For instance, current standards regulate that the level of safety-criticality of each function has to be assessed and suitable methods must be implemented to minimize the risks caused by malfunctions, c.f., ISO 26262 [15]. Moreover, automotive design guidelines (e.g., [9]) require that safety-critical content must be displayed in defined display areas and while driving potentially distracting content (like video playback) must not be displayed to the driver. Additionally, country-specific laws must be fulfilled, e.g., as regulated by German law (StVZO §57 [17]), in a moving car the speedometer must be visible.

Since display sharing results in scenarios where safety-critical applications, share the same display with uncritical applications, concepts for the safe sharing of displays between applications are required. Specifically, display areas have to be isolated such that it is guaranteed that the output of different applications does not interfere. For instance, the brake warning light may indicate a potentially severe hydraulic problem in the brake system and being covered by other application windows could be critical to the safety of the driver. Therefore, the output of safety-critical applications must be guaranteed to be always visible if required by

SACMAT'14, June 25–27, 2014, London, Ontario, Canada.
Copyright 2014 ACM 978-1-4503-2939-2/14/06 ...$15.00.
http://dx.doi.org/10.1145/2613087.2613104.

the status of the car or traffic conditions. Since this also applies to third-party applications, it is the responsibility of the OEMs to ensure that graphical outputs from different applications do not interfere. One approach to ensure this is to test and certify the correct behavior of all applications by the OEM. However, such a certification process is expensive and cumbersome. Therefore, technical solutions are required to ensure the isolation of display areas.

A naïve approach is to provide isolation for window placement by defining a static mapping in which the IC applications only access the IC display and the HU applications access the HU display and, additionally, the IC display within a reserved area. However, this approach lacks flexibility since only a predefined number of applications can be supported, and sharing is restricted to pre-defined display areas. Therefore, more flexible dynamic display sharing is required.

In this paper, we present a novel access control model for sharing graphical displays to offer flexibility without compromising safety. Basically, our model grants applications dynamic permissions to draw to certain display areas. To support the decentralized software development process involving OEMs and subcontractors and possibly third-party developers, permissions are managed based on a delegation hierarchy such that applications can pass permissions to subcomponents, e.g., third-party or subcontractor components. In detail, we make the following contributions in this paper: 1. A formal definition of the access control model and the required properties such as isolation. 2. A formal proof of correctness for this model. 3. A proof-of-concept implementation to show the feasibility of this approach.

The rest of this paper is structured as follows. In Sec. 2 we present our system model and requirements. Sec. 3 defines our access control model and presents properties for the model with the proof in Sec. 4. We present our implementation in Sec. 5, and related work in Sec. 6. We conclude with a summary and an outlook on future work in Sec. 7.

2. SYSTEM MODEL & REQUIREMENTS

In this section, we describe the components, assumptions and requirements of our system for display access control in an automotive HMI system.

2.1 System Model

The components of our system are depicted in Fig. 1. First of all, we assume that the available *display surface* consists of multiple **displays**. The display surface is shared between all applications. We define a *display area* as a subset of the pixels of the display surface. Each pixel of the display surface is indexed by x and y coordinates and is unambiguously identifiable by its position.

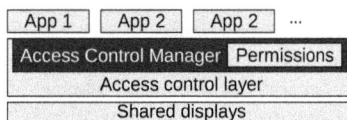

Figure 1: System model

Applications communicate with an Access Control Layer to get access to display areas. We assume that all applications can be unambiguously identified, e.g., by using Universally Unique Identifiers (UUID). Moreover, the usage of the displays by applications is restricted by the context of the

car. For instance, video playback is permitted only if the car is not in motion. Applications can be deployed or removed dynamically during runtime. Applications provided by the OEM or third-party developers are stored on a backend server infrastructure (cf. Fig. 2, [20]). To deploy or update an application in the car, the vehicle establishes a secure connection to the backend server to download binaries, a list of permissions, and certificates from the server.

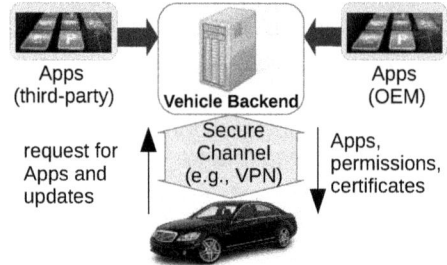

Figure 2: App deployment

The **Access Control Layer** restricts access to the display surface. Since there is no static mapping between applications and display areas, the mapping is performed by the *Access Control Manager*. Before an application can access a display area, it needs a permission from the Access Control Manager that centrally manages all granted permissions.

2.2 Requirements

In the following, we present our requirements targeting access control of the display surface which need to be fulfilled to ensure safety in automotive HMI systems.

Req. 1 – Dynamic permissions: An application shall be allowed to access a display area if, and only if, there exists a corresponding permission. A permission shall be grantable and revocable during runtime of the system to meet the different demands of the applications which can be influenced by the status of the car or traffic conditions.

Req. 2 – Priorities: Applications shall have priorities assigned. Priorities can depend on importance, urgency, criticality, and legal requirements for displaying graphical content. If multiple applications want to access the same display area, access shall depend on their priorities.

Req. 3 – Safe access: Each pixel shall be mapped to *exactly* one application. This requirement consists of the following two sub requirements.

Req. 3.1 – Exclusive access: Each pixel shall be mapped to *at most* one application. Thus, an application that has access to a pixel is guaranteed to be visible.

Req. 3.2 – Completeness: Each pixel shall be mapped to *at least* one application. For each pixel there exists an application that has a permission to set its content and can grant access to it, and "dead" pixels are avoided.

Req. 4 – Delegation: To facilitate the software development process, the OEM may pass usage permissions for display areas to software development companies or even individual developers, which again can pass usage permissions to others. Passing usage permissions must happen in a way that the OEM can ensure to meet all safety-relevant requirements without being a central certification authority for all applications. For instance, as depicted in Fig. 3, the OEM passes different usage permissions to Company 1. Company 1 decides to pass a subset of its permissions to

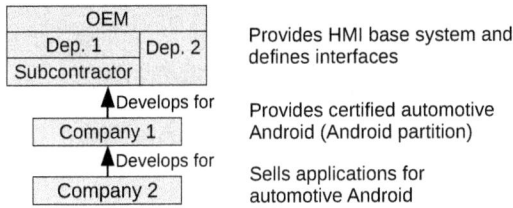

Figure 3: Software development hierarchy scenario

Company 2. This example of permissions requires a *delegation relation* between the parties for exchanging permissions. More precisely, we assume a *decentralized development process* as it is commonly applied in today's car industry, e.g., by service-based software development [18]. This process involves different departments of the OEM, subcontractors, as well as third-party developers like application developers for a (future) app store for vehicular apps. In the scenario depicted in Fig. 3, the OEM software development is done by different departments and subcontractors. The OEM provides the HMI base system, interface definitions, and certification policy. Company 1 is independent from the OEM and provides an Android partition—running isolated from the OEM applications, e.g. within QNX [3]—with an automotive app menu which is compatible and certified for the OEM's HMI system. This app menu uses display areas dedicated by the OEM to display Android applications. Company 2 sells automotive Android applications that enhance the features of the car. For instance, an application which display relevant information about service stations nearby the current position of the car.

As becomes obvious from this scenario, our system has to support the delegation of permissions to access display areas between the involved parties to facilitate the decentralized development process.

3. ACCESS CONTROL MODEL

We now present the first main contribution of this paper: an access control model for automotive HMI systems. We first give an overview of the model, before we formally define the model and verify its properties.

3.1 Overview

In general, an access control mechanism controls which subjects can access which objects. In our context, subjects correspond to *applications* and objects to *display areas* whose pixels are modified by the application. We use *permissions* to define that a certain application is granted access to a certain display area. Since permissions can be granted and revoked dynamically, we need a formal model that can express this dynamic behavior. To this end, we introduce *states* that model the mapping of permissions to applications at a certain point in time. *Transitions* between states are triggered, whenever a permission is granted or revoked, i.e., whenever the mapping of permissions to applications changes. The state transitions over time can be modeled as a *graph*, where states correspond to vertices and transitions to edges. We introduce the notion of a *safe state*. A safe state obeys all requirements of Sec. 2.2. A system is safe, if it starts in a safe state and every transition that occurs over time leads to a safe state. In order to ensure that only safe states can occur, we define which transitions are allowed. As stated

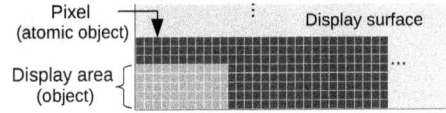

Figure 4: Entities: Pixels and display areas

in our requirements, our system should support granting of permissions where an application passes on a permission for a display area to another application. In order for a transition to be valid, an application can only pass a permission for a display area if it owns the permission for this area.

To further control the transfer of permissions, we introduce a *delegation relation* between applications. This relation is defined based on the decentralized development process where the OEM might delegate the development of a certain application component to a contractor, contractors might delegate parts of the application to subcontractors, etc. In order to show the GUI of a component, the actual developer can receive the permission to draw into a certain display area if he is in a delegation relation with the grantor. If a permission has been granted, the grantor cannot access the display area anymore. However, he can *revoke* a granted permission to get access to the corresponding display area again. Based on the rules to transfer permissions, we can then prove the correctness of our model by complete induction showing that the initial state is valid and each transition from a valid state leads again to a valid state.

Next, we present formal definitions of our model and an outline of the proof.

3.2 Subjects and Objects

A display area is defined as a set of pixels as depicted in Fig. 4. The smallest possible area consists of a single pixel, i.e., an *atomic object*. The complete display area is called the *display surface* and consists of all pixels.

Definition 1. $AO = \{ao_1, ..., ao_n\}$ *is a finite set of pixels (atomic objects). A display area is a subset of the set of pixels, formally a display area o is an object $o \in O = \mathcal{P}(AO) \backslash \emptyset$ with O representing the set of all display areas.*

Definition 2. $S = \{s_1, ..., s_n\}$ *is a set of applications (subjects) with $n \geq 1$.*

3.3 States

Each *state* of our model is represented by the currently valid *permissions* and *delegation relations*.

Definition 3. *A permission grants an application access to a certain display area. Formally, $P = \mathcal{P}(S \times O)$ represents the set of all possible combinations of permissions.*
$B = \{f : S \to P \times P\}$ *maps to each application in S two sets of sets of permissions ($P \times P$), representing the permissions an application has* received *from other applications and permissions it has* granted *to other applications.*

Let $b \in B, s \in S$. Set $received(b, s) := \{r | (r, g) \in b(s)\}$ denotes the set of permissions that application s has received. And set $granted(b, s) := \{g | (r, g) \in b(s)\}$ denotes the set of permissions application s has granted. Accordingly, $(s, o) \in received(b, s')$ indicates that application s' has received the permission to access display area o from

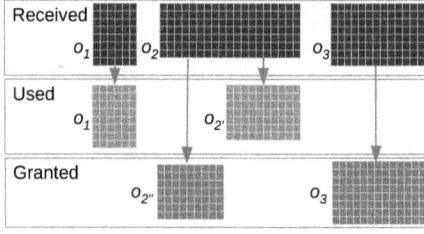

Figure 5: Example for a set of received, granted, and used display areas of an application

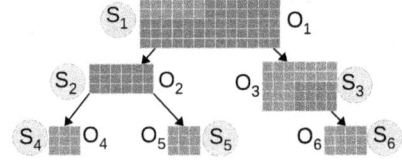

Figure 6: Example for permissions dependencies

application s. $(s,o) \in granted(b,s')$ indicates that application s' has granted the permission to access display area o to application s.

We distinguish between received permissions for display areas and actually *used* display areas. A display area o is used by an application if it is setting the graphical content of o. A display area is in the set of used display areas of an application if the display area is in the set of received display areas and it must not be granted to other applications. Applications can only set the graphical content of display areas which are part of their set of used display areas.

Definition 4. *used* : $B \times S \to \mathcal{P}(O)$ *is a function which returns the set of display areas used by an application. Let $o \in O, s \in S, b \in B$. We define $o \in used(b,s) \Leftrightarrow$*

$$\exists(\hat{s},\hat{o}) \in S \times O : (\hat{s},\hat{o}) \in received(b,s) \wedge o \subseteq \hat{o} \wedge \quad (4.1)$$

$$\forall(s',o') \in S \times O : (s',o') \in granted(b,s) \Rightarrow o \cap o' = \emptyset \quad (4.2)$$

In Fig. 5 we depict an example of the sets of received, granted, and used display areas. The application received the display areas o_1, o_2, and o_3 and decided to grant o_3 and part of o_2 to another application. Therefore, the display areas $o_{2''}$ and o_3 are in the set of granted display areas. Hence, o_1 and $o_{2'}$ are in the set of used display areas and the application can set their graphical content.

We say an application s' that received a display area o from another application s *depends on* that application since it can revoke display area o at any time. If display area o will be granted by s' to another application s'', then s'' also depends on application s since revoking of display area o by s will recursively revoke o from application s''. Fig. 6 depicts the hierarchical dependencies between applications. Application s_1 granted part of its display area o_1 to the applications s_2 and s_3 keeping only a small display area in the upper left corner to set its graphical content. The applications s_4 and s_5 received each a part of the display area s_2 received from s_1. Similarly, s_6 received part of the display area which s_3 received from s_1. Hence, the applications s_4, s_5, and s_6 indirectly depend on s_1 since revoking of the display areas granted to s_2 and s_3 would also revoke the display areas of these applications.

We introduce the operator $<_o$ that denotes if an application depends on another applications directly or indirectly according to a display area. More precisely, $s <_o s'$ means, application s has received o either directly from s' or by using a chain of intermediate applications, i.e., s depends on s' according to o. The formal definition is in Sec. A, Def. 10.

For instance, in Fig. 6 application s_3 depends on s_1 according to display area o_3, i.e., $s_3 <_{o_3} s_1$. Hence, application s_6 depends on s_3 and s_1 according to o_6, i.e., $s_6 <_{o_6} s_3$ and

$s_6 <_{o_6} s_1$. Let $s,s' \in S$. We define $s \neq_o s' \Leftrightarrow \nexists o \in O : s <_o s' \vee s' <_o s$. That is, application s and s' do not have a dependency due to any display area $o \in O$. For instance, in Fig. 6 the applications s_2 and s_3 do not have any display areas granted directly or indirectly, i.e., $s_2 \neq_o s_3$.

Applications will only grant permissions to or receive permissions from applications they are in a delegation relation with. Each application can be in a delegation relation with one or more other applications. To prevent granting of permissions from non-safety-critical applications to safety-critical applications a delegation relation is only established if a mutual agreement between the applications exists.

Definition 5. *We map to each application the set of applications it allows to be in a delegation relation with. This mapping is performed by a function $dr \in DR = \{dr : S \to \mathcal{P}(S)\}$. Applications s and $\tilde{s}$ are in a delegation relation with each other if, and only if, $s \in dr(\tilde{s})$ and $\tilde{s} \in dr(s)$.*

The delegation relations correspond to the development hierarchy, cf. Sec. 2.1. Hence, the delegation relations between applications restrict the propagation of permissions. To support dynamic deployment of applications during runtime, applications are allowed to dynamically declare with which applications they want to be in a delegation relation.

After we introduced permissions and delegation relations, we formally define states.

Definition 6. *A state consists of active permissions and delegation relations between applications. Formally, $v \in V$ is a state in $V = B \times DR$.*

3.4 Properties of States

States have properties that represent the requirements of Sec. 2.2. First, we define Ω_{used} as the union set of all pixels in the sets of used display areas in b. Ω_{used} represents all display areas whose graphical content is set by applications.

Definition 7. $\Omega_{used} : B \to \mathcal{P}(O)$ *is a function which returns a set of all used areas according to $b \in B$. We define*

$$\Omega_{used}(b) \Leftrightarrow \bigcup\{o \in O | \exists s \in S : o \in used(b,s)\}$$

Additionally, set $\Phi(b,s) := \bigcup used(b,s)$ denotes the union set of all pixels in the sets of used display areas of an application s in b.

Next, we define three *properties* that determine the consistency of our model and correspond to Req. 3 and Req. 4 introduced in Sec. 2.2. A state is called *safe*, if, and only if, it satisfies all three properties.

Exclusive Access Property (EAP): In a state that satisfies EAP, each display area is used by at most one application. Let $v = (b,dr) \in V$. v satisfies EAP $\Leftrightarrow$ $\forall s,s' \in S : s \neq s' \Rightarrow \Phi(b,s) \cap \Phi(b,s') = \emptyset$.

This means, the sets of used display areas of all applications are intersection-free. Therefore, competing access to display areas is precluded and Req. 3.1 fulfilled.

20

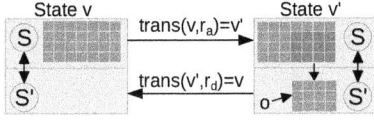

Figure 7: Example of a transition from state v to v'

Completeness Property (CP): In a state that satisfies CP, each pixel is used by at least one application. Let $v = (b, dr) \in V$. v satisfies CP $\Leftrightarrow \Omega_{used}(b) = AO$.
All pixels must be in $\Omega_{used}(b)$ which represents all pixels of all used display areas. That is, for each pixel there exists an application that sets the pixels color, which fulfills Req. 3.2.

Delegation Property (DP): In a state that satisfies DP, permissions are only granted between applications having a delegation relation. Let $v = (b, dr) \in V$.
v satisfies DP $\Leftrightarrow$

$$\forall s, s' \in S, \forall o \in O : s \neq s' \wedge s <_o s' \Rightarrow \quad \text{(DP.1)}$$

$$\exists s_0, ..., s_{n+1} \in S : s_0 = s \wedge s_{n+1} = s' \wedge \quad \text{(DP.2)}$$

$$\forall i \in \{0, ..., n\} \subset \mathbb{N}_0 : s_i <_o s_{i+1} \wedge$$
$$s_i \in dr(s_{i+1}) \wedge s_{i+1} \in dr(s_i) \quad \text{(DP.3)}$$

(DP.1) implies that for all applications which depend on another application according to a display area, a chain of applications exists (DP.2), for which every application is in a delegation relation with its predecessor and successor (DP.3). Since permissions are only granted if a delegation relation exists, Req. 4 is fulfilled.

3.5 Transitions

Transitions between states are triggered by application requests. In more detail, four requests might trigger state changes: Requests for granting or revoking permissions, and requests for adding or deleting an application to or from a delegation relation. Next, we define these four requests.

Definition 8. *A transition is triggered by a request to add or delete permissions or delegation relations. The operation mode is determined by $RA = \{append, discard\}$. To alter permissions the set of requests RO is used. A request $r \in RO$ consists of operation mode, grantor, grantee and the display area; formally, $RO = RA \times S \times S \times O$.*
To alter delegation relations the set of requests RD is used. A request $r \in RD$ consists of operation mode and the two applications of which the first wants to establish or withdraw a delegation relation with the second; formally, $RD = RA \times S \times S$. The set of all requests is the set $R = RO \cup RD$.

Next, we formally define transitions between states.

Definition 9. *$trans : V \times R \to V$ is a function which represents the transition from one state to another state initiated by a request $r \in R$.*

As described in Sec. 3.4, states must fulfill all three properties to be safe states. A transition changes from one state to another. Transition rules ensure that the new state is also a safe state. Therefore, we say a sequence of transitions from safe state to safe state is called *safe state sequence*.

Since applications can request to trigger a transition to add or delete permissions or delegation relations, we need four rules to restrict transitions for the two operation modes on permissions and delegation relations.

In the following, we define Rule 1.1 and Rule 1.2 to describe how permissions can be changed, and Rule 2.1 and Rule 2.2 to describe how delegation relations can be changed.

Rule 1.1 If application s' wants to have a permission for display area o from application s, this is expressed by the request $r_a \in RO$ with $r_a = (append, s, s', o)$. If application s decides to grant a permission, $trans(v, r_a)$ is executed as depicted in Fig. 7. In detail, $trans$ calls a function $add_{so}(b, s, s', o)$ (cf. Def. 11 in Sec. A), which adds o to the set of granted permissions of s, and adds it to the set of received permissions of s' if the following condition for R1.1 is satisfied. Condition $cond_1$ is satisfied, if

(1) request r is in RO and operation mode ra is *append*.
(2) different s and s' have a delegation relation.
(3) the application s' does not receive a permission for a display area which is part of a display area granted by s', thus, preventing cyclic grants.
(4) display area o is in the set of used display areas of s.

Formally, we define

$$cond_1 = r \in RO \wedge ra = append \wedge \quad (1)$$

$$s \neq s' \wedge s' \in dr(s) \wedge s \in d(s') \wedge \quad (2)$$

$$\exists \hat{o} \in O : \hat{o} \in used(b, s) \wedge o \subseteq \hat{o} \wedge \quad (3)$$

$$\nexists (\tilde{s}, \tilde{o}) \in granted(b, s') : o \subseteq \tilde{o} \quad (4)$$

Rule 1.2 An application s can revoke a permission for display area o from another application s'. This is expressed by the request $r_d \in RO$ with $r = (discard, s, s', o)$ as depicted in Fig. 7. In this case, $trans$ calls a function $del_{so}(b, s, s', o)$ (cf. Def. 12 in Sec. A), which removes o from the set of granted permissions of s and removes it from the set of received permissions of s' with $trans(v', r_d) = v$ if the following condition for R1.2 is satisfied. Condition $cond_2$ is satisfied if (1) request r is in RO, operation mode ra is *discard*, and (2) revoking of display area o was previously granted by application s to s' and $s \neq s'$. Formally, we define

$$cond_2 = r \in RO \wedge ra = discard \quad \wedge \quad (1)$$

$$s \neq s' \wedge (s', o) \in granted(b, s) \wedge (s, o) \in received(b, s') \quad (2)$$

If s' has granted permissions that contain part of o, the function del_{so} will recursively revoke all these permissions. Therefore, del_{so} removes all permissions with display areas that are part of o from the sets of granted and received permission if the applications depend on s. Furthermore, the permission which s granted to s' is removed from the set of granted permissions of s. The sets of permission of all applications that do not depend on s will not be changed.

Rule 2.1 The set of delegation relations DR can be changed by using transitions. If application s wants to be in a delegation relation with application s', this is expressed by the request $r \in RD$ with $r = (append, s, s')$. Then $trans$ calls function $add_{dr}(dr, s, s')$ (cf. Def. 13 in Sec. A), which adds the new relation $s \to s'$ to dr if the request r is in RD, the operation mode ra is *append*, and $s \neq s'$, i.e., no self-referencing delegation relation can be created. Formally, Condition $cond_3 = r \in RD \wedge ra = append \wedge s \neq s'$.

Granting of permissions is restricted to applications which are in a delegation relation. For instance, in Fig. 6 application S_1 has to be in a delegation relation with application S_2 before permissions can be granted between them.

Rule 2.2 Similarly, if application s no longer wants to be in a delegation relation with application s', this is expressed by the request $r \in RD$ with $r = (discard, s, s')$. In this case, $trans$ calls function $del_{dr}(dr, s, s')$ (cf. Def. 14 in Sec. A), which removes the delegation relation $s \rightarrow s'$ from dr if the following condition is satisfied. Condition $cond_4$ is satisfied if (1) request r is in RD, operation mode ra is $discard$, and (2) application s revoked or returned all permissions granted between s and s' beforehand and $s \neq s'$. Formally, we say

$$cond_4 = r \in RD \wedge ra = discard \quad \wedge \quad (1)$$

$$s \neq s' \wedge \forall o \in O : s \neq_o s' \quad (2)$$

Next, we formally define $trans$ using the four rules. Let $v = (b, dr) \in V$, and $r \in R$ with $r = (ra, s, s', o) \in RO$ or $r = (ra, s, s') \in RD$. We define

$$trans(v, r) = \begin{cases} (add_{so}(b, s, s', o), dr) & \text{if } cond_1 \quad \text{(R1.1)} \\ (del_{so}(b, s, s', o), dr) & \text{if } cond_2 \quad \text{(R1.2)} \\ (b, add_{dr}(dr, s, s')) & \text{if } cond_3 \quad \text{(R2.1)} \\ (b, del_{dr}(dr, s, s')) & \text{if } cond_4 \quad \text{(R2.2)} \\ v & \text{otherwise} \end{cases}$$

If none of the conditions of Rule 1.1, Rule 1.2, Rule 2.1, and Rule 2.2 are fulfilled, then the state v does not change.

4. SYSTEM VERIFICATION

In this section, we verify our model against the requirements in Sec. 2.2. Req. 1 (Dynamic permissions) is directly given by the granting and revoking of permissions by applications. The hierarchical dependencies between applications represent priorities according to Req. 2. The three properties Exclusive Access, Completeness, and Delegation (cf. Sec. 2.2) correspond to Req. 3.1 (exclusive access), Req. 3.2 (completeness), and Req. 4 (delegation), respectively.

While Req. 1 and Req. 2 are given by design of the model, Req. 3 and 4 are properties which we prove using complete induction. In this section we describe the main steps of our proof using Lemmas whose proofs can be found in Sec. B.

First, we define a *system* that consists of *sequences of states and requests*. We use this system to define propositions which we prove by using complete induction over the states. Finally we prove that a system is *safe* if the initial state fulfills the properties EAP, CP, and DP.

4.1 System

We prove the correctness of our system using complete induction over a sequence of transitions. Therefore, we define a *system* which represents all possible sequences of transitions between states reachable from a given initial state. First, we denote a sequence of $n - 1$ requests as $x_r := (r_0, ..., r_{n-1})$ and a sequence of n states as $x_v := (v_0, ..., v_n)$ with $n \in \mathbb{N}_0$. A system $\Psi(v_0)$ consists of all possible transitions between states using requests, starting with initial state v_0. That is, in such a system each sequence of states x_v triggers $n-1$ transitions traversing the states x_v, denoted as $(x_r, x_v) \in \Psi(v_0)$. Furthermore, we denote $(v_x, r_x, v_y) \gg \Psi(v_0)$ if a sequence of states and requests beginning from state v_0 exists in the system, and contains the state v_x, where, using request r_x a transition to v_y is performed. The formal definition can be found in Sec. A, Def. 15 to 18.

A system is *safe* if all states in that system are safe states. That is, a system consists only of states that satisfy the properties EAP, CP, and DP.

4.2 Propositions

Since the states and transitions of our model consist of mathematical formulations we can define propositions that correspond with our properties defined in Sec. 3.4. We define three propositions that correspond to the properties and help us to prove the safety of our model. Let $v, v', v_0 \in V$; $v' = (b', dr')$; $v = (b, dr)$ and $r \in R$.

Proposition 1: All sequences in $\Psi(v_0)$ satisfy EAP for any v_0 which satisfies EAP $\Leftrightarrow \forall (v, r, v') \in V \times R \times V : (v, r, v') \gg \Psi(v_0) \Rightarrow v, v'$ satisfy EAP

Proposition 2: All sequences in $\Psi(v_0)$ satisfy CP for any v_0 which satisfies CP $\Leftrightarrow \forall (v, r, v') \in V \times R \times V : (v, r, v') \gg \Psi(v_0) \Rightarrow v, v'$ satisfy CP

Proposition 3: All sequences in $\Psi(v_0)$ satisfy DP for any v_0 which satisfies DP $\Leftrightarrow \forall (v, r, v') \in V \times R \times V : (v, r, v') \gg \Psi(v_0) \Rightarrow v, v'$ satisfy DP

Proposition 1 says that all sequences in a system $\Psi(v_0)$ satisfy EAP if, and only if, for all states v' which can be directly generated from any state v with one request, implies that states v and v' also satisfy EAP. Proposition 2 and Proposition 3 are similar to the Proposition 1 but they target CP, and DP. By proving these three propositions we can conclude that every system $\Psi(v_0)$ is a safe system if state v_0 satisfies our properties in Sec. 3.

4.3 Proof by Complete Induction

To prove the correctness of Proposition 1, Proposition 2, and Proposition 3, we define a lemma for each of them. Additionally, we define Lemma 1 and 2 for the similar proofs of Lemma EAP and CP. Finally, we use complete induction over the system states to prove the propositions. We present the formal proofs of Lemma 1, Lemma 2, Lemma EAP in Sec. B. Due to space restrictions the proofs of Lemma CP and Lemma DP are published in [13].

We first define Lemma 1, which states that after a transition using (R1.1) with $add_{so}(b, s, s', o)$ the display area o moved from the used display areas of application s to s'.

Lemma 1: Let $v_0 \in V$, $\Psi(v_0)$ be a system and $(v, r, v') \in V \times R \times V$ with $(v, r, v') \gg \Psi(v_0)$. Let $v = (b, dr)$ satisfy EAP and $ra = append$ and $cond_1 \Rightarrow trans(v, r) = (b', dr) \in V$ with $b' = add_{so}(b, s, s', o)$.

$$\Phi(b', s) = \Phi(b, s) \backslash o \quad \text{(L1.1)}$$

$$\Phi(b', s') = \Phi(b, s') \cup \{o\} \quad \text{(L1.2)}$$

The following Lemma 2 says that after a transition using rule (R1.2) with del_{so} each display area o' (being a subset of the display area o) moves from the set of used display areas of application s' to that of application s.

Lemma 2: Let $v_0 \in V$, $\Psi(v_0)$ be a system and $(v, r, v') \in V \times R \times V$ with $(v, r, v') \gg \Psi(v_0)$. Let $v = (b, dr)$ satisfy EAP and $ra = discard$ and $cond_2 \Rightarrow trans(v, r) = (b', dr) \in V$ with $b' = del_{so}(b, s, s', o)$:

$$\forall \hat{s} \in S \backslash \{s\} : used(b', \hat{s}) = used(b, \hat{s}) \backslash$$
$$\{o' \in O | o' \subseteq o \wedge \hat{s} <_{o'} s\} \quad \text{(L2.1)}$$

$$\Phi(b', s) = \Phi(b, s) \cup o \quad \text{(L2.2)}$$

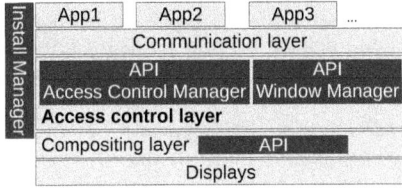

Figure 8: Implemented architecture

Lemma 1 and 2 say that a transition with an add_{so} or a del_{so} do not modify the union set of used display areas of all applications. The proofs are in Sec. B.

Next, we define the Lemma EAP, which states that a transition from a state which satisfies EAP will always end in a state which also satisfies EAP.

Lemma EAP: Let $v_0 \in V$, $\Psi(v_0)$ be a system and $(v, r, v') \in V \times R \times V$ with $(v, r, v') \gg \Psi(v_0)$. $v = (b, dr)$ satisfies EAP $\Rightarrow v' = (b', dr')$ satisfies EAP. The proof is in Sec. B.

The following Lemma CP states that a transition from a state which satisfies CP and EAP will always end in a state which also satisfies CP.

Lemma CP: Let $v_0 \in V$, $\Psi(v_0)$ be a system with $(v, r, v') \in V \times R \times V$ and $(v, r, v') \gg \Psi(v_0)$: $v = (b, dr)$ satisfies CP, and EAP $\Rightarrow v' = (b', dr')$ satisfies CP.

Next, we define the Lemma DP, which states that a transition from a state which satisfies DP will always end in a state which also satisfies DP.

Lemma DP: Let $v_0 \in V$ and $\Psi(v_0)$ be a system. Let $(v, r, v') \in V \times R \times V$ with $(v, r, v') \gg \Psi(v_0)$: v satisfies DP $\Rightarrow v'$ satisfies DP.

Finally, we prove Proposition 1, 2, and 3 by complete induction. Without loss of generality, we assume initial state $v_0 \in V$ with $v_0 = (\{(s_{root}, (\{(s_{root}, AO)\}, \emptyset))\}, \emptyset)$. That is, v_0 maps the permission to access the whole display area to the root application s_{root}. Since the permission has not been granted by another application, we set both, grantor and grantee, to s_{root} and no delegation relation exists.

Base: v_0 satisfies EAP and CP, since only s_{root} has a permission, and has access to all pixels. DP is satisfied, since $\nexists s, s' \in S : s \neq s' \wedge s <_o s'$ (cf., DP.1).

Induction hypothesis: v_i satisfies EAP, CP, and DP— with $(x_r, x_v) \in \Psi(v_0)$ and v_i a state of sequence x_v.

Induction step: Let v_i satisfy EAP, CP, and DP. From the Lemmas EAP, CP, and DP follows $v_{i+1} = trans(v_i, r_i)$ satisfies EAP, CP, and DP. $\square$

We follow that $\Psi(v_0)$ is a safe system, i.e., our rules do not violate EAP, CP, or DP.

5. IMPLEMENTATION

We implemented a proof-of-concept prototype which demonstrates the feasibility to implement our access control system. First, we introduce our system architecture.

5.1 Implemented Architecture

The system architecture of our Linux-based implementation is depicted in Fig. 8. To demonstrate the functionality of our access control system we used typical Instrument Cluster (IC) and Head Unit (HU) *Applications*. The *Communication Layer* provides session-based FIFO communication between applications, *Access Control Manager (ACM)*, and *Window Manager (WM)*. The access control layer contains the two components ACM and WM. The ACM is the access control unit that performs access decisions in the access control layer. The WM is responsible for creating, destroying, and positioning of windows. Applications that want to create, modify, or move a window send a request to the WM. We implemented a client API for access control management and window management that can be used by the applications to interact with the ACM and the WM. We implemented the *Compositing Layer* that provides an API which allows for resizing and mapping of windows. Each time the WM applies changes to windows it updates the screen by initiating the respective API call to the compositing layer. The implemented compositing layer uses the driver API of the Image Processing Unit (IPU) provided by the i.MX6 board for bit-blit operations in framebuffers. The *Install Manager* is responsible for the deployment of applications, XML-based permissions, and delegation relations.

We deployed our implementation in the cockpit demonstrator depicted in Fig. 9. As HCI devices the demonstrator uses two automotive 12" displays each with a resolution of 1440×540 pixels, which are connected to an embedded i.MX6 platform from Freescale Semiconductor. We also connected the steering wheel buttons and the central control knob, which are used to control the applications.

Next, we describe the main system components in detail.

5.2 Applications

To demonstrate automotive scenarios, we use 15 applications like speedometer, tachometer, check engine indicator, phone, and navigation software. In addition, we use two Linux applications that represent an Android menu and an Android application. Each application has a unique id called App_{id} and an application class $AppClass_{id}$ (e.g., an application class for indicators or video playing applications). Applications receive notifications about event changes, e.g., if the car starts moving. The deployment of an application includes the deployment of an application certificate to the ACM which is required to verify the authenticity of the application. The certification authority is either the OEM or a trusted third-party company, e.g., hosting an automotive Android app store. A certificate contains information about the application, i.e., the App_{id}, $AppClass_{id}$, company, public key, certification authority, and issue date (cf. X.509 [16]). The ACM stores the certificate of each application. An application can request a connection to the ACM via the Communication Layer. This requires the authentication of the application against the ACM which can be done by using a certificate-based authentication technique like described in ISO/IEC 9594-8 [16]. Each application has a set of XML files which contain the App_{id} and the $AppClass_{id}$ of the applications they want to be in a delegation relation with. In addition, the XML files can contain restrictions according to the display area an application shall get. For instance, the IC shall only grant a small display area to the requesting phone application which wants to display information like phone number in case of an incoming phone call. We determined the hierarchical dependency of applications in two steps. First, we assigned each application to one of the three classes *IC*, *HU*, and *Android*. Class *IC* contains IC applications which are normally safety-critical like the indicators and therefore have the highest priority. Class *HU* contains OEM applications like navigation. Class *Android* contains third-party applications which have the smallest

23

Figure 9: Cockpit demonstrator

priority. As second step, we determined the hierarchical dependency within a class according to given requirements (e.g., automotive ISO standards [9], legal restrictions [17]) or designed the dependencies between the applications according to HMI usability. In order to deploy an application, it is passed to the Install Manager. The deployment of an application consists of the application binaries, the XML files, and updates to XML files of already existing applications (e.g., to establish a delegation relation to an existing application). To prevent malicious modifications of the XML files, these are digitally signed, cf. [16].

5.3 Access Control Manager

According to our access control concept, permissions are centrally managed by the ACM. Each application is connected to the ACM and can send requests which the ACM forwards to the application specified in the request or which is responsible for the requested display area. If the receiving application grants a permission to the requesting application, it sends it to the ACM. The ACM denies all requests in case the application is not authenticated or the receiving and requesting applications are not in a delegation relation. Otherwise, the ACM checks if the granted permission is valid and does not violate existing permissions. Then it updates its permission mapping tables and notifies the client. All permissions are only valid if they can be derived from a root permission by a chain of grants. The root permission covers the whole display surface and is initialized by the ACM at startup of the system. This initial state is safe, since it fulfills the properties in Sec. 3.4, cf. Sec. 4. The ACM has always a consistent view of all granted permissions and can ensure consistency by preventing invalid permission exchanges.

In the following we describe the four access control API functions which correspond to the rules of our model.

Grant a permission (R1.1) Applications can grant permissions to other applications by using the request $GrantPermissions(DisplayArea\ o, App_{id}\ id)$. The requesting application specifies the display area o for which the application with id shall get a permission.

Revoke a permission (R1.2) For revoking a permission, $RevokePermissions(DisplayArea\ o, App_{id}\ id)$ is used. The requesting application specifies the display area o for which the permission shall be revoked from id.

Create a delegation relation (R2.1) To create a delegation relation to another application id, an application uses the request $CreateDelegationRel(App_{id}\ id)$ and is implicitly pending while waiting for the confirmation from the ACM. The ACM stores id in a table of the requesting application. If application id did not request a delegation relation, yet, the ACM notifies it with $DelegationRelPending(App_{id}\ id)$. A delegation relation is only established if both applications have requested the delegation relation. The ACM sends

$ConfirmDelegationRel(App_{id}\ id)$, where id is the application a delegation relation is established with.

Delete a delegation relation (R2.2) An application requests the deletion of a delegation relation by calling $DeleteDelegationRel(App_{id}\ id)$. If there exists any granted permission between those two applications the ACM denies the request. Otherwise it deletes the entry in the according table and notifies both applications.

5.4 Window Manager

The WM is the only process that can access the compositing layer. Thus, the WM checks, by calling the ACM, if the a request for creating a window by an application matches existing permissions of the requesting application and initiates the creating or moving of the window by performing respective API calls to the compositing layer. Next, we describe the three API functions for interaction with the WM.

Create a window Applications need a window mapped to the screen to display graphical content. To this end, after receiving a permission an application can issue the request $CreateWindow(Window\ w)$ to map a window to the display area it previously received a permission for. The parameter w specifies the size and the position of the window. The WM sends the request $Verify(Window\ w, App_{id}\ id)$ to the ACM, which verifies that a permission of application id matches window w and responds with $ResponseVerify(Ack\ ack)$. If an appropriate permission exists the WM sends an acknowledgment and the window id in response with $ResponseCreateWindow(Ack\ ack, Window_{id}\ id)$.

Modify a window Furthermore, permission changes can require applications to modify windows using the request $ModifyWindow(Window\ w)$ with new window parameters w. The WM also verifies if a permission exists by sending a request $Verify(Window\ w, App_{id}\ id)$ to the ACM which replies $ResponseVerify(Ack\ ack)$. Finally, the WM confirms the modify request with $ResponseModifyWindow(Ack\ ack)$.

Delete a window Applications can delete their windows by using the request $DeleteWindow(Window\ w)$. In case the necessary permission to display a window is revoked, the ACM notifies the application by sending $DeletePermission(DisplayArea\ o)$ and it sends the WM a notification about the permission change by using $NotifyPermChanged(DisplayArea\ o, App_{id}\ id)$. Then, the WM starts a timeout. If the application does not have any further permissions or does not modify the window to switch to another permission by using the request $ModifyWindow(Window\ w)$, the window will be deleted by the WM after the timeout expires. The WM notifies the application about the deleted window by sending $WindowDeleted(Window\ w)$.

Implemented Scenarios

Next, we describe two implemented scenarios where an application uses—depending on the current state—either a display area on the IC display or the HU display.

In the first scenario, we demonstrate granting and revoking of permissions to display an application *Media*. The required request-response calls are depicted in Fig. 10. If the car reaches parking position ❶, the (yet hidden) application *Media* gets notified and, in order to display the last presented video in full-screen on the HU display, requests

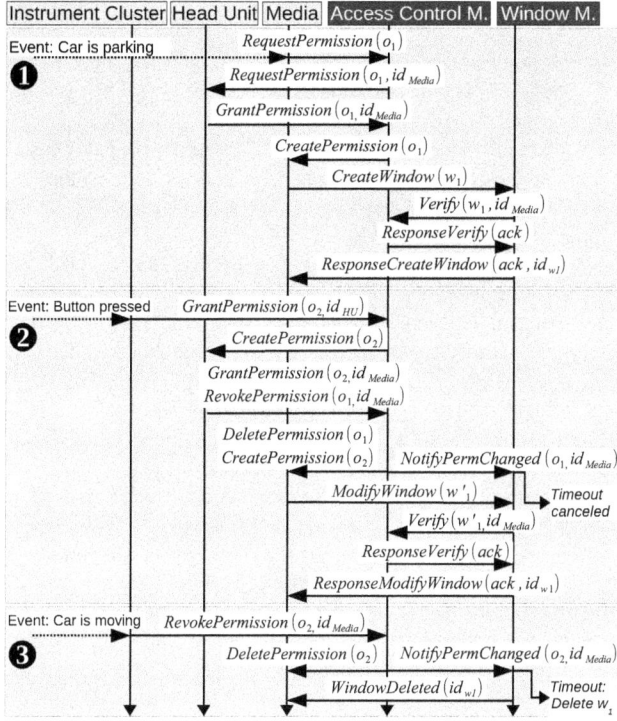

Figure 10: Sequence of operations for scenario 1

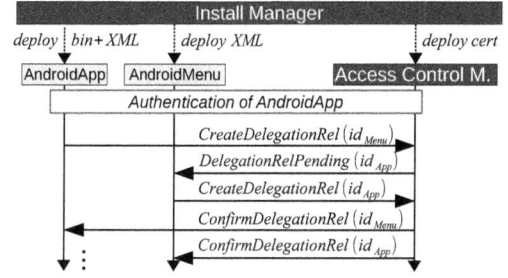

Figure 11: Sequence of operations for scenario 2

a permission for display area o_1 ($RequestPermission(o_1)$) from the ACM. $RequestPermission(o_1, id_{Media})$ is then forwarded to the HU application which grants a permission to $Media$ ($GrantPermission(o_1, id_{Media})$) since the car is not in motion. The ACM checks if the HU application has a valid permission which covers o_1 and creates a permission for $Media$ by using $CreatePermission(o_1)$. Then, $Media$ sends $CreateWindow(w_1)$ to the WM to create a window. With $Verify(w_1, id_{Media})$ the WM lets the ACM check if w_1 matches a permission of $Media$. Then, the WM confirms the creation of the window and sends back the window id id_{w_1}. Now, $Media$ has a valid window and can present the video in full-screen on the HU display.

Then, the driver decides to shift $Media$ to the IC display and to watch the video in full-screen. This requires the modification of the window position and therefore the granting of a new permission for the IC display. To perform the shift, the driver presses a button ❷ which triggers the IC to grant a permission ($GrantPermission(o_2, id_{HU})$) for its display area to the HU since no car related content like speedometer needs to be displayed while the car is not moving. Then, the ACM creates a permission with $CreatePermission(o_2)$ for the HU. The HU replaces the permission previously granted to $Media$ by a new one which covers the display area of the IC using the calls $GrantPermission(o_2, id_{Media})$ and $RevokePermission(o_1, id_{Media})$. The ACM in response creates a new permission and deletes the old one by using $CreatePermission(o_2)$ and $DeletePermission(o_1)$.

Deleting a permission requires a notification of the WM ($NotifyPermChanged(o_1, id_{Media})$) since the window w_1 has no valid permission anymore. Therefore the WM hides the window and starts a timeout after which the window will be deleted if still no appropriate permission exists. Since

$Media$ got a new permission for o_2, it modifies its window id_{w_1} by sending the request $ModifyWindow(w_1')$ to the WM. In response the WM stops the timeout and lets the ACM check with $Verify(w_1', id_{Media})$ if the w_1' is covered by a permission of $Media$. Finally, the WM confirms the modification with $ResponseModifyWindow(ack, id_{w_1})$. Now, the video is presented in full-screen on the IC display.

After watching part of the video, the driver starts the engine and accelerates the car. Therefore, $Media$ is no longer allowed to present the video. The IC receives a notification about that state change ❸. Since $Media$ belongs to an application class known to display videos, the IC calls $RevokePermission(o_2, id_{Media})$ to revoke the current permission. In addition, the IC would now grant the permissions to IC applications like speedometer, tachometer, and indicators, which is not depicted in Fig. 10. The ACM deletes the permission with $DeletePermission(o_2)$ and sends $NotifyPermChanged(o_2, id_{Media})$ to the WM. Finally, the WM deletes the window id_{w_1} after the timeout.

In the second scenario we focus on the deployment of the new application $AndroidApp$. As described in Sec. 2 we assume Company 1 provides an Android partition for the OEM infotainment system and implemented an application $AndroidMenu$ designed for usage in vehicles. Company 2 implemented an application $AndroidApp$ which shall be deployed on a vehicle. Company 2 negotiates with Company 1 about a permission for displaying the $AndroidApp$ which shall be selectable in $AndroidMenu$. Company 1 defines an XML file which contains the information about the $AndroidApp$ and the display area that shall be granted to it. Company 2 also defines an XML file which contains the information about $AndroidMenu$ and creates a certificate for $AndroidApp$. The XML files, the binary of $AndroidApp$, and its certificate are uploaded on the vehicle backend server and get deployed on the vehicle by the $Install\ Manager$ on request of the user. As soon as $AndroidApp$ is loaded it sends a request for authentication to the ACM. The ACM can verify the authenticity by using the certificate of $AndroidApp$ and applying an authentication procedure as described in ISO/IEC 9594-8 [16]. Then the $AndroidApp$ requests a delegation relation to $AndroidMenu$ by sending $CreateDelegationRel(id_{Menu})$. The ACM sends $DelegationRelPending(id_{App})$ since the $AndroidMenu$ did not send a delegation request, yet. As soon as $AndroidMenu$ receives the XML file, it also requests the creation of a delegation relation to $AndroidApp$. Then, the ACM calls $ConfirmDelegationRel$ with the parameters id_{App} and id_{Menu} to confirm the delegation relation. Now, $AndroidMenu$ can grant permissions to $AndroidApp$.

6. RELATED WORK

So far, there exists no fine-grained access control for displays or graphics resources. Feske et al. provide a concept for overlay management [10] of application windows executed in different virtual machines and a minimized secure graphical user interface called Nitpicker [11] with focus on low-level mechanisms to address security issues caused by spyware or Trojan horses. Hansen proposes a display system called Blink [14] which allows multiplexing of graphical content from different virtual machines safely onto a single GPU. However, both works neglect restrictions in window management. Similarly, Epstein et al. address security issues like weak authentication, unlimited sharing of X resources, between applications or overlapping windows in X11 [8] and propose mechanisms [7] to prevent them. However, they do not enforce permission based display access restrictions.

Protection of shared resources by using access control has been researched almost since the beginnings of operating systems [19]. Although later work (e.g., [22]) is based on hierarchical permissions, related work does not support priority-based access control using hierarchical granting and revoking of permissions. Birget et al. [5] unify a user and a resource hierarchy based on access relations into a single one which simplifies access control management but this technique is only applicable when the system changes slowly.

Bell and LaPadula [4] defined a model for secure information sharing and information flow control. The model is defined as a state-based system for enforcing access control and uses an access control matrix for restricting access to data in order to provide confidentiality of information. Restrictions are enforced for access of users or applications to files or resources concering the sensitivity level and security level. Therefore, their model does not guarantee exclusive access on resources. Additionally, it does not support decentralized permission management and consequently cannot be used for a decentralized development process. Related work [21]—based on the Bell and LaPadula model—extends the model for hierarchical organizations and distinguishes between read access and write access. They therefore target the flow of information, but do not support permission granting with exclusive access.

7. SUMMARY AND FUTURE WORK

In this paper, we presented an access control model which can be used for safety-critical automotive HMI systems. Our model supports hierarchical granting of display permissions and allows applications to be dynamically added and removed during runtime without modifying the access control layer. We proved the correctness of our model and showed that it fulfills all requirements we consider to be relevant for safe automotive HMI systems. Finally, we described our proof-of-concept implementation showing its feasibility in an automotive cockpit demonstrator. In future work we want to extend our model for context handling and constraints. Additionally, we want to improve our implementation by using a virtualized Android partition which is running applications using our API. Furthermore, we want to analyze overhead and performance of our implementation.

8. ACKNOWLEDGMENT

This paper was supported by the ARAMiS project of the German BMBF with funding ID 01IS11035.

9. REFERENCES

[1] Mercedes-Benz F125. http://www.motorauthority.com /news/1070046_mercedes-benz-ponders-the-future-of-in-car-tech, 2014.

[2] Mercedes-Benz integration of iPhone App in A-Class. http://www.iphone-ticker.de/mercedes-benz-iphone-integration-a-klasse-30952/, 2014.

[3] New Version of QNX CAR Platform. http://www.qnx.com/news/pr_5602_1.html, 2013.

[4] D. E. Bell and L. J. LaPadula. Secure Computer System: Unified Exposition and MULTICS Interpretation. Tech. Report ESD-TR-75-306, 1976.

[5] J.-C. Birget, X. Zou, G. Noubir, and B. Ramamurthy. Hierarchy-based access control in distributed environments. In *Communications, 2001. ICC 2001*.

[6] C. Ebert and C. Jones. Embedded software: Facts, figures, and future. *Computer*, 42(4):42–52, April 2009.

[7] J. Epstein et al. A prototype B3 trusted X Window System. In *Proceedings of the 7th Annual Computer Security Applications Conference*, Dec. 1991.

[8] J. Epstein and J. Picciotto. Trusting X: Issues in building Trusted X window systems – or – what's not trusted about X. In *Proc. of the 14th National Computer Security Conference*, volume 1, Oct. 1991.

[9] ESOP. *On safe and efficient in-vehicle information and communication systems*. Commission of the European Communities, 2008.

[10] N. Feske and C. Helmuth. Overlay window management: User interaction with multiple security domains, 2004.

[11] N. Feske and C. Helmuth. A Nitpicker's guide to a minimal-complexity secure GUI. In *Proceedings of the 21st ACSAC*, pages 85–94, Dec. 2005.

[12] Ford. Software development kit (SDK). https://developer.ford.com/develop/openxc/, 2013.

[13] S. Gansel et al. An Access Control Concept for Novel Automotive HMI Systems. Tech Report 2013/02, University of Stuttgart, IPVS, Germany, 2013.

[14] J. G. Hansen. Blink: Advanced Display Multiplexing for Virtualized Applications. In *Proceedings of the 17th NOSSDAV*, 2007.

[15] ISO 26262. *Road vehicles – Functional Safety*. ISO, Geneva, Switzerland, Nov. 2011.

[16] ISO/IEC 9594-8. *The Directory: Public-key and attribute certificate frameworks*. Switzerland, 2008.

[17] H. Janker. *Straßenverkehrsrecht: StVG, StVO, StVZO, Fahrzeug-ZVO, Fahrerlaubnis-VO, Verkehrszeichen, Bußgeldkatalog*. C.H. Beck, 2011.

[18] I. Krüger et al. Service-Based Software Development for Automotive Applications. In *Proceedings of the CONVERGENCE 2004. CTEA*, Jan. 2004.

[19] B. W. Lampson. Protection. *SIGOPS Oper. Syst. Rev.*, 8(1):18–24, Jan. 1974.

[20] M. Stümpfle and H. Kohler. Die Konnektivität als Kernmerkmal von Premium-Fahrzeugen. Xpert.press, pages 125–144. Springer Berlin Heidelberg, 2013.

[21] J. Wang, L. Zhou, and C. Tan. A BLP-Based Model for Hierarchical Organizations. In *Proc. of the 2009 Second IWCSE*, pages 456–459, 2009.

[22] E. Wilde and N. Nabholz. Access Control for Shared Resources. In *Pro. of the CIMCA-IAWTIC'06*, 2005.

APPENDIX

A. FORMAL DEFINITIONS

Definition 10. *We define the transitive operator $<_o$ that denotes whether an application has granted a given display area to another application.*
Let $s, s' \in S; o \in O; b \in B$. We define $s <_o s' \Leftrightarrow$

$$\exists s_1, ..., s_n \in S; \exists o_1, ..., o_{n-1} \in O : \qquad (10.1)$$

$$s_1 = s' \wedge s_n = s \wedge o \subseteq o_{n-1} \wedge \qquad (10.2)$$

$$\forall i : 1 \leq i < n : (s_i, o_i) \in received(b, s_{i+1}) \wedge \qquad (10.3)$$

$$\forall i : 1 \leq i < n - 2 : o_{i+1} \subseteq o_i \qquad (10.4)$$

Definition 11. *Function $add_{so} : B \times S \times S \times O \rightarrow B$ is defined as follows. Let $b, b' \in B; s, s' \in S; o \in O$. We define $b' = add_{so}(b, s, s', o) \Leftrightarrow$*

$$b'(s) = (received(b, s), granted(b, s) \cup \{(s', o)\}) \wedge \quad (11.1)$$

$$b'(s') = (received(b, s') \cup \{(s, o)\}, granted(b, s')) \wedge \quad (11.2)$$

$$[\forall s_3 \in S \backslash \{s', s\} : b'(s_3) = b(s_3)] \qquad (11.3)$$

Definition 12. *Function $del_{so} : B \times S \times S \times O \rightarrow B$ is defined as follows. Let $b, b' \in B; s, s' \in S; o \in O$. We define*

$$b' = del_{so}(b, s, s', o) \Leftrightarrow [\forall \hat{s} \in S : \hat{s} <_o s \Rightarrow \qquad (12.1)$$

$$received(b', \hat{s}) = received(b, \hat{s}) \backslash \qquad (12.2)$$
$$\{(\tilde{s}, o') \in S \times O | o' \subseteq o \wedge \hat{s} <_{o'} \tilde{s}\} \wedge$$

$$granted(b', \hat{s}) = granted(b, \hat{s}) \backslash \qquad (12.3)$$
$$\{(\tilde{s}, o') \in S \times O | o' \subseteq o \wedge \tilde{s} <_{o'} \hat{s}\}] \wedge$$

$$b'(s) = (received(b, s), granted(b, s) \backslash \{(s', o)\}) \wedge \quad (12.4)$$

$$\forall s'' \in S \backslash \{s', s\}; \forall o' \in O : o' \subseteq o \wedge s'' \neq_{o'} s \qquad (12.5)$$
$$\vee s <_o s'' \Rightarrow b'(s'') = b(s'')$$

Definition 13. *Function $add_{dr} : DR \times S \times S \rightarrow DR$ is defined as follows. Let $dr, dr' \in DR; s, s' \in S$. We define $dr' = add_{dr}(dr, s, s') \Leftrightarrow dr'(s) = dr(s) \cup \{s'\} \wedge \forall \hat{s} \in S : \hat{s} \neq s \Rightarrow dr'(\hat{s}) = dr(\hat{s})$*

Definition 14. *Function $del_{dr} : DR \times S \times S \rightarrow DR$ is defined as follows. Let $dr, dr' \in DR; s, s' \in S$. We define $dr' = del_{dr}(dr, s, s') \Leftrightarrow dr'(s) = dr(s) \backslash \{s'\} \wedge \forall \hat{s} \in S : \hat{s} \neq s \Rightarrow dr'(\hat{s}) = dr(\hat{s})$*

Next, we give formal definitions for the sequence of states and the system. We define $I^n \subset \mathbb{N}_0$ with $I^n = \{0, 1, 2, ..., n\}$.

Definition 15. *Operator $\succ$ denotes whether an element is part of a sequence of states. The set of sequences of states is a set of n-tuples defined as $X^{I^n} = \{(x_0, ..., x_i, ..., x_n) | x_i \in X \wedge i \in I^n \wedge x_i = f(i) \text{ with } f : I^n \rightarrow X\}$.*
$(x_0, x_1, ..., x_n) \in X^{I^n}$ is a sequence with $x_0 := x_0 \in X$, $x_1 := x'_1 \in X, ..., x_n := x_n^{(n)} \in X$. Let $(x_0, x_1, ..., x_n) \in X^{I^n}$. We define $x \succ (x_0, x_1, ..., x_n) \Leftrightarrow \exists i \in I^n : x = x_i$.

Based on Def. 15, we next define the sequences of requests, the sequences of states and a distinct mapping between these sequences by using transitions.

Definition 16. *For a sequence of requests $(r_0, ..., r_{n-1}) \in R^{I^{n-1}}$ the sequence of states generated by $(r_0, ..., r_{n-1})$ is given as $(v_0, v_1, ..., v_n) \in V^{I^n}$ with*
$\forall i \in I^{n-1} : v_{i+1} = trans(v_i, r_i)$.

Definition 17. *A system generated by $v_0 \in V$ is stated as $\Psi(v_0) \subset R^{I^n} \times V^{I^n}$. Let $x_r = (r_0, ..., r_{n-1}) \in R^{I^{n-1}}$, $x_v = (v_0, ..., v_n) \in V^{I^n}$. We define $(x_r, x_v) \in \Psi(v_0) \Leftrightarrow \forall i \in I^n \backslash \{0\} : v_i = trans(v_{i-1}, r_{i-1})$. Let $(v, r, v') \in V \times R \times V$, $v_0 \in V$. We define $(v, r, v') \gg \Psi(v_0) \Leftrightarrow$*

$$\exists x_r \in R^{I^{n-1}}, \exists x_v \in V^{I^n}, \exists i \in I^n \backslash \{0\} : \qquad (17.1)$$

$$(x_r, x_v) \in \Psi(v_0) \wedge v_i \succ x_v \wedge v_{i+1} \succ x_v \wedge r_i \succ x_r \wedge \quad (17.2)$$

$$(v, r, v') = (v_{i-1}, r_{i-1}, v_i). \qquad (17.3)$$

(v, r, v') is part of a system if a sequence of requests and states (17.1) exists of which v, r and v' are part of (17.2), and, a transition from state v to v' by request r (17.3) exists.

Definition 18. *$v \in V$ is a safe state $\Leftrightarrow v$ satisfies EAP and CP and DP. $(v_0, ..., v_n) \in V^{I^n}$ is a safe state sequence $\Leftrightarrow \forall i \in I^n : v_i$ is a safe state. A system $\Psi(v_0) \subset V^{I^n} \times R^{I^n}$ with $x_r \in R^{I^{n-1}}$ and $x_v = (v_0, ..., v_n) \in V^{I^n}$ is a safe system $\Leftrightarrow \forall (x_r, x_v) \in \Psi(v_0) : x_v$ is a safe sequence.*

B. PROOFS

Proof for Lemma 1

We first show (L1.1): Let $\hat{o} \in used(b, s)$ be the display area in $(cond_1)$ with $o \subseteq \hat{o}$. We have to prove:

$$o \not\subseteq \Phi(b', s) \qquad (i)$$

$$(\hat{o} \backslash o) \subseteq \Phi(b', s) \qquad (ii)$$

Due to $\hat{o} \cap o = o$, for (i) we only have to show $\hat{o} \not\subseteq \Phi(b', s)$.
  (i): Due to (11.1), we know $(s', o) \in granted(b', s)$ after a transition to state v'. Since $o \subseteq \hat{o}$, it follows $\hat{o} \cap o = o \neq \emptyset$. Thus, the condition (4.2) is no longer valid for b' which proves (i). This means, all subsets of $\hat{o}$ are not in the set of used display areas of application s in b'.
  (ii): To prove statement (ii) we have to show that display area $(\hat{o} \backslash o)$ fulfills the condition of Def. 4. Therefore we prove the following two conditions:

$$(\hat{o} \backslash o) \subseteq \Lambda(b', s) \qquad (a)$$

$$(\hat{o} \backslash o) \cap \Gamma(b', s) = \emptyset \qquad (b)$$

(a): Due to $\hat{o} \subseteq \Phi(b, s)$, we know $\hat{o} \subseteq \Lambda(b, s)$. After a transition with add_{so} to v' we conclude with (11.1) $\Lambda(b, s) = \Lambda(b', s)$. Hence, $(\hat{o} \backslash o) \subseteq \hat{o} \subseteq \Lambda(b, s) = \Lambda(b', s)$ and therefore (a) is true.
(b): We know that $\hat{o} \in used(b, s)$ is true. Since we assume EAP is satisfied in $v = (b, tr)$ we conclude $\hat{o} \cap \Gamma(b, s) = \emptyset$. With (11.1) we conclude $\Gamma(b', s) = \Gamma(b, s) \cup o$ and therefore (b) is true in state v'.

$$(\hat{o} \backslash o) \cap \Gamma(b', s) = (\hat{o} \backslash o) \cap (\Gamma(b, s) \cup o) \qquad (6.1)$$
$$= ((\hat{o} \backslash o) \cap (\Gamma(b, s))) \cup$$
$$((\hat{o} \backslash o) \cap o) \qquad \text{(Distr. law)}$$
$$= \emptyset \cup ((\hat{o} \backslash o) \cap o) = \emptyset \quad (\hat{o} \cap \Gamma(b, s) = \emptyset)$$

Therefore, we conclude statement (ii) $(\hat{o} \backslash o) \subseteq \Phi(b', s)$.
We show (L1.2): We need to prove that the display area o fulfills the conditions of (Def. 4) for b'. Therefore we show in a similar approach like in the proof of L1.1 that the following two conditions are satisfied:

$$o \subseteq \Lambda(b', s') \qquad (i)$$

$$o \cap \Gamma(b', s') = \emptyset \qquad (ii)$$

(i): We directly follow $received(b', s') = received(b, s') \cup \{o\}$ due to (11.2).

(ii): We know that $\Gamma(b, s) \cap o = \emptyset$ is valid in b. We conclude $\Gamma(b, s') \cap o = \emptyset$ from the following: We assume $\Gamma(b, s') \cap o \neq \emptyset$. Then we conclude $o \subseteq \Lambda(b, s')$ which leads to $\Gamma(b, s) \cap o \neq \emptyset$. But this is in contradiction to $\Gamma(b, s') \cap o = \emptyset$. Hence, $\Gamma(b, s') \cap o = \emptyset$ is valid. With $Def.\ 11.2$ we know $\Gamma(b', s') = \Gamma(b, s')$ and we conclude $\Gamma(b', s') \cap o = \Gamma(b, s') = \emptyset \cap o$. The sets of granted and received display areas of all other applications are unmodified due to (11.3).

Hence, the conditions of Def. 4 and therefore (L1.2) are satisfied. □

Proof for Lemma 2

We first prove (L2.1): Let $s \neq s'$ and state v satisfies EAP. In Def. 12 all display areas o' which are a subset of o are removed from the sets of received display areas of all applications depending on s according to o'. We follow $\forall \hat{s} \in S \backslash \{s\} : \Lambda(b', \hat{s}) = \Lambda(b, \hat{s}) \backslash \bigcup \{o' \in O | o' \subseteq o \wedge \hat{s} <_{o'} s\}$. This means, (4.1) is violated and the display area o' are no longer in the set of used display areas of the according applications. Hence, we can directly conclude statement (L2.1).

We prove (L2.2): Due to (R1.2), we know that $(s', o) \in granted(b, s)$ which leads to $o \subseteq \Lambda(b, s)$. Hence, (4.1) is satisfied. With (12.1) we conclude $\Gamma(b', s) = \Gamma(b, s) \backslash o$.

Next, we show $o \cap \Gamma(b', s) = \emptyset$, which means (4.2) is satisfied:

$$o \cap \Gamma(b', s) = o \cap (\Gamma(b, s) \backslash o) \quad (7.4)$$
$$= (o \cap \Gamma(b, s)) \backslash (o \cap o) \quad \text{(Distr. law)}$$
$$= (o \cap \Gamma(b, s)) \backslash o = \emptyset \quad \text{(since } o \cap \Gamma(b, s) \subseteq o\text{)}$$

Hence, we conclude statement (L2.2). □

Proof for Lemma EAP: The request r is either in RD or in RO (Def. 9). The case $r \in RD$ is trivial, since $b' = b$ due to v = v' (Def. 9 Rule 2) and changes of dr do not affect Lemma EAP. In case $r = (ra, s, s', o) \in RO$, there are the following three subcases:

(R1.1): Let $ra = append$ and $cond_1$ be fulfilled. It follows $trans(v, r) = (b', dr) \in V$ with $b' = add_{so}(b, s, s', o)$. The set of permissions and used display areas of all applications beside s and s' do not change in v' (11.3). Hence, $\forall \hat{s} \in S \backslash \{s, s'\} : \big(used(b', \hat{s}) = used(b, \hat{s})\big)$ due to $b'(\hat{s}) = b(\hat{s})$.

Since v satisfies EAP, we conclude $\forall \hat{s}, \tilde{s} \in S \backslash \{s, s'\} : \hat{s} \neq \tilde{s} \Rightarrow \Phi(b', \hat{s}) \cap \Phi(b', \tilde{s}) = \emptyset$. This means we only have to prove EAP in v' for s and s'. To this end, we show the following statements:

$$\Phi(b', s) \cap \Phi(b', s') = \emptyset \quad (i)$$
$$\forall \hat{s} \in S \backslash \{s, s'\} : \Phi(b', s) \cap \Phi(b', \hat{s}) = \emptyset \quad (ii)$$
$$\forall \hat{s} \in S \backslash \{s, s'\} : \Phi(b', s') \cap \Phi(b', \hat{s}) = \emptyset \quad (iii)$$

We prove (i), (ii) and (iii) by using Lemma 1 and 2.

(i): $\Phi(b', s) \cap \Phi(b', s')$
$$= (\Phi(b, s) \backslash o) \cap \Phi(b', s') \quad (L1.1)$$
$$= (\Phi(b, s) \backslash o) \cap (\Phi(b, s') \cup o) \quad (L1.2)$$
$$= ((\Phi(b, s) \backslash o) \cap \Phi(b, s')) \quad \text{(Dist. law)}$$
$$\quad \cup ((\Phi(b, s) \cap o) \backslash (o \cap o))$$
$$= ((\Phi(b, s) \backslash o) \cap \Phi(b, s')) \cup (o \backslash o)$$
$$= ((\Phi(b, s) \backslash o) \cap \Phi(b, s')) \quad (R1.1)$$

$$= (\Phi(b, s) \cap \Phi(b, s')) \backslash (o \cap \Phi(b, s')) \quad \text{(Dist. law)}$$
$$= \emptyset \backslash (o \cap \Phi(b, s')) = \emptyset \quad \text{(EAP)}$$

(ii): Let $s'' \in S \backslash \{s, s'\}$ be arbitrary, then follows:

$\Phi(b', s) \cap \Phi(b', s'')$
$$= (\Phi(b, s) \backslash o) \cap \Phi(b', s'') \quad (L1.1)$$
$$= (\Phi(b, s) \backslash o) \cap \Phi(b, s'') \quad (11.3)$$
$$= (\Phi(b, s) \backslash \Phi(b, s'')) \backslash (o \cap \Phi(b, s'')) \quad \text{(Dist. law)}$$
$$= \emptyset \backslash (o \cap \Phi(b, s'')) = \emptyset \quad \text{(EAP)}$$

(iii): Let $s'' \in S \backslash \{s, s'\}$ be arbitrary, then follows:

$\Phi(b', s') \cap \Phi(b', s'')$
$$= (\Phi(b, s') \backslash o) \cap \Phi(b', s'') \quad (L1.2)$$
$$= (\Phi(b, s') \backslash o) \cap \Phi(b, s'')$$
$$= (\Phi(b, s') \backslash \Phi(b, s'')) \cup (o \cap \Phi(b, s'')) \quad (11.3)$$
$$= \emptyset \cup (o \cap \Phi(b, s'')) = \emptyset \quad \text{(Dist. law, EAP)}$$

(R1.2): Let $ra = discard$ and $cond_2$ be satisfied. Hence, $trans(v, r) = (b', dr) \in V$ with $b' = del_{so}(b, s', s, o)$. In this case, we have to consider those applications which are in relation according to a display area $o' \subseteq o$ (12.5). We know with (L2.1) that $\forall \hat{s} \in S \backslash \{s\} : \Phi(b', \hat{s}) \subseteq \Phi(b, \hat{s})$. Since state v satisfies EAP we only have to prove EAP for applications s and s' in state v', namely:

$$\Phi(b', s) \cap \Phi(b', s') = \emptyset \quad (i)$$
$$\forall \hat{s} \in S \backslash \{s, s'\} : \Phi(b', s) \cap \Phi(b', \hat{s}) = \emptyset \quad (ii)$$
$$\forall \hat{s} \in S \backslash \{s, s'\} : \Phi(b', s') \cap \Phi(b', \hat{s}) = \emptyset \quad (iii)$$

(i): $\Phi(b', s') \cap \Phi(b', s)$
$$= (\Phi(b, s') \backslash o) \cap \Phi(b', s) \quad (L2.1)$$
$$= (\Phi(b, s') \backslash o) \cap (\Phi(b, s) \cup o) \quad (L2.2)$$
$$= ((\Phi(b, s') \backslash o) \cap \Phi(b, s))$$
$$\quad \cup ((\Phi(b, s') \cap o) \backslash (o \cap o)) \quad \text{(Distr. law)}$$
$$= ((\Phi(b, s') \backslash o) \cap \Phi(b, s)) \cup ((\Phi(b, s') \cap o) \backslash o)$$
$$= ((\Phi(b, s') \backslash o) \cap \Phi(b, s)) \quad ((\Phi(b, s') \cap o) \subseteq o)$$
$$= (\Phi(b, s') \cap \Phi(b, s)) \backslash (\Phi(b, s) \cap o) \quad \text{(Distr. law)}$$
$$= \emptyset \backslash (\Phi(b, s) \cap o) = \emptyset \quad \text{(EAP)}$$

(ii): Let $\hat{s} \in S \backslash \{s, s'\}$ be arbitrary then follows:

$\Phi(b', s) \cap \Phi(b', \hat{s})$
$$= (\Phi(b, s) \backslash o) \cap \Phi(b', \hat{s}) \quad (L2.2)$$
$$= (\Phi(b, s) \backslash o) \cap \Phi(b, \hat{s}) \quad (12.2)$$
$$= (\Phi(b, s) \backslash \Phi(b, \hat{s})) \backslash (o \cap \Phi(b, \hat{s})) \quad \text{(Distr. law)}$$
$$= \emptyset \backslash (o \cap \Phi(b, \hat{s})) = \emptyset \quad \text{(EAP)}$$

(iii): Let $\hat{s} \in S \backslash \{s, s'\}$ be arbitrary then follows:

$\Phi(b', s') \cap \Phi(b', \hat{s})$
$$= (\Phi(b, s') \backslash o) \cap \Phi(b', \hat{s}) \quad (L1.2)$$
$$= (\Phi(b, s') \backslash o) \cap \Phi(b, \hat{s}) \quad (12.1)$$
$$= (\Phi(b, s') \backslash \Phi(b, \hat{s})) \cup (o \cap \Phi(b, \hat{s})) \quad \text{(Distr. law)}$$
$$= \emptyset \cup (o \cap \Phi(b, \hat{s})) = \emptyset \quad \text{(EAP)}$$

(otherwise): Since $v' = v$ and v satisfy EAP, v' also satisfies EAP. □

Monitor Placement for Large-Scale Systems

Nirupama Talele
Penn State University
IST,University Park
State College, PA-16802
nrt123@psu.edu

Jason Teutsch
Penn State University
IST,University Park
State College, PA-16802
teutsch@cse.psu.edu

Robert Erbacher
Army Research Lab
2800 Powder Mill Rd
Adelphi, MD-20783
robert.f.erbacher.civ@mail.mil

Trent Jaeger
Penn State University
IST,University Park
State College, PA-16802
tjaeger@cse.psu.edu

ABSTRACT

System administrators employ network monitors, such as traffic analyzers, network intrusion prevention systems, and firewalls, to protect the network's hosts from remote adversaries. The problem is that vulnerabilities are caused primarily by errors in the host software and/or configuration, but modern hosts are too complex for system administrators to understand, limiting monitoring to known attacks. Researchers have proposed automated methods to compute network monitor placements, but these methods also fail to model attack paths within hosts and/or fail to scale beyond tens of hosts. In this paper, we propose a method to compute network monitor placements that leverages commonality in available access control policies across hosts to compute network monitor placement for large-scale systems. We introduce an equivalence property, called *flow equivalence*, which reduces the size of the placement problem to be proportional to the number of unique host configurations. This process enables us to solve mediation placement problems for thousands of hosts with access control policies containing of thousands of rules in seconds (less than 125 for a network of 9500 hosts). Our method enables administrators to place network monitors in large-scale networks automatically, leveraging the actual host configuration, to detect and prevent network-borne threats.

Categories and Subject Descriptors

D.4.6 [**Operating Systems**]: Security and Protection—*Access Control*

Keywords

Monitor Placement; Information flow graph scalability; Large scale systems

1. INTRODUCTION

System administrators are responsible for the security of all the hosts in their networks. They aim to prevent the software on their hosts from being compromised and to protect critical organizational data from leakage and/or unauthorized modification. System administrators often leverage *network monitoring* in the form of firewalls [9], traffic analysis tools [3], and network intrusion prevention systems [34] to block attacks. Such tools examine packets destined for networked processes in the host and packets produced by those processes to detect malicious input data and leaked secret data, respectively.

The problem for system administrators is to determine how to leverage network monitoring to protect their hosts effectively. There are two challenges. First, system administrators must determine where to place network monitoring. A naive approach would be to monitor at each networked device, but monitoring incurs a cost, both towards deployment (e.g., configuring monitoring) and in terms of performance (e.g., overhead of monitoring). Second, system administrators must determine which rules to enforce at each monitor. While system administrators often leverage community knowledge (e.g., Snort rule bases) about known malicious behavior to detect or block attacks at monitors, these rules may not pertain to that monitoring location or be specific to different configurations, and therefore miss some attacks. Also, system administrators must be careful when modifying such rule bases to avoid introducing false positives.

Researchers have explored methods to both reason about adversary attack paths and to place monitoring to cover all known paths. Attack trees [21] and attack graphs [33, 29, 1] model possible actions of adversaries that may lead to the compromise of a valuable resource. However, building either attack trees or attack graphs currently requires knowledge about the likely vulnerabilities on individual hosts, which may be incomplete (i.e., previously-unknown vulnerabilities may be missed) and brittle (i.e., vulnerabilities may be patched). Alternatively, researchers have developed methods to place security monitoring to block or limit adversary access to prevent attacks based on classical problems [27, 30, 17]. These methods focus on only one layer of the system, such as the network, a single host, or a single program because the size of the graphs becomes prohibitive. A recent work that reasons about data flows in distributed systems only handles systems with tens of hosts [23]. As a result, such methods are not usable for organizations with several networks containing many hosts.

In this paper, our goal is to develop a method that enables the placement of network monitoring for the actual threats present in an organization-wide deployment. This work is motivated by Talele *et al.* who build summaries of individual hosts to improve scalability to networks of tens of hosts with fine-grained access control policies [37], such as the SELinux reference policy that contains over 50,000 rules [28]. We identify several insights that enable additional, significant improvements in scalability. First, many hosts are launched from the same OS distribution, which today come pre-configured with an access control policy, consequently all hosts running that OS distribution have the *same access control policy*. Second, many hosts assume the same "role" in an organization, such as network (e.g., DHCP or DNS) server, web server, database, web client, often resulting in the *same information flows per host*. Third, we find that network connections among hosts are often equivalent from a security standpoint, in which case we obtain the *same threats for hosts with equivalent network connections*. Using these insights, we define three equivalence relations for hosts that enable merging of equivalent host graphs. Further, we prove that one equivalence property, called *flow equivalence*, reduces the size of the placement problem to be proportional to the number of unique host configurations, rather than the number of hosts.

We use these equivalence properties to examine how to produce network monitor placements in large-scale, heterogeneous networks. First, we develop a method for computing merged graphs from network configurations, host access control policies, and target applications of the hosts. We show that solutions can be produced for the merged graphs that are equivalent to those that would be computed from the original graph using standard algorithms. Second, we demonstrate the impact of our approach on a heterogeneous network configuration [25], finding that it works well for all types of networks except ad hoc (i.e., where connections cannot be predicted). In this example, merging enables a significant reduction in the sizes of graphs, from millions of nodes to a few thousand, enabling network monitor placements to be computed in 1-2 minutes, where the entire process of generating the merged systems and computing placements takes 10-40 minutes. While we do not produce specific monitor placement code, we produce the placement of network monitoring and the associated security requirements, which correspond approximately to network monitoring rules. Generating specific network monitor rules is future work.

In this work, we make the following contributions.

- We define three equivalence relations among hosts, called *concrete*, *label*, and *flow equivalence*, that enable all hosts in an equivalence class to be represented by a single *merged* host in a mediator placement problem without loss of information flow semantics.

- We show that by using these equivalence relations the size of a mediator placement problem is dependent on the number of unique host configurations, not the number of hosts. Thus, networks with significant redundancy among host configurations will see significant benefits.

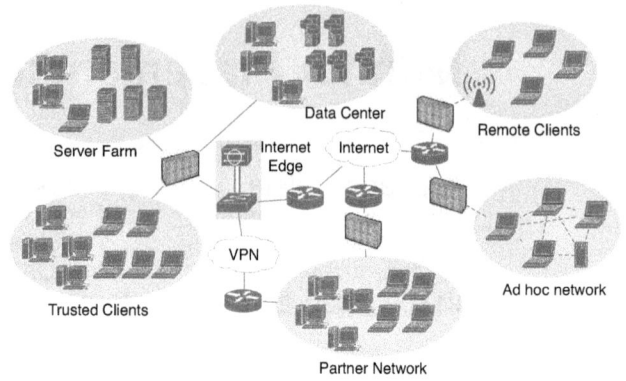

Figure 1: Example Organization's System: Containing six networks, two server and four client networks (one is wireless and one is ad hoc)

- We use the method to show that graphs representing the information flows in networks containing nearly 10,000 hosts can be compressed from millions of nodes and edges to just a few thousand without any loss of information flow semantics. Using this method, monitor placement for such networks can be computed in slightly over 2 minutes.

The rest of the paper is as follows. In Section 2, we identify the challenges and goals in network monitor placement. In Section 3, we review the formal model for reasoning about network monitor placement and highlight the challenges in solving the problem. In Section 4, we outline the proposed approach to producing network monitor placements in large-scale networks and define three equivalence relations for merging host information flow models. In Section 5, we outline a method for computing network monitor placements that leverages the merging offered by these equivalence classes. In Section 6, we evaluate the method analytically and experimentally. In Section 7, we compare our approach to related work. We conclude by summarizing our approach and results in Section 8.

2. EXAMPLE SCENARIO

Figure 1 shows an example of an organization's computing system. In this example, the organization deploys a set of web applications across six networks, two server networks and four client networks. While the exact deployments vary, the server-side deployments of the web applications generally utilize edge servers (e.g., firewalls, load balancers, etc.) that forward requests to one or more web servers (e.g., Apache, IIS), which may then leverage application servers (e.g., Tomcat) to implement the core application functionality by retrieving the necessary data from database servers. The server-side deployments are almost exclusively wired networks with a well defined network topology and extensive connectivity among the server layers.

On the other hand, the clients may access server applications through more varied network configurations. Client networks may be wired or wireless, and the wireless networks may be 802.11, cellular, or ad hoc (e.g., MANETs). Clients on organization networks are protected by firewalls and may be isolated by technologies, such as VLANs, but otherwise the structure of such networks is relatively flat.

For clients outside organizational networks, organizations often offer their employees services to access internal applications (e.g., VPNs).

Modern organizations often control the configuration of their internal hosts. For convenient management, it is often common for server hosts performing the same task to be configured identically. For example, all web servers may be configured using the same OS distribution and many may support the same web applications to enable load balancing. In addition, while organizational clients may be deployed on a variety of platforms, including traditional hosts (e.g., desktops and laptops) and a variety of new devices (e.g., phones, tablets, etc.), organizations often control the applications (and versions) that run on these devices to ease management as well. In many cases, client users are not allowed to download new applications to organizational machines.

System administrators are concerned with a variety of threats to the confidentiality, integrity, and availability of their application processing throughout their organization. Threats may originate externally, from other internal networks, and from hosts within the same network. While external hosts may be treated as fully untrusted, our particular interest is in tracking attacks that may be propagated from within organizational networks. A common problem is that unprivileged processes on one host are compromised and then used as a stepping stone to more advanced attacks compromising security-critical hosts that impact all hosts on the network (e.g., a Windows domain controller). Thus, we aim to account for data flows among processes on hosts, as well as data flows among hosts across entire organizations.

In this work, we propose to develop automated methods to place network monitors to log and/or block unsafe communications for large-scale (organizational) networks. Conceptually, the goal is to produce a minimal cost monitor placement that blocks all access to vulnerabilities (i.e., no false negatives), that does not block any legitimate functionality (i.e., no false positives), and does not include any spurious monitoring (i.e., no unnecessary overhead). In practice, such goals are ideal, but experience has shown that false positives must be prevented, while spurious monitoring and false negatives must be minimized.

3. MEDIATOR PLACEMENT PROBLEM

The problem of determining where to place network monitoring to block or log all possible attack paths is an instance of the *mediator placement problem* [18, 30]. The mediator placement problem aims to resolve all information flow errors, as defined in an information flow model, such as the one below (adopted from Talele *et al.* [37]).

DEFINITION 1. *An* information flow model, $\mathcal{I} = (\mathcal{G}, \mathcal{L}, \mathcal{M})$, *consists of the following concepts:*

1. *A directed data flow graph $G = (V, E)$ consisting of a set of nodes V connected by edges E.*

2. *A lattice $\mathcal{L} = \{L, \preceq\}$. For any two labels $l_i, l_j \in L$, $l_i \preceq l_j$ means that l_i 'can flow to' l_j.*

3. *A label mapping function $M : V \rightarrow \mathcal{P}^L$ where $\mathcal{P}^L$ is the power set of L (i.e., each node is mapped either to a set of labels in L or to $\emptyset$).*

4. *The lattice imposes security constraints on the information flows enabled by the data flow graph. Each*

pair $u, v \in V$ s.t. $[u \hookrightarrow_G v \wedge (\exists l_u \in M(u), l_v \in M(v). \; l_u \npreceq_{\mathcal{L}} l_v)]$, *where $\hookrightarrow_G$ means there is a path from u (source) to v (sink) in G, represents an* information flow error.

In this model, the possible data flows are edges that propagate labels representing the security requirements on system data among nodes that represent system resources (subjects and objects). The lattice of labels represents the legal flows of labeled data that every operation of the system must satisfy. While lattice policies are traditionally associated with multilevel security [5, 6], more general policies are possible, such as policies constructed from sets of individual security requirements [19, 42] that we will leverage in this paper. When data with incompatible labels reach the same node, an information flow error results. It has been shown that information flow errors [24, 16, 32, 8] can be found automatically using such a model.

A solution that resolves all information flow errors mediates all paths to those errors by imposing security requirements (i.e., labels required by the sink). An *edge mediator* (or simply, mediator), $R = ((u, v), l)$, where $(u, v) \in E$ is an edge and $l \in L$ is the label of the data propagated on that edge. In general, the *mediator placement problem* is to find the minimal cost placement of mediators that resolve all errors in an information flow model.

Researchers have explored methods for solving the mediator placement problem to monitor security in networks [27], hosts [23, 30], and individual programs [18, 13, 20]. These techniques convert the operations authorized by network policies, network topology, host policies, and program code, respectively, into *data flow graphs*. They then identify threats and security requirements of the system, define the legal information flows as a *lattice* of labels representing these threats and security requirements, and define a *label mapping function* to associate the threats and security requirements with their sources and sinks, respectively. The security requirements at sinks are mostly domain-specific, and may be added by OS distributors and/or system administrators. Researchers have demonstrated that the mediator placement problem can be reduced to well-known graph problems, such as directed multicut (i.e., graph cut for multiple pairs of terminals) and vertex cover. Although these problems are NP-complete, several greedy algorithms are available (e.g., union the solution to individual cut problems). In fact, the equivalence between such problems has been shown formally [18].

The main limitation of the above approaches is scalability. Organizations may consist of thousands of hosts. In addition, each host may run many processes each with complex interactions. The policy that governs how Linux processes may legally communicate contains tens of thousands of rules [28]. Finally, individual programs also implement complex data flows. As a result, most prior methods for solving mediator placement problems only reason about one level of the system, such as the network [27], hosts [23, 30], or individual programs [13, 20, 18]. When researchers consider all these layers, the problem was limited to a small number of machines [23]. Talele *et al.* proposed a method whereby summaries of individual hosts are produced [37], yet only problems consisting of tens of hosts could be solved. Our goal is to develop methods for reasoning about organizational networks in their entirety.

4. MERGING REDUNDANT HOSTS

The key to placing network monitors in large-scale networks is removing the redundancy from instances of the information flow model of Definition 1. In this section, we leverage the insight that there is potentially a significant amount of redundancy among hosts. The commonality assumption is based on the understanding of various information available on the corporate and university networks studied. Using this insight, we propose three, progressively more ambitious equivalence relationships among hosts, *concrete*, *label*, and *flow equivalence*, that enable the merging of hosts that satisfy those relations.

4.1 Redundant Host Information Flows

We make the observation that in a distributed system, the system is composed from a set of interconnected hosts. Thus, we distinguish the contributions to the system information flow model of each host as a *host information flow model* (HIFM), where a HIFM for host i is defined as $\mathcal{I}_i = (G_i, \mathcal{L}, M_i)$, where $G_i = (V_i, E_i)$, security lattice $\mathcal{L}$ and label mappings $M_i : V_i \rightarrow \mathcal{P}^L$.

Viewing a system's single host at a time also requires a distinction of input and output between hosts. Input nodes are the nodes in a HIFM's data-flow graph that only receive input from nodes outside the data-flow graph, and output nodes are nodes in a HIFM's data-flow graph that only send output to nodes outside the data-flow graph. Formally, an edge (u, v) is an *input edge* for an HIFM data-flow graph G_i if $v \in V_i$ and $u \notin V_i$. v is then said to be an *input node* for host graph i, and for all edges (u, v) for an input node v imply that $u \notin V_i$. The set of input nodes of G_i are $I_i \subseteq V_i$. Second, an edge (v, u) is an *output edge* for G_i if $v \in V_i$ and $u \notin V_i$. v is then said to be an *output node* for G_i, and for all edges (v, u) for an output node v imply that $u \notin V_i$. The set of output nodes of G_i are $O_i \subseteq V_i$. The combination of input and output edges and nodes are called *I/O edges* and *I/O nodes*, respectively.

Our goal is to identify HIFMs that are equivalent with respect to the mediator placement problem. Intuitively, two HIFMs are equivalent if any equivalent mediator placement will either resolve all the information flow errors in both HIFMs or will fail to resolve at least one information flow error. If so, we find that we can *merge* the two HIFMs into one merged HIFM that represents all the information flows of both, reducing the size of the data-flow graph by removing one host sub graph. In some cases, some effort must be undertaken to ensure that the outputs produced by the merged HIFM is equivalent to that of the individual nodes. We discuss these requirements below, but detail the merging methods for each equivalence relation in Section 5.3.

We find that there is a significant redundancy among hosts in conventional systems because many hosts are now deployed from the same image. For example, many organizations produce a master image for hosts with specific roles in the organization, such as application-specific servers (e.g., web server and database) and employee clients. Using a single master image makes it easier to install hosts and also gives administrators more control over the security of the hosts.

From our perspective, the main impact of the use of master images is that the security policies of several hosts may be identical, potentially resulting in the same information flows. In modern systems, many OS distributions include a mandatory access control (MAC) policy [28, 4, 35, 41]. Researchers have previously shown that MAC policies define the possible data flows on a host [38, 16]. If the images are the same, then they will implement the same firewall policy dictating the I/O of the host. For hosts deployed for the same purpose (e.g., a generic client host or a specific server application), then the firewall policies will often allow only the same I/O. As a result, we find that many hosts implement the same data flows. We define the *data-flow equivalence* relation below, which we will use as a foundation for the later equivalence classes used for merging below.

DEFINITION 2. *Two HIFMs* $\mathcal{I}_1 = (G_1, \mathcal{L}, M_1)$ *and* $\mathcal{I}_2 = (G_2, \mathcal{L}, M_2)$ *are said to be* data-flow equivalent $\mathcal{I}_1 \equiv_{df} \mathcal{I}_2$ *if:*

1. **Same data-flow graph**: *There is a graph isomorphism between G_1 and G_2. Implied by the graph isomorphism is a bijection $f : V_1 \rightarrow V_2$, which maps nodes from graph G_1 to G_2. A node in one graph that is bijectively-mapped to a node in the other graph is said to* correspond.

2. **Corresponding inputs**: *For every input node $i \in I_1$ in G_1 the corresponding node $f(i) = j$ that is an input node in G_2, such that $j \in I_2$.*

3. **Corresponding outputs**: *For every output node $o \in O_1$ in G_1 the corresponding node $f(o) = p$ that is an output node in G_2, such that $p \in O_2$.*

It is easy to see that the data-flow equivalence relation reflexive, symmetric, and transitive, so it is an equivalence relation.

The key insight in this paper is that if many hosts have the same data flows, then many will face different versions of essentially the same mediator placement problem. While different HIFMs with the same data flow graphs may still have different label mappings in general, we find that in many cases installations that are configured for same application can apply the same label mapping. In addition, if the labels are distinct, applications dictate that label mappings be applied on the same subjects and objects in the MAC policy (i.e., the same nodes in the data flow graph). The rest of this section, we leverage this idea to define three equivalence relations for HIFMs that imply that the hosts have the same impact on the solution of the mediator placement problem.

4.2 Concrete Equivalence

We begin by defining a basic equivalence relation between HIFMs that serves as a foundation for the more subtle equivalence relations defined later. Intuitively, the idea is that if two hosts have the same data-flow graphs, label mapping functions, and the same input and output connections, then they will produce the same information flows along all corresponding edges. We call this *concrete equivalence* because the HIFM of the two hosts must be identical.

DEFINITION 3. *Two HIFMs* $\mathcal{I}_1 = (G_1, \mathcal{L}, M_1)$ *and* $\mathcal{I}_2 = (G_2, \mathcal{L}, M_2)$ *are said to satisfy* concrete equivalence $\mathcal{I}_1 \equiv_c \mathcal{I}_2$ *if:*

1. $\mathcal{I}_1$ *and* $\mathcal{I}_2$ *satisfy data-flow equivalence.*

2. **Corresponding input edges**: *If $i_1 \in I_1$, $(u, i_1) \in E$ and $f(i_1) = i_2$, then $(u, i_2) \in E$.*

3. **Corresponding mappings**: *If $M_1(v_1) = L$ and $f(v_1) = v_2$, then $M_2(v_2) = L$.*

4. **Corresponding output edges**: *If $o_1 \in O_1$, $(o_1, v) \in E$ and $f(o_1) = o_2$, then $(o_2, v) \in E$.*

This definition places many restrictions on equivalent hosts: two hosts have the same data flow graph, I/O nodes and edges, and, label mapping function. That is these are hosts that enforce the same security policies (same data flow), configured within the same network to the same other hosts (same I/O), and are applied to the same application security requirements (same label mapping). Clearly, in this case, these two hosts will have the same information flow error paths (since all the paths are the same).

Finally, note that the requirement for output equivalence can be relaxed. HIFMs that satisfy concrete equivalence requirements 1-3 above will always produce data of the same label at the corresponding output nodes. Thus, we can merge two HIFMs with different output edges by unioning these edges to the merged HIFM. HIFMs that satisfy only concrete equivalence requirements 1-3 are said to satisfy *concrete input equivalence*.

Example: Suppose two web servers have the same input connections (from edge servers and databases) and output connections (with databases and edge servers). If they also enforce the same MAC policy, then they satisfy concrete equivalence and can be represented by a single host sub graph. If the web servers had different output connections, then could still be merged because they satisfy concrete input equivalence.

4.3 Label Equivalence

While concrete equivalence will enable merging of hosts in the same network, it is not suitable for merging hosts in different networks. In that case, the hosts do not have the same concrete connections in the network topology. We find that two HIFMs that receive data of the same label at corresponding input nodes, also produce equivalent information flow errors. We call this *label equivalence*.

DEFINITION 4. *Two HIFMs $\mathcal{I}_1 = (G_1, \mathcal{L}, M_1)$ and $\mathcal{I}_2 = (G_2, \mathcal{L}, M_2)$ are said to satisfy* label equivalence $\mathcal{I}_1 \equiv_l \mathcal{I}_2$ *if:*

1. *$\mathcal{I}_1$ and $\mathcal{I}_2$ satisfy data-flow equivalence.*

2. **Equivalent input mappings**: *If $M_1(i_1) = L$ and $f(i_1) = i_2$, then $M_2(i_2) = L$.*

3. **Corresponding mappings**: *If $M_1(v_1) = L'$ and $f(v_1) = v_2$, then $M_2(v_2) = L'$.*

In this case the main difference between concrete input equivalence is that we replace the corresponding input edges by equivalent input label mappings (requirement 2). This implies that if the labels of the data received at the input node is known and is same at each input, then the two HIFMs satisfy information-flow equivalence. In this case, the input labels, data flows, and label mappings are the same, so the information flow error paths will be the same.

Example: To understand when this would be applicable consider the following case. Suppose clients in two different offices depend on the same services (DHCP, DNS, etc.) administered by the same trusted party and are limited to the same set of web applications. In this case, the labels of the data that can be received by these clients could be determined in advance. Assuming that the two clients further enforce the same MAC policy and host firewall policy (e.g., use the same OS distribution) and run the same internal applications over the same data (i.e., same label mappings), then these clients satisfy label equivalence.

4.4 Flow Equivalence

While label equivalence abstracts hosts from their specific network connections, hosts have to enforce exactly the same security requirements (label mappings) against exactly the same threats (input labels). However, in many cases, the same programs may be used for different deployments, where we know that may face threats at the same input location, but the exact nature of the threat may vary (i.e., input label may differ). In addition, the exact security requirements that a program may need to enforce may also vary although the program must still defend itself against threats from the same paths (i.e., label mapping may differ). In this section, we show that HIFMs can be equivalent even if the specific label mappings do not match; instead, only the sources and sinks of information flow errors must match.

The intuition is that external threats are received at input nodes, and the question is simply whether two hosts have information flow errors at the same sinks, regardless of the specific labels mapped to input nodes or sinks. If so, the hosts' HIFMs still have information flow errors along the same path (see Definition 1, item 4).

Conceptually, the key insight is that information flow errors are not borne of specific labels, but of the paths that lead to errors. If the corresponding paths lead to errors, then corresponding mediator placements will resolve those errors. The actual label of the mediator can be determined later. Based on this insight, we define *flow equivalence* between HIFMs.

DEFINITION 5. *Two HIFMs $\mathcal{I}_1 = (G_1, \mathcal{L}, M_1)$ and $\mathcal{I}_2 = (G_2, \mathcal{L}, M_2)$ are said to satisfy* flow equivalence $\mathcal{I}_1 \equiv_f \mathcal{I}_2$ *if:*

1. *$\mathcal{I}_1$ and $\mathcal{I}_2$ satisfy data-flow equivalence.*

2. **Corresponding info flow errors**: *If node $u_1 \in V_1$ is a source of an information flow error at $v_1 \in V_1$ if and only if the corresponding node $f(u_1) = u_2 \in V_2$ is a source of an information flow error at the corresponding node $f(v_1) = v_2 \in V_2$.*

Flow equivalence is the first equivalence class for which some non-trivial computation is necessary to validate equivalence. In theory, computing all the sources of constraint violations could be expensive[1], but there are several factors that mitigate this expense. First, we only need to focus on input nodes as sources, as other errors could be computed in advance. In practice, input nodes form a small fraction of the number of nodes in a host's data-flow graph. Second, we compute the paths after the host graphs are summarized, which already eliminated spurious paths [37].

Example: Suppose two web servers implement two different web applications on behalf of their clients. The labels of the application data are l_1 and l_2, respectively. Note that the web servers must protect their application data from untrusted clients, whose label c is below (recall that we are focusing on integrity) that of the application data $c < l_1$ and $c < l_2$. If the two web servers are deployed using the same OS distribution and web server, the untrusted clients will submit requests through corresponding input nodes in the two servers (sources), leading to information flow errors (as $c < l_1$ and $c < l_2$) in the corresponding web applications

---

[1]Information flow errors can be detected in linear time in the worst case [31], but identifying all sources that may cause all errors is $O(|V| * |E|)$ in worst-case.

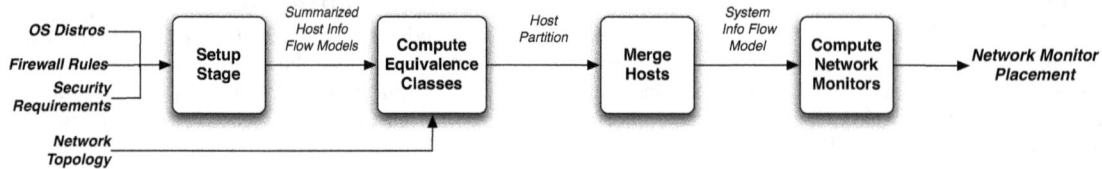

Figure 2: Network Monitor Placement Method

(sinks). Since such information flow errors in both servers can be resolved anywhere along the corresponding paths, the corresponding mediator placement can resolve both errors. That is, if the merged HIFM mediator is $((u, v)l)$ this can be mapped to respective mediators $((u_1, v_1)l_1)$ and $((u_2, v_2)l_2)$ for the web servers. Thus for networks with diverse configurations, we can still perform merging, since the flow equivalence is not based on the concrete connections and labels. Our method boils down the minimal required constraint for information flow error equivalence. In hosts where we don't have information flow error equivalence, merging is not feasible in those cases and have to be solved separately.

Reduction in mediation placement problem size. One key question is what the impact of flow equivalence is on the size of the mediation placement problem. In theory, the size of the merged network is the same as the number of flow-equivalence classes of hosts, as each host in an equivalence class can be represented by a single HIFM. In practice, flow equivalence dictate that any hosts with the same MAC policy (OS distribution), firewall policy, and target application(s) has the potential of being merged. Thus, as described above, all web servers hosted on the same OS distribution are candidates for equivalence.

4.5 Leveraging Network Mediation

Merging individual HIFMs based on flow equivalence provides the potential for the greatest reduction of the three relations, but it does not take into account the protection that can be provided by the network nodes on paths to hosts. Suppose that a network node provides the data to a set of web server hosts, if the web servers all satisfy flow equivalence, then a mediator may be placed in each of the web server hosts at the corresponding edges. However, since the network node is on the data flow path to the web server hosts, we could place a single mediator at the network node obviating the need for the per host mediation. A naive application of flow equivalence will lead to a larger number of mediators by not utilizing network nodes effectively.

The fundamental problem is that flow equivalence enables us to merge a set of hosts that are in different networks. If one of the hosts is in a network that lacks the ability to do network mediation, then mediators will be placed inside the merged host and be applied to *all* hosts represented by the merged host, including those hosts that have network nodes capable of the required mediation. As a result, we will produce a worse solution than we would without the merging.

Fortunately, there is a simple solution to this problem. Instead of merging based solely on hosts, we can include the nodes for the network devices that may provide mediation in the HIFM's data flow graph. Thus, if the network deployments differ in their mediation, then the hosts will not

be merged, enabling utilization of network mediation for all hosts where it is possible.

Of course, the network nodes must be capable of performing whatever mediation is required. In practice, a network node must be capable of changing the security requirements of the network data to satisfy the needs of the sink. As such security requirements are expressed in terms of labels, likewise mediation capabilities can be defined in terms of the labels that can be achieved by nodes. In this work, we associate each network node and host with a lattice label defining the LUB of mediation, called the *capability label*, where each capability label is in the set of lattice labels of the system information flow model. In theory, the node can mediate to any label dominated by its capability label.

5. PLACING NETWORK MONITORS

In this section, we discuss how to use the equivalence relations defined above to compute a network monitor placement from host information flow models and network topologies for the system. Figure 2 shows the steps in our proposed method. First, we describe a setup stage that produces the host information flow models from security policies and network topologies, using an existing method to produce summaries. Second, we partition the set of summarized HIFMs into equivalence classes using the three types of equivalence relations from the previous section. Third, given a set of equivalence classes and the network topologies for the system, we produce a merged system information flow model. Fourth, we leverage known methods for solving the mediator placement problem for the merged system information flow graph.

5.1 Setup Stage: Host Summaries

Our method produces network monitor placements from host information flow models and network topologies. However, since hosts are not configured directly as host information flow models, these have to be produced. Fortunately, researchers have developed several automated methods for computing elements of the information flow model. While some manual configuration of host information flow models may still be required, the task can be significantly reduced. In addition, host information flow models of modern OS distributions may be quite complex themselves, so we leverage previously proposed methods for producing summarized host information flow models, which we call *host summaries*.

Host information flow models consist of a data flow graph, lattice, and label mapping function as specified in Definition 1, but automated techniques are available to generate each of the above elements. First, modern OS distributions now provide pre-configured software packages, host firewall policies, and mandatory access control (MAC) policies from which data flow graphs can be constructed[2]. One issue is connecting the data flows between network nodes and the host processes, but some OS distributions (e.g., RedHat) leverage labeled networking [10] (e.g., Secmark [22]) and researchers have explored methods to relate access control policies to system call sites [15]. Network topologies express flows among network nodes.

Second, instead of using lattices to express traditional multilevel security policies [5, 6], we envision using lattices to represent security requirements as sets of labels, as in Decentralized Information Flow Control [14] (DIFC). Security requirements are predicates on nodes that must be satisfied to prevent compromise. For example, one security requirement would be a limit for the number of allowed entries in an HTTP Range query at the web server. Such a requirement can be encoded as a label, where only data satisfying that requirement may be assigned that label. Our approach is agnostic to the source of security requirements. Some requirements may be derived from known vulnerabilities and others from software testing.

In general, all web servers may want to enforce the HTTP Range requirement highlighted above, so that label can be mapped to any web server in any deployment. Thus, we can automatically assign this label mapping to any host targeted as a web server deployment. However, some security requirements may be deployment-specific. For example, many organizations deploy their own custom software on OS distributions, such as web applications. Fortunately, MAC policies support such customizations. For example, system administrators use the `mod_selinux` module for Apache to generate separate web application processes with distinct permissions. However, the system administrators (or web application developers) will have to assign specific labels for their web application, if the web application has any special data requirements. This is the main manual effort in setup.

Finally, researchers have found that host information flow models themselves can be large, with thousands of nodes and edges. This observation inspired Talele *et al.* to produce *host summaries* that retain only the nodes and edges necessary to preserve the attack path semantics of the original host information flow model [37]. Such summarization is analogous to building function summaries for static program analysis [7]. For some server host configurations, they found that they could reduce the number of nodes by 65-80% and the number of edges by approximately 85%.

5.2 Compute Equivalence Classes

Given the HIFM summaries computed above, we aim to partition these summaries into equivalence classes using the equivalence relations defined in Section 4 and then merge the equivalent hosts. The challenge is that not all the equivalence classes are the same from a merging perspective. Concrete equivalence requires the fewest graph changes, followed by label equivalence, and finally flow equivalence. Thus, we want to design a method that prefers concrete equivalence to others, where possible, but still enables subsequent merging using label and flow equivalence.

---

[2]The typical method is to create a node for each subject and object and edges as follows: for each authorized read-like operation by subject u upon object v create edge (v, u) and for each authorized write-like operation by subject u upon object v create edge (u, v).

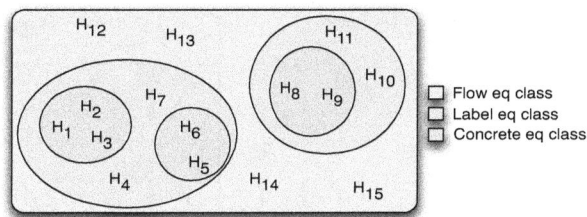

Figure 3: Equivalence Class Dominance: Flow Equivalence creates classes that are a superset of Label Equivalence, which in turn creates classes that are a superset of Concrete Equivalence

We find that the three proposed equivalence relations satisfy a set-dominance relation themselves.

DEFINITION 6. *If two hosts information flow models $\mathcal{I}_1$ and $\mathcal{I}_2$ are concrete-equivalent $\mathcal{I}_1 \equiv_c \mathcal{I}_2$ (i.e., they belong to the same concrete equivalence class), then they are also label-equivalent $\mathcal{I}_1 \equiv_l \mathcal{I}_2$ and flow-equivalent $\mathcal{I}_1 \equiv_f \mathcal{I}_2$. Similarly, if two hosts are label-equivalent then they are also flow-equivalent.*

By definition concrete equivalence implies that equivalent hosts have equivalent information flow models and connect to the same external nodes (input and output). As a result, they are guaranteed to receive input data of the same label, which along with the equivalent information flow models satisfies label equivalence. Further, hosts that satisfy label equivalence must violate constraints at the same sinks since they have the same input labels, label mapping functions, and lattice. Also, the corresponding sources will contribute atoms (data of offending labels) that violate constraints at those sinks for the same reason. Since label-equivalent hosts also have equivalent host information flow graphs, they satisfy flow equivalence as well. Concrete-equivalent are also flow-equivalent as can be seen.

The Venn diagram shown in Figure 3 demonstrates this subsumption relationship among three equivalence classes. As Section 5.3 shows, flow equivalence is the most expensive case to merge, so this subsumption relation is helpful because we can merge concrete and label cases to reduce the cost associated with merging for flow equivalence. As a result, our method checks for concrete equivalence, followed by label, and lastly flow equivalence. Also, we avoid checking for equivalence for obviously distinct cases, such as those hosts with different OS distributions and different applications with label mappings.

5.3 Merge Hosts

Merge operation uses the equivalence classes produced in previous section and leverages the hierarchy of equivalence properties to execute the merge. Figure 4 shows a method for merging the summarized HIFMs (simply HIFMs in this section) for the three equivalence properties. We merge from finest (concrete) to coarsest (flow) equivalence classes.

First, concrete equivalence classes consist of HIFMs that have the same input and output links, so merging these HIFMs is straightforward. We produce one representative HIFM for each class and eliminate the rest. The solution produced for the merged HIFM will be applicable to all members of the equivalence class. In Figure 3, we see that

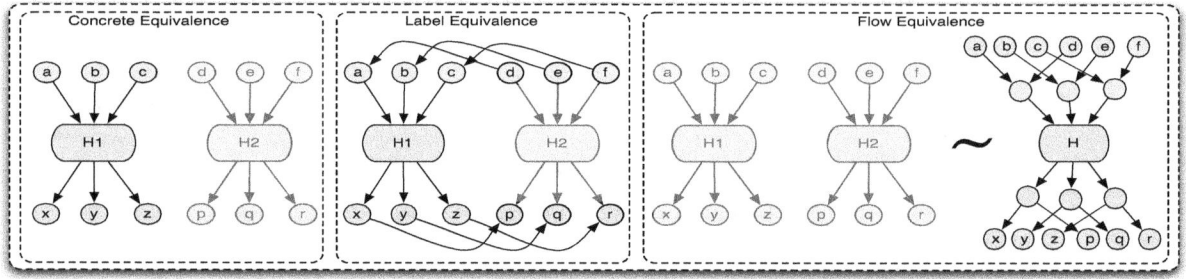

Figure 4: Host Merging for Concrete, Label, and Flow Equivalence (left to right)

HIFMs H_1, H_2 and H_3 can be represented using H_1, thus we keep one HIFM and discard the others. If we have two HIFMs that satisfy only concrete input equivalence, we union the output edges (not shown).

Figure 4 shows the merging operation performed for label-equivalent HIFMs. For label equivalence, we again create one merged HIFM for each equivalence class, but we have to address the problem that the network links are different. Since the HIFMs all receive data of the same label, it is sufficient to union the I/O edges of the individual HIFMs into the merged HIFM. Again referring to Figure 3, we have H_1 and H_5 as representatives of two concrete equivalence classes contained in the same label equivalence class with two additional HIFMs H_4 and H_7. We then perform the merge operation on these four HIFMs to create one merged HIFM. The I/O edges for all four HIFMs are unioned and are added to the corresponding nodes of the merged HIFM in this case.

We merge HIFMs of the same flow equivalence classes as represented in Figure 4. If HIFMs are flow-equivalent, then they have the same data-flow graphs and hence each of the HIFMs can be represented using any one of the HIFM's data-flow graphs. However, since each HIFM's input nodes may expect data of different labels, we augment the data-flow graph with a second layer of dummy input nodes for each unique input label, which we call *constraint nodes* because they require satisfaction of a label mapping. Each input edge to one of the merged HIFMs is connected to one of the new input constraint nodes instead, enabling detection of information flow errors should the input not comply with the expected constraints from their label mappings.

A similar approach is taken to handle the output nodes and their connections[3] as represented in Figure 4. In this case, we create an output constraint node for each combination of corresponding output node and expected label for that node to transmit output of an expected output label along the output edges. In order to create these output constraint nodes, we need to predict the expected output labels correctly. Normally, this is not a problem, as the target application is responsible for most outputs and must obey specific security requirements (i.e., label mappings). However, some data may simply "flow through" the HIFM, so we cannot predict the label associated to that data. We remove HIFMs from the merge if we cannot predict the labels of the data at all output nodes.

We then have to construct the label mapping function for the merged HIFM based on the HIFMs that satisfy flow equivalence. Since flow equivalence requires that all the label mappings for each of the HIFMs merged result in the same error paths, we can use any one HIFM as a template to produce the merged HIFM's label mapping function. Thus, we create a dummy lattice corresponding to the labels used in one HIFM and their information flow relationships and map those to the corresponding nodes in the equivalent HIFMs. Input and output constraint nodes "translate" between the dummy labels and the actual labels to maintain the correct input and output information flows.

5.4 Compute Network Monitor Placement

In the last step, we compute a network monitor placement that satisfies the system's security requirements. This resultant network monitors may be chosen to enforce secrecy, integrity, and/or availability requirements. Finally, the security requirements must be converted into equivalent rules for the network monitors to enforce those requirements.

We compute network monitor placements by solving the mediator placement problem for the system's information flow model. Recall from Section 3 that the mediator placement problem can be formulated as a graph problem. We solve the directed multicut problem [11] using a greedy algorithm that unions solutions to individual cut problems.

Since security requirements are simply sets of individual requirements, we can represent requirements for integrity, secrecy, and availability independently. In general, such requirements may not be orthogonal, however. An integrity requirement to filter data may cause a denial of service. In order to prevent conflicts, we separate the security requirements into those that are known unsafe (to block) or not known to be safe (to log). Thus, if the integrity requirement above is for a known unsafe case, then blocking it denies an adversary and prevents a likely compromise.

6. EVALUATION

In this section we aim to evaluate the two claims made in this paper. First, we examine how the concrete, label, and flow equivalence relations enable reductions in the size of the information flow model. We find that one host information flow model (HIFM) per distinct host configuration can represent large systems, thus considerably reducing the sizes of mediator placement problems. Second, we examine the variation in the cost of computing mediator placement while keeping the number of equivalence class constant but increasing the host count. We observe that the results substantiate our claim that the size of a mediator placement

---

[3]Note that we must precompute the label on each output constraint node in order to propagate data of the expected label as the original host would have.

Table 1: Example Network from Figure 1: Network types: "wired"=regular wired office network with routers and switches; "wireless"=wireless network with access point acting as monitor; "adhoc"=network with no specific access point. Network protected values: "yes"= network devices can mediate to any label; "limited capability"=can only mediate some errors; "no"=no mediation on the network device.

Network	Client	Admin Client	Web Server 1	Web Server 2	DB Server	DNS Server	Network Type	Network Devices	Network Protected	Total
Trusted Clients	400	400	100	-	-	1	wired	router, IDPS, firewall	yes	901
Server Farm	-	100	400	400	-	1	wired	router, IDPS, firewall	yes	901
Data Center	-	-	100	100	600	1	wired	router, IDPS, firewall	yes	801
Partner Clients	150	150	-	-	-	1	wired	router, firewall	limited capability	301
Remote Clients	300	100	-	-	-	1	wireless	router, access point	limited capability	401
Adhoc Network	300	-	-	-	-	-	ad hoc	network connected host	no	300
Total	1150	750	600	500	600	5				3605

problem depends on the number of distinct HIFMs and not the number of hosts.

We perform the evaluation on the network shown in Figure 1, which is described elsewhere [25] and covers several aspects of a typical corporate network. The details of the different host configurations and network properties for this experiment network are provided in Table 1. The columns specify distinct host data flow configurations representing different applications, the network architectures, the network devices in each network, and the mediation capability for the available network devices. Each host system enforces SELinux MAC policies [28]. The networks also include other servers such as DHCP and DNS servers. The network communication for each host is defined by the network topology and the firewall iptable rules enforced in the hosts and network.

6.1 Information Flow Model Merging Results

Table 2 shows the experimental results of merging in four organizational networks with variations in the unique host configurations and the network configuration. The fourth row describes the example network detailed in Table 1. The first column in Table 2 shows the total number of hosts in the sample network, followed by how many unique host data flows (MAC/firewall policies/applications) are given for each host. Each host can have multiple label mapping functions represented in third column. These configurations of unique host data flows and their various mapping functions generate unique host configurations identified in the next column. The distribution of these unique host configurations among the number of subnets forms the basis of the merging capability of the system.

The columns for concrete and label equivalence classes in Table 2 show the equivalence classes computed in each of the subnets of the system and then the number of classes for the whole system. The label equivalence classes will always be greater than or similar to the unique host configurations in the system. The next column shows the flow equivalence classes computed across all the networks in the system. The flow equivalence is independent of the actual labels mapped to the hosts as discussed earlier, which enables compression to lower number of equivalence classes than the unique host

configurations. We discussed in Section 4.5 that mediator placement solutions may be degraded when the network mediation capability is not considered. The final column shows the merging possible when accounting for network mediation capabilities using flow equivalence. As expected, the number of equivalence class increases, but the number of mediators required decreases, as the table shows.

Table 3 shows an example of the impact of merging on the total number of nodes and edges in a system-wide information flow model for the network detailed in Table 1. We see a reduction of three orders of magnitude, even relative to the summarized hosts [37], using the proposed method, reducing the number of nodes from millions to approximately 3500. As the graph cut method has a worst-case cost $O(|E|f)$, where f is the maximum flow in the graph, such a reduction will have a significant impact on compute time.

Table 3: Reduction in the Data Flow Graph

	Whole Network	Summarized	Merged hosts
Nodes	9 million	1.5 million	3540
Edges	19 million	3.8 million	20819

By computing mediator placement solutions for each merged system we show that flow-equivalent merges that include the network devices capable of mediation reduce the size of the placement solution. For instance, the network in the fourth row in Table 2 with 18 flow-equivalent hosts results in a solution requiring 3213 host mediators using the method described in Section 5.4. The mediator placement computed from the 22 hosts including network mediation results in only 2709 host mediators and 4 network mediators. Thus the 4 network nodes can reduce the host mediation necessary by over 100 mediators per network mediator.

6.2 Performance Analysis

Table 4 shows the compute times for each step in the process of computing monitor placement for a network system. The experiments were performed on a 2.80GHz intel dual core machine running Linux kernel 2.6.31. The first two columns in the table show the average time required for computing the data flow graph and the summaries for one

Table 2: Equivalence Analysis Results: *-300 ad hoc network hosts

Host Count	Unique Data Flows	Unique Mappings	Unique Host Configs	Subnets in System	Concrete Eq (Hosts per Subnet/Sys)	Label Eq (Hosts per Subnet/Sys)	Flow Eq (Hosts per System)	Host Mediators	Flow Eq+Net (Hosts per System)	Host+Network Mediators
3600	5	2	11	5	2.8/14	2.6/13	9	1644	11	1319+3
6000	5	4	15	5	5.2/26	3.6/18	13	2326	14	1768+3
9500	5	30	120	5	26/130	24.3/121	112	20416	118	16718+3
3600	5	6	21	6	53.3/320*	4/24	18	3213	22	2709+4

Table 4: Compute Times for the Method Steps

Network Size	Build host model per host (sec)	Summarize host per host (sec)	Compute Equivalence (min)	Merge hosts (min)	Compute Placement (min)
3600	3.5	25	5.03	3.43	1.25
6000	3.5	25	11.45	6.43	1.47
9500	3.5	25	21.36	12.27	2.06

host, these steps can be performed independently of each other and hence can be parallelized easily. The computation of the equivalence classes and merge operation is performed on the entire information flow model using flow-equivalence accounting for network mediation. The computation has a worst case complexity of $O(n^2)$ where n is the number of total hosts in the system. The computation for data flow equivalence is optimized in cases where the policy applied to the host is known to be same. Once the equivalence classes have been identified, the processing of each HIFM can be done independently from the others and then merged together. Computing mediator placements for an individual HIFM given the host summary takes about 4-6 seconds on average.

7. RELATED WORK

The research in the network and system security has mostly followed a parallel path in finding and fixing the security vulnerabilities. We have various policy based system security approaches [28, 37] which address the security requirement in the system. Network security typically consists of placing the network intrusion detection systems [12, 36] and efficiently tracking the traffic between hosts. These methods do not take into account internal hosts processes to identify the actual nature of data being transmitted. The attack graph [33, 29] and attack tree [21] approaches bring the network and the host states closer to identify an exploit, but they rely on previous knowledge of the vulnerability. As the size of the system increases the approach faces the problem of state space explosion and soon becomes intractable. There has been much work done in the area of performing efficient attack graph based analysis [27, 1, 40, 26, 2]. These techniques are mostly based on various heuristics and knowledge of previous attacks to determine the attack behavior. The work in [40] does vulnerability analysis based on the topology, temporal property and received alerts to predict possible future alerts. The method used in [1] is an extension of above method and employs a temporal abstraction of the attack graph to determine relevant sequences in order to perform scalable detection. The work in [26] also employs forensic analysis of attack strategies in order to predict and defend future attacks. Rather than basing the detection on earlier attack strategies and heuristics we proactively model the host data flow to block all possible

attack paths by providing complete mediation. There have been efforts to assure complete mediation while identifying the optimal placement using classical approaches like vertex cover [27] and graph cut problems [30, 17]. These efforts have been mostly either in the context of host or network mediation, but not for both.

Another work on network reduction [39] for the purpose of efficient analysis, is based on reducing the number of network nodes by unifying them such that the key network protocol correctness properties are not violated. The work takes an Border Gateway Protocol (BGP) instance of the protocol and utilizes the Stable Paths Problem(SPP) to identify the nodes that can be unified to reduce the network size prior to performing analysis for anomaly diagnosis. The method displays a similar idea on reduction of the graph for analysis and is specific to network and does not deal with host data flow connections.

This work is closer to the host data flow summarization method done in [37], where they show that summaries maintain the fine grained data flow properties needed for complete mediation while making it more efficient to analyze. Though the method performed some reduction at host level for efficient analysis, it was not able to handle more than hundred hosts. We leverage their work further to address the redundancy across the network and achieve further summarization and are able to address thousands of hosts efficiently.

8. CONCLUSION

In this paper we have successfully introduced the method to model large network systems in scalable manner to enable information flow analysis. We presented three key equivalence concepts that enable us to preserve the information flow error paths in the reduced system model. The model can then be analyzed for security errors and the placement solution thus obtained can solve the security errors in the entire systems. This work considers the fine-grained flow properties in every host while scaling the analysis to huge corporate networks. The results show that this method can achieve substantial reduction in the system graphs where such reduction depends on the amount of *redundancy among host configurations and network topologies* rather than the actual number of hosts and network flows. We demonstrate how near-optimal and efficient network monitor placement can be done considering the host flows for typical configurations of large corporate networks.

9. ACKNOWLEDGMENTS

This research was sponsored by the Army Research Laboratory and was accomplished under Cooperative Agreement Number W911NF-13-2-0045 (ARL Cyber Security CRA). The views and conclusions contained in this document are those of the authors and should not be interpreted as representing the official policies, either expressed or implied, of the Army Research Laboratory or the U.S. Government. The U.S. Government is authorized to reproduce and distribute reprints for Government purposes notwithstanding any copyright notation here on.

10. REFERENCES

[1] M. Albanese, S. Jajodia, A. Pugliese, and V. S. Subrahmanian. Scalable detection of cyber attacks. In N. Chaki and A. Cortesi, editors, *CISIM*, volume 245 of *Communications in Computer and Information Science*, pages 9–18. Springer, 2011.

[2] H. M. J. Almohri, D. Yao, L. T. Watson, and X. Ou. Security optimization of dynamic networks with probabilistic graph modeling and linear programming. Technical report, Virginia Tech, 2014.

[3] P. Barford, J. Kline, D. Plonka, and A. Ron. A signal analysis of network traffic anomalies. In *Proceedings of the 2nd ACM SIGCOMM Workshop on Internet measurment*, IMW '02, pages 71–82, New York, NY, USA, 2002. ACM.

[4] M. Bauer. Paranoid penguin: An introduction to novell apparmor. *Linux J.*, 2006(148):13–, Aug. 2006.

[5] D. E. Bell and L. J. LaPadula. Secure Computer System: Unified Exposition and Multics Interpretation. Technical Report ESD-TR-75-306, Deputy for Command and Management Systems, HQ Electronic Systems Division (AFSC), March 1976.

[6] K. J. Biba. Integrity Considerations for Secure Computer Systems. Technical Report MTR-3153, MITRE, April 1977.

[7] A. J. Bik and H. A. Wijshoff. Implementation of fourier-motzkin elimination. In *Proceedings of the first annual Conference of the ASCI*, pages 377–386. Citeseer, 1994.

[8] H. Chen, N. Li, and Z. Mao. Analyzing and comparing the protection quality of security enhanced operating systems. In *NDSS*, 2009.

[9] W. R. Cheswick, S. M. Bellovin, and A. D. Rubin. *Firewalls and Internet security: repelling the wily hacker*. Addison-Wesley Longman Publishing Co., Inc., 2003.

[10] Introduction to labeled Networking in Linux. `http://www.linuxfoundation.jp/jp_uploads/seminar20080709/paul_moore-r1.pdf`.

[11] E. Dahlhaus, D. S. Johnson, C. H. Papadimitriou, P. D. Seymour, and M. Yannakakis. The complexity of multiterminal cuts. *SIAM J. Comput.*, 23:864–894, August 1994.

[12] P. Garcia-Teodoro, J. Diaz-Verdejo, G. Maciá-Fernández, and E. Vázquez. Anomaly-based network intrusion detection: Techniques, systems and challenges. *computers & security*, 28(1):18–28, 2009.

[13] S. Gulwani and A. Tiwari. Computing procedure summaries for interprocedural analysis. In *ESOP*, 2007.

[14] W. R. Harris, S. Jha, and T. Reps. Difc programs by automatic instrumentation. In *Proceedings of the 17th ACM conference on Computer and communications security*, pages 284–296. ACM, 2010.

[15] M. Howard, J. Pincus, and J. Wing. Measuring relative attack surfaces. In *Computer Security in the 21st Century*, pages 109–137. 2005.

[16] T. Jaeger, R. Sailer, and X. Zhang. Analyzing integrity protection in the SELinux example policy. In *USENIX Security Symposium*, Aug. 2003.

[17] D. King, S. Jha, T. Jaeger, S. Jha, and S. A. Seshia. Towards automated security mediation placement. Technical Report NAS-TR-0100-2008, Network and Security Research Center, Department of Computer Science and Engineering, Pennsylvania State University, University Park, PA, USA, November 2008.

[18] D. King, S. Jha, D. Muthukumaran, T. Jaeger, S. Jha, and S. A. Seshia. Automating security mediation placement. In A. D. Gordon, editor, *ESOP*, volume 6012 of *Lecture Notes in Computer Science*, pages 327–344. Springer, 2010.

[19] M. N. Krohn, A. Yip, M. Brodsky, N. Cliffer, M. F. Kaashoek, E. Kohler, and R. Morris. Information flow control for standard OS abstractions. In *Proceedings of the 21st ACM Symposium on Operating Systems Pr inciples*, pages 321–334, Oct. 2007.

[20] B. Livshits and S. Chong. Towards fully automatic placement of security sanitizers and declassifiers. In *Proceedings of the 40th ACM SIGPLAN-SIGACT Symposium on Principles of Programming Languages*, pages 385–398, New York, NY, USA, Jan. 2013. ACM Press.

[21] S. Mauw and M. Oostdijk. Foundations of attack trees. In *International Conference on Information Security and Cryptology, ICISC 2005. LNCS 3935*, pages 186–198. Springer, 2005.

[22] J. Morris. New Secmark-based network controls for SELinux. `http://james-morris.livejournal.com/11010.html`.

[23] D. Muthukumaran, S. Rueda, N. Talele, H. Vijayakumar, T. Jaeger, J. Teutsch, and N. Edwards. Transforming commodity security policies to enforce Clark-Wilson integrity. In *ACSAC*, 2012.

[24] A. C. Myers and B. Liskov. A decentralized model for information flow control. *ACM Operating Systems Review*, 31(5):129–142, Oct. 1997.

[25] Network based intrusion detection configuration. `http://www.cisco.com/en/US/docs/solutions/Enterprise/Data_Center/ServerFarmSec_2.1/8_NIDS.pdf`.

[26] P. Ning and D. Xu. Learning attack strategies from intrusion alerts. In *Proceedings of the 10th ACM conference on Computer and communications security*, CCS '03, pages 200–209, New York, NY, USA, 2003. ACM.

[27] S. Noel and S. Jajodia. Advanced vulnerability analysis and intrusion detection through predictive attack graphs. In *Critical Issues in C4I, Armed Forces Communications and Electronics Association (AFCEA) Solutions Series*. International Journal of Command and Control, 2009.

[28] Security-enhanced linux. `http://www.nsa.gov/research/selinux/`.

[29] X. Ou, W. F. Boyer, and M. A. McQueen. A scalable approach to attack graph generation. In *Proceedings of the 13th ACM Conference on Computer and*

Communications Security, pages 336–345, New York, NY, USA, 2006. ACM.

[30] L. Pike. Post-hoc separation policy analysis with graph algorithms. In *Workshop on Foundations of Computer Security (FCS'09). Affiliated with Logic in Computer Science (LICS)*, August 2009.

[31] J. Rehof and T. A. Mogensen. Tractable constraints in finite semilattices. *Sci. Comput. Program.*, 35(2-3):191–221, 1999.

[32] B. Sarna-Starosta and S. D. Stoller. Policy analysis for Security-Enhanced Linux. In *WITS*, April 2004.

[33] O. Sheyner, J. W. Haines, S. Jha, R. Lippmann, and J. M. Wing. Automated generation and analysis of attack graphs. In *IEEE Symposium on Security and Privacy*, pages 273–284, 2002.

[34] Snort Intrusion Detection/Prevention System. http://www.snort.org/.

[35] Sun Microsystems. Trusted Solaris operating environment - a technical overview. http://www.sun.com.

[36] Suricata Intrusion Detection/Prevention System. http://suricata-ids.org/.

[37] N. Talele, J. Teutsch, T. Jaeger, and R. F. Erbacher. Using security policies to automate placement of network intrusion prevention. In *ESSoS*, pages 17–32, 2013.

[38] Tresys. SETools - Policy Analysis Tools for SELinux. Available at http://oss.tresys.com/projects/setools.

[39] A. Wang, C. L. Talcott, A. J. T. Gurney, B. T. Loo, and A. Scedrov. Reduction-based formal analysis of bgp instances. In C. Flanagan and B. König, editors, *TACAS*, volume 7214 of *Lecture Notes in Computer Science*, pages 283–298. Springer, 2012.

[40] L. Wang, A. Liu, and S. Jajodia. Using attack graphs for correlating, hypothesizing, and predicting intrusion alerts. *Computer Communications*, 29(15):2917–2933, Sept. 2006.

[41] R. N. M. Watson. TrustedBSD: Adding trusted operating system features to FreeBSD. In *Proceedings of the FREENIX Track: 2001 USENIX Annual Technical Conference*, pages 15–28, 2001.

[42] N. Zeldovich, S. Boyd-Wickizer, E. Kohler, and D. Mazières. Making information flow explicit in HiStar. In *OSDI*, 2006.

Anomaly Detection and Visualization in Generative RBAC Models

Maria Leitner[†*]
maria.leitner@univie.ac.at

Stefanie Rinderle-Ma[†]
stefanie.rinderle-ma@univie.ac.at

[†]University of Vienna, Faculty of Computer Science, Vienna, Austria
[*]SBA Research, Vienna, Austria

ABSTRACT

With the wide use of Role-based Access Control (RBAC), the need for monitoring, evaluation, and verification of RBAC implementations (e.g., to evaluate ex post which users acting in which roles were authorized to execute permissions) is evident. In this paper, we aim at detecting and identifying anomalies that originate from insiders such as the infringement of rights or irregular activities. To do that, we compare prescriptive (original) RBAC models (i.e. how the RBAC model is expected to work) with generative (current-state) RBAC models (i.e. the actual accesses represented by an RBAC model obtained with mining techniques). For this we present different similarity measures for RBAC models and their entities. We also provide techniques for visualizing anomalies within RBAC models based on difference graphs. This can be used for the alignment of RBAC models such as for policy updates or reconciliation. The effectiveness of the approach is evaluated based on a prototypical implementation and an experiment.

Categories and Subject Descriptors

D.4.6 [**Operating Systems**]: Security and Protection—*Access controls*; K.6.4 [**Management of Computing and Information Systems**]: System Management—*Management audit*

General Terms

Measurement, Security

Keywords

access control; anomaly detection; audit; graph edit distance; inexact graph matching; RBAC; similarity

1. INTRODUCTION

Enterprise management systems use Role-based Access Control (RBAC) as de facto standard to enforce access control policies (cf. [11]). Currently, there are two general

SACMAT'14, June 25–27, 2014, London, ON, Canada
Copyright 2014 ACM 978-1-4503-2939-2/14/06 ...$15.00.
http://dx.doi.org/10.1145/2613087.2613105.

approaches to establish RBAC models. In the *top-down* approach, the RBAC models are typically derived by analyzing e.g., business processes and artifacts in order to obtain roles that can fulfill the business operations adequately (cf. [22]). In the *bottom-up* approach, role mining techniques are used to automatically generate RBAC models based on an access control configuration (e.g., a set of user-permissions) such as in [14, 24, 18]. These generative RBAC models contain roles that may indicate job functions or organizational entities.

Recent developments show that generative RBAC models can be derived from event logs (e.g., [2, 19]). For example, Molloy et al. [19] apply role mining techniques on event logs to generate RBAC models. Another approach in Baumgrass et al. [2] proposes to derive role engineering artifacts from event logs. These generative (current-state) RBAC models contain which users in which roles have actually invoked which permissions i.e., they reflect operational reality. Hence, these access snapshots can be used for an ex post analysis and evaluation of RBAC implementations.

In this paper, we aim at detecting potential anomalies in RBAC models that originate from insiders. Anomalies represent patterns in event logs that do not conform to the specified notion of normal behavior (cmp. [6]). In our case, the normal behavior is specified in an original (prescriptive) RBAC model (i.e. it specifies how users are expected to work) and we compare it with a generative model (i.e. how users actually work) obtained with e.g., role mining techniques. The generative model might deviate from the prescriptive model that has been deployed in the enterprise management system. These deviations may occur due to e.g., policy errors, misconfiguration or changed user behavior (which might indicate insider threats).

Anomalies can be distinguished into *point*, *contextual*, and *collective* anomalies (see [6]). In this paper, we center on the detection of point and contextual anomalies. Point anomalies occur due to structural modifications between prescriptive and generative RBAC models. Examples are new role-permission or user-role assignments. Such point anomalies can be detected based on comparing the *structures* of prescriptive and generative RBAC models. We provide measures based on set-based and graph-based representations of RBAC models.

Contextual anomalies go beyond structural differences between RBAC models, i.e., it is possible that two RBAC models differ structurally, but not in a contextual manner. Assume, for example, that in the prescriptive RBAC model a user u has role r which is assigned two permissions p_1 and p_2. Assume further that in the generative RBAC model, role r is split into two roles r_1 with permission p_1 and role r_2 with permission p_2 and u is assigned both roles r_1 and r_2. Then prescriptive and generative RBAC model obviously differ structurally, but from a point of view of user u she still has the same set of permissions as before. Analyzing contextual anomalies on top of structural differences can yield insights on the actual effects of the deviations of the generative RBAC model from the prescriptive one.

In order to analyze and interpret the differences between RBAC models with respect to anomalies it is crucial to convey the information about the differences to the analyst. For this we elaborate on techniques for visualizing the difference between RBAC models. We employ difference models [1] as means to build RBAC difference as well as similarity models.

Our approach is outlined as follows: In Section 2, we define the fundamentals of RBAC models and their transformation onto directed acyclic graphs. We provide different similarity metrics for measuring structural differences in Section 3 and contextual differences between RBAC models in Section 4 along with their algorithmic realization in Section 5. Section 6 provides implementation details, visualization techniques, and experimental results. Related work is outlined in Section 7. Section 8 concludes the paper.

2. PRELIMINARIES

We base our approach on the NIST standard RBAC model (cf. Definition 1) [11] and its administrative operations such as `addUser` or `assignUser` (further called edit operations) as defined in [11]. The edit operations provide one option to describe differences between two RBAC models. The other option is to capture the differences based on the graph representation in a set-based manner.

DEFINITION 1 (RBAC MODEL). *Based on Ferraiolo et al. [11], an RBAC model RBAC is defined as $RBAC :=$ (U, R, P, UA, PA, RH) with: U is a set of users, R is a set of roles, P is a set of permissions, $UA \subseteq U \times R$ is a many-to-many relation between users and roles, $PA \subseteq R \times P$ is a many-to-many mapping between roles and permissions, and $RH \subseteq R \times R$ is an inheritance relation where $r_1 \succeq r_2$ only if all permissions of r_2 are also permissions of r_1 and all users assigned to r_1 are also users authorized to r_2.*

Based on RBAC models, a set of review functions [11] is useful for defining similarity metrics later. We summarize these functions in the appendix in Definition 7.

For comparison and particularly visualization reasons, we transform RBAC models into graphs (cmp. [12]). In particular, we will transform an RBAC model into a directed acyclic graph (DAG) (see [9]) in order to specify role hierarchy relations (i.e., the direction from senior roles to junior roles).

DEFINITION 2 (GRAPH-TRANSFORMED RBAC MODEL). *Let $RBAC := (U, R, P, UA, PA, RH)$ be an RBAC model. Then the graph-transformed RBAC model is defined as $RM := (N, E)$ with:*

- *$N := \{U \cup R \cup P\}$ is a set of nodes*

- *$E := \{UA \cup PA \cup RH\}$ is a set of edges*

In our approach, we assume that the graph-transformed RBAC models utilize **unique** labels. This is justified by

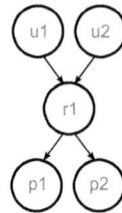

Figure 1: Example: Graph-transformed Representation of an RBAC model

the application as access control systems use unique IDs for users, roles, and permissions. In addition, the labels of edges are represented by the labels of the (two) nodes the edges (n, m) interconnect.

For example, Figure 1 shows a graph-transformed representation of an RBAC model with two users u_1 and u_2, one role r_1, and two permissions p_1 and p_2. The users are assigned role r_1 by directed edges (u_1, r_1) and (u_2, r_1) and role r_1 is assigned two permissions by edges (r_1, p_1) and (r_1, p_2).

Furthermore, we claim that graph RM does not contain isolated nodes. In this paper, we assume that the basis for generative RBAC models are event logs which consist typically of user-permission tuples (cf. [2]). Hence, in our approach, each node must have a relation with another node, i.e. a user or permission node cannot exist without a role assignment and a role node cannot exist without the assignment of a user and permission.

3. STRUCTURAL ANALYSIS

In this paper, we focus on identifying insider threats from advanced users that are typically trusted individuals who know the internal organization and application systems. Their application use is recorded in an event log. Based on the data, we derive a generative RBAC model and analyze patterns that differ from the normal behavior (as defined in the prescriptive RBAC model).

In this section, we tackle the problem in two ways: in Section 3.1, we analyze potential anomalies between graph-transformed representations of two RBAC models in a set-based manner. In Section 3.2, we investigate the application of graph matching techniques for the graph-transformed representations of RBAC models for analysis of similarities and differences between the underlying RBAC models.

3.1 Potential Point Anomalies

As can be seen in Figure 2, we target at three types of modifications in RBAC models: missing vertices, additional nodes, and connectivity change in graph-transformed RBAC models. We also show how these anomalies can be detected based on the graph-transformed representation of RBAC models.

Missing Vertices.

As generative RBAC models reflect operational reality, they only consist of actually "used" roles, permissions, and users. For example, if employees are on vacation, their users might not show up in the generative RBAC model. Furthermore, permissions may not be included or are "missed" because they have not been in use. Given a prescriptive RBAC model with graph-transformed representation $RM_1 = (N_1, E_1)$ and a generative RBAC model with graph-transformed

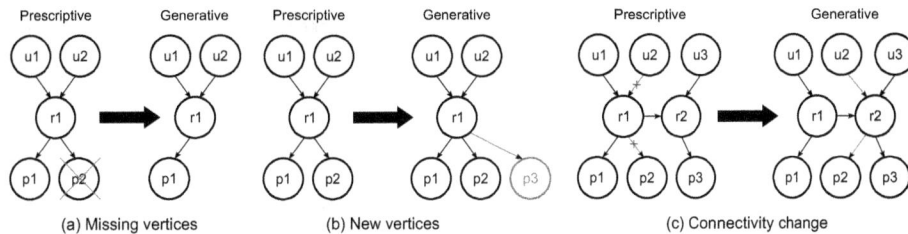

Figure 2: Potential Anomalies in Generative RBAC Models

representation $RM_2 = (N_2, E_2)$, the set of missing nodes or vertices N_{mis} can be determined by $N_{mis} := N_1 \setminus N_2$.

For example, the president has the entitlement to order the use of nuclear weapons (permission p_2) as shown in Figure 2(a). Albeit he might not make use of the entitlement, he/she still has the "permission". However, the permission p_2 is not shown in the generative RBAC model as it has not been utilized (cf. Figure 2(a)). Hence, as generative models might not contain a full set of access control policies (as defined in the prescriptive models), a missing node might not automatically be evaluated as anomaly but more as a deficiency/ absence of permissions. In other cases, the absence of permissions might indicate abnormal (intended) behavior for e.g., permissions that are executed in daily business processes.

New Vertices.

Anomalies that stem from the infringement of rights may result into new vertices in the RBAC graph. Given a prescriptive RBAC model with graph-transformed representation $RM_1 = (N_1, E_1)$ and a generative RBAC model with graph-transformed representation $RM_2 = (N_2, E_2)$, the set of new nodes or vertices N_{new} can be determined by $N_{new} := N_2 \setminus N_1$.

For example, new vertices (that cannot be matched to the original model) may stand for new employees (users) or new functional roles. However, in some cases they may represent the use of "fake" user profiles (users) or roles. Furthermore, new permissions (assigned to roles) may indicate that roles are granted more privileges (e.g., the use of new applications) or that the role has been empowered illicitly. As shown in Figure 2(b), role *r1* is empowered by granting an additional privilege p_3. Hence, users u_1 and u_2 are authorized to perform p_3.

Connectivity Change.

Connectivity change in an RBAC graph can result from e.g., rights infringement or changing user behavior (due to e.g., promotions, demotions). Given a prescriptive RBAC model with graph-transformed representation $RM_1 = (N_1, E_1)$ and a generative RBAC model with graph-transformed representation $RM_2 = (N_2, E_2)$, connectivity changes can be determined by the set of missing or new edges in RM_2, i.e., $E_{cch} := (E_1 \setminus E_2) \cup (E_2 \setminus E_1)$.

In Figure 2(c), the role membership of user u_2 and the permission assignment of p_2 changes. Reasons for this connectivity change can be such as promotions (e.g., user u_2 has been promoted to role r_2), new projects (e.g., user u_2 is now part of project r_2), or security violations (e.g., user u_2 has illicitly acquired role r_2). A connectivity change may look simple but can have a large effect on the RBAC model. It may be harder to interpret than e.g., missing or new vertices.

Analyzing the missing and new nodes and connectivity change in the RBAC models can indicate potential anomalies. However, to identify potential anomalies as actual insider threats is a challenging task. To do that, the final evaluation of anomalies and their interpretation such as insider threats, violations, or organizational changes can only be performed with a certain level of domain knowledge. However, with our approach we want to support the selection of potential anomalies for further investigation.

3.2 Graph-matching Distance Measures

Based on the graph-transformed RBAC representation (cf. Definition 2), the structure of the RBAC model can be also investigated using graph matching techniques. We evaluated *exact* and *inexact* graph matching techniques (see [8]). While *exact* matching techniques require a strict correspondence between two graphs being matched, *inexact* graph matching techniques do not require two graphs to be identical i.e., the comparison of completely different graphs is possible. As we aim to compare not completely identical graph-transformed RBAC models, *inexact* graph matching techniques are highly suitable for the structural analysis of RBAC models. In fact, we could apply the problems graph isomorphism, subgraph isomorphism, and the maximum common subgraph (cf. [5, 9]) for the purpose of comparing two RBAC models.

Graph isomorphism determines whether there exists a bijective mapping between the node and edges sets of the graph-transformed representations of two RBAC models, i.e., it can be used to check whether two RBAC models are "the same". As we assume a unique node labeling for RBAC models and their graph-transformed representations, we can check equality of node and edge sets, i.e., for a prescriptive RBAC model with graph-transformed representation $RM_1 = (N_1, E_1)$ and a generative RBAC model with graph-transformed representation $RM_2 = (N_2, E_2)$, $RM_1 = RM_2$ holds if $N_1 = N_2$ and $E_1 = E_2$.

Interpretation: If $RM_1 = RM_2$ holds, no deviations from the prescriptive model have occurred, i.e., no anomalies within the generative models are detected.

Subgraph isomorphism can be utilized to identify if a graph-transformed representation of an RBAC model is a part of a graph-transformed representation of another RBAC model. Assume that a prescriptive RBAC model with graph-transformed representation $RM_1 = (N_1, E_1)$ and a generative RBAC model with graph-transformed representation $RM_2 = (N_2, E_2)$ are given. We can determine that $RM_1 \subset RM_2$ if $N_1 \subset N_2$ and $E_1 \subset E_2$ (and vice versa) assuming unique node labeling.

Interpretation: If $RM_1 \subset RM_2$, new vertices and connectivities have been added to RM_1. This corresponds to anomaly (b) – new vertices – as depicted in Figure 2. If $RM_2 \subset RM_1$,

43

parts of RM_1 have been "removed", i.e., vertices are missing corresponding to anomaly (a) as shown in Figure 2.

The maximum common subgraph can be used to compare the similarity of two graphs even if they are not isomorph or subgraph isomorph. For a prescriptive RBAC model with graph-transformed representation $RM_1 = (N_1, E_1)$ and a generative RBAC model with graph-transformed representation $RM_2 = (N_2, E_2)$, the maximum common subgraph $mcs(RM_1, RM_2)$ is a subgraph of RM_1 and RM_2 and there exists no subgraph of RM_1 and RM_2 that is larger than $mcs(RM_1, RM_2)$. For a formal definition we refer to [4]. Interpretation: The larger the maximum common subgraph is, the higher is the similarity between two graphs. This can be seen as a general indicator of how similar two RBAC models are or, in turn, how much they differ from each other.

In the following, we will analyze distance measures for the maximum common subgraph problem in order to compare different graph-transformed representations of RBAC models. The first measure is the *graph edit distance* $d_{ged}(RM_1, RM_2)$ for graph-transformed RBAC models RM_1 and RM_2 that is the minimal number of graph edit operations necessary to transform RM_1 into RM_2 [4]. Edit operations may include node/edge insertions and deletions. In our approach, we consider the RBAC edit operations outlined in Section 2 as graph edit operations. For this, [4] suggest the following formula that transforms the calculation of the graph edit distance to computing the maximum common subgraph:

$$d_{ged}(RM_1, RM_2) = |RM_1| + |RM_2| - 2 |mcs(RM_1, RM_2)| \tag{1}$$

Interpretation: Based on edit operations, it can be precisely stated which modifications have been applied to transform RM_1 to RM_2. Hence, the shorter the sequence is to transform one graph to another, the greater is their similarity. If RM_1 was transformed into RM_2 intentionally by, for example, executing some optimizations on RM_1 and if the edit operations were logged, they can easily be analyzed. However, if we derive generative RBAC models from logs, we do not know the edit operations that might have transformed the prescriptive model into the generative one. Then, $d_{ged}(RM_1, RM_2)$ has to be determined on basis of RM_1 and RM_2.

Furthermore, determining the graph edit operations indicates how many operations it would take to transform the prescriptive into the generative RBAC model but does not express the similarity of the two models. In relation to the previous measure, another distance metric d_{mcs} based on the maximum common subgraph is defined in [5] as follows:

$$d_{mcs}(RM_1, RM_2) = 1 - \frac{|mcs(RM_1, RM_2)|}{max(|RM_1|, |RM_2|)} \tag{2}$$

where mcs is the maximum common subgraph, $|\ldots|$ is the size of a graph[1], and $max(\ldots)$ is the maximum operation. Another distance measure is based on the idea of graph union in [26]:

$$d_{gu}(RM_1, RM_2) = 1 - \frac{|mcs(RM_1, RM_2)|}{|RM_1| + |RM_2| - |mcs(RM_1, RM_2)|} \tag{3}$$

Interpretation: The distance metrics d_{mcs} and d_{gu} provide a value, i.e., how much the generative RBAC model deviates

---

[1] The size of a graph-transformed representation RM can be determined by $|RM| := |N| + |E|$.

from the prescriptive one, but not the exact graph edit operations. Having both measures is an asset for the anomaly analysis.

In later sections, we will show how these measures are used to identify point anomalies.

4. SEMANTIC ANALYSIS

When we first investigated the similarity of RBAC models, we discovered that not only the structure can indicate anomalies and security violations, but also the semantic aspects of RBAC models are important such as the semantic meaning of roles (cf. [14, 18]) as they are typically designed for a purpose such as to fulfill a job function. For instance, Figure 3 displays two RBAC models which look very similar at first glance. In *RBAC1*, users u_1 and u_2 are assigned to roles r_1 and r_2. However, in *RBAC2* user u_1 is only assigned to role r_1 and user u_2 only to r_2. It can be seen by evaluating the review functions (see Definition 7 in the appendix) that both models differ structurally and have a different role composition. However, an evaluation of the access control configurations shows that they are identical (i.e. both models have the same set of user-permissions). Even tough both models differ structurally, they enable the same "behavior" for users because of the same user-permissions. Hence, these contextual aspects should be considered when comparing RBAC models semantically.

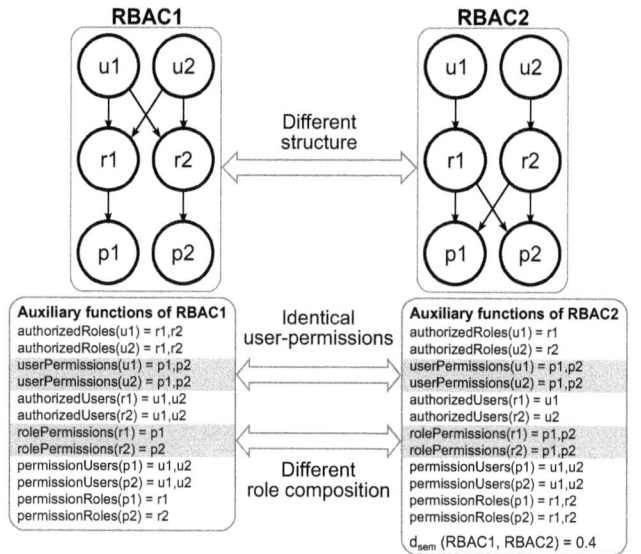

Figure 3: Example for Semantic Differences

In our analysis, we compare "the composition" of RBAC models; we investigate the associations of users, roles and permissions in the RBAC models. For example, for each user node in the generative model we analyze if the user has the same authorized roles and permissions as in the original model (cf. Figure 3). If these authorized roles and permissions deviate from the original model, these semantic differences can be identified as potential *contextual* anomalies. We were inspired by [25, 23] who measure the similarity between role sets with the Jaccard coefficient. We further adapt it to analyze not only the similarity of roles but also of users and permissions which are further used to compute the semantic similarity of RBAC models.

Approach

In the following, we will assess the semantic similarity for RBAC models: a predictive RBAC model $RBAC_1 = (U_1, R_1, P_1, UA_1, PA_1, RH_1)$ and a current-state RBAC model $RBAC_2 = (U_2, R_2, P_2, UA_2, PA_2, RH_2)$. Thereby, we will compare model $RBAC_2$ with model $RBAC_1$ in order to determine semantic anomalies. We will use the Jaccard Coefficient which is a well known similarity metric (cf. [24, 23]) to compare the similarity between node sets. For the computation of a semantic similarity measure between RBAC models, we calculate the similarity of each node in the model and use them to calculate the semantic similarity. The overall approach is outlined as follows:

1. In the first step, the nodes of models $RBAC_2$ and $RBAC_1$ are matched by their (unique) labels.

2. For each matched node, the node similarity is calculated. For each "unmatched" node, the similarity is set to a threshold value. In this approach, we set the similarity value for unmatched nodes to zero.

3. Then, we calculate the similarity measure for each user, role, and permission node.

4. Finally, we compute the average semantic similarity measure based on the node similarity measures.

In the next paragraphs, we will describe the computation of the semantic similarity measure between $RBAC_1$ and $RBAC_2$ in detail. Recall Definition 7 in the appendix for review functions on RBAC models.

User Node Analysis.

In the first step, the similarity of all user nodes are analyzed based on their authorized roles and user-permission assignments. For each pair of matched user nodes (u_i, u_j) (i.e., $u_i = u_j, i \neq j$), we determine the user-role similarity $simUR$ and the user-permission similarity $simUP$. The user-role similarity measure $simUR$ between users u_i and u_j is defined by the authorized roles for users:

$$simUR(u_i, u_j) = \frac{|\texttt{authorizedRoles}(u_i) \cap \texttt{authorizedRoles}(u_j)|}{|\texttt{authorizedRoles}(u_i) \cup \texttt{authorizedRoles}(u_j)|}$$

The function $\texttt{authorizedRoles}(u_i)$ returns a set of authorized roles for user $u_i \in U_1$ of model RM_1 and $\texttt{authorizedRoles}(u_j)$ returns a set of authorized roles for user $u_j \in U_2$ of model RM_2 (cf. Definition 7).

The user-permission similarity $simUP$ between users u_i and u_j (if $u_i = u_j, i \neq j$) is defined based on the user permissions where $\texttt{userPermissions}(u_i)$ is the set of all permissions authorized for user $u_i \in U_1$ and $\texttt{userPermissions}(u_j)$ is the set of all permissions authorized for user $u_j \in U_2$ (cf. Definition 7):

$$simUP(u_i, u_j) = \frac{|\texttt{userPermissions}(u_i) \cap \texttt{userPermissions}(u_j)|}{|\texttt{userPermissions}(u_i) \cup \texttt{userPermissions}(u_j)|}$$

Furthermore, we will combine these measures to specify the similarity measure between two user nodes.

DEFINITION 3 (USER-USER SIMILARITY). *The user-user similarity userSim for two users u_i and u_j with $u_i = u_j, i \neq j$ is the weighted sum of the user-role and the user-permission similarity:*

$$userSim(u_i, u_j) = w_{ur} * simUR + w_{up} * simUP$$

where $w_{ur}, w_{up} \in [0; 1] \wedge w_{ur} + w_{up} = 1$

In our paper, we specified the weights as $w_{ur} = w_{up} = \frac{1}{2}$. The function $userSim$ returns a value between 0 and 1. If two user nodes are identical (i.e. have the same associations with roles and permissions) the similarity is 1. The more identical both user nodes are (i.e. have the same set of authorized roles and user-permissions) the higher is their similarity. Furthermore, we can compute the distance between user nodes as $d_{user}(u_i, u_j) = 1 - userSim(u_i, u_j)$.

Role Node Analysis.

In a next step, we investigate all role nodes. To do that, we adapted the role-permission, role-user, role hierarchy relation, and role-role similarity measure defined in [23] to our approach. In the following, we will describe the role-user similarity $simRU$, role hierarchy relation $simRH$ and role-permission $simRP$ similarity and use them as a composite measure for the similarity between roles.

The role-user similarity between two roles r_i and r_j (for a match $r_i = r_j, i \neq j$) is specified based on the authorized users for roles [23]; the function $\texttt{authorizedUsers}(r_i)$ returns a set of authorized users for role $r_i \in R_1$ and $\texttt{authorizedUsers}(r_j)$ returns a set of authorized users for role $r_j \in R_2$ (cf. Definition 7).

$$simRU(r_i, r_j) = \frac{|\texttt{authorizedUsers}(r_i) \cap \texttt{authorizedUsers}(r_j)|}{|\texttt{authorizedUsers}(r_i) \cup \texttt{authorizedUsers}(r_j)|}$$

The role hierarchy relation similarity $simRH$ is defined based on the hierarchy relations (senior and junior roles) for roles [23]. The function $\texttt{senior}(r_i)$ returns a set of senior roles of role r_i and $\texttt{junior}(r_i)$ returns a set of junior roles of role r_i. While in [23] only immediate senior and junior roles are returned, in our approach full inheritance (comp. [18]) is applied i.e., all senior and junior roles associated to a role are returned (cf. Definition 7).

$$simRH(r_i, r_j) = w_{sen} * \frac{min(|\texttt{senior}(r_i)|, |\texttt{senior}(r_j)|)}{max(|\texttt{senior}(r_i)|, |\texttt{senior}(r_j)|)}$$
$$+ w_{jun} * \frac{min(|\texttt{junior}(r_i)|, |\texttt{junior}(r_j)|)}{max(|\texttt{junior}(r_i)|, |\texttt{junior}(r_j)|)}$$
$$\text{where } w_{sen}, w_{jun} \in [0; 1], w_{sen} + w_{jun} = 1$$

The role-permission similarity $simRP$ is specified based on the set of permissions each role has [23]. The function $\texttt{rolePermissions}(r_i)$ returns all permissions role $r_i \in R_1$ has and $\texttt{rolePermissions}(r_j)$ returns all permissions associated to role $r_j \in R_2$ (cf. Definition 7).

$$simRP(r_i, r_j) = \frac{|\texttt{rolePermissions}(r_i) \cap \texttt{rolePermissions}(r_j)|}{|\texttt{rolePermissions}(r_i) \cup \texttt{rolePermissions}(r_j)|}$$

Based on these measures, we determine the similarity measure between two matching roles, i.e., $r_i = r_j, i \neq j$.

DEFINITION 4 (ROLE-ROLE SIMILARITY). *We combine the role-user, role hierarchy relation and role-permission similarity to specify the role-role similarity roleSim (cf. [23]).*

$$roleSim(r_i, r_j) = w_{ru} * simRU + w_{rh} * simRH + w_{rp} * simRP$$
$$\text{where } w_{ru}, w_{rh}, w_{rp} \in [0; 1] \wedge w_{ru} + w_{rh} + w_{rp} = 1$$

In our approach, we set the weights $w_{ru} = w_{rh} = w_{rp} = \frac{1}{3}$. The function $roleSim \in [0, 1]$ returns a value between 0 and 1. If two role nodes are identical their similarity is 1. Role nodes with only some common features have a value between 0 and 1. Role nodes have a high similarity if they have a large set of identical authorized users, role-permissions, and hierarchy relations. Additionally, we can define the distance between role nodes as $d_{role}(r_i, r_j) = 1 - roleSim(r_i, r_j)$.

Permission Node Analysis.

In the next step, the similarity of matched permission nodes (p_i, p_j) with $p_i = p_j, i \neq j$ is computed based on users and roles that are authorized to access the permission. The permission-user similarity $simPU$ is specified based on the authorized users to a permission; `permissionUsers`(p_i) returns a set of authorized users for permission $p_i \in P_1$ and `permissionUsers`(p_j) returns a set of authorized users for permission $p_j \in P_2$.

$$simPU(p_i, p_j) = \frac{|\mathtt{permissionUsers}(p_i) \cap \mathtt{permissionUsers}(p_j)|}{|\mathtt{permissionUsers}(p_i) \cup \mathtt{permissionUsers}(p_j)|}$$

Furthermore, we compute the permission-role similarity $simPR$ based on the authorized roles to a permission. The function `permissionRoles`(p_i) returns a set of authorized roles for permission $p_i \in P_1$ and `permissionRoles`(p_j) returns a set of authorized roles for permission $p_j \in P_2$.

$$simPR(p_i, p_j) = \frac{|\mathtt{permissionRoles}(p_i) \cap \mathtt{permissionRoles}(p_j)|}{|\mathtt{permissionRoles}(p_i) \cup \mathtt{permissionRoles}(p_j)|}$$

Based on these measures, we compute the similarity between two permissions.

DEFINITION 5 (PERMISSION-PERMISSION SIMILARITY). *The similarity for any two permissions $p_i \in P_1$ and $p_j \in P_2$ with $p_i = p_j, i \neq j$ is specified as the weighted sum of the permission-users simPU and the permission-roles simPR similarity.*

$$permSim(p_i, p_j) = w_{pu} * simPU + w_{pr} * simPR \text{ where } w_{pu} + w_{pr} = 1$$

The function $permSim$ returns a value between 0 and 1. The similarity of corresponding permission nodes increases the more user-permission and permission-roles are matched. Subsequently, we can specify the distance between permission nodes as $d_{perm}(p_i, p_j) = 1 - permSim(p_i, p_j)$.

Based on these similarity measures of the users, roles, and permissions, we can further specify the semantic similarity.

DEFINITION 6 (SEMANTIC SIMILARITY).

$$semSim(RBAC_1, RBAC_2) = \frac{1}{m} \sum_{i=0}^{m} sim(n_i)$$
$$\text{where } n_i \in U_1 \cup U_2 \cup R_1 \cup R_2 \cup P_1 \cup P_2 \qquad (4)$$

See Definition 8 in the appendix for a specification of $sim(n_i)$.

Accordingly, the more the user, role, and permission nodes of one model correspond to the nodes in the other model, the higher is their semantic similarity. The similarity function $semSim(RBAC_1, RBAC_2) \in [0, 1]$ has value 1 if $RBAC_1$ and $RBAC_2$ are identical and value 0 if $RBAC_1$ and $RBAC_2$ share no common features. Furthermore, we can define the semantic distance between two RBAC models as $d_{sem}(RBAC_1, RBAC_2) = 1 - semSim(RBAC_1, RBAC_2)$.

With determining the semantic similarity between two RBAC models, we aim to detect anomalies in the composition of RBAC models. Missing or new vertices and connectivity changes (cf. Section 3.1) affect each node similarity and therefore also the semantic similarity ($semSim$). For example, the user-user similarity ($simU$) incorporates if a user node is newly connected to a role or "misses" a role (by the user-role similarity $simUR$).

In the next sections, we will show how the semantic analysis is utilized to detect and identify potential anomalies.

5. ALGORITHMS

This section outlines the algorithms proposed for the structural and semantic metrics that were described in previous sections.

The algorithm to compute the distance measures for the structural analysis is straightforward. Because of the assumption that graph-transformed RBAC models use unique labels, the implementation of the distance measures requires only the intersection of sets and a function that returns the cardinality of a set. Hence, to compute the distance measures, all vertices and edges have to be analyzed in both RBAC models which takes $O(|E_1| + |E_2|)$ time.

Furthermore, the algorithm to compute the semantic distance between two RBAC models is displayed in the appendix in Algorithm 1 and basically summarizes the semantic analysis from the previous section. In the first step, the labels of all nodes are matched between RBAC models RM_1 and RM_2. For each node that has been matched, the node similarity is computed. In particular, the user-user similarity for user nodes, the role-role similarity for role nodes, and the permission-permission similarity for permissions. For each unmatched node, the similarity is set to a threshold value. Then, the average of all similarity values is calculated and the semantic distance is computed by subtracting one from the average.

The review functions (cf. Definition 7 in the appendix) to analyze the relations of the nodes such as `authorizedRoles`, `authorizedUsers`, and `userPermissions` return the cardinality of a set of nodes. We implemented each function as a depth-first search (DFS). For example, to determine the user-user similarity for user u_1 in the predictive RBAC model in Figure 2(c), we have to analyze the authorized roles and the user-permissions with a DFS. The DFS analyzes the associated (outgoing) edges of user node u_1 which leads to role r_1. In the next steps, the outgoing edges of r_1 are analyzed and p_1, p_2, and r_2 are discovered. Subsequently, permission p_3 (associated with r_2) is discovered. Hence, for user u_1 the authorized roles are r_1 and r_2 and the user-permissions are p_1, p_2, and p_3. These authorized roles and user-permissions of the predictive model are compared to the authorized users and user-permissions from the generative model (`authorizedRoles`: r_1, r_2, `userPermissions`: p_1, p_2, p_3) and the user-user similarity for node u_1 is computed ($userSim(P.u_1, G.u_1) = 1$). Unfortunately, the use of DFS and the matching of nodes increases the time to compute the semantic distance measure to $O(N^3)$ with $N := N_1 + N_2$. However, this opens the possibility for further optimizations such as with approximate solutions in future research.

6. EVALUATION

This section describes the implementation, visualization and experimental results of this approach.

6.1 Implementation

We used graph-tools (cf. `http://graph-tool.skewed.de/`), an efficient Python module for manipulation and statistical analysis of graphs to implement our approach. In particular, we have implemented the proposed structural and semantic analysis of RBAC models. Furthermore, the prototype represents RBAC models as graphs as shown in Example 1.

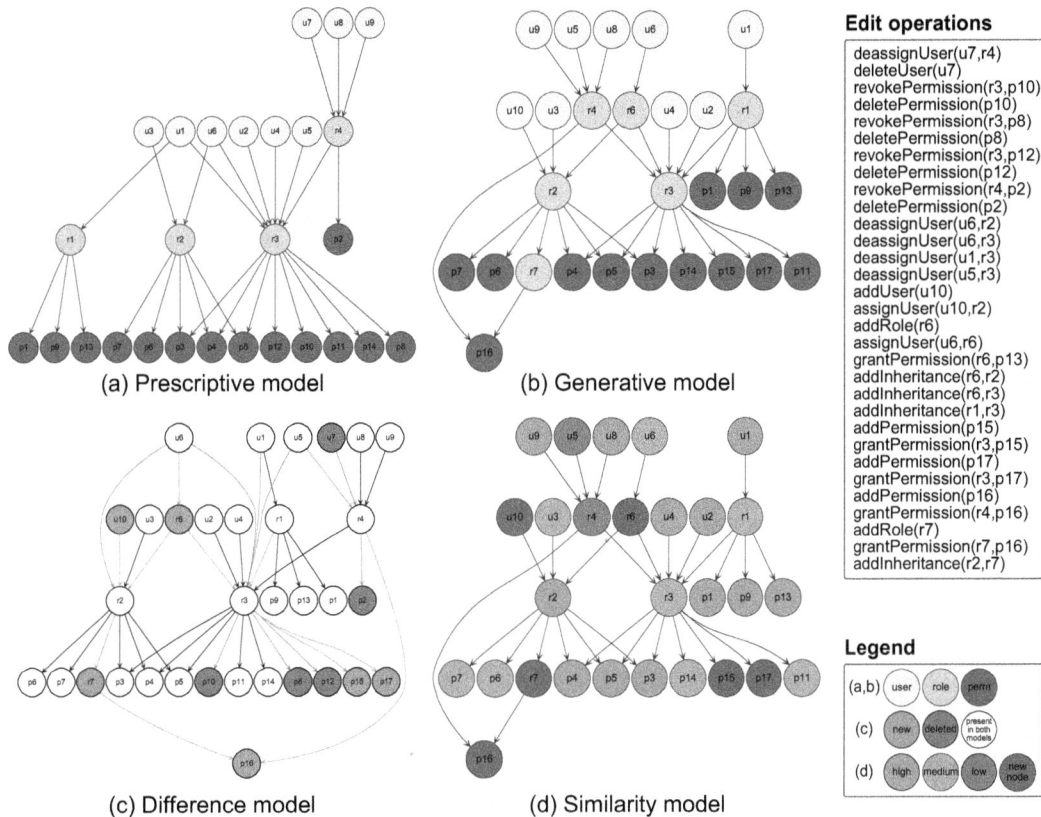

Edit operations

deassignUser(u7,r4)
deleteUser(u7)
revokePermission(r3,p10)
deletePermission(p10)
revokePermission(r3,p8)
deletePermission(p8)
revokePermission(r3,p12)
deletePermission(p12)
revokePermission(r4,p2)
deletePermission(p2)
deassignUser(u6,r2)
deassignUser(u6,r3)
deassignUser(u1,r3)
deassignUser(u5,r3)
addUser(u10)
assignUser(u10,r2)
addRole(r6)
assignUser(u6,r6)
grantPermission(r6,p13)
addInheritance(r6,r2)
addInheritance(r6,r3)
addInheritance(r1,r3)
addPermission(p15)
grantPermission(r3,p15)
addPermission(p17)
grantPermission(r3,p17)
addPermission(p16)
grantPermission(r4,p16)
addRole(r7)
grantPermission(r7,p16)
addInheritance(r2,r7)

Figure 4: Example 1 consists of (a) a Predictive RBAC Model and (b) a Generative RBAC model and their (c) Difference Model and (d) Similarity Model

Example 1. The example in Figure 4 displays a prescriptive RBAC model in Figure 4(a) and a generative RBAC model in (b). As can be seen from the figures, both models contain user, role, and permission nodes. Edges represent user-role assignments (UA), role hierarchy relations (RH), and role-permission assignments (PA). In addition, we use shades of blue to distinguish between the type of node: user, role, and permission (only for the purpose of representation).

For illustration reasons, we selected an RBAC model of small size as example. However, as RBAC models can become very complex, the visualization of RBAC models is a challenging task. We are aware that the visualization of large-scale RBAC models might result into very large and complex images. In this case, a section of the RBAC model (e.g., visualize only a set of roles and their assignments) can reduce the complexity for illustration purposes or other visualizations might be more applicable (e.g., [28, 3]).

When comparing the RBAC models in Figure 4(a) and (b), it is noticeable that there are differences between them. However, it is hard to clearly detect the structural differences just by looking at both figures. Furthermore, it is even tougher to identify if there are semantically similar or not. That is why we developed visualizations to display structural and semantic differences between RBAC models.

6.2 Visualization of Potential Anomalies

With the use of a visualization, we aim to support the easier identification and understanding of potential anomalies in order to evaluate insider threats (see [16]). Furthermore, the visualization should facilitate the investigation of RBAC differences such as policy updates or reconciliation. In this paper, we propose two models to display anomalies in RBAC models of moderate size: a difference model that highlights *point* anomalies and a similarity model that reveals *contextual* anomalies.

Difference Model.

Typically, a difference model is utilized to contrast or compare two distinct models (e.g., [1, 13]). In our paper, we use it to display the graph edit operations necessary to transform one model into the other (i.e. to visualize structural differences). Let $RM_1 = (N_1, E_1)$ and $RM_2 = (N_2, E_2)$ be two graph-transformed RBAC models (cf. Section 2). The difference model DM can be specified as:

$$DM := (N_1 \cup N_2, E_1 \cup E_2, M_N, M_E) \qquad (5)$$

The markings of nodes M_N and edges M_E of the difference model describe if a node/an edge is changed, i.e., if a node/an edge is added or deleted. The node markings distinguish between (0) a node with the same label exists in both models, (1) a node that exists only in the generative model RM_2 (i.e. it has been added), or (-1) a node that exists only in the predictive model RM_1 (i.e. it has been deleted). For each node $n \in N_1 \cup N_2$ the marking is defined as follows:

$$M_N(n) = \begin{cases} 0 & \text{if } n \in N_1 \wedge n \in N_2 \\ 1 & \text{if } n \in N_2 \wedge n \notin N_1 \\ -1 & \text{if } n \in N_1 \wedge n \notin N_2 \end{cases}$$

Similarly, the marking for each edge $e \in E$ is specified as:

$$M_E(e) = \begin{cases} 0 & \text{if } e \in E_1 \land n \in E_2 \\ 1 & \text{if } e \in E_2 \land n \notin E_1 \\ -1 & \text{if } e \in E_1 \land n \notin E_2 \end{cases}$$

An example of the difference model is shown in Figure 4(c) and the visual elements of the difference model are specified in the appendix in Table 3. As shown in Figure 4(c), the difference graph uses the color red for deleted nodes and edges and the color green to represent new nodes and edges (i.e. are potential point anomalies). Nodes with white background color represent nodes that exist in both models. It can be seen from Figure 4(c) that structural differences are distinctively observable with this visualization.

Similarity Model.

In addition, we propose the similarity model to visualize the semantic node similarity for each node in the generative RBAC model. Let $RM_1 = (N_1, E_1)$ and $RM_2 = (N_2, E_2)$ be two graph-transformed RBAC models. The similarity model can be specified as:

$$SM := (N_2, E_2, S_N) \tag{6}$$

Hence, we examine the generative RBAC model to identify abnormal semantical changes. The node markings S_N of the similarity model distinguish if a node exists in both models $(sim(n))^2$ or if a node is newly added to RM_2 (t):

$$S_N(n) = \begin{cases} sim(n) & \text{if } n \in N_1 \land n \in N_2 \\ t & \text{if } n \in N_2 \land n \notin N_1 \end{cases}$$

In our approach, we set the threshold value t to zero. An example of the similarity graph is visualized in Figure 4(d) using the elements listed in the appendix in Table 4. As can be seen from Figure 4(d), the red-colored nodes indicate that the semantic similarity compared to the nodes in the predictive model is very low. Green and orange nodes have a high and medium similarity. Furthermore, blue nodes represent (new) nodes (i.e. they did not exist in the prescriptive model). For example, user u_5 in Figure 4(d) differs highly from its corresponding node in the original model and can be identified as potential contextual anomaly. From the difference graph in Figure 4(c) it can be inferred that this is because of a role change of user u_5 (from role r_3 to r_4). Hence, the combination of both visualizations facilitate the identification and understanding of potential anomalies.

6.3 Experimental Results

In this section, we will evaluate the structural and semantical distance measures with an example data set. Furthermore, we analyze our findings in the context of point and context anomalies.

6.3.1 Data Set

For our evaluation, we analyzed the data sets from [10] provided in *RMiner* [17]. In particular, we used the data sets *firewall2*, *firewall1*, and *university_large* and applied the *HierarchicalMiner* [18] to generate an RBAC model. The results of data sets *firewall1* and *university_large* are not described in this paper due to page limitations however they

yield very similar results. For each data set, the resulting RBAC model was converted into a graph-transformed RBAC model and transferred into our prototype.

Based on this original RBAC model RM_1, we injected anomalies to derive RBAC model RM_2 — a "corrupted" version of the original RBAC model. In particular, we injected three types of anomalies: new vertices, missing vertices and connectivity changes (cf. Section 3.1). The algorithms for injecting anomalies into generative RBAC models are outlined in Appendix E. The use of generative models as input is common practice, for example, generative models are produced in Molloy et al. [19]. In the following, we compare the original RBAC model with the corrupted versions based on their unique labels. For example, role r_1 in the original model is matched with the role r_1 in the corrupted version, user u_1 with u_1 and so on. Furthermore, we investigate the impact of the injected anomalies by analyzing the structural and semantic distance of the two RBAC models and sensitivity of the measures to anomalies.

6.3.2 Detecting Anomalies

Example 2. In order to compare RBAC models, we first generated three corrupted (generative) RBAC models of the data set *firewall2* for three types of point anomalies. For point anomaly *new vertices*, we created three corrupted versions where we inserted new nodes (and corresponding edges) that increased the node count by approximately 3.5%, 7%, and 14% of its original vertices. We refer to the resulting RBAC models as $RM_{new,100-p\%}$ where p stands for the percentage increase of vertices (compared to the original model). For the anomaly *missing vertices*, we generated three corrupted RBAC models $RM_{mis,100-p\%}$ by deleting nodes (and their corresponding edges) that approximately account for 3.5%, 7%, and 14% of its vertices. In case of the anomaly *connectivity change*, we created three corrupt versions $RM_{cha,100-p\%}$ where we modified the edge connectivity of the original model in p percent of its edges. In particular, we re-assigned users to roles and permissions to roles. Table 1 shows the key data of the original RBAC model RM_1 and the corrupted models with new vertices ($RM_{new,100-p\%}$), missing vertices ($RM_{mis,100-p\%}$), and connectivity changes ($RM_{cch,100-p\%}$). In addition, it contains the weighted structural complexity (WSC) that sums up the number of relationships in an RBAC state (see Molloy et al. [18] for a specification).

In the following, we will use the models in Example 2 to compute the structural and semantic distance measures and analyze the measures for point and contextual anomalies.

Point Anomalies.

We evaluate point anomalies at two levels. First, we calculate the graph-matching distance measures that indicate the structural difference at *model level*. Secondly, we analyze and visualize point anomalies on *node and edge level* with the difference model as outlined in Section 6.2.

Table 2 displays the distance measures at model level that are represented as bar chart in Figure 5. As can be seen from the figure and table, the more anomalies are injected, the higher is the structural distance to the original model (see d_{mcs} and d_{gu}). Interestingly, in case of new or missing vertices, the distance measures d_{mcs} and d_{gu} are identical. However, in case of changes of the connectivity (see d_{mcs} and d_{gu} in $RM_{cch,100-p\%}$ in Figure 5), the distance based

---

[2]See Definition 8 in the appendix.

Table 1: Key Information about the Data Sets in Examples 1 and 2

Data set	No. of Nodes			No. of Edges	WSC
	$|U|$	$|R|$	$|P|$		
Fig. 4(a)	9	4	14	29	33
Fig. 4(b)	9	6	13	31	37
RM_1	365	85	720	1312	1397
$RM_{new,96.5}$	384	85	742	1353	1438
$RM_{new,93}$	409	85	759	1395	1480
$RM_{new,86}$	452	85	804	1483	1568
$RM_{mis,96.5}$	337	85	707	1266	1351
$RM_{mis,93}$	320	85	684	1225	1310
$RM_{mis,86}$	290	85	641	1142	1227
$RM_{cch,96.5}$	365	85	720	1312	1397
$RM_{cch,93}$	365	85	720	1312	1397
$RM_{cch,86}$	365	85	720	1312	1397

Table 2: Overview of Distance Measures: Graph Edit Distance d_{ged}, mcs Distances d_{mcs}, Graph Union Distance d_{gu}, Semantic Distance d_{sem} of the Compared RBAC Models $G1$ and $G2$

$G1$	$G2$	d_{ged}	d_{mcs}	d_{gu}	d_{sem}
Fig. 4(a)	Fig. 4(b)	31	0.28814	0.42466	0.48666
RM_1	$RM_{new,96.5}$	82	0.03198	0.03198	0.04934
RM_1	$RM_{new,93}$	166	0.06269	0.06269	0.09361
RM_1	$RM_{new,86}$	342	0.12111	0.12111	0.17742
RM_1	$RM_{mis,96.5}$	87	0.03505	0.03505	0.04833
RM_1	$RM_{mis,93}$	168	0.06769	0.06769	0.09624
RM_1	$RM_{mis,86}$	324	0.13054	0.13054	0.17799
RM_1	$RM_{cch,96.5}$	76	0.01531	0.03016	0.05000
RM_1	$RM_{cch,93}$	156	0.03143	0.06094	0.09453
RM_1	$RM_{cch,86}$	302	0.06084	0.11470	0.30928

on the idea of graph union d_{gu} increases stronger than the distance based on the maximum common subgraph d_{mcs}. Accordingly, we can convey that the change of vertices of $p\%$ also increases the distance between the models to approximately $p\%$. However, only in the case of reassignments of edges ($RM_{cch,100-p\%}$), the distance d_{mcs} increases $\frac{p}{2}\%$.

Hence, structural distance measures indicate the structural modifications between RBAC models. However, they do not give information on the semantical changes. In the following, we will investigate these (contextual) changes.

Contextual Anomalies.

The identification and investigation of contextual anomalies is challenging as contextual anomalies are influenced by point anomalies (e.g., new vertices or changes in the connectivity of edges). In our approach, we evaluate the contextual anomalies at two levels. First, we evaluate the semantic similarity on *model level* by computing the similarity measure between two RBAC models. Secondly, we investigate contextual anomalies on *node level* by analyzing the semantic similarity for each node in a graph-transformed RBAC model. Furthermore, we visualize the node similarity in the similarity model (see Section 6.2).

The results of the semantic distance measure d_{sem} is shown in Table 2 and Figure 5. It can be seen from the figure that structural modifications can lead to semantic changes in the composition of the RBAC model. We can infer that the more anomalies are injected, the higher is their semantic distance. In Example 2, the reassignment of 14% of edges (i.e. user-role and role-permission assignments) leads to a steep increase in the semantic distance (see d_{sem} for

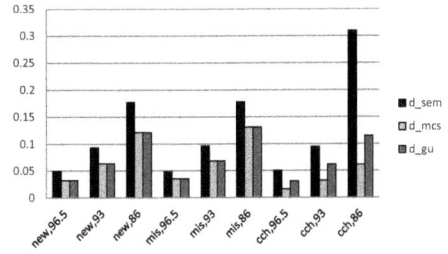

Figure 5: Example2: Distance Measures of Corrupted RBAC Versions compared to the Original RBAC Model

$RM_{cch,86}$ in Figure 5). By analyzing the difference graph $DM(RM_1, RM_{cch,86})$, we identified that $RM_{cch,86}$ contains many user-role and role-permission assignments that were in the original model RM_1 connected to roles in the upper hierarchy and are in $RM_{cch,86}$ associated with roles in the lower hierarchy. We discovered similar effects in the data sets *university_large* and *firewall1*. Subsequently, modifications in the upper hierarchy have a strong impact on the semantic similarity. We will evaluate the impact of changes in upper hierarchy levels in future research.

When comparing the measures with the WSC, it can be seen that structural changes can increase or decrease the WSC (see Table 1). However, the metric is limited when RBAC changes are injected and the WSC of the prescriptive and generative model is identical (see models $RM_{cch,100-p\%}$). In this case, the structural and semantical RBAC changes (e.g., in $RM_{cch,86}$ or $RM_{cch,93}$) cannot be exposed as WSC summarizes the RBAC state.

7. RELATED WORK

Anomaly detection is an important problem that has been researched in many areas of application domains such as intrusion detection or statistics (see [6]). Furthermore, graphs can be used for anomaly detection such as in Noble et al. [20] where anomalous substructures or subgraphs are detected. In case of RBAC, Park et al. [21] provide a role-oriented profile analysis in order to monitor insiders using frequency patterns. In this paper, we use graph-transformed RBAC models to analyze the behavior of insiders by analyzing structural and semantic differences.

Generative RBAC models have gained increased attention from the research community (e.g., [19, 3, 7]). For example in Baumgrass et al. [3], model matching techniques are used to migrate a generative RBAC model to a target-state RBAC model. Here, the migration is performed via edit operations to transform one model to another. Our approach aims to investigate anomalies between RBAC models to identify insider threats. Therefore, we use edit operations to compute the distance measures between graphs. Another example for RBAC comparison is the delta analysis in Leitner [15] that aims to compare two RBAC models in order to detect errors or violations in RBAC configurations. In this paper, we propose structural and semantic measures that can be used for delta analysis.

Moreover, graph representations of RBAC models are used such as in Koch et al. [12] that provide a formalization of RBAC models using graph transformations. Another example in Zhang et al. [29] uses RBAC graphs for role engineering. Furthermore, research has provided several metrics to analyze characteristics of RBAC such as the WSC in Molloy et al. [18] or the accuracy or coverage of roles in Zhang et al. [27]. For example, the accuracy and coverage are metrics to identify similarities for role sets and user-permission sets. In our approach, we investigate similarities on node (user, role, and permission) and model level. Moreover, [24, 23] measure the similarity between two role sets with the Jaccard coefficient. We adapt this approach to evaluate the semantic similarity between roles.

8. CONCLUSION

This paper provided an approach to identify anomalies in RBAC models that may indicate insider threats. Thereby, we compare a prescriptive RBAC model to a generative RBAC model (e.g., derived from event logs). Furthermore, we provide metrics for structural and semantic differences between RBAC models. In addition, we provide visualization techniques to evaluate our metrics with an experimental setup and examples. Our approach not only identifies and exposes potential anomalies in RBAC models but also can be used for RBAC alignments. As this was an initial step towards anomaly detection in RBAC models, for future work, we plan to investigate semi-supervised techniques and to discover collective anomalies.

9. ACKNOWLEDGMENTS

The research was funded by COMET K1, FFG - Austrian Research Promotion Agency.

10. REFERENCES

[1] M. Alanen and I. Porres. Difference and union of models. In *UML '03*, number 2863 in LNCS, pages 2–17. Springer, Jan. 2003.

[2] A. Baumgrass. Deriving current-state RBAC models from event logs. In *ARES '11*, pages 667–672, 2011.

[3] A. Baumgrass and M. Strembeck. Bridging the gap between role mining and role engineering via migration guides. *Information Security Technical Report*, 17(4):148–172, May 2013.

[4] H. Bunke. On a relation between graph edit distance and maximum common subgraph. *Pattern Recognition Letters*, 18(8):689–694, 1997.

[5] H. Bunke and K. Shearer. A graph distance metric based on the maximal common subgraph. *Pattern Recognition Letters*, 19(3–4):255–259, Mar. 1998.

[6] V. Chandola, A. Banerjee, and V. Kumar. Anomaly detection: A survey. *ACM Comput. Surv.*, 41(3):15:1–15:58, July 2009.

[7] S. Chari, I. Molloy, Y. Park, and W. Teiken. Ensuring continuous compliance through reconciling policy with usage. In *SACMAT '13*, page 49–60. ACM, 2013.

[8] D. Conte, P. Foggia, C. Sansone, and M. Vento. Thirty years of graph matching in pattern recognition. *Int. Journal of Pattern Recognition and Artificial Intelligence*, 18(03):265–298, May 2004.

[9] P. J. Dickinson, H. Bunke, A. Dadej, and M. Kraetzl. Matching graphs with unique node labels. *Pattern Analysis and Applications*, 7(3):243–254, Dec. 2004.

[10] A. Ene, W. Horne, N. Milosavljevic, P. Rao, R. Schreiber, and R. E. Tarjan. Fast exact and heuristic methods for role minimization problems. In *SACMAT '08*, page 1–10. ACM, 2008.

[11] D. F. Ferraiolo, R. Sandhu, S. Gavrila, D. R. Kuhn, and R. Chandramouli. Proposed NIST standard for role-based access control. *ACM Trans. Inf. Syst. Secur.*, 4(3):224–274, 2001.

[12] M. Koch, L. V. Mancini, and F. Parisi-Presicce. A graph-based formalism for RBAC. *ACM Trans. Inf. Syst. Secur.*, 5(3):332–365, Aug. 2002.

[13] S. Kriglstein, G. Wallner, and S. Rinderle-Ma. A visualization approach for difference analysis of process models and instance traffic. In *BPM*, pages 219–226. Springer, 2013.

[14] M. Kuhlmann, D. Shohat, and G. Schimpf. Role mining - revealing business roles for security administration using data mining technology. In *SACMAT '03*, page 179–186. ACM, 2003.

[15] M. Leitner. Delta analysis of role-based access control models. In *EUROCAST '13*, volume 8111 of *LNCS*, pages 507–514. Springer, 2013.

[16] M. Leitner and S. Rinderle-Ma. A systematic review on security in process-aware information systems – constitution, challenges, and future directions. *Information and Software Technology*, 56:273–293, 2014.

[17] R. Li, H. Li, W. Wang, X. Ma, and X. Gu. RMiner: a tool set for role mining. In *SACMAT '13*, page 193–196. ACM, 2013.

[18] I. Molloy, H. Chen, T. Li, Q. Wang, N. Li, E. Bertino, S. Calo, and J. Lobo. Mining roles with semantic meanings. In *SACMAT '08*, page 21–30. ACM, 2008.

[19] I. Molloy, Y. Park, and S. Chari. Generative models for access control policies: applications to role mining over logs with attribution. In *SACMAT '12*, page 45–56. ACM, 2012.

[20] C. C. Noble and D. J. Cook. Graph-based anomaly detection. In *KDD '03*, page 631–636. ACM, 2003.

[21] J. Park and J. Giordano. Role-based profile analysis for scalable and accurate insider-anomaly detection. In *IPCCC '06*, 2006.

[22] M. Strembeck. Scenario-driven role engineering. *Security Privacy, IEEE*, 8(1):28 –35, Feb. 2010.

[23] H. Takabi and J. B. Joshi. StateMiner: an efficient similarity-based approach for optimal mining of role hierarchy. In *SACMAT '10*, page 55–64. ACM, 2010.

[24] J. Vaidya, V. Atluri, and Q. Guo. The role mining problem: finding a minimal descriptive set of roles. In *SACMAT '07*, page 175–184. ACM, 2007.

[25] J. Vaidya, V. Atluri, Q. Guo, and N. Adam. Migrating to optimal RBAC with minimal perturbation. In *SACMAT '08*, page 11–20. ACM, 2008.

[26] W. D. Wallis, P. Shoubridge, M. Kraetz, and D. Ray. Graph distances using graph union. *Pattern Recognition Letters*, 22(6–7):701–704, May 2001.

[27] D. Zhang, K. Ramamohanarao, T. Ebringer, and T. Yann. Permission set mining: Discovering practical and useful roles. In *ACSAC '08*, pages 247–256, 2008.

[28] D. Zhang, K. Ramamohanarao, S. Versteeg, and R. Zhang. RoleVAT: visual assessment of practical need for role based access control. In *ACSAC '09*, pages 13–22, 2009.

[29] D. Zhang, K. Ramamohanarao, S. Versteeg, and R. Zhang. Graph based strategies to role engineering. In *CSIIRW '10*, page 25:1–25:4. ACM, 2010.

APPENDIX

A. REVIEW FUNCTIONS

The review functions required in this paper are defined as follows (based on [11]):

DEFINITION 7 (REVIEW FUNCTIONS ON RBAC MODELS). Let $RBAC := (U, R, P, UA, PA, RH)$ be an RBAC model. Then we define the following review functions:

- $d\_senior : R \mapsto 2^R$ with
  $d\_senior(r) = \{r' \in R \mid \exists(r', r) \in RH\}$

- $senior : R \mapsto 2^R$ with
  $senior(r) = \{r' \mid r' \in d\_senior(r) \vee \exists r'' \in d\_senior(r) : r' \in senior(r'')\}$

- $d\_junior : R \mapsto 2^R$ with
  $d\_junior(r) = \{r' \in R \mid \exists(r, r') \in RH\}$

- $junior : R \mapsto 2^R$ with
  $junior(r) = \{r' \mid r' \in d\_junior(r) \vee \exists r'' \in d\_junior(r) : r' \in junior(r'')\}$

- $authorizedUsers : R \mapsto 2^U$ with
  $authorizedUsers(r) = \{u \in U \mid \exists ua \in UA \text{ with } ua = (u, r) \vee ua = (u, senior(r))\}$

- $authorizedRoles : U \mapsto 2^R$ with
  $authorizedRoles(u) = \{r \in R \mid \exists ua \in UA \text{ with } ua = (u, r) \vee ua = (u, junior(r))\}$

- $userPermissions : U \mapsto 2^P$ with
  $userPermissions(u) = \{p \in P \mid \exists ua \in UA, pa \in PA \text{ with } (ua = (u, r) \wedge pa = (r, p)) \vee (ua = (u, junior(r)) \wedge pa = (junior(r), p))\}$

- $permissionsUser : P \mapsto 2^U$ with
  $permissionsUser(p) = \{u \in U \mid \exists ua \in UA, pa \in PA \text{ with } (ua = (u, r) \wedge pa = (r, p)) \vee (ua = (u, senior(r)) \wedge pa = (senior(r), p))\}$

- $rolePermissions : R \mapsto 2^P$ with
  $rolePermissions(r) = \{p \in P \mid \exists pa \in PA \text{ with } pa = (r, p) \vee pa = (junior(r), p)\}$

- $permissionRoles : P \mapsto 2^R$ with
  $permissionRoles(p) = \{r \in R \mid \exists pa \in PA \text{ with } pa = (r, p) \vee pa = (senior(r), p)\}$

B. SIMILARITY FUNCTION

For the computation of the semantic similarity, the similarity function is defined as follows:

DEFINITION 8 (SIMILARITY FUNCTION). *The similarity function $sim(n)$ returns the node similarity for a node n.*

$$sim(n) = \begin{cases} userSim(u_i, u_j) \ for \ n = u_j \\ roleSim(r_i, r_j) \ for \ n = r_j \\ permSim(p_i, p_j) \ for \ n = p_j \end{cases} \quad (7)$$

C. ALGORITHM SEMANTIC DISTANCE

Algorithm 1 computes the semantic distance between two RBAC models.

D. VISUALIZATION

The visualization of the difference graph requires the definition of the visual elements as shown in Table 3. Furthermore, Table 4 outlines the visual elements used in the similarity graph. See Appendix B for a definition of the function sim. For x, y, we specify $0.0 < x < y < 1.0$.

E. ALGORITHMS FOR ANOMALY INJECTION

Algorithm 2 injects new vertices and Algorithm 3 injects "missing" vertices into a graph-based representation of an

---

Algorithm 1 Semantic Distance: $dSem(RM_1, RM_2)$

Require: Two RBAC models: RM_1, RM_2.
Require: Weights $w_{ur}, w_{up}, w_{ru}, w_{rh}, w_{rp}, w_{sen}, w_{jun}, w_{pu}, w_{pr}$.
Require: Threshold t.

$sumSemSim \leftarrow 0$
$count \leftarrow 0$
$nodeSim \leftarrow 0$
$matchedNodes = N_1 \cap N_2$
for each $n \in N_1 \cup N_2$ **do**
  if $n \in matchedNodes$ **then**
    if n is a user node **then**
      $simUR \leftarrow \frac{|\text{authorizedRoles}(n_1) \cap \text{authorizedRoles}(n_2)|}{|\text{authorizedRoles}(n_1) \cup \text{authorizedRoles}(n_2)|}$
      $simUP \leftarrow \frac{|\text{userPermissions}(n_1) \cap \text{userPermissions}(n_2)|}{|\text{userPermissions}(n_1) \cup \text{userPermissions}(n_2)|}$
      $nodeSim \leftarrow w_{ur} * simUR + w_{up} * simUP$
    else if n is a role node **then**
      $simRU \leftarrow \frac{|\text{authorizedUsers}(n_1) \cap \text{authorizedUsers}(n_2)|}{|\text{authorizedUsers}(n_1) \cup \text{authorizedUsers}(n_2)|}$
      $simRH \leftarrow w_{sen} * \frac{min(|\text{senior}(n_1)|, |\text{senior}(n_2)|)}{max(|\text{senior}(n_1)|, |\text{senior}(n_2)|)} + w_{jun} * \frac{min(|\text{junior}(n_1)|, |\text{junior}(n_2)|)}{max(|\text{junior}(n_1)|, |\text{junior}(n_2)|)}$
      $simRP \leftarrow \frac{|\text{rolePermissions}(n_1) \cap \text{rolePermissions}(n_2)|}{|\text{rolePermissions}(n_1) \cup \text{rolePermissions}(n_2)|}$
      $nodeSim \leftarrow w_{ru} * simRU + w_{rh} * simRH + w_{rp} * simRP$
    else if n is a permission node **then**
      $simRP \leftarrow \frac{|\text{permissionRoles}(n_1) \cap \text{permissionRoles}(n_2)|}{|\text{permissionRoles}(n_1) \cup \text{permissionRoles}(n_2)|}$
      $simPU \leftarrow \frac{|\text{permissionUsers}(n_1) \cap \text{permissionUsers}(n_2)|}{|\text{permissionUsers}(n_1) \cup \text{permissionUsers}(n_2)|}$
      $nodeSim \leftarrow w_{pr} * simRP + w_{pu} * simPU$
    end if
    $sumSemSim \leftarrow sumSemSim + nodeSim$
    $count \leftarrow count + 1$
    $nodeSim \leftarrow 0$
  else
    $nodeSim \leftarrow t$
    $sumSemSim \leftarrow sumSemSim + nodeSim$
    $count \leftarrow count + 1$
  end if
end for
return $\left(1 - \frac{sumSemSim}{count}\right)$

RBAC model. Algorithm 4 injects connectivity changes into an RBAC model; it reassigns user or permission nodes to role nodes. In the following, we describe the utilized functions in the algorithms:

- $createRandomUserPermVertex()$ creates a new user or permission node,

- $selectRandomEdge(E)$ returns a random edge from a edge set E,

- $selectRandomVertex(N)$ returns a random vertex from a node set N,

- $selectRandomVertexSet(N)$ returns a random set of vertices from a node set N,

- $source()$ returns the source node and $target()$ returns the target node of a directed edge,

- and $outNeighbors()$ returns a set of out-neighbors of a vertex, and $inNeighbors()$ returns a set of in-neighbors of a vertex.

Table 4: Representation of Nodes/ Edges in the Similarity Model

Symbol	Meaning	Description
Green node	High similarity	$\forall n \in N_2 \wedge n \in N_1$ where $sim(n) \geq y \wedge sim(n) \leq 1.0$
Orange node	Medium similarity	$\forall n \in N_2 \wedge n \in N_1$ where $sim(n) \geq x \wedge sim(n) < y$
Red node	Low similarity	$\forall n \in N_2 \wedge n \in N_1$ where $sim(n) \geq 0.0 \wedge sim(n) < x$
Blue node	New node	$\forall n \in N_2 \wedge n \notin N_1$ where $sim(n) = t$

Table 3: Representation of Nodes/ Edges in the Difference Model

Symbol	Meaning	Description
(id)	New node	$\forall n \in N_2$ for $M_N(n) = 1$
(id)	Deleted node	$\forall n \in N_2$ for $M_N(n) = -1$
⟶	New edge	$\forall e \in E_2$ for $M_E(n) = 1$
⟶	Deleted edge	$\forall e \in E_2$ for $M_E(n) = -1$

Algorithm 2 Injection of new vertices: $injectNewVertices(RM, p)$

Require: RBAC model: $RM = (U, R, P, UA, PA, RH)$.
Require: Percentage p.

$numNewVertices \leftarrow \frac{|U|+|R|+|P|}{100} * p$
for $i = 1$ to $numNewVertices$ **do**
  $n \leftarrow createRandomUserPermVertex()$
  $r \leftarrow selectRandomVertex(R)$
  if n is a user node **then**
    $U \leftarrow U \cup \{n\}$
    $RS \leftarrow selectRandomVertexSet(R)$
    for each $r \in RS$ **do**
      $UA \leftarrow UA \cup \{(n, r)\}$
    end for
  else if n is a permission node **then**
    $P \leftarrow P \cup \{n\}$
    $RS \leftarrow selectRandomVertexSet(R)$
    for each $r \in RS$ **do**
      $PA \leftarrow PA \cup \{(r, n)\}$
    end for
  end if
end for
return RM

Algorithm 3 Injection of "missing" vertices: $injectMisVertices(RM, p)$

Require: RBAC model: $RM = (U, R, P, UA, PA, RH)$.
Require: Percentage p.

$numMisVertices \leftarrow \frac{|U|+|R|+|P|}{100} * p$
for $i = 1$ to $numMisVertices$ **do**
  $n \leftarrow selectRandomVertex(U \cup P)$
  if n is a user node **then**
    for each $(n, r) \in UA$ **do**
      $UA \leftarrow UA \setminus \{(n, r)\}$
    end for
    $U \leftarrow U \setminus \{n\}$
  else if n is a permission node **then**
    for each $(r, n) \in PA$ **do**
      $PA \leftarrow PA \setminus \{(r, n)\}$
    end for
    $P \leftarrow P \setminus \{n\}$
  end if
end for
return RM

Algorithm 4 Injection of connectivity changes: $injectCChanges(RM, p)$

Require: RBAC model: $RM = (U, R, P, UA, PA, RH)$.
Require: Percentage p.

$numCchEdges \leftarrow \frac{|U|+|R|+|P|}{100} * p$
for $i = 1$ to $numCchEdges$ **do**
  $e \leftarrow selectRandomEdge(UA \cup PA)$
  $sourceVertex \leftarrow e.source()$
  $targetVertex \leftarrow e.target()$
  if $e \in UA$ **then**
    $RS \leftarrow R \setminus \{targetVertex\}$
    $RS \leftarrow RS \setminus \{sourceVertex.outNeighbors()\}$
    $r \leftarrow selectRandomVertex(RS)$
    $UA \leftarrow UA \setminus \{e\}$
    $UA \leftarrow UA \cup \{(sourceVertex, r)\}$
  else if $e \in PA$ **then**
    $RS \leftarrow R \setminus \{sourceVertex\}$
    $RS \leftarrow RS \setminus \{targetVertex.inNeighbors()\}$
    $r \leftarrow selectRandomVertex(RS)$
    $PA \leftarrow PA \setminus \{e\}$
    $PA \leftarrow PA \cup \{(r, targetVertex)\}$
  end if
end for
return RM

Reduction of Access Control Decisions

Charles Morisset
Centre for Cybercrime and Computer Security
Newcastle University, U.K.
charles.morisset@newcastle.ac.uk

Nicola Zannone
Eindhoven University of Technology
n.zannone@tue.nl

ABSTRACT

Access control has been proposed as "the" solution to prevent unauthorized accesses to sensitive system resources. Historically, access control models use a two-valued decision set to indicate whether an access should be granted or denied. Many access control models have extended the two-valued decision set to indicate, for instance, whether a policy is applicable to an access query or an error occurred during policy evaluation. Decision sets are often coupled with operators for combining decisions from multiple applicable policies. Although a larger decision set is more expressive, it may be necessary to reduce it to a smaller set in order to simplify the complexity of decision making or enable comparison between access control models. Moreover, some access control mechanisms like XACML v3 uses more than one decision set. The projection from one decision set to the other may result in a loss of accuracy, which can affect the final access decision. In this paper, we present a formal framework for the analysis and comparison of decision sets centered on the notion of decision reduction. In particular, we introduce the notion of safe reduction, which ensures that a reduction can be performed at any level of policy composition without changing the final decision. We demonstrate the framework by analyzing XACML v3 against the notion of safe reduction. From this analysis, we draw guidelines for the selection of the minimal decision set with respect to a given set of combining operators.

Categories and Subject Descriptors

D.4.6 [**Security and Protection**]: Access controls

General Terms

Security, Theory

Keywords

Policy evaluation, access decision, XACML, formal analysis

SACMAT'14, June 25–27, 2014, London, Ontario, Canada.
Copyright 2014 ACM 978-1-4503-2939-2/14/06 ...$15.00.
http://dx.doi.org/10.1145/2613087.2613106.

1. INTRODUCTION

An access control mechanism can generally be seen as a system taking as input an access query from the environment (typically submitted by a user) and deciding whether to allow this query or not, possibly by collecting the current contextual information. Although such a mechanism can also decide to modify the query to make it acceptable, or to request some obligations to be fulfilled at runtime, it should eventually decide whether to allow the query or not.

An access control mechanism usually relies on one or several *access control policies*, which are functions associating access queries with decisions. In other words, given a set of queries Q and a set of decisions D, a policy is a function $\pi : Q \to D$. Whenever the range of a policy π is a subset of $\{1, 0\}$, indicating that a query should be allowed and denied, respectively, we say π is *enforceable*, i.e., an access control mechanism can directly enforce this policy without the need of interpreting the decision. For instance, a trivial example of enforceable policy is a function π_1 such that for any query q, $\pi_1(q) = 1$, i.e., the policy allowing every possible query.

However, defining a single enforceable policy for a large set of queries can be quite challenging: a simple enumeration of the allowed (or denied) queries is likely to contain mistakes, especially when the system changes. Hence, the usual approach to define an enforceable policy is compositional, i.e., sub-policies corresponding to different concerns are first defined, and then composed together. Each sub-policy can also be defined in a compositional way. For instance, a security designer might want to define: a confidentiality policy over read accesses and an integrity policy over write accesses; a different policy for each business role in a company; a regular policy and an emergency policy, and so on.

It is therefore often useful to introduce decisions beyond 1 and 0 in order to represent the possible interactions between the different policies. For instance, a typical decision is "not-applicable" (denoted here $\bot$), which indicates that a policy cannot be applied to a query. In the previous examples, a policy regulating the read accesses to a file is not applicable to queries for write access, and thus it cannot make any *conclusive* decision for such queries. Similarly, the policy for a nurse might not be applicable to a physician or an administrator. We present in Section 2 several examples of decision sets, which usually come with specific decision operators, describing how to compose decisions.

Although a larger set of decisions provides more flexibility to compose sub-policies, it also implies that the access control mechanism might not know how to interpret decisions which are neither 1 nor 0. For instance, a mechanism having to control a query q for which the policy returned $\perp$ is facing two options: it could deny q, interpreting $\perp$ as "providing no evidence that the query should be granted", or allow q, interpreting $\perp$ as "providing no evidence that the query should be denied". In addition, different access control mechanisms might need to interact together in order to provide the final decision, and if they use different decision sets, it is not directly possible to combine their decisions.

It is therefore useful, when introducing new decisions, to also introduce a *reduction* function, which defines how to reduce a decision set to a smaller one. Such a function serves several purposes: it allows the mechanism to make a conclusive decision by reducing inconclusive ones; it allows to reuse on a smaller set of decisions operators defined on a larger set; it provides a common ground for different mechanisms to interact. A reduction function between decision sets, however, can introduce weaknesses in the access control mechanism. Indeed, it might change the intended semantics of a policy. In particular, applying a reduction function to different stages of the policy evaluation process may result in a different decision. These considerations raise the main research question addressed in this paper: *How (and when) to reduce a decision set while preserving the policy semantics?*

The main contribution of this paper is a formal framework around the notion of reduction between decision sets. In particular, we introduce the notion of *safe reduction*, which ensures that a reduction can be performed at any level of policy composition without changing the final decision. We illustrate the framework by analyzing XACML v3 [2], the de facto standard for the specification and enforcement of access control policies. What makes XACML v3 an interesting access control mechanism to investigate is that it uses two decision sets. In particular, it uses the four-valued decision set of XACML v2 [1] in which indeterminacy is represented using a single decision value; in addition, it introduces an extended set for indeterminacy to represent the potential decision to be returned if there would not have been an error causing the indeterminacy. Combining operators in XACML v3 are defined over either a decision set or the other. Therefore, decision values have to be projected from one decision set to the other depending on the used operator. We show that the reduction between these two sets defined in [2] may lead to counter-intuitive results. Based on this analysis, we provide guidelines for the selection of the minimal decision set preserving the policy semantics with respect to a given set of combining operators.

The remainder of the paper is organized as follows. The next section provides an overview of the decision sets defined in the literature. Section 3 introduces the notion of decision reduction and discusses the issues that can arise when a decision set is reduced using some examples. Section 4 formalizes the notion of safe reduction. Section 5 presents an analysis of XACML v3 against the notion of safe reduction and provides guidelines for the selection of the minimal decision set. Finally, Section 6 concludes the paper.

2. DECISION SET

To the best of our knowledge, there is no related work specifically on the reduction of one decision set to another. There is, however, a rich literature on the definition of different decision sets, in order to represent different problems. In this section, we present an overview of some of these decision sets. In general, a decision set is a set $\mathcal{D} = \{d_1, \ldots, d_n\}$,

where each d_i represents a distinct decision that can be returned by a policy. For the sake of clarity, we refer to 1 and 0, representing allow and deny respectively, as conclusive decisions, since they can be directly enforced by an access control mechanism.

2.1 Two-valued

Historically, the decision set was simply $\mathcal{D}_2 = \{0, 1\}$. For instance, Lampson [15] introduces the notion of access matrix, where a subject can access an object if and only if the corresponding access right exists in the matrix. Similarly, the protection matrix of the HRU model [13] explicitly denies or allows accesses. Bell-Lapadula [5] and Chinese Wall [6] models extends the notion of access matrix by considering a lattice of levels of security and conflict of interest classes, respectively, but still define a strict partition of accesses between those allowed and those denied. Similarly, the RBAC model [12] introduces more flexibility with the notion of role, but an access is allowed if the subject has a role with the corresponding decision, and denied otherwise.

The classical Boolean operators can be used when composing access control policies ranging in $\mathcal{D}_2$.

2.2 Three-valued

Specifying and managing access control policies is a difficult and error-prone task which may lead to grant permissions to the wrong users. To this end, policy languages should allow the specification of exceptions to make it explicit in which cases access should not be granted. The concept of exception has led to the differentiation between positive and negative policies [11], where positive policies are used to represent privileges and negative policies are used to represent restrictions. This idea has been further extended by the introduction of structured languages to define security policies [21]. Although this allows the specification of fine-grained access control policies and facilitates policy management, it introduces some challenges.

An access control policy unlikely covers all possible queries that can be specified. This results in situations in which any (positive or negative) policy that matches a given query does not exist. In addition, a query may be *incomplete*, i.e., there is not enough available information to determine whether an access should be granted or denied [21]. To capture these situations, it is necessary to introduce a decision that indicates that a policy is not applicable.

On the other hand, the adoption of structured languages allows the specification of composite policies. Intuitively, a policy can be formed of sub-policies, where each sub-policy corresponds to a different concern of the protection system or represent the same concerns from the perspective of a different authority. In this setting, more than one sub-policy may be applicable to a given query. Therefore, it is necessary to have mechanisms to combine the decisions returned by different applicable policies.

Crampton and Huth [9] consider the set $\mathcal{D}_3 = \{1, 0, \perp\}$, where $\perp$ stands for the non-applicable decision. To combine decisions obtained by applying different applicable policies, they provide a characterization of combining operators over $\mathcal{D}_3$. A binary operator $\oplus$ is said to be a $\sqcup$-operator when $x \oplus \perp = x = \perp \oplus x$, for any decision x. Similarly, an operator $\oplus$ is said to be a $\sqcap$-operator when $x \oplus \perp = \perp = \perp \oplus x$, for any x. Rao et al. [18] define the Fine-grained Integration Algebra, which supports policies ranging in $\mathcal{D}_3$. Furthermore,

$\sqcap$	1	0	$\bot$
1	1	0	$\bot$
0	0	0	$\bot$
$\bot$	$\bot$	$\bot$	$\bot$

(a) Weak conjunction

$\sqcup$	1	0	$\bot$
1	1	1	$\bot$
0	1	0	$\bot$
$\bot$	$\bot$	$\bot$	$\bot$

(b) Weak disjunction

$\tilde{\sqcap}$	1	0	$\bot$
1	1	0	$\bot$
0	0	0	0
$\bot$	$\bot$	0	$\bot$

(c) Strong conjunction

$\tilde{\sqcup}$	1	0	$\bot$
1	1	1	1
0	1	0	$\bot$
$\bot$	1	$\bot$	$\bot$

(d) Strong disjunction

Figure 1: Binary operators over $\mathcal{D}_3 = \{1, 0, \bot\}$

X	$\neg X$	$\sim X$
1	0	1
0	1	0
$\bot$	$\bot$	0

Figure 2: Unary operators over $\mathcal{D}_3 = \{1, 0, \bot\}$

they prove that their algebra is complete, i.e., it can express all possible ways of integrating policies. The language EPAL [4], an XML-based language for privacy policies, also uses non-applicable as third value.

Crampton and Morisset [10] use a three-valued logics for the evaluation of policy targets in PTaCL, based on Kleene algebra. Figures 1 and 2 define some operators for the three-valued logic over $\mathcal{D}_3$: $\sqcap$ and $\sqcup$ represent the weak conjunction and disjunction, respectively; $\tilde{\sqcap}$ and $\tilde{\sqcup}$ represent the strong conjunction and disjunction, respectively; $\neg$ is the negation operator; and $\sim$ is a "weakening" operator, transforming $\bot$ into 0. Jobe [14] proved that the set of operators $\{\tilde{\sqcup}, \neg, \sim\}$ is functionally complete.

2.3 Four-valued

Many factors may influence an access decision; capturing these factors in the decision requires extending the decision set. Two main factors have led to the extension of $\mathcal{D}_3$ with an additional value: (i) the notion of conflict and (ii) errors which can occur in policy evaluation.

2.3.1 Conflict

As said above, traditional access control models, such as those described in Section 2.1 only allow the specification of "positive" policies (i.e., policies that specify the actions that a user can perform on an object). Intuitively, an access is denied unless there exists a policy which matches the access query.

In contrast, structured languages allow the specification of composite policies comprising both positive and negative sub-policies to regulate the access to sensitive resources and data. This may result in conflicts during policy evaluation, as some policies can grant permission and others deny the very same permission.

Many policy algebras especially rooted on $\mathcal{D}_3$ aim to resolve conflicts, i.e., choosing between 1 or 0 when both decisions are returned by different sub-policies, for instance using the conjunction or disjunction operator. However, in some cases it is desirable to record that a conflict occurred. To this end, a more fine-grained decision set is needed. For instance, Bruns and Huth [7] introduce a new decision, denoted as $\top$, to allow for an explicit notion of conflict.

The new decision set $\mathcal{D}_4 = \{1, 0, \bot, \top\}$ can be intuitively obtained by considering the powerset of the two-valued decision set. In particular, the powerset of $\mathcal{D}_2$ is defined as $\wp(\mathcal{D}_2) = \{\emptyset, \{0\}, \{1\}, \{0, 1\}\}$. The meaning of each of these decisions can be understood as follows:

- $\emptyset$ indicates that the decision is neither 0 nor 1. In other words, the policy cannot reach any conclusive decision. This is modeled as the decision $\bot$ in [7], and can be interpreted as the non-applicable decision.

- $\{0\}$ and $\{1\}$ indicates that the policy reached the conclusive decision 0 and 1, respectively.

- $\{0, 1\}$ indicates that the policy reached the decision that the query should be both allowed and denied. This is modeled as decision $\top$ in [7], and can be interpreted as the conflict decision.

Intuitively, a decision in $\mathcal{D}_4$ corresponds to *all* the decisions in the set, and therefore the operators defined for $\mathcal{D}_2$ can be extended to $\mathcal{D}_4$ in a point-wise way, i.e., given any operator $op : \mathcal{D}_2 \times \mathcal{D}_2 \to \mathcal{D}_2$ and any sets $X, Y \subseteq \mathcal{D}_2$, we define operator $\overline{op} : \mathcal{D}_4 \times \mathcal{D}_4 \to \mathcal{D}_4$ as

$$\overline{op}(X, Y) = \{op(x, y) \mid x \in X \wedge y \in Y\}$$

According to [20], a language ensuring that no policy can return $\emptyset$ is said to be total, while a language ensuring that no policy can return $\{0, 1\}$ is said to be deterministic.

2.3.2 Indeterminate

Conflicts are not the only case where a conclusive decision cannot be made. Errors occurring in policy evaluation also introduce uncertainty into decision-making. A policy language which introduces a decision to indicate the occurrence of errors in the policy evaluation process is XACML v2 [1]. In particular, XACML v2 uses decision set {Permit, Deny, NA, Indeterminate}, where Permit represents the permit decision, Deny the deny decision, NA represents that the policy is not applicable to the given query, and Indeterminate indicates that the policy decision point is unable to evaluate the query because of some error (e.g., missing attributes, division by zero, network errors while retrieving policies, syntax errors in the query or in the policy). This decision set corresponds to $\mathcal{D}_4 = \{1, 0, \bot, \top\}$, where $\top$ now stands for the decision representing indeterminacy. XACML v2 also provides a number of combining algorithms to make a decision when more than one policy is applicable: permit-overrides, deny-overrides, first-applicable, only-one-applicable. Intuitively, these algorithms define procedures to evaluate composite policies based on the order of the sub-policies and priorities between decisions.

It is worth mentioning that even though, strictly speaking, XACML v2 considers a four-valued decision set, some combining algorithms distinguish the case where Indeterminate is obtained from a permit rule and the case where Indeterminate is obtained from a deny rule; however, such a distinction is not explicit. In other words, the semantics of decision Indeterminate might change according to the effect of the policy that returned it. As we show in the next section, XACML v3 clarifies this semantics by introducing the extended set for the Indeterminate decision.

Li et al. formalize in [16] the notion of policy combining algorithms as defined in XACML v2, and as such also considers the set $\mathcal{D}_4 = \{1, 0, \bot, \top\}$, where $\top$ stands for the Indeterminate decision. In addition to the XACML operators, they also define consensus and majority operators, using linear constraints. Finally, Arieli and Avron define in [3] the operators $\neg$, $\oplus$ and $\supset$, intuitively corresponding to the negation, non-deterministic choice and implication, respectively, and prove that $\{\neg, \oplus, \supset, \bot, \top\}$ is functionally complete for $\mathcal{D}_4$.

2.4 Six-valued

XACML v3 [2] uses two decision sets. Besides the decision set of XACML v2, XACML v3 refines the notion of indeterminacy by introducing the Indeterminate extended set: Indeterminate{P}, Indeterminate{D} and Indeterminate{PD}. Intuitively, the new Indeterminate decisions indicate the evaluation of a policy if an error would not have occurred. This results in the set $\mathcal{D}_6 = \{$Permit, Deny, NA, Indeterminate{P}, Indeterminate{D}, Indeterminate{PD}$\}$. The choice of the decision set depends on the algorithm used to combine policies. In particular, permit-overrides and deny-overrides are defined using the Indeterminate extended set and therefore over $\mathcal{D}_6$; in contrast, the other combining algorithms – first-applicable, permit-unless-deny, deny-unless-deny and only-one-applicable – are defined over $\mathcal{D}_4$.

2.5 Seven-valued

The intuition behind the extended set defined in XACML v3 is that an indeterminate decision effectively corresponds to several decisions. For instance, Indeterminate{P} indicates that a policy could have either evaluated to NA or to Permit, but not to Deny.

The language PTaCL [10] makes this intuition explicit by considering $\mathcal{D}_7 = \wp(\mathcal{D}_3) \setminus \emptyset$ as the decision set, i.e., a decision is a non-empty subset of $\mathcal{D}_3 = \{1, 0, \bot\}$, representing all the possible decisions. In this case, Indeterminate{P} is encoded as $\{1, \bot\}$. In a similar way than operators over $\mathcal{D}_2$ can be extended in a point-wise way to operators over $\mathcal{D}_4$, operators over $\mathcal{D}_3$ can be extended over $\mathcal{D}_7$. For instance, Figure 4 presents the definition of weak conjunction $\sqcap$ over $\mathcal{D}_7$.

2.6 Other decision sets

A decision set can also be defined in a more general way. For instance, the D-algebra [17] uses multi-valued logics, such as the Lukasiewicz logic, to represent the decision set. The D-algebra is defined for a non-empty set of decisions, and the operators, which intuitively correspond to negation, strong disjunction and test for equality, are algebraically specified.

A decision can also be defined as a risk value [8], i.e., as the probability of an event to happen if this decision is enforced multiplied by the impact of this event.

In general, there is no strict limit to the way a decision set can be defined. The definition of the decision set depends on the specific needs of the system in which the access control mechanism is deployed.

3. DECISION REDUCTION

As illustrated in the previous section, there is a large variety of access decision sets in the literature, typically introduced to address a specific problem to be addressed by the corresponding access control language. For instance, a language handling uncertainty in the environment might use the XACML decision Indeterminate, in order to represent that something unexpected occurred, or a language requiring an explicit notion of conflict might use the decision $\top$, as defined in PBel [7].

However, this multiplicity of decision sets raises several issues. First, it is not always clear how non-conclusive decisions (i.e., neither 1 nor 0) should be treated at the enforcement point. In addition, languages can evolve over time, adding new decisions to handle new aspects (e.g., XACML from v2 to v3), and it could be desirable to ensure that the operators defined over the new set are compatible with the former set. Finally, access control systems using different decision sets might need to interact in order to make a decision, in which case they need to have a common ground. For instance, systems of systems (SoS) are dynamic coalitions of distributed, autonomous and heterogeneous systems that collaborate to achieve a common goal, and each system in the SoS can use a different access control model along with a different decision set [19].

In order to address these issues, we introduce here the notion of *decision reduction*, such that, intuitively speaking, a decision set is reduced into a smaller one. We focus here on the size of the decision sets, making the implicit assumption that two decision sets with the same size are equivalent. This is clearly an over-simplification, and it can be argued that the two different four-valued sets presented in Section 2.3 associate a different meaning with the fourth value, one being for conflict, the other for indeterminacy. However, we focus here on operators, which are defined similarly on both sets. A rigorous approach would be to define a notion of abstract set, for instance $\mathcal{D}_4 = \{0, 1, 2, 3\}$, and then to consider different interpretations, mapping each abstract decisions to a concrete one, for instance $\mathcal{D}_{\text{XACML}} = \{0 \mapsto \text{Deny}, 1 \mapsto \text{Permit}, 2 \mapsto \text{NA}, 3 \mapsto \text{Indeterminate}\}$ for the decision set of XACML v2. We believe there is little to be gained by adopting a rigorous approach here, and for the sake of simplicity, we do not make the distinction between abstract and concrete sets whenever it is clear from the context. In particular, we assume that the decision set of XACML v2, $\mathcal{D}_4$, is included into that of XACML v3, $\mathcal{D}_6$, such that Indeterminate and Indeterminate{PD} are just different interpretations of the same abstract decision. We argue that this assumption is reasonable: the XACML specification states that "the output of a combining algorithm which does not track the extended set of Indeterminate values MUST be treated as Indeterminate{PD} for the value Indeterminate by a combining algorithm which tracks the extended set of Indeterminate values" [2, C.1].

Hence, we now define the notion of reduction, which maps all decisions of a set to decisions of a subset, while leaving the decisions in the subset unchanged.

DEFINITION 1 (DECISION REDUCTION). *Given two decision sets $\mathcal{D}_n$ and $\mathcal{D}_m$ such that $\mathcal{D}_m \subseteq \mathcal{D}_n$, a reduction is a function $\rho : \mathcal{D}_n \to \mathcal{D}_m$ such that for any $d \in \mathcal{D}_m$, $\rho(d) = d$.*

Given two decision sets, more than one reduction function can be defined, corresponding to different interpretations of the reduced decisions. For instance, when reducing from $\mathcal{D}_3$ to $\mathcal{D}_2$, the decision $\bot$ can be projected either to 1 or to 0, corresponding to a less restrictive or a more conservative approach, respectively. Accordingly, we have re-

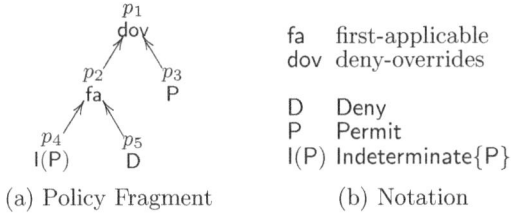

(a) Policy Fragment   (b) Notation

Figure 3: Policy Example

ductions ρ_{32}^1 and ρ_{32}^0 where $\rho_{32}^1(\bot) = 1$, $\rho_{32}^0(\bot) = 0$ and $\rho_{32}^1(d) = \rho_{32}^0(d) = d$ for $d \in \{0,1\}$.

A reduction from one set to another, however, may result in an unnecessary loss of accuracy, which has an effect on the final access decision. In particular, it might lead to accept a query that would have been intuitively denied, or conversely. In the remainder of the section, we discuss some examples in which decision reductions have an impact on the final access decision using some sample reductions.

XACML v3.

As mentioned in Section 2.4, XACML v3 is defined over two decision sets: $\mathcal{D}_4$ in which indeterminacy is modeled as a single decision Indeterminate, and $\mathcal{D}_6$ in which indeterminacy is modeled using the Indeterminate extended set. The Indeterminate extended set is only used for combining algorithms permit-overrides and deny-overrides. The other combining algorithms are defined over $\mathcal{D}_4$. Intuitively, decisions Indeterminate{P}, Indeterminate{D} and Indeterminate{PD} are projected onto decision Indeterminate when the policy has to be evaluated with respect to first-applicable, permit-unless-deny, deny-unless-permit, only-one-applicable. As said above, Indeterminate is considered equivalent to Indeterminate{PD} when the policy has to be evaluated with respect to permit-overrides and deny-overrides.

Consider the policy fragment in Figure 3. Policy p_1 consists of policies p_2 and p_3 which are combined using deny-overrides (dov, see Section 5 for its full definition). In turns, p_2 consists of policies p_4 and p_5 which are combined using first-applicable (fa). Suppose now that p_3 is evaluated to Permit, p_4 to Indeterminate{P}, and p_5 to Deny. Because of first-applicable, XACML v3 projects the decision of p_4 to Indeterminate, and thus $p_2 = \mathsf{fa}(p_4, p_5)$ evaluates to Indeterminate. The decision of p_2 is then projected to Indeterminate{PD}, and thus $p_1 = \mathsf{dov}(p_2, p_3)$ evaluates to Indeterminate{PD}. Now assume that the Indeterminate extended set is used with every combining algorithm. For instance, first-applicable can be intuitively extended over $\mathcal{D}_6$ by returning the decision of the first applicable policy (see Section 5 for a definition of first-applicable over $\mathcal{D}_6$). In this case, $p_2 = \mathsf{fa}(p_4, p_5)$ evaluates to Indeterminate{P}. Hence, $p_1 = \mathsf{dov}(p_2, p_3)$ evaluates to Permit.

From XACML v3 to XACML v2.

As another example of the loss of accuracy introduced by the extended set of XACML v3, consider the behavior of the operator dov with respect to the Indeterminate values, depending on whether evaluated in the context of XACML v2 or XACML v3. XACML v2 employs two versions of dov, one for combining rules and one for combining policies [1,

C.1]. The operator dov for policy is based on a single interpretation of Indeterminate and has the following behavior:

$$\mathsf{dov}(\mathsf{Indeterminate}, \mathsf{Permit}) = \mathsf{Deny}$$

In contrast, dov for rules takes into account the effect of the rule in which the error occurred in order to make a decision. In particular, it has the following behavior:

$$\mathsf{dov}(\mathsf{Indeterminate}, \mathsf{Permit}) = \mathsf{Permit} \qquad \text{if } e(I) = \mathsf{Permit}$$
$$\mathsf{dov}(\mathsf{Indeterminate}, \mathsf{Permit}) = \mathsf{Indeterminate} \qquad \text{if } e(I) = \mathsf{Deny}$$

where $e(I)$ indicates the effect of the rule which returns Indeterminate.

XACML v3 uses a single operator dov for both rules and policies [2, C.2], which generalizes dov for rules of XACML v2. Formally,

$$\mathsf{dov}(\mathsf{Indeterminate}\{P\}, \mathsf{Permit}) = \mathsf{Permit}$$
$$\mathsf{dov}(\mathsf{Indeterminate}\{D\}, \mathsf{Permit}) = \mathsf{Indeterminate}\{PD\}$$
$$\mathsf{dov}(\mathsf{Indeterminate}\{PD\}, \mathsf{Permit}) = \mathsf{Indeterminate}\{PD\}$$

Evaluating dov in the context of XACML v2 or XACML v3 poses some issues. It is evident that the semantics of dov for policy in XACML v2 is different from the one of dov in XACML v3. This difference has a significant impact on policy evaluation. Suppose we need to evaluate expression dov(Indeterminate{P}, Permit) in the context of XACML v2, where the value Indeterminate{P} needs to be reduced. We obtain different decisions depending on the point at which we apply the reduction. In particular, if we apply the reduction at the top level (i.e., first decisions are combined using dov of XACML v3 and then the decision is reduced), we obtain Permit; on the other hand, if we apply it at the sub-policy level (i.e., first decisions are reduced and then they are combined using dov of XACML v2), we obtain Deny (when dov for policy is used). Although we cannot necessarily decide which behavior is the correct one, we can analyze the operator dov to detect such inconsistencies, through the notion of *safe reduction*, introduced in Section 4.

From PTaCL to XACML v3.

PTaCL uses decision set $\mathcal{D}_7 = \wp(\{1, 0, \bot\}) \setminus \{\emptyset\}$, while XACML v3 uses decision set $\mathcal{D}_6 = \{\mathsf{Permit}, \mathsf{Deny}, \mathsf{NA}, \mathsf{Indeterminate}\{P\}, \mathsf{Indeterminate}\{D\}, \mathsf{Indeterminate}\{PD\}\}$. To reduce $\mathcal{D}_7$ to $\mathcal{D}_6$, one needs to project two decisions in $\mathcal{D}_7$ onto one decision in $\mathcal{D}_6$. Intuitively, the 3-valued logic $\{1, 0, \bot\}$ is used to represent Permit, Deny and NA, respectively. The notion of indeterminacy is modeled in PTaCL by considering *sets of decisions*, instead of single decisions. Thus, we have the following reduction $\rho_{76}^{\mathsf{I(PD)}}$:

$\{1\} = \mathsf{Permit}$	$\{1, \bot\} = \mathsf{Indeterminate}\{P\}$
$\{0\} = \mathsf{Deny}$	$\{0, \bot\} = \mathsf{Indeterminate}\{D\}$
$\{\bot\} = \mathsf{NA}$	$\{1, 0\}, \{1, 0, \bot\} = \mathsf{Indeterminate}\{PD\}$

We now show that such a reduction may have an undesirable behavior with respect to operators used to combine decisions. Consider, for instance, the weak conjunction operator $\sqcap$ in Figure 1a extended to $\mathcal{D}_7$ in a point-wise way (Section 2.3). Figure 4 shows the encoding of weak conjunction in PTaCL.

An encoding of weak conjunction in XACML v3 (Figure 5) can be obtained by applying the reduction presented above

$\sqcap$	1	0	$\bot$	$1,\bot$	$0,\bot$	$1,0$	$1,0,\bot$
1	1	0	$\bot$	$1,\bot$	$0,\bot$	$1,0$	$1,0,\bot$
0	0	0	$\bot$	$0,\bot$	$0,\bot$	0	$0,\bot$
$\bot$	$\bot$	$\bot$	$\bot$	$\bot$	$\bot$	$\bot$	$\bot$
$1,\bot$	$1,\bot$	$0,\bot$	$\bot$	$1,\bot$	$0,\bot$	$1,0,\bot$	$1,0,\bot$
$0,\bot$	$0,\bot$	$0,\bot$	$\bot$	$0,\bot$	$0,\bot$	$0,\bot$	$0,\bot$
$1,0$	$1,0$	0	$\bot$	$1,0,\bot$	$0,\bot$	$1,0$	$1,0,\bot$
$1,0,\bot$	$1,0,\bot$	$0,\bot$	$\bot$	$1,0,\bot$	$0,\bot$	$1,0,\bot$	$1,0,\bot$

Figure 4: Weak conjunction in PTaCL

$\sqcap$	P	D	NA	I(P)	I(D)	I(PD)
P	P	D	NA	I(P)	I(D)	I(PD)
D	D	D	NA	I(D)	I(D)	D,I(D)
NA	NA	NA	NA	NA	NA	NA
I(P)	I(P)	I(D)	NA	I(P)	I(D)	I(PD)
I(D)	I(D)	I(D)	NA	I(D)	I(D)	I(D)
I(PD)	I(PD)	D,I(D)	NA	I(PD)	I(D)	I(PD)

Figure 5: Weak conjunction in XACML v3. In the figure, P stands for Permit, D for Deny, NA for non-applicable, I(P) for Indeterminate{P}, I(D) for Indeterminate{D}, and I(PD) for Indeterminate{PD}.

	K_{Id}	K_0	K_1	$K_\bot$	$\sqcap_0$	$\sqcup_1$	$\tilde{\sqcap}_\bot$	$\tilde{\sqcup}_\bot$	$\neg$	$\sim$
1	1	0	1	$\bot$	0	1	$\bot$	1	0	1
0	0	0	1	$\bot$	1	0	$\bot$	0	1	0
$\bot$	$\bot$	0	1	$\bot$	1	1	$\bot$	$\bot$	$\bot$	0
ρ^1_{32}	✓	✓	✓	✓	✕	✓	✓	✓	✕	✕
ρ^0_{32}	✓	✓	✓	✓	✓	✕	✓	✓	✕	✓

Figure 6: Unary operators and safety of ρ^1_{32} and ρ^0_{32}

	$\tilde{\sqcap}_1$	$\tilde{\sqcap}_0$	$\tilde{\sqcap}_\bot$
1	1	0	$\bot$
0	0	0	0
$\bot$	$\bot$	0	$\bot$

	$\sqcap_1$	$\sqcap_0$	$\sqcap_\bot$
1	1	0	$\bot$
0	0	0	$\bot$
$\bot$	$\bot$	$\bot$	$\bot$

(a) Unary operators for $\tilde{\sqcap}$ (b) Unary operators for $\sqcap$

Figure 7: Modeling binary operators using unary operators

to Figure 4. It is worth noting that two possible values are possible when combining Deny and Indeterminate{PD}. This is due to the interpretation of Indeterminate{PD}: if Indeterminate{PD} corresponds to $\{1,0\}$, the decision is Deny; otherwise, if Indeterminate{PD} corresponds to $\{1,0,\bot\}$, the decision is Indeterminate{D}. This different interpretation can lead to inaccurate or even incorrect authorization decisions.

In the next section we study the conditions under which a reduction is safe for an operator, i.e. the reduction does not change the semantics of a (composite) policy.

4. SAFE REDUCTION

As shown in the previous section, a reduction can lead to risks of inaccurate or even incorrect authorization decisions. To avoid such risks, the reduction of a decision set should be "safe". Intuitively, a reduction is safe if projecting onto decision set $\mathcal{D}_m$ the decision obtained by applying an operator op to two decisions in decision set $\mathcal{D}_n$ returns the same decision obtained by first projecting the two decisions onto $\mathcal{D}_m$ and then applying op to the resulting decisions.

In this section, we first study the safety of a reduction with respect to a combining operator. Then, we analyze the safety of a reduction with respect to a set of operators as well as the safety of a composition of reductions. The proofs of the propositions are given in Appendix.

4.1 Single operators

To understand when the reduction of a decision set is safe, we first focus on unary operators, i.e., functions $\alpha : \mathcal{D} \to \mathcal{D}$ where $\mathcal{D}$ is a decision set. For instance, the negation operator $\neg$ and the weakening operator $\sim$ over $\mathcal{D}_3$ are defined in Figure 2. Intuitively, a reduction is safe for α if the operator behaves similarly under reduction when the argument is reduced and when it is not.

DEFINITION 2 (SAFE REDUCTION). *Let $\mathcal{D}_n$ and $\mathcal{D}_m$ be two decision sets such that $\mathcal{D}_m \subseteq \mathcal{D}_n$, $\rho : \mathcal{D}_n \to \mathcal{D}_m$ a*

decision reduction, and $\alpha : \mathcal{D}_n \to \mathcal{D}_n$ a unary operator. We say that ρ is safe for α if and only if

$$\forall d \in \mathcal{D}_n \quad \rho(\alpha(d)) = \rho(\alpha(\rho(d))) \qquad (1)$$

Note that if $\mathcal{D}_m$ is closed under α, Eq. (1) can be simplified to $\rho(\alpha(d)) = \alpha(\rho(d))$. Figure 6 presents some unary operators together with the safety of reductions ρ^1_{32} and ρ^0_{32} defined in Section 3 with respect to these operators. We can observe that reduction ρ^1_{32} is safe neither for $\neg$ nor for $\sim$, while ρ^0_{32} is safe for $\sim$ but not for $\neg$. In practice, this means that if we have to reduce the decision set of a policy using the operator $\neg$ over sub-policies that can evaluate to $\bot$, then the result will be different whether the reduction is applied at the top-level or at the sub-policy level.

Using currying, any binary operator $\beta : \mathcal{D} \times \mathcal{D} \to \mathcal{D}$ can be defined as an ordered set of unary operators $\beta = \{\alpha_1, \ldots, \alpha_n\}$, where each α_i is a unary operator. For each $d_i \in \mathcal{D}$ we write $\beta[d_i]$ for α_i such that $\beta(d_i, d_j) = \beta[d_i](d_j) = \alpha_i(d_j)$.[1] For instance, the binary strong conjunction $\tilde{\sqcap}$ can be defined as $\tilde{\sqcap} = \{\tilde{\sqcap}_1, \tilde{\sqcap}_0, \tilde{\sqcap}_\bot\}$ and the weak conjunction as $\sqcap = \{\sqcap_1, \sqcap_0, \sqcap_\bot\}$ where each $\tilde{\sqcap}_x$ and $\sqcap_x$ are defined in Figure 7a and Figure 7b, respectively.

This approach can be inductively extended to other operators: an operator $\gamma : \mathcal{D}^k \to \mathcal{D}$ with arity k can be defined as an ordered set $\{\gamma_1, \ldots, \gamma_n\}$, where each γ_i is an operator of arity $k-1$ corresponding to the decision $d_i \in \mathcal{D}$, such that $\gamma(d_1, \ldots, d_k) = \gamma[d_1](d_2, \ldots, d_k)$. The definition of safe reduction for unary operators can be easily extended to k-ary operators.

DEFINITION 3 (SAFE REDUCTION). *Let $\mathcal{D}_n$ and $\mathcal{D}_m$ be two decision sets such that $\mathcal{D}_m \subseteq \mathcal{D}_n$, $\rho : \mathcal{D}_n \to \mathcal{D}_m$ a decision reduction, and $\gamma : \mathcal{D}_n^k \to \mathcal{D}_n$ a k-ary operator. We say that ρ is safe for γ if and only if*

$$\forall d_1, \ldots, d_k \in \mathcal{D}_n \quad \rho(\gamma(d_1, \ldots, d_k)) = \rho(\gamma(\rho(d_1), \ldots, \rho(d_k)))$$

Figure 8 presents the safety of ρ^1_{32} and ρ^0_{32} for the conjunctive and disjunctive operators over $\mathcal{D}_3$ (defined in terms of the unary operators presented in Figure 6). We say that two operators are ρ-equivalent when they behave similarly under ρ. For instance, we can observe that the strong and weak conjunctions over $\mathcal{D}_3$ are ρ^0_{32}-equivalent, while strong

---

[1] For the sake of readability, we do not use the notation $\beta(d_i)(d_j)$ which, although correct, could be confusing.

	$\sqcap$	$\sqcup$	$\tilde{\sqcap}$	$\tilde{\sqcup}$
1	K_{Id}	$\sqcup_1$	K_{Id}	K_1
0	$\sqcap_0$	K_{Id}	K_0	K_{Id}
$\bot$	$K_\bot$	$K_\bot$	$\tilde{\sqcap}_\bot$	$\tilde{\sqcup}_\bot$
ρ_{32}^1	$\times$	$\checkmark$	$\checkmark$	$\checkmark$
ρ_{32}^0	$\checkmark$	$\times$	$\checkmark$	$\checkmark$

Figure 8: Binary operators and safety of ρ_{32}^1 and ρ_{32}^0

	$\mathsf{pov_P}$	$\mathsf{pov_D}$	$\mathsf{pov_{NA}}$	$\mathsf{pov_{I(P)}}$	$\mathsf{pov_{I(D)}}$	$\mathsf{pov_{I(PD)}}$
P	P	P	P	P	P	P
D	P	D	D	I(PD)	D	I(PD)
NA	P	D	NA	I(P)	I(D)	I(PD)
I(P)	P	I(PD)	I(P)	I(P)	I(PD)	I(PD)
I(D)	P	D	I(D)	I(PD)	I(D)	I(PD)
I(PD)	P	I(PD)	I(PD)	I(PD)	I(PD)	I(PD)
$\rho_{64}^\bot$	$\checkmark$	$\times$	$\checkmark$	$\checkmark$	$\checkmark$	$\checkmark$

Figure 9: Unary operators for permit-overrides and safety of $\rho_{64}^\bot$

and weak disjunctions over $\mathcal{D}_3$ are ρ_{32}^1-equivalent, which intuitively can be read as: if $\bot$ is treated as 0, then there is no difference between the weak and strong conjunctions, and if $\bot$ is treated as 1, then there is no difference between the weak and strong disjunctions. More formally:

DEFINITION 4. *Let γ and γ' be two operators of arity k, and $\rho : \mathcal{D}_n \to \mathcal{D}_m$ a decision reduction. We say that γ and γ' are ρ-equivalent, denoted as $\gamma \equiv_\rho \gamma'$, if and only if, for any decisions $d_1, \ldots, d_k \in \mathcal{D}_n$, we have:*

$$\rho(\gamma(d_1, \ldots, d_k)) = \rho(\gamma'(d_1, \ldots, d_k))$$

We are now in position to prove that the safety of a reduction for an operator γ of arity k can be obtained from the safety of the same reduction for the operators of arity $k-1$ that are defining γ. In practice, this result means that in order to prove the safety of a reduction for an operator, which can be quite complex for large arity, can be inductively reduced to prove the safety of the reduction for unary operators, which are simpler to analyze.

PROPOSITION 1. *Given an operator $\gamma : \mathcal{D}_n^k \to \mathcal{D}_n$ of arity k, and a decision reduction $\rho : \mathcal{D}_n \to \mathcal{D}_m$, ρ is safe for γ if and only if ρ is safe for $\gamma[d_i]$ for each $d_i \in \mathcal{D}_m$ and $\gamma[d_j] \equiv_\rho \gamma[\rho(d_j)]$ for each $d_j \in \mathcal{D}_n \setminus \mathcal{D}_m$.*

It is worth observing that it might be possible to have a safe operator γ using a non-safe operator for a decision d_j as long as both $d_j \notin \mathcal{D}_m$ and $\gamma[d_j] \equiv_\rho \gamma[\rho(d_j)]$.

Figure 8 shows that ρ_{32}^1 is not safe for $\sqcap$ and ρ_{32}^0 is not safe for $\sqcup$. Based on Proposition 1, the (un)safety of these reductions can be explained by analyzing their safety with respect to the unary operators forming $\sqcap$, $\sqcup$, $\tilde{\sqcap}$, and $\tilde{\sqcup}$. For instance, reduction ρ_{32}^1 is safe for $\sqcap[1] = K_{Id}$, but not for $\sqcap[0] = \sqcap_0$, and therefore it is not safe for $\sqcap$ (in addition, $\sqcap[\bot] = K_\bot$ is not ρ_{32}^1-equivalent to K_{Id}). On the other hand, ρ_{32}^1 is safe for $\tilde{\sqcap}[1] = K_{Id}$, safe for $\tilde{\sqcap}[0] = K_0$, and $\tilde{\sqcap}[\bot] = \tilde{\sqcap}_\bot$ is ρ_{32}^1-equivalent to K_{Id}, so it is safe for $\tilde{\sqcap}$. These examples illustrate the constructiveness of our approach: for $\sqcap$, we can directly pinpoint where the problem comes from, i.e., operator $\sqcap_0$ treats decisions 1 and $\bot$ differently, while ρ_{32}^1 projects $\bot$ to 1. Thus, we can conclude ρ_{32}^1 is not safe for $\sqcap$ because it is not safe for $\sqcap_0$.

4.2 Composition of operators

Typically, access control models provides more than one operator for combining decisions. We now study the safety of a reduction for a set of operators.

PROPOSITION 2. *Given operators $\gamma, \gamma_1, \ldots, \gamma_j : \mathcal{D}_n^k \to \mathcal{D}_n$ and decision reduction $\rho : \mathcal{D}_n \to \mathcal{D}_m$, if ρ is safe for $\gamma, \gamma_1, \ldots, \gamma_j$, then ρ is safe for any combination of $\gamma, \gamma_1, \ldots, \gamma_j$.*

This result shows that, when more than one operator is used to combine decisions, it is sufficient to study the safety of the operators individually in order to determine whether a decision set can be safely reduced. For the sake of clarity, Proposition 2 is limited to the case where every operator has the same arity k. The proposition can be trivially extended to the case where every operator has an arbitrary arity.

4.3 Composition of reductions

Reductions can be composed together, in order to reduce successively a decision. For instance, consider the reduction $\rho_{43}^\bot : \mathcal{D}_4 \to \mathcal{D}_3$, which reduces $\top$ to $\bot$, i.e., $\rho_{43}^\bot(\top) = \bot$ and $\rho_{43}^\bot(d) = d$, for $d \neq \top$. We may now wish to compose this reduction with ρ_{32}^1 or ρ_{32}^0, in order to obtain a reduction from $\mathcal{D}_4$ to $\mathcal{D}_2$.

PROPOSITION 3. *Given three decisions set $\mathcal{D}_l \subseteq \mathcal{D}_m \subseteq \mathcal{D}_n$, a reduction $\rho_1 : \mathcal{D}_n \to \mathcal{D}_m$ and a reduction $\rho_2 : \mathcal{D}_m \to \mathcal{D}_l$, an operator γ defined over $\mathcal{D}_n$ and closed under $\mathcal{D}_m$ (i.e., for any $\bar{d} \in \mathcal{D}_m^k$, $\gamma(\bar{d}) \in \mathcal{D}_m$), if both ρ_1 and ρ_2 are safe for γ, then their composition $\rho_2 \circ \rho_1$ is also safe for γ.*

5. ANALYSIS OF XACML V3

XACML v3 uses two decision sets, namely $\mathcal{D}_4$ and $\mathcal{D}_6$. Decisions are projected from one decision set to the other depending on the combining algorithm used to evaluate a composite policy. In Section 3, we showed that this can affect the final decision returned by the policy decision point, and thus the overall security provided by the employed access control mechanism. In this section, we analyze the combining operators provided by XACML v3 against the notion of safe reduction and provide guidelines for the selection of the minimal decision set to be used.

The reduction function used in XACML v3 from $\mathcal{D}_6$ to $\mathcal{D}_4$ projects the Indeterminate extended set to a single Indeterminate value (i.e., I). As discussed in Section 3, XACML v3 considers I to be equivalent to I(PD) (we use the abbreviations defined in Figure 5). More formally, reduction $\rho_{64}^\bot$ is defined as $\rho_{64}^\bot(I(P)) = \rho_{64}^\bot(I(D)) = \rho_{64}^\bot(I(PD)) = I(PD)$, and $\rho_{64}^\bot(d) = d$ for $d \in \{P, D, NA\}$.

Figures 9 and 10 present the encoding of combining algorithms permit-overrides and deny-overrides, respectively, using unary operators along with the safety of $\rho_{64}^\bot$. We can observe that some unary operators encoding these combining algorithms are not safe (i.e., $\mathsf{pov_D}$ for permit-overrides and $\mathsf{dov_P}$ for deny-overrides). Indeed, we have:

$$\rho_{64}^\bot(\mathsf{pov_D}(I(D))) = D \qquad \rho_{64}^\bot(\mathsf{pov_D}(\rho_{64}^\bot(I(D)))) = I(PD)$$
$$\rho_{64}^\bot(\mathsf{dov_P}(I(P))) = P \qquad \rho_{64}^\bot(\mathsf{dov_P}(\rho_{64}^\bot(I(P)))) = I(PD)$$

	$\mathsf{dov_P}$	$\mathsf{dov_D}$	$\mathsf{dov_{NA}}$	$\mathsf{dov_{I(P)}}$	$\mathsf{dov_{I(D)}}$	$\mathsf{dov_{I(PD)}}$
P	P	D	P	P	I(PD)	I(PD)
D	D	D	D	D	D	D
NA	P	D	NA	I(P)	I(D)	I(PD)
I(P)	P	D	I(P)	I(P)	I(PD)	I(PD)
I(D)	I(PD)	D	I(D)	I(PD)	I(D)	I(PD)
I(PD)	I(PD)	D	I(PD)	I(PD)	I(PD)	I(PD)
ρ^l_{64}	×	✓	✓	✓	✓	✓

Figure 10: Unary operators for deny-overrides and safety of ρ^l_{64}

In addition, $\mathsf{pov_{I(D)}}$ and $\mathsf{dov_{I(P)}}$ are not ρ^l_{64}-equivalent to $\mathsf{pov_{I(PD)}}$ and $\mathsf{dov_{I(PD)}}$, respectively. Based on the results presented in the previous section, it follows that ρ^l_{64} is safe neither for permit-overrides nor for deny-overrides. Thereby, XACML v3 lacks an unambiguous and well-defined semantics, which can have an impact on the final decision.

In order for XACML v3 to be founded on an unambiguous and well-defined semantics, it should use only one decision set, namely $\mathcal{D}_6$. The other combining algorithms – first-applicable (fa), deny-unless-permit (dup), permit-unless-deny (pud), and only-one-applicable (ooa) – can be easily extended to $\mathcal{D}_6$ based on their semantics on $\mathcal{D}_4$.

We now define the unary operators for each of these operators, for decision set $\{P, D, NA, I(P), I(D), I(PD)\}$. Remark that a k-ary operator can be represented as an ordered set of $k-1$-ary operators. The order of operators is defined by the order of decisions in the decision set above.

deny-unless-permit: for any $x \in \mathcal{D}_6$, let $K_P(x) = P$, and let $\mathsf{dup_D}(x) = P$ if $x = P$ and $\mathsf{dup_D}(x) = D$ otherwise; then $\mathsf{dup} = \{K_P, \mathsf{dup_D}, \mathsf{dup_D}, \mathsf{dup_D}, \mathsf{dup_D}, \mathsf{dup_D}\}$.

permit-unless-deny: for any $x \in \mathcal{D}_6$, let $K_D(x) = D$, and let $\mathsf{pud_P}(x) = D$ if $x = D$ and $\mathsf{pud_P}(x) = P$ otherwise; then $\mathsf{pud} = \{\mathsf{pud_P}, K_P, \mathsf{pud_P}, \mathsf{pud_P}, \mathsf{pud_P}, \mathsf{pud_P}\}$.

first-applicable: for any $x \in \mathcal{D}_6$ and any $y \in \mathcal{D}_6$, let $\mathsf{fa}_x(y) = x$ if $x \neq NA$, and $\mathsf{fa}_x(y) = y$ otherwise; then $\mathsf{fa} = \{\mathsf{fa_P}, \mathsf{fa_D}, \mathsf{fa_{NA}}, \mathsf{fa_{I(P)}}, \mathsf{fa_{I(D)}}, \mathsf{fa_{I(PD)}}\}$.

only-one-applicable: for any $x \in \mathcal{D}_6$, let $K_{Id}(x) = x$, and for any $y \in \mathcal{D}_6$, let $\mathsf{ooa}_y(x) = y$ if $x = NA$, and $\mathsf{ooa}_y(x) = I(PD)$ otherwise; then $\mathsf{ooa} = \{\mathsf{ooa_P}, \mathsf{ooa_D}, K_{Id}, \mathsf{ooa_{I(P)}}, \mathsf{ooa_{I(D)}}, \mathsf{ooa_{I(PD)}}\}$.

Note that the semantics of only-one-applicable with respect to indeterminacy is undefined over $\mathcal{D}_6$; thus, different interpretations can be used to define only-one-applicable over the Indeterminate extended set. For instance, an alternative interpretation of only-one-applicable in XACML v3, hereafter denoted as $\overline{\mathsf{ooa}}$, is to record the decision of the policies that caused the indeterminacy. For instance, $\overline{\mathsf{ooa}}_P(P) = I(P)$, $\overline{\mathsf{ooa}}_P(D) = I(PD)$, $\overline{\mathsf{ooa}}_P(I(P)) = I(P)$, etc. ($\overline{\mathsf{ooa}}$ behaves as ooa if at most one policy is applicable) In the rest of the section, we consider both interpretations.

The question is whether $\mathcal{D}_6$ is the most appropriate decision set for XACML v3. Ideally, the decision set should be the smallest as possible in order to reduce the complexity of the policy evaluation process and thus facilitate the task of making a conclusive decision. On the other hand, it should be expressive enough to capture the semantics of combining operators. Based on these observations, we say that a decision set is *minimal* for a (set of) operator(s) if there exists no safe reduction to a smaller decision set.

fa	1	0	⊥
1	1	1	1
0	0	0	0
⊥	1	0	⊥

(a) first-applicable over $\mathcal{D}_3$

$\overline{\mathsf{fa}}$	1	0	⊥	1,⊥	0,⊥	1,0	1,0,⊥
1	1	1	1	1	1	1	1
0	0	0	0	0	0	0	0
⊥	1	0	⊥	1,⊥	0,⊥	1,0	1,0,⊥
1,⊥	1	1,0	1,⊥	1,⊥	1,0,⊥	1,0	1,0,⊥
0,⊥	1,0	0	0,⊥	1,0,⊥	0,⊥	1,0	1,0,⊥
1,0	1,0	1,0	1,0	1,0	1,0	1,0	1,0
1,0,⊥	1,0	1,0	1,0,⊥	1,0,⊥	1,0,⊥	1,0	1,0,⊥

(b) Operator $\overline{\mathsf{fa}}$ over $\mathcal{D}_7$

Figure 11: Defining an operator resembling first-applicable over $\mathcal{D}_7$

	pov	dov	fa	dup	pud	ooa	$\overline{\mathsf{ooa}}$	$\overline{\mathsf{fa}}$	⊓	⊔	⊓̃	⊔̃
$\rho^{I(PD)}_{76}$	✓	✓	✓	✓	✓	✓	✓	✓	×	×	✓	✓
ρ^l_{64}	×	×	✓	✓	✓	✓	✓	×	×	×	×	×

Figure 12: Safety of reduction functions with respect to operators over $\mathcal{D}_6$ and $\mathcal{D}_7$

We use an operator $\overline{\mathsf{fa}}$ over $\mathcal{D}_7$ resembling first-applicable in XACML to discuss the minimality of the decision set for XACML v3. To define this operator, we can first define first-applicable in $\mathcal{D}_3$ (Figure 11a) and then extend it to $\mathcal{D}_7$ in a point-wise way as described in Section 2.3.1. The decision table for $\overline{\mathsf{fa}}$ over $\mathcal{D}_7$ is presented in Figure 11b. We can observe that $\overline{\mathsf{fa}}$ returns a conclusive decision in cases where fa returns an Indeterminate decision. In particular, $\overline{\mathsf{fa}}(\{1, \perp\}, \{1\}) = 1$ while $\mathsf{fa}(I(P), P) = I(P)$; also $\overline{\mathsf{fa}}(\{0, \perp\}, \{0\}) = 0$ while $\mathsf{fa}(I(D), D) = I(D)$. Intuitively, this means that, if the first applicable policy is evaluated to Permit (Deny resp.) in case an error would not have occurred and the next applicable policy is evaluated to Permit (Deny resp.), then we have sufficient evidence to grant permission. Notice that this intuition is already adopted in XACML v3 for the target evaluation. In particular, if at least one element ⟨AllOf⟩ matches the query, then the element ⟨AnyOf⟩ containing that ⟨AllOf⟩ evaluates to 'Match' regardless if an error occurs in another element ⟨AllOf⟩ of the same ⟨AnyOf⟩ [2, p. 81-82]. We argue that the semantics of $\overline{\mathsf{fa}}$ is preferable to the one of fa as it provides a conclusive decision in more cases without changing the intended semantics of the composite policy. Let now consider the reduction from $\mathcal{D}_7$ to $\mathcal{D}_6$ defined in Section 3, hereafter denoted $\rho^{I(PD)}_{76}$. We can easily verify that $\rho^{I(PD)}_{76}$ is safe with respect to $\overline{\mathsf{fa}}$. This might confirm that $\mathcal{D}_6$ is the appropriate decision set for XACML v3 also if operator $\overline{\mathsf{fa}}$ is used instead of fa.

In general, the choice of the decision set to be used depends on the employed operators. Figure 12 shows the safety of reduction functions $\rho^{I(PD)}_{76}$ and ρ^l_{64} for a number of operators. Operators fa, dup, pud, ooa and $\overline{\mathsf{ooa}}$ can be defined over $\mathcal{D}_7$ as we did for $\mathcal{D}_6$. Operators pov and dov can be defined over $\mathcal{D}_7$ in a point-wise way. It is worth noting that a point-wise definition of pov and dov over $\mathcal{D}_7$ behaves as pov and dov as defined in XACML.

Based on Figure 12, we can conclude that $\mathcal{D}_6$ is the minimal decision set with respect to the operators used in XACML v3. Indeed, $\mathcal{D}_7$ can be safely reduced to $\mathcal{D}_6$ with respect to these operators. However, if we want to extend XACML with additional operators already defined for a larger decision set, it is necessary to determine the safety of the reduction function with respect to the new operators. For instance, suppose we want to support weak conjunction ($\sqcap$) and weak disjunction ($\sqcup$) in XACML. Reduction $\rho_{76}^{\mathsf{I(PD)}}$ is not safe with respect to these operators. Therefore, the minimal decision set that preserves the semantics of a policy would be $\mathcal{D}_7$. Conversely, $\mathcal{D}_4$ is sufficient to support an access control model with operators fa, dup, pud, and ooa (or $\overline{\mathsf{ooa}}$).

The different reductions presented up to now can be chained together; for instance, we can reduce from $\mathcal{D}_7$ to $\mathcal{D}_6$ with $\rho_{76}^{\mathsf{I(PD)}}$; from $\mathcal{D}_6$ to $\mathcal{D}_4$ with ρ_{64}^{I}; from $\mathcal{D}_4$ to $\mathcal{D}_3$ with $\rho_{43}^{\perp}$; and from $\mathcal{D}_3$ to $\mathcal{D}_2$ with ρ_{32}^{0}. Hence, we can observe that since all reductions are safe for the operators pud and dup, then the composite reduction $\rho_{72}^{0} = \rho_{32}^{0} \circ \rho_{43}^{\perp} \circ \rho_{64}^{\mathsf{I}} \circ \rho_{76}^{\mathsf{I(PD)}}$ is also safe for these operators, following Proposition 3. Note that this proposition is not an equivalence, and we can observe that ρ_{72}^{0} is safe for $\sqcap$ even though ρ_{64}^{I} and $\rho_{76}^{\mathsf{I(PD)}}$ are not.

6. CONCLUSIONS

Although reducing a decision set may be needed, for instance to obtain a conclusive decision, it may change the semantics of a composite policy, leading to accept a query that would have been intuitively denied (or vice versa). This paper has presented a formal framework centered on the notion of decision reduction for determining whether a decision reduction preserves the intended semantics of a policy. We demonstrated the framework by analyzing XACML v3, the de facto standard for the specification and enforcement of access control policies. XACML v3 defines combining operators over two decisions sets, namely $\mathcal{D}_4$ and $\mathcal{D}_6$. Depending on the operator used to evaluate a policy, a decision set is projected onto the other set. Our analysis shows that the reduction function used in XACML v3, which projects the Indeterminate extended set to a single Indeterminate value, may result in an unnecessary loss of accuracy, which affects the final access decision. In particular, this reduction is not safe with respect to permit-overrides and deny-overrides. We show that the choice of the decision set depends on the combining operators used in the access control model. For instance, extending an access control model by reusing an operator defined over a larger decision set requires ensuring that the reduction does not change the semantics of the operator, i.e. the reduction is safe for that operator.

Acknowledgement This work has been partially funded by the EDA project IN4STARS2.0, the ITEA2 project FedSS, and the ARTEMIS project ACCUS, the NWO CyberSecurity programme under the PriCE project, the Dutch national program COMMIT under the THeCS project and the Choice Architecture for Information Security project, EPSRC Grant EP/K006568/1.

7. REFERENCES

[1] eXtensible Access Control Markup Language (XACML) Version 2.0. OASIS Standard, OASIS, 2005.

[2] eXtensible Access Control Markup Language (XACML) Version 3.0. OASIS Standard, OASIS, 2012.

[3] O. Arieli and A. Avron. The value of the four values. *Artificial Intelligence*, 102(1):97–141, 1998.

[4] P. Ashley, S. Hada, G. Karjoth, C. Powers, and M. Schunter. Enterprise Privacy Authorization Language (EPAL). Technical report, IBM Research, Rüschlikon, 2003.

[5] D. E. Bell and L. J. LaPadula. Secure computer systems: A mathematical model, Volume II. *Journal of Computer Security*, 4(2/3):229–263, 1996.

[6] D. F. C. Brewer and M. J. Nash. The Chinese Wall Security Policy. In *Proceedings of Symposium on Security and Privacy*, pages 329–339. IEEE, 1989.

[7] G. Bruns and M. Huth. Access control via Belnap logic: Intuitive, expressive, and analyzable policy composition. *TISSEC*, 14(1):9, 2011.

[8] P.-C. Cheng, P. Rohatgi, C. Keser, P. A. Karger, G. M. Wagner, and A. S. Reninger. Fuzzy multi-level security: An experiment on quantified risk-adaptive access control. In *Proceedings of Symposium on Security and Privacy*, pages 222–230. IEEE, 2007.

[9] J. Crampton and M. Huth. An authorization framework resilient to policy evaluation failures. In *Computer Security*, LNCS 6345, pages 472–487. Springer, 2010.

[10] J. Crampton and C. Morisset. PTaCL: A language for attribute-based access control in open systems. In *Proceedings of POST*, LNCS 7215, pages 390–409. Springer, 2012.

[11] S. De Capitani Di Vimercati, S. Foresti, P. Samarati, and S. Jajodia. Access control policies and languages. *Int. J. Comput. Sci. Eng.*, 3(2):94–102, 2007.

[12] D. F. Ferraiolo and D. R. Kuhn. Role-based access control. In *Proceedings of the 15th National Computer Security Conference*, pages 554–563, 1992.

[13] M. Harrison, W. Ruzzo, and J. Ullman. Protection in operating systems. *Commun. ACM*, 19(8):461–471, 1976.

[14] W. Jobe. Functional completeness and canonical forms in many-valued logics. *Journal of Symbolic Logic*, 27(4):409–422, 1962.

[15] B. W. Lampson. Protection. *SIGOPS Oper. Syst. Rev.*, 8(1):18–24, 1974.

[16] N. Li, Q. Wang, W. H. Qardaji, E. Bertino, P. Rao, J. Lobo, and D. Lin. Access control policy combining: theory meets practice. In *Proceedings of 14th ACM SACMAT*, pages 135–144. ACM, 2009.

[17] Q. Ni, E. Bertino, and J. Lobo. D-algebra for composing access control policy decisions. In *Proceedings of ACM AsiaCCS*, pages 298–309. ACM, 2009.

[18] P. Rao, D. Lin, E. Bertino, N. Li, and J. Lobo. An algebra for fine-grained integration of XACML policies. In *Proceedings of 14th ACM SACMAT*, pages 63–72. ACM, 2009.

[19] D. Trivellato, N. Zannone, M. Glaundrup, J. Skowronek, and S. Etalle. A semantic security

framework for systems of systems. *Int. J. Cooperative Inf. Syst.*, 22(1), 2013.

[20] M. C. Tschantz and S. Krishnamurthi. Towards reasonability properties for access-control policy languages. In *Proceedings of 11th ACM SACMAT*, pages 160–169. ACM, 2006.

[21] T. Y. C. Woo and S. S. Lam. Authorizations in distributed systems: A new approach. *Journal of Computer Security*, 2(2-3):107–136, 1993.

APPENDIX

A. PROOFS

In this section we provide the proofs of the propositions in Section 4.

PROOF (PROPOSITION 1). Let us first observe that for any decision $d_i \in \mathcal{D}_m$, since $d_i = \rho(d_i)$ by definition of ρ, we trivially have $\gamma[d_i] \equiv_\rho \gamma[\rho(d_i)]$.

($\Leftarrow$) Given $d_1, \ldots d_k \in \mathcal{D}_n$,:

$$\rho(\gamma(d_1, \ldots, d_k)) = \rho(\gamma[d_1](d_2, \ldots, d_k))$$
$$\text{(definition of } \gamma)$$
$$= \rho(\gamma[\rho(d_1)](d_2, \ldots, d_k))$$
$$(\gamma[\rho(d_1)] \equiv_\rho \gamma[d_1])$$
$$= \rho(\gamma[\rho(d_1)](\rho(d_2), \ldots, \rho(d_k)))$$
$$(\rho(d_1) \in \mathcal{D}_m, \text{ so } \rho \text{ is safe for } \gamma[\rho(d_1)])$$
$$= \rho(\gamma(\rho(d_1), \rho(d_2), \ldots, \rho(d_k)))$$
$$\text{(definition of } \gamma)$$

($\Rightarrow$) Let γ be a safe operator. Let us first prove that, for any $d_i \in \mathcal{D}_m$, $\gamma[d_i]$ is safe. Given $d_1, \ldots, d_{k-1} \in \mathcal{D}_n$, we have:

$$\rho(\gamma[d_i](d_1, \ldots, d_{k-1})) = \rho(\gamma(d_i, d_1, \ldots, d_{k-1}))$$
$$\text{(definition of } \gamma)$$
$$= \rho(\gamma(\rho(d_i), \rho(d_1), \ldots, \rho(d_{k-1})))$$
$$(\rho \text{ is safe for } \gamma)$$
$$= \rho(\gamma[\rho(d_i)](\rho(d_1), \ldots, \rho(d_{k-1})))$$
$$\text{(definition of } \gamma)$$
$$= \rho(\gamma[d_i](\rho(d_1), \ldots, \rho(d_{k-1})))$$
$$(d_i = \rho(d_i) \text{ by definition of } \rho)$$

Now, given $d_j \in \mathcal{D}_n \setminus \mathsf{D}_m$, let us prove that $\gamma[d_j] \equiv_\rho \gamma[\rho(d_j)]$. Let $d_1, \ldots, d_{k-1} \in \mathcal{D}_n$:

$$\rho(\gamma[d_j](d_1, \ldots, d_{k-1})) = \rho(\gamma(d_j, d_1, \ldots, d_{k-1}))$$
$$\text{(definition of } \gamma)$$
$$= \rho(\gamma(\rho(d_j), \rho(d_1), \ldots, \rho(d_{k-1})))$$
$$(\rho \text{ is safe for } \gamma)$$
$$= \rho(\gamma[\rho(d_j)](\rho(d_1), \ldots, \rho(d_{k-1})))$$
$$\text{(definition of } \gamma)$$
$$= \rho(\gamma[\rho(d_j)](d_1, \ldots, d_{k-1}))$$
$$(\rho(d_j) \in \mathcal{D}_m, \text{ so } \rho \text{ safe for } \gamma[\rho(d_j)])$$

$\square$

PROOF (PROPOSITION 2). Let us denote $\bar{d}$ the arguments of an operator γ_i, i.e. $\gamma_i(\bar{d})$ stands for $\gamma_i(d_1, \ldots, d_k)$. Also, we write $\rho(\bar{d})$ for $\rho(d_1), \ldots \rho(d_k)$. We have:

$$\rho(\gamma(\gamma_1(\bar{d}), \ldots, \gamma_k(\bar{d}))) = \rho(\gamma(\rho(\gamma_1(\bar{d})), \ldots, \rho(\gamma_k(\bar{d}))))$$
$$(\rho \text{ safe for } \gamma)$$
$$= \rho(\gamma(\rho(\gamma_1(\rho(\bar{d}))), \ldots, \rho(\gamma_k(\rho(\bar{d})))))$$
$$(\rho \text{ safe for } \gamma_1, \ldots, \gamma_k)$$
$$= \rho(\gamma(\gamma_1(\rho(\bar{d})), \ldots, \gamma_k(\rho(\bar{d}))))$$
$$(\rho \text{ safe for } \gamma)$$

$\square$

PROOF PROPOSITION 3. Let $\bar{d} \in \mathcal{D}_n^k$:

$$\rho_2(\rho_1(\gamma(\bar{d}))) = \rho_2(\rho_1(\gamma(\rho_1(\bar{d})))) \qquad (\rho_1 \text{ safe for } \gamma)$$
$$= \rho_2(\gamma(\rho_1(\bar{d}))) \qquad (\mathcal{D}_m \text{ closed under } \rho_1)$$
$$= \rho_2(\gamma(\rho_2(\rho_1(\bar{d})))) \qquad (\rho_2 \text{ safe for } \gamma)$$
$$= \rho_2(\rho_1(\gamma(\rho_2(\rho_1(\bar{d}))))) \qquad (\mathcal{D}_m \text{ closed under } \rho_1)$$

$\square$

Sorting Out Role Based Access Control

Wouter Kuijper
Nedap N.V.
Parallelweg 2, Groenlo
the Netherlands, 7141 DC
wouter.kuijper@nedap.com

Victor Ermolaev
Nedap N.V.
Parallelweg 2, Groenlo
the Netherlands, 7141 DC
victor.ermolaev@nedap.com

ABSTRACT

Role-based access control (RBAC) is a popular framework for modelling access control rules. In this paper we identify a fragment of RBAC called *bi-sorted role based access control* (RBÄC). We start from the observation that "classic" RBAC blends together subject management aspects and permission management aspects into a single object of indirection: a *role*. We posit there is merit in distinguishing these administrative perspectives and consequently introducing two distinct objects of indirection: the *proper role* (which applies solely to subjects) and the *demarcation* (which applies solely to permissions). We then identify a third administrative perspective called *access management* where the two are linked up. In this way we enhance organisational scalability by decoupling the tasks of maintaining abstractions over the set of subjects (assignment of subjects into proper roles), maintaining abstractions over the set of permissions (assignment of permissions into demarcations), and maintaining abstract access control policy (granting proper roles access to demarcations). Moreover, the latter conceptual refinement naturally leads us to the introduction of *negative roles* (and, dually, *negative demarcations*). The relevance of the four-sorted extension called *polarized, bi-sorted role based access control* (R$^{\pm}$BÄC), in a semantic sense, is further supported by the existence of Galois connections between sets of subjects and permissions and between positive and negative roles.

Categories and Subject Descriptors

H.1 [**Models and principles**]: General—*RBAC*; H.4 [**Information Systems Applications**]: Miscellaneous—*physical access control*

General Terms

Mathematical foundations of RBAC, Galois connections

Keywords

RBAC; Organizational Structure; Physical Access Control; Scalability; Positive Specification; Negative Specification; Galois Connections; Domain Specific Languages

1. INTRODUCTION

In the present paper we introduce a fragment of *role based access control* (RBAC), this fragment is called *bi-sorted role based access control* (RBÄC). RBÄC suggests to treat permissions via *demarcations* separately from subjects via *proper roles*. Being a fragment implies that RBÄC might be directly used with existing RBAC implementations. Nonetheless RBÄC has an added value which lies mainly in the conceptual boundaries that it introduces. As a first step towards validating this we have built a prototype implementation of our access control scheme on top of the graph database Neo4j (cf. Appendix A).

In the remainder of the paper we explain how the added value of RBÄC derives from the fact that permission and subject management are decoupled and a new higher level administrative level for access management is introduced. For practitioners working in physical access control such a decoupling implies that:

- The human resources team can be purely concerned with personnel management placing designation on individual subjects that make semantic sense without becoming overly concerned with the actual physical spaces that these roles grant/withhold.

- The site management team controlling the physical space of the company would designate certain areas as public, general-use, sensitive, etc. These *demarcations* stand in a hierarchy (in much the same way as do roles on the subject side), e.g. access to sensitive areas will probably imply access to the public ones. They do this without getting overly concerned with the actual employees that these demarcations invite/ban.

- The team of security officers then will set up the actual access control rules on an abstraction level suitable to their responsibilities without getting bogged down by either subject or permission management issues.

We will show how RBÄC enables many–to–many administrative mutations and ultimately leads to more organisational scalability. Besides that we speculatively state that in practice such an approach might be beneficial in the following senses:

- The elimination of communication errors between different teams trying to blend all aspects of AC into roles.

- Increased level of employees' privacy: only HR department directly works with employees' data.

- Less exposed infrastructure: only demarcations need be exposed; the actual building plans, they are mapped on, are only accessible to the relevant site managers.

In addition, we introduce natural and useful extension of RBÄC called R$^\pm$BÄC which makes use of *negative* counterparts of RBÄC's proper roles and demarcations. Introduction of negative counter parts is further supported by the existence of a Galois connection between the negative and positive part of the specification, Definition 4. Our design of R$^\pm$BÄC governed by the found regularities excludes combinations of negative and positive permissions in a *single* object of indirection (this has been an issue in the widely-accepted NIST RBAC [19]).

For practitioners this typically means, that, when an exception arises, instead of exercising in transformations of logical expressions and consequent rewriting of existing AC rules, security officers can *generalise* the exception, and cleanly and compositionally adapt the previous AC specification touching far fewer rules (for very practical examples see [1]). For that matter we shall give an extensive example on how and why negative objects of indirection could work in practice. In particular, professionals working in the subject management perspective can rest assured the following will always hold:

- assigning a positive role will not, inadvertently, revoke permissions from the subject;

- assigning a negative role will not, inadvertently, reassign permissions to the subject.

On the other hand, professionals working in the permission management perspective can rest assured that:

- assigning a positive demarcation will not, inadvertently, ban subjects from the permission;

- assigning a negative demarcation will not, inadvertently, invite subjects to the permission.

At the same time, the third administrative perspective (access management) allows security officers degrees of freedom on an abstraction level suitable for their responsibilities. The only small price to pay by the security officers for having the framework be such well-behaved to the people they delegate subject/permission management tasks to is that they may never use a positive object of indirection in a negative context or use a negative object of indirection in a positive context. Which, in fact, forces them to make clear design trade-offs as to what aspects of the security policy are handled positively and which are handled negatively.

In general, we take an approach that somewhat breaks with the trend of extending RBAC. Even though we will present the section on language first and the section on Galois connections second, in our approach we actually went back to first principles first and developed the language(s) second. In particular once the Galois connections were clear it became rather straightforward to uncover the, so far unexploited, symmetries in existing RBAC which finally led to RBÄC and then to $R^\pm$BÄC.

2. ACCESS CONTROL

Access control (AC) is all about *who* gets to do *what*. As such it involves at least two domains. We distinguish the set of *subjects* S (the *who*), the set of *permissions* P (the *what*), and the *access relation* $SP \subseteq S \times P$ (*who* gets to do *what*). In Figure 1a this situation is depicted using an entity relationship diagram[1]

This very limited conceptual framework suffices in practice only as long as S and P are relatively small sets. If the cardinalities of S and P are too large there are too many pairs in $S \times P$ to consider. We call this the *subject–permission explosion problem*.

In order to deal with the subject–permission explosion we can turn to the framework of *role–based access control* (RBAC) [18]. In this framework an extra layer of indirection in the form of a set of *roles* R is introduced. Now permissions are not assigned directly to subjects anymore, they are instead assigned to roles which are, in turn, assigned to subjects. This situation is shown in Figure 1b, the two white diamonds represent the *subject assignment* and *permission assignment* relations, the grayed out diamond still represents the *access relation* which now *follows* from the subject assignment and the permission assignment relations, i.e.: it is a *computed* relation. As can be seen from Figure 1b: we do not (yet) have the desirable square domain structure where we would be able to recover the access relation *on the abstract level*.

Nevertheless, assuming that the set of roles remains small, classic RBAC is an adequate solution to the subject–permission explosion. There is, however, an important extra dimension to consider when evaluating the merit of an access control scheme. In practice it is rarely the case that an access control policy is written once from scratch and remains static from that moment onwards, citing [18]:

> The ability to modify policy to meet the changing needs of an organization is an important benefit of RBAC.

Yet, RBAC is rather limited where it concerns administrative degrees of freedom. We can distinguish the following four basic RBAC mutations:

1. Enroll a subject $s \in S$ to role $r \in R$, i.e.: add (s, r) to SR.

2. Disenroll a subject $s \in S$ from role $r \in R$, i.e.: remove (s, r) from SR.

3. Assign a permission $p \in P$ to role $r \in R$, i.e.: add (p, r) to PR.

4. Unassign a permission $p \in P$ from role $r \in R$, i.e.: remove (p, r) from PR.

In the first case the effect on the access relation SP is that a *single* subject gains (potentially) *many* permissions. In the second case the effect on the access relation SP is that a

---

[1]Entity relationship diagrams are often used to describe relational databases, here we use them on a more conceptual level. Please note that this is, in fact, the original intent in [6]

[2]Strictly speaking $\langle RH \rangle$, $\langle RH^+ \rangle$ and $\langle DH^+ \rangle$ are reflexive relations that can be drawn inside their own diamonds, however, for presentation purposes, we write them directly after the entity names.

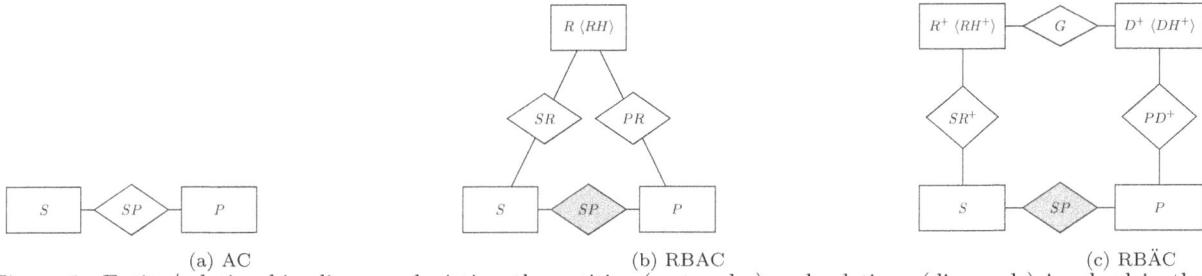

Figure 1: Entity/relationship diagram depicting the entities (rectangles) and relations (diamonds) involved in the various access control schemes discussed in the paper.[2]

single subject loses (potentially) *many* permissions. In the third case the effect on the access relation SP is that (potentially) *many* subjects gain a *single* permission. In the fourth case the effect on the access relation SP is that (potentially) *many* subjects lose a *single* permission. In short, the effect of an atomic RBAC mutation on SP is always *either* one–to–many *or* many–to–one, never *many–to–many*. We call this the *administrative micro-stepping problem*. We see that, in order to obtain administrative scalability we need to break away from individual subjects and individual permissions, hence, at the very least, mutations with a many–to–many effect on the access relation must be enabled.

It would be inaccurate to claim that RBAC does *not* allow many–to–many mutations in the aforementioned sense. It does so, however, in a counterintuitive way, namely through the *inheritance* relation: RH. Combined with items 1 up to 4 above the following completes the *exhaustive* list of possible RBAC mutations:

5. Make a role r a senior role with respect to role r', i.e.: add (r, r') to RH.

6. *Unmake* a role r as a senior role of r', i.e.: *remove* (r, r') from RH.

For case 5 the effect on the access relation is that (potentially) *many* subjects gain (potentially) *many* permissions; for case 6 the effect on the access relation is that (potentially) *many* subjects lose (potentially) *many* permissions.

The inheritance relation RH is, by design, something that has a *static* flavor: for a properly engineered set of roles it is desirable that the inheritance relation is fixed at the time the set of roles is fixed and does not change *dynamically* (it should typically only change in response to new roles being added or old ones being removed). As an example consider the role manager $\in R$ and employee $\in R$ such that (manager, employee) $\in RH$, i.e.: manager is senior role with respect to employee. The latter entails that the manager role inherits all the permissions of the employee role, and, vice versa, the employee role inherits all the subjects of the manager role. Over time it may well be the case that the manager and/or employee roles gain and/or lose new permissions and/or subjects. However we would expect that the latter is realized by introducing/removing pairs from PR and/or SR and *not* by introducing/removing pairs from RH. In particular we would not expect the inheritance relation between managers and employees to be removed as the latter could have many more unpredictable effects both upward as well as downward in the entire role hierarchy.

So we may conclude that, although, in principle, RBAC supports many–to–many administrative mutations, in prac-

tice, it does not provide the necessary safeguards to do so effectively[3]. In the rest of this paper we present a solution to this problem in the form of a safe, two–sorted fragment of RBAC (RBÄC), which, at the same time, can be seen as a conceptual enrichment. In particular we partition the set of roles R into *proper roles* R^+ and *demarcations* D^+ and stipulate that proper roles can only have subjects assigned to them and demarcations can only have permissions assigned to them. This then leads to a corresponding partition on RH into *proper role inheritance, demarcation inheritance*, and *grant–rule–pairs*, the latter being suitable for *dynamic* many–to–many administrative mutations.

As it turns out, the two–sorted fragment of RBAC naturally leads us to a proper extension with *negative roles*. So far, in the literature, negative roles have definitely been explored yet usually dismissed on grounds of being too *confusing*, [19, subsection 7.3], the later standard [10] avoids discussing negative permissions or roles. We show how negative roles are introduced in a clean way into RBÄC whilst avoiding much of the confusion that would occur in the case of adding them to classic RBAC directly.

We support our observations with a thorough mathematical analysis. In particular we identify two Galois connections between the domains of subjects and permissions and between the domains of positive (grant) sets and negative (withhold) sets. We interpret these results as additional confirmation that there is structure on the underlying semantic domain to justify the additional conceptual distinctions that we make (roles vs. demarcations, positive vs. negative roles).

3. LANGUAGE

3.1 Role Based Access Control

The formalism we discuss in this section was previously introduced in [18] as RBAC$_1$. The only difference is that we will not concern ourselves here with the distinction between *having* a role and *activating* it [17] (i.e.: we simply assume a subject will always activate all of its roles).

Definition 1 (RBAC). The following two sets form the *principal semantic domains* underlying RBAC:

- Let S be a set of *subjects* (sometimes notions of *users*, [17, 18], or *principals*, [2], are used).

---

[3]In fact, intuition suggests that not having a rather stable role hierarchy will amplify the problem of "maintaining a good understanding of the currently implemented policy", a common problem among practitioners [4].

- Let P be a set of *permissions* (sometimes introduced as *actions on objects*).

The following primitives form the *syntax* of RBAC meaning that these are entities which the *user* of RBAC (policy designer/security officer) *directly manipulates*:

- Let R be a set of *roles*.
- Let $SR \subseteq S \times R$ be a subject–role assignment relation.
- Let $PR \subseteq P \times R$ be a permission–role assignment relation.
- Let $RH \subseteq R \times R$ be a role–hierarchy relation, RH is required to be *acyclic*.

The following definitions lay down the *semantics* of RBAC, meaning they map the syntactical constructs into the principal semantic domains.

- We define $\geq$ as the transitive reflexive closure of RH. For two roles $r, r' \in R$ such that $r > r'$ we say r is a *senior* role of r', or, vice versa, r' is a *junior* role of r.
- We define the *access relation* $SP \subseteq S \times P$ such that $(s, p) \in SP$ iff there exists roles r, r' in R such that the following conditions are fulfilled:

  1. $(s, r) \in SR$, i.e.: subject s is a member of role r.
  2. $r \geq r'$, i.e.: $r = r'$ or r is senior role of r'.
  3. $(p, r') \in PR$, i.e. permission p is part of role r'.$\diamond$

The numbered conditions of the last definition can be visualized superimposed on the triangle in Figure 1b: one must traverse the north–west and north–east sides in order to prove a tuple (s, p) belongs to SP (the south side).

Example 1 (RBAC). We consider a simple example where:

$$R = \{\mathsf{manager}, \mathsf{employee}\}, \quad RH = \{(\mathsf{manager}, \mathsf{employee})\},$$
$$SR = \{(s_1, \mathsf{manager}), (s_2, \mathsf{employee})\},$$
$$PR = \{(p_1, \mathsf{manager}), (p_2, \mathsf{employee}), (p_3, \mathsf{employee})\}$$

In Figure 2a we show this policy graphically. $\triangle$

In the diagramming style of Figure 2a the dotted lines represent the subject–role and permission–role assignment relations and the solid lines represent the role–hierarchy relation. By convention the senior roles are drawn towards the top of the diagram and the more junior roles are drawn towards the bottom of the diagram. Because subjects are inherited top–down they are drawn one level up from the roles they are assigned, and because permissions are inherited bottom–up they are drawn one level down from the roles they are assigned to. It now becomes possible to follow the paths through the diagram starting from some subject and always going down and/or to the right in order to derive which subject–permission pairs are in the access relation. For this example those are:

1. (s_1, p_1) using path: $s_1, \mathsf{manager}, p_1$
2. (s_1, p_2) using path: $s_1, \mathsf{manager}, \mathsf{employee}, p_2$
3. (s_1, p_3) using path: $s_1, \mathsf{manager}, \mathsf{employee}, p_3$
4. (s_2, p_2) using path: $s_2, \mathsf{employee}, p_2$
5. (s_2, p_3) using path: $s_2, \mathsf{employee}, p_3$

As can be seen the final semantics of the policy become:

$$SP = \{(s_1, p_1), (s_1, p_2), (s_1, p_3), (s_2, p_2), (s_2, p_3)\}$$

The example also demonstrates the limited administrative degrees of freedom for RBAC. Consider, for example, the case where we want to remove permission (s_2, p_2) this means we would need to perform *two* actions. First we must remove $(p_2, \mathsf{employee})$ from PR, next we must *add* $(p_2, \mathsf{manager})$ to PR (otherwise also (s_1, p_2) would be cancelled from SP). This is shown in Figure 2b.

3.2 Two–sorted Role Based Access Control

Definition 2 (RBÄC). We let the principal semantic domains S and P be as in Definition 1. The following forms the *syntax* of RBÄC meaning that these are entities which the *users* of RBAC (policy designer/security officer, HR–dept., IT–dept./Infrastructure–dept.) *directly manipulate*:

- Let R^+ be a set of *proper roles* and let D^+ be a set of *demarcations*, both sets are required to be disjoint.
- Let $SR^+ \subseteq S \times R^+$ be a subject–role assignment relation and let $PD^+ \subseteq P \times D^+$ be a permission–demarcation assignment relation.
- Let $RH^+ \subseteq R^+ \times R^+$ be a proper–role–hierarchy relation, and let $DH^+ \subseteq D^+ \times D^+$ be a demarcation–hierarchy relation, both DH^+ and RH^+ are required to be *acyclic*.
- Let $G \subseteq R^+ \times D^+$ be a *grant* relation.

The following definitions lay down the *semantics* of RBÄC meaning they map the syntactical constructs into the principal semantic domains.

- We define $\geq_r^+$ as the transitive reflexive closure of RH^+ and $\geq_d^+$ as the transitive reflexive closure of DH^+.
- We define the *access relation* $SP \subseteq S \times P$ such that $(s, p) \in SP$ iff there exists roles $r, r' \in R^+$ and demarcations $d, d' \in D^+$ such that the following conditions hold:

  1. $(s, r) \in SR^+$, i.e.: subject s is a member of proper role r.
  2. $r \geq_r^+ r'$, i.e.: $r = r'$ or r is senior role of r'.
  3. $(r', d') \in G$, i.e.: proper role r' is granted access to demarcation d'.
  4. $d' \geq_d^+ d$, i.e. $d = d'$ or d is a sub-demarcation of d'.
  5. $(p, d) \in PD^+$, i.e. permission p is part of demarcation d.$\diamond$

The enumerated conditions of the last definition can be visualized superimposed on the square in Figure 1c: one must traverse the west, north and east sides in order to prove a tuple (s, p) belongs to SP (the south side).

Example 2 (RBÄC). We consider a simple example where:

$$R^+ = \{\mathsf{manager}, \mathsf{employee}\}, \quad RH^+ = \{(\mathsf{manager}, \mathsf{employee})\},$$
$$D^+ = \{\mathsf{red}, \mathsf{amber}, \mathsf{green}\},$$
$$DH^+ = \{(\mathsf{red}, \mathsf{amber}), (\mathsf{amber}, \mathsf{green})\},$$
$$SR^+ = \{(s_1, \mathsf{manager}), (s_2, \mathsf{employee})\},$$
$$PD^+ = \{(p_1, \mathsf{red}), (p_2, \mathsf{amber}), (p_3, \mathsf{green})\},$$
$$G = \{(\mathsf{manager}, \mathsf{red}), (\mathsf{employee}, \mathsf{green}), (\mathsf{employee}, \mathsf{amber})\}$$

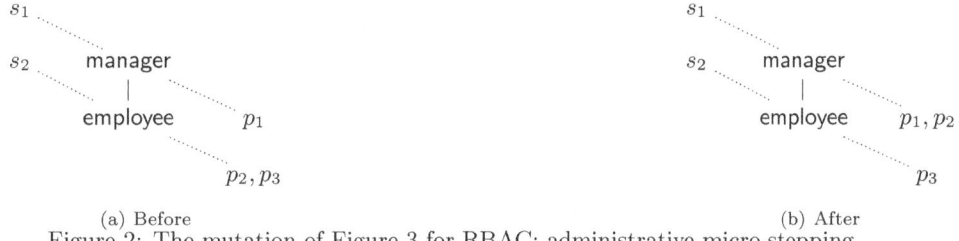

Figure 2: The mutation of Figure 3 for RBAC: administrative micro-stepping.

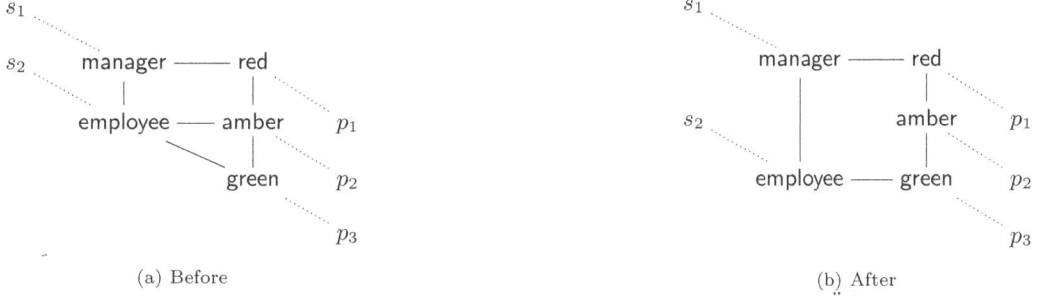

(a) Before (b) After

Figure 3: Lowering the access–level of the employee proper role in the RBÄC case.

(a) Before (b) After

This situation is shown in Figure 3a. $\triangle$

The first thing to note from the diagram in Figure 3a is the redundancy in deriving SP pairs, e.g. for a pair (s_1, p_3) for example, there are three ways to prove this pair belongs in the access relation SP. The first is through the path $s_1, \mathsf{manager}, \mathsf{red}, \mathsf{amber}, \mathsf{green}, p_3$, the second is through the path $s_1, \mathsf{manager}, \mathsf{employee}, \mathsf{amber}, \mathsf{green}, p_3$ and the third is through the path $s_1, \mathsf{manager}, \mathsf{employee}, \mathsf{green}, p_3$. The latter type of redundancy would be easy to remove by tool support: we could simply warn the user that the pair (employee, green) is subsumed by the pair (employee, amber) so removing the former would be cleaner. But what about the remaining redundancy: the square manager, red, amber, employee? We posit this type of redundancy is not harmful, in fact it is crucial to administrative scalability. The formal reason is that both horizontal edges constitute fixed points in the Galois connection that exists between subject and permission sets and neither can be removed without changing SP (cf. Example 4). A more conceptual reason, perhaps, is that all four pairs express a distinct *intent* and, from that perspective, neither pair subsumes any of the others. Let us evaluate the four pairs to see what their intents are:

1. (manager, red) $\in G$: managers need red security clearance to do their job.

2. (red, amber) $\in DH^+$: red is a strictly higher security clearance than amber.

3. (employee, amber) $\in G$: employees need amber security clearance.

4. (manager, employee) $\in RH^+$: managers can do anything that employees can.

What would happen if, in the example, we find out that item 3 is inaccurate: actually all employees can perform all their responsibilities having only green security clearance. In that case the principle of least privilege dictates to lower the security clearance of employees to green. Now an administrative mutation has to be addressed and we see how the

aforementioned redundancy actually plays out to our advantage: (employee, amber) can be simply removed from G and *all the other intents, 1, 2 and 4, remain valid*. The result is shown in Figure 3b. Note that the redundancy that was in the diagram ensures that the impact of this *local* change remains limited to the proper role employee: the proper role manager is not affected.

Contrast this to the classic situation in Figure 2. In that case the mutation required examination of individual permissions, i.e.: the change occurred on the micro–level. Moreover the change violated locality because it impacted the proper role manager.

3.3 Positive and Negative Roles and Demarcations

Definition 3 ($\mathrm{R}^{\pm}\mathrm{B\ddot{A}C}$). We let the principal semantic domains S and P be as in Definition 1. The *syntax* of $\mathrm{R}^{\pm}\mathrm{B\ddot{A}C}$ is defined analogously to Definition 2 except for the fact that we introduce *positive* and *negative* versions for all the relevant types.

- Let R^+ be a set of *(positive) proper roles*, let R^- be a set of *negative proper roles* (also called *castes*), let D^+ be a set of *(positive) demarcations* and let D^- be a set of *negative demarcations* (also called *delimitations*).

- Let $SR^+ \subseteq S \times R^+$ and $SR^- \subseteq S \times R^-$ be the positive and negative subject–role assignment relations and let $PD^+ \subseteq P \times D^+$ and $PD^- \subseteq P \times D^-$ be the positive and negative permission–demarcation assignment relations.

- Let $RH^+ \subseteq R^+ \times R^+$ and $RH^- \subseteq R^- \times R^-$ be the positive and negative proper–role–hierarchy relations, and let $DH^+ \subseteq D^+ \times D^+$ and $DH^- \subseteq D^- \times D^-$ be the positive and negative demarcation–hierarchy relations, all four hierarchies are required to be *acyclic*.

- Let $T = \{\langle G_1, W_1 \rangle, \dots \langle G_n, W_n \rangle\}$ be an indexed set of *specification tuples* for each $i \leq n$ consisting of a grant relation $G_i \subseteq R^+ \times D^+$ and a withhold relation $W_i \subseteq R^- \times D^-$.

The following definitions lay down the *semantics* of R$^\pm$BÄC meaning they map the syntactical constructs into the principal semantic domains.

- We define $\geq_r^+$, $\geq_r^-$, $\geq_d^+$ and $\geq_d^-$ as the transitive reflexive closure of RH^+, RH^-, DH^+, and DH^- respectively.

- We define the *access relation* $SP \subseteq S \times P$ such that $(s, p) \in SP$ iff there exists a specification tuple $\langle G, W \rangle \in T$ such that there exist positive proper roles $r, r' \in R^+$ and positive demarcations $d, d' \in D^+$ for which conditions 1. up to 5. of Definition 2 hold, *and*, in addition, there do *not* exist negative proper roles $r, r' \in R^-$ and negative demarcations $d, d' \in D^-$ for which the following conditions hold:

  6. $(s, r) \in SR^-$, i.e.: subject s is a member of negative proper role r.

  7. $r \geq_r^- r'$, i.e.: $r = r'$ or r is a negative senior role of r'.

  8. $(r', d') \in W$, i.e.: negative proper role r' is withheld access to d'.

  9. $d' \geq_d^- d$, i.e. $d = d'$ or d is a negative subdemarcation of d'.

  10. $(p, d) \in PD^-$, i.e. permission p is part of negative demarcation d. $\diamond$

Conditions 6 to 10 are completely analogous to conditions 1 to 5 in Definition 2. It is important to note that the negative aspects of the language are kept completely separate from the positive aspects on all levels. In this definition, withhold pairs always override grant pairs. It is possible to reverse this w.l.o.g. throughout the paper, however in the definitions that follow we implicitly assume that withhold pairs override grant pairs.

Example 3 (R$^\pm$BÄC). As an example of negative rules we consider the policy shown in Figure 3a, the extensions of all the relevant (positive) domains are given in Example 2.

Now let us assume we are in the position of a security officer who was issued a request to change a security policy: subject s_2 (John) should no longer have permission p_2 (Root–Access).

As a general principle we would like to keep the security policy general, i.e. with no explicit references to particular subjects or permissions. Hence, we shall try to elicit *why* it is the case that John should no longer have root permission. Our goal is to generalize this and embed this knowledge into our organization's security policy, applying the same rule to all the other subjects and permissions under our control. Assume that instead of refactoring the existing (positively specified) policy into a new set of positive rules, we prefer to express the change with a withhold clause and avoid touching the present positive specification.

To do so, we consult with the HR dept. about *what the defining property of John is, that makes him unsuitable for wielding root permission*, and with the IT dept. about *what the property of the root permission is, which makes it off-limits to someone like John*. Let us assume the HR dept. identifies the problem as John lacking the *certified* system

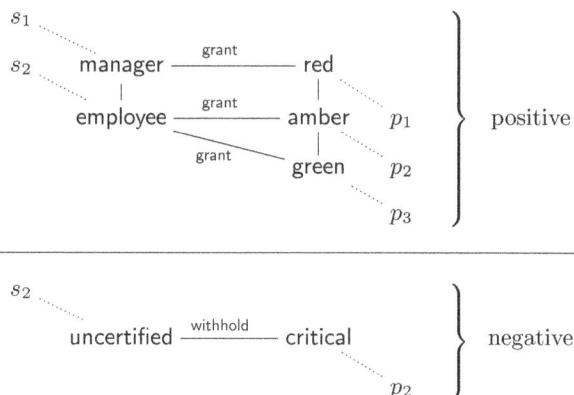

Figure 4: Example with a combination of positive and negative specification styles.

administrator training diploma, and the IT dept. identifies the problem as root permission being a security *critical* permission.

After having figured out the identifying features, a new negative role $R^- = \{$uncertified$\}$ and a new negative demarcation $D^- = \{$critical$\}$ are introduced. The HR and IT departments are henceforth instructed to maintain these designations accurately for *all* relevant subjects and *all* relevant permissions in the organization. For the moment this results in $(s_2,$ uncertified$) \in SR^-$ and $(p_2,$ critical$) \in PD^-$. The complete policy is shown in Figure 4. $\triangle$

There are two reasons why in R$^\pm$BÄC the introduction of negative roles is less confusing than is the case in RBAC. The first reason lies in the fact that R$^\pm$BÄC does not mix positive and negative concepts. The framework is fully *monotone* with respect to positive proper roles and demarcations, and it is fully *antitone* with respect to negative proper roles and demarcations, i.e.: assigning a positive proper role is guaranteed to only *add* permissions, while assigning a negative proper role is guaranteed to only *remove* permissions from the subject. Similarly, assigning a positive demarcation is guaranteed to only *invite* subjects to use the permission, while assigning a negative demarcation is guaranteed only to *ban* subjects from using the permission. These two separate perspectives are illustrated in Figure 5.

The second reason lies in the fact that R$^\pm$BÄC does not mix subject and permission concepts. As is shown in the example: when a negative (withhold) rule is used there is always a property of the subject (i.e.: uncertified) and a property of the permission (i.e.: critical) involved. In RBAC these two aspects have to be mapped onto one and the same object of indirection which makes it hard to elicit meaningful negative roles.

4. RBÄC AND R$^\pm$BÄC IN RELATION TO RBAC

To properly understand the relationship between RBAC and RBÄC we need to distinguish at least three levels: the formal, the conceptual and the expressive. On the formal level RBÄC is a fragment of RBAC because we do not allow roles that simultaneously connect subjects and permissions. On the conceptual level RBÄC is an enrichment of RBAC because we make conceptual distinctions that RBAC simply does not make. Finally, in terms of expressiveness both for-

Subject: John	
Positive Roles	Negative Roles
employee	uncertified
...	...

(a) Subject Management Perspective

Permission: Root–Access	
Demarcations	Delimitations
amber	critical
...	...

(b) Permission Management Perspective

Figure 5: Example for the two administrative perspectives that act at micro level.

malisms are equivalent because there are one–to–one translations in both directions.

Theorem 1. *There exists a linear translation from RBAC to RBÄC and, vice versa, there exists a linear translation from RBÄC back to RBAC.*

Proof. We give a constructive proof. First we consider the case of translating RBAC to RBÄC. For this we proceed by mapping each role to a proper role and demarcation.

$$R^+ = \{\mathsf{proper}[r] \mid r \in R\}$$
$$D^+ = \{\mathsf{demarc}[r] \mid r \in R\}$$
$$SR^+ = \{(s, \mathsf{proper}[r]) \mid (s, r) \in SR\}$$
$$PD^+ = \{(p, \mathsf{demarc}[r]) \mid (p, r) \in PR\}$$
$$RH^+ = \{(\mathsf{proper}[r], \mathsf{proper}[r']) \mid (r, r') \in RH\}$$
$$DH^+ = \{(\mathsf{demarc}[r], \mathsf{demarc}[r']) \mid (r, r') \in RH\}$$
$$G = \{(\mathsf{proper}[r], \mathsf{demarc}[r]) \mid r \in R\}$$

it is clear that the size of the new policy is linear in the size of the original policy and defines the same access relation.

Next we consider the case of translating RBÄC to RBAC. For this we proceed by identifying concepts: proper roles are roles that are not (directly) assigned any permissions and demarcations are roles that are not (directly) assigned any subjects:

$$R = R^+ \cup D^+ \qquad RH = RH^+ \cup DH^+ \cup G$$
$$SR = SR^+ \qquad PR = PD^+$$

clearly the size of the new policy is linear in the size of the original policy and defines the same access relation. □

As can be seen the first case in the proof completely fixes G, i.e.: the only reasonable choice is to set the map as it is was defined, which implies there are no degrees of freedom left. This demonstrates clearly that in RBAC the access management administrative perspective (north side of Figure 1c) is not present. Which, in turn, constitutes formal confirmation of the observations that we detailed in the introduction: in RBAC it is not possible to perform many-to-many administrative mutation on an abstract level unless we do this through the role–hierarchy relation (but this is not desirable for obvious reasons).

The case of R$^\pm$BÄC is different: there is no straightforward translation from R$^\pm$BÄC to RBAC because the former allows a (restricted form) of negation and the latter does not. Clearly, in the other direction, it is trivial to translate RBAC to R$^\pm$BÄC using the first part of Theorem 1.

5. ACCESS CONTROL SEMANTICS

This section discusses the tacit connections between subjects and their permissions and between the positive (grant) and negative (withhold) style of specification.

In the remainder of this section we show the existence of two Galois connections. The first between subject sets and permission sets and the second between grant sets and withhold sets (which can be seen as the positive and negative semantic objects corresponding to the positive and negative parts of an R$^\pm$BÄC specification). In this section we will follow a technique

Figure 6: Interpretation of a Galois connection as an inherent trade–off, [22].

whereby we assume some target access relation that may be implicit in the organization but at least still needs to be elicited and formalized. We then analyse w.r.t. this target access relation what are the tacit structures on S and P that can potentially be exploited for writing concise access control policies. First and foremost this is a syntax-agnostic analysis that acts entirely on the semantic domains.

Definition 4 (Target Access Relation). We let S be some fixed background set of subjects, we let P be some fixed background set of permissions, and we let $SP_\odot \subseteq S \times P$ be some fixed, target access relation. ◇

5.1 Galois Connection: Subjects–Permissions

Definition 5 (Powersets). Let $\mathcal{S} = 2^S$ be the set of sets of subjects and $\mathcal{P} = 2^P$ be the set of sets of permissions. These sets are partially ordered w.r.t. set-inclusion ordering. ◇

Using the full powersets over the principal semantic domains we look at what are possible grant pairs for the *given target* access relation: we define for any given set of subjects the greatest common set of granted permissions, and, vice versa, for any given set of permissions the greatest common set of invited subjects.

Definition 6 (Subject/Permission Adjoints). We define the *greatest common granted permission adjoint* $\mathcal{SP} : \mathcal{S} \to \mathcal{P}$ and the *greatest common invited subject adjoint* $\mathcal{PS} : \mathcal{P} \to \mathcal{S}$ as follows:

$$\mathcal{SP}(\hat{S}) = \bigcup\{\hat{P} \in \mathcal{P} \mid \hat{S} \times \hat{P} \subseteq SP_\odot\},$$
$$\mathcal{PS}(\hat{P}) = \bigcup\{\hat{S} \in \mathcal{S} \mid \hat{S} \times \hat{P} \subseteq SP_\odot\}$$

A *grant pair* $(S', P') \in \mathcal{S} \times \mathcal{P}$ is a *fixed–point* pair iff it holds that $S' = \mathcal{PS}(P')$ and $P' = \mathcal{SP}(S')$. ◇

Theorem 2 (Subject/Permission Connection). $\langle \mathcal{SP}, \mathcal{PS} \rangle$ *is an anti-tone Galois connection between $\mathcal{S}$ and $\mathcal{P}$.*

Proof. Connection $\langle \mathcal{SP}, \mathcal{PS} \rangle$ is a particular case of *relation-generated* Galois connections class. A general proof is at hand from [20, Theorem 2.5.1], [15, Theorem 13]. □

Intuitively this means that there exists an inherent trade–off between abstracting over the set of subjects and abstracting over the set of permissions: if a grant pair is very general with respect to the subject set, it must be very specific with respect to the permission set and, vice versa, if a grant pair is very general with respect to the permission set it must be very specific with respect to the subject set. The necessity to balance the left– and the right–hand–side in order to arrive at beautiful (concise, readable, understandable, maintainable) specifications is illustrated in Figure 6.

Example 4 (Subject/Permission Fixed–Point Pairs). Let us consider once more the RBÄC specification of Example 2. By applying the upper and lower adjoint we can compute the fixed point pairs over SP. For the example the following are fixed–point pairs: $(\{s_1, s_2\}, \{p_2, p_3\})$, and $(\{s_1\}, \{p_1, p_2, p_3\})$. These grant pairs precisely correspond to the proper–role/demarcation pairs (employee, amber) and (manager, red). $\triangle$

5.2 Galois Connection: Positive–Negative

For reasons of exposition in this section we simplify the situation with respect to grant and withhold pairs. In the previous section we treated grant pairs as consisting of a *set* of subjects and a *set* of permissions, in this way there are many possible combinations that lead to the same access relation, in this section we will assume w.l.o.g. that the subject set and the permission set are always *singleton*. Note that it is always possible to normalize any set of grant/withhold pairs to such a set of singleton grant/withhold pairs.

Definition 7 (Grant/Withhold Set). A *grant set* $\mathsf{G} \subseteq \{\mathsf{grant}\} \times S \times P$ consists of a marked set of subject/permission pairs written as terms: $\mathsf{grant}[s, p] \in \mathsf{G}$, with $\mathcal{G}$ we denote the set of all such grant sets. We define a partial order $\sqsupseteq$ on $\mathcal{G}$ such that $\mathsf{G} \sqsupseteq \mathsf{G}'$ iff for all $\mathsf{grant}[s, p] \in \mathsf{G}'$ there exists $\mathsf{grant}[s, p] \in \mathsf{G}$ we say G is *more permissive* than G', for two grant sets G, G' we define their join $\mathsf{G} \sqcup \mathsf{G}'$ as the (set theoretical) union. A *withhold set* $\mathsf{W} \subseteq \{\mathsf{withhold}\} \times S \times P$ consists of a marked set of subject/permission pairs written as terms: $\mathsf{withhold}[s, p] \in \mathsf{W}$, with $\mathcal{W}$ we denote the set of all withhold sets. We define a partial order $\sqsupseteq$ on $\mathcal{W}$ such that $\mathsf{W} \sqsupseteq \mathsf{W}'$ iff for all $\mathsf{withhold}[s, p] \in \mathsf{W}$ there exists $\mathsf{withhold}[s, p] \in \mathsf{W}'$ we say W is *more permissive* than W', for two withhold sets W, W' we define their join $\mathsf{W} \sqcup \mathsf{W}'$ as the (set theoretical) intersection. Note that we overloaded $\sqsupseteq$ and $\sqcup$ for grant and withhold sets, it will be clear from the context which lattice is intended. For a given grant set G and a given withhold set W we define the corresponding access relation $SP(\mathsf{G}, \mathsf{W}) = \{(s, r) \in S \times R \mid \mathsf{grant}(s, r) \in \mathsf{G}, \mathsf{withhold}(s, r) \notin \mathsf{W}\}$. $\diamond$

Definition 8 (Grant/Withhold Adjoints). We define the *negative correcting adjoint* $\mathcal{GW} : \mathcal{G} \to \mathcal{W}$ and the *positive correcting adjoint* $\mathcal{WG} : \mathcal{W} \to \mathcal{G}$ as follows:

$$\mathcal{GW}(\mathsf{G}) = \bigsqcup\{\mathsf{W} \in \mathcal{W} \mid SP(\mathsf{G}, \mathsf{W}) \subseteq SP_\odot\},$$

$$\mathcal{WG}(\mathsf{W}) = \bigsqcup\{\mathsf{G} \in \mathcal{G} \mid SP(\mathsf{G}, \mathsf{W}) \subseteq SP_\odot\}$$

A *grant/withhold specification pair* $(\mathsf{G}, \mathsf{W}) \in \mathcal{G} \times \mathcal{W}$ is a *fixed–point* pair iff it holds that $\mathsf{W} = \mathcal{GW}(\mathsf{G})$ and $\mathsf{G} = \mathcal{WG}(\mathsf{W})$. $\diamond$

Theorem 3 (Grant/Withhold Connection). $\langle \mathcal{GW}, \mathcal{WG} \rangle$ is an antitone Galois connection between $\mathcal{G}$ and $\mathcal{W}$.

Proof. Identical to the proof of Theorem 2. $\square$

Intuitively, if we are more permissive in the positive part of a specification tuple this means that we must be less permissive in the negative part of the specification tuple and, vice versa, if we are more permissive in the negative part of the specification tuple we must be less permissive in the positive part of the specification.

6. RELATED WORK

The research on RBAC was initiated in the 90s [18]. The standard was introduced in [7, 10, 19]. Since then the conceptual core of RBAC has remained stable. Only few authors reported on work that goes beyond the conceptual framework as given in the standard.

Oh and Park [14] were, to our knowledge, the first who realized that permissions should be grouped independently of roles. They called such grouped permissions *tasks*. Tasks were then assigned to roles making their model well-tailored for enterprise environment where work-flow has to be controlled. Task inheritance is not directly addressed. The findings of [14] underline how the need for a separate concept for grouping on the permission side arises naturally in practice.

The more recent critique of the ANSI standard of RBAC [12] contained several suggestions for improving the standard. We draw reader's attention to Suggestion 5 "The semantics of role inheritance should be clearly specified and discussed". Li et al. [12] rightly observed that role hierarchies can be viewed differently as RBAC combined different entities (subjects and permissions) into a single concept of a role. This observation allowed them to describe several peculiarities when role hierarchy was used solely for either user inheritance or permission inheritance. The authors of the ANSI standard for RBAC replied [8] on the aforementioned critique as follows: "...(the) proposal to interpret hierarchies differently in different circumstances is not conducive to conceptual simplicity in the model and is likely to lead to considerable confusion among practitioners". We agree on this point, but, moreover, we identify the reason for such a confusion as having *several* different hierarchies for *one* set of roles. Our first model (RBÄC) splits the concept of a role into a proper role and demarcation and introduces separate hierarchies for both of them therefore preventing the very cause of any possible confusion for interpretation of hierarchies.

The work by Kern et al. [11] on enterprise role-based access control clearly demonstrates the practicality of maintaining two distinct role hierarchies. The terminology they use is *enterprise* role on the enterprise level and *functional* role on the level of target systems. Our proposal is different from enterprise role-based access control in that we advocate a conceptual split right down the middle through the core of the access control model. Indeed in the latter work the triangular domain structure of RBAC remains untouched. Our goals are also slightly different in that we try to address administrative scalability (by preventing administrative microstepping) rather than trying to tie together disjoint access control models (i.e.: Oracle, UNIX, RACF) as per Kern's work. However, the fact that the same mechanism arises naturally in that context we consider as additional confirmation of the relevance of our work.

The work by Nyanchama and Osborn [13] on role graph models underlines once more the relevance of the dichotomy between roles and demarcations that we point out. At the same time roles are still presented as the central object of indirection resulting in a slightly skewed but essentially still triangular domain structure. Another important difference is that Role Graphs are emergent, i.e.: their structure is *defined* in terms of permission (privilege) inclusion. More precisely the is-junior (is-senior) relation is *partly* computed based on privilege inclusion and *partly* given in the form of hints.

Due to the opinion, common in the community, that ". . . negative permission can be very confusing, especially in presence of general hierarchies" [19, subsection 7.3] and that it is better to "base decisions on permissions rather than exclusion" [16], very few researchers addressed the use of negative permissions. Alfaro et al. [1] ". . . point out the necessity of full expressiveness for combining both negative and positive conditions". However authors solely focus on the use of negative and positive rules in firewall languages, provide no formal analysis why mixing positive and negative styles is beneficial for AC management and, thus, argue about pros of such a mixture on a meta-level purely.

Tripunitara and Li [21] introduce a theory for comparing the expressive power of access control models. Their approach is to formalize an access control scheme as a state transition system and to define an expressivity ordering among schemes based on simulation relations. Of course an important point is then how strong or weak we require these simulation relations to be. They demonstrate this clearly by showing pathological cases such as the simulation of RBAC into DAC.

One point that is not addressed in the aforementioned work is *simplicity* (or alternatively: a cap on complexity). Tripunitara and Li [21]'s approach is used in [9] to prove that all existing access control schemes can be simulated by their *tag based access control* scheme but for that they use very liberal formalisation of their labeled transition systems, basically allowing the user to write arbitrary logic sentences and even to choose the actual logic (proof system). In contrast: under the most natural formalisation of an labeled transition system for the RBÄC scheme it may well turn out that RBÄC is *less* expressive (in the strict Tripunitara and Li [21] sense) than RBAC, while under a more liberal formalisation (based on Theorem 1) they would turn out to be equivalent.

In general the key to comparing access control languages cannot lie, solely, in their expressivity. If the latter were true then this problem would already have been solved by using some powerful variant of first or even second order logic. Yet there are many reports in the literature that indicate the problem instead arises on a conceptual level as users are struggling to specify clearly and concisely, to cope with changing policies over time and to keep an overview on the policy that is actually in effect at any given time [3–5].

7. CONCLUSION

As has been shown in the previous section, the problem with role hierarchies was identified by a number of researchers, but no formal analysis was carried out to investigate it. In this respect we can compare the common RBAC approach with macro physics which manipulates with pressure, temperature, etc. and our approach with statistical physics which starts with simple micro interactions (i.e. $\mathcal{SP}$ and $\mathcal{PS}$ adjoints) and, besides reproducing all macroscopic quantities, improves understanding of the analyzed system

providing new insight and a firmer base for future developments. This new knowledge allowed us to introduce negative permissions in a non-confusing manner. In the rest of the section we sum up our findings.

One of the challenges in AC is designing a model which allows to manage a large number of permissions and subjects. While the set of subjects and permissions may considered as a given, a first logical step to take is to apply a "divide et impera" strategy: introduction of RBÄC is a natural progress in this direction. The discussed model RBÄC makes a clear distinction between subject and permission and in doing so introduces a number novel of concepts in access management.

It is often a challenge to design roles and demarcations which are no subject to exclusions. There are two main reasons for that: 1)when all factors influencing the role design are known, it renders very possible to have an unnecessarily granular role structure, and 2)when some factors are not known or missed, a re-factoring of the actual role structure may be very difficult in terms of refining roles and demarcations, re-assigning subjects and permissions and, finally altering access control rules. Introduction of negative counterparts of proper roles and demarcation in RBÄC resulted in R$^\pm$BÄC which addresses the mentioned issues. Therefore there are two ways a negative configuration can be used: 1)avoid micro-granular roles and have human-understandable roles, or/and 2) manage exclusions in a hustle-free manner.

We agree with [19] on that, although RBAC generally allows negative permissions, combination of positive and negative permissions can lead to an unpredictable AC decisions, especially if hierarchies are used. We feel that an anecdotal example comparing negative permissions to generally harmless sleeping pills which may trigger death if not used correctly is appropriate here. To avoid possible unpleasant side effects we give a prescription of how to use them:

- *use two different levels of indirections for subjects and permissions;*
- *maintain polarities: proper roles can only add permissions, positive demarcations can only invite subjects, proper negative roles can only withdraw permissions, negative demarcation can only ban subjects.*

Put formally, we claim that the monotonicity of the access relation defined through positive roles and positive demarcations, and the antitonicity of the access relation in the case of negative roles and negative demarcations are desirable properties that are relied upon by (and hence become particularly important from) the decoupled subject management and permission management perspectives.

7.1 Economy of Roles/Demarcation Split

Although the economy of the approach remains to be validated there are a number of concerns that, in absence of quantitative data, can be preliminarily addressed based on the theoretical analysis developed in the present paper.

One possible concern with the approach advocated here can be paraphrased as saying "more layers implies more things to engineer and sustain". We would like to point out here that this is primarily a question about economy of scale. As mentioned in the introduction, for smaller problem instances, or problem instances that are otherwise well-behaved, a different, simpler type of access control scheme might well be sufficient and therefore better suitable purely on the merit of being *simpler*. In general it is true that the best solution to any problem is the *simplest* solution that qualifies as an adequate solution to the *whole* problem (in all of its facets).

It is therefore true that also bi-sorted role based access control must target a particular sweet spot of domain complexity. Our analysis suggest that the two main prerequisites on the organisation willing to adopt such a scheme will be:

- The organisation is of a certain minimum size, such that the three administrative perspectives (*subject*, *permission* and *access* management) are clearly discernible and are delegated to distinct teams or at least to distinct individuals.

- The organisation experiences a rate of administrative changes (*policy flux*) which merits the extra overhead in implementing the proposed decoupling and which overweights the cost of maintaining a more traditional static policy.

7.2 Economy of Positive/Negative Split

In a similar vein as the split between roles and demarcations we can discuss concerns about the split between positive and negative objects of indirection.

One such concern can be paraphrased as saying "in the presence of negation, policies can quickly become inconsistent." Inconsistency is a notion that is important for *logical specification* where the set of models characterized by a set of formulae can easily become empty if two or more of these formulae lead to a logical contradiction. Note that in our case the situation is different: there is always exactly one well-defined model (the access relation). That model is completely and unambiguously fixed by the policy specification. In fact it only makes sense to withhold a permission after it has first been granted. Inconsistency, in the strict logical sense, does not arise.

As soon as one starts considering constraints or invariants (written in some logical language) that are to hold *over* a given policy specification, consistency becomes important again and is a good candidate property to check for during static analysis of the constraints and invariants.

7.3 Economy of Graphical Languages

We would like to point out that although we use *graphical* language throughout the paper to explain and illustrate the *symbolic* expressions, in no way this means we advocate the exclusive use of graphical language in this context.

In general, simple examples denoted using graphical languages have the advantage to be more immediately intuitive. Perhaps because they appeal more directly to spatial pattern recognition abilities of the user. However this apparent advantage is offset by the fact that complexity of real–life problem instances rather quickly surpasses these same spatial pattern recognition abilities. In other words: graphs quickly get too cluttered, thereby limiting the utility of graphical languages.

At the same time, as shown in Appendix A, graphical languages can be rather intuitive for presenting query results where only a small portion of the graph is shown, i.e.: only the portion that is relevant to the query parameters.

7.4 Future Work

There are several avenues to consider for future work. The first, practical avenue, is to build an actual AC system employing all the introduced primitives and do a case study. We have already taken the first steps in this direction by building a prototype on top of the Neo4j graph database (cf. Appendix A).

On the theoretical side it is interesting to consider the introduction of *constraints*. Already explored for RBAC we know that constraints are a useful addition there. The situation for RBÄC (and R$^{\pm}$BÄC) we expect to be even more interesting with respect to constraints because of the two (four) sorted nature of the languages. As an example we can mention, besides the usual static and dynamic separation of duties, the introduction of bi–sorted *implication* constraints. With such a constraint one might for example say that some proper role intern implies a *negative* proper role uncertified.

Constraints are not to be confused with inheritance. A user of the AC language may, in principle set an inheritance relation between any two roles and/or demarcations and, in doing so, alter the resulting access function. There is no notion of an inheritance relation either *holding* or *not holding* for a given specification (it is *part of* the specification).

As mentioned before in the context of *consistency*: a logical constraint serves the purpose of restricting the possible role/demarcation assignments and it can either hold or not for a given set of assignments. As such, a second, more pragmatic, question to consider here would be how such constraints are best enforced or how a user can best be guided in satisfying them. This ties in with work on model-checking entire policy specifications.

8. ACKNOWLEDGEMENTS

We would like to thank Albert Dercksen for valuable input, Prof. Ninghui Li for constructive feedback and useful pointers to literature, and our anonymous reviewers for indicating points of improvement.

References

[1] J. Alfaro, F. Cuppens, and N. Cuppens-Boulahia. Management of exceptions on access control policies. In *New Approaches for Security, Privacy and Trust in Complex Environments*, pages 97–108. Springer, 2007.

[2] M. Barletta, S. Ranise, and L. Viganò. Automated Analysis of Scenario-based Specifications of Distributed Access Control Policies with Non-Mechanizable Activities (Extended Version). *arXiv preprint arXiv:1206.3180*, 2012.

[3] L. Bauer, L. Cranor, R. Reeder, M. Reiter, and K. Vaniea. A user study of policy creation in a flexible access-control system. In *Proceedings of the twenty-sixth annual SIGCHI conference on Human factors in computing systems*, pages 543–552. ACM, 2008.

[4] L. Bauer, L. Cranor, R. Reeder, M. Reiter, and K. Vaniea. Real life challenges in access-control management. In *Proceedings of the 27th international conference on Human factors in computing systems*, pages 899–908. ACM, 2009.

[5] D. Botta, R. Werlinger, A. Gagné, K. Beznosov, L. Iverson, S. Fels, and B. Fisher. Towards understanding IT security professionals and their tools. In *Proceedings of the 3rd symposium on Usable privacy and security*, pages 100–111. ACM, 2007.

[6] P. P.-S. Chen. The entity-relationship model — toward a unified view of data. *ACM Transactions on Database Systems*,

1(1):9–36, Mar. 1976. ISSN 0362-5915. doi: 10.1145/320434. 320440. URL http://doi.acm.org/10.1145/320434.320440.

[7] D. Ferraiolo, R. Sandhu, S. Gavrila, D. Kuhn, and R. Chandramouli. Proposed NIST standard for role-based access control. *ACM Transactions on Information and System Security (TISSEC)*, 4(3):224–274, 2001.

[8] D. Ferraiolo, R. Kuhn, and R. Sandhu. RBAC standard rationale: Comments on "Comments on a Critique of the ANSI Standard on Role-Based Access Control". *Security & Privacy, IEEE*, 5(6):51–53, 2007.

[9] T. L. Hinrichs, W. C. Garrison III, A. J. Lee, S. Saunders, and J. C. Mitchell. TBA : A Hybrid of Logic and Extensional Access Control Systems. In G. Barthe, A. Datta, and S. Etalle, editors, *Formal Aspects of Security and Trust*, volume 7140 of *Lecture Notes in Computer Science*, pages 198–213. Springer Berlin Heidelberg, 2012. ISBN 978-3-642-29419-8. doi: 10.1007/978-3-642-29420-4_13. URL http://dx.doi.org/10.1007/978-3-642-29420-4_13.

[10] A. INCITS. INCITS 359-2004. Role Based Access Control. *Role based access control*, 2004.

[11] A. Kern, A. Schaad, and J. Moffett. An administration concept for the enterprise role-based access control model. In *Proceedings of the eighth ACM symposium on Access control models and technologies*, pages 3–11. ACM, 2003. URL http://www.moffett.me.uk/jdm/pubs/AdminRBAC_SACMAT2003.pdf.

[12] N. Li, J. Byun, and E. Bertino. A critique of the ANSI standard on role-based access control. *Security & Privacy, IEEE*, 5(6):41–49, 2007.

[13] M. Nyanchama and S. Osborn. The role graph model and conflict of interest. *ACM Transactions on Information and System Security (TISSEC)*, 2(1):3–33, 1999. URL http://www.matunda.org/wp-content/uploads/2006/12/p3-nyanchama1.pdf.

[14] S. Oh and S. Park. Task–role-based access control model. *Information Systems*, 28(6):533–562, 2003.

[15] O. Ore. Galois connexions. *Transactions of the American Mathematical Society*, pages 493–513, 1944.

[16] J. H. Saltzer and M. D. Schroeder. The protection of information in computer systems. *Proceedings of the IEEE*, 63 (9):1278–1308, 1975.

[17] R. Sandhu. Role activation hierarchies. In *Proceedings of the third ACM workshop on Role-based access control*, pages 33–40. ACM, 1998.

[18] R. Sandhu, E. Coyne, H. Feinstein, and C. Youman. Role-based access control models. *Computer*, 29(2):38–47, 1996. ISSN 0018-9162. doi: 10.1109/2.485845.

[19] R. Sandhu, D. Ferraiolo, and R. Kuhn. The NIST model for role-based access control: towards a unified standard. In *Proceedings of the fifth ACM workshop on Role-based access control*, pages 47–63, 2000.

[20] P. Smith. The Galois connection between syntax and semantics. *University of Cambridge*, 2010. URL http://logicmatters.net/resources/pdfs/Galois.pdf.

[21] M. V. Tripunitara and N. Li. Comparing the expressive power of access control models. In *Proceedings of the 11th ACM conference on Computer and communications security*, CCS '04, pages 62–71, New York, NY, USA, 2004. ACM. ISBN 1-58113-961-6. doi: 10.1145/1030083.1030093. URL http://doi.acm.org/10.1145/1030083.1030093.

[22] WikiMedia Commons. Libra. http://en.wikipedia.org/wiki/File:Libra2.jpg, January 2011. This work is in the public domain.

APPENDIX

A. PROTOTYPE IMPLEMENTATION

Neo4j is an open–source graph database that has been gaining popularity in the community. In this appendix we outline a prototype implementation of a bi-sorted role based access control engine built on top of the Neo4j graph database. The goal is to specify the entire policy as a graph and evaluate the access function purely using the graph database query language. In this way we are effectively leveraging the database engine to take care of the heavy lifting (query planning, indexing, caching, etc.)

In addition we will show how this implementation allows for clear feedback from the access control engine to the policy designer by asking the right type of queries and presenting the result back as a graph. The latter is especially useful when combining the positive and negative style of specification.

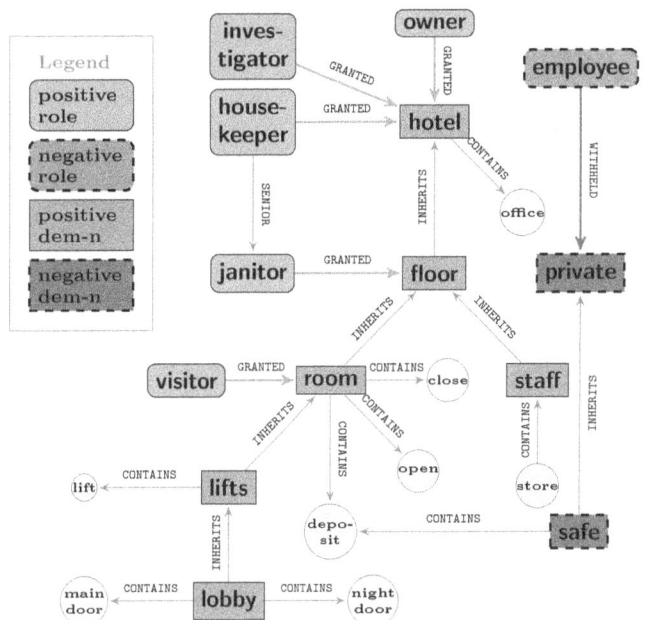

Figure 8: Roles and demarcations

We consider an anecdotal case of a small hotel. Assume that owner does not know much of Role-Based Access Control, but he understands challenges and regulations involved in such business:

- he, as owner, has to have access everywhere in the hotel;

- visitors have to have access to their rooms and all appliances there — let there be a safe, where one can deposit things in;

- there must be a janitor at each floor responsible for cleaning rooms at that floor, janitors are coordinated by a housekeeping office;

- according to city regulations, policemen, after having shown a search warrant, have to have access everywhere.

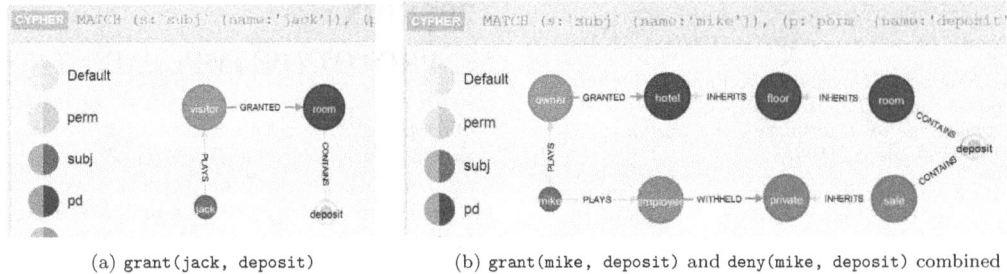

(a) `grant(jack, deposit)`   (b) `grant(mike, deposit)` and `deny(mike, deposit)` combined

Figure 7: Two examples of graphical explanations of a computed AC relation

In this case the best candidate for demarcations hierarchy is the actual physical division of the hotel into rooms and floors. Having considered all the factors he comes up with a green part (left part) of the sketch given in Figure 8. We see that this part is, in fact, very similar to the regular RBAC: members of senior roles are also members of their respective juniors and permissions of junior roles are accessible for members of senior ones. One can apply the result of Theorem 1 to reconstruct the corresponding RBAC model. Nevertheless we can immediately see the benefits of the RBÄC scheme: roles of owner, housekeeper and investigator have the *same* permission set, though these roles are conceptually distinct. Quickly the positive design shows its flaw: employees can deposit things in safes, thus open and close them. Now instead of redefining the positive hierarchy, he introduces a single negative role "employee" and a single negative demarcation "safe" which include exactly one permission. Withdrawal of access rights to the safe demarcation from employees fixes the flaw. Now Figure 8 depicts the complete AC design (note the similarities to Figure 4).

We have implemented the hotel AC design with some floors and rooms in graph database Neo4j. There are two types of entities in Neo4j: nodes and relationships. The former are usually written in lower case letters surrounded with round brackets, e.g. `(node)`, relationships are usually written in capitals surrounded with square brackets, e.g. `[:RELATIONSHIP]`. Two nodes can be connected with such a relationship in a directional manner. Cypher query language of Neo4j allows to condition a length of a relation path between two nodes, e.g. `[:RELATIONSHIP*1..20]`. These features will allow us to compute AC decisions in a rather simple way.

In our example we assigned `mike` to `owner` and, thus, `employee` roles and `jack` to visitor role in some room. To find out if a subject can carry out some permission, simple Cypher queries, Listings 1 and 2, must be executed. Placeholders `subject` and `permission` need be replaced with actual subject and permission names. Logically, access is granted if grant *is not* empty and deny *is* empty, denied — in all other cases. It is possible to combine the last two queries, but we preferred to state them separately for the sake of clarity. The grant query requires the db engine to first match a certain subject and permission we are interested in. Second, a match for a role directly assigned to the given subject is looked for. Next we try to trace (via `[:SENIOR]` relation to some junior roles) a role which is directly granted access to a demarcation which, in turn, inherits (via `[:INHERITS]` relation to some junior demarcations)

the given permission. These results combined form a (non-unique) `grant` path from the subject to permission.

```
MATCH (s:subj {name:'subject'}),
      (p:perm {name:'permission'}),
grant=
    (s)-[:PLAYS]->(PosRole:pr)-[:SENIOR*0..]->
    (somePosRole:pr)-[:GRANTED]->
    (somePosDemn:pd)<-[:INHERITS*0..]-
    (PosDemn:pd)-[:CONTAINS]->(p)
RETURN grant
```

Listing 1: Grant query

We relax the condition on the number of relations in-between the nodes and allow it to be absent. Similar procedure holds when a (non-unique) `deny` path is looked for.

```
MATCH (s:subj {name:'subject'}),
      (p:perm {name:'permission'}),
deny=
    (s)-[:PLAYS]->(NegRole:nr)-[:SENIOR*0..]->
    (someNegRole:nr)-[:WITHHELD]->
    (someNegDemn:nd)<-[:INHERITS*0..]-
    (NegDemn:nd)-[:CONTAINS]->(p)
RETURN deny
```

Listing 2: Deny query

Assume `jack` would like to `deposit` some personal belongings in a safe, then `grant(jack, deposit)` yields a path given in Figure 7a and `deny(jack, deposit)` expectedly produces an empty path. It is more interesting to see if `mike` can exercise the permission, for that we execute `grant(mike, deposit)` and `deny(mike, deposit)`, the result of combination of the two outputs is given in Figure 7b. We see that the `mike`'s granted `deposit` right is cancelled with his membership in the negative `employee` role.

In a practical setting it is very important to provide high quality feedback (*explanations*) to a policy designer. Arguably this is an even more fundamental requirement than expressivity of the AC language. Our framework has excellent properties in this respect. As an example take the case outlined above. Imagine a scenario where Mike wants to deposit something in an hotel room safe. Being precluded to do so Mike calls the security officer responsible complaining that he cannot access the safe. The security officer asks the AC system to explain to him the access request (`mike`, `deposit`), the result is shown graphically in Figure 7b. Following the blue path it is clear that Mike in principle has access to the safe by virtue of holding the *owner* role. However, following the red path it becomes clear that this privilege is withdrawn because as an employee he has no access to private belongings of hotel guests.

Towards More Usable Information Flow Policies for Contemporary Operating Systems

Wai Kit Sze, Bhuvan Mital and R. Sekar
Stony Brook University
Stony Brook, NY, USA

ABSTRACT

There has been a resurgence of interest in information flow based techniques in security. A key attraction of these techniques is that they can provide strong, principled protection against malware, regardless of its sophistication. In spite of this advantage, most advances in information flow control have not been adopted in mainstream operating systems since a strict application of information flow can limit system functionality and usability. Permitting dynamic changes to subject labels, as proposed in the low-watermark model, provides better usability. However, it suffers from the *self-revocation* problem, whereby read/write operations on already open files are denied because the label of the subject performing these operations has been downgraded. While most applications deal gracefully with security failures on file open operations, they are unprepared to handle security violations on subsequent reads/writes. As a result, subject downgrades may lead to crashes or malfunction. Even those applications that deal with read/write errors may still leave output files in a corrupted or inconsistent state since write permissions were taken away in the midst of producing an output file. To overcome these drawbacks, we propose a new approach for dynamic downgrading that eliminates the self-revocation problem. We show that our approach represents an optimal combination of functionality and compatibility. Our experimental evaluation shows that our approach is efficient, incurring an overhead of a few percentage points, is compatible with existing applications, and provides strong integrity protection.

1. Introduction

Operation Aurora [2] and Stuxnet [7] signified the arrival of an era of targeted attacks by sophisticated malware. Their pace has only quickened in the past two years, as malware attack campaigns are revealed on major organizations at alarmingly regular intervals.

Security in contemporary operating systems such as Windows and various flavors of UNIX is based on discretionary access control (DAC) that relies on userids. It suffers from the well-known weakness that DAC cannot distinguish a malicious user from a malicious program. As a result, if a legitimate user happens to run a malicious program, this program can co-opt all of the user's privileges to defeat or circumvent system security. Worse, malware need not even be executed by the user in most cases, as it can take the form of malicious data that hijacks a vulnerable benign application. According to Trend Micro [29], at least 70% of targeted malware attacks compromised victim systems using non-executable content such as PDF or JPEG.

The weaknesses of userid-based DAC has prompted a resurgence of interest in mandatory access control (MAC) [17, 4, 13, 26, 30, 6, 5, 14, 18, 28, 8]. Information-flow approaches such as the Biba model [4] are particularly attractive in the context of malware threats, as they can prevent low-integrity (untrusted and potentially malicious) data or code from ever influencing high-integrity data or applications. It not only prevents malware from directly corrupting important system files, but also stops indirect attacks that operate by corrupting some intermediate data consumed by other high integrity processes that can update important system files.

A drawback of the Biba model is that its strict separation between high and low-integrity objects and subjects, which impacts its usability. Consider a utility application such as a word-processor that needs to operate on both high and low integrity files. It would be necessary to have two versions of every such application, one for operating on high-integrity files and another for low-integrity files. It is cumbersome to install and maintain two versions of every application. Worse, a user needs to be careful in selecting the correct version of an application for each task — choosing a high-integrity version of an application for processing low-integrity files (or vice-versa) will lead to security failures and/or application crashes.

The low-watermark policy [4] can avoid these drawbacks of the strict policy by permitting subject integrity to be downgraded at runtime. In particular, this policy allows applications to be invoked with high integrity, and the integrity level to be downgraded if the application subsequently reads a low integrity object. Fraser [8] argues eloquently why low watermark policy provides significantly better compatibility with existing software as compared to the strict model. However, prior to this project, the low watermark policy was not very popular because of the *self-revocation* problem [8]. Specifically, consider a subject that has already opened a high integrity file for writing. If this subject subsequently opens a low integrity file for reading, it is downgraded. At this point, the subject cannot be permitted to write the high integrity file any more. Applications expect and handle security failures when opening files, but once opened, they assume that subsequent read and write operations will not fail. When this assumption is invalidated, applications may malfunction or crash.

The LOMAC project [8] does not attempt to solve the self-revocation problem in its entirety, but focuses on two common instances

†This work was supported in part by grants from NSF (CNS-0831298, CNS-1319137) and AFOSR (FA9550-09-1-0539).

that involve pipes and shared memory abstractions. Pipes are particularly nasty, because downgrading of one process in a pipeline can prevent it from writing to the pipe, which in turn will cause the next process in the pipeline to fail because it does not get any input. LOMAC avoids this problem by permitting pipe communications only within a UNIX process group, and ensuring that all processes within this group are at the same level. This notion of a group is further extended to include all processes that share memory. Since all processes within a group are at the same level at all times, there is no need to restrict communication among them, and hence pipes and shared memory operations don't ever have to be denied. Unfortunately, self-revocation problem still remains when dealing with files, as well as other IPC mechanisms such as sockets.

In this paper, we propose a more general solution to the self-revocation problem in all cases. Our specific contributions are:

- We develop a model (Section 2) to compare different integrity policies in terms of their functionality (i.e., the behaviors that they permit) and failure compatibility (i.e., ability to map security failures newly introduced by the policy into those that are already handled by an application). We show that among these policies, low-watermark policy is the best in terms of functionality, but the worst in terms of compatibility.

- We then define a new policy, called *Self-Revocation-Free Dynamic Downgrading (SRFD)* that combines the best features of different information flow policies.

- We present a design for enforcing SRFD on contemporary operating systems. (See Section 3.) Our design uses a novel constraint propagation technique to identify file open operations that introduce a potential for future self-revocations, and denies them. Our design is general, and avoids self-revocation involving files as well as interprocess communication.

- We formally show that SRFD eliminates self-revocations. We also show that unless future inter-process communications can be predicted accurately, it is not possible to improve on the functionality of SRFD without incurring self-revocation.

- We present an implementation of SRFD on Ubuntu Linux 13.10 in Section 4. Our experimental evaluation (Section 5) shows that our implementation is fast, incurring a maximum overhead under 6% and average overhead below 2% across several macro-benchmarks. The evaluation also demonstrates that SRFD provides very good compatibility, while thwarting malware attacks.

An open source implementation of SRFD can be found at [27].

2. Model

In this section, we consider information-flow policies that are commonly used in the context of integrity preservation: strict integrity policy and (two flavors of) dynamic downgrading policy. We propose a model to compare these security policies. Specifically, we show that a policy that supports dynamic downgrading of subjects provides better functionality than the strict integrity model. However, more functionality does not always translate to better compatibility or user experience. We therefore formalize the notion of compatibility, and proceed to define a new dynamic downgrading policy that provides an optimal combination of functionality and compatibility among the commonly-used integrity policies.

We model process execution in terms of the sequence of actions $\mathbf{A} = A_1 \ldots A_n$ performed by a process. Each action A_i can be:

- an invocation (*I*), typically, the execution of another program;
- an observation (*O*), typically, a file read operation; or
- a modification (*W*), typically, a file write operation.

In order to simplify terminology and description, we consider only two integrity levels in this paper: high (Hi) and low (Lo). Objects (typically files) as well as subjects (processes) have one of these integrity levels.

DEFINITION 1 (INTEGRITY-PRESERVING EXECUTIONS). *Such executions ensure that the content of all high integrity objects are derived entirely from other high integrity objects and subjects.*

A strong integrity-preservation policy, such as the Biba's strict integrity policy and the low-watermark policy, will ensure that all executions are integrity preserving. In particular, this means that low-integrity data and programs cannot influence the contents of integrity-critical (data or program) files on the system. Today's remote exploits and malware attacks all rely on modifying critical files using data or code from untrusted sources, and hence can be definitively blocked by enforcing these integrity policies, provided we ensure that only data/code from trustworthy sources is given a high integrity label.

When a security policy is enforced, it can alter an execution sequence in one of two ways. First, it can disallow an operation A_i, denoted as $\not{A}_i$. There are several possibilities here, including (a) silent suppression of A_i, (b) suppressing A_i and returning an error to the process performing this operation, and (c) replacing A_i with another allowable action. In the rest of this paper, we primarily focus on the alternative (b).

A second avenue for the enforcement engine is to downgrade a subject before A_i, denoted $\downarrow A_i$. Note that such a downgrade may be an internal operation within a reference monitor enforcing the policy, and hence we may not explicitly show it in some instances.

Executions without any failed operations are called *permitted* or *successful executions*, while the rest are called *failed executions*. The more execution sequences that a security policy permits, the less functionality will be lost as a result of security policy enforcement. This leads to the following definition comparing the functionality supported by security policies.

DEFINITION 2 (FUNCTIONALITY). *A security policy P_1 is said to be more functional than P_2, denoted $P_1 \supseteq_F P_2$, if and only if every execution sequence permitted by P_2 is also permitted by P_1.*

Note that functionality defines a partial order on security policies, and hence two policies could be incomparable in terms of functionality. By permitting more executions, a more functional policy would seem to provide weaker security than a less functional policy, thus capturing the tension between functionality and security.

2.1 Integrity policies

We can now classify actions into two categories: *high integrity actions* (A_H) that can be performed by high integrity subjects, and *low integrity actions* (A_L) that can be performed by low integrity subjects. Specifically, A_H includes all actions except read-down (O_L), i.e., read a low-integrity input, and invoke-down (I_L), i.e., executing a program that has low integrity. A_L includes all actions except write-up (W_H). Note that I_H is permitted in A_L because we interpret it as the execution of a high integrity file within a low integrity subject. (In contrast, the term "invoke-up" is used in Biba model to refer to the execution of a high integrity subject.)

Integrity-preserving execution sequences can be achieved by confining high integrity processes to perform only A_H, and low integrity processes to perform only A_L. Since W_H exists only in A_H and O_L exists only in A_L, it is clear that low-integrity objects and subjects cannot affect high-integrity objects.

Since we want to protect the integrity of critical files, revisions to object integrity levels are disallowed in most systems. However, subject integrity label can be revised down as long as the down-

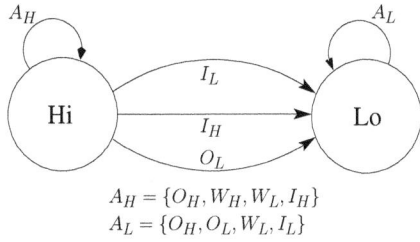

$$A_H = \{O_H, W_H, W_L, I_H\}$$
$$A_L = \{O_H, O_L, W_L, I_L\}$$

Figure 1: State machine for integrity-preserving executions.

graded subject is restricted to perform A_L after the downgrade. This leads to the following variants that all preserve integrity.

No Downgrading (ND). This policy, which corresponds to the Biba strict policy, permits no privilege revision (NPR): labels are statically assigned to subjects and objects, and they cannot change. With this strict interpretation, every program has to be labeled as high or low integrity, and a high integrity program cannot be used to process low integrity data, even if all outputs resulting from such use flow only to low-integrity files or low-integrity subjects.

Eager downgrading (ED). This policy permits subject labels to be downgraded, but only when executing another process. This approach, also called *privilege revision on invocation* (PRI), allows more executions as compared to the no-downgrading policy. With the PRI policy, a subject wishing to operate on low-integrity files should know ahead of time (i.e., prior to execution) that it needs to consume low-integrity file, and drop its privilege before execution. This is why we call it *eager downgrading*.

Lazy downgrading (LD). The final policy is the low watermark policy for subjects, where downgrades can happen before any observe operation, or an invoke operation. We call it lazy (or just-in-time) downgrading since downgrading operation would typically be delayed until the very last step, which must be the consumption of a low-integrity input.

Figure 1 shows a simple state-machine model that captures the above three policies. With the ND policy, none of the transitions between H and L states are available. With the ED policy, only the transitions on I_L and I_H are enabled. Note that while it is mandatory to transition to Lo on I_L, I_H may or may not cause a transition to Lo. When it does, it corresponds to the use of a high-integrity application to process low-integrity data.

With the LD policy, only the I_L and O_L transitions from Hi to Lo are enabled. There is no need to make a transition from Hi to Lo on I_H, as the downgrade can be deferred until the next operation to read low-integrity data. As a result, LD avoids one of the difficulties of ED, namely, the need to predict ahead of time whether a certain process will need to read low-integrity data.

2.2 Comparing functionalities of integrity policies

It is easy to see the motivation for the LD policy: when the actions performed by an application are disallowed, it can lead to errors and failures, and hence loss of functionality. In contrast, downgrading has the potential to permit the application to continue to provide its function. In fact, we can formally state:

THEOREM 3. $LD \supset_F ED \supset_F ND$

Proof: This theorem simply states that LD is strictly more functional than ED, which, in turn, is more functional than ND. From the definition of the three policies, and Figure 1, it is easy to see that all three policies accept the same set A_L^* of execution sequences for low-integrity subjects. (We are using a regular expression syntax to succinctly capture the set of execution sequences permitted by a policy.) Thus, we can limit our comparisons to the execu-

tion sequences permitted for high-integrity subjects. Note that ND accepts only sequences of the form A_H^* for high subjects. ED accepts $(I_L|I_H)A_L^*$ for subjects started with high, in addition to the set A_H^*. Finally, LD accepts $A_H^*(I_L|O_L)A_L^*$, which is a strict superset of sequences accepted by ED. ∎

2.3 Compatibility

Increased functionality does not always translate to a better user experience, or better compatibility with existing software. Self-revocation is a prime example of the compatibility problem posed by LD, an approach that maximizes functionality over other integrity policies. In contrast, ED provides less functionality as compared to LD, but is intuitively perceived as being more compatible.

Self-revocation occurs when a subject is initially granted access to a resource, but this access is revoked subsequently; and the revocation is the result of some of the other actions performed by the subject itself. More concretely, self-revocation manifests itself as follows in the context of file system APIs provided by modern operating systems: a process successfully opens a file, but a subsequent write operation using that file handle is denied. Although self-revocation is more commonly identified with failures of writes, it can also happen on read operations. In both cases, self-revocation raises several compatibility issues:

- The file system API is designed to perform security checks on open operations, but not on reads and writes. As a result, there is usually no way to even communicate a security failure to the subject performing the read or write[1]. Thus, security failures have to be mapped into other failures that can occur on reads/writes, such as an attempt to read a file before opening it. Such remapping has obvious drawbacks because applications may misinterpret the error code and respond inappropriately.

- Even if an error code is returned on reads and writes, many applications may not check them at all. This is because failures of these operations are rare and unexpected, so many applications may not contain code for checking these error cases, or undertaking any meaningful error recovery.

- Even if the application checks the error and undertakes recovery, data loss or corruption may be unavoidable at this point. Consider an application that was updating a file. If its write access is taken away when it is half-way through the update, that may lead to the file being truncated, leading to data loss, inconsistency or corruption.[2]

For this reason, we develop the following notion of failure-compatibility, or simply, compatibility of security policies.

DEFINITION 4 (COMPATIBILITY). *We say that a security policy P is compatible if all actions disallowed by it can return a valid permission failure error to the subject.*

With contemporary file APIs, this means that a compatible policy would deny open's but not reads/writes. We show that in terms of compatibility, the results are inverted from that of functionality:

THEOREM 5. *LD is not failure-compatible, whereas ND and ED are both failure compatible.*

Proof: Recall that for subjects that start at low integrity, all three policies allows A_L^*. It is clear that this sequence permits the same

---

[1]For instance, on UNIX, there are no error codes related to permissions that can be returned by read and write system calls.

[2]With buffered I/O, even the data that an application believes to have written prior to the self-revoking action may be lost — such data may be held in the program's internal buffers, which may be flushed much later, at which point, the write system call would fail.

set of operations throughout, so self-revocation is not possible. For high integrity subjects, ND accepts A_H^* — again, the set of operations permitted remain constant throughout the subject's lifetime, and hence there will be no self-revocation. For ED, the sequences accepted are of the form A_H^* or A_L^*. For each alternate, it is easy to see that all of the actions permitted towards the beginning of the sequence are also permitted later on, once again ruling out the possibility of self-revocation. Finally, we have already explained how LD suffers from self-revocation. ∎

2.4 Maximizing functionality *and* compatibility

The results above lead to the following question: can there be an approach that is preferable in terms of both functionality and compatibility? Our answer in this paper is affirmative. We begin by positing the existence of a new dynamic downgrading policy that combines LD's functionality with the compatibility of ED.

DEFINITION 6 (SELF-REVOCATION-FREE DOWNGRADING). *SRFD accepts the same set of execution sequences as LD. Every sequence that is modified by LD is also modified by SRFD, but unlike LD, SRFD only modifies (i.e., denies) open operations.*

So, the next natural question is whether SRFD is realizable. Conceptually, we can synthesize execution sequences accepted/modified by SRFD from the acceptance and modification actions of LD as follows. If LD accepts a sequence, then SRFD will accept the same sequence. If LD modifies a sequence, let A_i be the first write operation denied by LD. SRFD will identify the open operation A_j preceding A_i that caused LD to downgrade the subject, and then SRFD will deny A_j.

Noting that LD denies only write operations on high-integrity files, this means that SRFD needs to predict whether a subject will perform future writes on any of the currently open file descriptors for accessing high-integrity files. If so, SRFD should not permit the subject to open any low-integrity file. In this manner, SRFD can prevent the subject from downgrading itself, and hence will not have to deny writes on one of these descriptors in the future.

This raises the final question: how can a reference monitor predict future actions of a subject? Often, questions regarding future behavior are answered by assuming that any thing that can happen will indeed happen. We formalize this by characterizing a class of programs that transfer data along every possible communication channel between communicating processes, and show that for this class, SRFD can indeed be realized.

Another way to characterize our result is as follows. Unless an oracle for predicting future behavior of a set of communicating processes exists, one cannot improve over the functionality of the design presented in the next section without risking self-revocation.

3. Our approach

Our approach represents a hybrid between ND that refuses to ever downgrade a subject, and LD which downgrades at the first open of a low-integrity file. The key idea is to deny these open operations when a subject already holds open file descriptors that write to high-integrity files. This task is simple enough for stand-alone subjects, but challenges arise when considering processes that interact with each other.

Note that many applications involve processes that communicate via pipes, sockets, shared memory and other IPC mechanisms. If we look at each process in isolation and allow one of them to be downgraded, it is possible that a future read by another process would have to be denied, since it is reading an output of the downgraded process. Since the goal of our approach is to avoid denials

of reads/writes, it would seem that we need better mechanisms to keep track of open file descriptors across collections of processes.

A simple approach to deal with collections of communicating processes is to treat them as a single unit, and downgrade them as a unit. LOMAC [8] uses this approach to avoid self-revocation due to IPC within a UNIX process group. However, this approach does not recognize the one-way nature of pipe-based communication, and hence would needlessly downgrade an upstream process when a downstream process opens a low-integrity file. To avoid this, it would seem that we need a mechanism to keep track of all output files held open by processes that are downstream from each process. Since this information is different for each process, keeping track of it can be messy as well as expensive, especially if the number of processes (or number of open files) grows large.

To overcome these problems, we develop a new approach that is based on propagating constraints about downgradability of processes. In particular, we keep track of the highest integrity of any output file that is held open by a process and any of the processes that it writes to. We call this `min_lbl` and propagate it "upstream" through pipes and other communication mechanisms. The result is an approach that relies on maintaining/propagating just this single quantity (`min_lbl`) for each process, instead of having to propagate a large amount of information concerning open file descriptors.

We now proceed to describe the key abstractions in our design and our constraint propagation mechanism. Although we have limited ourselves to just two integrity levels, the design described below is quite general and can support any lattice of integrity labels. While our design is fully compatible with unmodified COTS applications, it does provide features that can be utilized by information-flow-aware applications to provide improved functionality. One such feature enables an application to explicitly request that it not be downgraded below a certain level. In particular, this means that any attempt to open files at a lower integrity than this specified level should be denied. Another feature allows trusted applications[3] to request selective, fine-grained exceptions to the information-flow policy. Although we do not discuss these features in depth in this paper due to space constraints, we point out that fully working systems need a handful of key administrative and helper applications that rely on these features.

3.1 Abstractions

Our design uses three entities: Objects, Subjects and Handles.

Objects. Objects consist of all storage and inter-process communication abstractions on an OS: files, pipes, sockets, message queues, semaphores, etc. These objects are divided into two categories: file-like and pipe-like. There is a fundamental difference between these classes. File-like objects are persistent, and have a fixed label assigned to them. Any data read from the file has this label, and writes to the file don't change the label. (The information flow policy ensures that any subject writing to it has a equal or higher label.) For a file-like object, the label of data read from it will be the same as that of data written into it. In contrast, for a pipe-like object, the label of data read from the object representing one end of the pipe is the same as the label of data written to the object representing the other end of the pipe (called a peer object). Examples of pipe-like objects include UNIX pipes and sockets.

Subjects and SubjectGroups. Subjects correspond to threads. Since the OS-level mechanisms used in our framework cannot mediate information flows that take place via shared memory, subjects

---

[3]These are applications that have been written carefully so as to protect themselves from low-integrity data, and hence can operate on them while retaining their high integrity.

that share memory are grouped into SubjectGroups. The idea is that all subjects within a SubjectGroup will have the same security label at any time.

Handles.   Handles provide a level of indirection between subjects and objects. They serve to link together objects and subjects that have an information flow relationship. There is a many-to-one mapping between handles and subjects, and many-to-one mapping between handles and objects.

Handles are conceptually similar to file descriptors, but there are some differences as well, e.g., a handle is unidirectional: a handle provides either a read or a write capability. (Obtaining both requires two handles.) The label of a read-handle is given by the label of the object that it reads from, while the label of a write-handle is given by the label of the subject holding the handle. When read (or write) operation takes place, the label of the handle will be passed to the corresponding subject (or object).

3.2   Information Flow Policies

A current label (`current_lbl`) field is associated with each object and subject, and it provides the basis for policy enforcement. In particular, no flow will be permitted from a source to a destination unless the source's current label is greater than or equal to that of the destination.

INVARIANT 7. *Any information flow from an entity A to another entity B must satisfy* `current_lbl`$(A) \geq$ `current_lbl`(B).

Instead of denying the operation when the above invariant does not hold, our system will attempt to dynamically downgrade the label of the destination. Since the model presented so far restricts downgrading to subjects, B must be a subject, and downgrade occurs when it reads from a handle A. B can protect itself from undesirable downgrades by setting its minimum label (called `min_lbl`). In particular, downgrading of `current_lbl` won't be attempted unless the following invariant holds after the downgrade:

INVARIANT 8. $\forall B$, `current_lbl`$(B) \geq$ `min_lbl`(B).

Since we do not downgrade the labels of file-like objects, their `min_lbl` will be the same as their `current_lbl`. For subjects and pipe-like objects, `min_lbl` is determined by constraint propagation, as described further in Section 3.4. Finally, handles do not have an independent value for their current label and minimum label; instead, these are derived from the corresponding values of objects and subjects associated with a handle.

Combining the above two invariants, we can say that our approach will permit information flow from A to B in all cases where `current_lbl`$(A) \geq$ `min_lbl`(B). Since self-revocation occurs precisely when such a data transfer is denied, we can say:

OBSERVATION 9. *A read (or write) operation that transfers data from an entity A to another entity B will be denied in our approach only if* `current_lbl`$(A) <$ `min_lbl`(B).

3.3   Forward information flows

Figure 2 illustrates the flow of information between objects and subjects via handles. In this figure, solid lines represent actual flow of information. There are two subjects S_1 and S_2. Flow of information between these two subjects occurs via a socket object O_1 (which is pipe-like), and a file object O_2.

Flow of information via file objects is simpler than that of pipe-like objects. In particular, an object created by a subject receives the label of that subject. This flow is handled by propagating the current label of subject S_2 to its write handle WH_2, and then from WH_2 to the object O_2. (If the object is already present, then its `current_lbl` should be less than or equal to that of the subject

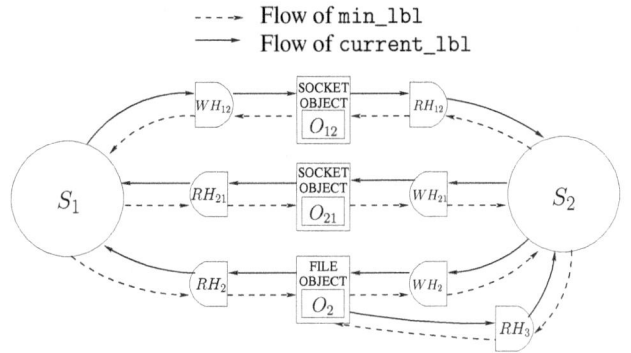

Figure 2: Illustration of Information Flow in our Framework

writing to it, and no propagation would be needed.) If S_1 subsequently reads from the object O_2, the label of O_2 will flow into S_1.

Since a socket is a pipe-like object representing two distinct flows, we split it into two objects: O_{12} that represents information flow from S_1 to S_2, and O_{21} that represents the information flow from S_2 to S_1. S_1 uses a read-handle RH_{21} and a write-handle WH_{12} to read from and write into the socket, while S_2 uses RH_{12} and WH_{21} respectively for the same purpose.

It is important to clarify the role of `open` versus `read` operations. Specifically, when a file is opened for reading, the file's `current_lbl` flows from the file to the handle. But since no data has yet been read by the subject, the propagation of `current_lbl` from the handle to the subject does not take place until the first `read` operation. (A similar comment applies to `write` operations as well.) This distinction between `open` and `read` operations is made for pipe-like objects as well, except that there are many open-like system calls, including `pipe`, `connect` and `accept`.

Delaying `current_lbl` propagation serves an important purpose: shells (e.g., bash) often open files for file redirection, and set up pipes for use by its child processes. The shell process does not perform any reads/writes on these objects. By deferring any downgrades until the first `read`, we prevent the shell from having to downgrade itself. Such a downgrade of shell's label is disastrous, as it prevents the shell from ever running high-integrity commands.

We note that for memory-mapped files, reads may happen implicitly when memory is read, and hence we don't support delayed propagation of labels as described above.

3.4   Constraint propagation

As noted earlier, self-revocation is avoided in our approach by propagating constraints on `min_lbl`. Figure 2 shows constraint propagation using dashed lines. Note that constraints propagate in the reverse direction of information flow.

Note that `min_lbl` represents the minimum label that needs to be maintained by a subject A. Any entity B from which information can flow to A needs to maintain a label higher than `min_lbl`(A) or else the flow from B to A may have to be cut-off. Since such cut-offs lead to self-revocation, we want to prevent them. This is accomplished by propagating `min_lbl`(A) to any handle from which A reads; and from this handle to the associated object; and so on. In other words, by propagating `min_lbl` in the inverse direction of information flow, we can ensure that every data producer upstream will be able ensure the integrity level required by A.

Whereas the forward flow of labels is normally delayed until an explicit read or write operation, constraint propagation is instantaneous, i.e., when a channel (representing file or pipe-like communication) for information flow from entity A to another entity B is opened, B's `min_lbl` is propagated immediately to A. Because of

79

Invariant 8, this propagation will fail if A's current label is already less than $\texttt{min\_lbl}(B)$. In this case, the $\texttt{open}$ operation is denied.

It is important to note that $\texttt{min\_lbl}$ is a quantity that is derived through constraint propagation. It should not be thought of as a variable whose value is increased each time a new communication channel is established. For this reason, $\texttt{min\_lbl}$ can either *increase* or *decrease* during the lifetime of a subject. Increases happen when a subject opens a new output handle, while decreases happen when a subject closes an output handle.

Due to constraint propagation, the following invariant holds:

INVARIANT 10. *If there is an information flow path (shown by solid lines in Figure 2) from A to B, $\texttt{min\_lbl}(A) \geq \texttt{min\_lbl}(B)$.*

Since constraint propagation increases a $\texttt{min\_lbl}$ value for an entity only if there is a constraint that requires it to be that high, and since files are the only entities that have a hard requirement for their $\texttt{min\_lbl}$ values, we can make the following observation:

OBSERVATION 11. *For an entity A, let $B_1, ..., B_k$ be all the open output files reachable from A while following the information flow paths. Then $\texttt{min\_lbl}(A)$ will be the maximum among $\texttt{min\_lbl}(B_1), ..., \texttt{min\_lbl}(B_k)$.*

This observation follows readily from our declarative definition of constraints and their propagation.

3.5 Properties

THEOREM 12. *There will be no self-revocations in our approach.*

Proof: The proof is by contradiction. Suppose that a self-revocation takes place on a $\texttt{read}$ or $\texttt{write}$ operation that transfers data from A to B. From Observation 9, self-revocation can happen only when $\texttt{current\_lbl}(A) < \texttt{min\_lbl}(B)$. Together with Invariant 8, this implies that $\texttt{min\_lbl}(A) < \texttt{min\_lbl}(B)$. However, note that it is invalid to issue a read or write operation before setting up the information flow path between A and B. (In this case, the path happens to be of length 1.) From Invariant 10, the condition $\texttt{min\_lbl}(A) \geq \texttt{min\_lbl}(B)$ must also hold, thus leading to a contradiction. ∎

DEFINITION 13 (FLOW-INDETERMINATE PROGRAMS). *A set of programs are said to be flow-indeterminate if for any set of communicating processes running them, the following condition holds: for every communication path p between any two processes, there will be data transfer operations that cause data to flow from the beginning to the end of this path.*

Flow-indeterminacy simply formalizes the idea that programs may exhibit any possible pattern of communication that is consistent with their current set of open file descriptors; and that there is no simple yet general way to delineate likely communications from those that are unlikely/impossible.

THEOREM 14. *For flow-indeterminate programs, any policy that accepts any execution rejected by SRFD will suffer from self-revocation.*

Proof: For an execution sequence rejected by our approach, consider the first operation A_i that is denied. From the description of the approach in Section 3.4, A_i must be an $\texttt{open}$ operation that would have created a path from entity A to B such that $\texttt{current\_lbl}(A) < \texttt{min\_lbl}(B)$. Now, suppose that there exists a correct integrity policy P that permits this $\texttt{open}$ operation. Then, because of the properties of flow-indeterminate programs, it can be seen that there will be a subsequent operation that transfers data from A to B. This will either have to be denied, or it will cause $\texttt{current\_lbl}(B)$ to fall below $\texttt{min\_lbl}(B)$. The former case corresponds to self-revocation, thus completing the proof. In the

latter case, from Observation 11, it can be seen that there is some output file B_i whose $\texttt{min\_lbl}$ is higher than $\texttt{current\_lbl}(B)$. Also, from properties of flow-indeterminate programs, there will be an actual data flow from B to B_i, which will cause the output file B_i's label to fall below its minimum value. This is not permissible in the model, and hence the more permissive policy P is simply invalid. Thus, in either case, we have established that the functionality offered by SRFD cannot be increased without risking self-revocation. ∎

Thus, for flow-indeterminate programs, we have shown that our approach allows the same successful executions as any other valid information-flow policy that is free of self-revocations. Thus, it represents the maximal functionality achievable without any self-revocations.

4. Implementation

We have implemented SRFD design as described in the previous section. Our implementation uses Linux Security Module (LSM) framework, and works on Ubuntu 13.10. Our code is primarily in the form of handlers for various LSM hooks. Although Linux kernel no longer allows loadable modules to use LSM hooks, there are work-arounds available [1] that we relied on. Structuring the system as a loadable module eases development and debugging, especially in the early stages of prototype development.

LSM hooks are used to enforce information flow policies, perform dynamic downgrading, and to track and maintain $\texttt{min\_lbl}$ constraints. Our implementation also uses an user-level component to provide some usability enhancing features, e.g., notifying users when a process is downgraded and shadowing accesses to preference files for low integrity processes. By maintaining separate preference files for high and low integrity processes, SRFD prevents processes from downgrading automatically due to consuming low integrity preference files. Note that these features do not allow a process to bypass kernel enforcement.

The overall size of our implementation is shown in Figure 3.

	C	Header	Python	Total
Kernel Code	3844	865	-	4709
Userland code	643	142	57	842
Total	4487	1007	57	5561

Figure 3: Implementation size

4.1 Subjects, Objects, and Handles

SRFD maps threads to subjects. Threads of the same process belong to the same subject group. Within the kernel, these correspond to $\texttt{task\_structs}$. Since LSM does not provide hooks to track process creation directly, our prototype relies on $\texttt{cred\_*}$ hooks instead. For each subject group, SRFD maintains information such as integrity level and a list of handles.

Objects are mapped into $\texttt{inodes}$ in the kernel. Our implementation maintains and updates object-related information, including labels, handles associated with each object, and constraints. LSM hooks on inodes are used for creating objects on demand, and deallocating objects when they are no longer needed. For file objects, integrity labels are stored on the disk using extended attributes provided by the file system.

Handles are similar to file descriptors but represent an unidirectional information flow between exactly one subject and one object. SRFD relies on LSM hooks such as $\texttt{file\_open}$, $\texttt{inode\_permission}$ and $\texttt{d\_instantiate}$ to maintain handles.

	Simple syscall	Simple read	Simple write	Simple stat	Simple open/ close	Select 10 fd's	Select 500 fd's	Pipe latency	AF_UNIX latency	Process fork+ exit	Process fork+ /bin/sh -c	**Geometric mean**
unprotected	0.375	0.477	0.517	1.104	2.591	0.624	8.935	12.854	8.812	235.4	1830	
protected	0.376	0.526	0.580	1.122	5.867	0.624	8.958	13.994	9.785	249.8	1963	
Overhead (%)	0.09%	10.28%	12.15%	1.62%	126%	-0.1%	0.26%	8.87%	11.04%	6.08%	7.27%	**12%**

Figure 4: lmbench Performance overhead

When an object is associated with a subject (as a result of a file open, pipe or socket creation), the object will be attached to the subject via at least one handle. When the association is broken, e.g., due to a `close` operation, the corresponding handle is destroyed.

4.2 Constraint propagation

When a subject A opens a file O for writing (or a socket connection with another process), constraints from the file (or target process) have to be propagated in the inverse direction of information flow, as described in Section 3.4. The open operation is permitted if the invariants regarding `current_lbl` and `min_lbl` can be satisfied after this propagation.

Note that constraint propagation can involve circular dependencies as illustrated in Figure 2. To deal with cycles, we use a fixpoint algorithm for constraint propagation. To detect a fixpoint, our algorithm stores the previous value of `min_lbl` in a variable called `last_min_lbl`. It then updates the value of `min_lbl` of A to be the maximum of `last_min_lbl` and the label of the file O. If $min\_lbl(A) = last\_min\_lbl(A)$ then a fixpoint has been reached, and our algorithm stops. If not, then the same process is used to propagate the new value of A's `min_lbl` to each of the subjects $S_1, \ldots, S_n$ that output to A, and the process continues. If any of the propagation steps fail because it results in a `min_lbl` exceeding the value of `current_lbl`, then the `open` operation is denied, and the values of `min_lbl` restored.

The same fixpoint algorithm is used even if A performs a `close` rather than an `open`. The only difference is that instead of computing the maximum of A's `min_lbl` and that of the new object being opened, we recompute `min_lbl` as the maximum of the labels of all the currently open write handles of A. However, in the presence of cycles, this simple algorithm will not always compute the least fixpoint. For this reason, our algorithm will retry constraint propagation from scratch before denying an open request. Note that (a) this retry step is unnecessary if no `close` operations have taken place since the last retry, and (b) constraint propagation itself is unnecessary for processes that are already at low integrity.

LSM provides no hooks on `close` operation: SRFD is not notified when a process closes a file. As a result, SRFD may have stale information regarding files opened. This requires SRFD to walk through the file descriptor table to prune out outdated handles when recomputing constraints. SRFD optimizes this by recomputing the constraints only when the current constraints cannot be satisfied.

4.3 Tracking subjects

Processes inherit a lot of rights from their parents, e.g., ability to write to a file. SRFD needs to be aware of these inherited rights to protect against self-revocation of these rights.

When a new process is created, SRFD duplicates the book-keeping information associated with the parent to the child. This approach automatically captures the communication between parent and child that happen using mechanisms such as pipes. The most common use of pipes occur in the context of shell processes, where the parent first creates a pipe with a readable-end and a writable-end. It then creates two child processes. At this point, the parent and children can all read and write from the pipes, so there is cyclic dependency between them. As a result, any constraint propagation will result in all three processes having the same `min_lbl`. However, in the next step, parent shell will close the two ends of the pipe, and then the first child will close the readable end of the pipe, while the second child will close the writable end of the pipe. After these close operations, there can be no flow between the children and the parent shell. Moreover, no information can flow from the second child to the first child. All of this is handled by our constraint propagation algorithm, which will correctly allow the second child to be downgraded (if necessary) without having to downgrade the first child or the parent.

4.4 Limitations

Our current prototype does not enforce its policies on operations relating to capabilities, file mount points, signals, message queue, and semaphores. In particular, low integrity processes performing these operations are not restricted. We also simply denies lower integrity processes to ptrace on higher integrity processes. We have left out these aspect since our experiments did not make use of these system calls. A complete implementation should also mediate these operations by propagating labels. It is part of our ongoing and future work to mediate them all.

For sockets, our prototype handles Unix domain sockets because the two ends of the socket connection are within the control of the OS. For sockets in the internet domain, their other end is typically outside the control of the OS. Hence SRFD does not attempt to enforce any policies on such internet sockets.

5. Evaluation

5.1 Performance

We evaluate the performance of our SRFD system using micro- as well as macro-benchmarks. All the evaluations are performed on a Ubuntu 13.10 VMware virtual machine allocated with one VCPU AMD Opteron Processor 4228 HE (2.8GHz) and 1GB RAM.

As a micro-benchmark, we use `lmbench`, which measures the overhead for making individual system calls. Figure 4 shows the overheads of our system for different classes of system calls. Note that the overheads are modest: the geometric mean is about 12%, and the arithmetic mean is 16%. Note that if we exclude open and close, which are typically less frequent than other calls such as read/write, the overheads are much smaller — less than 5%.

It is natural for `open` and `close` to have higher overheads because of constraint propagation, but that does not explain a doubling of execution time. It occurs in our prototype because LSM does not provide hooks for `close`, and as a result, our implementation has to walk through the list of open file descriptors while propagating constraints. In contrast, because there can be no failures on read and write, no additional checking is needed, and the only work is to blindly copy `current_lbl` from the source to destination.

Micro-benchmarks help to understand and explain the the overheads of kernel-based defenses such as ours, but they tend to overestimate the overheads because most applications spend only a minority of their time in the kernel. Macro-benchmarks are better at estimating overheads experienced by real users in practice. For this

| | Unprotected | Protected |
	Time (s)	Overhead
400.perlbench	554.41	-0.21%
458.sjeng	865.29	-0.23%
462.libquantum	1032.35	-0.23%
471.omnetpp	543.24	0.27%
473.astar	738.29	0.16%
433.milc	875.47	-0.14%
Average		0.04%

Figure 5: SPEC2006 Overhead (showing top 6), `ref` input size

| | Protected |
	Overhead
Openssl	-0.08%
dpkg -b coreutils	2.93%
dpkg -b am-utils	1.22%
Firefox	4.89%
Postmark	5.74%

Figure 6: Overhead on other benchmarks

reason, we used several macro-benchmarks, including the CPU-intensive SPEC 2006 and openssl, file-system intensive `Postmark`, and commonly used programs such as browsers and software builds.

From Figures 5 and 6, it is clear that overheads on CPU-intensive programs such as SPEC and openssl are negligible — the overheads are below measurement errors/noise.

Package builds, which represent a combination of CPU and I/O load, show a slightly higher overhead of 1% to 3%. Specifically, our benchmark built Debian Linux packages for `coreutils` and `am-utils` from source code. Another mixed load consists of Firefox, whose overhead was measured using `pageloader`, a benchmarking tool from Mozilla. Top 3000 Alexa sites were prefetched in this experiment so as to eliminate the effects of network latency. (If this was not done, then the overheads will be even smaller.) The overhead experienced was 5%.

Finally, the I/O-intensive `Postmark` was configured to create 500 files with size between 500 bytes and 500 Kbytes. The overhead reported was 6%.

5.2 Experience

As noted in the introduction, our work is motivated by a continuing trend in sophisticated and adaptive malware attacks, and our desire to provide principled defenses against them. Existing approaches rely on techniques such as sandboxing a few key applications such as browsers and email readers that have the most exposure to malware. While sandboxing these applications can prevent some attacks, e.g., those that try to mount a code injection attack on an email reader (or other document viewers invoked by a browser), more sophisticated attacks can often get around these defenses. For instance, users may save a document on their desktop, and subsequently open it with their favorite document editor/viewer application. Since the application is typically not sandboxed in this usage scenario, the attack can succeed. In contrast, an information-flow based approach would mark such files as untrusted, and regardless of the number of applications that process them, or how many intermediate steps they go through, untrusted files will always be operated on by low integrity processes. Since such processes can only output low integrity files, and cannot modify high integrity files or interfere with high-integrity subjects, their attempts to compromise system integrity will continue to fail.

Although these theoretical benefits of information-flow based integrity protection are well-known, these techniques have not found widespread use on modern operating systems as they often pose compatibility challenges. In this section, we walk through several illustrative and common usage scenarios to demonstrate that SRFD can work well on contemporary operating system distributions, without posing major compatibility problems. Naturally, our focus will be on illustrating features specific to SRFD, as opposed to information-flow based techniques in general.

In these scenarios, we assume that the default OS installation consists of only high-integrity files; and that low integrity files enter the system when it begins to be used, and new files are created by untrusted subjects. We assume that browsers and email readers are run as low integrity processes.

5.2.1 Self-revocations involving files, pipelines and sockets

The scenarios discussed here illustrate the benefits of accurate information-flow dependency tracking in SRFD, and how that permits us to provide more functionality as compared to previous approaches (specifically, LOMAC [8]), while avoiding self-revocation.

One of the challenges in SRFD is to track communications between processes. This can be nontrivial when a deep pipeline is involved. Consider the command:

```
cat lowI | grep... | sed | ... | sort | uniq » highI
```

It is necessary to propagate labels across the pipeline to ensure that information from low-integrity file `lowI` is prevented from contaminating a high integrity file `highI`. Opportunities for self-revocation abound, especially if the shell opens `highI` before `cat` gets a chance to open `lowI`. Even otherwise, self-revocation is possible since intermediate commands such as `grep` may begin execution as high integrity processes, and then be prevented from reading their input pipes, or they may be downgraded and prevented from writing on their output pipes. LOMAC [8] avoids self-revocation on pipes by downgrading process groups at a time — in this case, all processes in the pipeline will be part of the same process group.

SRFD accurately captures information flow dependencies between the processes in the pipeline, and can avoid self-revocation, while preserving usability. In particular, depending on the order in which processes are scheduled, `cat` may be permitted to downgrade. In this case, SRFD will deny the open operation on `highI`. Alternatively, if `highI` is opened first, SRFD will deny `cat`'s attempt to open `lowI`.

Another example that illustrates the strength of SRFD is:

```
cat high1 | tee high2 | lowP
```

where `lowP` is a low integrity utility program. SRFD will run this pipeline successfully: both `cat` and `tee` will be remain at high integrity, and be able to output to high integrity file `high2`, while `lowP` will run at low integrity. LOMAC requires all processes in the pipeline to be at the same level, and hence cannot run this.

SRFD supports sockets, and can avoid self-revocation on processes that make use of these features. When a server program has a high integrity file opened for writing, SRFD will deny connections from a low integrity client, as the establishment of such a connection would violate the constraints on `min_lbl`. Moreover, any client that is already connected to such a server will be prevented from opening a low integrity file, or connecting to any other low-integrity process. LOMAC will experience self-revocation.

5.2.2 Commonly used applications

SRFD is implemented on a Ubuntu 13.10 desktop system. This system runs a large number of applications and servers, including a number of daemons, X-server, GNOME desktop environment, and so on. All these applications work with SRFD, but this is unsurprising: in our tests, these applications did not access low integrity files, and so SRFD does not constrain them in any way.

In the same manner, applications that don't modify high integrity files will run without any problems, as SRFD imposes no constraints on them. Most complex applications can be run this way — for instance, we run web browsers and email readers in this mode.

Most command-line programs can run as high or low integrity without any problems. Common utilities such as tar, gzip, make, compilers, and linkers can be run without any problems on low integrity files. Composing these command line applications using pipelines works as described in the preceding section. Thus, we focus the rest of this section on more complex GUI applications that need to access a combination of low and high integrity files.

Document viewers. Document viewers such as evince and Acrobat Reader can be used in SRFD without any issues. These programs can be used to open high and low integrity documents simultaneously. However, once the viewer has opened a low integrity file, it will not be able to overwrite a high integrity file.

Editors. GUI editors (e.g., gedit, OpenOffice, GIMP) impose additional challenges for dynamic downgrading systems like SRFD. When users select files to edit using file selection dialogs, applications tend to open every file to generate a preview, regardless of the integrity of the files. When users open a directory containing low integrity files, the editors will automatically be downgraded to low integrity even if the users did not intend to open low integrity files.

To prevent editors from downgraded accidentally, we can allow editors to be downgraded only when demanded by users. We can rely on the "implicit-explicit" mechanism suggested in [28] to identify file accesses that are requested explicitly by users, and only allow editors to be downgraded on opening these files. Other low integrity files can be denied when accessed implicitly.

Media Editors. We consider media editors (e.g., f-spot and audacity) separately because they usually do not modify the original media files directly. Instead, they edit copies of the media files. As a result, these media editors can be used without usability issues.

5.2.3 Defense against malware

We downloaded a rootkit ark from [3]. The tar file was labeled as low integrity when downloaded into the system by a web browser. The user then untars the file by invoking tar. SRFD started tar as a high integrity process, with current_lbl = Hi, min_lbl = Lo because it has no constraints on its output files and it has not been contaminated with any low integrity information. tar started by loading libraries like ld.so.cache and libc − 2.17.so. The tar process was then downgraded to low integrity when reading the rootkit tar file. tar process then spawned gzip as low integrity to decompress the file. After decompressing, the tar process continued to untar. All of the new files created are automatically labeled as low integrity.

With these integrity labels in place, SRFD can easily preserve system integrity. Specifically, system directories are labeled as high integrity and hence system utility rootkits cannot be placed in the system directories. However, it is possible for users to accidentally invoke these rootkits by placing them in some user-specific search paths. SRFD protects the system integrity by downgrading processes when these rootkits are executed or used, including executions by root processes. Hence, when a user process executes a low integrity binary or loads library, the process will be downgraded and is prevented from damaging system integrity.

SRFD also intercepts LSM hooks related to kernel modules. Low integrity kernel modules cannot be loaded even by root processes.

6. Related Work

A number of related works, including classical work on information flows and integrity protection were discussed in the introduction and the main body of the paper. We focus this section on related works that haven't been discussed before, and on providing a more in-depth comparison of works that are most closely related.

LOMAC [8] argues that a central reason for non-adoption of conventional information flow techniques is that of compatibility. They consider information flow systems that support privilege revision (such as dynamic downgrades) and those that don't, and conclude that former class provides increased compatibility.

They point out that policies such as low-watermark policy had not received much attention because of the self-revocation problem. They proceeded to address this problem in a particularly common case, namely, the pipelines created by shell processes. As noted earlier, their solution relied on the shell's use of UNIX process groups to run each pipeline, and ensuring that all processes within such a group had identical integrity labels. In this manner, there will never be a need to restrict communications within a process group, and thus self-revocation involving pipes is prevented. They remark that they "cannot entirely remove this pathological case without also removing the protective properties of the model." Indeed, the solution they present does not attempt to address revocations involving files, sockets, etc. Our work is inspired by their comments, and shows that it is in fact possible to retain the security benefits of integrity protection, as well as the compatibility benefits of privilege revision without incurring the cost of self-revocation.

Promoting early failure, as we do in this paper, is not the only way to solve the self-revocation problem. An alternative approach is to build recovery mechanisms to "roll back" failed executions. This is not always easy to do in general. One-way isolation [24] supports roll back as the default choice, while providing primitives to commit executions that the user determines to be secure. However, it is problematic to rely on users to decide what is secure. Not only does it demand considerable time, effort and skill on the part of users, but also suffers from the fact that users could be easily fooled. Thus, roll-back techniques coupled with automated procedures for determining secure executions are needed. Such automated procedures require full specification of what is secure — this itself is too difficult a task to be accomplished in general. However, it may be possible to specify detailed and accurate policies for secure execution in special cases. One example of this is the secure software installation [25] work, where a policy for determining secure installations was specified and checked automatically.

Roll-back based approaches complement our work. In particular, a complete SRFD system needs to support secure installation of untrusted code, and a technique such as SSI [25] can do this for us.

There has been a resurgence of interest in information-flow control in the last several years. Some of the techniques start off from classical *centralized* information-flow techniques, while others have targeted *decentralized* information flow control (DIFC). UMIP [14], IFEDAC [18], PPI [26] and PIP [28] belong to the first category. Another common thread among these approaches is that they target contemporary OSes, specifically, Linux. UMIP, IFEDAC and PPI all support dynamic downgrading of subject labels (i.e., LD). UMIP and IFEDAC do not address the problem of self-revocation, perhaps expecting that the applications will have mechanisms to deal with the problem. PPI relies on training for determining whether a certain access should be denied, or result in subject downgrade. Thus, it can eliminate some downgrades where training suggests that it will lead to failures. PIP uses early downgrading (ED) and hence does not suffer from self-revocation problem. However, as noted earlier, ED restricts functionality over LD

— thus, PIP avoids self-revocation at the cost of increased security failures. Furthermore, PIP relies on userid for policy enforcement, and hence cannot support low integrity root processes.

Some of the works that pursue the DIFC model include HiStar [30] and Asbestos [6], which redesign the operating systems to provide finer-granularity information flow control. Flume [13] provides DIFC within the context of standard OS abstractions. All of these works require nontrivial application or OS modifications in order to take advantage of information flow control. Changes to cope with self-revocations would be a small part of these modifications, and so self-revocation is not explicitly treated in these works.

Schneider [22] formulates enforceable security policies using the formalism of security automata. These automata make transitions that are entirely based on a subject's own operations, such as open's, read's and write's. Whereas these automata can only accept or reject an execution sequence, Ligatti et al [16] proposed a more powerful automata called *edit automata* that could also suppress or modify a subject's actions. We also use automata to compare different downgrading schemes for information flow systems, but the transitions in our automata are not only dependent on the subject's actions, but also the state of the file system. This is because whether an operation opens a high or low integrity file is a function of the file system state. Indeed, Ligatti et al [16] explicitly specify that security properties in their model are those that are purely functions of the operation sequence.

Policy-based confinement [5, 10, 11, 17, 21, 23] has been studied and widely deployed as a defense against malicious code. A runtime monitor allows or denies actions of processes based on a pre-defined policy. Depending on the enforcement mechanism used, the implementation can be tricky [9, 12] due to TOCTTOU attacks. The most difficult part of applying these techniques is to have a good policy to identify bad behaviors [19]. A policy that is too permissive would let malicious programs to compromise the system, while a policy that is restrictive would impair usability.

Isolation [15, 25, 24, 20] is another commonly used technique to protect system integrity. By running potentially malicious code in an isolated environment, the host system integrity can be preserved. It is simpler than policy-based confinement because there is no application-specific policy required. All resources are isolated. A main drawback of isolation is fragmentation of the file system namespace into several distinct "isolated" namespaces. When a user wants to access a file, they first need to recall which container has this file. Moreover, if they want to combine information across multiple containers, it is not only cumbersome, but opens an avenue for malicious code or data in one container to infect another.

7. Conclusion

We categorized information flow policies into No Downgrading (ND), Eager Downgrading (ED) and Lazy Downgrading (LD). We proposed a formal model to compare these information flow policies in terms of functionality and compatibility. Our model shows that LD is more functional than ED, which, in turn, is more functional than ND. However, LD poses compatibility problems due to self-revocation, whereas ND and ED do not suffer from this drawback. We therefore proposed SRFD, which combines LD's functionality with the compatibility of ED. We formally showed that SRFD does not suffer from self-revocation. We also showed that unless an oracle was available to predict future behaviors of programs, it is not possible to further improve SRFD, i.e., accept more executions without compromising integrity or risking self-revocation. Our prototype shows that SRFD provides very good performance, and can support a variety of benign usage scenarios while providing principled defense against malware attacks. We

believe that this work represents a promising step that can contribute to some mainstream adoption of information-flow based integrity protection techniques. To further this cause, we are releasing the source code for our prototype [27].

8. References

[1] Akari, http://akari.sourceforge.jp/.
[2] Operation Aurora, http://en.wikipedia.org/wiki/Operation_Aurora.
[3] Packet Storm, http://packetstormsecurity.com.
[4] K. J. Biba. Integrity Considerations for Secure Computer Systems. In *Technical Report ESD-TR-76-372, USAF Electronic Systems Division, Hanscom Air Force Base, Bedford, Massachusetts*, 1977.
[5] C. Cowan, S. Beattie, G. Kroah-Hartman, C. Pu, P. Wagle, and V. Gligor. SubDomain: Parsimonious Server Security. In *LISA*, 2000.
[6] P. Efstathopoulos, M. Krohn, S. VanDeBogart, C. Frey, D. Ziegler, E. Kohler, D. Mazières, F. Kaashoek, and R. Morris. Labels and Event Processes in the Asbestos Operating System. In *SOSP*, 2005.
[7] N. Falliere, L. Murchu, and E. Chien. W32. Stuxnet Dossier. *White paper, Symantec Corp., Security Response*, 2011.
[8] T. Fraser. LOMAC: Low Water-Mark Integrity Protection for COTS Environments. In *S&P*, 2000.
[9] T. Garfinkel. Traps and Pitfalls: Practical Problems in System Call Interposition Based Security Tools. In *NDSS*, 2003.
[10] T. Garfinkel, B. Pfaff, and M. Rosenblum. Ostia: A Delegating Architecture for Secure System Call Interposition. In *NDSS*, 2004.
[11] I. Goldberg, D. Wagner, R. Thomas, and E. A. Brewer. A Secure Environment for Untrusted Helper Applications (Confining the Wily Hacker). In *USENIX Security*, 1996.
[12] K. Jain and R. Sekar. User-Level Infrastructure for System Call Interposition: A Platform for Intrusion Detection and Confinement. In *NDSS*, 2000.
[13] M. Krohn, A. Yip, M. Brodsky, N. Cliffer, M. F. Kaashoek, E. Kohler, and R. Morris. Information Flow Control for Standard OS Abstractions. In *SOSP*, 2007.
[14] N. Li, Z. Mao, and H. Chen. Usable Mandatory Integrity Protection for Operating Systems . In *S&P*, 2007.
[15] Z. Liang, W. Sun, V. N. Venkatakrishnan, and R. Sekar. Alcatraz: An Isolated Environment for Experimenting with Untrusted Software. In *TISSEC 12(3)*, 2009.
[16] J. Ligatti, L. Bauer, and D. Walker. Edit Automata: Enforcement Mechanisms for Run-Time Security Policies. *International Journal of Information Security*, 4(1-2):2–16, 2005.
[17] P. Loscocco and S. Smalley. Meeting Critical Security Objectives with Security-Enhanced Linux. In *Ottawa Linux symposium*, 2001.
[18] Z. Mao, N. Li, H. Chen, and X. Jiang. Combining Discretionary Policy with Mandatory Information Flow in Operating Systems. In *TISSEC 14(3)*, 2011.
[19] C. Parampalli, R. Sekar, and R. Johnson. A Practical Mimicry Attack Against Powerful System-Call Monitors. In *ASIACCS*, 2008.
[20] S. Potter and J. Nieh. Apiary: Easy-to-Use Desktop Application Fault Containment on Commodity Operating Systems. In *USENIX conference on USENIX annual technical conference*, 2010.
[21] N. Provos. Improving Host Security with System Call Policies. In *USENIX Security*, 2003.
[22] F. B. Schneider. Enforceable Security Policies. In *TISSEC 3(1)*, 2000.
[23] R. Sekar, V. Venkatakrishnan, S. Basu, S. Bhatkar, and D. C. DuVarney. Model-Carrying Code: A Practical Approach for Safe Execution of Untrusted Applications. In *SOSP*, 2003.
[24] W. Sun, Z. Liang, V. N. Venkatakrishnan, and R. Sekar. One-Way Isolation: An Effective Approach for Realizing Safe Execution Environments. In *NDSS*, 2005.
[25] W. Sun, R. Sekar, Z. Liang, and V. N. Venkatakrishnan. Expanding Malware Defense by Securing Software Installations. In *DIMVA*, 2008.
[26] W. Sun, R. Sekar, G. Poothia, and T. Karandikar. Practical Proactive Integrity Preservation: A Basis for Malware Defense. In *S&P*, 2008.
[27] W. K. Sze and B. Mital. Self-Revocation Free Downgrading (SRFD). http://www.seclab.cs.sunysb.edu/seclab/srfd.
[28] W. K. Sze and R. Sekar. A Portable User-Level Approach for System-wide Integrity Protection. In *ACSAC*, 2013.
[29] TrendLabs APT Research Team. Spear-Phishing Email: Most Favored APT Attack Bait. 2012.
[30] N. Zeldovich, S. Boyd-Wickizer, E. Kohler, and D. Mazières. Making Information Flow Explicit in HiStar. In *OSDI*, 2006.

Attribute Based Access Control for APIs in Spring Security

Alessandro Armando
DIBRIS, U. of Genova, Italy
and
Security and Trust Unit,
FBK-Irst, Trento, Italy
armando@fbk.eu

Roberto Carbone
Security and Trust Unit,
FBK-Irst, Trento, Italy
carbone@fbk.eu

Eyasu Getahun Chekole
Security and Trust Unit,
FBK-Irst, Trento, Italy
chekole@fbk.eu

Silvio Ranise
Security and Trust Unit,
FBK-Irst, Trento, Italy
ranise@fbk.eu

ABSTRACT

The widespread adoption of Application Programming Interfaces (APIs) by enterprises is changing the way business is done by permitting the implementation of a multitude of apps, customized to user needs. While supporting a more flexible exploitation of available data, services and applications developed on top of APIs are vulnerable to a variety of attacks, ranging from SQL injection to unauthorized access of sensitive data. Available security solutions must be re-used and/or adapted to work with APIs.

In this paper, we focus on the development of a flexible access control mechanism for APIs. This is an important security mechanism to guarantee the enforcement of authorization constraints on resources while invoking their API functions. We have developed an extension of the Spring Security framework, the standard for securing services and apps built in the popular (open source) Spring framework, for the specification and enforcement of Attribute-Based Access Control (ABAC) policies. We demonstrate our work with scenarios arising in a smart energy eco-system.

Categories and Subject Descriptors

D.4.6 [**Security and Protection**]: Access controls

Keywords

Attribute-based Access Control; Spring Security; Energy@Home

1. INTRODUCTION

Software is becoming more and more pervasive in our life and permeates almost every industry, ranging from hardware/software companies—offering combinations of hardware devices with software operating systems, applications, and cloud services—to sports clothing companies—setting up sports social networks to support targeted applications to customers. This is the result of the widespread development and adoption of apps, that can be used from a variety of devices and permit the reuse of existing information assets while adding value. For instance, Nike+[1] aggregates data from hundreds of thousands of users every day, collected from a variety of devices (e.g., sport watches) and apps (e.g., the Running App) that allow for tracking sport activities, comparing performances with friends, etc. The idea is that purchasing a product is not the end but the beginning of the marketing cycle by offering consumers a wide range of products and services tailored to their individual needs.

The flexibility for developing tailored apps is offered by the increasing adoption of Application Programming Interfaces (APIs), which are interfaces allowing for invoking software components over a communication network using standard technologies (e.g., HTTP). APIs are used both internally and externally of an enterprise and turn out to be beneficial in both contexts. Internally, APIs reduce complexity by providing a single set of functionalities that can be invoked from clients on any platform, and simplify change management by identifying a core set of services on top of which several others can be fine tuned according to the evolving business needs. Externally, independent developers can think of innovative (sometimes unexpected) ways of using APIs in value-added applications without the need for the enterprise to invest in app development. Indeed, this is made possible only if the enterprise provides an adequate eco-system in which APIs can be exploited. For instance, the Nike Fuel Lab[2] aims at fostering interest in leveraging the Nike+ technology by other companies. However, making APIs available to developers is a difficult task that must address a variety of issues such as developer management, adequate documentation, community forums, portals, and a set of well-engineered techniques to securing apps. For this reason, infrastructures to design and develop APIs are being proposed by IT companies such as Layer7[3] and WSO2.[4] A substantial part of these infrastructures aim to provide means to protect services and apps built on top of APIs

SACMAT'14, June 25–27, 2014, London, Ontario, Canada.
Copyright 2014 ACM 978-1-4503-2939-2/14/06 ...$15.00.
http://dx.doi.org/10.1145/2613087.2613109.

---

[1] http://nikeplus.nike.com
[2] http://www.nikefuellab.com
[3] http://www.layer7tech.com and http://www.apify.co
[4] http://wso2.com/products/api-manager

from known web vulnerabilities (e.g., SQL injection) as well as new exploits deriving from insights obtained by analyzing the available API documentation. Following a basic rule in security, API infrastructures provide means to mitigate these vulnerabilities by re-using and adapting available security solutions for, e.g., confidentiality, integrity, authentication, and authorization at various levels.

In this paper, we consider the problem of realizing a flexible access control mechanism for APIs on top of the popular (open source) Spring Security framework,[5] which is used to secure applications developed in the Spring framework.[6] The latter provides a comprehensive programming and configuration model for modern Java-based enterprise applications and supports the development of (RESTful Web) APIs. We present the Attribute-Based Access Control (ABAC) model and argue why it is suitable for APIs (Section 2). We then present the architecture of the enforcement mechanism for ABAC policies in the Spring Security framework (Section 3). Finally (Section 4), we describe a demonstration of our enforcement mechanism for scenarios arising in a smart energy platform, that we are contributing to secure, in the context of the activity "SecSES Secure Energy Systems" of the action line ASES Smart Energy Systems of the EIT ICT Labs. The platform is developed by Energy@Home,[7] a non-profit association of companies with the mission of developing and promoting techniques for energy efficiency in smart homes.

2. API AND ABAC

In [4], ABAC has been identified as the "right" access control model for applications based on the Service Oriented Architecture (SOA) paradigm. Classical access control models are mostly static and coarsely grained since authorization decisions are taken by considering identities or roles. Such models are thus not well-suited for SOA applications where users are not easily authenticated, security-related information is distributed and frequently evolves over time. In contrast, ABAC bases authorization decisions on security-relevant properties (called attributes in ABAC) that can be easily distributed and updated. Furthermore, by suitably defining attributes, ABAC allows security experts not only to simulate and combine classical access control models but also refine them so as to supplement and combine—rather than supplanting—available access schemas; see [2] for a discussion on these and related issues.

It is natural to choose ABAC as the reference access control model also for APIs, since these share many basic architectural principles with SOA. We believe that the flexibility of ABAC can be even more crucial for securing APIs as these are meant to be more open and easily consumable than SOA applications, thereby posing more stringent requirements in terms of expressiveness to support a wide range of authorization requirements. For instance, ABAC permits to express access conditions on the data (called resources in ABAC) on which the API functionalities operate by means of their attributes. As observed in [3], this is beneficial since expressing access condition directly on resources is often more convenient than indirectly encoding them via the permissions of invoking API functions, as done, e.g., in Java Enterprise

[5] http://projects.spring.io/spring-security
[6] http://projects.spring.io/spring-framework
[7] http://www.energy-home.it

Edition (JEE) 2 applications using roles. The obvious precondition to use ABAC for securing APIs is the availability of suitable mechanisms for enforcing policies. In Section 3 below, we describe the architecture of one of such mechanisms for Java APIs, integrated in the popular (open source) Spring Security framework. In the rest of this section, we briefly recall the main notions underlying ABAC.

ABAC in a nutshell. The ABAC model allows for granting access rights according to the attributes of the entities involved in access control, namely subjects (e.g., users or applications), actions (e.g., read, write, update), resources (e.g., a file, a document, or a database record), and environments (i.e. contextual information such as location or time of day). For simplicity, in this paper, we will omit environments although the discussion can be easily generalized to handle them.

An ABAC policy $P(s, a, r)$ is a Boolean-valued function on the sets of attributes of the subjects s, actions a, and resources r. We assume that ABAC policies can be written as Boolean assertions. For instance,

$$s.subjectId = r.resourceOwnerId \land a.name = view \qquad (1)$$

expresses the authorization condition that any subject s can view the content of any resource r provided that s is the owner of r. An attribute assignment for a subject, an action, or a resource is a mapping of its attributes to appropriate values. For instance, assume that $Paolo$ is a subject and that $subjectId$ is one of its attributes: an attribute assignment v_{Paolo} can map $subjectId$ to the integer 1434234278 and similarly for all its other attributes. Given attribute assignments $v_{\bar{s}}$, $v_{\bar{a}}$, and $v_{\bar{r}}$, we say that subject $\bar{s}$ can execute action $\bar{a}$ on resource $\bar{r}$ according to the ABAC policy P iff $true$ is the value of P on the attribute values specified by $v_{\bar{s}}$, $v_{\bar{a}}$, and $v_{\bar{r}}$, written as $v_{\bar{s}}, v_{\bar{a}}, v_{\bar{r}} \models P$. For instance, $v_{Paolo}, v_{view}, v_{Doc} \models$ (1) for $v_{Paolo}(subjectId) = 1434234278$, $v_{view}(name) = view$, and $v_{Doc}(resourceOwnerId) = 1434234278$.

3. SPRING ENFORCEMENT OF ABAC POLICIES FOR API

The Spring Security framework provides comprehensive and extensible support for both authentication and authorization to Spring-based applications. Here, we discuss some software techniques used in Spring Security that are relevant to our implementation of the enforcement mechanism for ABAC policies. In particular, we focus on method-level security, i.e. how the invocation of Java methods can be mediated by access control, that we customize to use ABAC policies.

Dependency injection (DI) is a software design pattern for which, instead of having an object instantiate its needed dependencies, the dependencies are given to the object by another object (usually called injector). The pattern is particularly useful for locating plugin components to customize the behavior of software components.

Decorator pattern for proxies. For method-level security, Spring Security uses proxies, i.e. methods are wrapped so that their behavior is extended without changing their original purpose. This is useful when we want to check authorization conditions before the invocation of a method. Syntactical support for the decorator pattern is given by authorization annotations that are added to a Java method m in order to evaluate policies and then decide to grant or deny

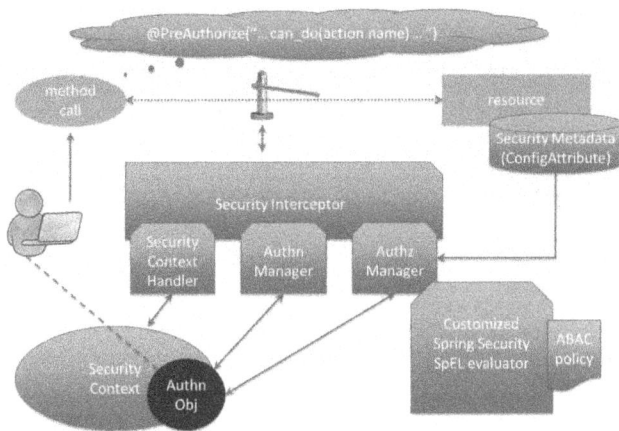

Figure 1: Spring Framework implementation of the ABAC enforcement mechanism for APIs

the permission to invoke m. We use the annotation `@PreAuthorize('`*SpEL expression*`')`, that should be placed immediately before the declaration of a method whose access is supposed to depend on the fact that the '*SpEL expression*' passed as argument is evaluated to true. The Spring Expression Language (SpEL) is a powerful language available in Spring with constructs for—among others—accessing properties, method invocation, the usual mathematical operators (e.g., addition and subtraction), relational operators (equality, less-than, etc.), and Boolean connectives (conjunction, disjunction, and negation). The Spring Security framework furtherly extends SpEL with constructs for access control lists and role-based policies. In the rest of this section, we discuss how DI and `@PreAuthorize` annotations are used for generating customized proxies of methods in an API capable of enforcing ABAC policies.

Enforcing ABAC policies for APIs in Spring Security. The architecture of our solution is depicted in Figure 1 and can be seen as a refinement of the classical schema in which subjects (e.g., users or applications) make requests to execute certain operations (encapsulated in a method) on an object (i.e. an instance of a Java class to which the method belongs). The enforcement mechanism decides whether the particular request is allowed; this is done by the Security Interceptor, which needs to know who is making the request (the subject), what the request is (the action), what the target of the request is (the resource), and which is the policy to be used to take the decision. In Spring Security, the request is specified in the `@PreAuthorize` annotation of the method whereas to determine the subject and the target of the request, the Security Interceptor uses modules Security Context Handler and Authorization Manager, respectively. The correctness of the enforcement mechanism is ensured by the fact that the Security Interceptor intercepts every request on the resource. In our implementation, this is done by extending—via the decorator pattern for proxies based on the `@PreAuthorize` annotation—every method with code for answering authorization queries and permit or deny method invocation.

By using the DI pattern, suitable instances of the Authn (authentication) and Authz (authorization) Managers are injected into the Security Manager when deploying the

application (typically by means of configuration files). Any of the methods for authentication available in Spring Security, (such as user-name and password or authentication protocols, e.g., OpenId) can be used. The Security Context Handler offers an interface to store and retrieve the Security Context, which contains security-relevant information including an Authn (authentication) object storing, among other security metadata, all the attributes of the subject. At every authorization request, the Security Context Handler checks the existence of an Authn object in the Security Context: if this is the case, it is passed to the Security Interceptor; otherwise, the Authn Manager is invoked so that the corresponding Authn object can be created.

After retrieving the Authn object, the Authz (authorization) Manager is invoked to establish if the Authn object has the right to perform the action—specified in the `@PreAuthorize` annotation—on the resource. (Notice that the resource is very easy to identify by establishing to which object is applied the invoked method.) The expression in the `@PreAuthorize` annotation is a conjunction of assertions of the form `can_do('`*action*`')`, where '*action*' is the name of a possible action such as 'read,' 'write,' or 'view' that can be performed on the resource. We allow conjunctions of `can_do` assertions since a method may require the subject to have several permissions on the resource; e.g., when reading from and writing to it. At this point, we have collected the attribute assignments for the subject, resource, and the actions, it is then possible to compute authorization decisions (one per action in the `@PreAuthorize` annotation) by invoking the Authz (authorization) Manager. Indeed, the invocation of the method is permitted if all the authorization queries are answered positively.

Spring Security offers some implementations of authorization decision algorithms to be used by the Authz Manager, among which is the customizable evaluator for SpEL expressions. We have written our version of the evaluator to support a syntax for ABAC policies which is quite similar to the one presented in Section 2. This is possible by exploiting the usual 'dot' notation of Java to dereference attributes of subjects, actions, and resources. For instance, the ABAC policy (1) can be written as the following SpEL expression:

```
(subject.subjectId == resource.resourceOwnerId)
        and (action.name == 'view')
```

where `subject` and `action` stand for the subject and action variables s and a, respectively. Our customization of the SpEL evaluator amounts to mapping `subject` to the user identified by the current Authn object, `resource` to the value of the variable `this`, which contains a reference to the object on which the method is invoked, and reading the ABAC policy from a file (specified in a configuration file). The specification of the policy in a separate file simplifies the process of changing the policy even while the API functionalities are invoked (it is sufficient to reload the file) without the need of re-compiling the code.

4. THE ENERGY@HOME SMART GRID DEMONSTRATION

Smart grids promise to optimize energy consumption. Key to this is the capability of collecting and sharing fine-grained energy consumption data by means of an advanced (smart) metering infrastructure for re-distributing energy according to the time-varying consumer needs. Designing and implementing the information infrastructure underlying smart metering is difficult and error prone. To simplify this, APIs are being increasingly adopted for sharing data among the involved stakeholders, namely consumers, utilities, and third-party services. As a result, the security of applications built on top of the APIs is dependent upon their security.

We have used the implementation of the ABAC enforcement mechanism of Section 3 to ameliorate the confidentiality, integrity, and availability of the API for the (open source) smart metering framework JEMMA (Java-based Energy Management Application).[8] This is part of the Energy@Home (E@H) platform, which is being actively developed by a non-profit association of companies (also called E@H) with the mission of developing and promoting techniques for energy efficiency in smart homes. We are contributing to secure the E@H platform in the context of the activity "SecSES Secure Energy Systems" of the action line ASES Smart Energy Systems of the EIT ICT Labs.

The architecture of the E@H platform is depicted in Figure 2. Smart metering data are collected by a Cloud Data Center (CDC) operated by Telecom Italia, which offers the API functionalities to enable customers and third-party providers (such as those in the Operations and Market domains) to exploit consumers data. Access must satisfy several authorization constraints. On the one hand, consumers own their consumption data and should be able to impose their own policies. Additionally, a number of legal constraints on the storing and processing of the data must be taken into account by the CDC, which should also be able to impose suitable policies supporting such constraints. On the other hand, third-party service providers (such as the operators in the Operations and Market domains) can access data according to the policies of consumers and the CDC, while constraining access to the data derived from their elaboration of smart metering data according to the contracts stipulated with users. We have discussed how to specify and combine ABAC policies to satisfy these constraints elsewhere [1]. During the demonstration, we will illustrate the policies for an example scenario and show how enforcement mechanism of Section 3 can support their enforcement.

More in details, the demonstration will be structured as follows. First, we discuss selected parts of the API, the authorization requirements of the main stakeholders (consumers, utilities, and third-party service providers), and identify the sets of attributes that characterize their profiles. Second, we show the SpEL expressions of the ABAC policies that ensure the authorization requirements previously identified. The results of evaluating some authorization queries will be shown by considering different stakeholders that use a simple web application built on top of the API functions. We also discuss how policies rules can be changed at run-time (simply by editing a policy file) according to some evolving needs, thus leading to different authorization decisions. Finally, we discuss how policies can be changed by consumers (usually not experts in writing authorization conditions and thereby using the policies provided by the CDC when signing the contract) via a dashboard. To understand this, consider

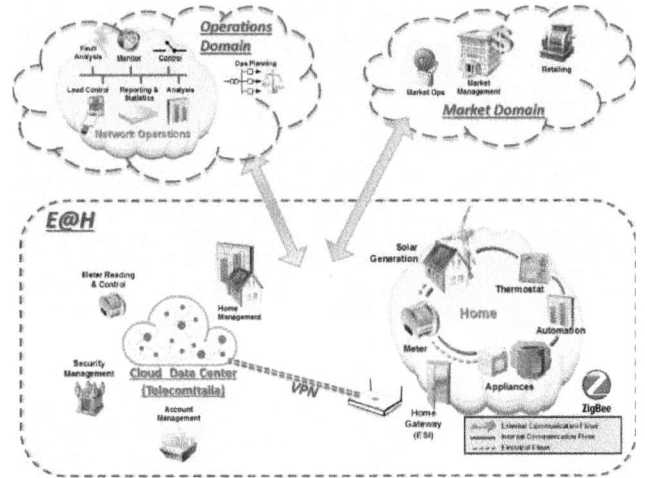

Figure 2: The Energy@Home Platform: overview

the following policy expression:

$$s.role = consumer \land r.owner = s.id \quad \land$$
$$releasableto(r.id, p) \land a.name = read$$

where *releasableto* checks whether the user has marked as releasable to the third-party service p a resource r which they own. The dashboard permits consumers to change the result returned by *releasableto* for all the resources they own so that authorization decisions for each resource can be tuned while leaving the policies unmodified.

5. ACKNOWLEDGMENTS

This work has partially been supported by the activity "SecSES Secure Energy Systems" of the action line ASES Smart Energy Systems of the EIT ICT Labs, and by the MIUR PRIN 2010-11 project "Security Horizons." We are grateful to Claudio Petrazzuolo and Andrea Ranalli from Telecom Italia for useful comments and discussions.

6. REFERENCES

[1] A. Armando, R. Carbone, E. G. Chekole, C. Petrazzuolo, A. Ranalli, and S. Ranise. Selective Release of Smart Metering Data in Multi-domain Smart Grids. In *2nd Open EIT ICT Labs Workshop on Smart Grid Security*, 2014.

[2] X. Jin, R. Krishnan, and R. Sandhu. A Unified Attribute-Based Access Control Model Covering DAC, MAC and RBAC. In *DBSec*, number 7371 in LNCS, pages 41–55, 2012.

[3] G. Naumovich and P. Centonze. Static Analysis of Role-based Access Control in J2EE Applications. *SIGSOFT Softw. Eng. Notes*, 29(5):1–10, Sept. 2004.

[4] E. Yuan and J. Tong. Attributed Based Access Control (ABAC) for Web Services. In *IEEE Int. Conf. on Web Services*, ICWS '05, pages 561–569. IEEE Computer Society, 2005.

---

[8] http://jemma.energy-home.org

Comprehensive Integrity Protection for Desktop Linux

Wai Kit Sze and R. Sekar
Stony Brook University
Stony Brook, NY, USA

ABSTRACT

Information flow provides principled defenses against malware. It can provide system-wide integrity protection without requiring any program-specific understanding. Information flow policies have been around for 40+ years but they have not been explored in today's context. Specifically, they are not designed for contemporary software and OSes. Applying these policies directly on today's OSes affects usability. In this paper, we focus our attention on an information-flow based integrity protection system that we implemented for Linux, with the goal of minimizing usability impact. We discuss the design decisions made in this system and provide insights on building usable information flow systems.

1. Introduction

Information flow has been proposed 40+ years ago for integrity protection. While these systems [2, 5, 9, 12, 3, 6, 7, 4] can provide principled protections against malware, they are rarely used in practice. This is because these systems often require (1) changing OSes to enforce information flow policies, and/or (2) rewriting applications to handle new security failures. These requirements limit practical adoption of information flow systems. In this paper, we discuss the techniques in making them usable. Our discussion is based on PIP [11], an information flow system focused on usability. Increased usability results from increased application compatibility, combined with the ability to preserve user experience on contemporary OSes that do not support integrity protection. We also propose some demo scenarios to show how our techniques work.

In Section 2, we give a brief overview of PIP. In Section 3, we focus on information flow policies that can improve usability. We describe a technique to distinguish between different types of files, and applying different policies based on these types. We also discuss how to deal with programs that need to handle high and low integrity data simultaneously. We summarize the implementation of PIP in Section 4. Demo scenarios and evaluation are presented in Section 5 and 6 respectively. Related works are presented in Section 7. The paper concludes in Section 8.

The main goal of this demo paper is to illustrate techniques to improve usability of information flow based integrity protection.

SACMAT'14, June 25–27, 2014, London, Ontario, Canada.
Copyright is held by the owner/author(s). Publication rights licensed to ACM.
ACM 978-1-4503-2939-2/14/06 ...$15.00.
http://dx.doi.org/10.1145/2613087.2613112.

2. Architecture Overview

Basic information flow policy for preserving system integrity is no-write-up and no-read-down. Low integrity processes are not allowed to modify high integrity files while high integrity processes are not allowed to read low integrity files.

PIP is a portable information flow system that has been implemented on Linux and BSD systems. It consists of three main components: existing multi-user support from OSes, a library, and a helper process. We provide an overview on the system architecture here. Details about the system can be found in [11].

PIP relies on existing multi-user support for labeling integrity and enforcing no-write-up on low integrity processes. For simplicity, we consider two integrity levels: high integrity (benign) and low integrity (untrusted). Low integrity subjects are run with a newly created userid called *untrusted*. By default, these untrusted processes have no permission to modify user data. This provides a robust enforcement of no-write-up policy.

No-read-down policy is enforced by a library. Although library enforcement is subject to bypass attacks, note that we are applying it only to benign processes. Such processes run benign code from trustworthy sources, and operate on benign data. It is therefore reasonable to assume that they will not actively seek to subvert policy enforcement, and hence library-based enforcement is reasonable.

To obtain a fully working system, a handful of administrative and utility applications need to be *trusted,* i.e., they should be able to consume untrusted input while continuing to have high integrity. Section 3.5 discusses these applications.

The basic policy outlined so far focuses on preserving integrity, but not usability of programs. For instance, untrusted processes may not be able to read user data as they are treated as a different user on the system. This is where the helper process component comes in: it runs with the privileges of the current user — also called *logged user*, and provides a mechanism for untrusted processes to request controlled access to the user's files. It will allow user files to be opened in read-only mode, and creating files in user directories.

By default, our system only protects integrity, and does not target confidentiality. However, it is possible to enhance the helper process and the rest of the system to enforce stricter policies.

3. Improving usability

3.1 Fine-grained policies

Traditional UNIX file permissions does not provide sufficient granularity that enables processes of the *untrusted* user to have read

---

†This work was supported in part by grants from NSF (CNS-0831298, CNS-1319137) and AFOSR (FA9550-09-1-0539).

access to all the files of the logged user. This deficiency can be rectified using Access Control Lists (ACL) on Linux. However, this interferes with normal use of file permissions, e.g., a manual permission change can negate the ability of untrusted code to access user files. Moreover, many applications are unaware of ACLs and may run into compatibility problems, e.g., they may be using `stat` or `eaccess` to check permissions. Finally, ACLs can only allow or deny accesses, but cannot support more complex policies, such as redirecting access to a shadow copy of a high-integrity file. For this reason, PIP uses library and helper process to fine-tune the coarse-grained policy captured by the DAC permission.

3.2 Policy Inference for File Accesses

The basic information flow policy focuses on preserving integrity, but not usability. PIP improves usability by supporting multiple policies. Instead of simply allowing or denying an access, PIP also supports shadowing. Shadowing is crucial for improving usability of untrusted processes: some files need to be read and written whenever a program is executed. Labeling these files as high integrity will prevent untrusted processes from using these files. Labeling them as untrusted will prevent benign processes from using them. Using only allow and deny policies break either benign or untrusted processes. Shadowing maintains two independent copies of the same file and transparently redirects accesses to the file copy based on the integrity of the process. This allows programs to be used as both benign and untrusted.

PIP does not apply shadowing to resolve all file access denials. This is because shadowing of data files causes confusion. Without realizing it, a user may accidentally invoke an untrusted application to edit a high integrity data file. With shadowing, this will work, but subsequently, if the user tries to view the file, a benign viewer will be redirected to the benign, unmodified copy, and the user is left confused as to what happened to the edits he/she made. For this reason, PIP uses the following technique to determine if a file represents a data access or a preference file, and applies different policies.

3.3 Determining file type

PIP relies on file type to determine what policies to apply. Figure 1 shows the file types in PIP. Code and configuration files are easy to identify based on how they are accessed. However, preference files and data files cannot be identified via permission. An important distinction that PIP relies on is how these files are accessed. Data files are specified explicitly by users, while preference files are accessed by programs implicitly.

File type	Permission	Access
code	R–X	-
configuration files	R– –	Implicit
preference files	RW–	Implicit
data	RW–	Explicit

Figure 1: File types in PIP

Implicitly accessed files are those that are not specified explicitly by users. PIP identifies these files by exclusion: the set of files accessed by the application but are not explicitly specified.

Typically, users specify data file accesses in these ways:

- arguments when executing the program
- environment variables
- file names returned by a file selection widget, which captures file names selected by a user from a file dialog box

Identifying explicitly accessed files can be posed as a taint-tracking problem with taint sources listed. Taint propagates in PIP according to the following rule: when a tainted directory is opened, all the file names inside the directory are marked as tainted. Every file access made by the application is then matched against the set of tainted values to identify explicitly accessed files. Implicitly accessed files are those that do not match with the tainted values. PIP relies on Aho-Corasick [1] algorithm to track and identify tainted values efficiently.

With information on whether a file is accessed implicitly by programs or explicitly by users, different policies can be applied to serve users better. While this section focuses on describing how this "implicit-explicit" technique can be used to infer file types and hence be used for shadowing policy, this technique can also be applied to limit the trust on programs that need to handle high and untrusted simultaneously (Section 3.5).

3.4 uudo Inference

By design, PIP does not allow subjects to change their integrity labels. PIP is a Privilege Revision on Invoke (PRI) system and it does not suffer from the problem of self-revocation [4]. Hence PIP avoids causing failures that applications cannot handle gracefully. In PIP, a benign (high integrity) process can read and write into high integrity files and write into untrusted files, but not read from untrusted files. On the other hand, an untrusted process can read and write untrusted files, but it can only read high integrity files. Since it does not allow subject integrity to change, a process has to decide ahead of time what integrity level it wants to be. uudo is a program that PIP provides to let users (and benign subjects) execute a program as untrusted.

Instead of requiring users to specify the integrity level for every program executed, PIP relies on uudo inference to infer what integrity level a process should be executed with. It involves predicting what files a program will use when executed: if users want to use a program with untrusted files, the process should be executed with userid *untrusted* to avoid violating the security policy. On the other hand, if no untrusted files are involved, the process can be executed with high integrity. By design, an incorrect choice of integrity level only affects usability, but not system integrity.

PIP determines the required integrity level of a process based on a simple technique. If any of the arguments or environment variables corresponds to a low integrity file, PIP would execute the program as untrusted. We found that this simple technique is very helpful because data are typically specified as program's input arguments. For instance, a lot of command line programs are not interactive and input files need to be specified as arguments. Even for GUI programs, they also accept input arguments to specify files to be opened. File explorers (e.g., nautilus) then act as front ends to interact with users: double-clicking on the icons cause them to be executed with file path arguments.

This technique, however, fails if files to be opened depend on the interaction with the programs. Since files to be accessed are not known when deciding process integrity, PIP cannot infer the use of uudo if high integrity programs are invoked without arguments.

3.5 Trusted programs

Applications that are designed to handle data from various sources simultaneously require special handling in information flow systems as this violates the basic information flow policy. We provide a discussion on how these applications are handled in PIP, so as to balance integrity protection and usability.

Web browsers.

We designated `Firefox` to protect itself from network inputs and inputs from local files selected using a file dialog by the user. Files selected by user using a file dialog are mainly used for uploading. These files are identified by the "implicit-explicit" mechanism described in Section 3.3, preventing `Firefox` from using untrusted files as non-data inputs. To ensure that downloaded files are associated with the right integrity labels, we developed a `Firefox` addon, which uses a database to map domains to integrity levels.

As a second alternative, we dedicated an instance of the web browser for benign sites. Using policies, the benign instance can be restricted from accessing untrusted sites. In PIP, we manually defined a whitelist of benign sites. A better alternative would use whitelists provided by third parties. Instead of blocking users from visiting untrusted sites, we can invoke the untrusted browser instance to load the pages directly.

Email clients.

Email clients introduce untrusted data into the system through message headers, content, and attachments. Our approach is to trust the email reader to protect itself from untrusted sources. However, attachments are given labels corresponding to the site from which the attachment was received. We developed an addon for `Thunderbird` for this purpose. However, the current email protocol (SMTP) does not protect against spoofing. To provide trustworthy labeling, we could either rely on digital signatures (when present), or on the chain of SMTP servers that handled the email. Such spoof-protection has not yet been implemented.

Software Installation.

Our system relies on correct integrity labeling when new files are introduced into the system. Of particular concern is the software installation phase, especially because this phase often requires administrative privileges. Solutions have previously been developed for securing software installation, such as SSI [8]. We are implementing an approach similar to SSI to protect the software installation phase and to label files introduced during the installation. PIP can then enforce the policies at run time based on the labels.

X-Server and DBus.

Malicious X-clients can abuse X-server APIs to harm other X-clients. One approach we provide is to redirect untrusted X-clients to `Xephyr`, a nested X-server. Another alternative uses X-security-extensions to designate untrusted processes as *untrusted X-client*, to restrict/disable accesses to certain X resources. Since this option trusts the X-server, it is not as secure as the first alternative, but integrates smoothly in terms of user experience.

We are also trusting DBus and some service daemons to handle requests from untrusted processes. For instance, we allow untrusted processes to send desktop notifications and play sounds. Same as X-server, we trust these applications to handle requests from untrusted processes, but not for consuming untrusted files.

File utilities.

Files belonging to different integrity levels co-exist. Utilities such as `mv`, `cp`, `tar`, `find`, `grep`, and `rm` may need to handle files of high integrity and untrusted *at the same time*. We designated these file utilities as able to protect themselves when dealing with untrusted data such that their functionalities can be preserved.

Instead of trusting these utilities to consume any untrusted data, PIP can further reduce the set of files by relying on the "implicit-explicit" technique described in Section 3.3. When users invoke a command, data files are specified as input arguments[1].

---

[1] When globbing is used in shell command, the shell process will expand it to the set of file names matching the pattern.

	LOC				
	C		header		Other
	Ubuntu	+PCBSD	Ubuntu	+PCBSD	Both
Shared	2208	130	737	27	39
helper	703	16	106		
uudo	68	52			
library	2206	163	492	30	74
Total	5185	361	1335	57	113

Figure 2: Code complexity on Ubuntu and PCBSD

A side effect of making these utilities as trusted is that their outputs have high integrity labels. This is not desirable for applications like `cp` and `tar` as integrity labels on original files are lost. We solved this problem by setting appropriate flags to preserve the integrity information. This is relatively easy as the integrity information is encoded as group ownership in PIP.

4. Implementation

We implemented the system on Ubuntu 10.04. A prototype is also developed for PCBSD 8.2. Figure 2 summarizes the implementation complexity. +PCBSD corresponds to the additional number of lines of code required in order to support PCBSD. Shared corresponds to code shared across multiple components.

5. Usage/Demo Scenario

Here are some scenarios to illustrate the usability of PIP.

Watching a movie.

We opened a movie torrent from an untrusted website. `Firefox` downloaded the file to the temporary directory and labeled it as untrusted. The default BitTorrent client, `Transmission`, was invoked as untrusted to start downloading the movie into the Download directory. Once the download completed, we double-clicked the movie to view it. `vlc` was started as untrusted to play the movie. Realizing that the movie had no subtitles, we located `subdownloader` for downloading subtitles. Since our installer considers Ubuntu's universe repository as untrusted, the application was installed as untrusted, and hence operated only in untrusted mode. We searched and found a match. Clicking on the match resulted in launching an untrusted `Firefox` instance. We went back to `subdownloader` to download the subtitle, and then loaded this file into `vlc` to continue watching the movie.

Compiling programs from students.

Some students submit their programming assignments. Teaching assistants for the course need to download their projects, extract them, compile them and execute the binaries in order to grade the assignments. In this experiment, we considered an attack that creates a backdoor by appending ssh key to `authorized_keys` so that a malicious student can break into TA's machine later.

With protection from PIP, when the TA received the submission as an attachment, it was marked untrusted. As the code was unpacked, compiled and run, this "untrusted" label stayed with it. So, when the code tried to append a public key, it was stopped.

Resume template.

We downloaded a compressed resume template from the Internet. When we double clicked on the tgz file, `FileRoller`, the default archive manager started automatically as untrusted because the file was labeled as untrusted by `Firefox`. We extracted the files to Documents directory. We then opened the file with `texmaker` by selecting "Open With", since `texmaker` was not the default handler for tex file. `texmaker` was started as untrusted and we started editing the file. We then compiled the latex file and viewed the dvi

Document Readers	Adobe Reader, dhelp, dissy, dwdiff, evince, F-spot, FoxitReader, Geegle-gps, jparse, naturaldocs, nfoview, pdf2ps, webmagick
Editor/ Office/ Document Processor	Audacity, Abiword, cdcover, eclipse, ewipe, gambas2, gedit, GIMP, Gnumeric, gwyddion, Inkscape, labplot, lyx, OpenOffice, Pitivi, pyroom, R Studio, scidavis, Scite, texmaker, tkgate, wxmaxima
Games	asc, gbrainy, Kiki-the-nano-bot, luola, OpenTTD, SimuTrans, SuperTux, supertuxkart, Tumiki-fighters, wesnoth, xdemineur, xtux
Internet	cbm, evolution, dailystrips, Firefox, flickcurl, gnome-rdp, httrack, jdresolve, kadu, lynx, Opera, rdiff, scp, SeaMonkey, subdownloader, Thunderbird, Transmission, wbox, xchat
Media	aqualung, banshee, mplayer, rhythmbox, totem, vlc
Shell-like	bochs, csh, gnu-smalltalk, regina, swipl
Other	apoo, arbtt, cassbeam, clustalx, dvdrip, expect, gdpc, glaurung, googleearth, gpscorrelate-gui, grass, gscan2pdf, jpilot, kiki, otp, qmtest, symlinks, tar, tkdesk, treil, VisualBoyAdvance, w2do, wmmon, xeji, xtrkcad, z88

Figure 3: Software tested

document with `evince` by clicking on the "View DVI" button in `texmaker`. We then viewed pdf and `AdobeReader` was automatically invoked as untrusted. The document was rendered properly.

Stock charting and analysis.

We wanted to study trend of a stock and we searched the Internet about how to analyze. We came across a tutorial on an unknown website with a `R` script. We installed `R` and downloaded the script. When we started `R`, we found that it is a command line environment and is not so user-friendly for beginners. We then installed `RStudio`, a front-end for `R`, from a deb file we found on another unknown website. Our installer installed `RStudio` as untrusted because `Firefox` labeled the deb file as untrusted. After we started `RStudio`, we loaded the script and realized that it required several `R` libraries. We installed the missing `R` libraries. These libraries were installed in a shadow directory since `R` implicitly accessed the library directory. After installing the libraries, we generated a graph. We saved the graph in the Pictures directory, and edited the graph with `GIMP`.

6. Evaluation

We tested about 100 software packages spanning multiple categories listed in Figure 3. All of these programs can run as benign, as well as untrusted. They all worked without any problems or perceptible differences. Usability of these programs depends on the type of programs. We focus our discussion on usability for the first two categories. More detailed discussions can be found in [11].

Benign document readers can only open high integrity files. Untrusted readers have no restriction in opening. We believe this does not affect usability because these document readers are usually invoked via file explorers (e.g., double-clicking an icon in nautilus). Our `uudo` inference technique (Section 3.4) can infer the required integrity level. A difference between benign and untrusted document readers is when performing a "SaveAs": Benign readers can create high integrity copies while untrusted readers can only create low integrity copies.

When invoking editors via file explorers, usability is preserved because PIP can infer reliably the files to be edited. However, editors can violate information flow policies when they are used to edit both high and low integrity files simultaneously. Usability depends on what integrity the editors are in. Benign editors cannot open low integrity files. On the other hand, untrusted editors tend to open high integrity files in read-only mode automatically when they cannot open them in writable-mode.

7. Related Work

Since the Biba [2] integrity model proposed, researchers have been working to improve usability of information flow systems. Low-water-mark is an extension to the Biba model that allows entities to downgrade from higher integrity to lower, such that more usage scenarios can be supported. LOMAC [4] improves on the low-water-mark model to address self-revocation problems.

Instead of focusing on usability, Decentralized Information Flow Control (DIFC) systems (HiStar [12], Flume [5], and Asbestos [3]) extend functionalities by allowing applications to create their own labels. This model, however, requires applications (or even the OS) to be rewritten in order to take advantage of the system.

UMIP [6], PPI [9] and IFEDAC [7] are more recent systems developed for Linux OS and compatible with existing applications. However, they do not address the usability issues discussed here.

8. Conclusion

PIP system being demonstrated provides systematic integrity protection for Linux. This paper presented the PIP system architecture, and describes in some depth the challenges posed by traditional information flow techniques, and the techniques we developed in PIP to address them. We also proposed some demo scenarios to illustrate how the techniques we introduced are useful in improving usability. PIP has been tested with hundreds of software packages. It is an open-source project, with the source-code as well as a virtual machine image being downloadable from our website [10].

9. References

[1] A. V. Aho and M. J. Corasick. Efficient String Matching: An Aid to Bibliographic Search. In *Communications of the ACM 18(6)*, 1975.

[2] K. J. Biba. Integrity Considerations for Secure Computer Systems. In *Technical Report ESD-TR-76-372, USAF Electronic Systems Division, Hanscom Air Force Base, Bedford, Massachusetts*, 1977.

[3] P. Efstathopoulos, M. Krohn, S. VanDeBogart, C. Frey, D. Ziegler, E. Kohler, D. Mazières, F. Kaashoek, and R. Morris. Labels and Event Processes in the Asbestos Operating System. In *SOSP*, 2005.

[4] T. Fraser. LOMAC: Low Water-Mark Integrity Protection for COTS Environments. In *S&P*, 2000.

[5] M. Krohn, A. Yip, M. Brodsky, N. Cliffer, M. F. Kaashoek, E. Kohler, and R. Morris. Information Flow Control for Standard OS Abstractions. In *SOSP*, 2007.

[6] N. Li, Z. Mao, and H. Chen. Usable Mandatory Integrity Protection for Operating Systems . In *S&P*, 2007.

[7] Z. Mao, N. Li, H. Chen, and X. Jiang. Combining Discretionary Policy with Mandatory Information Flow in Operating Systems. In *TISSEC 14(3)*, 2011.

[8] W. Sun, R. Sekar, Z. Liang, and V. N. Venkatakrishnan. Expanding Malware Defense by Securing Software Installations. In *DIMVA*, 2008.

[9] W. Sun, R. Sekar, G. Poothia, and T. Karandikar. Practical Proactive Integrity Preservation: A Basis for Malware Defense. In *S&P*, 2008.

[10] W. K. Sze. Portable Integrity Protection System (PIP). http://www.seclab.cs.sunysb.edu/seclab/pip.

[11] W. K. Sze and R. Sekar. A Portable User-Level Approach for System-wide Integrity Protection. In *ACSAC*, 2013.

[12] N. Zeldovich, S. Boyd-Wickizer, E. Kohler, and D. Mazières. Making Information Flow Explicit in HiStar. In *OSDI*, 2006.

Game Theoretic Analysis of Multiparty Access Control in Online Social Networks

Hongxin Hu
Clemson University
Clemson, SC 29634
hhu@desu.edu

Gail-Joon Ahn
Arizona State University
Tempe, AZ 85287
gahn@asu.edu

Ziming Zhao
Arizona State University
Tempe, AZ 85287
ziming.zhao@asu.edu

Dejun Yang
Colorado School of Mines
Golden, CO 80401
djyang@mines.edu

ABSTRACT

Existing online social networks (OSNs) only allow a single user to restrict access to her/his data but cannot provide any mechanism to enforce privacy concerns over data associated with multiple users. This situation leaves privacy conflicts largely unresolved and leads to the potential disclosure of users' sensitive information. To address such an issue, a MultiParty Access Control (MPAC) model was recently proposed, including a systematic approach to identify and resolve privacy conflicts for collaborative data sharing in OSNs. In this paper, we take another step to further study the problem of analyzing the strategic behavior of rational controllers in multiparty access control, where each controller aims to maximize her/his own benefit by adjusting her/his privacy setting in collaborative data sharing in OSNs. We first formulate this problem as a multiparty control game and show the existence of unique Nash Equilibrium (NE) which is critical because at an NE, no controller has any incentive to change her/his privacy setting. We then present algorithms to compute the NE and prove that the system can converge to the NE in only a few iterations. A numerical analysis is also provided for different scenarios that illustrate the interplay of controllers in the multiparty control game. In addition, we conduct user studies of the multiparty control game to explore the *gap* between game theoretic approaches and real human behaviors.

Categories and Subject Descriptors

D.4.6 [**Security and Protection**]: Access controls; H.2.7 [**Information Systems**]: Security, integrity, and protection

Keywords

Multiparty Access Control, Social Networks, Game Theory

1. INTRODUCTION

Online social networks (OSNs) have experienced explosive growth in recent years and become a *de facto* portal for hundreds of mil-

lions of Internet users. Facebook, for example, claims that it has more than 1.2 billion monthly active users [2]. As the popularity of OSNs continues to grow, a huge amount of possibly sensitive and private information has been uploaded to OSNs. To protect such a large volume of sensitive information, access control has received considerable attention as a central feature of OSNs [1, 3].

Today, nearly 4 out of 5 active Internet users visit OSNs [4], leading to a fundamental shift in the patterns of information exchange over the Internet. Users in OSNs are now required to be content *creators* and *managers*, rather than just being content *consumers*. Even though OSNs currently provide privacy control mechanisms allowing users to regulate access to information contained in their *own* spaces, users, unfortunately, have no control over data residing *outside* their spaces [8, 28, 34, 36]. For instance, if a user posts a comment in a friend's space, s/he cannot specify which users can view the comment. In another case, when a user uploads a photo and tags friends who appear in the photo, the tagged friends cannot restrict who can see this photo. Since multiple associated users may have different privacy concerns over the shared data, *privacy conflicts* occur and the lack of collaborative privacy control increases the potential risk in leaking sensitive information by friends to the public. In addition, federal and state government sectors have been leveraging social networks to exchange information and establish specialized groups/communities/task forces [27]. Even IT professionals started adopting social networks to look for solutions and best practices for their daily tasks while willingly sharing their tasks over OSNs [37]. Also, social networks have been widely accepted by a wide variety of patients who need to search for medical advices and exchange their experiences and other relevant information [15]. Such environments desperately need to protect and control the shared data due to its potential sensitivity and criticality. Therefore, it is essential to accommodate the special privacy control requirements coming from multiple associated users for collaboratively managing the shared data in OSNs.

To address such an issue, we recently proposed a multiparty access control (MPAC) model [22] to capture the core features of multiparty authorization requirements, which have not been accommodated by other access control systems for OSNs (e.g., [10, 11, 16, 17]). In particular, we introduced a systematic conflict detection and resolution approach [21] to cope with privacy conflicts occurring in collaborative management of data sharing in OSNs, balancing the need for privacy protection and the users' desire for information sharing by quantitative analysis of privacy risk and sharing loss. However, the proposed privacy conflict resolution mechanism assumes that all controllers are *well-behaved* to provide their privacy settings for collaborative sharing. In practice, users may attempt to *selfishly* maximize their own profits without respecting the benefit of the entire system.

In this paper, we take a further step toward analyzing the strategic behaviors of rational users who aim to maximize their own benefits in collaborative data sharing in OSNs. To this end, we formulate a multiparty control game, which models the interaction of controllers in multiparty access control. In addition, we derive the conditions and expressions of Nash Equilibrium (NE) for such a game. At an NE, no controller has an incentive to adjust her/his privacy setting when others fix their strategies. Moreover, we introduce two interactive adjustment algorithms to calculate the NE with respect to two different conditions, synchronous adjustment and non-synchronous adjustment, respectively. Our experimental analysis illustrates the system can converge to an NE in only a few iterations. We also provide a numerical analysis of the multiparty control game in terms of several different situations that reflect different incentives for controllers to change their privacy settings. Furthermore, we carry out user studies of the multiparty control game and articulate the gap between our game model and real human behaviors. We believe our game theoretic analysis provides important implications for the design of future collaborative sharing systems in OSNs.

The rest of the paper is organized as follows. In Section 2, we overview the multiparty access control mechanism, focusing on privacy conflict detection and resolution. In Section 3, we discuss our game model, along with the Equilibrium analysis and the convergence of our game. The details about evaluation results are described in Section 4. We overview the related work in Section 5. Section 6 discusses several important issues and our future work. We conclude this paper in Section 7.

2. OVERVIEW OF MULTIPARTY ACCESS CONTROL

Users in OSNs can post statuses and notes, upload photos and videos in their own spaces, tag others to their content, and share the content with their friends. On the other hand, users can also post content in their friends' spaces. The shared content may be connected with multiple users. For example, consider a photograph contains three users, Alice, Bob and Carol. If Alice uploads it to her own space and tags both Bob and Carol in the photo, Alice is called the *owner* of the photo, and Bob and Carol *stakeholders* of the photo. In another case, if this photo is posted by Alice to Bob's space, Alice is called the *contributor* of the photo. In addition, if Alice views a photo in Bob's space and decides to share this photo with her friends, the photo will be in turn posted to her space and she can authorize her friends to see this photo. In such a case, Alice is a *disseminator* of the photo. In all these cases, all associated users may be desired to specify privacy policies to control over who can see this photo. However, current online social networks, such as Facebook and Google+, only allow the data *owner* to fully control the shared data, but lack a mechanism to specify and enforce the privacy concerns from other associated users, leading to privacy conflicts being largely unresolved and sensitive information being potentially disclosed to the public. In order to enable a collaborative management of data sharing in OSNs, the multiparty access control (MPAC) model [22] was recently proposed.

When two users disagree on whom the shared data item should be exposed to, it causes a *privacy conflict*. The essential reason leading to the privacy conflicts is that multiple associated users of the shared data item often have different privacy concerns over the data item. For example, assume that Alice and Bob are two con-

trollers of a photo. Each of them defines a privacy policy stating only her/his friends can view this photo. Since it is almost impossible that Alice and Bob have the same set of friends, privacy conflicts may *always* exist considering collaborative control over the shared data item. A systematic conflict detection and resolution mechanism has been presented in [21] to cope with privacy conflicts occurring in collaborative management of data sharing in OSNs, balancing the need for privacy protection and the users' desire for information sharing by quantitative analysis of privacy risk and sharing loss.

Privacy Conflict Identification: Through specifying the privacy policies to reflect the privacy concern, each controller of the shared data item defines a set of trusted users who can access the data item. The set of trusted users represents an *accessor space* for the controller. In [21], a space segmentation approach was provided to partition accessor spaces of all controllers of a shared data item into disjoint segments. Then, conflicting accessor space segments called *conflicting segments*, which contain accessors that some controllers of the shared data item do not trust, are identified. Each conflicting segment contains at least one privacy conflict.

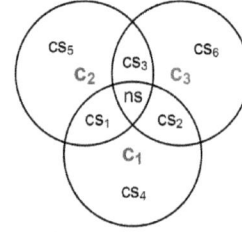

Figure 1: Privacy Conflict Identification

Figure 1 gives an example of identifying privacy conflicts based on accessor space segmentation. Circles are used to represent accessor spaces of three controllers, c_1, c_2 and c_3, of a shared data item. This example illustrates that three of accessor spaces overlap with each other, indicating that some accessors within the overlapping spaces are trusted by multiple controllers. After performing the space segmentation, seven disjoint accessor space segments are generated as shown in Figure 1. The accessor space segments are classified into two categories: *non-conflicting* segments and *conflicting* segments. A *non-conflicting* segment covers all controllers' access spaces, which means that any accessor within the segment is trusted by all controllers of the shared data item, indicating no privacy conflict occurs. A *conflicting* segment does not contain all controllers' access spaces, which means that accessors in the segment are untrusted by some controllers. Each *untrusting* controller points out a privacy conflict. In Figure 1, the segment ns is a *non-conflicting* segment, and cs_1 through cs_6 are *conflicting* segments, where cs_1, cs_2 and cs_3 indicate *one* privacy conflict, respectively, and cs_4, cs_5 and cs_6 are associated with *two* privacy conflicts, respectively.

Once multiparty privacy conflicts are identified, a systematic approach for resolving privacy conflicts is needed. The process of privacy conflict resolution makes a decision to allow or deny the accessors within the conflicting segments to access the shared data item. In general, allowing the assessors contained in conflicting segments to access the data item may cause *privacy risk*, but denying a set of accessors in conflicting segments to access the data item may result in *sharing loss*.

Measuring Privacy Risk: The privacy risk of a conflicting segment is an indicator of potential threat to the privacy of controllers in terms of the shared data item: the higher the privacy risk of a conflicting segment, the higher the threat to controllers' privacy. The basic premises for the measurement of privacy risk for a conflicting segment are: (a) the lower the number of controllers who trust the accessors within the conflicting segment, the higher the privacy risk; (b) the stronger the general privacy concerns of controllers, the higher the privacy risk; (c) the more sensitive the shared data item, the higher the privacy risk; and (d) the wider the data item spreads, the higher the privacy risk. In order to measure the overall privacy risk of a conflicting segment α denoted by $PR(\alpha)$, the following equation is used to aggregate the privacy risks of α due to different untrusting controllers.

$$PR(\alpha) = \sum_{\beta \in controllers_{ut}(\alpha)} (pc_\beta \times sl_\beta) \times n_\alpha \quad (1)$$

where function $controllers_{ut}(\alpha)$ returns all untrusting controllers of a conflict segment α, pc_β denotes the general privacy concern of an untrusting controller β $(0 \leq pc_\beta \leq 1)$, sl_β denotes the sensitivity level of the shared data item explicitly chosen by an untrusting controller β $(0 \leq sl_\beta \leq 1)$, and n_α denotes visibility of the data item with respect to a conflicting segment captures how many accessors are contained in the segment α.

Measuring Sharing Loss: When the decision of privacy conflict resolution for a conflicting segment is "deny", it may cause losses in potential data sharing since there are controllers expecting to allow the accessors in the conflicting segment to access the data item. The overall sharing loss $SL(\alpha)$ of a conflicting segment α is computed as follows:

$$SL(\alpha) = \sum_{\beta \in controllers_t(\alpha)} (1 - pc_\beta) \times (1 - sl_\beta) \times n_\alpha \quad (2)$$

where function $controllers_t(\alpha)$ returns all trusting controllers of a segment α.

Conflict Resolution Based on Privacy Protection and Data Sharing: An optimal solution for privacy conflict resolution should cause lower privacy risk when allowing the accessors in some conflicting segments to access the data item, and get lesser loss in data sharing when denying the accessors to access the shared data item. Thus, for each conflict resolution solution r, a resolving score $RS(r)$ can be calculated using the following equation:

$$RS(r) = \frac{1}{\lambda \sum_{\alpha_1 \in CS_p^r} PR(\alpha_1) + (1 - \lambda) \sum_{\alpha_2 \in CS_d^r} SL(\alpha_2)} \quad (3)$$

where CS_p^r and CS_d^r denote *permitted* conflicting segments and *denied* conflicting segments respectively in the conflict resolution solution r. And λ and $1 - \lambda$ are preference weights for the privacy risk and the sharing loss, $0 \leq \lambda \leq 1$, reflecting the privacy-sharing tradeoff. λ can be calculated in terms of the average of sensitivity levels of all controllers. That is, $\lambda = \frac{\sum_{\beta \in controllers(d)} sl_\beta}{\ell \times n}$, where $controllers(d)$ returns all controllers of the shared data item d, and n is the number of these controllers. Then, the optimal conflict resolution CR_{opt} on the tradeoff between privacy risk and sharing loss can be the maximum resolving score, $CR_{opt} = \max_r RS(r)$.

To find the maximum resolving score, the privacy risk ($PR(\alpha)$) and the sharing loss ($SL(\alpha)$) are first calculated for each conflict segment (α), individually. Finally, the following equation can be utilized to make the decisions for privacy conflict resolution.

$$Decision = \begin{cases} \text{Deny} & \text{if } \lambda PR(\alpha) \geq (1 - \lambda) SL(\alpha) \\ \text{Permit} & \text{if } \lambda PR(\alpha) < (1 - \lambda) SL(\alpha) \end{cases} \quad (4)$$

3. GAME MODEL

The privacy conflict resolution mechanism for multiparty access control presented in Section 2 assumes that all controllers are *well-behaved* to provide their privacy settings for collaborative sharing. However, in practice, controllers may attempt to *selfishly* maximize their own profits without respecting the benefit of entire system. For example, if a controller in the multiparty control system notices that the current privacy-sharing tradeoff (represented by λ in Equation 3) for the conflict resolution is lower than her/his expectation, s/he may set a much stronger privacy preference to make the privacy-sharing tradeoff close to her/his expectation. In this section, we first introduce the basic game theory concepts and then articulate our multiparty control game model.

3.1 Basic Concepts in Game Theory

Game theory [31] is a discipline aiming at modeling situations where decision makers have to choose specific actions that have mutual or possibly conflicting consequences. A game consists of a set $\mathcal{P} = \{1, 2, ..., n\}$ of players. Each player $i \in \mathcal{P}$ has a nonempty strategy set Π_i. Let $s_i \in \Pi_i$ denote the selected strategy by i. A strategy profile s consists of all the players' strategies, i.e., $s = (s_1, ..., s_n)$. Obviously, we have $s \in \Pi = \times_{i \in \mathcal{P}} \Pi_i$. Let s_{-i} denote the strategy profile excluding s_i. Hence, we then have $s = (s_i, s_{-i})$. The utility function $u_i(s)$ of i measures i's valuation on strategy profile s. We say that i prefers s_i to s_i' if $u_i(s_i, s_{-i}) > u_i(s_i', s_{-i})$.

Given other players' strategies s_{-i}, i can select a strategy, denoted by $\rho_i(s_{-i})$, which maximizes its utility function. Such a strategy is known as *best response* [31] in game theory, which can be formally defined as follows:

DEFINITION 1. *(Best Response). Given other player's strategies s_{-i}, a best response strategy of i is a strategy $s_i \in \Pi_i$ such that $\rho_i(s_{-i}) = arg \max_{s_i \in \Pi_i} u_i(s_i, s_{-i})$, where Π_i is the strategy space of i.*

To study the interactions of players, we adopt the concept of *Nash Equilibrium* (NE) [31], which is formally defined as follows:

DEFINITION 2. *(Nash Equilibrium). A strategy profile $s^{ne} = (s_1^{ne}, ..., s_n^{ne})$ is called a Nash Equilibrium, if for every play i, we have $u_i(s_i^{ne}, s_{-i}^{ne}) \geq u_i(s_i, s_{-i}^{ne})$ for every $s_i \in \Pi_i$.*

In an NE, none of the players can improve its utility by unilaterally deviating from its current strategy. Mathematically, it means $\rho_i(s_{-i}^{ne}) = s_i^{ne}$ for all $i \in \mathcal{P}$.

3.2 Multiparty Control Game

We model and study the interaction of controllers as a *multiparty control game* where each controller tries to maximize her/his own utility function. We derive conditions and expressions for the NE. This consists of the privacy setting strategy of each controller, such that no controller can benefit in terms of improving the utility by unilaterally deviating from the NE.

Consider a set of controllers, $\mathcal{P} = \{1, 2, ..., n\}$, who collaboratively control the sharing of a data item in a social network. The *multiparty control game* is played among n controllers in the set $\mathcal{P}$. Each controller $i \in \mathcal{P}$ can specify her/his privacy policy. Then, conflict detection and resolution mechanisms in the system are performed to discover and resolve privacy conflicts. Feedbacks of the conflict resolution are in turn provided to associated controllers. Based on the feedbacks, controllers can adjust their privacy settings to maximize their own utilities. For simplicity, we assume that the feedback returned to each controller indicates the privacy-sharing tradeoff, and the controller adjusts her/his privacy setting through changing the sensitivity level, sl_i, for the shared data item. The goal for each controller to adjust her/his privacy setting is to make the privacy-sharing tradeoff close to her/his expectation, ep_i. However, changing privacy setting may also result in the utility loss of the controller. For example, if a controller increases the sensitivity level for the shared data item, sharing loss values (calculated by Equation (2)) of the conflicting segments contained in this controller's access space are reduced. That means these conflicting segments have a higher chance to be denied due to such a privacy setting change, implying potential sharing loss for the controller. Therefore, we present the utility function of controller i as follows:

$$u_i(sl_i, sl_{-i}) = -\mu_i(ep_i - \frac{\sum_{j \in \mathcal{P}} sl_j}{n})^2 - \tau_i(sl_i - ep_i)^2 . \quad (5)$$

In this utility function, if sl_i is greater than ep_i, which means the controller i strengthens her/his privacy setting, μ_i denotes the number of accessors in the conflicting segments *untrusted* by the controller i, and τ_i is the number of accessors in the conflicting segments *trusted* by the controller i. Otherwise, in case the controller i weakens her/his privacy setting, μ_i and τ_i in this utility function indicate the numbers of *trusted* and *untrusted* accessors in conflicting segments, respectively. The *first term* in the utility function quantifies the utility gained by the controller i and the *second term* in the utility function represents the utility loss of the controller i when s/he changes her/his privacy setting. For instance, if the privacy-sharing tradeoff is lower than the controller's expectation in current system state, this means the controller's privacy risk is higher than her/his expectation after resolving privacy conflicts. The controller may increase the sensitivity level sl_i of the shared data item to make the privacy-sharing tradeoff close to her/his expectation for reducing her/his privacy risk. At the same time, such a privacy setting change may also cause the sharing loss of the controller.

The set of controllers $\mathcal{P}$, the strategy space Π, and the utility function $\mathcal{U}$ define together the multiparty control game, $\mathcal{G}(\mathcal{P}, \Pi, \mathcal{U})$. In this game, each controller i maximizes her/his own utility u_i by choosing a *best response* strategy (privacy setting) $sl_i \in \Pi_i$, given the strategies (privacy settings) of others sl_{-i}, i.e.,

$$\rho_i(sl_{-i}) = arg \max_{sl_i \in \Pi_i} u_i(sl_i, sl_{-i}) . \quad (6)$$

3.3 Equilibrium Analysis

Based on the definition of NE (Definition 2), each controller plays her/his best response strategy in an NE. In other words, no controller has any incentive for changing her/his own strategy while the other controllers fix their strategies. To study the best response strategy of controller i, we calculate the derivatives of u_i with respect to sl_i:

$$\frac{\partial u_i(sl_i, sl_{-i})}{\partial sl_i} = \frac{2\mu_i}{n}(ep_i - \frac{\sum_{j \in \mathcal{P}} sl_j}{n}) - 2\tau_i(sl_i - ep_i) . \quad (7)$$

$$\frac{\partial^2 u_i(sl_i, sl_{-i})}{\partial sl_i^2} = -\frac{\mu_i}{n^2} - \tau_i < 0 . \quad (8)$$

Since the second-order derivative of u_i is negative, the utility u_i is a *strictly concave function* in sl_i. Therefore, given any strat-

egy profile sl_{-i} of the other controllers, the best response strategy $\rho_i(sl_{-i})$ of controller i is unique, if it exists. Setting the first derivative of u_i to 0, we obtain

$$\frac{\mu_i}{n}(ep_i - \frac{\sum_{j \in \mathcal{P}} sl_j}{n}) - \tau_i(sl_i - ep_i) = 0 . \quad (9)$$

Solving for sl_i in (9), we get

$$sl_i^* = \frac{(\mu_i n + \tau_i n^2)ep_i - \sum_{j \in \mathcal{P} \setminus \{i\}} sl_j^*}{\mu_i + \tau_i n^2} . \quad (10)$$

If all controllers have the same numbers of trusted/untrusted accessors in conflicting segments, i.e. $\mu_i = \mu$ and $\tau_i = \tau$ where $\forall i \in \mathcal{P}$, an explicit expression can be calculated for the unique NE. Through simple algebraic manipulations, we get

$$(1 + \frac{1}{\mu + \tau n^2})sl_i^* = \frac{(\mu n + \tau n^2)ep_i - \sum_{j \in \mathcal{P}} sl_j^*}{\mu + \tau n^2} . \quad (11)$$

and

$$\sum_{j \in \mathcal{P}} sl_j^* = \frac{\mu n + \tau n^2}{\mu + \tau n^2 + n - 1} \sum_{j \in \mathcal{P}} ep_j . \quad (12)$$

Then, the unique NE of the game is gotten as

$$sl_i^{ne} = \frac{(\mu n + \tau n^2)(ep_i - \frac{1}{\mu + \tau n^2 + n - 1} \sum_{j \in \mathcal{P}} ep_j)}{\mu + \tau n^2 - 1} . \quad (13)$$

Even though the controllers have different numbers of trusted/untrusted accessors in conflicting segments, we can still get the unique NE. The best response functions of the controllers can be expressed at the sl^* in matrix form

$$sl^* = A sl^* + B, \quad (14)$$

where $B = (b_1, b_2, ..., b_n)$ and $b_i = \frac{(\mu_i n + \tau_i n^2)ep_i}{\mu_i + \tau_i n^2}$, and

$$A = \begin{pmatrix} 0 & -\frac{1}{\mu_1 + \tau_1 n^2} & \cdots & -\frac{1}{\mu_1 + \tau_1 n^2} \\ -\frac{1}{\mu_2 + \tau_2 n^2} & 0 & \cdots & -\frac{1}{\mu_2 + \tau_2 n^2} \\ \vdots & \vdots & \ddots & \vdots \\ -\frac{1}{\mu_n + \tau_n n^2} & -\frac{1}{\mu_n + \tau_n n^2} & \cdots & 0 \end{pmatrix}$$

Thus, the NE is

$$sl^* = (I - A)^{-1}B, \quad (15)$$

where I is the identity matrix and $(.)^{-1}$ indicates the matrix inverse.

3.4 Converging to Nash Equilibrium

In the multiparty control game, the controllers interact with each other and adjust their privacy settings, unless the system is at the Nash equilibrium. They usually cannot reach a stable status in a single round. We model controller dynamics with interactive adjustment algorithms.

Synchronous Adjustment: In synchronous adjustment (SA), controllers adjust their privacy settings simultaneously at a time step $t = 1, 2, ..., n$ in terms of their own best response functions derived from (10):

$$sl_i(t+1) = \begin{cases} \frac{(\tau_i n + \mu_i n^2)ep_i - (\overline{sl} - sl_i(t))}{\tau_i + \mu_i n^2}, & \text{if } ep_i > \frac{\overline{sl}}{n}; \\ sl_i(t), & \text{if } ep_i = \frac{\overline{sl}}{n}; \quad (16) \\ \frac{(\mu_i n + \tau_i n^2)ep_i - (\overline{sl} - sl_i(t))}{\mu_i + \tau_i n^2}, & \text{if } ep_i < \frac{\overline{sl}}{n}. \end{cases}$$

where $\overline{sl} = \sum_{j \in \mathcal{P}} sl_j$.

From (16), we can notice that if a controller's privacy expectation (ep_i) is higher than the current privacy-sharing tradeoff ($\frac{\overline{sl}}{n}$), the controller strengthens her/his privacy setting (sl_i). If a controller's privacy expectation is lower than the current privacy-sharing tradeoff, the controller weakens her/his privacy setting. Otherwise, the controller keeps her/his privacy setting. Algorithm 1 shows the pseudocode of SA algorithm.

Algorithm 1: Synchronous Adjustment (SA)

  Input: Initial sensitivity level $sl(0)$, convergence threshold ψ.
  Output: NE of the game.
1 /* Initialize time step, t, and privacy expectation, ep */
2 $t \leftarrow 0$;
3 **foreach** $i \in \mathcal{P}$ **do**
4     $\lfloor \ ep_i \leftarrow sl_i(0)$;
5 /* Find the stable state */
6 **repeat**
7     $\overline{sl}(t) \leftarrow \sum_{i \in \mathcal{P}} sl_i$
8   **foreach** $i \in \mathcal{P}$ **do**
9   **if** *controller i adjusts* **then**
10   **if** $ep_i \geq \frac{\overline{sl}(t)}{n}$ **then**
11             $\lfloor \ sl_i(t+1) = \frac{(\tau_i n + \mu_i n^2)ep_i - (\overline{sl}(t) - sl_i(t))}{\tau_i + \mu_i n^2}$.
12   **else**
13             $\lfloor \ sl_i(t+1) = \frac{(\mu_i n + \tau_i n^2)ep_i - (\overline{sl}(t) - sl_i(t))}{\mu_i + \tau_i n^2}$.
14   **else**
15           $\lfloor \ sl_i(t+1) = sl_i(t)$.
16     $t \leftarrow t+1$;
17 **until** *There is no controller satisfying the condition*: $|sl(t) - sl(t-1)| > \psi$;

---

non-synchronous Adjustment: In practice, it is hard to require all controllers to update their privacy settings simultaneously. Therefore, a more realistic solution is to design a non-synchronous adjustment (NA) algorithm for practical collaborative sharing scenarios. In non-synchronous adjustment, we consider that controllers adjust their privacy settings one by one at one time step. The NA algorithm for the controller i is formally defined with the same function as (16), but $\overline{sl}$ is defined as

$$\overline{sl} = \sum_{j<i} sl_j(t+1) + \sum_{j\geq i} sl_j(t). \qquad (17)$$

The pseudocode of NA algorithm is shown in Algorithm 2.

4. EVALUATION

In this section, we present our evaluation results for our multiparty control game including both experimental analysis and user studies.

4.1 Experimental Analysis

To explore the convergence to the Nash equilibrium of our multiparty control game, we implemented and analyzed two interactive adjustment algorithms discussed above in a simulation system. We also presented a numerical analysis of the multiparty control game based on three different situations with respect to the number of untrusted accessors (μ) and the number of trusted accessors (τ) in the conflicting segments.

4.1.1 Convergence Analysis

To view the process of system convergence, we ran the simulation on a 10-controller environment with initial sensitivity levels ranging from 0.1 to 1 in increments of 0.1, and considered all

---

Algorithm 2: non-synchronous Adjustment (NA)

  Input: Initial sensitivity level $sl(0)$, convergence threshold ψ.
  Output: NE of the game.
1 /* Initialize time step, t, and privacy expectation, ep */
2 $t \leftarrow 0$;
3 **foreach** $i \in \mathcal{P}$ **do**
4     $\lfloor \ ep_i \leftarrow sl_i(0)$;
5 /* Find the stable state */
6 **repeat**
7   **foreach** $i = 1$ *to* n **do**
8         $\overline{sl} = \sum_{j<i} sl_j(t+1) + \sum_{j \geq i} sl_j(t)$
9   **if** $ep_i \neq \frac{\overline{sl}(t)}{n}$ **then**
10   **if** $ep_i \geq \frac{\overline{sl}(t)}{n}$ **then**
11             $\lfloor \ sl_i(t+1) = \frac{(\tau_i n + \mu_i n^2)ep_i - (\overline{sl}(t) - sl_j(t))}{\tau_i + \mu_i n^2}$.
12   **else**
13             $\lfloor \ sl_i(t+1) = \frac{(\mu_i n + \tau_i n^2)ep_i - (\overline{sl}(t) - sl_j(t))}{\mu_i + \tau_i n^2}$.
14   **else**
15           $\lfloor \ sl_i(t+1) = sl_i(t)$.
16     $t \leftarrow t+1$;
17 **until** *There is no controller satisfying the condition*: $|sl(t) - sl(t-1)| > \psi$;

---

controllers have 20 untrusted accessors ($\mu = 20$) and 20 trusted accessors ($\tau = 20$).

For a synchronous scenario (each controller adjusts the sensitively level simultaneously), the interactive adjustment of sensitivity levels is depicted in Figure 2(a). We can observe that the speed of convergence to Nash equilibrium values is very fast (within 5 steps) in this scenario.

Regarding a non-synchronous scenario, a similar result occurs as shown in Figure 2(b). However, the convergence takes more steps (approximately 20 steps), since only one controller can update the sensitively level per step in such a scenario.

4.1.2 Numerical Analysis

For the numerical analysis of our multiparty control game, we only focused on the initial and final (Nash equilibrium) sensitivity levels of the controllers under three different conditions.

In the first scenario, we studied a condition in which controllers have untrusted accessors more than trusted accessors ($\mu > \tau$). In this case, a controller with an expected (initial) sensitivity level higher than the privacy-sharing tradeoff (the average sensitivity level) has a strong incentive to enlarge her/his sensitivity level for reducing her/his privacy risk. However, a controller with an expected sensitivity level lower than the privacy-sharing tradeoff is reluctant to deviate too much from her/his initial sensitivity level due to the small number of trusted accessors in conflicting segments. Setting all controllers with 30 untrusted accessors ($\mu = 30$) and 10 trusted accessors ($\tau = 10$), Figure 3(a) illustrates the initial and final sensitivity levels of all controllers.

The second scenario studies the case when all controllers have the same number of untrusted accessors and trusted accessors ($\mu = \tau$). In such a case, the controllers with higher and lower initial sensitivity levels have similar intentions to change their sensitivity levels. Figure 3(b) shows the results of numerical analysis regarding 20 untrusted accessors and 20 trusted accessors for each controller.

In case that all controllers have untrusted accessors fewer than trusted accessors in conflicting segments ($\mu < \tau$), a controller with an initial sensitivity level lower than the privacy-sharing tradeoff has a much stronger incentive to deviate from her/his initial sensitivity level for mitigating her/his sharing loss. Considering 10 un-

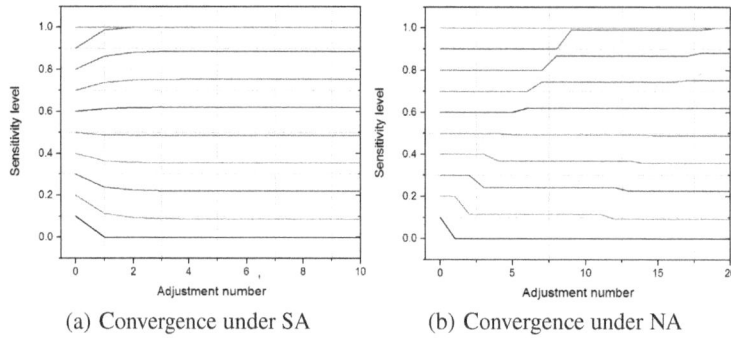

(a) Convergence under SA   (b) Convergence under NA

Figure 2: Convergence to NE

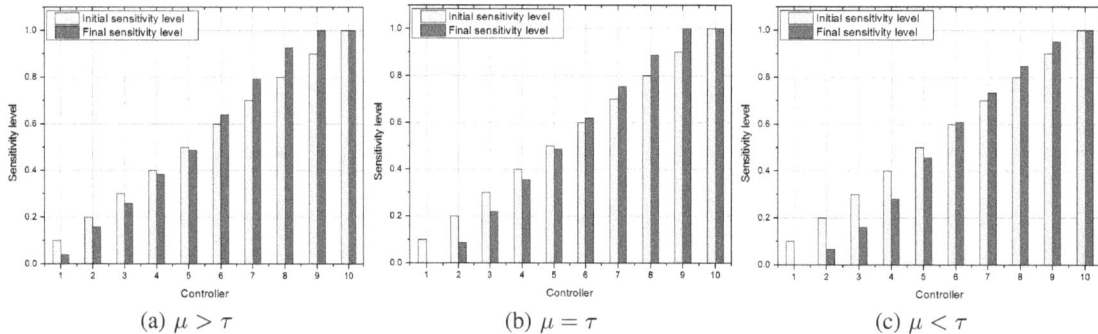

(a) $\mu > \tau$ (b) $\mu = \tau$ (c) $\mu < \tau$

Figure 3: Initial and Final Sensitivity Levels of Controllers in Numerical Analysis

trusted accessors and 30 trusted accessors for each controller, the results of numerical analysis are depicted in Figure 3(c).

4.2 User Study

We conducted user studies of the multiparty control game with respect to real human behaviors. The purpose of user studies is to verify if users behave as our game theoretical model expected. If there are some deviations of their behaviors from the model's predictions, we attempt to capture the factors that may cause such deviations.

4.2.1 User Study Design and Setup

We designed two different kinds of user studies, which are approved by our institute's IRB. One is a multiple-round game (MRG) where participants set their sensitivity levels of photos at each round and they are told the average sensitivity levels after all participants finished inputting values. Another is a single-round game (SRG) where participants are told how many friends (trusted accessors) and non-friends (untrusted accessors) can view their photos after they initiate their sensitivity level settings, and they are only provided one chance to change their sensitivity levels.

As part of the user studies, we first explained the motivation of our user studies to the participants, which is 'On Facebook or similar online social networks, a person who uploads a photo can tag other people and get control over who can see this photo. However, people tagged in the photo have no control over it. We are proposing a system that allows everyone tagged in a photo to collaboratively control the shared photo'. Therefore, they can better understand what is the purpose of our proposed system and behave more rationally. No matter which type of games they are in, the participants were asked to finish surveys before and after the games. The survey before a game asks some general questions about themselves and their experiences and feelings towards photo sharing and tagging in OSNs. The survey after a game asks why a participant makes certain choices in the game.

For both types of games, we did not use actual photos, because they may introduce privacy violations. Also, we did not leverage the real-world social network platforms, since it is hard to force all people in specific photos to take part in our games simultaneously. Instead, our current games use imaginary scenes by describing a photo to the participants and explaining them that this photo is shared through a social networking site and s/he is tagged in it. Since each participant's sensitivity levels, which are associated with their personalities and other factors, for different photos may be different, we designed several storylines of photos, for which we believe may enable participants to make different choices. The storyline of each photo describes: 1) who are in the photo; 2) where they are; and 3) what they are doing. The storylines are carefully designed so that each involved individual is to be equal in position. The complete storylines used in our games are listed in Table 1.

For the multiple-round games, in each round, each participant is asked to specify a sensitivity level of an imaginary photo based on our description of the photo content. In order to make the participants a more intuitive understanding of the concept of sensitivity level, they are allowed to choose a value between 0.1 and 1, where 0.1 denotes 'the photo is not sensitive to me at all and I want to share it with the public', 0.4 denotes 'the photo is kind of sensitive and I want to share it with my friends', 0.7 denotes 'the photo is very sensitive and I only share it with my close friends', 1 denotes 'the photo is extremely sensitive and I hope only tagged people can see it', and the other numbers denote more fine-grained levels accordingly. The participants are also told that, after everyone specifies her/his sensitivity level, the average of the imputed sensitivity levels is leveraged for making the final decision of photo sharing. Then, we compute the average of sensitivity levels, which is also a number between 0.1 and 1. The number is additionally rounded to the nearest tenth and its corresponding meaning is presented to the participants, where 0.1 denotes 'the photo will be public' and 1 denotes 'only tagged people can see this photo'. Each game con-

98

Table 1: Storylines of the Imaginary Photos

Number	Storyline
1	This is a photo about you and your colleagues working in the office
2	This is a photo about you and your classmates in the commencement
3	This is a photo about you and your family members in the commencement
4	This is a photo about you having drinks with your friends in a party
5	This is a photo about you having drinks with strangers in a bar

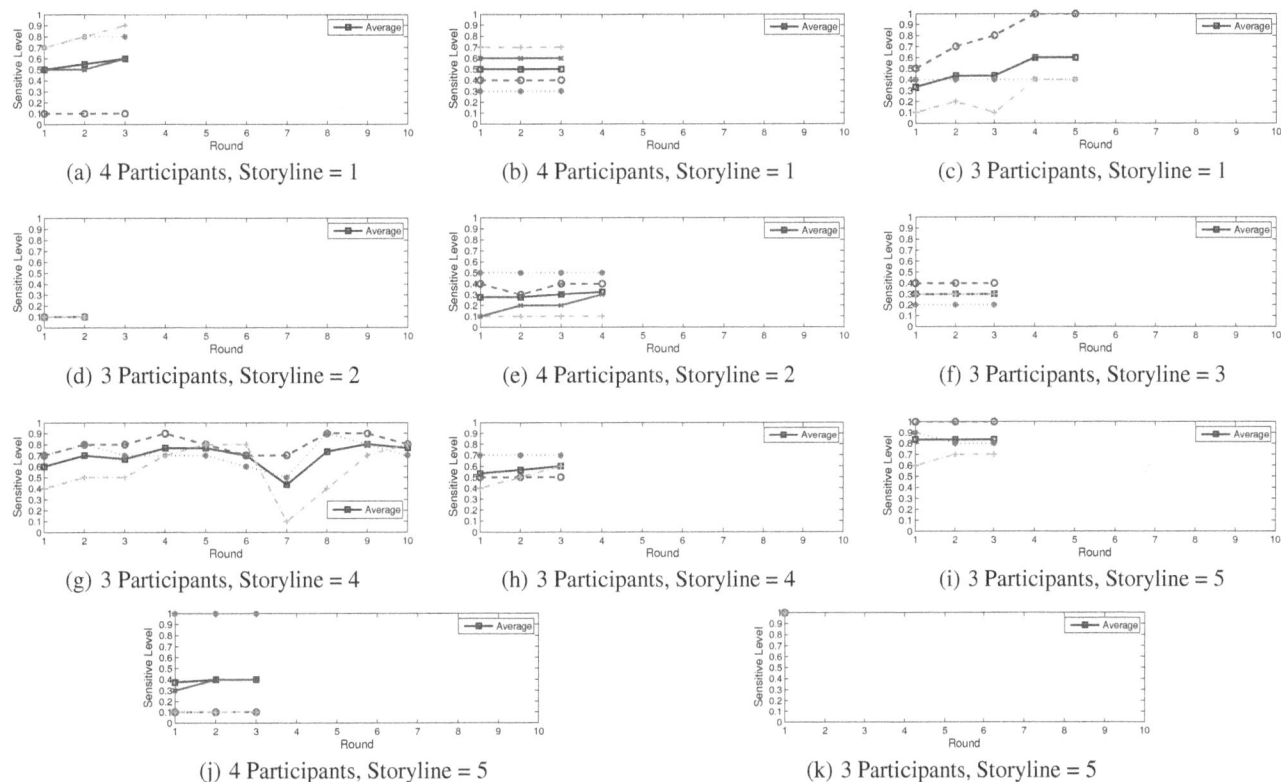

(a) 4 Participants, Storyline = 1   (b) 4 Participants, Storyline = 1   (c) 3 Participants, Storyline = 1

(d) 3 Participants, Storyline = 2   (e) 4 Participants, Storyline = 2   (f) 3 Participants, Storyline = 3

(g) 3 Participants, Storyline = 4   (h) 3 Participants, Storyline = 4   (i) 3 Participants, Storyline = 5

(j) 4 Participants, Storyline = 5   (k) 3 Participants, Storyline = 5

Figure 4: Multiple Round Game Results. Each game continues for at most 10 rounds or stops when an equilibrium has been reached.

tinues for at most 10 rounds or terminates when an equilibrium has been reached.

For the single-round games, we first describe a photo to all the participants as same as the multiple-round game and ask all the participants to set their sensitivity levels. After that, instead of giving them an average of sensitivity levels, they are told how many of their friends and non-friends can view the photo at that moment. We provide one of the three different scenarios, which are 1) 30 friends and 10 non-friends, 2) 20 friends and 20 non-friends, and 3) 10 friends and 30 non-friends, to the participants in each game. Then, each of them has one chance to change her/his sensitivity level of the photo. No further feedback is shown to the participants.

We invited 20 participants who are all students in our institution to take part in our user studies. We divided participants into several groups where all group members know each other in a social network. All games were played by participants in person and they were not allowed to interact with other participants directly. We played MRG 11 times and SRG 5 times, and obtained survey results from all participants. Even though we have conducted limited number of experiments and the participants in the games may share similar background, their tendencies could still provide us significant insights into users' decision making in our games.

4.2.2 User Study Results and Findings

We now present the user study results and our findings based on participants' choices and survey answers. The results of MRG and SRG are depicted in Figures 4 and 5, respectively.

Finding 1: **Users agree that everyone in a photo should have the right to decide who can view it.**

According to the participants' answers on 'Do you believe all the people in a photo that is posted in an online social network should give a say about who can view it?', 100% participants in our studies believe so and they are not satisfied with the current options for photo sharing and tagging in Facebook and Google+. A more detailed question revealed that 27% participants allow their friends to tag them without their approvals, another 55% participants allow friends to tag them but sometimes remove those tags, 9% participants only allow tagging with their approvals, and another 9% participants never allow friends to tag them.

Finding 2: **Games reach an equilibrium in a timely manner.**

As shown in Figure 4, 8 out of 11 multiple-round games reached an equilibrium in only three rounds in our experiments, which indicates that a game-based multiparty control approach as proposed in this paper could produce acceptable results for all participants in a timely manner. Even though users' choices may not always follow

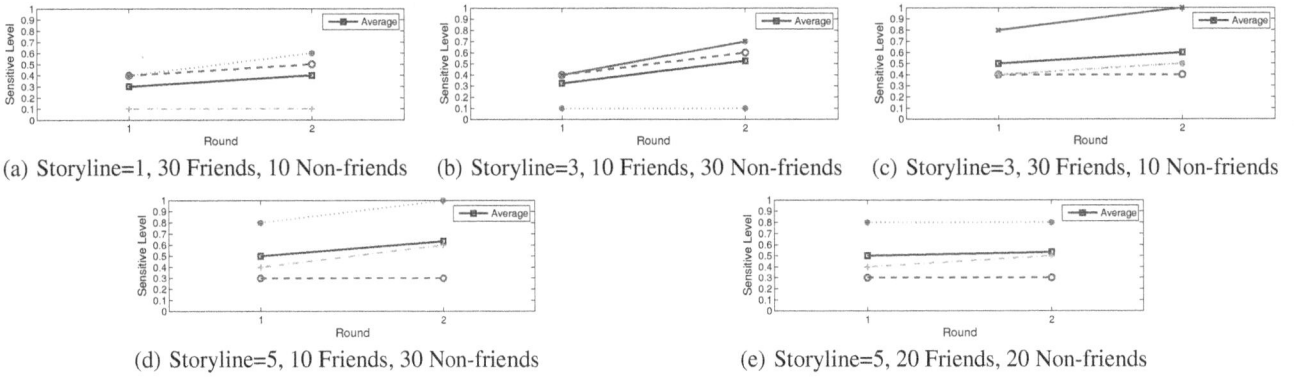

(a) Storyline=1, 30 Friends, 10 Non-friends (b) Storyline=3, 10 Friends, 30 Non-friends (c) Storyline=3, 30 Friends, 10 Non-friends

(d) Storyline=5, 10 Friends, 30 Non-friends (e) Storyline=5, 20 Friends, 20 Non-friends

Figure 5: Single Round Game Results. Participants have only one chance to change their sensitivity levels after the initial settings.

the best strategy in terms of our game theoretic analysis, we found that our game-based approach could help all the people in a photo to collaboratively control who can view the picture.

Finding 3: **A user' sensitivity level settings are highly related to the content of photos.**

When we asked if a user cares more about sharing with friends or forbidding non-friends to view a photo, 55% participants replied that it depends on the photo. Another 27% participants answered they care more about their privacy. We computed the average sensitivity levels for all users' inputs on each photo storyline. Storyline 2 received the lowest average sensitivity level that is 0.24. Most participants believe such a photo is not so sensitive and they agree to share it with some strangers. Storyline 4 got the highest average sensitive level which is 0.66. Most participants only want to share such a photo with their close friends.

Finding 4: **Users tend to change their sensitivity levels in order to make the averages closer to their expected sensitivity levels.**

According to the survey answers, 50% participants in our games claim that they have the experiences to change their sensitivity levels to make the averages closer to their own original sensitivity levels and attempt to maximize their own benefits. Such behaviors are consistent with what our game theoretic model predicts. We computed the number of such changing behaviors in our collected data. If the multiplication of a user's current sensitivity level setting minus her/his last round setting and the average of last round minus his/her current setting is negative, denoted as $(sl_{now} - sl_{last}) \times (average_{last} - sl_{now}) < 0$, we say this change is towards her/his own sensitivity level instead of the average. In our collected data, 18.6% sensitivity level changes belong to this category, which is an evidence that users' behaviors do follow our game theoretic patterns in some cases.

Finding 5: **Sometimes users may not adopt the best strategies when making decisions.**

To measure whether a sensitive level change is towards the average of last round or other directions, we used the criteria that the multiplication of a user's current sensitivity level setting minus her/his last round setting and the average of last round minus her/his current setting is positive, denoted as $(sl_{now} - sl_{last}) \times (average_{last} - sl_{now}) > 0$, to indicate such cases. It turns out 28.3% sensitivity level changes fall into this category. Based on the survey answers and in-person discussions with the participants, we observed several reasons behind such human behaviors:

- *Reason 1: Users may not always maximize their own benefits without respecting others' benefits.* Some participants indicated that the average sensitivity levels received from the

last round made them reconsider their own choices. And they were willing to change their sensitivity levels towards the last averages, because such behaviors show their respects to their peers.

- *Reason 2: Users seem to be honest and use our system more for the negotiation than the manipulation.* Our game theoretic model suspects that users may choose more extreme sensitivity values to make the averages closer to their expectations. In those cases, the sensitivity values chosen by users may not reflect their true sensitivity levels of the shared photos. Even though, as discussed in Find 3, such behaviors did exist and 50% participants did admit they had such experiences in the games, we found the participants were unwilling to manipulate the system by deviating from their expected sensitivity levels. Two evidences support such a conclusion based on our survey: 1) 60.0% participants said their sensitivity value settings always reflect their true sensitivity values; and 2) 53.2% sensitivity value settings are consistent with the previous setting values, which indicates participants would rather stick to what they have initially chosen.

- *Reason 3: Users care more about others' privacy protection than their own data sharing.* In most cases, users who chose low sensitivity values tended to increase their sensitivity levels to reach agreements with others. Participants showed strong tendencies with this pattern, because they believed respecting others' privacy concerns is more important than maintaining their own sharing intentions. In our collected data, 85% average sensitive levels are increased from the last rounds.

In summary, our user studies showed that our game theoretic model could capture many features of the human decision making process in multiparty access control systems. However, the proposed model still needs to be refined. Especially, we should consider more fine-grained quantification of utility gain and loss in our model with respect to some other aspects, such as peers' privacy concerns, for more accurate analysis of user behaviors in multiparty access control.

5. RELATED WORK

Several access control schemes for OSNs have been introduced (e.g., [10, 11, 16, 17, 24]). Carminati et al. [10] introduced a rust-based access control model, which allows the specification of access rules for online resources, where authorized users are denoted in terms of the relationship type, depth, and trust level between users in OSNs. They also introduced a semi-decentralized discretionary access control model and a related enforcement mechanism for controlled sharing of information in OSNs [11], and proposed a semantic web based access control framework for social networks. Fong et al. [17] presented an access control model that formalizes and generalizes the access control mechanism implemented in Facebook, admitting arbitrary policy vocabularies that are based on theoretical graph properties. Carrie [12] claimed relationship-based access control as one of new security paradigms that addresses unique requirements of Web 2.0. Then, Fong [16] formulated this paradigm called a Relationship-Based Access Control (ReBAC) model that bases authorization decisions on the relationships between the resource owner and the resource accessor in an OSN. However, none of these work could accommodate privacy control requirements with respect to the *collaborative* data sharing in OSNs.

The need of collaborative management for data sharing, especially photo sharing, in OSNs has been addressed by some recent research [8, 20, 25, 34, 36]. Also, game theory as a rich set of mathematical tools has been used to model and analyze the interactions of agents in security and privacy problems [5, 6, 13, 18, 19, 29, 32, 33]. Alpcan et al. [6] introduced a game theoretic model to study the evolution of trust for digital identity in online communities. Chen et al. [13] presented a weighted evolutionary game-theoretic model to study the behavior of users in OSNs regarding how they choose their privacy settings. In particular, Squicciarini et al. [34] proposed a solution for collective privacy management for photo sharing in OSNs that adopted Clarke-Tax mechanism [14] to enable the collective enforcement of privacy preferences and game theory to evaluate the scheme. However, the auction process adopted in their approach indicates only the winning bids could finally determine who was able to access the data, instead of accommodating all stakeholders' privacy preferences. In contrast, we propose a simple but flexible mechanism for collaborative management of shared data in OSNs. And game theory is leveraged in this paper to model and analyze the strategic interaction of users in multiparty access control.

Measuring privacy risk in OSNs has been recently addressed by several work [7, 26, 35]. Becker et al. [7] presented *PrivAware*, a tool to detect and report unintended information loss through quantifying privacy risk associated with friend relationship in OSNs. Talukder et al. [35] discussed a privacy protection tool, called *Privometer*, which can measure the risk of potential privacy leakage caused by malicious applications installed in the user's friend profiles and suggest self-sanitization actions to lessen this leakage accordingly. Liu et al. [26] proposed a framework to compute the privacy score of a user, indicating the user's potential risk caused by her/his participation in OSNs. Their solution also focused on the privacy settings of users with respect to their profile items. Compared with those work, the multiparty access control can help measure the privacy risk caused by different privacy concerns from multiple users.

6. DISCUSSION AND FUTURE WORK

As we have discussed before, our game theoretic model should be enhanced to consider more fine-grained quantification of utility gain and loss for accurate analysis of user behaviors. In addition, the current utility function in our model only captures the privacy setting adjustment through changing the sensitivity level of shared data item, and the utility gain and loss with respect to trusted and untrusted accessors of each controller. Further development of our game theoretic model will be investigated to better reflect reality and capture more sophisticated factors, such as accessor space changes for adjusting privacy settings, controllers' general privacy concerns, and trust levels of accessors, which may also significantly influence user behaviors in multiparty access control. Besides, we

will study other alternative game theoretic approaches [29] for formulating our game model.

We will also conduct more extensive user studies of the multiparty control game to analyze the strategic interactions of users in *real-world* social network platforms, considering a variety of factors, such as the numbers of trusted/untrusted accessors in conflicting segments, different trust levels of accessors and controllers, and different relationships among controllers. Those experimental studies can additionally articulate the *gap* between game theoretic approaches and real human behaviors [9], and potentially help us capture some missing aspects of our game-theoretic model.

Another issue for multiparty privacy control is that a group of users could *collude* with one another so as to manipulate the final decision. Consider an attack scenario, where a set of malicious users may want to make a shared photo available to a wider audience. They could collude with each other to assign a very low sensitivity level for the photo and specify policies to grant a wider audience to access the photo. We will also investigate a game theoretic mechanism to tackle collusion activities in multiparty privacy control in OSNs with the consideration of the proposed approaches in the recent work [23, 30, 38].

7. CONCLUSION

In this paper, we investigated the problem of analyzing the strategic behavior of rational controllers in multiparty access control, where each controller aims to maximize her/his own benefit by adjusting her/his privacy setting in collaborative data sharing in OSNs. We formulated such a problem as a multiparty control game and proved the existence of unique NE of this game. In addition, we introduced interactive update algorithms to compute the NE. Moreover, a numerical analysis was provided for several scenarios that illustrate the interplay of controllers in multiparty access control in OSNs. We further carried out user studies of the multiparty control game to examine the gap between game theoretic approaches and real human behaviors. We believe our game theoretic analysis and additional insights gained from this study would help identify important implications in designing the enhanced multiparty access control systems in OSNs.

Acknowledgments

The work of H. Hu, G.-J. Ahn and Z. Zhao was partially supported by the grants from National Science Foundation (NSF-IIS-0900970 and NSF-CNS-0831360) and Department of Energy (DE-SC0004308).

8. REFERENCES

[1] Facebook Privacy Policy. http://www.facebook.com/policy.php/.

[2] Facebook Statistics. http://www.statisticbrain.com/facebook-statistics/.

[3] Google+ Privacy Policy. http://http://www.google.com/intl/en/+/policy/.

[4] The State of Social Media 2011: Social is the new normal, 2011. http://www.briansolis.com/2011/10/state-of-social-media-2011/.

[5] T. Alpcan and T. Başar. *Network security: A decision and game-theoretic approach.* Cambridge University Press, 2010.

[6] T. Alpcan, C. Örencik, A. Levi, and E. Savaş. A game theoretic model for digital identity and trust in online communities. In *Proceedings of the 5th ACM Symposium on Information, Computer and Communications Security*, pages 341–344. ACM, 2010.

[7] J. Becker and H. Chen. Measuring privacy risk in online social networks. In *Proceedings of the 2009 Workshop on Web*, volume 2. Citeseer.

[8] A. Besmer and H. Richter Lipford. Moving beyond untagging: Photo privacy in a tagged world. In *Proceedings of the 28th international conference on Human factors in computing systems*, pages 1563–1572. ACM, 2010.

[9] C. Camerer. *Behavioral game theory: Experiments in strategic interaction*. Princeton University Press, 2003.

[10] B. Carminati, E. Ferrari, and A. Perego. Rule-based access control for social networks. In *On the Move to Meaningful Internet Systems 2006: OTM 2006 Workshops*, pages 1734–1744. Springer, 2006.

[11] B. Carminati, E. Ferrari, and A. Perego. Enforcing access control in web-based social networks. *ACM Transactions on Information and System Security (TISSEC)*, 13(1):1–38, 2009.

[12] E. Carrie. Access Control Requirements for Web 2.0 Security and Privacy. In *Proc. of Workshop on Web 2.0 Security & Privacy (W2SP)*. Citeseer, 2007.

[13] J. Chen, M. R. Brust, A. R. Kiremire, and V. V. Phoha. Modeling privacy settings of an online social network from a game-theoretical perspective. In *Collaborative Computing: Networking, Applications and Worksharing (Collaboratecom), 2013 9th International Conference Conference on*, pages 213–220. IEEE, 2013.

[14] E. Clarke. Multipart pricing of public goods. *Public choice*, 11(1):17–33, 1971.

[15] C. B. et al. The power of social networking in medicine. *Nature biotechnology*, 27(10):888–890, 2009.

[16] P. Fong. Relationship-Based Access Control: Protection Model and Policy Language. In *Proceedings of the First ACM Conference on Data and Application Security and Privacy*. ACM, 2011.

[17] P. Fong, M. Anwar, and Z. Zhao. A privacy preservation model for facebook-style social network systems. In *Proceedings of the 14th European conference on Research in computer security*, pages 303–320. Springer-Verlag, 2009.

[18] J. Freudiger, M. H. Manshaei, J.-P. Hubaux, and D. C. Parkes. On non-cooperative location privacy: a game-theoretic analysis. In *Proceedings of the 16th ACM conference on Computer and communications security*, pages 324–337. ACM, 2009.

[19] J. Grosslags, N. Christin, and J. Chuang. Secure or insure?: a game-theoretic analysis of information security games. In *Proceedings of the 17th international conference on World Wide Web*, pages 209–218. ACM, 2008.

[20] H. Hu and G. Ahn. Multiparty authorization framework for data sharing in online social networks. In *Proceedings of the 25th annual IFIP WG 11.3 conference on Data and applications security and privacy*, DBSec'11, pages 29–43. Springer, 2011.

[21] H. Hu, G. Ahn, and J. Jorgensen. Detecting and resolving privacy conflicts for collaborative data sharing in online social networks. In *Proceedings of the 27th Annual Computer Security Applications Conference*, ACSAC'11, pages 103–112. ACM, 2011.

[22] H. Hu, G. Ahn, and J. Jorgensen. Multiparty access control for online social networks: model and mechanisms. *IEEE Transactions on Knowledge and Data Engineering*, 15(7):1614–1627, 2013.

[23] H. Kargupta, K. Das, and K. Liu. Multi-party, privacy-preserving distributed data mining using a game theoretic framework. *Knowledge Discovery in Databases: PKDD 2007*, pages 523–531, 2007.

[24] S. Kruk, S. Grzonkowski, A. Gzella, T. Woroniecki, and H. Choi. D-FOAF: Distributed identity management with access rights delegation. *The Semantic Web–ASWC 2006*, pages 140–154, 2006.

[25] A. Lampinen, V. Lehtinen, A. Lehmuskallio, and S. Tamminen. We're in it together: interpersonal management of disclosure in social network services. In *Proceedings of the 2011 annual conference on Human factors in computing systems*, pages 3217–3226. ACM, 2011.

[26] K. Liu and E. Terzi. A framework for computing the privacy scores of users in online social networks. *ACM Transactions on Knowledge Discovery from Data (TKDD)*, 5(1):6, 2010.

[27] T. Lohman. Federal government embracing gov 2.0. *Computerworld*, 2011.

[28] M. Madejski, M. Johnson, and S. Bellovin. The Failure of Online Social Network Privacy Settings. Technical Report CUCS-010-11, Columbia University, NY, USA. 2011.

[29] M. Manshaei, Q. Zhu, T. Alpcan, T. Basar, and J. Hubaux. Game theory meets network security and privacy. *ACM Computing Survey*, 45(3), 2013.

[30] D. Niyato and E. Hossain. Competitive pricing for spectrum sharing in cognitive radio networks: Dynamic game, inefficiency of nash equilibrium, and collusion. *Selected Areas in Communications, IEEE Journal on*, 26(1):192–202, 2008.

[31] M. Osborne. *An introduction to game theory*, volume 3. Oxford University Press New York, NY, 2004.

[32] A. C. Squicciarini and C. Griffin. An informed model of personal information release in social networking sites. In *Privacy, Security, Risk and Trust (PASSAT), 2012 International Conference on and 2012 International Confernece on Social Computing (SocialCom)*, pages 636–645. IEEE, 2012.

[33] A. C. Squicciarini, C. Griffin, and S. Sundareswaran. Towards a game theoretical model for identity validation in social network sites. In *Privacy, security, risk and trust (PASSAT), 2011 ieee third international conference on and 2011 ieee third international conference on social computing (SocialCom)*, pages 1081–1088. IEEE, 2011.

[34] A. C. Squicciarini, M. Shehab, and F. Paci. Collective privacy management in social networks. In *Proceedings of the 18th international conference on World wide web*, pages 521–530. ACM, 2009.

[35] N. Talukder, M. Ouzzani, A. Elmagarmid, H. Elmeleegy, and M. Yakout. Privometer: Privacy protection in social networks. In *Proceedings of 26th International Conference on Data Engineering Workshops (ICDEW)*, pages 266–269. IEEE, 2010.

[36] K. Thomas, C. Grier, and D. Nicol. unFriendly: Multi-party Privacy Risks in Social Networks. In *Privacy Enhancing Technologies*, pages 236–252. Springer, 2010.

[37] S. Weglage. How it professionals are using social media. *IT World*, 2010.

[38] Y. Wu, B. Wang, K. Liu, and T. Clancy. A scalable collusion-resistant multi-winner cognitive spectrum auction game. *Communications, IEEE Transactions on*, 57(12):3805–3816, 2009.

102

Scalable and Precise Automated Analysis of Administrative Temporal Role-Based Access Control

Silvio Ranise
Security & Trust, FBK-Irst,
Trento, Italia
ranise@fbk.eu

Anh Truong
Security & Trust, FBK-Irst,
Trento, Italia
DISI, U. of Trento, Italia
tatruong@fbk.eu

Alessandro Armando
Security &Trust, FBK-Irst,
Trento, Italia
DIBRIS, U. of Genova, Italia
armando@fbk.eu

ABSTRACT

Extensions of Role-Based Access Control (RBAC) policies taking into account contextual information (such as time and space) are increasingly being adopted in real-world applications. Their administration is complex since they must satisfy rapidly evolving needs. For this reason, automated techniques to identify unsafe sequences of administrative actions (i.e. actions generating policies by which a user can acquire permissions that may compromise some security goals) are fundamental tools in the administrator's tool-kit.

In this paper, we propose a precise and scalable automated analysis technique for the safety of administrative temporal RBAC policies. Our approach is to translate safety problems for this kind of policy to (decidable) reachability problems of a certain class of symbolic transition systems. The correctness of the translation allows us to design a precise analysis technique for the safety of administrative RBAC policies with a finite but unknown number of users. For scalability, we present a heuristics that allows us to reduce the set of administrative actions without losing the precision of the analysis. An extensive experimental analysis confirms the scalability and precision of the approach also in comparison with a recent analysis technique developed for the same class of temporal RBAC policies.

Categories and Subject Descriptors

D.2 [**Software Engineering**]: Software/Program Verification

Keywords

Administrative Access Control; Temporal Role-Based Access Control; Automated Safety Analysis

1. INTRODUCTION

Today, the administration of access control policies is key to the security of many IT systems that need to evolve in rapidly changing environments and dynamically finding the

best trade-off among a variety of needs. Permissions to perform administrative actions must be restricted since security officers can only be partially trusted. In fact, some of them may collude to, inadvertently or maliciously, modify the policies so that untrusted users can get sensitive permissions. Taking into consideration the effect of all possible sequences of administrative actions is a difficult task. Thus, push-button analysis techniques are needed to identify *safety* issues, i.e. administrative actions generating policies by which a user can acquire permissions that may compromise some security goals. This is known as the *safety problem*, which amounts to establish whether there exists a (finite) sequence of administrative actions, selected from a set of available ones, that applied to a given initial policy, yield a policy in which a user gets a certain permission. Several important policy analysis problems can be reduced to safety problems, e.g., deciding if the set of users having a given permission is a sub-set of that having another permission (containment), computing the minimal sets of permissions that a user should have so as to make another policy reachable by means of a finite sequence of administrative actions (weakest preconditions), and others (see, e.g., [9]). This makes automated techniques capable of solving safety problems even more valuable to understand the subtle interplay among the actions performed by several administrators.

In general, the safety problem is undecidable [12]. A first step towards the development of automated techniques is to identify classes of policies for which the safety problem is decidable. Several such techniques have been proposed for administrative models of Role-Based Access Control (RBAC) policies [22]. This is so because RBAC is one of the most widely adopted access control models in the real world. The reason for this is the fact that the notion of role allows for simplifying policy management by decomposing user-permission assignment into user-role and role-permission assignments. For example, a new employee joining an organization is assigned to a role and this is sufficient for him/her to automatically acquire all the permissions associated to that role. Similarly, when someone is promoted or demoted, it is sufficient to update the roles with which he/she is associated to make available the permissions required by the new position. The role-permission assignment rarely changes since this implies a change in the organization. These observations lead researchers to study safety problems for administrative RBAC (ARBAC) models—the most important one is the URA97 model [21]—in which administrative actions can only update the user-role assignment relation (see, e.g., [15, 24, 13, 5, 9]).

103

Available analysis techniques for RBAC are not readily applicable to extensions of RBAC in which authorizations depend also on contextual information, such as time, that are widely used in real-world applications. For instance, two temporal extensions of RBAC are reported in [7, 14]. These models impose temporal constraints on roles being enabled or for them to be assigned to users. In these models, the executability of administrative actions is also restricted by temporal constraints. To the best of our knowledge, only two works [16, 26] have proposed techniques for the automatic analysis of safety problems for Administrative Temporal RBAC (ATRBAC) models. In [16], the safety problem for ATRBAC policies is reduced to verification problems of timed automata [2], whose solution is supported by the model checker UPPAAL.[1] The approach supports the verification of a variety of properties, not only those for safety, but has the drawback of assuming a fixed set of users; every time the set of users changes, the analysis must be re-run. Additionally, the size of the state space to be explored by the model checker grows exponentially in the number of users, making the technique difficult to scale. The approach proposed in [26] amounts to decomposing safety of ATRBAC policies into reachability problems for policies that can be expressed in a model that is (close to) URA97. In this way, existing tools (such as RBAC-PAT [11] or VAC [9]) for the safety of URA97 administrative policies can be re-used. One of the main advantages of [26] is the possibility to leverage recent advances in the analysis of ARBAC policies. The main disadvantage is the state-space explosion since several safety problems for URA97 must be solved and the complexity of many restricted versions of this problem is known to be NP-hard [23]. To cope with this problem, [26] identifies situations under which the generated safety problems for ARBAC policies can be simplified, either by reducing the number of administrative actions or by simplifying their applicability conditions. For example, separate administration is assumed whereby the set of administrative roles are separate from that of regular roles, an administrative action can only be executed by a user with an administrative role and can modify the membership of regular roles only. Such an assumption is known to be unrealistic in many real-world scenarios (see e.g., [24] for a discussion of this and related issues), thereby making the results of the analysis less useful. On the other hand, available implementations of safety analysis techniques for temporal RBAC (TRBAC) policies are dramatically confronted with the state-space explosion problem and performing simplifying assumptions, even at the price of a loss of precision, is somehow necessary for the analysis to scale up.

In this paper, we present an automated technique for solving safety problems for ATRBAC policies that goes beyond the limitations of available approaches by reusing the symbolic model checking technique in [19]. Preliminarily (Section 2), we discuss and formalize a temporal RBAC model, the administrative actions, and the safety problem along the lines of [26]. We also briefly overview (Section 3) the symbolic model checking technique in [19] that uses a class of first-order formulae, called Bernays-Shönfinkel-Ramsey (BSR) [18], to represent transition systems and compute the fix-point of the set of (backward) reachable states by Satisfiability Modulo Theories (SMT) solvers (see, e.g., [6]).

Our **first contribution** (Section 4) is a translation from safety problems for ATRBAC policies to reachability problems of BSR transition systems. By re-using the decidability result in [19] for BSR-transition systems and arguing the correctness of the translation, we are able to state the first—to the best of our knowledge—decidability result for the safety of ATRBAC policies (Theorem 2). The result paves the way to a *precise* automated analysis technique since it assumes neither separate administration nor any other simplifying (unrealistic) assumption. In fact, we solve the safety problem considering a finite but unknown number of users in the TRBAC policies manipulated by the administrative actions. In other words, our technique for safety analysis is capable of certifying safety by taking into account that users may join or leave the organization in which the TRBAC policies are administered since the certificate holds for any (finite) number of users. Similarly, it can discover the number of users required for a certain sequence of administrative actions to turn the initial policy into one violating a security goal. This dramatically enlarges the scope of applicability of the analysis and thus the usefulness of its results.

Although desirable, precision hinders performances. Suitable heuristics must be devised in order to make the analysis scalable. Our **second contribution** is a heuristics designed as a pre-processing phase to the computation of the set of (backward) reachable states aiming at reducing the number of administrative actions that must be taken into account (Section 5). The heuristics identifies *useful* actions by transitively propagating dependencies on the roles that are mentioned in a security goal. The check to establish the usefulness of an action is computationally cheap but does not guarantee that an action considered useful will be retained when computing the set of backward reachable states. However, if an action is not useful, it is guaranteed not to contribute to the computation of the set of backward reachable states and can thus be discarded without degrading the precision of the analysis. The **third contribution** of the paper is an extensive experimental evaluation (Section 5) confirming that our technique is *scalable*. We also perform a comparison with the implementation of the approach in [26] showing how our approach is both more precise and scalable. In particular, the experiments confirm the crucial role played by the heuristics for identifying useful actions to alleviate the state-space explosion problem.

2. TEMPORAL RBAC POLICIES AND ADMINISTRATION

The idea underlying RBAC [22] is to regulate access by assigning users to roles which, in turn, are granted permissions to perform certain operations. Formally, we assume a (finite) set U of users, a (finite) set R of roles, a (finite) set P of permissions, a user-role assignment relation $UA \subseteq U \times R$, and a permission-role assignment relation $PA \subseteq P \times R$. For simplicity, we ignore the role hierarchy (i.e. a partial order on R). A user u is a member of role r when $(u, r) \in UA$. A user u has permission p if there exists a role $r \in R$ such that $(p, r) \in PA$ and u is a member of r. A *RBAC policy* is a tuple (U, R, P, UA, PA).

In many scenarios, authorization conditions depend on contextual information such as the time of the day. For instance, a part time employee of an enterprise should be authorized to access the IT system only during working hours,

---

[1]http://www.uppaal.org

e.g., between 8am to 12pm. Before being able to specify authorization conditions that depend on temporal constraints, we need to introduce a model of time. As observed in [26], a simple model is sufficient for expressing time-dependent authorization conditions. In fact, temporal constraints are usually specified by means of intervals periodically repeating time intervals, such as day/night-time (two intervals repeating daily), each hour (twenty-four intervals again repeating daily), or each day (seven intervals repeating weekly).

A model of time. Let T_{MAX} be a positive integer and a a non-negative integer such that $a + 1 \leq T_{MAX}$. A *time slot* is a pair $(a, a + 1)$; to ease the readability of the examples in the following of the paper, we will use, e.g., *(8am, 4pm)*, *(4pm, 12am)*, and *(12am, 8am)* to denote time slots $(0, 1)$, $(1, 2)$, and $(2, 3)$, respectively. The set of all time slots is $TS_{T_{MAX}} = \{(a, a + 1) \mid 0 \leq a < T_{MAX}\}$. We will often write TS in place of $TS_{T_{MAX}}$. A *time instant* is a non-negative real number. A time instant t *belongs to a time slot* $(a, a + 1)$ iff $a \leq (t \bmod T_{MAX}) < a + 1$ where mod is the usual modulo operator, i.e. $t' = t \bmod T_{MAX}$ iff there exists a non-negative integer k such that $t = t' + k \cdot T_{MAX}$.

We are now ready to formalize a simplified version of the Temporal RBAC model along the lines of [26]. The idea is to make RBAC policies depend on periodic constraints based on the notion of time introduced above.

Temporal RBAC. From now on, we assume that T_{MAX} is given so that the set TS of all time slots is fixed. TRBAC extends RBAC by adding the *role status* relation $RS \subseteq R \times TS$ and replacing the user-role assignment UA with the *temporal user-role assignment* relation $TUA \subseteq U \times R \times TS$. For the sake of simplicity, following [26], we neglect role hierarchies.

A role r *is enabled at time instant* t iff there exists a time slot ts such that t belongs to ts and $(r, ts) \in RS$. A user u *is a member of role* r *at time instant* t iff r is enabled at t and there exists a time slot ts such that t belongs to ts and $(u, r, ts) \in TUA$. A user u *has permission* p *at time instant* t iff there exists role r such that $(p, r) \in PA$ and u is a member of r at t. (The fact that u is a member of r at t implies that r is enabled at t.) A *TRBAC policy* is a tuple (U, R, P, RS, TUA, PA).

Following [26], we extend ARBAC to Administrative TRBAC policies by considering two groups of administrative actions: those that enable or disable a role r by modifying the time slots associated to r in the RS relation and those that change the time slots associated to a user-role pair in the TUA relation.

Administrative TRBAC. A *signed role* is an expression of the form r or of the form $\overline{r}$. A *condition* is a (finite) set of signed roles. A signed role σ in a condition C is *positive* (*negative*, resp.) when there exists a role r such that $\sigma = r$ ($\sigma = \overline{r}$, resp.). A *schedule* is a set of time slots. A time instant t *belongs to schedule* s iff there exists a time slot ts in s such that t belongs to ts.

Let C be a condition, RS be a role status relation, and TUA be a temporal user-role assignment relation. A time slot ts *satisfies* C *under* RS iff $(r, ts) \in RS$ for each r in C and $(r, ts) \notin RS$ for each $\overline{r}$ in C; i.e. when the positive roles in C are enabled in ts and the negative roles in C are not enabled in ts. A schedule s *satisfies* C *under* RS iff ts satisfies C under RS for each ts in s. A user u and time slot ts *satisfy* C *under* TUA iff $(u, r, ts) \in TUA$ for each r in C and $(u, r, ts) \notin TUA$ for each $\overline{r}$ in C. A user u and schedule s *satisfy* C *under* TUA iff u and ts satisfy C under

TUA for each ts in s. A user u and time slot ts *satisfy a condition* C *at time instant* t *under the role status relation* RS *and the temporal user role assignment relation* TUA iff t belongs to ts, ts satisfies C under RS, and u, ts satisfy C under TUA. A user u and schedule s *satisfy a condition* C *at time instant* t *under the role status relation* RS *and the temporal user role assignment relation* TUA iff u and ts satisfy C at t under RS and TUA for each ts in s.

In the following, let $\alpha = (U, R, P, RS, TUA, PA)$ be a TRBAC policy. An *administrative action* is a tuple $(C_a, s_{rule}, C, s_r, r)$ where C_a and C are conditions, s_{rule} and s_r are schedules, and r is a role. There are four types of administrative actions: role *enabling* or *disabling* and user *assign* or *revoke*. Role enabling and disabling (assign and revoke, resp.) have effects on the role status relation RS (TUA, resp.) in α. An administrative action $(C_a, s_{rule}, C, s_r, r)$ *can be executed at time instant* t *in* α (regardless of its type) iff there exists user u_{ad} and schedule $s_{ad} \subseteq s_{rule}$ such that u_{ad} and s_{ad} satisfy C_a at t under RS and TUA.

A *role enabling/disabling* administrative action $\tau = (C_a, s_{rule}, C, s_r, r)$ *can be executed at time instant* t *with respect to a schedule* $\hat{s} \subseteq s_r$ *in* α iff τ can be executed at t in α and $\hat{s}$ satisfies C under RS. An *assign/revoke* administrative action $\tau = (C_a, s_{rule}, C, s_r, r)$ *can be executed at time instant* t *with respect to a user* u *and a schedule* $\hat{s} \subseteq s_r$ *in* α iff τ can be executed at t in α and u together with $\hat{s}$ satisfy C under TUA.

An *ATRBAC system* is a tuple (α_0, ψ) where α_0 is the *initial* TRBAC policy and ψ is the (disjoint) union of the following sets of administrative actions *can_enable*, *can_disable*, *can_assign*, and *can_revoke* of type role enabling, role disabling, assign, and revoke, respectively. A *state* of an ATRBAC system is a pair (α, t) where α is a TRBAC policy and t is a time instant, called the *current time*. Since the administrative actions depend on and affect only the relations RS and TUA, in the following, we abbreviate a TRBAC policy (U, R, P, RS, TUA, PA) as (RS, TUA) and write (RS, TUA, t) for a state instead of $((RS, TUA), t)$. We define the effect of executing an administrative action in ψ by defining a binary relation $\rightarrow_\psi$ on the states of the ATRBAC system as follows: $(RS, TUA, t) \rightarrow_\psi (RS', TUA', t)$ iff there exists an administrative action $\tau = (C_a, s_{rule}, C, s_r, r)$ in ψ of type

- role enabling (disabling, resp.) that can be executed at t with respect to some $\hat{s} \subseteq s_r$, $TUA' = TUA$, and $RS' = RS \cup \{(r, \widehat{ts}) \mid \widehat{ts} \in \hat{s}\}$ ($RS' = RS \setminus \{(r, \widehat{ts}) \mid \widehat{ts} \in \hat{s}\}$, resp.) or

- assign (revoke, resp.) that can be executed at t with respect to some u and some $\hat{s} \subseteq s_r$, $RS' = RS$, and $TUA' = TUA \cup \{(u, r, \widehat{ts}) \mid \widehat{ts} \in \hat{s}\}$ ($TUA' = (TUA \setminus \{(u, r, \widehat{ts}) \mid \widehat{ts} \in \hat{s}\}$, resp.).

We illustrate the definitions with an example inspired to the hospital scenario in [26].

Example 1 *Let* $U = \{u_1, u_2, u_3\}$, $R = \{EMP$ *(Employee)*, DDR *(Day Doctor)*, NDR *(Night Doctor)*, PRC *(Practitioner)*, NRS *(Nurse)*, SEC *(Secretary)*, CHR *(Chairman)*$\}$,

$TS = \{(8am, 4pm), (4pm, 12am), (12am, 8am)\}$, and

$$(CHR, \{ts_1\}, \{NDR\}, \{ts_3\}, PRC) \in can\_enable \quad (1)$$
$$(SEC, \{ts_2\}, \{EMP, NDR\}, \{ts_3\}, NRS) \in can\_disable \quad (2)$$
$$(CHR, \{ts_1\}, \{EMP, \overline{NRS}\}, \{ts_2\}, DDR) \in can\_assign \quad (3)$$
$$(CHR, \{ts_3\}, \{EMP, \overline{NRS}\}, \{ts_3\}, NDR) \in can\_assign \quad (4)$$
$$(CHR, \{ts_2\}, \emptyset, \{ts_2\}, SEC) \in can\_revoke \quad (5)$$

where ts_1 stands for $(8am, 4pm)$, ts_2 for $(4pm, 12am)$, and ts_3 for $(12am, 8am)$. Assume that the initial state is $\alpha_0 = (RS_0, TUA_0, 8am)$ where

$$RS_0 = \{\ (CHR, ts_1), (CHR, ts_3), (DDR, ts_2), (NDR, ts_3)\ \}$$
$$TUA_0 = \{\ (u_1, CHR, ts_1), (u_1, CHR, ts_3), (u_2, EMP, ts_2)\ \}$$

Let us consider actions (1) and (3). It is easy to check that: (i) schedule $s_{rule} = \{ts_1\}$ satisfies condition $C_a = \{CHR\}$ under RS_0 (e.g., $(CHR, ts_1) \in RS_0$); (ii) user u_1 and s_{rule} satisfy C_a under TUA_0 since $(u_1, CHR, ts_1) \in TUA_0$; (iii) user u_1 and s_{rule} satisfy C_a at 9am (under RS_0 and TUA_0) because 9am belongs to s_{rule} and (i) and (ii); (iv) schedule $s_{r1} = \{ts_3\}$ satisfies condition $C_1 = \{NDR\}$ under RS_0 (e.g., $(NDR, ts_3) \in RS_0$); and (v) user u_2 together with $s_{r2} = \{ts_2\}$ satisfy $C_2 = \{EMP, \overline{NRS}\}$ since $(u_2, EMP, ts_2) \in TUA_0$ and $(u_2, NRS, ts_2) \notin TUA_0$. Action (1) ((3), resp.) can be executed at 9 am w.r.t. schedule s_{r1} (user u_2 and schedule s_{r2}, resp.) because of (iii) and (iv)—(iii) and (v), resp. The effect of executing action (1) on the initial state is that $(RS_0, TUA_0, 9am) \rightarrow_\psi (RS', TUA', 9am)$ where $RS' = RS_0 \cup \{(PRC, ts_3)\}$ and $TUA' = TUA_0$. Similarly, we also have the relation $(RS_0, TUA_0, 9am) \rightarrow_\psi (RS'', TUA'', 9am)$ where $RS'' = RS_0$ and $TUA'' = TUA_0 \cup \{(u_2, DDR, ts_2)\}$ by executing (3). □

Administrative actions do not modify the current time of the state of the ATRBAC system, i.e. administrative actions are assumed to occur instantaneously. To model the passing of time, we extend the definition above by adding the following clause: $(\alpha, t) \rightarrow_\psi (\alpha, t')$ iff $t' > t$ for any TRBAC policy α and any set ψ of administrative actions. Notice that the passing of time does not modify the TRBAC policy in the state of the ATRBAC system.

A *run* of an ATRBAC system (α_0, ψ) is a (possibly infinite) sequence $(\alpha_0, 0), ..., (\alpha_i, t_i), (\alpha_{i+1}, t_{i+1}), ...$ of states such that $(\alpha_i, t_i) \rightarrow_\psi (\alpha_{i+1}, t_{i+1})$ and $t_i \leq t_{i+1}$ for $i = 1, ..., n-1$ with $n > 1$. If the run is finite, i.e. it is of the form $(\alpha_0, 0), ..., (\alpha_n, t_n)$ for some $n \geq 0$, we say that (α_n, t_n) is the *final state* of the run.

Despite the fact that administrators can only execute a given set of administrative actions, it is still quite difficult to foresee all possible interleavings of actions that a group of administrators can perform together with their effect on an initial TRBAC policy. As a consequence, it may be the case that an untrusted user can acquire, in some time interval, a permission that he/she should not acquire. Being able to identify this situation amounts to solving the following analysis problem.

A *reachability problem* for an ATRBAC system (α_0, ψ) is identified by a tuple (u, C_f, s_f) and amounts to checking if there exists a finite run of the ATRBAC system whose final state (α_f, t_f) is such that user u and schedule s_f satisfy condition C_f under TUA_f and s_f satisfies C_f under RS_f, where $\alpha_f = (RS_f, TUA_f)$.

Our definitions of administrative action and reachability problem generalize those in [26], which assumes $C_a = \{r_a\}$ in $\tau = (C_a, s_{rule}, C, s_r, r)$ and $C = \{r\}$ in (u, C, s). In general, there is no efficient reduction from our version of the reachability problem to that in [26]. This is so because C_a can be any (finite) sub-set of the set $R \cup \{\overline{r} | r \in R\}$ of (signed) roles; thus, there are at most $2^{2 \cdot |R|}$ of such conditions. To encode this by a singleton C_a as in [26], we must introduce a "fresh" role for each such condition, i.e. the number of new roles is in $O(2^{2 \cdot |R|})$.

Finally, we observe that [26] introduces a timed version of the reachability problem in which the final state should be reached within a given time instant. For lack of space, we do not consider this problem here but we claim that our approach can be easily extended to handle also this problem.

3. REACHABILITY OF A CLASS OF SYMBOLIC TRANSITION SYSTEMS

Following [19], we reduce reachability problems for ATR-BAC systems to a (finite) sequence of constraint satisfaction problems. Here, we briefly recall the main notions underlying the approach in [19].

A well-known constraint satisfaction problem is Boolean satisfiability. It consists of establishing whether a formula—obtained by combining Boolean variables with logical connectives—can be made true (equivalently, is satisfiable) by assigning appropriate values to its Boolean variables. Our approach reduces reachability problems for ATRBAC systems to sequences of constraint satisfaction problems that are more easily and compactly described by using a richer language, called *Bernays-Schönfinkel-Ramsey* (BSR) formulae (see, e.g., [19]). The constraint satisfaction problem for BSR formulae is to determine the satisfiability of formulae of the form $\exists \underline{x}.\forall \underline{y}.\varphi(\underline{x}, \underline{y})$, where φ is a quantifier-free formula, i.e. a Boolean combination of atomic sub-formulae built out of equality, predicates, constants (functions are not allowed), and variables in the tuples $\underline{x}, \underline{y}$. When $\underline{x}$ ($\underline{y}$, resp.) is empty and $\underline{y}$ ($\underline{x}$, resp.) is not, the BSR formula is *universal* (*existential*, resp.). When both $\underline{x}$ and $\underline{y}$ are empty, the BSR formula is quantifier-free.

As shown in [17], BSR formulae can be used in many verification scenarios. For instance, the following BSR formulae

$$e_i \neq e_j \text{ for distinct } i, j \text{ in } \{1, ..., n\} \quad (6)$$
$$\forall x.(x = e_1 \vee \cdots \vee x = e_n) \quad (7)$$

characterize an enumerated data-type with n elements. The formulae in (6) constrain the constants $e_1, ..., e_n$ to be pairwise distinct ($e_i \neq e_j$ abbreviates $\neg(e_i = e_j)$) while (7) considers at most n distinct elements.

The satisfiability problem for BSR formulae can be reduced to Boolean satisfiability by an instantiation procedure [18]. Unfortunately, this process may yield a Boolean formula that is exponentially larger than the original. (The satisfiability problem for BSR formulae is known to be NEX-PTIME complete.) To alleviate this problem, alternative approaches (see, e.g., [17]) have been proposed that avoid the up-front reduction by reasoning on the extended (with respect to Boolean logic) language. These techniques have been implemented in *Satisfiability Modulo Theories* (SMT) solvers, that are extensions of Boolean solvers capable of establishing the satisfiability of formulae in decidable fragments of first-order logic (e.g., the BSR fragment) and decidable theories (e.g., Linear Arithmetics). SMT solvers are receiving a lot of attention because of their effectiveness in solving SMT problems derived from several application areas, such as hardware verification, program analysis, and scheduling; see, e.g., [6] for an introduction to SMT solving and its applications. In the following, we show how SMT solvers can be used to support the reachability analysis of a class of symbolic transition systems.

An *adequate BSR symbolic transition system* (*adequate BSR-STS*, for short) is a tuple $\langle \underline{s}, Ax, In, Tr \rangle$, where $\underline{s}$ is a (finite) sequence of predicates, called the *state variables*, Ax is a (finite) set of BSR formulae, called *axioms*, $In(\underline{s})$ is a universal BSR formula,[2] called the *initial state formula*, and Tr is a (finite) disjunction of BSR formulae of the form

$$\exists \underline{x}. \left(G(\underline{s}) \wedge \bigwedge_{s \in \underline{s}} \forall \underline{y}. \left(s'(\underline{y}) \;\Leftrightarrow\; U_s(\underline{s}, \underline{y}) \right) \right), \qquad (8)$$

called *transition formulae*, where $\underline{s}'$ is the sequence obtained from $\underline{s}$ by priming each element, $\underline{x}$ and $\underline{y}$ are tuples of variables, $G(\underline{s})$ is a quantifier-free BSR formula—called the *guard*, containing the variables in $\underline{x}$ as free variables, and where each occurrence of the predicate symbols in $\underline{s}$ are applied to variables in $\underline{x}$, and $U_s(\underline{s}, \underline{y})$ is a quantifier-free BSR formula—called the *update*, containing the variables in $\underline{x}, \underline{y}$ as free variables, the length of $\underline{y}$ matches the arity of s, and each occurrence of the predicate symbols in $\underline{s}$ is applied to variables in $\underline{x}, \underline{y}$.

The *reachability problem* for an adequate BSR-STS $\langle \underline{s}, Ax, In, Tr \rangle$ and an existential BSR formula $\gamma(\underline{s})$, called the *goal*, consists of establishing whether there exists an integer $n \geq 0$ such that

$$In(\underline{s}_0) \wedge \tau(\underline{s}_0, \underline{s}_1) \wedge \cdots \wedge \tau(\underline{s}_{n-1}, \underline{s}_n) \wedge \gamma(\underline{s}_n) \wedge Ax \qquad (9)$$

is satisfiable where $\tau(\underline{s}, \underline{s}') := \bigvee_{tr \in Tr} tr(\underline{s}, \underline{s}')$ and the sequence $\underline{s}_i$ is obtained from $\underline{s}$ by uniquely renaming each of its element by appending the suffix i (for $i = 0, ..., n$). For clarity, if $\phi(\underline{s})$ is a formula containing symbols from $\underline{s}$, then $\phi(\underline{s}_i)$ is the formula obtained from ϕ by pairwise replacement of each element in $\underline{s}$ with the corresponding one in $\underline{s}_i$.

A *monadic BSR-STS* is an adequate BSR-STS whose predicates are unary.

Theorem 1 ([19]) *The reachability problem for monadic BSR-STSs is decidable.*

The proof of this result amounts to proving the termination of a symbolic backward reachability procedure. The idea is to find the value of n for which the formula (9) is satisfiable (if possible) by computing increasingly precise under-approximations $R_0(\underline{s}), ..., R_n(\underline{s})$ of the formula $R(\underline{s})$ representing the set of states from which it is possible to reach a state of the goal $\gamma(\underline{s})$ by applying $0, ..., n$ times, respectively, the transition $Tr(\underline{s}, \underline{s}')$. In order to stop computing formulae in the sequence $R_0(\underline{s}), ..., R_n(\underline{s})$, there are two criteria. First, we can check whether $R_n(\underline{s}) \wedge In(\underline{s}) \wedge Ax$ is satisfiable: in this case, the formula (9) is satisfiable and there exists a finite sequence of transitions that leads the system from an initial state to one in γ. Second, we can check whether $Ax \rightarrow (R_n(\underline{s}) \rightarrow R_{n-1}(\underline{s}))$ is valid (or, equivalently by refutation, if $Ax \wedge R_n(\underline{s}) \wedge \neg R_{n-1}(\underline{s})$ is unsatisfiable): in

---

[2] From now on, we consider BSR formulae to be built over the symbols in Ax and $\underline{s}$.

this case, the sequence $R_0(\underline{s}), ..., R_n(\underline{s})$ has reached a fix-point at n. SMT solvers can be used to automatically solve the SMT problems underlying these two criteria. The tool described in Section 5 implements the procedure above and use an SMT solver to tackle the SMT problems encoding the two termination criteria.

To simplify the technical development, we consider a simple extension of the notion of monadic BSR-STS. Preliminarily, we introduce the many-sorted version of BSR formulae: each symbol is associated with sorts denoting the sets of values over which the arguments of the symbol range. It is well-known that many-sorted first-order logic is as expressive as first-order logic without sorts (see, e.g., [8]). Thus, all the results above carry over to sorted BSR formulae. Notationally, if S is a sort symbol, then $Enum(\{e_1, ..., e_n\}, S)$ stands for the set of formulae (6) and (7) above with $x, e_1, ..., e_n$ of the *enumerated* sort S. An *effectively monadic* BSR-STS is an adequate BSR-STS whose predicate symbols are n-ary for $n \geq 0$ and such that at least $n - 1$ arguments range over enumerated datatypes. It is always possible to transform an effectively monadic BSR-STS to a monadic BSR-STS.

Corollary 1 *The reachability problem for effectively monadic BSR-STSs is decidable.*

In [19], this result has been applied to the safety analysis of ARBAC policies. Section 4 will explain how to apply it to the analysis of ATRBAC systems. There are two main advantages in developing safety analysis based on Corollary 1. First, the user-role reachability problem is solved with respect to a finite but unknown number of users in the policies manipulated by the administrative actions; see [19] for a detailed discussion on this issue. Thus, when the goal is unreachable, the safety certification takes into account the fact that users may join or leave the organization in which the policies are administered. Instead, when the goal is reachable, the technique is capable of establishing the number of users needed for some sequence of administrative actions to transform the initial policy into one satisfying the goal (usually obtained by negating a security goal). In this way, our safety analysis technique can go beyond the separate administration assumption adopted by many approaches available in the literature, such as [11, 13]. The second advantage of developing a safety analysis on the backward reachability procedure on which Corollary 1 is based is the possibility to integrate heuristics that dramatically reduce the state-space explosion problem as shown in [20] for ARBAC policies. Section 5 will discuss an adaptation of an heuristics in [20] to ATRBAC systems whose impact on performances will be illustrated by the experiments of Section 5.1.

4. SOLVING REACHABILITY PROBLEMS FOR ATRBAC SYSTEMS

Let U be a set of users, R of roles, and $TS_{T_{MAX}}$ of time slots. We now show how to translate a reachability problem (u, C, s) for an ATRBAC system (α_0, ψ) to a reachability problem of an effectively monadic BSR-STS $\langle \underline{s}_{ATRBAC}, Ax_{ATRBAC}, In_{ATRBAC}, Tr_{ATRBAC} \rangle$ as specified in Figure 1. In the following, we first argue its correctness and then use Corollary 1 to derive the decidability of reachability problems for ATRBAC systems. Preliminary, we make a simple but important observation on the role of time.

Abstracting away time. We observe that, in order to solve reachability problems for ATRBAC systems, we do

State variables in $\underline{s}_{ATRBAC}$	rs: first argument of sort *Role*, second of sort *TimeSlot* tua: first argument of sort *User*, second of sort *Role*, third of sort *TimeSlot* at: one argument of sort *TimeSlot*
Initial TRBAC policy $\alpha_0 = (RS_0, TUA_0, ts_0)$	$\forall x, y, z. \begin{bmatrix} rs(y,z) & \Leftrightarrow & \bigvee_{(r,ts) \in RS_0}(y = r \wedge z = ts) & \wedge \\ tua(x,y,z) & \Leftrightarrow & \bigvee_{(u,r,ts) \in TUA_0}(x = u \wedge y = r \wedge z = ts) & \wedge \\ at(z) & \Leftrightarrow & z = ts_0 & \end{bmatrix}$
Administrative action in ψ: $\tau = (C_a, \{ts_{rule}\}, C, \{ts_r\}, r)$	transition formula of the form (8): $\exists \underline{x}.(G(\underline{s}) \wedge \bigwedge_{s \in \underline{s}} \forall \underline{y}.(s'(\underline{y}) \Leftrightarrow U_s(\underline{s}, \underline{y})))$ where $\underline{s}$ is replaced with $\underline{s}_{ATRBAC}$, $\quad \underline{x} := u_{ad}, u, ts$ of sort *User*, *User*, and *TimeSlot*, respectively Guard: $G := G_t \wedge G_a \wedge G_u$ where $\quad G_t := at(ts) \wedge ts = ts_{rule}$ $\quad G_a := ts\text{-}sat_{RS}(ts_{rule}, C_a) \wedge ts\text{-}sat_{TUA}(u_{ad}, ts_{rule}, C_a)$ $\quad G_u := \begin{cases} ts\text{-}sat_{RS}(ts_r, C) & \text{if } \tau \text{ is role enabling/disabling} \\ ts\text{-}sat_{TUA}(u, ts_r, C) & \text{if } \tau \text{ is assign/revoke} \end{cases}$ Update for role enabling/disabling: $\quad U_{rs}(\underline{s}, \underline{x}, \underline{y}) := \begin{cases} rs(y,z) \vee (y = r \wedge z = ts_r) & \text{if } \tau \text{ is role enabling} \\ rs(y,z) \wedge \neg(y = r \wedge z = ts_r) & \text{if } \tau \text{ is role disabling} \end{cases}$ $\quad U_{tua}(\underline{s}, \underline{x}, \underline{y}) := tua(x,y,z)$ $\quad U_{at}(\underline{s}, \underline{x}, \underline{y}) := at(z)$ Update for assign/revoke: $\quad U_{rs}(\underline{s}, \underline{x}, \underline{y}) := rs(y,z)$ $\quad U_{tua}(\underline{s}, \underline{x}, \underline{y}) := \begin{cases} tua(x,y,z) \vee (x = u \wedge y = r \wedge z = ts_r) & \text{if } \tau \text{ is assign} \\ tua(x,y,z) \wedge \neg(x = u \wedge y = r \wedge z = ts_r) & \text{if } \tau \text{ is revoke} \end{cases}$ $\quad U_{at}(\underline{s}, \underline{x}, \underline{y}) := at(z)$
Time passing	if $j + 1 < T_{MAX}$, then $\exists ts. \begin{bmatrix} at(ts) \wedge ts = (j, j+1) & \wedge \\ \forall y,z.rs'(y,z) \Leftrightarrow rs(y,z) \wedge \forall x,y,z.tua'(x,y,z) \Leftrightarrow tua(x,y,z) & \wedge \\ \forall z.at'(z) \Leftrightarrow (z = (j+1, j+2)) & \end{bmatrix}$ otherwise: $\exists ts. \begin{bmatrix} at(ts) \wedge ts = (T_{MAX}-1, T_{MAX}) & \wedge \\ \forall y,z.rs'(y,z) \Leftrightarrow rs(y,z) \wedge \forall x,y,z.tua'(x,y,z) \Leftrightarrow tua(x,y,z) & \wedge \\ \forall z.at'(z) \Leftrightarrow (z = (0,1)) & \end{bmatrix}$
Goal tuple (u, C_f, s_f)	$\exists x.x = u \wedge \bigwedge_{ts_f \in s_f} ts\text{-}sat_{TUA}(x, ts_f, C_f) \wedge ts\text{-}sat_{RS}(ts_f, C_f)$
Abbreviations	$ts\text{-}sat_{RS}(ts, C) := \bigwedge_{r \in C} rs(r, ts) \wedge \bigwedge_{\overline{r} \in C} \neg rs(r, ts)$ $ts\text{-}sat_{TUA}(u, ts, C) := \bigwedge_{r \in C} tua(u, r, ts) \wedge \bigwedge_{\overline{r} \in C} \neg tua(u, r, ts)$

Figure 1: Symbolic representation of reachability problems for ATRBAC systems

not need to keep track of the current time t in the state (RS, TUA, t) of (α_0, ψ) but only the time slot ts to which t belongs to. In fact, for any time instants t, t' belonging to the same time slot ts, we can easily show that

- a role enabling/disabling action $(C_a, s_{rule}, C, s_r, r)$ can be executed at t with respect to a schedule $\hat{s} \subseteq s_r$ iff $(C_a, s_{rule}, C, s_r, r)$ can be executed at t' with respect to $\hat{s} \subseteq s_r$, and

- an assign/revoke action $(C_a, s_{rule}, C, s_r, r)$ can be executed at t with respect to a user u and a schedule $\hat{s} \subseteq s_r$ iff $(C_a, s_{rule}, C, s_r, r)$ can be executed at t' with respect to u and $\hat{s} \subseteq s_r$.

For this reason, without loss of generality, we assume that the state of any ATRBAC system is of the form (RS, TUA, ts) where ts is a time slot.

We consider many-sorted BSR formulae built out of the following symbols: sorts *User*, *Role*, and *TimeSlot*; a constant of sort *User* for each element in U; a constant of sort *Role* for each element in R; and a constant of sort *TimeSlot* for each element in $TS_{T_{MAX}}$. We also assume that $Ax_{ATRBAC} = En(R, Role) \cup En(TS_{T_{MAX}}, TimeSlot)$.

Representing states. Typically, the relations RS_0 and TUA_0 in an initial state α_0 are finite since only finitely many users, roles, and time slots are considered. Thus, α_0 can be represented by a universal BSR formula, denoted with $[\alpha_0]$, as shown in Figure 1. In general, $[\alpha]$ denotes a universal BSR formula representing the state α of an ATRBAC system.

Example 2 *We recall that the initial state of the system in Example 1 is $\alpha_0 = (RS_0, TUA_0, 8am)$ and that $8am$ belongs to time slot $ts_1 = (8am, 4pm)$. Then, the formula $[(RS_0, TUA_0, ts_1)]$ is*

$$\forall x, y, z. \begin{bmatrix} rs(y,z) \Leftrightarrow \begin{pmatrix} (y = CHR \wedge z = ts_1) \vee \\ (y = CHR \wedge z = ts_3) \vee \\ (y = DDR \wedge z = ts_2) \vee \\ (y = NDR \wedge z = ts_3) \end{pmatrix} \wedge \\ tua(x,y,z) \Leftrightarrow \begin{pmatrix} (x = A \wedge y = CHR \wedge z = ts_1) \vee \\ (x = A \wedge y = CHR \wedge z = ts_3) \vee \\ (x = B \wedge y = EMP \wedge z = ts_2) \end{pmatrix} \wedge \\ at(z) \Leftrightarrow z = ts_1 \end{bmatrix}$$

(We recall from Example 1 that ts_2 stands for $(4pm, 12am)$ and ts_3 for $(12am, 8am)$.) Clearly, this is a universal BSR formula. $\square$

Before describing how administrative actions are translated to transition formulae of the form (8), we observe that it is possible to consider, without loss of generality, actions in which time schedules contain a single time slot, i.e. actions of the form $(C_a, \{ts_{rule}\}, C, \{ts_r\}, r)$, for ts_{rule} and ts_r time slots. In fact, an action whose time schedules contain more than one time slot can be easily transformed to a finite set of actions whose time schedules are singleton sets. We illustrate how this can be done on a simple example since the generalization to arbitrary actions is easy. The administrative action $(C_a, \{ts_1, ts_3\}, \{r_1, \overline{r_2}\}, \{ts_5\}, r)$ can be transformed into the following two actions: $(C_a, \{ts_1\}, \{r_1, \overline{r_2}\}, \{ts_5\}, r)$ and $(C_a, \{ts_3\}, \{r_1, \overline{r_2}\}, \{ts_5\}, r)$ for ts_i a time slot $(i = 1, 3, 5)$. This means that using schedules for the specification of administrative TRBAC actions does not increase expressiveness, it only allows for more compact specifications. For this reason, in the following, we consider administrative actions of the form $(C_a, \{ts_{rule}\}, C, \{ts_r\}, r)$.

Representing transitions. Figure 1 shows that an administrative action $(C_a, \{ts_{rule}\}, C, \{ts_r\}, r)$ can be mapped to a transition formula (8). The guard G is obtained as the conjunction of three formulae: G_t requires the action to be executed in the time slot ts_{rule}, G_a that the chosen administrator satisfies the condition C_a, and G_u that the time slot ts_r satisfies the condition C in case of a enabling/disabling action or the selected user with the time slot ts_r satisfy the condition C in case of assign/revoke action. The updates of an enabling/disabling action modify the state variable rs only by adding/deleting the pair (r, ts_r) whereas the updates of an assign/revoke action modify the state variable tua only by adding/deleting the triple (u, r, ts_r). We explain this more in detail below.

Consider the abbreviations $ts\text{-}sat_{RS}$ and $ts\text{-}sat_{TUA}$ at the bottom of Figure 1. Given a state $\alpha = (RS, TUA, ts)$, it is easy to see that

- ts satisfies a condition C under RS iff

  $[\alpha] \land ts\text{-}sat_{RS}(ts, C) \land Ax_{ATRBAC}$ is satisfiable and

- a user u and ts satisfy a condition C under TUA iff

  $[\alpha] \land ts\text{-}sat_{TUA}(u, ts, C) \land Ax_{ATRBAC}$ is satisfiable.

These imply that an administrative action $(C_a, \{ts_{rule}\}, C, \{ts_r\}, r)$ can be executed in state α—at any time instant t of the time slot ts_{rule}—iff there exists user u_{ad} such that

$$[\alpha] \land ts = ts_{rule} \land ts\text{-}sat_{RS}(ts_{rule}, C_a) \land \quad (10)$$
$$ts\text{-}sat_{TUA}(u_{ad}, ts_{rule}, C_a) \land Ax_{ATRBAC}$$

is satisfiable. Notice how—according to Figure 1—(10) can be re-written as $[\alpha] \land G_t \land G_a \land Ax_{ATRBAC}$. Additionally, we have that a role enabling/disabling action can be executed in α (w.r.t. ts_r) iff

$$(10) \land [\alpha] \land ts\text{-}sat_{RS}(ts_r, C) \quad (11)$$

is satisfiable and an assign/revoke action can be executed in α (w.r.t. some user u and ts_r) iff

$$(10) \land [\alpha] \land ts\text{-}sat_{TUA}(u, ts_r, C). \quad (12)$$

is satisfiable. Notice how—according to Figure 1—(11) and (12) can be re-written as $[\alpha] \land G_t \land G_a \land G_u \land Ax_{ATRBAC}$.

All these observations show that the executability of an administrative actions $(C_a, \{ts_{rule}\}, C, \{ts_r\}, r)$ in a state α

is equivalent to the satisfiability of the conjunction of $[\alpha]$, Ax_{ATRBAC}, and the guard G defined in Figure 1.

Concerning the updates U_{rs}, U_{tua}, and U_{at} defined in Figure 1, observe that all four types of administrative actions update in the same way the state variable at (i.e. its value is left unchanged) since they are assumed to be instantaneous. When considering role enabling/disabling actions, the state variable tua is updated identically whereas rs is added/deleted the pair (r, ts_r) by using disjunction or conjunction and negation. Similarly, when considering assign/revoke actions, the state variable rs is updated identically whereas tua is added/deleted the pair (u, r, ts_r). These show that the effects of administrative actions of ATRBAC systems are faithfully modeled by the update functions U_{rs}, U_{tua}, and U_{at} defined in Figure 1.

Example 3 *We show two transition formulae corresponding to two administrative actions of Example 1.*
For $(CHR, \{ts_1\}, \{EMP, \overline{NRS}\}, \{ts_2\}, DDR) \in can\_assign$, *the translation in Figure 1 generates the following instance of (8):*

$$\exists u_{ad}, u, ts. \begin{bmatrix} at(ts) \land ts = ts_1 \land \\ rs(CHR, ts_1) \land tua(u_{ad}, CHR, ts_1) \land \\ tua(u, EMP, ts_2) \land \neg tua(u, NRS, ts_2) \land \\ \forall y, z. rs'(y, z) \Leftrightarrow rs(y, z) \land \\ \forall x, y, z. tua'(y, z) \Leftrightarrow \begin{bmatrix} tua(x, y, z) \lor \\ \begin{bmatrix} x = u \land \\ y = DDR \land \\ z = ts_2 \end{bmatrix} \end{bmatrix} \land \\ \forall z. at'(z) \Leftrightarrow at(z) \end{bmatrix}$$

where the first line is G_t, the second is G_a, the third is G_u, the fourth contains the update U_{rs}, the fifth contains the update U_{tua}, and the last the update U_{at}.
For $(CHR, \{ts_1\}, \{NDR\}, \{ts_3\}, PRC) \in can\_enable$, *the translation in Figure 1 generates the following instance of (8):*

$$\exists u_{ad}, ts. \begin{bmatrix} at(ts) \land ts = ts_1 \land \\ rs(CHR, ts_1) \land tua(u_{ad}, CHR, ts_1) \land \\ rs(NDR, ts_3) \land \\ \forall y, z. rs'(y, z) \Leftrightarrow \begin{bmatrix} rs(y, z) \lor \\ [y = PRC \land z = ts_3] \end{bmatrix} \land \\ \forall x, y, z. tua'(x, y, z) \Leftrightarrow tua(x, y, z) \land \\ \forall z. at'(z) \Leftrightarrow at(z) \end{bmatrix}$$

where the first line is G_t, the second is G_a, the third is G_u, the fourth contains the update U_{rs}, the fifth contains the update U_{tua}, and the last the update U_{at}. □

As already observed in Section 2, the administrative actions do not modify time. Correspondingly, the state variable at is updated identically by the transition formulae in Figure 1 associated to an administrative action $(C_a, \{ts_{rule}\}, C, \{ts_r\}, r)$. To model the passing of time, Figure 1 shows two transition formulae of the form (8) that update identically the state variables rs and tua while modifying the value of at so that it stores time slot $(j+1, j+2)$ after storing time slot $(j, j+1)$. To see why it is sufficient to model the flow of time from time slot $(j, j+1)$ to $(j+1, j+2)$, it is sufficient to observe that the set of enabled administrative actions is fixed for any time instant in a given time slot.

Example 4 *Consider again Example 1 and recall that the set $TS_{T_{MAX}}$ of time slots is $\{ts_1, ts_2, ts_3\}$, where ts_1 is $(8am,$*

$4pm$), ts_2 is $(4pm, 12am)$, and ts_3 is $(12am, 8am)$. *Figure 1 generates the following instances of (8) to model the passing of time:*

$$\exists ts.[at(ts) \wedge ts = ts_1 \wedge \forall z.at'(z) \Leftrightarrow (z = ts_2) \wedge ID(rs, tua)]$$

$$\exists ts.[at(ts) \wedge ts = ts_2 \wedge \forall z.at'(z) \Leftrightarrow (z = ts_3) \wedge ID(rs, tua)]$$

$$\exists ts.[at(ts) \wedge ts = ts_3 \wedge \forall z.at'(z) \Leftrightarrow (z = ts_1) \wedge ID(rs, tua)]$$

where $ID(rs, tua)$ is the conjunction of $\forall y, z.rs'(y, z) \Leftrightarrow rs(y, z)$ and $\forall w, y, z.tua'(w, y, z) \Leftrightarrow tua(w, y, z)$. The first formula above formalizes the passing of time from a time instant in ts_1 to one in ts_2, the second from an instant in ts_2 to one in ts_3, and the last formula from an instant in ts_3 to one in ts_1 after T_{MAX} units of time have elapsed. □

Reachability problems. The translation in Figure 1 generates an adequate BSR-STS: the axioms are BSR formulae, the initial formula is a universal BSR formula, and the transition formulae are all of the form (8). It is not difficult to see that it is effectively monadic since the arguments of both rs and at range over sorts whose cardinality is bounded while tua has two, out of three, arguments that range over sorts whose cardinality is bounded. In fact, only the first argument of tua may assume an unknown number of values since the interpretation of $User$ is left unconstrained by the axioms in Ax_{ATRBAC}. In terms of the original model, this allows our safety analysis technique to consider a finite but unknown number of users in the temporal RBAC policies manipulated by the administrative actions.

To be able to apply Corollary 1, we are left with the problem of checking that the goal formula obtained by applying the translation described in Figure 1 to the reachability problem (u, C_f, s_f) is an existential BSR formula. Indeed, this is the case as a simple inspection of the penultimate row of the figure reveals.

Theorem 2 *The reachability problem (u, C_f, s_f) for ATRBAC systems is decidable (even when considering a finite but unknown number of users).*

At a closer look, it is possible to solve a *generalized reachability problem* (C_f, s_f) that requires to establish whether there exists a user u (we are not interested in who is the one, a priori) such that u and s_f satisfy C_f. To see why this is the case, it is sufficient to observe that the translation of (C_f, s_f) is the existential BSR formula

$$\exists x. \bigwedge_{ts_f \in s_f} \text{ts-sat}_{TUA}(x, ts_f, C_f) \wedge \text{ts-sat}_{RS}(ts_f, C_f),$$

obtained from that in Figure 1 by simply dropping the conjunction $x = u$. This version of the problem is useful to establish—among other things—availability, i.e. ensuring that an authorized user is able to acquire a certain set of permissions (via a given set of roles).

Theorem 3 *The generalized reachability problem (C_f, s_f) for ATRBAC systems is decidable (even when considering a finite but unknown number of users).*

Both Theorems 2 and 3 are immediate consequences of Corollary 1 since the translation in Figure 1 yields BSR-STSs. Since the proof of Theorem 1 (and thus also Corollary 1) is constructive by showing the backward reachability procedure sketched in Section 3 terminates on every BSR-STSs, we design the following two-phase technique for the

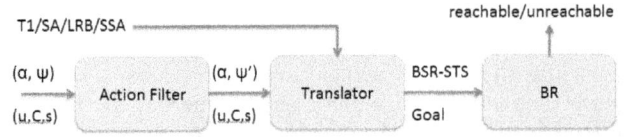

Figure 2: Our technique for solving reachability problems of ATRBAC systems

solution of a reachability problem for an ATRBAC system: first use the translation in Figure 1 and then run the backward reachability procedure in Section 3 on the resulting BSR-STS. Since the interpretation of $User$ is left unconstrained by the axioms in Ax_{ATRBAC}, the backward reachability procedure supports the solution of reachability problems for a finite but unknown number of users. As it is common for model checking procedures, backward reachability suffers from the state-space explosion problem. In Section 5, we discuss a general heuristics to alleviate this problem and refine the two-phase technique by adding a pre-processing phase whose goal is to reduce the number of administrative actions to consider while not degrading the precision of the analysis. We also illustrate the impact of the heuristics on the performance of an implementation of our approach in Section 5.1.

5. TECHNIQUE AND EXPERIMENTS

Our safety analysis technique is depicted in Figure 2. It takes as input a reachability problem (u, C, s) for an ATRBAC system (α, ψ) and returns either 'reachable' or 'unreachable'. When returning 'reachable', it outputs a finite sequence of actions in ψ that leads the ATRBAC system from α to a state in which (u, C, s) is satisfied.

The modules 'Translator' and 'BR' in Figure 2 correspond to the translation in Figure 1 and the backward reachability procedure sketched in Section 3, respectively. The module 'Action Filter' in Figure 2 corresponds to a heuristics aiming to identify a (hopefully small) sub-set ψ' of the administrative actions in ψ, that is sufficient to show whether (u, C, s) is reachable or not. The intuition underlying the heuristics is to identify—in a computationally cheap way—the actions in ψ that are likely to be applied in successive iterations of the backward reachability procedure, i.e. first those giving the set S_1 of states from which it is possible to reach the goal in one step, then those giving set S_2 of states from which a state of S_1 can be reached in one step, and so on. This is formalized by the notion of useful action. Let (u, C, s) be a reachability problem for an ATRBAC system ψ, an administrative action $\tau = (C_a, \{ts_{rule}\}, C_\tau, \{ts_r\}, r)$ in ψ is *useful* iff there exists a non-negative integer k such that τ is k-useful, where τ is

- 0-*useful* iff $r \in C$ and ts_r is in s or

- k-*useful* with $k > 0$ iff it is $(k-1)$-useful or there exists a $(k-1)$-useful action $(C'_a, \{ts'_{rule}\}, C', \{ts'_r\}, r')$ such that r occurs (possibly negated) either in C' and $ts'_r = ts_r$ or in C'_a and $ts'_{rule} = ts_r$.

Since there are finitely many administrative actions in ψ, there must exist a non-negative integer k^* such that an administrative action in ψ is useful iff it is k^*-useful. The 'Action Filter' in Figure 2 computes k^* by first identifying the set of all 0-useful actions, then the set of all 1-useful actions, and so on until the set of $(k^* + 1)$-useful actions is the same of that of k^*-useful actions, i.e. the fix-point ψ' has been obtained.

Property 1 *Let (u, C, s) be a reachability problem for an ATRBAC system (α, ψ) and ψ' be the set of useful actions computed by the 'Action Filter' in Figure 2. Then, (u, C, s) is reachable by using the actions in ψ iff it is so by using the actions in ψ'.*

This heuristics is an extension of the one designed for AR-BAC policies in [20]. The proof of Property 1 is an adaptation of that in [20] of a similar result for ARBAC policies; it is omitted for space constraints. The correctness of the translation (discussed in Section 4) and Property 1 imply that (u, C, s) is reachable by the ATRBAC system (α, ψ) iff the technique in Figure 2 returns 'reachable'.

The heuristics for useful actions and the related discussion extends straightforwardly to the case in which the input to our technique is a generalized reachability problem (C, s), as defined in Section 4. To see why this is the case, it is sufficient to observe that the definition of useful action does not depend on the user u in the reachability problem (u, C, s).

5.1 Implementation and Evaluation

We have implemented the technique of Figure 2 in a tool called ASASPTIME: the module 'BR' re-uses (off-the-shelf) the SMT-based model checker MCMT [10] and the modules 'Action Filter' and 'Translator' have been implemented in Python.

Description of the benchmark problems. We consider three benchmark classes—identified in the following by (a), (b), and (c)—comprising synthetic reachability problems: (a) and (b) assume separate administration whereas (c) does not. Benchmark class (a) contains the problems used in [26] whereas benchmark classes (b) and (c) contain reachability problems for ATRBAC systems that we have created by "temporalizing" (i.e. randomly adding the rule and role schedules to administrative actions of) the ARBAC policies in [24] and [9], respectively. Although our technique is capable of handling an arbitrary reachability problem (u, C_f, s_f), the three benchmark classes contain problems in which both C_f and s_f are singletons. The reason for this choice are two-fold. First, it simplifies the comparison with the tool described in [26], denoted in the following with TRED,[3] whereby reachability problems with only singleton condition and schedule set are considered. Second, observe that it is possible to reduce a reachability problem (u, C_f, s_f) with non-singleton set s_f of schedules to the set of problems $\{(u, C_f, \{t_f\}) \mid t_f \in s_f\}$. When the condition $C_f = \{\sigma\}$ is a singleton set for some signed role σ, this reduction enables our analysis technique to report whether σ can (or cannot, according to its sign) be assigned to the user u at each time slot in s_f. This is similar to what is done in one of the variants (called the "role schedule approach") of the technique in [26] and provides more detailed information on a certain reachability problem than simply reporting that the user u can (or cannot) be assigned to σ in *some* of the time slots in s_f. Indeed, the price to pay for the higher precision of

the analysis is a linear increase—in the number of time slots in s_f—of the reachability problems to be solved. Also in this case, the behavior of ASASPTIME on the problems in benchmark class (a) is similar to those in Figure 3 thanks to the heuristics based on useful actions. When the condition C_f is not a singleton set, the situation is more complex since we need to establish if it is possible to reach a TRBAC policy in which the user u can (or cannot) be assigned to each (signed) role of C_f. This situation is already computationally more expensive for ARBAC policies as observed in [1, 19]. To cope with this, we believe it is possible to adapt the sub-goaling technique in [1] for ARBAC policies to the ATRBAC systems considered in this paper. We leave this and the related experimental evaluation to future work. Here, instead, we prefer to study the behavior of our technique for different values of the parameters characterizing the size of (the set of) administrative actions. The values of such parameters for the three benchmark classes are shown in Table 1. The first column lists the parameters of an ATR-BAC system (α_0, ψ) for a reachability problem in any one of the three benchmark classes: Ro is the number of roles in the TRBAC policy α_0, Ru is the number of administrative actions in ψ, TS is the number of time slots of the ATRBAC system (α_0, ψ), AC is the cardinality of C_a, and C is the cardinality of C for an administrative action (C_a, s_{rule}, C, s_r) in ψ. The remaining three columns of Table 1, each one corresponding to a benchmark class, contains the value Z or the range $[X..Y]$ of values that a parameter p can take.

Experimental evaluation. All the experiments were performed on an Intel QuadCore (3.6 GHz) CPU with 16 GB Ram running Ubuntu 11.10.

Benchmark class (a) contains instances of the reachability in which the role status and the timed user-assignment relations in the initial TRBAC policy are empty and the administrative actions are randomly generated under separate administration [26]. Because of this assumption, we can safely ignore the condition C_a in each administrative action (C_a, s_{rule}, C, s_r), i.e. AC = 0 in Table 1, as there exists an administrator capable of executing any action anytime. The goal of these reachability problems is to understand how performances vary for increasing values (namely, 100, 300, 500, 700, and 1,000) of one of the three parameters Ro, Ru, and TS and leaving the other two fixed values (both at 200). For increasing values of each parameter, 15 instances are considered and the average of the times taken to solve each problem is shown in the three plots of Figure 3. Blue squares with solid lines identifies the performances of ASASPTIME. Dark blue diamonds with dashed lines and dark blue triangles with dash-dotted lines are the performances of two versions of TRED, resulting from two strategies with which it reduces a reachability problem for an ATRBAC system to several instances of the reachability problem for (variants of) ARBAC policies and then re-use (adapt) existing tools for ARBAC

---

[3]We thank the authors of [26] for making available to us the latest version of TRED together with the benchmarks in (a). We also gratefully acknowledge the support of Emre Uzun with running the tool.

Table 1: Values of parameters in the experiments

	(a)	(b)	(c)
Ro	$[100..1,000]$	$[10..32]$	$[15..34]$
Ru	$[100..1,000]$	$[229..1,076]$	$[127..994]$
TS	$[100..1,000]$	$[5..100]$	$[5..40]$
AC	0	0	1
C	$[1..10]$	$[1..6]$	$[1..8]$

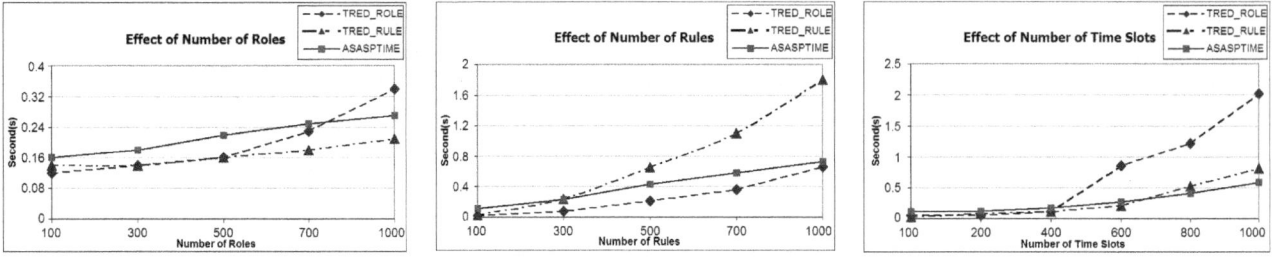

Figure 3: Results on benchmark class (a)

analysis. We denote by TRED_RULE and TRED_ROLE the two versions of TRED that work by splitting the reachability problem according to s_{rule} and s_r, respectively, in each administrative action $(C_a, s_{rule}, C, s_r, r)$. For details on the techniques underlying TRED, the reader is pointed to [26].

The plots of Figure 3 shows that the growth of ASASP-TIME performance closely follows that of the best version of TRED: it is linear when the number of roles or of time slots increases and it is linear (not exponential as it is the case for TRED, according to what has been already observed in [26]) when the number of administrative actions increases. The heuristic based on useful actions described above is key to this result because it helps in greatly reducing (even of 99%) the number of administrative actions. We observe that both tools find the problems in this class rather easy, as all timings are under 2 seconds.

Benchmark class (b) contains problems obtained by temporalizing the ARBAC policies in [24] under separate administration (AC = 0 in Table 1). For the values of the parameters Ro and Ru fixed by the underlying ARBAC policies, we generate an ATRBAC system by considering a value for TS from the set $\{5, 10, 20, 30, 40, 60, 80, 100\}$. The cluster bars plot in Figure 4 shows the performances of TRED_ROLE (black bar) and ASASPTIME (white bar) on this benchmark class: the y-axis shows average time (in seconds) taken by the tools to solve 15 user-role reachability problems obtained by randomly generated goals for each ATRBAC system considered above while the x-axis reports the tuples of values Ro/Ru (Us)/TS for Us the number of useful actions computed by the heuristics illustrated above. (Notice how more than one values of the parameters Ro, Ru, and TS may vary from one data point to the next one on the x-axis.) Although the problems in this benchmark class are more difficult than those in benchmark class (a)—compare the values on the y-axis of the plots in Figure 3 with those in the plot of Figure 4—clearly, ASASPTIME performs better than TRED_ROLE and shows a linear behavior for increasing values of the parameter TS instead of the exponential behavior of TRED_ROLE. (We do not report the results of TRED_RULE because it seg-faults for all but one problem in class (b); we have informed the authors of [26] about this problem and they are currently fixing it.) The heuristic based on useful actions is—as before—the key to explain the superior performances of ASASPTIME over TRED—compare the value of Ru with that of Us for each point on the x-axis: the alleviation of the state-space explosion problem is quite substantial.

Benchmark class (c) contains problems obtained by temporalizing the ARBAC policies in [9] without assuming separate administration (AC = 1 in Table 1). The problems are gen-

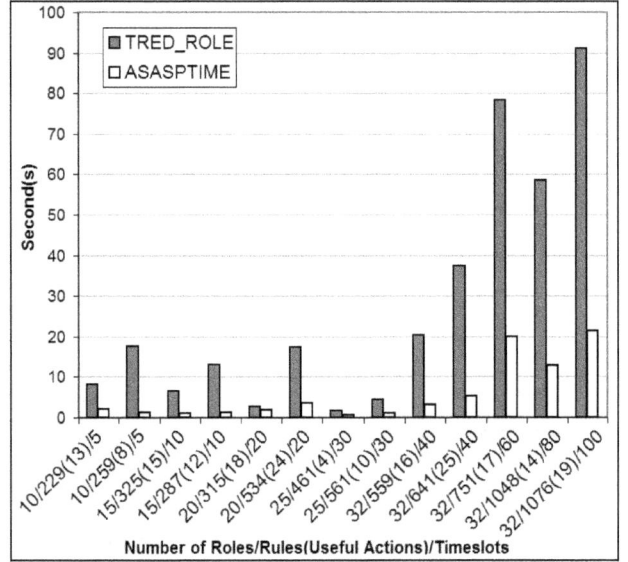

Figure 4: Results on benchmark class (b)

erated in the same way of those in benchmark class (b). The average time taken by ASASPTIME to solve the 15 problem instances per generated ATRBAC system are shown in Table 2. It is not possible to perform a comparison with TRED on this benchmark class since it does not fully support non-separate administration [25]. This is only an implementation issue, not a theoretical limitation of the approach in [26]. A first step in the direction of tackling reachability problems without separate administration is reported in [26] by considering so-called "multi-user reachability problems." These seem to be more general than problems under separate administration but not yet fully beyond it. We conclude by observing the importance of the heuristics based on useful actions for the scalability of ASASPTIME also on benchmark class (c)—compare the value of Ru with that in the column 'Useful actions:' as for the previous two benchmark classes, the alleviation of the state-space explosion problem is substantial.

6. CONCLUSIONS

We have described a precise and scalable automated analysis technique for solving reachability problems of ATRBAC systems. The approach amounts to translating safety problems to (decidable) reachability problems of BSR-STSs [19] and leveraging an existing symbolic model checking tool, MCMT [10], to solve them. We have also argued the correctness of the translation and shown that the analysis technique built on top of it can solve reachability problems for ATRBAC systems with a finite but unknown number of users. In this way, our technique is capable of certifying safety by taking into account that users may join or leave the organization in which the TRBAC policies are administered since the certificate holds for any (finite) number of users. Similarly, it can discover the number of users required for a certain sequence of administrative actions to turn the initial policy into one violating a security goal. This dramatically enlarges the scope of applicability of the analysis and thus the usefulness of its results. For example, it allows us to go beyond unrealistic assumptions, such as separate-administration. To the best of our knowledge, it is the first time that the decidability of the reachability problem for this class of ATRBAC systems is proved.

Concerning complexity, reachability problems of ATRBAC systems are PSPACE-hard. In fact, it is easy to reduce user-role reachability problems of administrative URA97 policies—which are in PSPACE [23]—to ATRBAC reachability problems, by ensuring that the temporal constraints are always satisfied. A more exhaustive characterization of the complexity of the general reachability problem for ATRBAC systems and its restrictions (e.g., under separate administration) is left as future work. In this paper, we have presented an extensive experimental analysis of the performances of our approach, that confirms its scalability and better behavior in comparison with the recent approach in [26]. Key to this is the heuristics (based on useful actions) that permits a substantial reduction of the set of administrative actions to be considered during model checking without losing precision. Since our heuristics is applied as a pre-processing step, we believe that it can be used also by other approaches to solve reachability problems for ATRBAC systems.

Another interesting line of research for future work is to study how to incorporate in our approach the notion of temporal role hierarchies [27]. Here, only time-independent role hierarchies have been considered (recall the beginning of Section 2) since they can be pre-processed away [23]. This can no more be done when the hierarchy is time-dependent, rising a new challenge for our safety analysis technique.

As a final remark, we would like to point out the problem of finding adequate benchmark sets that we have faced several times in our efforts for this paper and previous works [3, 1, 5, 4, 20, 19] for the design of safety analysis techniques in access control. As in many other papers in the literature (see, e.g., [24, 13, 9]), the evaluation is based on benchmarks derived from synthetic policies. In many cases, these are generated by identifying a realistic policy (e.g., for a bank or a hospital) together with some parameters that can be increased so that larger and larger instances of the same policy can be generated. Indeed, the goal is to evaluate the scalability of the proposed techniques. Unfortunately, the significance of the experimental results obtained in this way is debatable. The results reported in this paper suffer from the same problem. We believe that a community effort is needed to build up a common database of benchmarks, derived from real-world policies, that can be used to evaluate and compare old and new analysis techniques. Similar initiative in other fields (e.g., SAT/SMT solving,[4] Planning,[5] and Verification[6]) have greatly contributed to their advance. We believe this is a great opportunity also for increasing the impact of the safety analysis of access control policies in security. We hope that these remarks will stimulate further discussion and work in the community.

7. REFERENCES

[1] F. Alberti, A. Armando, and S. Ranise. Efficient Symbolic Automated Analysis of Administrative Role Based Access Control Policies. In *ASIACCS*. ACM Pr., 2011.

[2] R. Alur and D. Dill. A theory of timed automata. *Theoretical Computer Science*, 126:183–285, 1994.

[3] A. Armando and S. Ranise. Automated Symbolic Analysis of ARBAC Policies. In *6th STM Workshop*, volume 6710 of *LNCS*, pages 17–33. Springer, 2010.

[4] A. Armando and S. Ranise. Automated and efficient analysis of role-based access control with attributes. In *DBSec'12: Proceedings of the 26th Annual IFIP WG 11.3 conference on Data and Applications Security and Privacy*, pages 25–40. Springer-Verlag, 2012.

[5] A. Armando and S. Ranise. Scalable Automated Symbolic Analysis of Administrative Role-Based Access Control Policies by SMT Solving. *J. of Computer Security*, 20(4):309–352, 2012.

[6] B. Beckert, C. A. R. Hoare, R. Hähnle, R. Smith, D. R. Green, S. Ranise, C. Tinelli, T. Ball, and S. K. Rajamani. Intelligent systems and formal methods in software engineering. *IEEE Int. Sys.*, 21(6):71–81, 2006.

[7] E. Bertino, P. Bonatti, and E. Ferrari. TRBAC: A Temporal Role Based Access Control Model. *ACM TISSEC*, 4(3):191–233, 2001.

[8] H. B. Enderton. *A Mathematical Introduction to Logic*. Academic Press, Inc., 1972.

Table 2: Results on benchmark class (c)

Test Case	Ro/Ru/TS	ASASPTIME Useful actions	ASASPTIME Verification time (s)
Hospital 1	15/127/5	6	**0.45**
Hospital 2	15/149/5	9	**0.56**
Hospital 3	15/267/10	8	**0.63**
Hospital 4	15/287/10	12	**0.89**
Hospital 5	15/365/20	16	**1.93**
Hospital 6	15/392/20	14	**2.06**
Hospital 7	15/367/30	13	**2.15**
Hospital 8	15/552/30	22	**6.58**
Hospital 9	15/479/40	17	**5.19**
Hospital 10	15/725/40	19	**6.81**
University 1	34/220/5	5	**0.59**
University 2	34/224/5	8	**0.83**
University 3	34/483/10	9	**0.95**
University 4	34/491/10	7	**1.39**
University 5	34/542/20	13	**2.71**
University 6	34/560/20	13	**2.21**
University 7	34/784/30	18	**6.79**
University 8	34/802/30	17	**4.01**
University 9	34/938/40	23	**6.96**
University 10	34/994/40	27	**9.92**

---

[4] http://www.satlive.org and http://www.smtlib.org
[5] http://ipc.icaps-conference.org
[6] http://sv-comp.sosy-lab.org/2014

[9] A. L. Ferrara, P. Madhusudan, and G. Parlato. Policy Analysis for Self-Administrated Role-based Access Control. In *TACAS*. Springer, 2013.

[10] S. Ghilardi and S. Ranise. MCMT: a Model Checker Modulo Theories. In *Proc. of IJCAR'10*, LNCS, 2010.

[11] M. I. Gofman, R. Luo, A. C. Solomon, Y. Zhang, P. Yang, and S. D. Stoller. Rbac-pat: A policy analysis tool for role based access control. In *TACAS*, volume 5505 of *LNCS*, pages 46–49. Springer, 2009.

[12] M. A. Harrison, W. L. Ruzzo, and J. D. Ullman. Protection in Operating Systems. *Communications of ACM*, 19(8):461–471, 1976.

[13] K. Jayaraman, V. Ganesh, M. Tripunitara, M. Rinard, and S. Chapin. Automatic Error Finding for Access-Control Policies. In *CCS*. ACM, 2011.

[14] J. B. D. Joshi, E. Bertino, U. Latif, and A. Ghafoor. A Generalized Temporal Role-Based Access Control Model. *In IEEE Trans. on Knowledge and Data Engineering*, 7(1):4–23, 2005.

[15] N. Li and M. V. Tripunitara. Security analysis in role-based access control. *ACM TISSEC*, 9(4):391–420, 2006.

[16] S. Mondal, S. Sural, and V. Atluri. Security analysis of GTRBAC and its variants using model checking. volume 30, pages 128–147, 2011.

[17] R. Piskac, L. de Moura, and N. Bjørner. Deciding Effectively Propositional Logic Using DPLL and Substitution Sets. *J. of Automated Reasoning*, 44(4):401–424, 2010.

[18] F. P. Ramsey. On a Problem of Formal Logic. *Proceedings of the London Mathematical Society*, s2-30(1):264–286, 1930.

[19] S. Ranise. Symbolic Backward Reachability with Effectively Propositional Logic—Applications to Security Policy Analysis. *FMSD*, 42(1):24–45, 2013.

[20] S. Ranise, T. A. Truong, and A. Armando. Boosting Model Checking to Analyse Large ARBAC Policies. In *8th STM Workshop*, volume 7783 of *LNCS*, pages 273–288. Springer, 2012.

[21] R. Sandhu, V. Bhamidipati, and Q. Munawer. The ARBAC97 model for role-based control administration of roles. *ACM TISSEC*, 1(2):105–135, 1999.

[22] R. Sandhu, E. Coyne, H. Feinstein, and C. Youmann. Role-Based Access Control Models. *IEEE Computer*, 2(29):38–47, 1996.

[23] A. Sasturkar, P. Yang, S. D. Stoller, and C.R. Ramakrishnan. Policy analysis for administrative role based access control. In *CSF*. IEEE Press, July 2006.

[24] S. D. Stoller, P. Yang, C.R. Ramakrishnan, and M. I. Gofman. Efficient policy analysis for administrative role based access control. In *CCS*. ACM Press, 2007.

[25] E. Uzun. Personal communication. By email, October 29, 2013.

[26] E. Uzun, V. Atluri, S. Sural, J. Vaidya, G. Parlato, and A. L. Ferrara. Analyzing Temporal Role Based Access Control Models. In *SACMAT*, pages 177–186. ACM, 2012.

[27] E. Uzun, V. Atluri, J. Vaidya, and S. Sural. Analysis of TRBAC with Dynamic Temporal Role Hierarchies. In *DBSeC XXVII*, volume 7964 of *LNCS*, pages 297–304. 2013.

Access Control Models for Geo-Social Computing Systems

Ebrahim Tarameshloo   Philip W. L. Fong
Department of Computer Science,
University of Calgary,
Calgary, Alberta, Canada
{ etarames, pwlfong }@ucalgary.ca

ABSTRACT

A Geo-Social Computing System (GSCS) allows users to declare their current locations, and uses these declared locations to make authorization decisions. Recent years have seen the emergence of a new generation of social computing systems that are GSCSs.

This paper proposes a protection model for GSCSs. The protection system tracks the current locations of users and a knowledge base of primitive spatial relations between locations. Access control policies can be formulated by the composition of primitive spatial relations. The model is extended to account for Geo-Social Network Systems (GSNSs), which track both a spatial knowledge base and a social network. A policy language for GSNSs is proposed for specifying policies that combine both social and spatial constraints.

Categories and Subject Descriptors

D.4.6 [**Security and Protection**]: Access Controls

Keywords

Protection Model, Geo-Social Computing Systems, Geo-Social Network Systems, Location-based Protection, Spatial Relation, Policy Language, Hybrid Logic.

1. INTRODUCTION

With the proliferation of the Internet and GPS enabled smartphones, *Geo-Social Computing Systems (GSCSs)* have seen widespread adoption. These systems empower mobile users with knowledge of their vicinity, and thus significantly promote social interactions in contexts including transportation, marketing, health, and the general cultivation of personal and professional relationships. For instance, in PulsePoint, a registered user with cardiopulmonary resuscitation (CPR) training will be notified if a cardiac emergency occurs in his or her neighborhood; in Sonar [37] and Banjo [7], users can meet with friends who are nearby; in Foursquare and Yelp, a user can locate not only nearby

friends, but also restaurants and stores with good reviews from friends and other users; in Waze [44], a user selects routes based on traffic reports by friends and other users.

What distinguishes social computing systems is not only the fact that users may contribute personal information to the systems, but also the fact that such user-contributed information is used as the basis of authorization decisions. For example, user relationships are used by social network systems for authorizing accesses [24, 23]. Similarly, a distinguishing feature of GSCSs is that a user may declare her current location (through a mechanism known as "check in"), and such location declarations are used as a basis of authorization (e.g., "allow access if nearby"). GSCS policies can be used for protecting user contributed information, such as photos, status updates, etc. As a special case, the location declaration of a user can also be protected by such policies, just like the friend list can be protected by a relationship-based policy. The focus of this work is the formulation and analysis of access control models in which authorization decisions are a function of location claims.

There has been a growing body of literature on spatially aware access control models [19, 5, 33, 42, 27, 10, 11, 16, 34, 2, 6, 21, 1, 30]. Building on these insights, this study of GSCSs aspires to further our understanding of spatially-aware access control in two areas.

Area 1: Composite Policies. In previous works, location-based policies are usually atomic. In this work, we study how *composite* location-based policies can be formulated in terms of primitive spatial relations. Supporting composite policies offers system designers the flexibility of adopting a larger policy vocabulary, and defining high-level spatial concepts out of low-level spatial relations. Consider a PulsePoint-like GSCS that authorizes a helper's involvement by considering not only the length of the route to the incident location, but also whether the route allows the helper to fetch a nearby AED (automated external defibrillator). This policy involves non-trivial composition of spatial relationships that goes beyond mere Boolean combinations. What kind of composition operators are useful for composing location-based policies? What properties must a composite policy observe in order to reflect common spatial concepts?

Area 2: Geo-Social Network Systems. To the best of our knowledge, there has been no prior work that studies location-based policies in the context of social computing, especially in the context of a *Geo-Social Network System (GSNS)*, in which authorization decisions are based on both location claims as well as user relationships. For example, in a Yelp-like GSNS, a restaurant may authorize a steep promotional discount (as electronic coupons) when a potential customer is not only nearby, but also co-located with three or more friends. What policy languages would support the seamless interleaving of both location and relationship requirements? What authorization architecture is desirable?

In this work, a generic protection model for GSCSs is proposed. Our model captures the two essences of GSCSs: (a) the protection system tracks the declared locations of the users; (b) the relationship between declared locations of the resource requester and the resource owner form the basis of authorization decisions. The spatial knowledge of the protection system is explicitly modelled as a spatial structure (i.e., a graph-like structure; cf. [8]). The latter captures the primitive spatial relationships between known locations. Access control policies can then be formulated by the composition of these primitive spatial relations. The result is a highly flexible theoretical framework for exploring the composition of location-based access control policies. Details of this first contribution are discussed in §3.

A second contribution of this work is presented in §4, in which we propose a classification of GSCSs based on the complexity of the spatial knowledge base. Based on this classification, we outline properties that are common among policies in each family, as well as the implementation strategy for each of the families.

As a third contribution, we identify in §5 the algebraic properties common to reasonable GSCS policies, including co-location, proximity, and policies that interoperate with a spatial hierarchy. Such properties can be used for verifying if a composite GSCS policy has been formulated properly.

These three contributions target **Area 1**.

As a fourth contribution, the GSCS protection model has been extended to account for GSNSs. A GSNS tracks both the declared locations and the declared social relationships of the users. We consider a novel kind of GSNS policies, which are formulated in terms of the social network induced by a spatial neighborhood. A policy language for specifying such policies is proposed, and a modular architecture for authorization is articulated. This contribution, which deepens our understanding of **Area 2**, is detailed in §6.

2. RELATED WORKS

Although the literature is relatively silent on the access control models for GSCSs and GSNSs, there is a vast literature on using location information for controlling access. Spatially aware access control mechanisms can be traced back to [19, 5] (which address the information sharing concerns of satellite images in Geographical Information Systems) or [33, 42] (which propose architectures for location-based applications in wireless local networks).

Generic location-based access control models [27, 11, 34, 21, 30] have been proposed as extensions to the Role-based Access Control (RBAC) [35]. Bertino *et al.* proposed GEO-RBAC [11] to enable RBAC to incorporate spatial restrictions. Specifically, they introduced the notion of *spatial roles*, such that every role is paired with a spatial extent (a set of static spatial boundaries). A spatial role can be enabled only when the user's position is contained in the role's spatial extent. Another extension, LRBAC by Ray *et al.* [34], adds spatial extents to both permissions and roles. Specifically, an object's location must be contained in a permission's spatial extent in order for access to be granted.

Kirkpatrick *et al.*, in their work on Prox-RBAC [30], proposed *proximity-based* location constraints to extend RBAC. Specifically, the locations of other users in the system are considered when the access request of a user is authorized. They adopt a spatial model that subdivides an indoor space into a set of *protected areas*. In Prox-RBAC, a proximity constraint considers the *presence* or *absence* of other users in a protected area as well as the continuity of constraint enforcement when users change their locations.

There are also spatiotemporal extensions of RBAC that include both temporal and spatial constraints [16, 2, 6, 1]. In STARBAC [2, 1], the spatial constraints consider only the containment of a physical location in a set of points (as a logical location) for role enabling and disabling. LoT-RBAC [16] is another spatiotemporal extension that employs separate spatial containment hierarchy for each physical and logical location in order to incorporate fine-grained spatial constraints into RBAC. Although the authors were aware of the five topological relations between 2D objects [20], only containment is exploited in their authorization model.

Ardagna *et al.* [3] proposed an access control model for location-based services. They identified three types of location-based conditions. The first type are position-based conditions on the locations of users (e.g., containment or proximity). The second type corresponds to movement-based conditions on the mobility of users (e.g., velocity, acceleration or direction). The third type includes interaction-based conditions among multiple users and entities (e.g., number of users within a given area). Their model supports only a fixed set of location predicate families: i.e., *inarea*, *disjoint* and *distance* for position-based conditions, *velocity* for movement-based conditions, and *density* for interaction-based conditions.

Belussi *et al.* [10] proposed a discretionary access control model for geographical maps stored in spatial databases. Spatial objects have geometric and topological properties. Authorization rules against objects can be specified at a very fine-grained level, and positive and negative authorizations can be propagated among spatial objects.

While the approaches above have made significant contributions in the development of location-based access control models, our work is distinctive in that it captures the richness of spatial reasoning by supporting the formulation of complex location-based policies through the composition of primitive spatial relations. We also demonstrate how this GSCS model can be extended to a GNSN model, thereby allowing us to explore the interplay between spatial awareness and social relationships.

We are aware of an orthogonal previous work [31] that has considered location privacy of members in using proximity services in GSNSs. Their proposed cryptographic-based protocol, only considers *proximity* as an atomic spatial relation between two users. In addition, the *friend* relation is only utilized for identifying the list of users that the secret key should be shared with for a given member.

In recent years, a great deal of attention has been focused on the area of access control models for social computing applications [24, 15, 39, 38, 18]. A Relationship-Based Access Control (ReBAC) model and a series of ReBAC policy languages have been proposed in [23, 25, 13]. There are two points of comparison between this work and that of ReBAC. First, while the spatial structure tracked by a GSCS is mathematically akin to the relational structure in ReBAC, a novelty of this paper lies in studying the common families of GSCSs (§4) and the common properties of GSCS policies (§5). Second, while hybrid logic is used as a policy language in both ReBAC and GSNS, a novelty of this paper (§6) lies in (a) considering policies that are formulated in terms of the social network induced by a spatial neighborhood, (b) proposing a modular architecture in which the location service is separated from the social network service, and (c) devising an enforcement mechanism for the policies in (a) under the architectural constraints of (b).

The notion of policies induced by path patterns in §5 can be seen as a special case of Fong *et al.*'s notion of inducing an FSNS or ReBAC policy using bi-rooted graph patterns [22, 25]. Cheng *et al.* employs regular expressions as a building block for specifying ReBAC policies that are path based [17]. In comparison, our notion is at the semantic level rather than syntactic level, and thus may capture path pattern set that is not regular.

Jin *et al.* [29] presented a comparative analysis of currently implemented access control mechanisms for the user check-in feature of four GSNSs. They enumerated privacy issues in these GSNSs. Their analysis highlighted the necessity of having a more flexible policy language for GSNSs.

3. A PROTECTION MODEL FOR GEO-SOCIAL COMPUTING SYSTEMS

There are two defining characteristics of a Geo-Social Computing System (GSCS). First, a user can declare her current location through a mechanism commonly known as "check-in." Second, the protection system has a prior notion of how locations are related geometrically, and it uses the relationship between the declared locations of the resource owner and the requester as a basis of authorization.[1] That is, if the declared location of the resource owner and that of the resource requester are related in a way mandated by the access control policy (e.g., co-location, close proximity, spatial containment, etc), then access is granted. The formal model presented below captures this paradigm of access control.

3.1 Notations

Sets and Functions.

We write $|S|$ for the cardinality of set S. Note that if S is infinite, then $|S|$ is a cardinal number [26]. We write 2^S for the powerset of S (i.e., the set of all subsets of S).

We write $\mathcal{F}(S,T)$ for the set of all functions $f : S' \to T$ such that $S' \subseteq S$. That is, $\mathcal{F}(S,T)$ is the set of all *partial* functions from S to T. We write $f : S \rightharpoonup T$ when f is such a partial function. We write $dom(f)$ and $ran(f)$ respectively for the domain and range of function f. Given $f : S \rightharpoonup T$, $s \in S$ and $t \in T$, we write $f[s \mapsto t]$ for the function that maps s to t but otherwise behaves just like f. We write id_S for the identity map over domain S, or simply id if S is known from the context.

Relational Structures.

Fixing a finite set $\mathcal{I}$ of indices, a *(binary) relational structure* is a pair $G = \langle V, \{R_i\}_{i \in \mathcal{I}} \rangle$, where V is a set of entities, and $\{R_i\}_{i \in \mathcal{I}}$ is an indexed family of binary relations such that $R_i \subseteq V \times V$. We write $V(G)$ for V and $R_i(G)$ for R_i. When the set V is finite, then the relational structure is also called a *graph* or a *network*. Then $u \in V$ is a *vertex* and $(u,v) \in R_i$ is an *edge* of type i. That is, a finite relational structure is an edge-labelled directed graph.

Given a finite set $\mathcal{I}$ and a carrier set $\mathcal{V}$, we write $\mathcal{G}(\mathcal{I}, \mathcal{V})$ for the set of all relational structures G with $\mathcal{I}$ as the index set and $V(G) \subseteq \mathcal{V}$. We also write $\mathcal{G}_{\mathsf{fin}}(\mathcal{I}, \mathcal{V})$ for the set of all graphs (i.e., finite relational structures) in $\mathcal{G}(\mathcal{I}, \mathcal{V})$.

Suppose $G, G' \in \mathcal{G}(\mathcal{I}, \mathcal{V})$. A bijective function $f : V(G) \to V(G')$ is called an *isomorphism* between G and G' iff $(u,v) \in R_i(G) \Leftrightarrow (f(u), f(v)) \in R_i(G')$. In this case, we say that G and G' are *isomorphic*, and write $G \equiv_f G'$, or simply $G \equiv G'$ if the identification of f is not important.

Suppose $G = \langle V, \{R_i\}_{i \in \mathcal{I}} \rangle$, and $\mathcal{I}' \subseteq \mathcal{I}$. We write $G \downarrow \mathcal{I}'$ for the graph $\langle V, \{R_i\}_{i \in \mathcal{I}'} \rangle$. That is, $G \downarrow \mathcal{I}'$ is the graph obtained from G by discarding the edges with labels in $\mathcal{I} \setminus \mathcal{I}'$.

Suppose $G = \langle V, \{R_i\}_{i \in \mathcal{I}} \rangle$, and $V' \subseteq V$. The *subgraph of G induced by V'* (denoted by $G[V']$) is the relational structure G' for which $V(G') = V'$ and $R_i(G') = R_i(G) \cap (V' \times V')$ for every $i \in \mathcal{I}$.

3.2 Spatial Structures

A GSCS tracks a knowledge base of known locations and their primitive spatial relationships. Access control policies are composed from these primitive relationships. We model the spatial knowledge base as a relational structure $G = \langle L, \{R_i\}_{i \in \mathcal{I}} \rangle$, where $\mathcal{I}$ is a finite set of *spatial relation identifiers*, and L is a set of known locations. We call G a *spatial structure*, or a *spatial network* in case L is finite. The following are examples of spatial structures.

EXAMPLE 1 (CITIES AND NEIGHBOURHOODS). *Let $\mathcal{I} = \{\mathsf{coloc}, \mathsf{in}, \mathsf{next}\}$ be a set of spatial relation identifiers. Consider a spatial structure $G = \langle L, \{R_i\}_{i \in \mathcal{I}} \rangle$. The locations in L represent either cities (coarser grained location labels) or neighbourhoods (finer grained location labels). R_{coloc} is the co-location relation (i.e., the equality relation, indicating same city or same neighborhood). Also, $(l_1, l_2) \in R_{\mathsf{in}}$ iff neighborhood l_1 is in city l_2. Two neighbourhoods are related by R_{next} whenever they are adjacent to one another. L is a finite set, and thus G is a spatial network.*

EXAMPLE 2 (INDOOR FLOOR PLANS). *An indoor floor plan specified by the space model of [30] can be captured by a spatial network $G = \langle L, \{R_i\}_{i \in \mathcal{I}} \rangle$, where $L = L_{pa} \uplus L_{ep}$ and $\mathcal{I} = \{\mathsf{coloc}, \mathsf{links}, \mathsf{encloses}\}$. The set L is partitioned into two sets. L_{pa} is the set of **protected areas**, which correspond to enclosed spaces such as rooms, floors, etc. L_{ep} is the set of **entry points**, which corresponds to, say, doors. The colocation relation R_{coloc} is simply equality. Given an entry point l_1 and a protected area l_2, $(l_1, l_2) \in R_{\mathsf{links}}$ whenever l_1 is an entry point of l_2. Every entry point links exactly two protected areas (i.e., a door links two areas). Given two protected areas l_1 and l_2, $(l_1, l_2) \in R_{\mathsf{encloses}}$ whenever l_1 encloses l_2, and there is no l' such that l_1 encloses l' and l' encloses l_2. R_{encloses} defines a forest.*

EXAMPLE 3 (GPS COORDINATES). *Consider the spatial structure $G = \langle L, \{R_i\}_{i \in \mathcal{I}} \rangle$, where L is the set of GPS coordinates of the form (latitude, longitude), and $\mathcal{I} = \{\mathsf{within\text{-}10}\}$.*

---

[1] The protection mechanism of a geo-social computing system may make use of other information, such as the interpersonal relationship between the resource owner and the requester, as a basis of authorization, but this section focuses on the self-declared location information.

$R_{\textsf{within-10}}$ *contains pairs of coordinates that are 10 kilometers apart. Note that L is an uncountable set.*

EXAMPLE 4 (SPATIAL OBJECTS AS POINT SETS). *[20] studies the spatial relationships between three particular kinds of spatial objects in 2-D spaces, namely, points, lines and areas. Examples of such objects may include points of attraction, roads and buildings. Using point set topology and modelling spatial objects as point sets, they show that every two such objects must be related in one of five binary relations:* touch, in, cross, overlap, disjoint. *A spatial knowledge base of a finite number of known 2-D spatial objects can therefore be represented by a spatial network $G = \langle L, \{R_i\}_{i \in \mathcal{I}} \rangle$, in which L is the set of known spatial objects, each of which is a point set, and $\mathcal{I} = \{$touch, in, cross, overlap, disjoint$\}$.*

Point-set topology has been applied for characterizing containment relationships between indoor objects [40] and relationships between spatial objects in an urban area [14].

3.3 Protection State

The protection state of a GSCS is the current location declarations of the users. These location claims are user contributed information, and thus change over time during the normal operation of the GSCS. Formally, if U is the set of all active users (see §3.5 for details), G is the spatial structure tracked by the GSCS, and $L = V(G)$ is the set of all legitimate locations, then the protection state is a function $\eta : U \to L$, which we call ***location assignment***.[2]

3.4 Access Control Policies

Recall that the essence of GSCSs is that authorization decisions are based on the relationship between the declared locations of the resource owner and requester. A "pure" GSCS policy depends only on this location relationship, but not on user identities, roles, attributes, or even interpersonal relationships. Such a "pure" GSCS policy specifies a binary relation between the two locations (that of the resource owner and requester) in the context of a spatial structure. We formalize these notions in the following.

Suppose $\mathcal{I}$ is the set of all spatial relation identifiers, $\mathcal{L}$ is the universe of all location labels, and $\mathcal{U}$ is the universe of all user identifiers. A GSCS policy is a function $P : \mathcal{G}(\mathcal{I}, \mathcal{L}) \times \mathcal{F}(\mathcal{U}, \mathcal{L}) \to 2^{\mathcal{U} \times \mathcal{U}}$, with some additional requirements to be specified below. The policy $P(G, \eta)$ takes two arguments: (i) a spatial structure $G \in \langle \mathcal{I}, \mathcal{L} \rangle$, and (ii) a function $\eta \in \mathcal{F}(\mathcal{U}, \mathcal{L})$ that assigns location labels to users. On return, $P(G, \eta) \subseteq \mathcal{U} \times \mathcal{U}$ is a binary relation over users. The additional requirements mentioned above are listed in the following. They are mainly for ensuring the policy behaves in a reasonable way.

1. $P(G, \eta) \subseteq dom(\eta) \times dom(\eta)$. (That is, the policy returns a binary relation over the users with location declarations.)
2. If $ran(\eta) \not\subseteq V(G)$, then $P(G, \eta) = \emptyset$. (That is, if the location assignment is not of the right type, then the policy returns an empty binary relation.)

---

[2]In some implemented GSCSs, an active user can elect not to declare her current location. Such systems can be modelled by introducing a special location nowhere to indicate an empty declaration. The location nowhere is naturally not related to any location (including itself) in terms of primitive spatial relations. The access control policies (§3.4) can be adjusted accordingly to prevent access if either the owner or requester is at nowhere.

Given an owner u and a requester v, authorization is granted by P iff $(u, v) \in P(G, \eta)$. We write $P(G, \eta)(u, v)$ to assert this condition. Lastly, we write $\mathcal{PO}(\mathcal{I}, \mathcal{L}, \mathcal{U})$ for the set of all GSCS policies satisfying the above requirements.

A GSCS policy P is ***identity independent*** iff for every spatial structure G, location assignment η, and bijective function $f : dom(\eta) \to dom(\eta)$, we have $P(G, \eta)(u, v)$ whenever $P(G, \eta \circ f^{-1})(f(u), f(v))$. (Here, $\eta \circ f^{-1}$ is the usual functional composition of η with f^{-1}, such that $(\eta \circ f^{-1})(u) = \eta(f^{-1}(u))$.) In other words, permuting user names does not alter authorization decisions. The authorization decisions of an identity-independent policy do not depend on user identities and attributes (e.g., roles).

EXAMPLE 5. *Let P be the following GSCS policy: "Allow access if the owner and the requester are co-located, and no other users are currently located at where they are." That is, $P(G, \eta)(u, v)$ iff $\eta(u) = \eta(v)$ and for every $u' \in dom(\eta)$, $\eta(u') = \eta(u)$ implies that either $u' = u$ or $u' = v$. Policy P is identity independent.*

In the example above, authorization depends not only on the locations of the owner and the requester, but also on the current locations of other users. Many GSCS policies are not like that. In particular, a "pure" GSCS policy authorizes by considering only the relationship between the owner and requester locations, but ignoring the locations of other users. To formalize this idea, we begin with the definition of an auxiliary concept. A ***spatial-relational concept*** is a function $P^* : \mathcal{G}(\mathcal{I}, \mathcal{L}) \to 2^{\mathcal{L} \times \mathcal{L}}$, such that $P^*(G) \subseteq V(G) \times V(G)$. That is, P^* maps a spatial structure G to a binary relation $P(G)$ defined over the locations in G. For brevity, we write $P^*(G)(u, v)$ whenever $(u, v) \in P^*(G)$.

A GSCS policy P is said to be ***pure*** iff there exists a spatial-relational concept P^* such that $P(G, \eta)(u, v)$ whenever $P^*(G)(\eta(u), \eta(v))$. By definition, a pure GSCS policy is identity independent.

As we shall see, pure policies are prominent in GSCS implementations. In the rest of this section, as well as in §4 and §5, we will focus on pure policies.

CONVENTION 6. *Unless stated otherwise, GSCS policies are assumed to be pure. For economy of expression, we will identify a spatial relational concept with the pure GSCS policy that the former induces. Therefore, we will assume that a GSCS policy has the same function signature as a spatial relational concept (i.e., $\mathcal{G}(\mathcal{I}, \mathcal{L}) \to 2^{\mathcal{L} \times \mathcal{L}}$), and we write $\mathcal{PO}(\mathcal{I}, \mathcal{L})$ for the universe of GSCS policies.*

A GSCS policy can be defined as compositions of primitive spatial relations. For example, policies can be formulated as boolean combinations of primitive spatial relations: i.e., union $(R_1 \cup R_2)$, intersection $(R_1 \cap R_2)$ and complement $(\overline{R})$.

EXAMPLE 7 (CITIES AND NEIGHBOURHOODS). *Suppose an access control policy P is to be formulated for the spatial network of Example 1. Specifically, P grants access if the owner and the requester are either co-located, or located in adjacent neighbourhoods.*

$$P(G) = R_{\textsf{coloc}}(G) \cup R_{\textsf{next}}(G) \qquad (1)$$

A composite policy can also be formulated via inverse (R^{-1}), relational composition $(R_1 \circ R_2)$, transitive closure (R^+) or reflexive transitive closure (R^*).

EXAMPLE 8 (INDOOR FLOOR PLANS). *Consider a policy P for the spatial network of Example 2, such that access is granted if the requester is located in either a protected area l accessible from the protected area in which the owner is located, or in a protected area contained in l.*

$$P(G) = (R_{\mathsf{links}}(G))^{-1} \circ R_{\mathsf{links}}(G) \circ (R_{\mathsf{encloses}}(G))^* \quad (2)$$

Two protected areas l_1 and l_2 are accessible from one another when there exists an entry point l such that $(l, l_1) \in R_{\mathsf{links}}(G)$ and $(l, l_2) \in R_{\mathsf{links}}(G)$. In other words, $(l_1, l_2) \in (R_{\mathsf{links}}(G))^{-1} \circ R_{\mathsf{links}}(G)$. A protected area l_2 is contained in protected area l_1 iff $(l_1, l_2) \in (R_{\mathsf{encloses}}(G))^*$.

CONVENTION 9. *For brevity, we specify policies by mentioning the spatial relation identifiers in place of the actual relations. That is, policies (1) and (2) could have been specified in the following shorthands.*

$$P = \mathsf{coloc} \cup \mathsf{next} \qquad P = \mathsf{links}^{-1} \circ \mathsf{links} \circ \mathsf{encloses}^*$$

CONVENTION 10. *A spatial relational concept or the policy it induces can be seen as a family of binary relations, indexed by spatial structures. Consequently, in this paper we will sometimes talk about spatial relational concepts or policies as if they are binary relations. For example, we might say, "P is reflexive." The intended meaning is that the relation $P(G)$ is reflexive for every G.*

A GSCS policy P is **topology based** iff $G \equiv_f G'$ implies that $P(G)(u, v) \Leftrightarrow P(G')(f(u), f(v))$. Topology-based policies are those for which authorization decisions are invariant over isomorphism. The policies in Examples 7 and 8 are both topology based. In §4, we will see that topology-based policies are actually exceptions rather than norms.

3.5 Putting It Together

A GSCS is specified in three "layers." A system schema specifies the ontology of the protection system (i.e., the basic entities that exist in the system). Components of a schema are constant in an installation of the GSCS. A configuration of the system specifies the current privacy settings of the GSCS. Components of a configuration are changed only by administrative operations, though configuration transition is not modelled in this work. Fixing a configuration, a protection state records the system components that may be changed as a result of regular social computing activities. Again, state transition is not the focus of this work.

3.5.1 System Schema

A **system schema** (or simply a **schema**) is a triple $\mathcal{M} = \langle \mathcal{I}, \mathcal{L}, \mathcal{U} \rangle$, where:
- $\mathcal{I}$ is a finite set of spatial relation identifiers
- $\mathcal{L}$ is a set of locations
- $\mathcal{U}$ is a countable set of user identifiers

The sets $\mathcal{I}$ and $\mathcal{L}$ specify the type of spatial relational structures the system tracks. The set $\mathcal{U}$ is the universe of user identifiers. As we shall see, not every user identifier is actively used in the protection state.

3.5.2 Privacy Configuration

A system can be configured with different privacy settings over its life cycle. A **privacy configuration** (or simply a **configuration**) is an abstraction of such settings. Intuitively, a configuration specifies (a) the access control policies

of user resources and (b) the spatial knowledge base that defines the spatial relationships among known locations. For part (a), we make the simplifying assumption that there is a single policy that controls the access of all resources owned by a given user. Generalization to per-resource policies is a trivial exercise that does not inspire.

Formally, given a schema $\mathcal{M} = \langle \mathcal{I}, \mathcal{L}, \mathcal{U} \rangle$, a configuration is a tuple $\mathcal{N} = \langle U, L, \{R_i\}_{i \in \mathcal{I}}, policy \rangle$, in which:
- $U \subseteq \mathcal{U}$ is a *finite* set of active users,
- $\langle L, \{R_i\}_{i \in \mathcal{I}} \rangle \in \mathcal{G}(\mathcal{I}, \mathcal{L})$ is a spatial relational structure,
- $policy : U \to \mathcal{PO}(\mathcal{I}, \mathcal{L})$ assigns a policy to each active user.

3.5.3 Protection State

Given a configuration $\mathcal{N} = \langle U, L, \{R_i\}_{i \in \mathcal{I}}, policy \rangle$ of a system schema $\mathcal{M} = \langle \mathcal{I}, \mathcal{L}, \mathcal{U} \rangle$, a **protection state** (or simply a **state**) is a function $\eta : U \to L$ that records the current declared locations of active users.

3.5.4 Authorization

An access request made by a requester v against a resource owned by u is granted if the following check succeeds:

$$P(G)(\eta(u), \eta(v))$$

where $P = policy(u)$ and $G = \langle L, \{R_i\}_{i \in \mathcal{I}} \rangle$. That is, the GSCS will (i) look up the current locations of u and v using the location assignment η, (ii) look up the access control policy $P = policy(u)$ of the resource owner, (iii) instantiate P by the spatial knowledge base $G = \langle L, \{R_i\}_{i \in \mathcal{I}} \rangle$ to obtain a binary relation $P(G)$, and (iv) check if the locations $\eta(u)$ and $\eta(v)$ are related according to binary relation $P(G)$.

3.5.5 A Word on Transitions

There are two levels of dynamism in a GSCS. A **configuration transition** occurs when the privacy settings of a system is reconfigured by administrative operations. This may involve (a) introduction or removal of active users in U, (b) introduction or removal of known locations in L, (c) changing the spatial relationships between known labels (i.e., mutating $\{R_i\}_{i \in \mathcal{I}}$), or (d) adopting a different policy $policy(u)$ for some user u. Fixing the system configuration, a **state transition** occurs when users change their declared locations in η. State and configuration transitions are not the focus of this paper. We leave this topic to future work.

4. COMMON GSCS FAMILIES

From the four examples of §3.2, we discern three typical families of GSCSs. The classification is based on the cardinality of $\mathcal{L}$, the universe of locations, and the cardinality of L, the set of locations tracked by the spatial knowledge base. We point out in the following the common properties of policies in each family, as well as outlining the implementation strategy of each.

4.1 Logical Locations

Definition. In this family of GSCSs, locations are discrete abstract labels of physical locations (e.g., "111 Lake Louise Drive") such as those in Examples 1 and 2. There are *countably* many such labels in $\mathcal{L}$, but the spatial knowledge base tracks only *finitely* many labels in L (i.e., $|\mathcal{L}| = |\mathbb{N}|$ and $|L| < |\mathbb{N}|$).

Examples. Factual examples of this family of GSCSs include Facebook Places, Foursquare, Yelp, Google Latitude,

Path and Full Circle. Users declare their current locations by selecting a logical label (e.g., a place name or an address) from a list provided by the application. If a user has declared his current location (via check-in), then he can explore friends and places that are in his proximity.

Policies. Policies in a GSCS with logical locations are mostly topology based (see Examples 7 and 8), as the spatial relations are logical rather than geometrical.

Implementation. A typical implementation of such a GSCS stores the entire spatial network. That is, on top of the declared location claims of the users, the graph-like spatial knowledge base is actually tracked by the GSCS in order to support the evaluation of policies. There are general-purpose, efficient procedures for evaluating complex ReBAC policies that are composed from primitive interpersonal relations [17, 13]. Such procedures can be readily adapted for evaluating composite spatial policies in this family.

4.2 Physical Coordinates

Definition. Locations of this family of GSCSs are physical points, such as GPS coordinates, or coordinates in a Euclidean space (Example 3). For these GSCSs, $|\mathcal{L}| = |L| = |\mathbb{R}^k| = |\mathbb{R}|$. That is, the spatial knowledge base is a model of uncountably infinitely many coordinates[3] (though users are located in only finitely many of them).

Examples. A factual example of this family is Sonar [37], which uses the GPS coordinate gathered from a user's smartphone to determine which Sonar users are in close proximity, and thus shall be made visible to that user.[4]

Policies. Policies in a GSCS with locations as physical coordinates are almost never topology-based. Consider the policy within-10 from Example 3. Projection of the GPS coordinates may not preserve the distance between two points.

Implementation. A typical implementation encodes the spatial structure as a set of procedures. Specifically, for each primitive spatial relation, a procedure is implemented for testing if two given points satisfy the primitive spatial relation. Unfortunately, with this implementation strategy, it is unlikely that there exists efficient procedures for evaluating the composition of such primitive spatial relations. The result is that every composition of primitive spatial relations requires a dedicated implementation. This stands in sharp contrast with the case of logical locations.

4.3 Point Sets

Definition. Locations in this third family are spatial objects that correspond to point sets (Example 4). While there are uncountably many possible point sets, the spatial knowledge base tracks only finitely many of them: i.e., $|\mathcal{L}| = |2^{\mathbb{R}}|$, $|L| < |\mathbb{N}|$.

Examples. Waze [44] can be seen as an example of this family. Users can report locations of accidents, traffic jams, speed traps, as well as road hazards and closures to their communities and friends. The reporting mechanism is akin to check-ins, except that the application maps the physical location of the reporting user to the nearest spatial object (i.e., road) as the incident's location. These reports can be

accessed by other users as they enter the areas of reported incidents.

Policies. Policies of this family may or may not be topology based. The topology-based policies rely only on the spatial relationships between objects to arrive at an authorization decision. Those that are not may rely on the geometric properties internal to the object itself (e.g., shape, dimensions or size) to make authorization decisions.

Implementation. A typical implementation would precompute the primitive spatial relations between the spatial objects in L, and thus the spatial network is stored as a graph, as in the case of the logical-location family. In this case, there are also general-purpose procedures for evaluating composite policies.

5. VERIFICATION OF GSCS POLICIES

This section discusses the common properties expected of reasonable GSCS policies, particularly those that are formulated in terms of the spatial concepts of proximity, co-location and spatial containment. The goal of this discussion is to provide algebraic tools for assisting a policy engineer in debugging a GSCS policy, by verifying if the draft policy satisfies the aforementioned properties. Detection of violation means that the policy formulation is buggy.

For GSCSs with physical coordinates (§4.2) and point sets (§4.3) as location labels, spatial properties are relatively well understood. For example, axiomatization of the concept of nearness via point-set topology can be found in [43]. The essence of proximity, co-location, and containment are not as well understood in GSCSs with logical location labels and spatial networks. As we shall demonstrate (Example 12), formulation of policies to capture such spatial concepts can be error-prone. Our discussion in this section will therefore focus on GSCSs with a finite universe of location labels.

5.1 Path Patterns

Inspired by [36], we define the notion of path patterns. Given a set $\mathcal{I}$ of relation identifiers, we write $\widetilde{\mathcal{I}}$ to be the set $\left\{ \overrightarrow{i} \mid i \in \mathcal{I} \right\} \cup \left\{ \overleftarrow{i} \mid i \in \mathcal{I} \right\}$. Here, $\overrightarrow{i}$ is a *forward edge pattern*, and $\overleftarrow{i}$ is a *backward edge pattern*. A *path pattern* is a finite string of edge patterns. That is, the set $\left(\widetilde{\mathcal{I}} \right)^*$ is the set of all path patterns based on spatial identifiers in $\mathcal{I}$. In particular, the *empty path pattern* is denoted by ϵ.

Given a relational structure $G \in \mathcal{G}_{\mathsf{fin}}(\mathcal{I}, \mathcal{V})$, a path p in G is a finite sequence $u_0 u_1 \ldots u_n$, such that $n \geq 0$ and $u_i \in V(G)$ for every $0 \leq i \leq n$. The path p is also called a (u_0, u_n)-*path*. The *length* of p is n. A *degenerate path* is a path with length 0.

We say that a path p *matches* a path pattern π in G if there are edges in G along the vertex sequence of p that match the edge patterns in p. Formally, a degenerate path u matches the empty path pattern ϵ; if $p = u_0 u_1 \ldots u_n$, $\pi = \overrightarrow{i} \cdot \pi'$, $(u_0, u_1) \in R_i(G)$, and $u_1 \ldots u_n$ matches π', then p matches π; if $p = u_0 u_1 \ldots u_n$, $\pi = \overleftarrow{i} \cdot \pi'$, $(u_1, u_0) \in R_i(G)$, and $u_1 \ldots u_n$ matches π', then p matches π. We write $p \models_G \pi$ when p matches π in G.

Path patterns can be used for specifying a GSCS policy. The GSCS policy *induced by* a path pattern set $\Pi \subseteq \left(\widetilde{\mathcal{I}} \right)^*$ is the policy P for which $(u, v) \in P(G)$ iff there exists a (u, v)-path p in G and a path pattern $\pi \in \Pi$ such that

---

[3]Actual GPS coordinates have limited resolution. Assuming the cardinality of $\mathcal{L}$ to be $|\mathbb{R}|$ underlines the intractability of implementing the spatial structure as a graph.

[4]In Sonar, one can also check in with logical labels (aka places), but that information is not used for access control.

$p \models_G \pi$. A policy induced by a path pattern set is always topology based.

The notion of a GSCS policy induced by a path pattern captures the intuition that many spatial policies grants access when the owner is "accessible" from the requester via a specific type of paths of spatial relationships. The existence of such a path is a proof of accessibility.

5.2 Proximity

A popular access control policy for GSCSs is the proximity policy, which grants access when the owner and the requester are in "close proximity". While there is no standard definition of proximity, there are certain properties that a reasonable proximity policy shall possess. Firstly, the policy must be reflexive: i.e., two co-located persons are in close proximity. Secondly, the policy must be symmetric: i.e., u is close to v if v is close to u. We say that a policy is a **formal proximity policy** if it is both reflexive and symmetric.

EXAMPLE 11. *Policy (1) in Example 7 is a formal proximity policy. So is the following policy for Example 3.*

$$P = \mathsf{within\text{-}10}$$

The following is a formal proximity policy for Example 2.

$$P = \mathsf{links}^{-1} \circ \mathsf{links} \tag{3}$$

That a GSCS policy is a formal proximity policy does not mean that it is intended to capture the notion of proximity. Yet, if a policy engineer intends to formulate a GSCS policy to capture the notion of proximity, then she should make sure that the policy is a formal proximity policy, or else the policy is likely to be flawed. Such an error is usually rare when one is working with GSCSs for which location labels are physical coordinates or point sets. When one is working with a GSCS with logical location labels, these types of errors can be subtle, and checking that a policy that is intended to capture proximity is indeed reflexive and symmetric is a first line of defence against errors.

Intuitively, if the requester's location l_2 is "close" to the owner's location l_1 according to a proximity policy P, then as the requester moves from l_2 towards l_1, the requester shall not lose access. We formalize this intuitive notion in the following definition. A GSCS policy P is a **material proximity policy** iff (a) P is a formal proximity policy, and (b) P is induced by a path pattern set Π that is prefix-closed. (A path pattern set Π is prefix-closed iff $\pi \in \Pi$ and $\pi = \pi_1 \cdot \pi_2$ jointly imply $\pi_1 \in \Pi$. That is, if a string belongs to a prefix-closed set, then all the prefixes of the string also belong to the set.) The intuition of the definition is that, if $(l_1, l_2) \in P(G)$, then there is a (l_1, l_2)-path that testifies to the "closeness" of l_1 and l_2. As the requester moves from l_2 towards l_1 along this path, all the intermediate vertices are also "close" to l_1. If a policy can be shown to be a material proximity policy, then its formulation is likely to be correct.

EXAMPLE 12. *Among the three policies in Example 11, the only policy that is not a material proximity policy is policy (3), which in turn is based on the indoor floor plan domain (Example 2). The policy is formally a proximity policy, and it is induced by a path pattern set $\Pi = \left\{ \overleftarrow{\mathsf{links}} \cdot \overrightarrow{\mathsf{links}} \right\}$. Nevertheless, Π is not prefix-closed.*

To obtain a material proximity policy, we consider the following revision.

$$P = \mathsf{coloc} \cup \mathsf{links} \cup \mathsf{links}^{-1} \cup (\mathsf{links} \circ \mathsf{links}^{-1})$$

The path pattern set Π to induce P is the prefix-closed set below.

$$\left\{ \epsilon, \overrightarrow{\mathsf{links}}, \overleftarrow{\mathsf{links}}, \overleftarrow{\mathsf{links}} \cdot \overrightarrow{\mathsf{links}} \right\}$$

The path pattern set to induce a material proximity policy has some further properties.

PROPOSITION 13. *Let P be a material proximity policy that is induced by the path pattern set Π.*
1. *$\epsilon \in \Pi$*
2. *Π is closed under **path pattern reversal**.*

A pattern set Π is closed under path pattern reversal iff $\pi \in \Pi$ implies $\pi^R \in \Pi$, where the reversal of path pattern π, written π^R, is defined as follows:

$$\epsilon^R = \epsilon \qquad \left(\overrightarrow{i} \cdot \pi \right)^R = \pi^R \cdot \overleftarrow{i} \qquad \left(\overleftarrow{i} \cdot \pi \right)^R = \pi^R \cdot \overrightarrow{i}$$

PROOF. The two properties follow immediately from the reflexivity and symmetry of P. $\square$

5.3 Co-location

Another popular access control policy adopted by simple GSCSs is co-location. A typical co-location policy grants access when the owner and the requester are situated at the same location: i.e., co-location is simply the equality relation. Sometimes, a GSCS may need to capture a less precise notion of co-location in order to promote information disclosure. As in the case of proximity policies, we define in the following reasonable properties that can be expected from policies that are intended to capture the concept of co-location, in GSCSs with logical location labels.

We say that a policy is a **formal co-location policy** iff it represents an equivalence relation (i.e., reflexive, symmetric and transitive).

EXAMPLE 14 (CITIES AND NEIGHBOURHOODS). *We formulate the following policy for the GSCS of Example 1, so that access is granted when the requester is located in the same city as the owner.*

$$P = \mathsf{coloc} \cup \mathsf{in} \cup \mathsf{in}^{-1} \cup (\mathsf{in} \circ \mathsf{in}^{-1}) \tag{4}$$

The above policy is a formal co-location policy. Each city, together with its neighbourhoods, form an equivalence class.

By definition, every formal co-location policy is also a formal proximity policy.

A GSCS policy P is a **material co-location policy** iff (a) P is a formal co-location policy, and (b) there exists $\mathcal{I}' \subseteq \mathcal{I}$ such that P is induced by the path pattern set $\left(\widetilde{\mathcal{I}'} \right)^*$. An alternative statement of (b) in graph-theoretic terms is that there exists $\mathcal{I}' \subseteq \mathcal{I}$ for which the equivalence classes induced by $P(G)$ are exactly the connected components of $G \downarrow \mathcal{I}'$ (ignoring the directionality of edges).

EXAMPLE 15 (CITIES AND NEIGHBOURHOODS). *Policy (4) in Example 14 is a material co-location policy.*

PROPOSITION 16. *Every material co-location policy is also a material proximity policy.*

PROOF. By definition, a material co-location policy is induced by the path pattern set $\Pi = \left(\widetilde{\mathcal{I}'} \right)^*$ for some $\mathcal{I}' \subseteq \mathcal{I}$. Π is prefix-closed. $\square$

The alternative characterization of material co-location policies given below is more convenient for verification.

PROPOSITION 17. *A GSCS policy P is a material co-location policy iff (a) P is a material proximity policy, and (b) P is transitive.*

The above statement implies that the real difference between a material proximity policy and a material co-location policy is transitivity.

PROOF. ($\Rightarrow$) Suppose P is a material co-location policy. Proposition 16 implies condition (a). That P is a formal co-location policy implies condition (b).

($\Leftarrow$) Suppose P satisfies conditions (a) and (b). Since P is a formal proximity policy (by (a)) and transitive (by (b)), P is also a formal co-location policy.

Since P is a material proximity policy, it is induced by a prefix-closed set Π of path patterns. We claim that if either $\overrightarrow{i}$ or $\overleftarrow{i}$ appears in some path pattern $\pi \in \Pi$, then both $\overrightarrow{i}$ and $\overleftarrow{i}$ belong to Π. Without loss of generality, say $\overrightarrow{i}$ appears in $\pi \in \Pi$. So $\pi = \pi' \cdot \overrightarrow{i} \cdot \pi''$ for some path patterns π' and π''. As Π is prefix-closed, $\pi' \cdot \overrightarrow{i} \in \Pi$. By Proposition 13, Π is closed under path pattern reversal, and thus $\overleftarrow{i} \cdot \pi'^R \in \Pi$. By prefix closure again, $\overleftarrow{i} \in \Pi$. Applying closure under path pattern reversal again, $\overrightarrow{i} \in \Pi$ also. In summary, if $\mathcal{I}'$ is the set of all spatial relation identifiers that appear as an edge pattern in Π, then $\widetilde{\mathcal{I}'} \subseteq \Pi$. Since P is reflexive, symmetric and transitive, Π is simply $\left(\widetilde{\mathcal{I}'}\right)^*$. $\square$

5.4 Containment

Spatial containment is a common feature in GSCSs. A *containment relation* over locations is (a) a partial ordering (i.e., reflexive, anti-symmetric and transitive), and (b) every location has at most one immediate container. In short, containment induces a spatial hierarchy.

In a GSCS for which its spatial network has a containment relation, policies should be formulated to promote the declaration of fine-grained locations: i.e., if l_1 contains l_2, then we prefer users to declare her current location as l_2 rather than l_1. In particular, a reasonable policy shall grant more access to requesters who declare a finer-grained location.

Suppose R is a containment relation. A policy P is a *R-consistent* iff the following holds.

$$P(G)(l_1, l_2) \wedge (l_2, l_2') \in R \Rightarrow P(G)(l_1, l_2')$$

If R is a containment relation for a GSCS, then it is expected that all policies used in the GSCS are R-consistent.

EXAMPLE 18 (INDOOR FLOOR PLANS). *Policy (2) in Example 2 is encloses*-consistent.*

6. A GSNS MODEL

A Geo-Social Network System (GSNS) is an extension of a Geo-Social Computing System (GSCS). A GSNS tracks not only the location claims of users, but also their interpersonal relationships. Both pieces of information will be the basis for authorization decisions. In this section, we will examine how the interplay of the spatial and social dimensions influences the design of a protection system. We will also explore the design of a policy language for specifying GSNS policies.

6.1 Access Control Policies

A GSNS tracks two relational structures: (a) a spatial structure $G = \langle L, \{R_i\}_{i \in \mathcal{I}} \rangle$, and (b) a *social network*. The latter is a *finite* relational structure $H = \langle U, \{R_j\}_{j \in \mathcal{J}} \rangle \in \mathcal{G}_{\mathsf{fin}}(\mathcal{J}, \mathcal{U})$, where the edge labels come from the set $\mathcal{J}$ of *social relation identifiers*, and the vertices are from the universe $\mathcal{U}$ of users. Each identifier $j \in \mathcal{J}$ denotes a type of interpersonal relation (e.g., friend, parent, physician, etc.). In addition to the two relational structures, a GSNS tracks also the declared location of each user in the social network. As before, this is modelled as a function $\eta : U \to L$. In the next subsection, we will articulate how these three components are assigned to the schema, configuration and state of a GSNS. Before that, we will specify what an access control policy of a GSNS looks like.

As usual, an access request consists of a requester v requesting access to a resource owned by an owner u. A GSNS policy is a function P with the following type signature

$$\mathcal{G}(\mathcal{I}, \mathcal{L}) \times \mathcal{G}_{\mathsf{fin}}(\mathcal{J}, \mathcal{U}) \times \mathcal{F}(\mathcal{U}, \mathcal{L}) \to 2^{\mathcal{U} \times \mathcal{U}} \qquad (5)$$

That is, P takes three arguments: (i) a spatial structure $G \in \mathcal{G}(\mathcal{I}, \mathcal{L})$, (ii) a social network $H \in \mathcal{G}(\mathcal{J}, \mathcal{U})$, and (iii) a function $\eta \in \mathcal{F}(\mathcal{U}, \mathcal{L})$ that assigns locations to users. On return, $P(G, H, \eta) \subseteq \mathcal{U} \times \mathcal{U}$ is a binary relation over $\mathcal{U}$. We further require the following of a policy.

1. $P(G, H, \eta) \subseteq dom(\eta) \times dom(\eta)$.
2. If $P(G, H, \eta) \neq \emptyset$ then η must have the function type $V(H) \to V(G)$.

Given an owner u and a requester v, authorization is granted iff $(u, v) \in P(G, H, \eta)$. We write $P(G, H, \eta)(u, v)$ to assert this condition. Lastly, we write $\mathcal{PO}(\mathcal{I}, \mathcal{L}, \mathcal{J}, \mathcal{U})$ for the set of all GSNS policies satisfying the above requirements.

Implicit in the above definition is the possibility for a policy to base authorization decisions on not only the declared locations of the owner and the requester, but also the declared locations of other users in the social network. Consider an alternative (hypothetical) definition of policies in which a policy has the following function type instead:

$$\mathcal{G}(\mathcal{I}, \mathcal{L}) \times \mathcal{G}(\mathcal{J}, \mathcal{U}) \to 2^{\mathcal{L} \times \mathcal{L} \times \mathcal{U} \times \mathcal{U}} \qquad (6)$$

That is, a policy takes a spatial network and a social network as input, and produces a 4-ary relation that relates an owner location, a requester location, an owner and a requester. In such a definition, only the locations of the owner and the requester inform the authorization decision. The declared locations of other users do not play a role. As the following example illustrates, there are indeed policies that will take into account the current locations of users other than the owner and the requester.

EXAMPLE 19. *Consider a GSNS akin to Facebook Places, with $\mathcal{I} = \{\mathsf{coloc}\}$ and $\mathcal{J} = \{\mathsf{friend}\}$. Consider the following GSNS policy:*

Policy A: Grant access if requester is both co-located with the owner and also a friend-of-friend of the owner.

This policy is simply a conjunction of a co-location policy and a friend-of-friend policy. Consider the following scenario, which is depicted in Figure 1.

Scenario S: *An owner u and a requester v share exactly one common friend w, such that $\eta(u) = \eta(v) \neq \eta(w)$.*

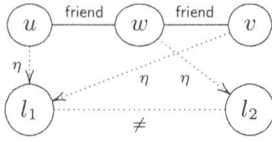

Figure 1: Scenario S

Policy A will grant access in Scenario S. For such kind of policies, the simplistic type signature of (6) would suffice.

In the emerging GSNS, Nextdoor [32], interpersonal relationships are spatially scoped, in the sense that an interpersonal relationship is articulated in the context of a spatial neighborhood (e.g., a city). Generalizing this idea of spatially scoped relationships, consider the GSNS policy below:

Policy B: Grant access if, in the social network of those users who are co-located with the owner, the requester is a friend-of-friend of the owner.

That is, access is only granted if (a) the requester is a friend-of-friend of the owner, and (b) both the requester and one of the common friends between the owner and the requester are co-located with the owner. For the owner u, requester v and common friend w in Scenario S, access will be denied by this policy, because w is not co-located with u. For this kind of policies, the more general type signature of (5) is required.

Policy B above requires that a certain social relationship (friend-of-friend) to hold between the owner and the requester in a spatially constructed social network: i.e., the subgraph of the original social network that is induced by the users co-located with the owner. Such a social network that is induced by a spatial neighborhood of the owner is called a *spatially scoped social network*. We believe that policies framed in terms of spatially scoped social networks represent a novel protection feature for GSNSs.

6.2 Schemas, Configurations, and States

The specification of the GSNS model closely parallels the three-layer organization of the GSCS model (§3.5). In the following, we highlight the differences between the schemas, configurations and states of GSNSs and those of GSCSs.

A GSNS *schema* is a 4-tuple $\mathcal{M} = \langle \mathcal{I}, \mathcal{J}, \mathcal{L}, \mathcal{U} \rangle$. The new component $\mathcal{J}$ is a finite set of social relation identifiers.

A GSNS *configuration* $\mathcal{N} = \langle U, L, \{R_i\}_{i \in \mathcal{I}}, policy \rangle$ has the same basic structure as its GSCS counterpart, except that *policy* now has the function type $U \to \mathcal{PO}(\mathcal{I}, \mathcal{L}, \mathcal{J}, \mathcal{U})$. In short, the configuration consists of the spatial structure and user privacy settings.

A GSNS *state* is a pair $\langle \eta, \{R_j\}_{j \in \mathcal{J}} \rangle$, where η is the usual location assignment function, and the second component $\{R_j\}_{j \in \mathcal{J}}$ is such that $\langle U, \{R_j\}_{j \in \mathcal{J}} \rangle$ forms a social network. While the spatial structure is a component of the configuration, the social network is a component of the state, which is changeable during the normal operation of the GSNS.

When a requester v attempts to access a resource of owner u, the authorization decision is obtained by evaluating $P(G, H, \eta)(u, v)$, where $P = policy(u)$, $G = \langle L, \{R_i\}_{i \in \mathcal{I}} \rangle$, and $H = \langle U, \{R_j\}_{j \in \mathcal{J}} \rangle$.

6.3 A GSNS Policy Language

We devise a policy language for expressing GSNS policies. The language is intended to be used by system designers and

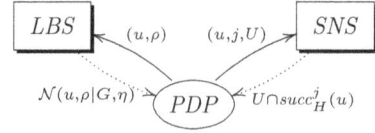

Figure 2: A modular architecture: the Policy Decision Point (PDP) can query a Location-Based Service (LBS) and a Social Network System (SNS).

administrators for specification of policies in GSNSs. In this endeavour, we have three design goals in mind. First, previous work [23, 13] has shown that modal logic [12] and hybrid logic [4] form a solid theoretical foundation for the design of a policy language for Relationship-Based Access Control (ReBAC). We therefore take it as a design goal to base the GSNS policy language on the hybrid language of [13], imposing as few perturbations to that language as possible. Second, the GSNS policy language shall support the expression of policies that are based on spatially scoped social networks (Example 19). Third, the language shall support a modular system architecture, in which the location service and the social network system may belong to two separate administrative domains [41].

6.3.1 System Model

We assume a modular design within the Policy Decision Point (PDP). Specifically, we assume the PDP can direct queries to two kinds of services, as shown in Fig. 2: (i) a location-based service (LBS) and (ii) a social network system (SNS). First, the PDP can submit a user u and a spatial relation ρ (e.g., $\mathsf{coloc} \cup \mathsf{in} \cup \mathsf{in}^{-1} \cup (\mathsf{in} \circ \mathsf{in}^{-1})$) to the LBS, and request the LBS to return the set of users v for which the declared locations of u and v are related by the spatial relation ρ (see (7) in §6.3.3). Second, the PDP can submit a user u, a social relation identifier j and a set U of users to the SNS, and request the SNS to return the set of users $v \in U$ for which u and v are related by relation type j (see (8) in §6.3.3). Implicit in this system model is the assumption that location information and social relationships are tracked by two separate subsystems. This arrangement allows a GSNS to selectively "outsource" either the LBS or the SNS (or both) to a different social computing provider [41].

6.3.2 Syntax

A GSNS policy is represented by a formula (ϕ) in a hybrid logic with the following abstract syntax:

$$\rho ::= i \mid -i \mid \bar{\rho} \mid \rho \cup \rho \mid \rho \circ \rho \mid \rho^*$$
$$\phi ::= \top \mid x \mid \neg\phi \mid \phi \wedge \phi \mid \langle j \rangle \phi \mid @_x\phi \mid \downarrow x . \phi \mid \rho : \phi$$

where $i \in \mathcal{I}$, $j \in \mathcal{J}$ and $x \in X$. The set X is a countably infinite set of variables. We assume that X contains two distinct members, own and req.

Except for the new construct "$\rho : \phi$" and the new syntactic category ρ, the rest of the policy language is essentially the same as the ReBAC policy language of [13]. Each formula ϕ expresses a binary relation between the owner and the requester in a social network. We refer the reader to §6.3.4 or [23, 13] for examples of how these constructs can be used for expressing ReBAC policies, including constraints on depth of friendship or number of common friends.

The newly introduced construct "$\rho : \phi$" is called *spatial scoping* (or simply *scoping*). It is the primary vehicle for expressing policies based on spatially scoped social networks. Each **neighborhood expression** ρ specifies a spatial relation, which is composed from primitive spatial relations (i) using converse ($-$), complement ($\bar{\cdot}$), union ($\cup$), relational composition ($\circ$), or reflexive transitive closure ($*$). As we shall see below, the semantics of a modal logic is defined via a crawler of the social network. At any point of model checking, the crawler is positioned at a vertex u in the social network. Intuitively, the formula "$\rho : \phi$" means: "*in the subgraph of the social network induced by user u as well as those users who are spatially related to u via the spatial relation ρ, the sub-policy ϕ holds.*"

6.3.3 Semantics

The semantics of our GSNS policy language is specified in three steps: the definition of (1) neighbourhoods, (2) the satisfaction relation, and (3) the authorization relation.

First, we define the meaning of neighborhood expressions. We begin by interpreting each neighborhood expression ρ as a binary relation in a given spatial structure G.

$$[\![i]\!]_G = R_i(G) \qquad\qquad [\![-i]\!]_G = R_i(G)^{-1}$$
$$[\![\bar{\rho}]\!]_G = \overline{[\![\rho]\!]_G} \qquad\qquad [\![\rho^*]\!]_G = ([\![\rho]\!]_G)^*$$
$$[\![\rho_1 \cup \rho_2]\!]_G = [\![\rho_1]\!]_G \cup [\![\rho_2]\!]_G \quad [\![\rho_1 \circ \rho_2]\!]_G = [\![\rho_1]\!]_G \circ [\![\rho_2]\!]_G$$

Now, the neighborhood of user u induced by the neighborhood expression ρ is the following set.

$$\mathcal{N}(u, \rho \mid G, \eta) =$$
$$\{v \in dom(\eta) \mid \eta(u) = \eta(v) \vee (\eta(u), \eta(v)) \in [\![\rho]\!]_G\} \quad (7)$$

In short, the neighborhood consists of users whose declared locations are related to the declared location of u through the reflexive closure[5] of $[\![\rho]\!]_G$. Neighbourhoods are essentially obtained by querying the LBS component of the system model (Fig. 2).

Second, we specify the satisfaction relation of hybrid logic: $G, H, \eta, g, U, u \models \phi$. Here, spatial network G, social network H and location assignment η are components from the configuration and state of a GSNS. The **variable assignment** $g : X \rightharpoonup V(H)$ interprets variables as users. The set U is a subset of $V(H)$, and $u \in U$ is a user. The definition of the satisfaction relation is specified inductively as follows.

- $G, H, \eta, g, U, u \models \top$ always holds.
- $G, H, \eta, g, U, u \models x$ iff $u = g(x)$[6].
- $G, H, \eta, g, U, u \models \neg\phi$ iff it is not the case that $G, H, \eta, g, U, u \models \phi$.
- $G, H, \eta, g, U, u \models \phi_1 \wedge \phi_2$ iff both $G, H, \eta, g, U, u \models \phi_1$ and $G, H, \eta, g, U, u \models \phi_2$.
- $G, H, \eta, g, U, u \models \langle j \rangle \phi$ iff there exists $u' \in U \cap succ_H^j(u)$ such that $G, H, \eta, g, U, u' \models \phi$. Here, $succ_H^j(u)$ is the set of type-j neighbours of u in the social network H.

$$succ_H^j(u) = \{v \in V(H) \mid (u, v) \in R_j(H)\} \quad (8)$$

As shown in Fig. 2, the set $U \cap succ_H^j(u)$ is obtained by a query to the SNS component of the system model. Note also that the set $U \cap succ_H^j(u)$ is essentially equivalent to $succ_{H[U]}^j(u)$.

- $G, H, \eta, g, U, u \models @_x\phi$ iff $g(x) \in U$ and $G, H, \eta, g, U, g(x) \models \phi$.
- $G, H, \eta, g, U, u \models \downarrow x . \phi$ iff $G, H, \eta, g[x \mapsto u], U, u \models \phi$.
- $G, H, \eta, g, U, u \models \rho : \phi$ iff $G, H, \eta, g, U', u \models \phi$ for $U' = U \cap \mathcal{N}(u, \rho \mid G, \eta)$.

Compared to the semantics of the ReBAC policy language of [13], there are three extensions.

1. The rule for scoping ($\rho : \phi$) reduces the current scope U to U', which is obtained by focusing on the spatial neighborhood $\mathcal{N}(u, \rho \mid G, \eta)$ induced by the spatial relation ρ. So the scoping parameter U delimits a smaller and smaller social network as recursion unfolds. Hence, having the scoped social network, the complexity of policy evaluation in our model is at most as hard as policy evaluation in [13].
2. The semantic rules for $\langle j \rangle \phi$ and $@_x\phi$ have been adapted (from their counterparts in [13]) to limit graph traversal within the induced subgraph $H[U]$.
3. Implicit in the semantic rule of x is the requirement that testing succeeds only when $g(x)$ is a vertex in the induced subgraph $H[U]$ (footnote 6).

Third, we specify the authorization relation $G, H, \eta, u, v \Vdash \phi$, which determines if a requester v may access a resource owned by user u, in the context of spatial structure G, social network H, and location assignment η. Specifically, $G, H, \eta, u, v \Vdash \phi$ holds iff $G, H, \eta, g_\star, V(H), u \models \phi$, where

$$g_\star = \{\mathsf{own} \mapsto u, \mathsf{req} \mapsto v\}$$

In short, the global variables own and req denote respectively the owner (u) and the requester (v), and the initial scope is the entire social network ($V(H)$).

6.3.4 Derived Forms and Examples

Standard derived forms can be defined as follows.

$$\rho_1 \cap \rho_2 \stackrel{def}{=} \overline{\bar{\rho_1} \cup \bar{\rho_2}} \qquad \rho^+ \stackrel{def}{=} \rho \circ \rho^*$$
$$\bot \stackrel{def}{=} \neg\top \qquad \phi_1 \vee \phi_2 \stackrel{def}{=} \neg(\neg\phi_1 \wedge \neg\phi_2) \qquad [j]\phi \stackrel{def}{=} \neg\langle j \rangle \neg\phi$$

The following example, taken from [23], reviews how basic modal constructs can be used for expressing interpersonal relationships.

EXAMPLE 20 (MODAL LOGIC CONSTRUCTS).
- *Grant access to the owner's spouse:* $\langle \mathsf{spouse} \rangle \mathsf{req}$.
- *Grand parents:* $\langle \mathsf{parent} \rangle \langle \mathsf{parent} \rangle \mathsf{req}$.
- *Parents, aunts and uncles:*

$$\langle \mathsf{parent} \rangle \mathsf{req} \vee \langle \mathsf{parent} \rangle \langle \mathsf{sibling} \rangle \mathsf{req} \vee$$
$$\langle \mathsf{parent} \rangle \langle \mathsf{sibling} \rangle \langle \mathsf{spouse} \rangle \mathsf{req}$$

- *A sibling who is not married:* $\langle \mathsf{sibling} \rangle (\mathsf{req} \wedge [\mathsf{spouse}]\bot)$.

The following example, adapted from [13], reviews how constructs from hybrid logic can be used for expressing complex graph constraints in the social network.

EXAMPLE 21. *Grant access if owner and requester share two distinct common friends:*

$$\langle \mathsf{friend} \rangle (\neg\mathsf{own} \wedge \neg\mathsf{req} \wedge \downarrow x . \langle \mathsf{friend} \rangle (\mathsf{req} \wedge$$
$$@_{\mathsf{own}} \langle \mathsf{friend} \rangle (\neg\mathsf{own} \wedge \neg\mathsf{req} \wedge \neg x \wedge \langle \mathsf{friend} \rangle \mathsf{req})))$$

The following example illustrates the use of spatial scoping and the @ operator to test simple spatial relation between the requestor and the owner.

EXAMPLE 22 (SIMPLE SPATIAL RELATION). *The formula below encodes policy (4) from Example 14.*

$$(\mathsf{coloc} \cup \mathsf{in} \cup (-\mathsf{in}) \cup (\mathsf{in} \circ (-\mathsf{in}))) : @_{\mathsf{req}}\top$$

Thanks to the extended semantic rule of $@_{\mathsf{req}}$, the latter can be used for testing if req *is in the spatial neighborhood induced by* $\mathsf{coloc} \cup \mathsf{in} \cup (-\mathsf{in}) \cup (\mathsf{in} \circ (-\mathsf{in}))$.

The following example illustrates the checking of a social constellation (i.e., friends of friends) within a spatially scoped social network.

EXAMPLE 23 (SPATIALLY SCOPED INTERMEDIARIES). *Consider again the GSNS in Example 19. Policy A can be expressed by the following formula.*

$$(\mathsf{coloc} : @_{\mathsf{req}}\top) \wedge \langle\mathsf{friend}\rangle\langle\mathsf{friend}\rangle\mathsf{req}$$

Policy B, which involves the notion of spatially scoped social networks, can be expressed by the following formula.

$$\mathsf{coloc} : \langle\mathsf{friend}\rangle\langle\mathsf{friend}\rangle\mathsf{req}$$

Due to the extended semantic rule of $\langle\mathsf{friend}\rangle$, intermediate vertices visited by $\langle\mathsf{friend}\rangle$ must fall within the spatial neighborhood induced by coloc.

The following example illustrates how the nesting of the scoping operator leads to the consideration of a smaller and smaller social network.

EXAMPLE 24 (NESTED SCOPING). *Suppose a restaurant owner is to offer promotional discount to a potential customers u who is (a) close to the restaurant, and (b) gathering (i.e., co-located) with three friends. The policy that specifies the availability of promotional discount is encoded by the following formula:*

$$\mathsf{near} : (@_{\mathsf{req}} (\mathsf{coloc} : clique_4))$$

The above formula first focuses on the spatially scoped social network induced by those users near *to the restaurant. It then checks if the requester is within that social network by repositioning the search to* req *(i.e., $@_{\mathsf{req}}$). Now the scope is further reduced to those users who are co-located with the requester (*coloc :*). Lastly it checks if the requester is situated in a clique of size four: i.e., co-located with three friends. The subformula $clique_4$ employs only ReBAC constructs (i.e., no further scoping).*

$$\downarrow x . \langle\mathsf{friend}\rangle(\neg x \wedge$$
$$\downarrow y . \langle\mathsf{friend}\rangle(\neg x \wedge \neg y \wedge (\langle\mathsf{friend}\rangle x) \wedge$$
$$\downarrow z . \langle\mathsf{friend}\rangle(\neg x \wedge \neg y \wedge \neg z \wedge$$
$$(\langle\mathsf{friend}\rangle x) \wedge (\langle\mathsf{friend}\rangle y))))$$

7. CONCLUSION AND FUTURE WORK

We proposed an access control model for GSCSs. Complex spatial policies can be composed from primitive spatial relations. We studied the algebraic properties of typical GSCS policies. We extended the model to account for GSNSs. We explored policies that are formulated in terms of spatially scoped social networks, and designed a policy language to capture this notion.

With the advent of Indoor Positioning Systems (IPS) [9] (or High Sensitivity GPS Receivers [46]), future GSCSs/GSNSs may come with much richer spatial models than what is available in existing, GPS-driven systems. We anticipate that future spatial models will involve complex spatial relations induced by indoor or urban settings. A future work is therefore to study the algebraic properties of access control policies in these novel settings.

We assumed that users do not cheat in their location declarations. Several known location verification techniques can be employed in the presence of malicious users [28]. A future direction is to perform location verification by way of social testimony of proximal individuals, and integrate such social testimony with our GSNS authorization scheme.

Another future work is to extend the GSCS/GSNS model to incorporate additional temporal and spatial parameters such as time, direction, orientation and movement [3]. We believe that such extensions would address the need for protection when users and resources are in motion [45].

Acknowledgments

This work is supported in part by an NSERC Discovery Grant and a Canada Research Chair.

8. REFERENCES

[1] S. Aich, S. Mondal, S. Sural, and A. Majumdar. Role Based Access Control with Spatiotemporal Context for Mobile Applications. In *Transactions on Computational Science IV*, volume 5430 of *LNCS*, pages 177–199. Springer Berlin Heidelberg, 2009.

[2] S. Aich, S. Sural, and A. Majumdar. STARBAC: Spatiotemporal Role Based Access Control. In *Proceedings of the OTM'07*, pages 1567–1582. Springer Berlin Heidelberg, Vilamoura, Portugal, 2007.

[3] C. Ardagna, M. Cremonini, S. Capitani di Vimercati, and P. Samarati. Access Control in Location-Based Services. In *Privacy in Location-Based Applications*, LNCS, pages 106–126. Springer Heidelberg, 2009.

[4] C. Areces and B. ten Cate. Hybrid logics. In *Handbook of Modal Logic*, chapter 14. Elsevier, 2007.

[5] A. V. Atluri, V. Atluri, and P. Mazzoleni. A Uniform Indexing Scheme for Geo-spatial Data and Authorizaions. In *Proceedings of the 16th IFIP WG*, pages 207–218. Kluwer Academic Publishers, 2002.

[6] V. Atluri and S. A. Chun. A Geotemporal Role-Based Authorisation System. *IJISC*, 1(1/2):143–168, 2007.

[7] Banjo, Inc. Banjo v3.3, http://www.ban.jo, Apr. 2013.

[8] C. Becker and F. Dürr. On Location Models for Ubiquitous Computing. *Personal and Ubiquitous Computing.*, 9(1):20–31, Jan. 2005.

[9] S. Bell, W. R. Jung, and V. Krishnakumar. WiFi-based Enhanced Positioning Systems: Accuracy Through Mapping, Calibration, and Classification. In *Proceedings of the 2nd ACM SIGSPATIAL*, ISA'10, pages 3–9, San Jose, California, 2010.

[10] A. Belussi, E. Bertino, B. Catania, M. L. Damiani, and A. Nucita. An Authorization Model for Geographical Maps. In *Proceedings of the 12th ACM GIS'04*, pages 82–91, Washington DC, USA, 2004.

[11] E. Bertino, B. Catania, M. L. Damiani, and P. Perlasca. GEO-RBAC: A Spatially Aware RBAC. In *Proceedings of the tenth ACM SACMAT*, pages 29–37, Stockholm, Sweden, 2005.

[12] P. Blackburn, M. de Rijke, and Y. Venema. *Modal Logic*. Cambridge University Press, New York, 2001.

[13] G. Bruns, P. W. L. Fong, I. Siahaan, and M. Huth. Relationship-based Access Control: Its Expression and Enforcement Through Hybrid Logic. In *Proceedings of the second ACM CODASPY*, pages 117–124, San Antonio, Texas, USA, 2012.

[14] Bucher, B., Falquet, G., Clementini, E., and Sester, M. Towards a Typology of Spatial Relations and Properties for Urban Applications. In *Usage, Usability, and Utility of 3D City Models*. European COST Action TU0801, 2012.

[15] B. Carminati, E. Ferrari, and A. Perego. Enforcing Access Control in Web-based Social Networks. *ACM TISSEC*, 13(1):1–38, Nov. 2009.

[16] S. M. Chandran and J. B. D. Joshi. LoT-RBAC: A Location and Time-Based RBAC Model. In *Proceedings of WISE'05*, pages 361–375. Springer Berlin Heidelberg, 2005.

[17] Y. Cheng, J. Park, and R. Sandhu. A User-to-User Relationship-based Access Control Model for Online Social Networks. In *Proceedings of DBSec'12*, pages 8–24. Springer Berlin Heidelberg, 2012.

[18] Y. Cheng, J. Park, and R. Sandhu. Relationship-Based Access Control for Online Social Networks: Beyond User-to-User Relationships. In *Privacy, Security, Risk and Trust (PASSAT)*, pages 646–655, 2012.

[19] S. A. Chun and V. Atluri. Protecting Privacy from Continuous High-resolution Satellite Surveillance. In *Proceedings of the 14 th IFIP TC11/ WG11.3*, pages 233–244, Deventer, Netherlands, 2001.

[20] E. Clementini, P. D. Felice, and P. v. Oosterom. A Small Set of Formal Topological Relationships Suitable for End-User Interaction. In *Proceedings of SSD'93*, pages 277–295, London, UK, 1993. Springer-Verlag.

[21] I. F. Cruz, R. Gjomemo, B. Lin, and M. Orsini. A Location Aware Role and Attribute Based Access Control System. In *Proceedings of 16th ACM SIGSPATIAL*, pages 84:1–84:2, Irvine, CA, 2008.

[22] P. W. L. Fong. Preventing Sybil Attacks by Privilege Attenuation: A Design Principle for Social Network Systems. In *Proceedings of the S&P'11*, pages 263–278, Oakland, CA, USA, May 2011.

[23] P. W. L. Fong. Relationship-Based Access Control: Protection Model and Policy Language. In *Proceedings of the first ACM CODASPY'11*, pages 191–202, New York, NY, USA, 2011.

[24] P. W. L. Fong, M. Anwar, and Z. Zhao. A Privacy Preservation Model for Facebook-style Social Network Systems. In *Proceedings of the ESORICS'09*, pages 303–320, Berlin, Heidelberg, 2009. Springer-Verlag.

[25] P. W. L. Fong and I. Siahaan. Relationship-based Access Control Policies and Their Policy Languages. In *Proceedings of the 16th ACM SACMAT'11*, pages 51–60, Innsbruck, Austria, 2011.

[26] P. R. Halmos. *Naive Set Theory*. Springer, 1974.

[27] F. Hansen and V. Oleshchuk. Spatial Role-Based Access Control Model for Wireless Networks. In *Proceedings of the 58th IEEE Vehicular Technology Conference*, volume 3, pages 2093–2097, 2003.

[28] W. He, X. Liu, and M. Ren. Location Cheating: A Security Challenge to Location-Based Social Network Services. In *Proceedings of the 31st ICDCS*, pages 740–749, Washington, DC, USA, 2011.

[29] L. Jin, X. Long, J. Joshi, and M. Anwar. Analysis of Access Control Mechanisms for Users' Check-ins in Location-Based Social Network Systems. In *13th IRI'12*, pages 712–717, 2012.

[30] M. S. Kirkpatrick, M. L. Damiani, and E. Bertino. Prox-RBAC: A proximity-based spatially aware RBAC. In *Proceedings of the 19th ACM SIGSPATIAL*, GIS'11, pages 339–348, Chicago, Illinois, 2011.

[31] S. Mascetti, D. Freni, C. Bettini, X. S. Wang, and S. Jajodia. Privacy in Geo-social Networks: Proximity Notification with Untrusted Service Providers and Curious Buddies. *VLDB*, 20(4):541–566, Aug. 2011.

[32] Nextdoor, Inc. http://nextdoor.com, Mar. 2013.

[33] J. Nord, K. Synnes, and P. Parnes. An Architecture for Location Aware Applications. In *Proceedings of HICSS'02*, pages 3805–3810, Washington, DC, USA, 2002. IEEE Computer Society.

[34] I. Ray, M. Kumar, and L. Yu. LRBAC: A Location-aware Role-based Access Control Model. In *Proceedings of the ICISS'06*, pages 147–161, Kolkata, India, 2006. Springer-Verlag.

[35] R. S. Sandhu, E. J. Coyne, H. L. Feinstein, and C. E. Youman. Role-Based Access Control Models. *Computer*, 29(2):38–47, Feb. 1996.

[36] L. Snyder. Theft and conspiracy in the take-grant protection model. *Journal of Computer and System Sciences*, 23(3):333–347, 1981.

[37] Sonar, Inc. Sonar v1.9.3, http://www.sonar.me, 2013.

[38] A. Squicciarini, F. Paci, and S. Sundareswaran. PriMa: An Effective Privacy Protection Mechanism for Social Networks. In *Proceedings of the 5th ACM ASIACCS*, pages 320–323, Beijing, China, 2010.

[39] A. C. Squicciarini, M. Shehab, and J. Wede. Privacy Policies for Shared Content in Social Network Sites. *The VLDB Journal*, 19(6):777–796, Dec. 2010.

[40] E.-P. Stoffel, K. Schoder, and H. J. Ohlbach. Applying Hierarchical Graphs to Pedestrian Indoor Navigation. In *Proceedings of the 16th ACM SIGSPATIAL*, GIS'08, pages 54:1–54:4, Irvine, California, 2008.

[41] E. Tarameshloo, P. W. Fong, and P. Mohassel. On Protection in Federated Social Computing Systems. In *Proceedings of the 4th ACM CODASPY'14*, pages 75–86, San Antonio, Texas, USA, 2014.

[42] U. Varshney. Location Management for Mobile Commerce Applications in Wireless Internet Environment. *ACM Transactions on Internet Technology*, 3(3):236–255, Aug. 2003.

[43] L. S. Viţă and D. S. Bridges. A Constructive Theory of Point-set Nearness. *Theoretical Computer Science - Topology in Computer Science*, pages 473–489, 2003.

[44] Waze, Inc. Waze v3.6, http://www.waze.com, 2013.

[45] M. Youssef, V. Atluri, and N. R. Adam. Preserving Mobile Customer Privacy: An Access Control System for Moving Objects and Customer Profiles. In *Proceedings of the 6th ACM MDM'05*, pages 67–76, Ayia Napa, Cyprus, 2005.

[46] P. A. Zandbergen and S. J. Barbeau. Positional Accuracy of Assisted GPS Data from High-Sensitivity GPS-enabled Mobile Phones. *Journal of Navigation, Cambridge University Press*, 64:381–399, 7 2011.

What Are the Most Important Challenges for Access Control in New Computing Domains, such as Mobile, Cloud and Cyber-physical Systems?

Lujo Bauer
Carnegie Mellon University
Pittsburgh, PA, USA
lbauer@cmu.edu

Florian Kerschbaum
SAP, Karlsruhe
Germany
florian.kerschbaum@sap.com

ABSTRACT

We are seeing a significant shift in the types and characteristics of computing devices that are commonly used. Today, more smartphones are sold than personal computers. An area of rapid growth are also cloud systems; and our everyday lives are invaded by sensors like smart meters and electronic tickets. The days when most computing resources were managed directly by a computer's operating system are over—data and computation is distributed, and devices are typically always connected via the Internet.

In light of this shift, it is important to revisit the basic security properties we desire of computing systems and the mechanisms that we use to provide them. A building block of most of the security we enjoy in today's systems is access control. This panel will examine the challenges we face in adapting the access control models, techniques, and tools produced thus far to today's and tomorrow's computing environments. Key characteristics of these new systems that may require our approach to access control to change is that in many (e.g., cloud) systems users do not directly control their data; that a vast population of users operating mobile and other new devices has very little education in their use; and that cyber-physical systems permeate our environment to the point where they are often invisible to their users.

Access control comprises enforcement systems, specification languages, and policy-management tools or approaches. In each of these areas the shifting computing landscape leaves us examining how current technology can be applied to new contexts or looking for new technology to fill the gap. Enforcement of access-control policy based on a trusted operating system, for example, does not cleanly translate to massively distributed, heterogeneous computing environments; to environments with many devices that are minimally administered or administered with minimal expertise; and to potentially untrusted clouds that hold sensitive data and computations that belong to entities other than the cloud owner. What technologies or system components should be the building blocks of enforcement in these settings?

Similarly, access-control models like RBAC and ABAC, and associated policy-specification languages, which have proven useful in many contexts, may no longer be sufficient. An increasing amount of data is subject to access control. Even for content that we are used to protecting, like files, access-control needs are becoming more demanding. Users are developing nuanced sharing preferences that involve granting fine-grained access to parts of files and sharing approximations rather than details; they also make access contingent on context such as the kind of device that is used to access data, the physical location from which data is being accessed, and the presence of other individuals near the individual who is attempting to access data. Data like sensor readings (e.g., from a heart-rate sensor) and social network updates are also increasingly being shared. What access-control models are the best fit for this wide variety of data that needs to be protected and for the complex access-control preferences that users are developing?

Finally, policy management—an issue that has historically been an area of weakness—is likely to be only more difficult in the future. Even trained system administrators regularly make mistakes when attempting to specify or update access-control policy. Such problems are likely to grow manyfold as every user becomes an administrator of the policies that protect their own data, particularly in light of the rapid growth of the number and type of data items and users. Policies that are too lax can cause valuable or sensitive private data to be leaked; policies that are too strict can cause access to critical resources (e.g., emergency medical care) to be denied. What techniques and approaches can we develop to help users, both experts and non-experts, manage the massive and complex policies of tomorrow?

This panel will identify and rank specific challenges within these areas. It will discuss the important aspects that research should address, but maybe does not today. The panel will attempt to answer questions like: What needs to be done to secure the systems of the future and how does access control need to change? What are the most relevant challenges that will need to be solved and which solutions are the ones that will likely have the most impact?

Categories and Subject Descriptors

D.4.6 [**Operating Systems**]: Security and Protection—*Access control*

Keywords

Panel; Access Control; Challenges

SACMAT'14, June 25–27, 2014, London, Ontario, Canada.
ACM 978-1-4503-2939-2/14/06.
http://dx.doi.org/10.1145/2613087.2613090.

Limiting Access to Unintentionally Leaked Sensitive Documents Using Malware Signatures

Mordechai Guri[1], Gabi Kedma[1], Buky Carmeli, Yuval Elovici[1,2]
[1]Department of Information Systems Engineering, Ben-Gurion University
[2]Telekom Innovation Laboratories at Ben-Gurion University
Ben-Gurion University of the Negev, 653 Beer-Sheva 8410501, Israel
{gurim, gabik, bukyc}@post.bgu.ac.il, elovici@bgu.ac.il

ABSTRACT

Organizations are repeatedly embarrassed when their sensitive digital documents go public or fall into the hands of adversaries, often as a result of unintentional or inadvertent leakage. Such leakage has been traditionally handled either by preventive means, which are evidently not hermetic, or by punitive measures taken after the main damage has already been done. Yet, the challenge of preventing a leaked file from spreading further among computers and over the Internet is not resolved by existing approaches. This paper presents a novel method, which aims at reducing and limiting the potential damage of a leakage that has already occurred. The main idea is to tag sensitive documents within the organization's boundaries by attaching a benign detectable malware signature (DMS). While the DMS is masked inside the organization, if a tagged document is somehow leaked out of the organization's boundaries, common security services such as Anti-Virus (AV) programs, firewalls or email gateways will detect the file as a real threat and will consequently delete or quarantine it, preventing it from spreading further. This paper discusses various aspects of the DMS, such as signature type and attachment techniques, along with proper design considerations and implementation issues. The proposed method was implemented and successfully tested on various file types including documents, spreadsheets, presentations, images, executable binaries and textual source code. The evaluation results have demonstrated its effectiveness in limiting the spread of leaked documents.

Categories and Subject Descriptors

D.4.6 [**Operating Systems**]: Security and Protection – *Invasive software*; K.6.5 [**Management of Computing and Information Systems**]: Security and Protection – *Unauthorized access*.

General Terms

Terms: Security, Privacy, Malware.

Keywords

Keywords: Data Leakage, Sensitive Document, Anti-Virus Program, Detectable Malware Signature.

1. INTRODUCTION

Unintentional leakage of sensitive digital documents is a problem, which cannot be overlooked by organizations, either governmental or commercial [1]. Incidents such as the loss of CD's containing the personal data of 25 million people in the UK [2] or the uploading of personal medical information in the USA [3] [4], which are often based on unintentional or inadvertent leakage, are a source of constant embarrassment and severe security damages to government agencies and other organizations around the world. The traditional way to handle this problem includes various measures of monitoring the organization's gates (both physical and virtual), legal sanctions, etc. Such measures are typically aimed at either preventing the leakage or at punishing the leaker after the damage was done and the leaker was somehow tracked. Detailed discussion of existing Data Leakage Prevention (DLP) solutions is provided by [1].

According to [20], approximately 80% of data leakage is accidental. A rough estimate of the economic importance of the problem can be derived from the annual cost due to theft of Intellectual Property (IP); this was estimated by [5] as £9.2bn, regarding the UK economy; (this can be roughly translated to $300bn in terms of a global economy). Even if unintentional leaks account for only a fraction of this sum, the potential damage still seems significant. Note however that the findings of [5] were heavily debated by [6] and others.

We use the term 'unintentional leakage' to denote cases where the leakage of sensitive data is not caused by intentionally malicious actions. This term encloses cases where an insider is unaware of the sensitivity of the data which he deals with, or is unaware that some classified material got mixed with the unclassified message or media which he prepares. Consequently, and despite common security measures, sensitive data may escape the organization's boundaries through an insider's unintentional or at least without deliberate malicious intention. We assume that the data may initially escape the organization's boundaries either online (e.g. by email, file sharing services), or offline (e.g. by removable media). We further assume that an ordinary person, who tries to open the leaked document outside the boundaries of the organization, will not mess with it if it appears to be contaminated. Such 'ordinary person' may be either the initial unintentional leaker, or someone else.

Note that, despite the rising popularity of "Bring Your Own Device" (BYOD), enterprise organizations are still greatly concerned about their sensitive data being accessed by an unauthorized device or a partially authorized BYOD [37].

1.1 Motivating Scenario

Before we proceed to present our concept, let us consider a possible scenario where Bob, a dedicated and trusted researcher at ACME Corporation, wishes to complete his urgent work at home; he loads his documents from his workstation to a removable flash disk or a similar portable device and then, at home, loads them onto his private computer. It is assumed that Bob's private computer and his home network are significantly less secure than the corporate's network. Even if we ignore malicious eavesdropping, there is the possibility of unintentional leakage. Suppose Bob inadvertently stores a sensitive document in a directory over the 'cloud' which he shares with, say, 5 fellow researchers from all over the world, or with 50 students of a class that he teaches at the local college.

Assuming that unintentional leaks of this type or similar ones are possible and that sensitive digital documents will somehow escape the corporate's boundaries through one security loophole or another, the corporate's CSO would like to contain the leakage and to minimize its scope.

1.2 Concept

The idea, as presented in this paper, is to attach a Detectable Malware Signature (DMS), to each sensitive document within the organization's boundaries, which - if leaked outside - will be detected by common Anti-Virus (AV) programs and cause the AV program to react as if a real threat was detected (see Figure 1). This may prevent the file from spreading over the Internet (including email), where AV programs monitor gateways, email-servers and similar junctions. Also, on an endpoint (a user's computer), where an AV program is installed, the file will be erased or quarantined and the user will be alerted whenever he tries to download the file, either from the Web, from email, or when inserting a portable storage device, which contains the document into his personal computer or notebook. In a best-case scenario, when our fictional Bob comes home and tries to load the file onto his private computer, he will get an alert from his AV program. Even if the AV program lets the user choose between deleting the suspicious file and loading it, a normal user will typically avoid loading or opening such a file.

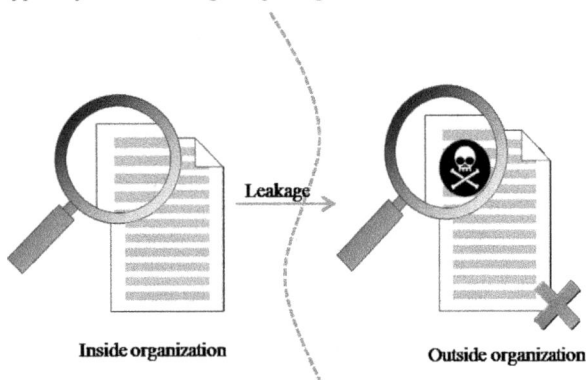

Figure 1: Conceptual illustration of the main components: The sensitive document inside the organization (left), the document outside the organization (right), DMS (crossbones label), and the AV program which deletes the file (magnifier glass).

The rest of this paper is structured as follows: Section 2 presents related work. In Section 3, we go on to present the basic design considerations. Next, in Section 4 we explain what it takes to get detected by an Antivirus program. We describe our new method

and its evaluation results in Section 5, and discuss some aspects of file-spreading related to our method in Section 6 right before concluding in Section 7. Appendix A presents, in a concise form, the behavior of the antivirus products which were tested in lab.

2. Related Work

Data Leakage Prevention (DLP), or Information Leakage Prevention (ILP), has been subjected to several researches and commercial products [20] [21], where major Information Security vendors struggle for developing innovative technologies. Often regarded as an 'insider threat', data leakage can be treated by employing honeypots or honey-tokens [22] [23]. Where sensitive data is distributed, data can be traced either by 'watermarking' or by unobtrusive techniques [24]. Previous mainstream works were focused on encountering data leakage at three stages. Endpoint solutions enforce access policies in desktop machines, and thus can prevent confidential documents from leaving the organization boundaries. Network traffic monitors continuously analyze the network communication to identify whether a sensitive file was sent while violating the security policies. File-level systems embed security-related information as a metadata in sensitive files [1] [7] [8]. Note that the aforementioned solutions are only effective within the organization's perimeter.

Another common solution is to encrypt sensitive files, preventing them from being opened in a readable form in a non-authorized environment. First, this paper contributes by presenting novel and completely different approach to encounter the DLP problem. Second, encryption based solutions do not prevent the file from being *spread* over the external network once it is leaked. The sensitive document can be sent freely, shared and accessed over the Internet, not only harming the organization's reputation but allowing a motivated adversary to decrypt it. Our method, on the other hand, may halt the initial leakage, and limit the propagation of the leaked document, by preventing access to it. Furthermore, our method may provide forensic evidence concerning the source and route of the tagged file, by analyzing related AV and security systems reports and logs, even outside the organization perimeter. In short, the presented solution can be used along with encryption-based methods to limit the harmful effects of unintentional data leakage.

One commercial solution is Microsoft Information Rights Management (IRM), for Office [9]. This solution prevents unauthorized users, within or outside the organization's boundaries, from reading a Microsoft Office document, which was unintentionally sent to them. However this kind of solution is limited to Microsoft Office documents and it does not prevent the file from spreading further on the external network once it is leaked. It also does not prevent a skilled hacker from attempting to decipher the contents of the file.

Here we consider another goal: assuming that a sensitive digital document has already leaked somehow, we shall consider a method of containing the leakage to minimize its scope and its damage. Our concept is aimed at a wide range of documents (preferably any kind of file), it aims at impeding and limiting the spreading of the leaked file beyond the organization's boundaries, and it aims at preventing access to the leaked file, preferably by having it deleted before unauthorized users access it.

Table 1. Applicability-range of various approaches

Solution	Initial leak	Further spreading
Network monitoring	Applicable	Not applicable
File System Monitoring	Applicable	Not applicable
Encryption	Not applicable	Not applicable
Watermarking	Applicable	Not applicable
IRM	Applicable	Not applicable
Presented method	Applicable	Applicable

Table 1 shows the applicability of various solutions to (a) the initial leak, and (b) further spreading of the leaked document. Our method is the only one which is applicable against further spreading, beyond the boundaries of the organization.

3. BASIC DESIGN CONSIDERATIONS

Before proceeding, we should examine some basic design considerations, which must be met to provide a feasible and safe solution.

1. **Limit the Damage from Unintentional Leakage**: Assume the user unintentionally moved confidential documents from the organizations secure perimeter to his home computer or to any other computer that is outside organizational reach. There is a need to develop a method that will limit the spread of the leaked documents.

2. **Coverage of Prevalent Document Types**: The goal is to design a method that will prevent the spread of approximately 90 percent of the documents used within a typical organization. Thus, in the case we have examined, the method was required to cover at least (a) Microsoft Office documents and (b) Adobe PDF documents. We assume that the corporate's CSO and the administrators have decent control over the applications used within the corporate's boundaries, and will not allow the installation of unauthorized applications. On the other hand, if we consider typical private computers outside the corporate's boundaries we should notice that many third party applications can read both Microsoft Office documents and Adobe PDF files. Thus, when considering the effects of our method on a computer outside the organization's boundaries, we should not solely rely on the behavior of Microsoft Word, for example, when opening a Word document or of Adobe Acrobat reader when opening a PDF file.

3. **Detectability Using Prevalent AV Programs**: Assume that the new method is based on attaching a Detectable Malware Signature (DMS), to each sensitive document within the organization's boundaries. The DMS should be detectable by major prevalent AV programs. We have decided to focus on the relevant products of the 'top ten' AV vendors as listed by [10], which account for 87.46% of the market together.

4. **Effective Action Taken by the AV Program**: Being detectable by the AV program is not enough. The DMS should also cause the AV program to take effective action. An effective action would be either deleting the whole document or putting it into quarantine. In the case of gateways such as mail servers with traffic filtering, the transmission of the document should be prevented. Preferably the user should not be given a permissive choice.

5. **Safe Exclusion Mechanism**: Within the corporate's boundaries, all active AV programs should be configured to exclude the given DMS from their detection lists or to override their default behavior when detecting the given DMS. Thus, the corporate's computers are not protected from the real threat mimicked by the DMS. It is therefore, essential that the chosen DMS does not affect the operating systems and applications, which are used within the corporate's boundaries. For example, if we use a DMS, which mimics an ancient MS-DOS virus (unable to function under modern Windows OS), its exclusion would be considered quite safe, assuming that the organization does not use any MS-DOS operated computers (or exclusion must not be applied to those specific machines). If a modern malware signature is used, it has to be attached in harmless way as discussed later. Note that when choosing modern malware signature as DMS, the exclusion rule will be applied only to the harmless form of the DMS, while the regular signature will be detected as malicious. In that case, harmless DMS will be avoided by AV, still the organization is protected against the real threat.

6. **Avoiding Malicious Abuse and Side Effects**: The implicit assumption behind this research is that the DMS alone should not cause any harm and should not bring about any predictably harmful side effects. This assumption is a mandatory requirement due to legal considerations. Further research should be done to examine possible security loopholes within the proposed method to eliminate them in advance.

7. **Transparent Deployment**: attaching the DMS to the sensitive file within the organization should be done automatically and in a manner, which is transparent to the user. This process should be applied to all endpoint computers within the organization's boundaries. The system should be able to attach the DMS to any document, which meets a certain level of classification. The system should be able to notice whenever such a document is saved to disk or 'printed' to a file (as in the case of a PDF when created from a Microsoft Office application). The system should be able to notice when the file is opened, closed, read or written, and handle such events transparently; it should be able to detect the application, which requests said operations, and to treat certain types of applications (e.g. Web browsers and email-clients), in a different manner. Preferably the system should be able to attach the DMS to the file when it is still opened within an application (such as Microsoft Word), and is locked from access by an external user-mode process. The system should also differentiate between tagged files and actual malware, possibly by means of a unique 'magic number' appended to the DMS. When the magic number is missing or incorrect, the DMS should be treated as actual malware. All these tasks should be carried on in computers, which are monitored by an active AV program and without affecting or disturbing the standard work of the user.

4. HOW AV PROGRAMS DETECT MALICIOUS FILES

To ensure that a file, which has leaked is detected as malicious by prevalent AV programs, even when the file is totally harmless, one should understand the basic detection mechanisms of typical AV programs. We shall focus on structural signatures (as opposed to behavioral signatures), which are based on static analysis of suspected files [11].

A typical AV program employs an updatable database of signatures of known malware, and a monitor, which scans new or modified files for the presence of such signatures. A signature may be as simple as the hash value or 'checksum' of a whole file, but modern viruses use polymorphic or metamorphic methods to change [12], so the signature should consist of fixed sequences within the file, which indicate malicious codes. Often the signature is like a regular expression, where some parts of the sequence may be fixed while others may vary [11].

The AV program scans executable files and certain types of data files, which may contain an executable code. Modern binary executable files such as PE on Microsoft Windows [13] or ELF on Linux [14] have a well-documented format, which is available to attackers and defenders alike. Malicious code may reside in various sections of the file, and a malicious executable may be packed or embedded within another executable (either as a 'resource' or otherwise). Malicious code may be prepended, inserted or appended to innocuous files. Thus, the filename extension is not enough to determine the true nature of a given file. Furthermore, certain kinds of data files, like Microsoft Office documents and Adobe PDF files (both having a well-documented format), may contain an executable code in the form of macros, embedded binary executables, embedded vulnerable files like Flash SWF, and shellcode (binary code sequences, which are not packaged as a standard binary executable). Other kinds of data files may contain shellcode, which is designed to execute upon a buffer overflow or a similar vulnerability's exploit. Malicious code may be packed, encoded or obfuscated to hinder its detection by malware analysts and AV programs [15].

Regarding the sophistication and obscurity of modern malware, an AV program may resort to heuristic detection methods or to machine-learning methods [30] with higher sensitivity rates, possibly overcoming new evasion techniques, at the cost of a lower specificity rate (i.e., such methods may raise false alarms). Upon detection of a suspicious file, the AV program will try to evaluate the reliability and the severity of the assumed threat, to determine the required reaction. Such a reaction may consist of automatic deleting or sandboxing the whole file, attempting to disinfect the file, or prompting the user for a decision in case of uncertainty. Often the user or the administrator can pre-configure the action upon detection of the AV program [16].

Having said all that, our goal is to provide the typical AV program with a signature, which looks specific enough to take automatic reactions and delete the whole file without disinfecting it all without user's intervention. Preferably, this reaction should be triggered automatically whenever the file is being downloaded (either from the network or from a removable storage device), without expecting the user to explicitly request a scan.

5. PROPOSED METHOD AND EVALUATION RESULTS

We separated the method design into the following main tasks:

- Searching for an optimal DMS
- Searching for an optimal DMS attachment method
- Building an engine to implement the proposed method

Those tasks are not completely orthogonal, since the DMS attachment method (and the DMS itself), affects the implementation of the method.

5.1 Optimal DMS

Various malware signatures can be found over the Internet at dedicated sites [27]. In searching for the optimal DMS we considered the following options:

- Nonfunctional malware. Those archaic viruses are still detected by most AV programs, although in general they do fails to run on modern operating systems, due to differences in memory management, executable files structure, and low-level behavior [29][12]. Among thousands of samples we choose Indos, a.k.a. AIDS virus [28] for testing. Similar options are old Windows 3.x viruses which are unable to run on modern 32/64 bits OS.
- A mixture of malware signatures, included as byte-arrays within an 'impostor' executable. The signatures strings are not harmful, and several hundreds of them can be included within an impostor executable to raise the probability of detection. The whole impostor executable is then used as a single DMS.
- Benign version of a generic attack pattern (e.g. heap-spray [25]). The source code of the program actually includes some well-known exploitation code which is detected by AVs, but does not use it for malicious purposes.
- Sterilized versions of malicious files. The binary code or the header of some well-known malware is modified to avoid malicious operations or overall execution.
- EICAR, a benign executable used to test AV programs compliance.
- Modern malware signature. These signatures generally have high detection rates, but raise serious security issues if they are not sterilized.

We have evaluated the alternatives according to several criteria, including their detectability by prevalent AV programs, the possibility of safe exclusion and other requirements as explained in Section 3. Size is also an important property, and we prefer the DMS to have a small footprint.

Following is a short discussion of each option.

1. An instance of 16-bit OS targeted malware's (Indos) was chosen due to its high detection rate and its inability to harm modern OS. Its size is approximately 10K (depending on variants), and it achieved a detection rate of approximately 40/46 (i.e., 40 positive detections with 46 AV programs) on VirusTotal when tested as a 'standalone' file (i.e., not attached to a document). We consider the Indos DMS to be benign for several reasons. This virus was originated in the early 1990s, targeting MS-DOS operating systems. In modern Microsoft Windows operating systems, such as XP or later versions, an old program like Indos is executed under severe restrictions, preventing the archaic program from interacting with the machine's resources through interrupts and effectively making it harmless. We tested this virus in our lab on a modern 32bit Windows OS and it simply failed to run, causing an incompatibility error message. Consequently, we consider this type of DMS to be safe for exclusion within the organization's boundaries, assuming it has no effect on the operating systems used within the organization.

2. The impostor cocktail, an executable containing a mixture of sterile signature-strings embedded inside, demanded approximately 18K bytes (with 288 signatures, each one 64 bytes), reached a detection rate of approximately 23/46 on VirusTotal, when tested as a 'standalone' file. Beyond that size, adding more signatures to the 'cocktail' did not seem to

improve the results. We consider this type of DMS to be benign, because the signature strings as included within the cocktail are harmless. However, safe exclusion of this DMS is quite problematic, since the cocktail may include hundreds of signature-strings, and we must guarantee that none of the viruses represented by these signatures can affect systems within the organization.

3. The benign attack pattern was tested and gave good detection rates. For example, a benign DMS with heap-spray code (but without a malicious payload), was detected by most prevalent AV programs. However it was frequently identified by the AV as 'generic' or 'looks-like', hence it would be hard to safely exclude this DMS (on the organization's computers), without opening the gates to its malicious relatives which have similar pattern.

4. Our sterilized versions of malicious files gave insufficient detection rates. This may indicate that most AV programs use quite advanced signatures. Enhanced sterilization methods may possibly improve the detection rate. Safe exclusion is possible but depends on the type of malware chosen.

5. The EICAR [17], a benign executable developed by the European Institute for Computer Antivirus Research and used to test AV programs compliance, gave good detection rates, comparable and even better than the Indos virus. However using EICAR as a DMS might be considered as an abuse of the original purpose of EICAR, and is therefore less practical.

6. Modern OS malware signatures were also proposed as DMS. These signatures are usually detected by most of the AV programs, and are simplest to find, since there are tens of thousands of samples publicly available [26]. However when considering such DMS, two points are important. (a) It should be guaranteed that malicious code will not be executed on the system (inside and outside the organization). For example, by embedding the DMS inside a PDF file as unspecified type of binary data, thus rendering the malware non runnable. (b) Another issue is adding a specific exclusion rule, to preserve the system protection against real malware. In the given PDF example, the exclusion mechanism should avoid the DMS only when it appears at a known offset in the PDF file. To this point we consider modern malware signatures to be an unacceptable solution, given the security loopholes it might open. Future work might suggest how to use modern malware signatures safely.

Table 2 summarizes the pros and cons of each DMS type. At this point, the preferable alternative for our purpose seems to be Indos (or a similar nonfunctional malware signature). This alternative was tested and compared to other options, as described in the following table.

Table 2. Comparison of DMS types

DMS type	Pros	Cons
Non-functional malware	Harmless high detectability, small size, Safe exclusion	
Impostor cocktail	Harmless	Insufficient detectability, relatively large size, problematic exclusion
Benign generic attack	Harmless, high detectability	Cautious exclusion
Sterilized malware	Harmless	Low detectability (depends on sterilization techniques)
EICAR	Harmless, high detectability, small, safe exclusion	Possible abuse
Modern OS malware	High detectability, Large selection	Cautious exclusion / Sterilization required

5.2 Optimal DMS Attachment Method

We have considered the following basic methods of DMS attachments.

- DMS-embedding: With various types of files (including Microsoft Office, Adobe PDF, and Windows PE), an object can be embedded within the target file without compromising its standard file structure.
- DMS-prepending: Another option is to prepend the DMS to the target file as a sequence of bytes, regardless of the target file's type.

We have evaluated the aforementioned basic attachment methods as follows:

1. Detection rate: a prepended DMS was more likely to be detected than an embedded DMS. The detection rate was tested on VirusTotal [18], a Web service which allows a user to upload suspicious files over the Internet and receive an answer online. VirusTotal employs a comprehensive list of AV programs, which is updated periodically.
2. Effectivity: most of the prevalent AV programs were able to disinfect a file with an embedded DMS, removing the DMS and passing the original file to the user. With a prepended DMS, however, virtually all the AV programs, which we tested failed or avoided disinfecting (or 'cleaning'), the tagged file. Hence, in most cases the tagged file, when detected as infected, was deleted / quarantined together with the DMS. Since VirusTotal does not provide this information, we tested the effectiveness rate in our lab, with the top-ten popular AV programs as listed by [10].
3. Tagging / untagging mechanism: embedding a DMS required a specialized mechanism for each type of file. Prepending, on the other hand, was performed with a rather unitary mechanism for all file types.
4. Readability of the tagged document: an embedded DMS, when ignored by the AV program, does nothing to prevent the user from reading the tagged document. On the other hand, a prepended DMS, which is not removed by the AV program, will typically make the tagged document unreadable for the average user.

Figure 2 presents the detection rates as tested on VirusTotal. The number of AV programs tested on VirusTotal was 46, and the highest score was 36 detections. Note that for certain file types, e.g. jpg and txt, embedding was not applicable. As can be seen, the DMS-prepending method, applied with the MS-DOS virus (Indos), gives the best results.

Also note that the weighted detection rate is considerably higher than the raw detection rate, considering the high performance of the top-ten AV programs which are far more ubiquitous than the rest of the programs, and dominate the market. Detailed calculations are provided in Section 6.1.

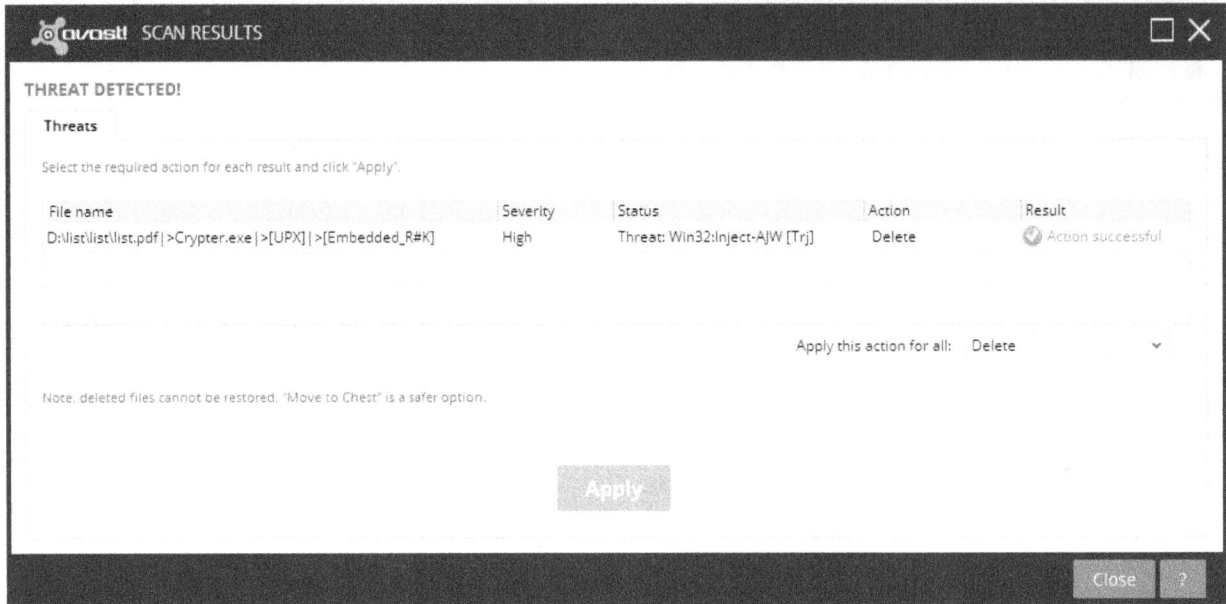

Figure 3: Deletion upon detection: As soon as the removable media is inserted into the computer (USB flash drive in this case), the Antivirus program (Avast! in this case) notifies the user that the whole document (list.pdf) was deleted because the file isn't cleanable.

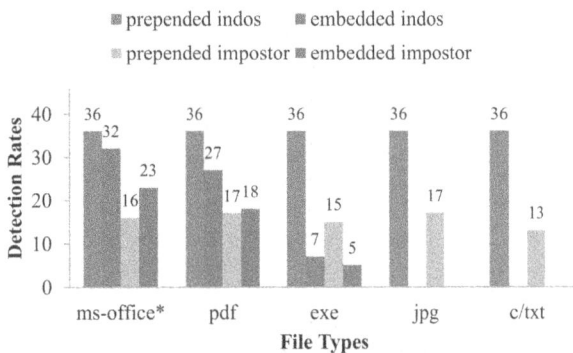

Figure 2: Detection rates, as tested on VirusTotal.
MS-Office files include docx, xlsx and pptx.

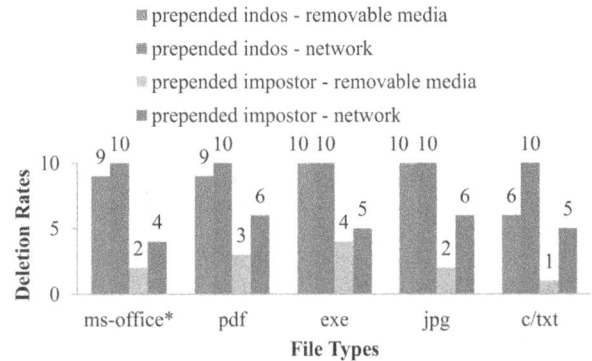

Figure 4: Deletion upon detection, tested in Lab with 'top-ten' AV programs. *MS-Office files include docx, xlsx and pptx.

Figure 4 presents the actual effectiveness of AV programs as tested in our lab, with the 'top-ten' AV programs (as listed by [10]). An effective AV, in our case, is one which deletes the whole file (not just the DMS), upon detection of a DMS. Furthermore, this behavior should be demonstrated automatically when the tagged file is being downloaded from an external source (e.g. email or removable disk). This behavior is illustrated in Figure 3. In our lab, we tested the behavior of the AV programs when downloading the tagged file (a) from a removable device, and (b) from the Internet. Note that lower results were recorded when downloading from a removable device; when downloading from the Internet, higher results were obtained. Further details are provided in Appendix A. Either way, as can be seen, the prepended Indos gives the best results.

Consequently, after trying both methods (i.e., prepending and embedding), we decided that DMS-prepending is better suited to our goals and constraints than DMS-embedding.

5.3 Testing the DMS on the Network

The DMS should limit the document's spread over the network. We tested the DMS with various popular email providers and various popular shared storage services.

With email, we first tried to send the tagged document from a browser-based client, and all tested email providers refused to send the tagged document (with the prepended Indos). Note that the sender's machine did not have an AV installed, so this behavior is attributed to the email provider, which checks the attachment online before the user sends the message. Then we tried to send the tagged document from a non-browser client (Microsoft Outlook); in this case the document was sent, but all tested targets refused to accept it. **Table 3** summarizes the results of our experiments with various email providers.

Table 3. DMS effectivity on email

	Browser-based client	Target
Gmail	Refuses to send	Refuses to accept
Hotmail	Refuses to send	Refuses to accept
Yahoo! Mail	Refuses to send	Refuses to accept

With shared storage, we first tried to upload a tagged document and share it among some authorized users; with local AV installed, it blocks the file from being uploaded and threat is as a virus (e.g. delete the file). When local AV was disabled, all tested shared-storage services let us upload and share the tagged document. We logged onto the shared storage as another authorized user and tried to open the tagged document; this step was carried out with an effective AV installed on the user's machine. The AV detected the DMS and refused to open the tagged document. We expect that the online storage service-providers will adapt malicious file filtering systems, as it already used by email-providers.

Table 4 summarizes the results of our experiments with various shared storage services.

Table 4. DMS effectivity on shared storage

	On upload and share (with local AV)	On upload and share (without local AV)	On open
DropBox	Blocked	Uploads and shares	Refuses to open/deleted from sharing
Google Drive	Blocked	Uploads and shares	Refuses to open/ deleted from sharing
SkyDrive	Blocked	Uploads and shares	Refuses to open/deleted from sharing

We also noted that when DropBox is installed as a directory on the user's machine and the user tries to open the tagged file (assuming the user has an effective AV installed), the AV offers deleting the tagged file; in which case, the file will be deleted from the service's shared directory and will no longer be available to other authorized users of the shared directory. With SkyDrive and Google-Drive, however, only the local files are deleted while the shared files stay intact.

5.4 Method Implementation

The implementation should handle file tagging and untagging within the organization's perimeter (by 'tagging' we mean attaching a DMS to a file). In general the method engine should ensure that every sensitive file on every computer within the organization will be tagged with a DMS. Applications reading the sensitive document will receive the untagged portion (the 'contents'), of the file, except for Internet browsers, email clients and their like, which will receive the whole tagged file. When an application writes to a sensitive file, the new or altered information should not overwrite the DMS. Said measures should be applied to a variety of file types, including Microsoft Office documents (e.g.: DOC, DOCX, XLS, XLSX), Adobe PDF files,

and binary executable files (EXE, DLL). The tagging mechanism should also be coordinated with the AV programs which are used within the organization, to avoid false alarms.

We have considered the following options for implementing the method engine:

- User mode monitor. This solution essentially requires listening to file modification events and constantly polling for file-close events to apply a DMS attachment, which normally cannot be performed when the file is opened by another program.
- Kernel mode filter driver. This solution utilizes the benefits of kernel-mode programs, which may intercept and hook native file-system calls, far beyond the capabilities of user-mode programs.

A user mode solution, if feasible, would have some benefits. First, it is probably the only feasible alternative if we consider DMS-embedding, which typically requires special user-mode libraries for each specific file type. Furthermore, a user-mode solution would not require special adjustments for each Windows release, it would not require special installation / removal procedures, it would not crash the whole system in case of unexpected bugs, and in general it seems easier to develop, to debug and to test (compared to a kernel mode solution).

Initially we started working on a user mode solution, utilizing the DMS-embedding method, yet we abandoned this direction when we discovered that DMS-embedding is unacceptable: in particular, an embedded DMS is easily disinfected by common AV programs, passing the untagged file to the user.

Since the alternative method (DMS-prepending), can be implemented in a generic way for virtually all file types, without requiring special user-mode libraries, we decided to use kernel-mode DMS-prepending.

Furthermore, a kernel-mode solution, implemented as a filter driver, can in principle be placed 'below' the kernel-mode component of an AV program. Thus, coordination with the AV is made almost trivial, since the DMS tagging / untagging operations are done transparently below the level of the AV, and we do not depend on the AV program's exclusion mechanism to exclude our specific DMS.

To develop the kernel mode solution we used Windows Driver Kit (WDK), 8, which is integrated with Visual Studio 2012, with Microsoft Windows 7 as the target platform. We built a kernel-mode minifilter, using the 'Filesystem Mini-filter' template as a starting point and adding our specific functionalities.

The conceptual architecture of the kernel mode filter is illustrated in Figure 5. Mini-filters (4, 5) are managed by the filter manager (3) and are placed at a given 'altitude' (the numerical level of a filter, relative to other drivers). Our filter (5) is placed lower than the AV filter (4). Figure 5 shows the response of our filter driver to a read or write request on a tagged file, where the request was made by a proper process and the requested operation is performed on the untagged contents. Please note that there are processes that will be provided with a tagged file since they be used unintentionally to leak the file. For example, processes such as Web browsers and Email clients, are blacklisted to avoid reading the file in untagged form.

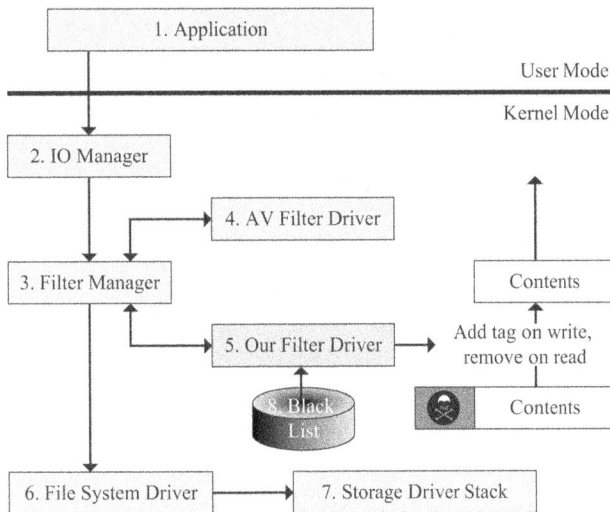

Figure 5: The filter's conceptual architecture, showing response to a read or write request on a tagged file (where the requesting process is not black-listed).

The following pseudo-code presents the schematic operation of the filter driver and its responses to various requests and various processes.

```
01: on FSevent(file, event)
02:    if (event == fileOpen) or (event ==
fileClose)
03:       if isFileSensitive(file)
04:          if not isFileTagged(file)
05:             do tagFile(file)
06:    else if (event == fileRead)
07:       if isFileTagged(file)
08:          getProcessName(event)
09:          if processName in blackList
10:             do readFileWithTag(file)
11:          else
12:             do seekTagOffset(file)
13:             do readFileContents(file)
14:       else
15:          do readFileNormally(file)
16:    else if (event == fileWrite)
17:       if isFileTagged(file)
18:          do seekTagOffset(file)
19:          do writeToFileContents(file)
20:       else
21:          do writeToFileNormally(file)
22: wait for next event
```

For the sake of clarity and brevity, this pseudo-code omits fine-grained details. It concentrates on the essential functionalities, i.e.: ensuring that each sensitive file is tagged, and ensuring that read and write operations on tagged files are appropriately performed. It does not go into the details of how a file is determined to be sensitive, or which processes are in the black-list.

5.5 System's Overhead

5.5.1 Storage overhead
Through DMS attachment, each document is inflated by a constant delta such that $V_T = V_O + V_D$ where V_T denotes the size of the tagged file, V_O denotes the size of the original file, and V_D denotes the size of the DMS.

The effect of V_D on the overall size of the tagged files essentially depends on the file-size distribution of the original files which are subject to tagging. Several distribution-types have been proposed for the overall population of files on a user's computer, including lognormal distribution and lambda distribution [36]. However, it is unclear if those distributions hold for the subpopulation of relevant files (i.e. only the files which are subject to tagging).

If we hypothetically apply Pareto principle to the relevant original documents size, then the largest 20% hold approximately 80% of the total size of the original files which we denote as $\sum V_O$. Hence the effect of V_D on $\sum V_T$ (the total size of the tagged files) would be practically higher than what would be expected with normal distribution.

However, if we assume that $V_D \ll \overline{V_O}$ where $\overline{V_O}$ denotes the average size of relevant original documents, regardless of the distribution, then the total volume required by the tagged files should not significantly exceed the total original volume of relevant files.

5.5.2 Performance overhead
The additional operations performed by our driver when reading and writing files are negligible ($O(1)$) regarding the size of the manipulated file as well as the number of manipulated files. We made several tests to corroborate this assumption, where files were created, written, read and deleted; the files' contents were randomized, to eliminate possible effects of caching. With 10,000 files of size 100,000 the performance with the driver was practically equal to the performance without the driver (2.85% difference).

5.6 Further Considerations
As noted earlier, the nonfunctional virus seems to provide optimal detection and deletion rates, while being effectively harmless in modern environments. However, with certain types of files, some other DMS may provide better automatic detection and deletion rates. As we have seen, some AV programs may require explicit scanning with certain file types, where an automatic response is required. Therefore, an optimal implementation may utilize more than one type of DMS, to handle all types of sensitive files.

One should also consider the potential overhead caused by the DMS concept. One aspect is the additional storage space required by attaching a DMS to every sensitive document within the organization. An overhead of 10K per file may seem acceptable with large documents or executable files, but some sensitive files (e.g. a C source code file), may be significantly smaller. Another aspect is the possible performance penalty inflicted by the implementation engine, which is assumed to be active continuously, monitoring and interfering with file IO operations. Related to this issue is the memory consumption of the implementation engine. Our experimental implementation engine does not seem to inflict noticeable performance overhead, but practical implementation may require some optimization.

In general, our experiments reveal a pattern, which appears to be common among different AV programs, concerning their reaction in varying situations. A typical AV program takes into account one or more of the following factors:

- The source of the suspected file. When the source is not physically external, many AV programs do not scan the file; this may happen when the file is transferred between a virtual guest machine and its host machine. With a removable storage device, most AV programs will scan the file. With an Internet source, all AV programs (at least among the top-ten), will scan the file. Furthermore, the source of the suspected file seems to be taken into consideration when the AV decides how to handle "positive" scan results.

- The type of the suspected file (our tagged document). With certain file types, notably docx and pdf, some AV programs do not perform scanning unless the file's source is the Internet. This is even more evident with tagged txt and c files. The type of the tagged document also affects the AV program's reaction (i.e., deleting or trying to disinfect), when the source is a removable storage device.

- The type of the infector (our DMS). Most AV programs (particularly among the top-ten), treat archaic viruses as a real threat. The specific type of the DMS also seems to affect the AV program's reaction (delete or disinfect).

This apparent pattern (regarding the source of the file, the file type, and the type of the infector) should be taken into consideration when designing a document-tagging framework. It should also be considered within the general malware-protection context.

Another consideration concerns the use of an extensible arsenal of alternative signatures, which will be plugged into the framework in a modular manner, on a temporal basis. Otherwise the method may eventually lose its effect and may possibly be abused. Using the same signature over elongated period of time may cause AV vendors to lower the risk associated with that signature, or even to ignore it. Furthermore, if the signature is not replaced, adversaries may learn to associate its occurrence with sensitive files, and may actively search for files bearing the overused signature.

6. DISCUSSION: FILE SPREADING

In this section we shall discuss the expected impact of our method on the spread of an unintentionally leaked document to friends of the leak source. Related issues include mathematical modelling of malware spreading over the Internet [31] and in mobile devices [32], modelling rumors spreading over social networks [33][34] and psychological aspects of rumor spreading [35]. However, an extensive coverage of these issues is beyond the scope of this paper and should be treated in future research. The following discussion is confined to the most elementary cases, as illustrated by Figure 6, where the topology is vastly simplified and each target node is approached only once.

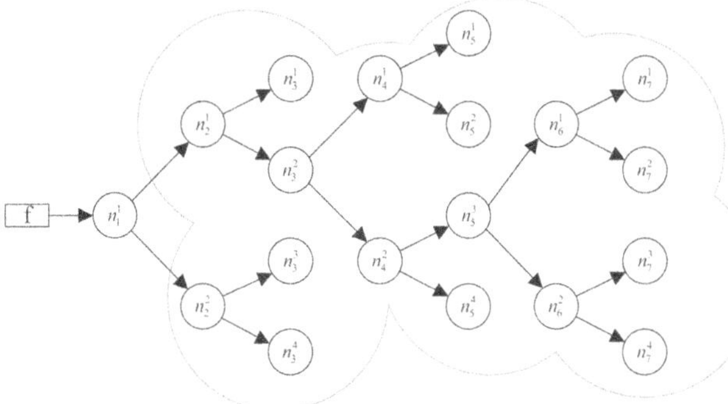

Figure 6: Spreading of a file over 7 hops, where each node has at most 2 friends.

Let S denote the number of nodes that received the leaked document. S is influenced by:

H Leakage propagation from the source node, measured by the maximal distance (or number of hops) that the

leaked document traveled in the graph (a tree in our simple case).

F Number of friends connected to each node in the tree.

L The probability that a node will leak the document to its friends.

P The probability that the leaked document will be detected and blocked by an AV. An approximation of P is given by $P = E \times I$, where E is the average effectiveness rate of AV programs (the rate of blocking a tagged file), and I is the installation rate of active AV programs over the network.

First we shall calculate P, considering our experimental results combined with available statistics of AV installations. Then we shall illustrate the spread S of a file over varying number of hops H, and examine the effect of our method.

6.1 Calculating P, the Probability that the Leaked Document will be Blocked

According to [1], the global percentage of computers which have an active AV program installed is approximately 84%. According to [10], the top ten AV vendors are (in top to bottom order), Avast, Avira, AVG, Microsoft, ESET, Symantec, Kaspersky, McAfee, Panda, and Trend Micro. Together, the top ten AV vendors hold 87.46% of the market, leaving merely 12.54% to 'others'. Note that the global percentage of AV installations is expected to increase over the next few years, due to growing awareness as demonstrated in the recent release of Microsoft Windows 8, with malware protection activated by default.

According to our results, the detection rate was approximately $\frac{36}{46}$ when tested on VirusTotal. This value refers to the prepended MS-DOS virus (Indos): the alternatives were either unacceptable (embedded Indos), or too low (prepended impostor). According to VirusTotal the detection rate among the top ten AV program was approximately $\frac{10}{10}$ (with Avira tested in lab), which implies a detection rate of $\frac{36-10}{46-10} \approx 0.72$ for the 'other' programs. Using these results, the weighed detection rate $D = \frac{\sum w_j d_j}{\sum w_j}$ is reduced to $\frac{87.46 \times 1.0 + 12.54 \times 0.72}{100} \approx 0.965$, considering both the top-ten and all other AV programs.

However when we tested the top ten AV programs in our lab to see if they automatically delete the whole file upon detection, along with the prepended DMS, we noticed that some file types (e.g. docx, pdf), achieved a deletion-rate of $\frac{9}{10}$ when downloaded from removable media, but were effectively blocked by all top-ten programs ($\frac{10}{10}$) when downloaded from the Internet. Consequently, with those file types the effectiveness rate P varies between $0.965 \times \frac{9}{10} \approx 0.87$ in the worst case (delivery by removable media), to $0.965 \times \frac{10}{10} = 0.965$ in the best case (spread over the Internet). Since spread by Internet is more frequent than spread by removable media it would be reasonable to accept the higher value as the representative value.

If we take those approximated calculations further, then the global percentage of computers with effective protection is $P = I \times E$ (where I is the global percentage with an AV installed, and E is the effectiveness rate). This value is between $84\% \times 0.87 \approx 73\%$ for spread over removable media and $84\% \times 0.965 \approx 81\%$ for spread over the Internet.

6.2 Evaluating the Spread of a Tagged File

Recall that S denotes the spread of the tagged file (measured by the number of nodes that received the leaked document). We assume that each target node is approached only once.

The number of nodes that receive the leaked document is given by

$$S = \sum_1^H ((1-P) \times L \times F)^H \qquad (1)$$

First let us examine the spread of the file when $P=0.00$; this is the case where the leaked file is not tagged with a DMS, and is free to spread without being blocked by AV programs across the network. We assume the probability of leakage L varies, and the number of friends $F=100$. This case is depicted in Figure 7, showing a steep diverging curve.

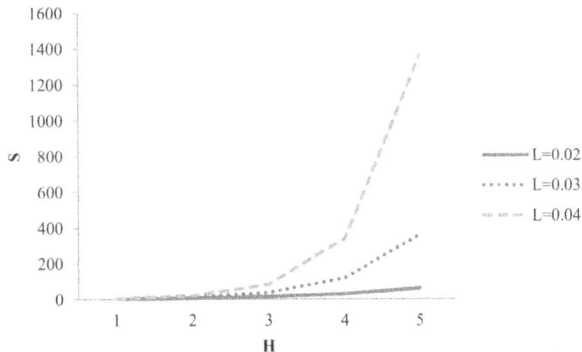

Figure 7: Spread S of a file across distance H for $P=0.00$, where L varies and $F=100$

Now let us examine the expected effect of our method, with $P=0.81$, related to spread over the Internet. Again we assume the probability of leakage L varies, and the number of friends $F=100$. This case is depicted in Figure 8, showing a converging curve.

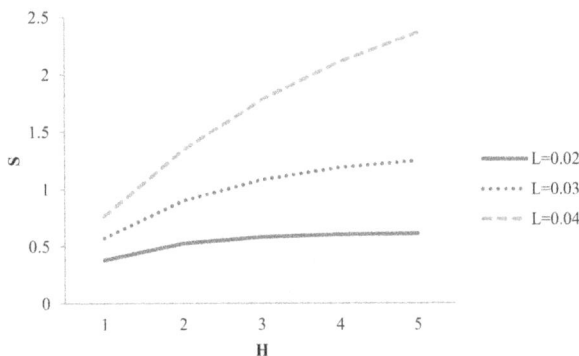

Figure 8: Spread S of a file across distance H for $P=0.81$, where L varies and $F=100$

As can be seen, our analysis suggests that our method can substantially reduce the spreading of a leaked document.

7. CONCLUSION

Unintentional data leakage is a serious problem, causing substantial financial loss, exposing sensitive information, and harming the reputation of the involved organization. Common technological solutions to this problem essentially are incapable of limiting the spread of a sensitive document once it had somehow leaked. In this paper we describe a new method, aiming to reduce this conceptual loophole. Our method involves tagging each sensitive file with a harmless malware signature, which is detected as a genuine threat by prevalent Antivirus (AV) programs, along with Intrusion Detection and Prevention systems. Consequently, the existing global infrastructure of installed AV programs outside the organization perimeter is employed to serve as remote sentinels and to halt the tagged leaked document, beyond the boundaries of the organization.

We conducted detailed experiments with various types of signatures and tagging methods, under various types of AV programs, to choose the optimal signature. Our current choice is based on an archaic virus, totally harmless on current operating systems yet effectively detected and halted by the majority of leading AV programs. We also developed a working deployment framework, capable of performing transparent tagging on various types of documents. Furthermore, our analysis, based on the experimental rate of effective detection and the current global rate of installed AV programs, suggests that our method can substantially reduce the spreading of a tagged leaked document.

The overhead inflicted by our method seems to be acceptable, in terms of the required additional storage as well as the performance penalty. The first was estimated theoretically, while the second was measured experimentally.

7.1 Future Research Directions

Future research directions include (a) refining the deployment framework, to reliably classify sensitive documents before tagging; (b) adding essential forensic information to the tagged file; (c) establishing standard protocols in coordination with the AV community, to enhance the acceptance and the applicability of our concept.

Following is a concise list of the main future directions, with some additional elaboration.

A. Refining the deployment framework involves a reliable mechanism which should classify documents according to their level of sensitivity, before applying the DMS tagging method. Additionally, such refinement may include a white list instead of the black list currently used to filter the processes which open a given file.

B. Adding essential forensic information to the tagged file involves details such as the user name, domain, machine identification, timestamp, and other information which may be helpful in a forensic investigation, when trying to track down the source of the leakage.

C. Establishing standard protocols in coordination with the AV community should enhance the acceptance and the applicability of our proposed concept. Such protocols should address various practical issues, e.g. the type of the DMS, the category of acceptable DMSs, particularly in case of a 'generic' type (as was discussed earlier in this paper, concerning a benign generic pattern like heap-spray). In addition, the kernel-mode drivers used by various AV vendors should remain on a higher lever (or 'altitude') above our DMS-handling driver, to ensure proper behavior of the system.

We assume that ongoing research, along with proper coordination efforts with the AV community, will assist in bringing our concept into the mainstream of leakage prevention methods.

8. REFERENCES

1. A. Shabtai, Y. Elovici and L. Rokach, "A Survey of Data Leakage Detection and Prevention Solutions," Springer, 2012.

2. BBC, "UK's families put on fraud alert," BBC NEWS, November 20, 2007. [Online]. Available: http://news.bbc.co.uk/2/hi/uk_news/politics/7103566.stm.

3. K. Sack, "Patient Data Posted Online in Major Breach of Privacy," The New York Times, 8 September 2011. [Online]. Available: http://www.nytimes.com/2011/09/09/us/09breach.html?_r=2 &ref=stanforduniversity&.

4. K. Stewart, "Utah Medicaid contractor loses job over data breach," The Salt Lake tribune, 17 Jan 2013 . [Online]. Available: http://www.sltrib.com/sltrib/news/55650800-78/health-medicaid-utah-breach.html.csp.

5. Detica and Office of Cyber Security and Information Assurance, "The Cost of Cyber Crime," 2011.

6. R. Anderson, C. Barton, R. Boehme, R. Clayton, M. van Eeten, M. Levi, T. Moore and S. Savage, "Measuring the Cost of Cybercrime," 2012.

7. Z. Xiaosong, L. Fei, C. Ting and L. Hua, "Research and Application of the Transparent Data Encpryption in Intranet Data Leakage Prevention," *Computational Intelligence and Security, 2009. CIS '09.* , vol. II, pp. 376-379, 2009.

8. C. Phua, "Protecting organisations from personal data breaches," *Computer Fraud & Security,* vol. 2009, no. 1, p. 13–18, 2009.

9. Microsoft, "About Information Rights Management," Microsoft Office Website, 2013. [Online]. Available: http://office.microsoft.com/en-us/help/about-information-rights-management-HP006220859.aspx.

10. OPSWAT, "Security Industry Market Share Analysis," OPSWAT, Inc., March 2012.

11. M. Christodorescu and J. Somesh, "Testing Malware Detectors," in *ACM SIGSOFT International Symposium on Software*, Boston, Massachusetts, USA., 2004.

12. P. Szor, "The art of computer virus research and defense," Addison Wesley, 2005.

13. Microsoft, "Microsoft Portable Executable and Common Object File Format Specification," Microsoft, 2010.

14. "elf - format of Executable and Linking Format (ELF) files," The Linux man-pages project, 2010. [Online]. Available: http://man7.org/linux/man-pages/man5/elf.5.html.

15. M. Sikorsky and A. Honig, "Practical malware analysis," No Starch Press, 2012.

16. Kaspersky, "File Anti-Virus: actions upon threat detection," Kaspersky PURE 2.0, [Online]. Available: http://utils.kaspersky.com/special/pure_2/46_pure_file_antivi r_actions_upon_threat_en.pdf. [Accessed 17 March 2013].

17. EICAR, "Anti-Malware testfile," European Institute for Computer Antivirus Research, 7 September 2006. [Online]. Available: http://www.eicar.org/86-0-Intended-use.html.

18. VirusTotal, "VirusTotal, Free online virus, malware and URL scanner," [Online]. Available: https://www.virustotal.com/. [Accessed Feb. 2013].

19. Kaspersky Lab, "Digital Consumer's Online Trends and Risks," Kapersky Lab, 2012.

20. Raschke, T. "The Forrester Wave ™: Data Leak Prevention, Q2 2008," Technical report, Forrester Research, Inc. 2008.

21. Lawton, G. "New technology prevents data leakage," Computer 41.9 (2008): 14-17.

22. Spitzner, L. "Honeypots: Catching the insider threat," Computer Security Applications Conference, 2003. Proceedings. 19th Annual. IEEE, 2003.

23. Storey, D. "Catching flies with honey tokens," Network Security 2009.11 (2009): 15-18.

24. Papadimitriou, P, and Garcia-Molina, H. "Data leakage detection," Knowledge and Data Engineering, IEEE Transactions on 23.1 (2011): 51-63.

25. Stevens, D. "Malicious PDF documents explained," IEEE Security & Privacy, Vol. 9. No. 1, p. 80-82, 2011.

26. Microsoft, "The evolution of malware and the threat landscape – a 10-year review," Microsoft Security Intelligence Report, special edition, 2012.

27. Lenny Seltzer, "Malware sample sources for researchers," [Online]. Available: http://zeltser.com/combating-malicious-software/malware-sample-sources.html.

28. Securelist, "Virus.DOS.Aids.552", [Online]. Available: http://www.securelist.com/en/descriptions/6880300/Virus.D OS.Aids.552.

29. Symantec, "Understanding virus behavior under Windows NT," Symantec Reasearch Center. [Online]. Available: http://www.symantec.com/avcenter/reference/virus.behavior. under.win.nt.pdf.

30. A. Shabtai, R. Moskovitch, Y. Elovici and C. Glezer, "Detection of malicious code by applying machine learning classifiers on static features: A state-of-the-art survey," *Information Security Technical Report,* vol. 14, no. 1, pp. 16-29, 2009.

31. Garetto, M., Gong, W., & Towsley, D. 2003. "Modeling malware spreading dynamics," In INFOCOM 2003. Twenty-Second Annual Joint Conference of the IEEE Computer and Communications. IEEE Societies (Vol. 3, pp. 1869-1879). IEEE.

32. Wang, P., González, M. C., Hidalgo, C. A., & Barabási, A. L. 2009. "Understanding the spreading patterns of mobile phone viruses," *Science*, 324(5930), 1071-1076.

33. Moreno, Y., Nekovee, M., & Pacheco, A. F. 2004. "Dynamics of rumor spreading in complex networks," Physical Review E, 69(6), 066130.

34. Chierichetti, F., Lattanzi, S., & Panconesi, A. 2009. "Rumor spreading in social networks," In *Automata, Languages and Programming* (pp. 375-386). Springer Berlin Heidelberg.

35. Bordia, P., & DiFonzo, N. 2005. "Psychological motivations," in *rumor spread. Rumor mills: The social impact of rumor and legend*, 87-101.

36. Evans, K. M., & Kuenning, G. H. 2002. "A study of irregularities in file-size distributions," In *Proceedings of the 2002 International Symposium on Performance Evaluation of Computer and Telecommunication Systems (SPECTS)*.

37. Scarfo, A. 2012. "New security perspectives around BYOD," In *Proceedings of the 2012 Seventh International Conference on Broadband, Wireless Computing, Communication and Applications* (pp. 446-451). IEEE Computer Society.

APPENDIX A

The following table presents, in a concise form, the behavior of the antivirus products (related to the top-ten vendors [10]) which were tested in lab. The relevant DMS is the prepended Indos. The numeric values indicate the step at which the file was deleted: transfer, open, or scan. Different colors indicate the transmission method: either networking or removable media.

	DLL		PDF		DOC/X		PPT/X		XLS/X		EXE		Text-file		.c (source code)		.JPG	
Avast!	1,2,3	1,2,3	1,2,3	1,2,3	1,2,3	2,3	1,2,3	2,3	1,2,3	2,3	1,2,3	1,2,3	1,2,3	2,3	1,2,3	2,3	1,2,3	1,2,3
AVG	1,2,3	1,2,3	1,2,3	1,2,3	1,2,3	1,2,3	1,2,3	1,2,3	1,2,3	1,2,3	1,2,3	1,2,3	1,2,3	2,3	1,2,3	2,3	1,2,3	1,2,3
Avira	1,2,3	1,2,3	1,2,3	1,2,3	1,2,3	1,2,3	1,2,3	1,2,3	1,2,3	1,2,3	1,2,3	1,2,3	1,2,3	2,3	1,2,3	2,3	1,2,3	1,2,3
NOD32	1,2,3	1,2,3	1,2,3	1,2,3	1,2,3	1,2,3	1,2,3	1,2,3	1,2,3	1,2,3	1,2,3	1,2,3	1,2,3	1,2,3	1,2,3	1,2,3	1,2,3	1,2,3
Kaspersky	1,2,3	1,2,3	1,2,3	1,2,3	1,2,3	1,2,3	1,2,3	1,2,3	1,2,3	1,2,3	1,2,3	1,2,3	1,2,3	1,2,3	1,2,3	1,2,3	1,2,3	1,2,3
McAfee	1,2,3	1,2,3	1,2,3	1,2,3	1,2,3	1,2,3	1,2,3	1,2,3	1,2,3	1,2,3	1,2,3	1,2,3	1,2,3	1,2,3	1,2,3	1,2,3	1,2,3	1,2,3
Microsoft	1,2,3	1,2,3	1,2,3	2,3	1,2,3	3	1,2,3	3	1,2,3	3	1,2,3	1,2,3	1,2,3	2,3	1,2,3	2,3	1,2,3	1,2,3
Norton	1,2,3	1,2,3	1,2,3	1,2,3	1,2,3	1,2,3	1,2,3	1,2,3	1,2,3	1,2,3	1,2,3	1,2,3	1,2,3	1,2,3	1,2,3	1,2,3	1,2,3	1,2,3
Panda	1,2,3	1,2,3	1,2,3	3	1,2,3	3	1,2,3	3	1,2,3	3	1,2,3	1,2,3	1,2,3	2,3	1,2,3	2,3	1,2,3	1,2,3
TrendMicro	1,2,3	1,2,3	1,2,3	1,2,3	1,2,3	1,2,3	1,2,3	1,2,3	1,2,3	1,2,3	1,2,3	1,2,3	1,2,3	1,2,3	1,2,3	1,2,3	1,2,3	1,2,3

(1) Delete file on transfer (download-file/copy-file)
(2) Delete file on open
(3) Delete file on scan

□	Internet / Network
□	USB / Removable media

Optimized and Controlled Provisioning of Encrypted Outsourced Data

Anis Bkakria
Télécom Bretagne
Rennes, France
anis.bkakria@telecom-bretagne.eu

Andreas Schaad
SAP AG
Karlsruhe, Germany
andreas.schaad@sap.com

Florian Kerschbaum
SAP AG
Karlsruhe, Germany
florian.kerschbaum@sap.com

Frederic Cuppens
Télécom Bretagne
Rennes, France
frederic.cuppens@telecom-bretagne.eu

Nora Cuppens-Boulahia
Télécom Bretagne
Rennes, France
nora.cuppens@telecom-bretagne.eu

David Gross-Amblard
Université de Rennes 1
Rennes, France
david.gross-amblard@irisa.fr

ABSTRACT

Recent advances in encrypted outsourced databases support the direct processing of queries on encrypted data. Depending on functionality (i.e. operators) required in the queries the database has to use different encryption schemes with different security properties. Next to these functional requirements a security administrator may have to address security policies that may equally determine the used encryption schemes. We present an algorithm and tool set that determines an optimal balance between security and functionality as well as helps to identify and resolve possible conflicts. We test our solution on a database benchmark and business-driven security policies.

Categories and Subject Descriptors

H.2.0 [**Database Management**]: General—*Security, Integrity, and Protection*; D.4.6 [**Operating Systems**]: Security and Protection—*Access control*

Keywords

Encrypted Database, Policy Configuration, Encryption Algorithm

1. INTRODUCTION

The IT world is facing an architectural shift where storage as well as processing capabilities are offered by cloud providers. We observe large platforms operated, for example, by Amazon, SAP or Microsoft successfully providing infrastructure, database-as-a-service, and entire cloud application offerings to some of the world's largest companies. Naturally, data security is a main concern and one general

answer is to use at-rest encryption technology to protect outsourced data. This, however, renders any offerings such as database-as-a-service useless when assuming that cloud companies may not be fully trusted [26] as encrypted data cannot be directly processed. A bizarre architectural setup is the result where customers have to encrypt large data sets before provisioning them to the cloud, but then retrieve them back to on-premise and decrypt them if they want to run any complex queries. How to securely store as well as process data in a cloud is thus a major question for companies willing to migrate to and benefit from cloud offerings.

However, encryption schemes have been proposed recently that allow to execute particular query operators over encrypted data and recent work by [24] shows that the general direct processing of encrypted data is an achievable goal, something recently confirmed in a larger industrial perspective [15]. Following the idea of encrypting cleartext in so called "onions" allows to balance and match data processing functionality, i.e. each layer of an onion supports some SQL operations, with security, i.e. an onion structure introduces a total order with respect to the security properties of the chosen schemes. Yet, it is not practical to encrypt all columns in a table with the same onion structure. For example, columns may not require any encryption as they do not contain any sensitive material. Other columns may, for company specific compliance regulations, require to always be encrypted using a specific scheme when outsourced.

We believe that in order to further promote the wider industrial adoption of directly processing encrypted data, a more flexible configuration management is required before outsourcing the data from on-premise to a database-as-a-service cloud. In this paper, we first present a policy-based configuration framework for encrypted data allowing the security administrator to specify the security policy to be applied over the outsourced data. Second, we propose an algorithm allowing to detect conflicts between security and utility requirements. Third, we prove that selecting the optimal combination of encryption schemes that fit the defined policies with respect to the data owner's functional requirements (e.g. SQL that should be executed over the encrypted data) is NP-hard. Fourth, we therefore propose a heuristic, polynomial-time algorithm for finding a combination of encryption schemes that satisfies a policy P and provides the best security level.

The rest of this paper is organized as follows, Section 2 describes the problem treated in this paper. Section 3 presents the modeling of the used system and the modeling of the policy to be applied over the outsourced database. We show, for a given policy, how to detect the conflict between security and utility requirements involved in the policy and how to choose the combination of encryption schemes that enforces it. Section 4 presents a use case showing the application and the benefits of our approach in practice. Section 5 discusses related work. Finally, Section 6 reports our conclusions.

2. PROBLEM DESCRIPTION

2.1 Adjustable Database Encryption

Encrypted databases can execute SQL queries over encrypted data. In this case data is never decrypted inside the database server, but always remains encrypted. The key to the encryption and decryption functions solely resides at the client.

The main idea to processing queries in this way is property-preserving encryption. In property-preserving encryption a function $f(E(x), E(y))$ on ciphertexts $E(x)$, $E(y)$ returns the same result as $f(x, y)$. Hacigümüs et al. have described this concept for deterministic encryption and equality as a function [16]. They realized that many database operators, particularly selection and join, often use equality. Each data value is separately deterministically encrypted. Those database operators can then be used unmodified on encrypted data.

A limitation of the initial approach was that inequality comparisons (range queries) were insufficiently supported. Agrawal et al. introduced order-preserving encryption [2]. Order-preserving encryption is property-preserving encryption for greater-than-or-equal comparisons. Using order-preserving encryption one can implement a large subset of SQL queries.

The security of order-preserving encryption and even deterministic encryption is still much debated. It is therefore better to choose the most secure encryption for a set of queries. If this set is unknown, then all data needs to be encrypted order-preservingly. Popa et al. presented a solution to this: adjustable (onion) encryption. Each data value is encrypted order-preservingly. This ciphertext is encrypted deterministically and the result is finally encrypted using standard randomized encryption secure against chosen plaintext attacks. Before a query is executed it is analyzed for the required encryption levels and the data values are adjusted (decrypted) to these levels. Hence, the most secure encryption can be chosen automatically.

2.2 Functional Requirements

As already mentioned the set of queries executed on the database pose a set of functional requirements. These requirements are captured as the functions executed on the ciphertext by the database operators.

In many cases a large subset of the queries to be executed is known. For example, when an application uses the database, one can analyse this application and extract the queries (maybe except for parameters). In many cases one can simply resort to the prepared SQL statements.

If this subset of queries is known in advance, then it would be unwise to adjust the encryption during run-time. Although the adjustment process is performed only once, it can be quite costly. Each data value of an entire column needs to be decrypted which can sum to several MByte or even GByte of data.

Instead, the database can be encrypted to a "prepared" state and the adjustment process avoided. This leads to a significant shortening of the phase from a cold to a hot database. Real systems can go faster into production.

Our approach is the first to support this analysis. We choose the appropriate encryption levels depending on the functional requirements of a set of queries.

2.3 Security Levels

The encryption levels of adjustable encryption correspond to different security levels. We claim that randomized encryption is at least as secure as deterministic encryption which is at least as secure as order-preserving encryption. We argue as follows.

Randomized encryption (RND) is semantically secure, i.e., it is secure against chosen plaintext attacks. We use AES in CBC for this encryption level. Clearly, then chosen plaintexts attacks are prevented.

Deterministic encryption (DET) allows chosen plaintext attacks, if the key is known or there is an encryption oracle. We only need symmetric encryption in encrypted database, such that it may be difficult to obtain the key or construct such an oracle. If a plaintext is encrypted and stored more than once, deterministic encryption also allows frequency attacks as in [18]. While not necessary, this may often – if not almost always – be the case in real databases. We therefore claim that deterministic encryption is less secure than randomized encryption. We use Pohlig-Hellman encryption, a symmetric key RSA variant, for this encryption level, in order to support proxy re-encryption [20].

Order-preserving encryption (OPE) is also deterministic, such that all attacks on deterministic encryption also work for order-preserving encryption. In addition, it preserves the order, which may enable many more attacks. It was concluded that order-preserving encryption leaks at least half of the plaintext bits [29]. Clearly, order-preserving encryption is the least secure choice. We use the scheme by Boldyreva et al. [5, 6] for this encryption level, which has been proven to be the optimally secure, immutable, order-preserving encryption scheme.

Next to these encryption levels we use homomorphic encryption (HOM) for aggregation. Specifically, we use Paillier encryption [22]. Homomorphic encryption is secure against chosen plaintext attacks as is randomized encryption. Since for processing queries both ciphertexts need to be offered in parallel, they can be safely assumed to provide the same security level. Furthermore, similar to onion encryption, homomorphic encryption can be downgraded to deterministic encryption. As in the approach by Bellare et al.[4], we can choose a deterministic randomization parameter. For downgrading we can simply select one ciphertext among the set of identical plaintexts. This has the added benefit that dictionary compression is as effective as on plaintext data [19].

2.4 Security Requirements and The Need for Policy Configuration

Considering the security levels from Section 2.3 The data owner may realize that certain queries may put his data at risk. These queries may adapt the encryption level to an unsafe state, e.g. order-preserving encryption, for a certain set of data. Even certain security standards, such as PCI-DSS, may require certain encryption levels.

Therefore the data owner may want to set certain policies on which encryption levels are allowed. He may want to prevent specific data from ever reaching a specific encryption state. For this he needs the approach for specifying policies we propose in this paper.

2.5 Policy Enforcement

The specified policies need to be enforced in the encrypted database. There is a crucial insight that enables prevention of certain encryption levels. If an encryption level is not present, it cannot be decrypted to. And vice versa, if an encryption should not be decrypted to, it does not need to be present. We therefore omit the encryption levels prevented by our policy. If one should not be able to decrypt to order-preserving encryption, the data value will not be encrypted order-preservingly. This has the positive side effect that ciphertexts may get smaller and encryption is more efficient.

The question remains what to do with queries that functionally require an encryption level that is prohibited by the security policy. In this case one ships the ciphertexts to the client, decrypts and executes the query on the client. The client query analysis algorithm of Kerschbaum et al. based on relational algebra, allows splitting a query into a local and a remote part [21]. This way only the minimally necessary part of the query according to the security policy will be executed on the client.

3. POLICY CONFIGURATION

In this section, we firstly present the modeling of the system and the specification of the policy. Afterwards, we present an algorithm allowing to detect conflicts between the constraints of the policy. We then propose an efficient algorithm allowing to enforce the policy while resolving the detected conflicts.

3.1 System modeling

In our approach, data to be outsourced is stored in a relational database $\mathcal{D}$, which is composed of a collection of relational tables $\mathcal{T} = \{T_1, \cdots, T_n\}$, with each of these relational tables T_i containing a collection of attributes $\mathcal{A}_{T_i} = \{a_{1,i}, a_{2,i}, \cdots\}$. The system contains a toolbox $\mathcal{E}$ composed of a set of m encryption schemes $\{E_1, \cdots, E_m\}$ that can be used to protect outsourced data. Each encryption scheme $E_i \in \mathcal{E}$ is characterized by a security level l_i that provides and a set of functionalities $F_i \subseteq \mathcal{F}$ that satisfies. Let $\mathcal{F}$ be the set of functional requirements that can be required over the data to be outsourced and $\mathcal{L}$ be the set of security levels provided by $\mathcal{E}$.

3.2 Policy modeling

We model, in a quite simple and powerful way, the requirements defined by the data owner. Those requirements are expressed through security and utility constraints. Security constraints are composed of confidentiality constraints and security threshold constraints.

Definition 1. (Confidentiality constraint) Given a relational table $T_i \in \mathcal{T}$ containing a list of attributes $\mathcal{A}_{T_i}$, a confidentiality constraint defined over T_i is a singleton set $CC = \{a\}$, where $a \in \mathcal{A}_{T_i}$.

Semantically speaking, a confidentiality constraint CC states that the value assumed by the attribute in CC is considered sensitive and therefore must be protected.

Definition 2. (Security threshold constraint) Given a relational table $T_i \in \mathcal{T}$ and an attribute $a \in \mathcal{A}_{T_i}$, a security threshold constraint TC_a over the attribute a is a security level l in $\mathcal{L}$. A security threshold constraint defined over the attribute a is well defined *iff* there exists a confidentiality constraint CC such that $a \in CC$.

Security threshold constraints allow the data owner to specify a security level threshold for each sensitive attribute. The semantics of a security threshold constraint TC is that the security level of the sensitive attribute a must be at least as much secure as the security level l of TC.

Definition 3. (Utility constraint) Given a relational table $T_i \in \mathcal{T}$ and an attribute $a \in \mathcal{A}_{T_i}$, an utility constraint UC_a over the attribute a is a set of functionality $F_a = \{f_1, \cdots, f_n\}$, where $F_a \subseteq \mathcal{F}$.

Confidentiality protection is provided at the expense of data utility. A utility constraint offers the data owner the ability to require that some functionalities on his data must be provided, otherwise the data is useless.

3.3 Policy conflict detection

Policy conflicts occur when the objectives of two or more constraints cannot be simultaneously satisfied. Conflict detection aims at checking whether a set of constraints contains conflicts. In our case, conflicts may occur between security constraints and utility constraints, more precisely, between security threshold constraints and utility constraints. To detect the conflicts, there are two steps. First, we must get for each security level $l \in \mathcal{L}$, the set of functionalities F_l which are satisfied by encryption schemes providing security levels that are at least as much secure as l. Then, for each sensitive attribute having $TC_a = l_a$ as a security threshold constraint and $UC_a = F_a$ as an utility constraint, we check if the set of functionalities F_{l_a} we got from the previous step for the level l_a is a superset of F_a, and if not, we deduce that there is a conflict between TC_a and UC_a. The set of conflicts in a defined policy are detected as described in Algorithm 1.

Example 1. Let $\mathcal{L} = \{RND, DET, OPE\}$ be the set of security level that can be provided from the set of encryption schemes $\mathcal{E} = \{E_1, E_2, E_3\}$. Suppose that the E_1, E_2 and E_3 provide respectively RND, DET and OPE, and satisfy respectively the functionalities $\emptyset$, $\{Equality, Join\}$ and $\{Min, Max\}$. Suppose that we want to enforce a policy composed of two constraints $TC_a = DET$ and $UC_a = \{Join, Min\}$. By performing the first step of Algorithm 1, we deduce that $F_{RND} = \emptyset$, $F_{DET} = \{Equality, Join\}$ and $F_{OPE} = \{Equality, Join, Min, Max\}$. The second step of Algorithm 1 gives that $UC_a \nsubseteq F_{DET}$, which allows to deduce that TC_a and UC_a are conflicting constraints.

```
input :
        A_s = {a_1, ⋯ , a_n}    /*sensitive attributes*/
        C_t = {TC_{a_1}, ⋯ , TC_{a_n}} /*security threshold
constraints*/
        C_u = {UC_{a_1}, ⋯ , UC_{a_n}} /*utility constraints*/
        E = {E_1, ⋯ , E_m} /*encryption schemes*/
        L = {l_1, ⋯ , l_p} /*security levels*/
output:
        I   /*set of conflicts*/
Main
I = ∅
/* First step */
foreach l_i in L do
 │ F_{l_i} = ∅
 │ foreach E_j in E do
 │  │ if (l_j is more secure or equal l_i) then
 │  │  │ F_{l_i} = F_{l_i} ∪ F_j
 │  │ end
 │ endfch
endfch
/* Second step */
foreach a_k in A_s do
 │ if ( UC_{a_k} ⊄ F_{TC_{a_k}} ) then
 │  │ I = I ∪ {(a_k, UC_{a_k}, TC_{a_k})}
 │ end
endfch
```

Algorithm 1: Conflict detection

3.4 Policy satisfaction

The policy to be enforced over the outsourced database is composed of security and utility constraints. Those constraints can be satisfied through the application of encryption schemes. Our main challenge is to find for each sensitive attribute a in the outsourced database, the *best combination of encryption schemes* that can satisfy the set of security and utility constraints defined over a.

Definition 4. (combination of encryption schemes) Let E be the set of available encryption schemes in the system, a combination of encryption schemes is a subset $C ⊆ E$.

Definition 5. Let $C = \{E_1, ⋯ , E_m\}$ be a combination of encryption schemes applied over the attribute a and l_i be the security level provided by the encryption scheme E_i, $1 ≤ i ≤ m$. The security level of the attribute a provided by the application of C is l, *iff* the following conditions hold:

- $l ∈ \{l_1, ⋯ , l_m\}$

- $∀l_j ∈ \{l_1, ⋯ , l_m\}$, l_j is at least as secure as l.

Note that the previous definition requires the security level provided by the combination of schemes in C to be the lowest security level provided by the application of each encryption schemes in C. A strategy to find the combination of encryption schemes that satisfy the chosen policy consists of finding the *best combination of encryption schemes*, that is, it provides the highest level of protection for sensitive data, while minimizing the number of involved encryption schemes. We formalize this problem as follows:

Problem 1. (best combination of encryption schemes) Let P be a policy, $C = \{C_1, ⋯ , C_n\}$ be a set of combinations of

encryption schemes that satisfy the policy P, and l_i be the security level provided by the application of the combination C_i, with $1 ≤ i ≤ n$. C_k is the best combination of encryption schemes in C that satisfy P *iff* the following conditions are satisfied:

- $∀C_j ∈ C$, l_k is at least as secure as l_j.

- $∀C_j ∈ C$, $|C_k| ≤ |C_j|$.

The problem of finding the best combination of encryption schemes is *NP-hard*. This is formally stated by the following theorem.

Theorem 1. The problem of finding the best combination of encryption schemes is *NP-hard*.

PROOF. We prove the previous theorem by a reduction from the NP-hard problem of minimum hypergraph coloring [13], which is formulated as follows: *given a hypergraph $G(V, E)$, determine a minimum coloring of G, that is, assign to each vertex in V a color such that adjacent vertices have different colors, and the number of colors is minimized.* We define the correspondence between finding the best combination of encryption schemes problem and the minimum hypergraph coloring problem as follows. Let a be a sensitive attribute, $TC_a = l$ be a security threshold constraint defined over a, $UC_a = \{f_{a_1}, ⋯ , f_{a_n}\}$ be a utility constraint defined over a, and $E_l = \{E_1, ⋯ , E_m\}$ the set of encryption schemes that provide a security level which is at least as secure as l. Any vertex $v_i ∈ V$ corresponds to a functionality $f_i ∈ F$. We denote e_a the edge in G which connects $v_{a_1}, ⋯ , v_{a_n}$, corresponds to the constraint UC_a. The combination of encryption schemes $C = \{E_{i_1}, ⋯ , E_{i_p}\}$, where $C ⊆ E$ and each $E_{i_j} ∈ C$ satisfies the set of functionalities $F_j = \{f_{j,1}, ⋯ , f_{j,k_j}\}$, satisfies the constraint UC_a correspond to a solution S for the corresponding hypergraph coloring problem. More precisely, S uses p colors. Vertices $\{v_{1,1}, ⋯ , v_{1,k_1}\}$ corresponding to the functionality satisfied by E_{i_1} are colored using the first color, vertices $\{v_{q,1}, ⋯ , v_{q,k_q}\}$ corresponding to the functionality satisfied by E_{i_q} are colored using the q-th color, and vertices $\{v_{p,1}, ⋯ , v_{p,k_p}\}$ corresponding to the functionality satisfied by E_{i_p} are colored using the p-th color. Therefore, any algorithm finding the combination of encryption schemes that involved the minimal number of encryption mechanism while satisfying the constraint UC_a can be used to solve the minimum hypergraph coloring problem.

Since the problem of finding the best combination of encryption schemes that satisfy a policy P is NP-hard, we cannot expect to be able to solve an instance of arbitrary size of this problem to optimality. Thus, heuristic resolution strategies are widely exploited to solve such a problem with a reasonable computational effort.

3.5 Heuristic search

We propose a near-optimal heuristic for finding a combination of encryption schemes that satisfy a policy P. Our heuristic is based on a constructive method consisting of building a solution to the problem step by step from scratch. The used constructive method is based on choosing for each iteration, the *best satisfier* of the chosen policy.

Definition 6. (best satisfier) Let P be a policy composed of two constraints: a security threshold constraint $TC_a = l$

and an utility constraint $UC_a = \{f_{a_1}, \cdots, f_{a_n}\}$. Both constraints are defined over the sensitive attribute a. Let $\mathcal{E} = \{E_1, \cdots, E_m\}$ be the set of available encryption schemes. $E_i \in \mathcal{E}$ is a best satisfier if the following conditions are satisfied:

- The security level l_{E_i} is at least as secure as l.

- $\forall E_j \in \mathcal{E}$, l_{E_j} is at least as secure as l and $|F_{E_i} \cap UC_a| \geq |F_{E_j} \cap UC_a|$, where F_E are the set of functionalities satisfied by E.

The second condition in the previous definition states that E_i is the *best satisfier* if it satisfies the highest number of functionalities in UC_a compared to other encryption schemes in $\mathcal{E}$ that satisfy TC_a.

Algorithm 2 shows our heuristic algorithm for computing for each sensitive attribute, a combination of encryption schemes that satisfy the constraints defined over it. The algorithm takes as input the set of attributes $\mathcal{A}$ in the database to be outsourced, the policy $\mathcal{P}$ to be enforced over the set of attributes $\mathcal{A}$, the set of available encryption schemes $\mathcal{E}$ that can be used to enforce the policy $\mathcal{P}$, the set of security levels $\mathcal{L}$, and returns as output the set of combinations of mechanisms $\mathcal{S}$ that efficiently enforce the policy $\mathcal{P}$. For conflicting constraints, the algorithm returns a set of propositions $\mathcal{CP}$ to aid in resolving the conflicts.

The algorithm first initializes $\mathcal{S}$, $\mathcal{CP}$, $\mathcal{A}_s$ to the empty set and execute the procedure *get_conflicting_constraints* which takes as parameters $\mathcal{P}$, $\mathcal{E}$, $\mathcal{L}$, and return the set of conflicts in the policy. The *get_conflicting_constraints* procedure is represented by the Algorithm 1. Based on the confidentiality constraints in $\mathcal{P}$, the algorithm performs the first **foreach** loop to get all sensitive attributes $\mathcal{A}_s$. Then, for each sensitive attribute a_i having an unconflicting constraint it tries to get the best combination of schemes in terms of the provided security level. In order to meet the previous goal, we use the **while** loop to run down the set of security levels in $\mathcal{L}$ which are at least as secure as ($\geq_s$) TC_i starting from the highest one. For each security level sec_lev, we get from $\mathcal{E}$ the set $\mathcal{E}_{sec\_lev}$ of encryption schemes that provide security levels which are at least as secure as sec_lev and which can satisfy functionalities in UC_i. Next, we copy the set of required functionalities UC_i to UC_{temp}, and at each iteration of the next **while** loop, we get the *best satisfier* E_{bs} from $\mathcal{E}_{sec\_lev}$ according to the Definition 6. E_{bs} will be next added to the combination Sol, removed from $\mathcal{E}_{sec\_lev}$, and the required functionalities satisfied by E_{bs} will be removed from UC_{temp}. This **while** loop is terminated if: (1) all required functionalities in UC_{temp} are satisfied, in this case the set Sol represents the combination allowing to satisfy the constraints defined over the attribute a_i; or (2) $\mathcal{E}_{sec\_lev}$ is empty, which means that there is no combination that satisfies UC_i in the security level sec_lev.

For each attribute a_i having a conflicting constraint, using the third outermost **foreach** loop, the algorithm gives additional proposition allowing to avoid the conflict. To meet this goal, we use the first **while** loop in the third outermost **foreach** loop to run down the set of security levels in $\mathcal{L}$ starting from TC_i. We perform the same operation as in the previous outermost **foreach** loop, except, for each sec_lev, we will add to the set of propositions $\mathcal{CP}$ the entry $(a_i, Prop, sat\_func, sec\_lev)$ stating that in the security level sec_lev, the combination of schemes $Prop$ is able to

---

```
input  : A = {a_1, ··· , a_n}    /*database attributes*/
         P = {CC_1, ··· , CC_l, TC_1, ··· , TC_l, UC_1, ··· , UC_l}
         E = {E_1, ··· , E_m} /*encryption schemes*/
         L = {l_1, ··· , l_p} /*security levels*/
output : S    /*Solution*/
         CP   /*Conflict resolution propositions*/
Main
S = ∅
CP = ∅
A_s = ∅
Conflicts = get_conflicting_constraints(P, E, L)
foreach CC in P do
 |  A_s = A_s ∪ CC
endfch
foreach a_i in A_s do
 |  if (not (a_i, TC_i, UC_i) in Conflicts) then
 |   |  sec_lev = get_the_highest_sec_lev(L)
 |   |  Sol = ∅
 |   |  while sec_lev ≥_s TC_i do
 |   |   |  Sol = ∅
 |   |   |  E_{sec_lev} = ∅
 |   |   |  foreach E in E do
 |   |   |   |  if (l_E ≥_s sec_lev and F_E ∩ UC_i ≠ ∅) then
 |   |   |   |   |  E_{sec_lev} = E_{sec_lev} ∪ E
 |   |   |   |  end
 |   |   |  endfch
 |   |   |  UC_{temp} = UC_i
 |   |   |  while (UC_{temp} ≠ ∅ and E_{sec_lev} ≠ ∅) do
 |   |   |   |  E_{bs} = get_first_elem(E_{sec_lev})
 |   |   |   |  foreach E in E_{sec_lev} do
 |   |   |   |   |  if (|F_E ∩ UC_i| ≥ |F_{E_{bs}} ∩ UC_i|) then
 |   |   |   |   |   |  E_{bs} = E
 |   |   |   |   |  end
 |   |   |   |  endfch
 |   |   |   |  Sol = Sol ∪ E_{bs}
 |   |   |   |  E_{sec_lev} = E_{sec_lev} \ {E_{bs}}
 |   |   |   |  UC_{temp} = UC_{temp} \ (F_{E_{bs}} ∩ UC_{temp})
 |   |   |  end
 |   |   |  if (UC_{temp} = ∅) then
 |   |   |   |  break
 |   |   |  end
 |   |   |  if (E_{sec_lev} = ∅) then
 |   |   |   |  sec_lev = get_next_best_level(sec_lev, L)
 |   |   |  end
 |   |  end
 |   |  S = S ∪ {(a_i, Sol, sec_lev)}
 |  end
endfch
foreach (a_i, TC_i, UC_i) in Conflicts do
 |  Prop = ∅
 |  sec_lev = TC_i
 |  while sec_lev ≠ NULL do
 |   |  Prop = ∅
 |   |  E_{sec_lev} = ∅
 |   |  foreach E in E do
 |   |   |  if (l_E ≥_s sec_lev and F_E ∩ UC_i ≠ ∅) then
 |   |   |   |  E_{sec_lev} = E_{sec_lev} ∪ E
 |   |   |  end
 |   |  endfch
 |   |  UC_{temp} = UC_i
 |   |  while (UC_{temp} ≠ ∅ and E_{sec_lev} ≠ ∅) do
 |   |   |  E_{bs} = get_first_elem(E_{sec_lev})
 |   |   |  foreach E in E_{sec_lev} do
 |   |   |   |  if (|F_E ∩ UC_i| ≥ |F_{E_{bs}} ∩ UC_i|) then
 |   |   |   |   |  E_{bs} = E
 |   |   |   |  end
 |   |   |  endfch
 |   |   |  Prop = Prop ∪ E_{bs}
 |   |   |  E_{sec_lev} = E_{sec_lev} \ {E_{bs}}
 |   |   |  UC_{temp} = UC_{temp} \ (F_{E_{bs}} ∩ UC_{temp})
 |   |  end
 |   |  sat_func = UC_i \ UC_{temp}
 |   |  CP = CP ∪ {(a_i, Prop, sat_func, sec_lev)}
 |   |  if (UC_{temp} = ∅) then
 |   |   |  break
 |   |  end
 |   |  if (E_{sec_lev} = ∅) then
 |   |   |  sec_lev = get_next_best_level(sec_lev, L)
 |   |  end
 |  end
endfch
```

Algorithm 2: Policy satisfaction

145

satisfy the set of functionalities sat_func required for the attribute a_i. These propositions may help the security administrator (data owner) to choose, from his point of view, the best trade off between security and utility.

Theorem 2. (Complexity) Given a set of p attributes $\mathcal{A}$, a policy $\mathcal{P}$ composed of n confidentiality constraints, n security threshold constraints, n utility constraints, a set of m encryption schemes $\mathcal{E}$, and a set of r security levels, the complexity of the policy satisfaction algorithm (Algorithm 2) is $O(m^2 \cdot n \cdot r + r \cdot m + 2n)$.

PROOF. (sketch) We suppose that we have p attributes having unconflicting constraints and q attributes having conflicting constraints, with $p + q = n$. According to Algorithm 1, the execution of the function $get\_conflicting\_constraints$ costs $O(r \cdot m + n)$. In Algorithm 2, the first *foreach* loop costs $O(n)$, the second *foreach* loop costs in the worst case $O(p \cdot r \cdot m^2)$, and the third *foreach* loop costs in the worst case $O(q \cdot r \cdot m^2)$. Finally, the overall time complexity of the Algorithm 2 is $O(m^2 \cdot n \cdot r + r \cdot m + 2n)$.

4. USE CASE

In this section, we present the use case. For our case study, we use a scenario based on the TPC-H [1] benchmark database. We first give an overview of the TPC-H benchmark database structure. Afterwards, we present the set of encryption schemes that can be used in our scenario, a set of functionalities required for processing the data, and policies to be applied over the TPC-H database. Finally, we illustrate the use of our previously presented policy satisfaction algorithm to enforce the chosen policy over the TPC-H database.

4.1 TPC-H database

The TPC-H database is composed of 8 tables. Each attribute in TPC-H tables represents data for industrial resource management. TPC-H provides 22 queries consisting of different kind of SQL operations such as select, join, order by, etc. Figure 1 represents the conceptual model of the TPC-H database which includes foreign key relationships.

4.2 System design

As described in 3.1, the used system is composed of a relational database $\mathcal{D}$, a set of security layers $\mathcal{L}$, a set of functional requirements $\mathcal{F}$, and a toolbox $\mathcal{E}$. In our case study, $\mathcal{D}$ represents the TPC-H benchmark database, $\mathcal{L}$ will be composed of three security layers as explained in 2.3: RND (random layer), DET (deterministic layer) and OPE (order preserving layer). As we work with relational databases, the set of utility requirements are composed of some SQL operators that can be used to query the database. In addition, we define the functionalities *computation* representing the numeric computation over the attributes (e.g., SET ATTR = ATTR + 30), and *order search* represeting the SQL operators ($>, \geq, <, \leq, between, min/max, order\ by$). Thus $\mathcal{F} = \{equality, join, group\ by, average, sum, computation, like, order\ search\}$. The toolbox $\mathcal{E}$ is composed of the following encryption schemes. For each encryption scheme, we extract and specify the provided security level and the set of satisfied functionalities as presented in 3.1.

AES-CBC. When used in CBC chaining mode, AES provides a probabilistic encryption which is semantically

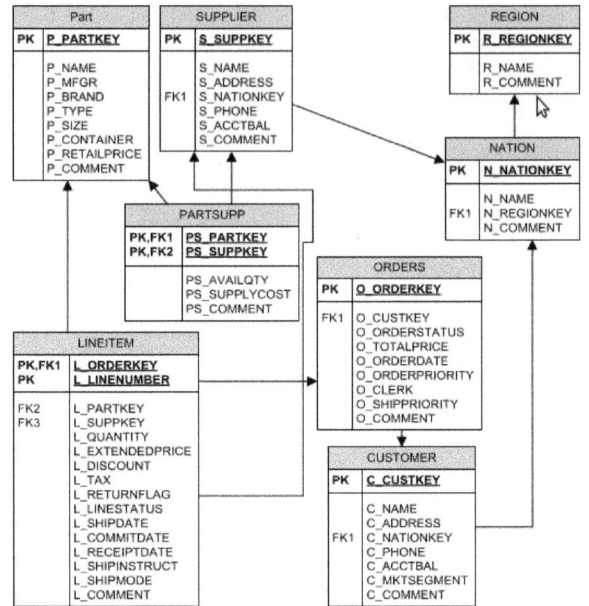

Figure 1: TPCH database

secure. Thus, it provides the security level RND. Despite that this encryption scheme does not leak any information about the plaintext values, it does not allow any efficient computation over encrypted data. Therefore, $l_{AES} = RND$ and $F_{AES} = \emptyset$.

Paillier [22]. It is based on secure probabilistic encryption which enables to perform computation aver encrypted data. A Paillier cryptosystem provides indistinguishability under an adaptive chosen-plaintext attack (IND-CPA). It provides the security level RND and allows to perform *sum*, *avg* operations over the encrypted data. Thus, $l_{Plr} = RND$ and $F_{plr} = \{sum, avg, computation\}$.

SSE [28]. SSE is a symmetric searchable encryption which is semantically secure (as long as there is no search token). It allows to perform search over encrypted data which gives the ability to perform MySQL's *like* operator. Based on these properties, the SSE can be specified by $l_{SSE} = RND$ and $F_{SSE} = \{like\}$.

Pohlig-Hellman. This is a deterministic encryption scheme allowing logarithmic time equality checks over ciphertexts. Pohlig-Hellman encryption cannot achieve the classical notions of security of probabilistic encryption because it leaks which encrypted values correspond to the same plaintext value. It provides the security level DET and allows to perform *equality*, *join*, and *group by* over the encrypted data. Thus, $l_{PH} = DET$ and $F_{PH} = \{equality, join, group\ by\}$.

Boldyreva [5, 6]. Boldyreva propose an order-preserving, deterministic encryption which allows performing order operations over encrypted data. As mentioned in 2.3, in addition to the information leaked by having the deterministic property, it reveals the order between encrypted values. The encryption scheme provides the security level OPE and allows to perform *equality*, *join*, *group by*, and *order search* operations. Thus, $l_{Bdv} = OPE$ and $F_{Bdv} = \{equality, join, group\,by, order\,search\}$.

4.3 The policy

In our scenario a security administrator (data owner) of the TPC-H benchmark database requires that the following security rules must be enforced:

1. The given discount for any Order should always remain *top secret*.

2. The account balance for a customer as well as our suppliers should always remain *top secret*.

3. The Name and Address of our suppliers should be *confidential*.

4. The supply cost of individual suppliers must be *confidential*.

5. Any pricing information must in general remain *secret*.

6. All other information in the database should be *unclassified*.

The security administrator used four levels to classify the data. The *top secret* classification levels means that any leaked information about the data will cause grave damage. The *secret* level means that some information about the data values can be leaked if they do not lead to reveal its values. The *confidential* level means that additional information about the data values can be leaked if they do not lead to reveal the values itselves. A *Unclassified* level implies that the data are not sensitive.

According to the properties of the security levels in $\mathcal{L}$ described in 2.3, we associate the *top secret* classification levels to the RND security level, the *secret* classification level to the DET security level, and the *confidential* classification level to the OPE security level. The previous rules are specified as follows:

Rule 1. It involves the attribute *L_DISCOUNT* of the table *LINEITEM*. This rule is specified using the folowing confidentiality and security threshold constraints:

- $CC_1 = \{L\_DISCOUNT\}, TC_1 = RND.$

Rule 2. This rule involves the attributes *C_ACCTBAL* and *S_ACCTBAL* from the tables *CUSTOMER* and *SUPPLIER*. It is specified using the following constraints:

- $CC_2 = \{C\_ACCTBAL\}, TC_2 = RND.$
- $CC_3 = \{S\_ACCTBAL\}, TC_3 = RND.$

Rule 3. It involves the attributes *S_NAME*, *S_ADDRESS*, and *S_NATIONKEY* from the table *SUPPLIER*. It is specified using the following constraints:

- $CC_4 = \{S\_NAME\}, TC_4 = OPE.$
- $CC_5 = \{S\_ADDRESS\}, TC_5 = OPE.$
- $CC_6 = \{S\_NATIONKEY\}, TC_6 = OPE.$

Rule 4. It involves the attribute *PS_SUPPLYCOST* from the table *SUPPLYCOST*. This rule is specified using the following constraints:

Sensitive attributes	Functionalities
L_DISCOUNT	*computation*(Q1,Q3,Q4) *sum*(Q1,Q3,Q4) *order search*(Q3)
C_ACCTBAL	*group by*(Q5) *sum*(Q8)
S_ACCTBAL	*order search*(Q2)
S_NAME	*order search*(Q2,Q7) *group by*(Q7)
S_ADDRESS	*like*(Q4)
S_NATIONKEY	*join*(Q2,Q4)
PS_SUPPLYCOST	*equality*(Q2)
P_RETAILPRICE	
L_EXTENDEDPRICE	*sum*(Q1,Q3) *computation*(Q3,Q4)
O_TOTALPRICE	*group by*(Q6) *order search*(Q6)

Table 1: **Required functionalities for sensitive attributes**

- $CC_7 = \{PS\_SUPPLYCOST\}, TC_7 = OPE.$

Rule 5. This rule involves the attributes *P_RETAILPRICE*, *L_EXTENDEDPRICE* and *O_TOTALPRICE* from tables *PART*, *LINEITEM* and *ORDERS*. It is specified using the following constraints:

- $CC_8 = \{P\_RETAILPRICE\}, TC_8 = DET$
- $CC_9 = \{L\_EXTENDEDPRICE\}, TC_9 = DET$
- $CC_{10} = \{O\_TOTALPRICE\}, TC_{10} = DET$

The security administrator gives examples of queries which should be executes efficiently over the TPC-H database. From these set of queries, we extract only the queries involving sensitive attributes described in the policy, which are illustrated in Figure 2. These queries enable us to extract the set of functionalities required for each sensitive attribute in the TPC-H database. Table 1 shows, for each sensitive attribute, the queries on which the attribute is involved and the set of required functionalities. These functional requirements are specified using the following utility constraints:

- $UC_1 = \{computation, sum, order\,search\}$
- $UC_2 = \{group\,by, sum\}$
- $UC_3 = \{order\,search\}$
- $UC_4 = \{order\,search, group\,by\}$
- $UC_5 = \{like\}$
- $UC_6 = \{join\}$
- $UC_7 = \{equality\}$
- $UC_8 = \emptyset$
- $UC_9 = \{sum, computation\}$
- $UC_{10} = \{group\,by, order\,search\}$

4.4 Policy enforcement results

Using the Algorithm 2, we get from the toolbox, for each sensitive attribute, the encryption scheme or the combination of encryption schemes that satisfies the policy. The results of the application of Algorithm 2 over our use case are the followings:

Q1:
SELECT L_RETURNFLAG, L_LINESTATUS,
  SUM(L_QUANTITY) AS SUM_QTY,
  SUM(L_EXTENDEDPRICE) AS SUM_BASE_PRICE,
  SUM(1-L_DISCOUNT) AS SUM_DISC_PRICE,
  AVG(L_QUANTITY) AS AVG_QTY,
FROM LINEITEM
WHERE
  L_SHIPDATE <= '2010-01-15'
GROUP BY L_RETURNFLAG, L_LINESTATUS
ORDER BY L_RETURNFLAG,L_LINESTATUS

Q2:
SELECT S_ACCTBAL, S_NAME, N_NAME, P_PARTKEY,
  P_MFGR, S_ADDRESS, S_PHONE, S_COMMENT
FROM PART, SUPPLIER, PARTSUPP, NATION, REGION
WHERE
  P_PARTKEY = PS_PARTKEY AND
  S_NATIONKEY = N_NATIONKEY
  PS_SUPPLYCOST = 1000
ORDER BY S_ACCTBAL DESC, N_NAME, S_NAME

Q3:
SELECT SUM(L_DISCOUNT) AS REVENUE
FROM LINEITEM
WHERE L_SHIPDATE >= '2010-01-01' AND
  L_SHIPDATE < '2010-01-01'
  AND L_DISCOUNT BETWEEN .06 - 0.01 AND .06 + 0.01
  AND L_QUANTITY < 24

Q4:
SELECT N_NAME AS NATION,
  L_EXTENDEDPRICE*(1-L_DISCOUNT) AS AMOUNT
FROM PART, SUPPLIER, LINEITEM, NATION
WHERE S_SUPPKEY = L_SUPPKEY
  AND S_NATIONKEY = N_NATIONKEY
  AND S_ADDRESS LIKE '%%RENNES%%'
Group By N_NAME.

Q5:
SELECT TOP 20 C_NAME, C_ACCTBAL,
  N_NAME, C_ADDRESS, C_PHONE, C_COMMENT
FROM CUSTOMER, ORDERS, LINEITEM, NATION
WHERE C_CUSTKEY = O_CUSTKEY AND
  L_ORDERKEY = O_ORDERKEY AND
  L_RETURNFLAG = 'R'
GROUP BY C_CUSTKEY, C_NAME, C_ACCTBAL, C_PHONE
ORDER BY C_NAME.

Q6:
SELECT C_NAME, O_ORDERDATE,
  O_TOTALPRICE, SUM(L_QUANTITY)
FROM CUSTOMER, ORDERS, LINEITEM
WHERE C_CUSTKEY = O_CUSTKEY AND
  O_ORDERKEY = L_ORDERKEY
GROUP BY C_NAME, C_CUSTKEY, O_TOTALPRICE
ORDER BY O_TOTALPRICE DESC.

Q7:
SELECT TOP 100 S_NAME, COUNT(*) AS NUMWAIT
FROM SUPPLIER, LINEITEM L1, ORDERS, NATION
WHERE S_SUPPKEY = L1.L_SUPPKEY AND
  O_ORDERKEY = L1.L_ORDERKEY AND
  L1.L_RECEIPTDATE> L1.L_COMMITDATE
GROUP BY S_NAME
ORDER BY NUMWAIT DESC, S_NAME.

Q8:
SELECT CNTRYCODE, COUNT(*) AS NUMCUST,
  SUM(C_ACCTBAL) AS TOTACCTBAL
FROM
  (SELECT SUBSTRING(C_PHONE,1,2) AS
  CNTRYCODE, C_ACCTBAL
  FROM CUSTOMER
  WHERE
  SUBSTRING(C_PHONE,1,2) IN ('13', '31', '23', '29'))
GROUP BY CNTRYCODE

Figure 2: Queries involving sensitive attributes

1. C_ACCTBAL: conflict detected (TC_2 and UC_2)
   Conflicts resolution propositions:
   - [*Paillier*] (RND), satisfied utility requirements: {*sum*} (Q8)
   - [*Paillier, Pohlig−Hellman*] (DET), satisfied utility requirements: {*group by, sum*} (Q8, Q5)

2. L_EXTENDEDPRICE: [*Paillier*] (RND), satisfied utility requirements: {*sum, computation*} (Q1,Q3,Q4).

3. PS_SUPPLYCOST: [*Pohlig − Hellman*] (DET), satisfied utility requirements: {*equality*} (Q2).

4. L_DISCOUNT: conflict detected (TC_1 and UC_1)
   Conflicts resolution propositions:
   - [*Paillier*] (RND), satisfied utility requirements: {*sum, computation*} (Q1,Q4).
   - [*Paillier, Boldyreva*] (OPE), satisfied utility requirements: {*sum, order search, computation*} (Q1,Q3,Q4).

5. S_ADDRESS: [*SSE*] (RND), satisfied utility requirements: {*like*} (Q4).

6. S_NAME: [*Boldyreva*] (OPE), satisfied utility requirements: {*order search, group by*} (Q2,Q7).

7. S_NATIONKEY: [*Pohlig−Hellman*] (DET), satisfied utility requirements: {*join*} (Q2,Q4).

8. S_ACCTBAL: conflict detected (TC_3 and UC_3)
   Conflicts resolution propositions:
   - [*AES − CBC*] (RND), satisfied utility requirements: ∅.
   - [*Boldyreva*] (OPE), satisfied utility requirements: {*order search*} (Q2).

9. P_RETAILPRICE: [*AES − CBC*] (RND).

10. O_TOTALPRICE: conflict detected (TC_{10} and UC_{10})
    Conflicts resolution propositions:
    - [*Pohlig − Hellman*] (DET), satisfied utility requirements: {*group by*}.
    - [*Boldyreva*] (OPE), satisfied utility requirements: {*group by, order search*} (Q6).

Result 1 shows the satisfaction of the constraints defined over the attribute C_ACCTBAL. A conflict between the constraints TC_2 and UC_2 has been detected. Thus, our algorithm gives the data owner two propositions in order to resolve the conflict. The first proposition states that the data owner can preserve the *RND* security level through the application of the *Paillier* encryption scheme, however only the *sum* functionality will be provided and therefore the query Q5 cannot be executed efficiently over the encrypted data. The second proposition gives the data owner the ability to decrease the required threshold security level to *DET* in order to allows the application of the combination [*Paillier, Pohlig − Hellman*] which satisfies the required utility constraints. Result 2 states that the encryption scheme *Paillier* can be applied to enforce the set of security and utility requirements defined over the attribute L_EXTENDEDPRICE. Result 3, shows that security and

148

utility constraints defined over the attribute PS_SUPPLYCOST can be enforced through the application of *Pohlig−Hellman* encryption scheme. Result 4 shows that there is a conflict between the constraints TC_1 and UC_1 and proposes two solution to reconcile the conflict. Result 5 states that the encryption scheme SSE can be applied to enforce the set of security and utility requirements defined over the attribute S_ADDRESS. Result 6 shows that the set of security and utility constraints defined over the attribute S_NAME can be enforced via the application of *Boldyreva* encryption scheme. Result 7 states that the encryption scheme *Pohlig − Hellman*, when applied, can enforce the of security and utility requirements defined over the attribute S_NATIONKEY. For this result, we remark that our algorithm has chosen the best encryption scheme in terms of provided security level, as the *Boldyreva* encryption scheme can also be used to enforce security and utility requirements defined over the attribute S_NATIONKEY. Result 8 shows the conflict detected between TC_3 and $UC3$ and proposes two solutions two overcome the conflict. Result 9 confirms that the application of $AES − CBC$ can enforce the constraints defined over the attribute P_RETAILPRICE. Finally, result 10 shows that there is a conflict between TC_10 and UC_10 and proposes two solution allowing to reconcile the conflict.

It is important to note that sequentially applying a combination of encryption schemes (e.g. [Paillier and Pohlig-Hellman] in one "onion") over an attribute may not provide the functionalities provided by each encryption scheme. This problem can be resolved by duplicating the values of the attribute over which the two mechanisms are to be applied and apply each mechanism separately.

5. RELATED WORK

5.1 Encrypted Databases

Hacigümüs et al. first introduced the concept of executing queries over encrypted data [16]. They used deterministic encryption for equality queries and binning for range queries. The binning concept was superseded by order-preserving encryption by Agrawal et al. [2]. Order-preserving encryption allows the processing of range queries also on encrypted data. Damiani et al. have presented an algorithm for optimizing the trade-off between security and performance of post-processing in encrypted databases [10]. Their algorithm combines deterministic ciphertexts if the security benefit outweighs the performance penalty. Popa et al. have recently presented CryptDB which introduces adjustable encryption as we use it [24]. This removes the need for analyzing all queries in advance, but also poses the policy configuration we solve in this paper.

The cryptographic community has further developed the encryption schemes used for processing queries. Bellare et al. introduce a concept for deterministic, public-key encryption [4]. They also note that only deterministic encryption can achieve sub-linear search. Boldyreva et al. propose a new order-preserving encryption scheme [5, 6]. Their scheme is as secure as any immutable, order-preserving encryption scheme can be. Popa et al. introduced an ideal-secure order-preserving encryption scheme [23]. Nevertheless, this scheme and adjustable "onion" encryption are not efficiently combinable. Recently, Gentry [14] presented fully homomorphic encryption. Implementing search in fully homomorphic encryption is difficult, since the result of the match is still encrypted. Therefore in a perfectly semantically secure search the database has to return all records completely annihilating the advantage of searching on the database. Instead, searchable encryption offers an almost as secure alternative. Song et al. introduced searchable encryption [28]. For equality searches indices achieve sub-linear time in the average case [7]. Still, they require an index for each searchable attribute which is currently still too inefficient in practice. The scheme of Shi et al. [27] performs range searches using logarithmically sized ciphertexts. Semantically secure range searches still always require a linear scan, i.e. linear time.

5.2 Policy Configuration

There are a couple of approaches to enforce and manage access control policies in encrypted databases. De Capitani di Vimercati et al. proposed over-encryption [12]: the layering of encryption to enforce policies by the user and the database. Again, De Capitani et al. presented an approach to selectively update the access control policies with minimal effort [11]. Damiani et al. have proposed selective encryption in order to also outsource the access control [9]. They presented the key management for this approach in [8]. Atallah et al. presented an efficient key management scheme for hierarchies [3]. Ion et al. use proxy re-encryptable, searchable encryption in order to enforce multi-user access policies [17]. An approach recently implemented for web applications is using a different scheme by Popa et al. [25].

All of these approaches implement access control for different users via encryption. Our approach and use of policies is different, albeit we also enforce confidentiality constraints. We configure the use of encryption in order to prevent unintended disclosure against the database provider (not other users of the database).

6. CONCLUSIONS AND FUTURE WORK

Searchable, yet encrypted databases appear to be one promising building block of a secure cloud offering. In order to help companies migrate data from on-premise to the cloud, tools are needed to help decide about the best acceptable trade-off between functionality and security requirements. In this paper we presented a set of algorithms which help to analyze functionality and security requirements when configuring an encrypted database following an onion-based approach. We reasoned about their formal characteristics as well as discussed their application in an enterprise use case on basis of the TPC-H benchmark. The assumption that data may be labelled as we proposed may appear oversimplified, but industrial experience shows that even in complex applications this is sufficient to cover the evaluation results of a typical 3x3 risk matrix. This work complements some earlier work of ours where we could show that in the context of some representative industrial customer datasets in the best case only 8 percent of all data ever had to be encrypted using an order-preserving scheme while still supporting all the required queries [15]. Future work will now concentrate on further tool support for building the optimal encrypted structures when outsourcing encrypeted searchable data. Even with our proposed optimizations, the initial, onion-based encryption of the plaintext data is computationally expensive and we are thus investigating on how to parallelize this. Thirdly, we are implementing support for splitting queries in local and remote parts [21].

7. ACKNOWLEDGMENTS

- This work has received a French government support granted to the CominLabs excellence laboratory and managed by the National Research Agency in the "Investing for the Future" program under reference ANR-10-LABX-07-01.

- This work has received a French government support granted to the Frag&Tag project and managed by the Dual Innovation Support Scheme (RAPID) under convention No 132906023.

- This work has received a support from EIT ICT Labs Doctoral School and the EIT ICT Labs Doctoral Training Center in Rennes.

8. REFERENCES

[1] Transaction processing performance council. benchmark h. http://www.tpc.org/.

[2] R. Agrawal, J. Kiernan, R. Srikant, and Y. Xu. Order preserving encryption for numeric data. In *Proceedings of the ACM International Conference on Management of Data*, SIGMOD, 2004.

[3] M. J. Atallah, M. Blanton, N. Fazio, and K. B. Frikken. Dynamic and efficient key management for access hierarchies. *ACM Trans. Inf. Syst. Secur.*, 12(3), 2009.

[4] M. Bellare, A. Boldyreva, and A. O'Neill. Deterministic and efficiently searchable encryption. In *Advances in Cryptology*, CRYPTO, 2007.

[5] A. Boldyreva, N. Chenette, Y. Lee, and A. O'Neill. Order-preserving symmetric encryption. In *Proceedings of the 28th International Conference on Advances in Cryptology*, EUROCRYPT, 2009.

[6] A. Boldyreva, N. Chenette, and A. O'Neill. Order-preserving encryption revisited: improved security analysis and alternative solutions. In *Proceedings of the 31st International Conference on Advances in Cryptology*, CRYPTO, 2011.

[7] R. Curtmola, J. Garay, S. Kamara, and R. Ostrovsky. Searchable symmetric encryption: improved definitions and efficient constructions. *Journal of Computer Security*, 19(5), 2011.

[8] E. Damiani, S. De Capitani di Vimercati, S. Foresti, S. Jajodia, S. Paraboschi, and P. Samarati. Key management for multi-user encrypted databases. In *Proceedings of the ACM Workshop on Storage Security and Survivability*, StorageSS, 2005.

[9] E. Damiani, S. De Capitani di Vimercati, S. Foresti, S. Jajodia, S. Paraboschi, and P. Samarati. Selective data encryption in outsourced dynamic environments. In *Proceedings of the Second International Workshop on Views on Designing Complex Architectures*, VODCA, 2007.

[10] E. Damiani, S. De Capitani di Vimercati, S. Jajodia, S. Paraboschi, and P. Samarati. Balancing confidentiality and efficiency in untrusted relational dbmss. In *Proceedings of the 10th ACM Conference on Computer and Communications Security*, CCS, 2003.

[11] S. De Capitani di Vimercati, S. Foresti, S. Jajodia, S. Paraboschi, and P. Samarati. A data outsourcing architecture combining cryptography and access control. In *Proceedings of the ACM Workshop on Computer Security Architecture*, CSAW, 2007.

[12] S. De Capitani di Vimercati, S. Foresti, S. Jajodia, S. Paraboschi, and P. Samarati. Over-encryption: Management of access control evolution on outsourced data. In *Proceedings of the 33rd International Conference on Very Large Data Bases*, VLDB, 2007.

[13] M. R. Garey and D. S. Johnson. *Computers and Intractability; A Guide to the Theory of NP-Completeness*. W. H. Freeman & Co., New York, NY, USA, 1990.

[14] C. Gentry. Fully homomorphic encryption using ideal lattices. In *Proceedings of the Symposium on Theory of Computing*, STOC, 2009.

[15] P. Grofig, M. Härterich, I. Hang, F. Kerschbaum, M. Kohler, A. Schaad, A. Schröpfer, and W. Tighzert. Experiences and observations on the industrial implementation of a system to search over outsourced encrypted data. In *Proceedings of the Conference of the GI Security Group*, SICHERHEIT, 2014.

[16] H. Hacigümüş, B. Iyer, C. Li, and S. Mehrotra. Executing sql over encrypted data in the database-service-provider model. In *Proceedings of the 2002 ACM International Conference on Management of Data*, SIGMOD, 2002.

[17] M. Ion, G. Russello, and B. Crispo. Enforcing multi-user access policies to encrypted cloud databases. In *Proceedings of the IEEE International Symposium on Policies for Distributed Systems and Networks*, POLICY, 2011.

[18] M. Islam, M. Kuzu, and M. Kantarcioglu. Access pattern disclosure on searchable encryption: ramification, attack and mitigation. In *Proceedings of the 19th Network and Distributed System Security Symposium*, NDSS, 2012.

[19] F. Kerschbaum, P. Grofig, I. Hang, M. Härterich, M. Kohler, A. Schaad, A. Schröpfer, and W. Tighzert. Adjustably encrypted in-memory column-store. In *Proceedings of the 20th ACM Conference on Computer and Communications Security*, CCS, 2013.

[20] F. Kerschbaum, M. Härterich, P. Grofig, M. Kohler, A. Schaad, A. Schröpfer, and W. Tighzert. Optimal re-encryption strategy for joins in encrypted databases. In *Proceedings of the IFIP Conference on Data and Applications Security and Privacy*, DBSec, 2013.

[21] F. Kerschbaum, M. Härterich, M. Kohler, I. Hang, A. Schaad, A. Schröpfer, and W. Tighzert. An encrypted in-memory column-store: The onion selection problem. In *Proceedings of the 9th International Conference on Information Systems Security*, ICISS, 2013.

[22] P. Paillier. Public-key cryptosystems based on composite degree residuosity classes. In *Proceedings of the 18th International Conference on Advances in Cryptology*, EUROCRYPT, 1999.

[23] R. A. Popa, F. H. Li, and N. Zeldovich. An ideal-security protocol for order-preserving encoding. In *34th IEEE Symposium on Security and Privacy*, S&P, 2013.

[24] R. A. Popa, C. M. S. Redfield, N. Zeldovich, and H. Balakrishnan. Cryptdb: protecting confidentiality with encrypted query processing. In *Proceedings of the 23rd ACM Symposium on Operating Systems Principles*, SOSP, 2011.

[25] R. A. Popa, E. Stark, S. Valdez, J. Helfer, N. Zeldovich, M. F. Kaashoek, and H. Balakrishnan. Securing web applications by blindfolding the server. In *Proceedings of the USENIX Symposium of Networked Systems Design and Implementation*, NSDI, 2014.

[26] P. Samarati and S. De Capitani di Vimercati. Data protection in outsourcing scenarios: issues and directions. In *ASIACCS*, pages 1–14, 2010.

[27] E. Shi, J. Bethencourt, H. T.-H. Chan, D. X. Song, and A. Perrig. Multi-dimensional range query over encrypted data. In *Proceedings of the 2007 Symposium on Security and Privacy*, S&P, 2007.

[28] D. X. Song, D. Wagner, and A. Perrig. Practical techniques for searches on encrypted data. In *Proceedings of the 21st IEEE Symposium on Security and Privacy*, S&P, 2000.

[29] L. Xiao, O. Bastani, and I.-L. Yen. Security analysis for order preserving encryption schemes. Technical Report UTDCS-01-12, Department of Computer Science, University of Texas Dallas, 2012.

User-Centric Identity as a Service-Architecture for eIDs with Selective Attribute Disclosure

Daniel Slamanig
Graz University of Technology
(IAIK)
daniel.slamanig@tugraz.at

Klaus Stranacher
E-Government Innovation
Center (EGIZ)
klaus.stranacher@egiz.gv.at

Bernd Zwattendorfer
E-Government Innovation
Center (EGIZ)
bernd.zwattendorfer@egiz.gv.at

ABSTRACT

Unique identification and secure authentication of users are essential processes in numerous security-critical areas such as e-Government, e-Banking, or e-Business. Therefore, many countries (particularly in Europe) have implemented national eID solutions within the past years. Such implementations are typically based on smart cards holding some certified collection of citizen attributes and hence follow a client-side and user-centric approach. However, most of the implementations only support all-or-nothing disclosure of citizen attributes and thus do not allow privacy-friendly selective disclosure of attributes. Consequently, the complete identity of the citizen (all attributes) are always revealed to identity providers and/or service providers, respectively. In this paper, we propose a novel user-centric identification and authentication model for eIDs, which supports selective attribute disclosure but only requires minimal changes in the existing eID architecture. In addition, our approach allows service providers to keep their infrastructure nearly untouched. Latter is often an inhibitor for the use of privacy-preserving cryptography like anonymous credentials in such architectures. Furthermore, our model can easily be deployed in the public cloud as we do not require full trust in identity providers. This fully features the Identity as a Service-paradigm while at the same time preserves citizens' privacy. We demonstrate the applicability of our model by adopting to the Austrian eID system to our approach.

Categories and Subject Descriptors

K.6.5 [**Management of Computing and Information Systems**]: Security and Protection—*Authentication*; K.4.1 [**Computers and Society**]: Public Policy Issues—*Privacy*

Keywords

Identity management; authentication; privacy; selective attribute disclosure; cloud computing; public cloud; Austrian eID; citizen card

1. INTRODUCTION

Identification and authentication play a vital role in numerous fields of application. Particularly, in areas such as e-Government, e-Banking, or e-Business these processes are highly security critical and complex. In order to cope with this complexity, various identity management systems such as SAML[1] or OpenID[2] have already evolved [2]. The main functions of identity management systems, besides secure and easy management of identities and corresponding attributes, are the handling of identification and authentication of users. Identity management systems usually target different horizons, e.g., the management of employees of a company or organization, or the management of the population of a whole country. For supporting the latter, many countries have already rolled-out national eID solutions. The aim of such solutions is to use authentic and qualified citizen attributes in sensitive electronic processes, where a high level of security is required.

1.1 Identity Management Models

An identity management system involves different stakeholders. Typically, *users* first need to identify themselves and authenticate at an *identity provider* before being able to access protected services and resources of a *service provider*. Thereby, the identity provider transfers authentic identity data of the user to the service provider in a structured form (either directly or via the user). Over time, different identity models have emerged, having differences in terms of user control or identity data storage location [20, 12, 13].

In the *central identity model*, user and identity data are stored centrally at the identity provider. Identity data provisioning is usually carried out by user registration at the identity provider prior first authentication. During an authentication process, identity data are transferred from the identity provider to the service provider. However, in this model the user usually is not aware which kind of data are actually stored in the identity provider's repositories and to whom it is released.

In the *federated identity model*, user and identity data are stored distributed across different identity providers. These data can be linked and exchanged if appropriate trust relationships exist amongst the identity providers. Trust relationships are usually established on organizational level whereas they are enforced on technical level. As above, in this model the user is usually not aware of the data stored

---
[1]Security Assertion Markup Language, http://saml.xml.org
[2]http://openid.net

at the identity provider and to whom the identity provider releases the data.

Finally, in the *user-centric identity model* identity data are directly stored in the user's domain, usually on a secure token such as a smart card. Identity data are only transferred to an identity provider or a service provider if the user explicitly gives her consent to do so. Hence, the user always remains in the sole control of her data. Many countries rely on this model for their national eID solutions. For instance, Austria stores citizens' identification data (e.g., unique identifier, name, data of birth) within a special data structure on the Austrian citizen card, the official eID in Austria [14]. This special data structure is signed by a trusted public authority to ensure integrity and authenticity of the data. Other countries such as Belgium, Estonia, Italy, or Spain include identity data (e.g., unique identifier and name) for their eID directly in an X.509 certificate, which is used for identification and authentication. Many other European countries follow the same or similar approaches for modeling electronic identities of their citizens. Details on the individual approaches can be found in [17, 7, 23].

1.2 Contribution

While all these national eID solutions are able to provide authentic and qualified identity attributes to service providers in a user-centric manner, they nearly all lack in selective disclosure possibilities as only the full eID can be revealed during an authentication process [18]. To close this gap and to better protect citizens' privacy as demanded by the EU data protection directive [8], a couple of approaches exist. However, in all these existing approaches several disadvantages can be identified limiting their practicality.

In this paper we propose a novel and practical identification and authentication model to be applied for eIDs, which keeps the advantages of user-centricity but allows for selective disclosure possibilities to better protect citizens' privacy compared to existing national eID solutions. In particular, it supports selective disclosure such that any service provider can still verify that the subset of revealed data has been certified by a trusted authority. Furthermore, our model can be easily deployed in semi-trusted environments such as the public cloud to fully benefit from their scalability and elasticity advantages. Semi-trusted thereby means *honest but curious*, i.e., such a party performs all tasks correctly, but processed or stored data may be leaked either due to adversarial insiders or security breaches. This is a reasonable adversarial model for public cloud providers. Finally, to demonstrate the applicability of our model, we apply it to the Austrian eID system.

1.3 Paper Outline

The paper is structured as follows. In Section 2 we overview approaches and existing systems enabling selective disclosure capabilities for electronic identities. In Section 3 we describe our abstract model, which enables user-centricity and selective disclosure for eIDs in a practical manner at the same time. After that, we apply our model to the current Austrian eID system in Section 4. Finally, we discuss our model – compared to existing approaches – based on selected criteria in Section 5.

2. SELECTIVE DISCLOSURE

To better protect citizens' privacy and to enable selective disclosure of authentic and qualified attributes of eIDs, different approaches have been proposed. In this section, we briefly review them. We distinguish between approaches based on the trust assumptions for the identity provider (identity provider is trusted or semi-trusted).

2.1 Trusted Identity Provider

A typical example for such an approach is the new German eID card [16]. The German eID card follows a user-centric approach enabling minimum data disclosure to the service provider. Each service provider gets issued a so-called access certificate which enables controlled access to a subset of identity data stored on the eID card. To facilitate the integration of eID functionality for service providers, an eID service acts as intermediary between the service provider and the eID card. The eID service manages the communication with the eID card and provides identity data from the eID to the service provider. While the citizen is able to select the data to be disclosed to the service provider on client-side through a client middleware, data are still available in plain form at the eID service and identity data not relevant for the eID service may be revealed to it. Hence, the eID service must be fully trusted in terms of privacy and data protection.

Another example for this approach is STORK[3] [15], which deals with eID federation and eID interoperability across EU countries. One interoperability model of STORK foresees a central gateway per country, which on the one side connects to the national eID infrastructure and, on the other side, transfers authentic identity data to national gateways of other countries in cross-border authentication scenarios. This national gateway only transfers the amount of data which has been requested by a foreign service provider and the citizen has given consent to. Thereby, the citizen gives her consent on the national gateway, hence on server-side. This implies that – depending on the national eID infrastructure – the national gateway may still get the full identity of the citizen before it releases only a subset of the identity data to a foreign country gateway. As above, the user can also not be sure that the correct subset of identity data is revealed. Therefore, the central gateway again needs to be fully trusted in terms of data protection and privacy.

2.2 Semi-Trusted Identity Provider

Privacy and data protection are particular issues in the (public) cloud, where cloud providers are able to inspect stored data if it is not encrypted. Thus, cloud providers can be seen as semi-trusted. This issue also holds for Identity as a Service (IDaaS) solutions, where the identity provider typically is operated in a public cloud.

To bypass this issue in IDaaS scenarios, Nuñez et al. [19] propose an approach to extend the OpenID protocol by using proxy re-encryption (cf. Section 3.3). Thereby, identity data are stored encrypted by the user at an OpenID provider, which is operated in a public cloud. If a service provider requires identity data for authentication, the identity data are re-encrypted for the service provider by the OpendID provider using a re-encryption key provided by

---

[3]Secure Identities Across Borders Linked, `http://www.eid-stork.eu`

the user. Consequently, the OpenID provider does not learn any of the user's identity data (attributes) in plaintext.

Anonymous credential systems are a typical example for a setting where the identity provider is not fully trusted. Thereby, the credential is issued in a way that issuing and showing of a credential cannot be related. Only claims of user attributes are transmitted to the service provider without revealing the full user identity. The generation of claims is usually carried out on client-side. Well known anonymous credential systems are for instance the multi-show (unlinkable showings) Idemix [6] and one-show (linkable showings) U-Prove [4] systems. While anonymous credential systems are valuable means to support selective disclosure of attributes in authentication scenarios, they still lack in practicability as the underlying cryptographic technologies are computationally expensive and put a lot of load onto the client-side software and smart card [3]. Furthermore, easy integration of anonymous credentials into existing identity protocols such as SAML or OpenID is still lacking. However, projects such as PRIME[4], PrimeLife[5], or ABC4Trust [22] put lots of efforts in cryptographic abstraction and standardization in order to make future integration easier. Nevertheless, if adopting such systems at the moment, service providers may have to significantly change their existing identification and authentication infrastructure.

Another approach for semi-trusted identity providers has been proposed by Zwattendorfer and Slamanig [25]. In fact, they actually propose three different approaches, all relying on different cryptographic technologies. The first approach uses fully homomorphic encryption, which can be considered impractical at the present time. The second approach bases on anonymous credentials, which still lack in deployment. The third approach uses a combination of proxy re-encryption and redactable signatures, which they concluded to be the most practical one. The third approach has also been applied in [26].

3. THE PROPOSED MODEL

In this section, we propose a new user-centric identification and authentication model, which is particularly applicable for semi-trusted environments (in terms of data protection and privacy) such as the public cloud. Our model allows the usage of both server-side and client-side approaches for user data storage, while still putting users under full control of their data, i.e., providing selective disclosure in both approaches.

3.1 Motivation

Many qualified eIDs issued and rolled-out by various countries miss the feature of selective disclosure in current implementations. This means that users usually have to reveal their full identity during an identification and authentication process even if a service provider only needs a subset of the identity for providing a service. To bypass this issue, several approaches support selective disclosure via non-cryptographic means. An obvious solution, e.g., implemented by the German eID card or by STORK, is to simply trust the identity provider (cf. Section 2.1). As mentioned, the drawback of this solution is that the identity provider needs to

---

[4]Privacy and Identity Management for Europe, `https://www.prime-project.eu`
[5]`http://primelife.ercim.eu`

be fully trusted, which makes a deployment in semi-trusted environments such as the public cloud impossible due to national data protection regulations.

In contrast to that, selective disclosure approaches such as anonymous credential systems allow the usage of semi-trusted environments. However, although a lot of research and work is going in that direction, they still lack in wide deployment and general acceptance. Other approaches supporting semi-trusted cloud environments, basically relying on proxy re-encryption, were proposed by Nuñez et al. [19] and Zwattendorfer and Slamanig [25]. While these approaches seem currently to be more practical compared to anonymous credential systems, they still have some drawbacks. The approach by Nuñez et al., for instance, is not applicable for qualified eIDs. In addition, a main drawback of the approach of Zwattendorfer and Slamanig is that their approach is strongly tailored to the Austrian eID system, which does not allow for general applicability. Furthermore, it requires quite cumbersome registration processes of identity providers and service providers. In addition, their approach is not fully user-centric as the user data are encrypted for a trusted third party and not the user herself.

The drawbacks of these existing solutions motivated us to design and develop an improved and more generic identification and authentication model for semi-trusted environments such as the public cloud.

3.2 Requirements

To be applicable for qualified eIDs, as currently in place in various countries, and to further extend their privacy capabilities, the model has to fulfill the following requirements. We distinguish between general requirements and requirements related to privacy.

General Requirements.

The following general requirements need to be fulfilled by our model:

Qualified and authentic identity data: The identity and the corresponding attribute data of a user has been verified and certified by a trusted authority and thus are of high quality. Every party that obtains (a subset of the) attribute data can verify that is has been certified by the trusted authority.

Semi-trusted identity providers: The model must be applicable to the semi-trusted identity providers approach, i.e., identity providers must not be considered as fully trustworthy.

Integration effort and complexity: The new model can be integrated into existing infrastructures without significant changes.

Privacy Requirements.

In addition, our model has to fulfill the following privacy requirements:

Privacy: The privacy of users' identity data must be preserved in the presence of an honest but curious (semi-trusted) identity provider, i.e., the identity provider must not learn anything about the identity attributes of a user.

User-centricity: The user always remains in full control over her identity data and solely the user can control which identity data will be revealed to other parties.

Selective Disclosure: The user can disclose only parts of her identity data to a service provider and the service provider does not learn anything about undisclosed attribute data.

3.3 Cryptographic Preliminaries

In this section we introduce the cryptographic building blocks that are required by our presented model. We provide an informal description here and refer the reader to Appendix A for a more formal description.

Proxy Re-Encryption.

A proxy re-encryption (PRE) scheme is a public key encryption scheme that allows a semi-trusted proxy to transform a ciphertext produced with a public key pk_A^{PRE} of party A into another ciphertext of another party B, which can be decrypted by the private key sk_B^{PRE}, using a re-encryption key $rk_{A\to B}^{PRE}$. Thereby, the proxy neither gets access to the plaintext nor to the decryption keys. We rely on 1) non-interactive, 2) unidirectional, and 3) single-use schemes [1]. Basically, this means that 1) a re-encryption key $rk_{A\to B}^{PRE}$ can be computed by A using the private key sk_A^{PRE} and the public key pk_B^{PRE}, 2) based on $rk_{A\to B}^{PRE}$ re-encryption from B to A is not possible, and 3) re-encryption can only be performed once to a given ciphertext (no transitivity).

Digital Signatures.

A digital signature scheme allows to produce a digital signature σ for a message M (using a private signing key sk^{DSS}) and given the signature σ, a message M and a public verification key pk^{DSS} anyone can check whether the signature has been issued for M (integrity) by the holder of the corresponding signing key (authenticity).

Redactable Signatures.

A redactable signature (RS) scheme [11, 24] is a malleable digital signature scheme that supports the *removal* of parts of a signed message by *any* party, without requiring access to the signer's secret key and without invalidating the original signature. Consequently, parts of a signed message can be blacked out without invalidating the signature.

Blank Digital Signatures.

Blank digital signatures (BDS) [10] allow an *originator* to delegate the signing rights for a certain *template* T to a *proxy*, where T is a sequence of non-empty sets of bitstrings T_i. Such sets T_i are either called *fixed* or *exchangeable*, depending on the cardinality of the respective set, i.e., exchangeable elements contain more than one bitstring, whereas fixed elements contain exactly one bitstring. Based on such a delegation, the *proxy* is able to issue a signature on an instance of the template on behalf of the *originator*. Such a valid instance needs to include all fixed elements and one choice for each exchangeable element. With the instance signature at hand, anyone is able to verify the validity of the instance signature, i.e., if it is a valid instantiation of the template and the delegation, whilst the original template, i.e., the unused values of the exchangeable elements of the template, cannot be determined by a verifier. Blank digital signatures can also be used as redactable signature scheme. That means the originator issues a signature for a template, whereas the exchangeable parts consist of a certain value and a symbol representing the redacted (empty) string. Thus, the proxy is able to choose the redacted string to perform the redaction. Compared to core redactable signature schemes, blank digital signatures do not require an additional signing of the instance M (representing the redacted message) as the proxy signs it in course of producing the instance signature.

3.4 The Model

Figure 1 illustrates the new identification and authentication model for eIDs, which is applicable as an Identity as a Service model in semi-trusted environments. The following entities are involved in this model:

Registration authority: The registration authority (RA) is a trusted entity which issues qualified and authentic identity data to the user. The identity data can be either stored on client-side, e.g., a secure token, or on server-side at a trusted identity and/or attribute provider.

User: The user wants to access protected resources of a service provider. For gaining access, the user can reveal selected identity data issued from the registration authority.

Service provider: The service provider (SP) offers different resources or services which require qualified identification and authentication using eIDs.

Identity provider: The identity provider (IdP) is deployed in the cloud, meaning in a semi-trusted environment. The identity provider manages the identification and authentication process for the service provider and provides the service provider with asserted data via well-known protocols such as SAML or OpenID.

Identity and/or attribute provider: This entity holds qualified and authentic identity data of the user on server-side.

In this proposed model for eIDs, identity data will be encrypted (using a proxy re-encryption scheme) by the registration authority for the user in such a way that only the user is able to decrypt the data. Encrypting attributes only for the user gives the user sole control to her data. This form of encryption and selective disclosure fulfills the requirement of *user-centricity* on the one side, and the support of *semi-trusted identity providers* on the other side, as only encrypted data are provided to the identity provider. The user can give a subset of re-encrypted attributes to a service provider such that it can only be decrypted by this service provider (*selective disclosure*). Furthermore, the encrypted identity data are digitally signed by the trusted registration authority using a malleable signature scheme (redactable or blank digital signatures). Signing the data has basically two functions. First, the data are authentic and integrity can be assured as the data are signed by the trusted registration authority. This meets the requirement of *qualified and authentic identity data*. Second, by using a malleable signature scheme, we can guarantee that only required (encrypted) attributes can be disclosed to the service provider without

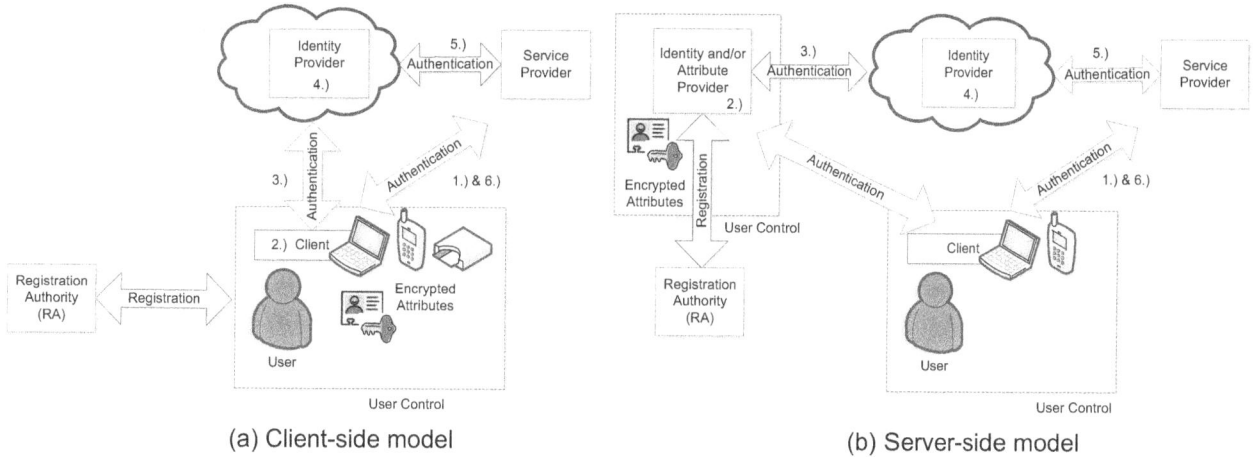

Figure 1: A user-centric and privacy-preserving Identity as a Service Model for eIDs.

invalidating the signature of the trusted registration authority. Finally, the requirement of *easy integration into existing infrastructures* can be met by this model as existing identity protocols already support the transfer of encrypted data and digital signatures out-of-the-box.

In the following, we give details on the registration process and the identification and authentication process when applying this model. The registration process has to be conducted only once, whereas the latter must be performed for each access to a protected resource.

Registration Process: Qualified and authentic identity data issuance is carried out by a trusted third party, the registration authority. Data provisioning is done during an appropriate registration process between the user and the registration authority. Details of the registration process are out of scope of this model and are dependent on the respective eID approach. Nevertheless, registered identity data are encrypted for the user using a proxy re-encryption scheme and signed by the registration authority using a redactable or blank digital signature scheme. The encrypted and signed data can be either stored on a secure token featuring a client-side approach or on a remote server modeling a server-side approach. However, irrespective of the underlying approach, identity data are always provided by a trusted authority in an authentic and qualified manner. This allows our approach to be used for national eID solutions.

Identification and Authentication Process: Figure 1 also illustrates the identification and authentication process when applying this model. For better illustration, we assume the identity provider to be running in a public cloud to fully feature the Identity as a Service paradigm. Basically, the identity provider in the public cloud has three main responsibilities: 1) user authentication and verification of authenticity of encrypted identity data, 2) re-encrypting the identity data for the service provider, and 3) structuring and transferring identity data to the service provider. To illustrate the individual responsibilities, we briefly describe an authentication process using our model.

1. The user wants to access a protected resource at the service provider who requires authentication. Authen-

tication is carried out by the identity provider. Hence, the user is forwarded there.

2. The user redacts all encrypted attributes which she does not want to disclose to the service provider. Depending on the underlying approach, this can be done on client-side or server-side. However, in both cases the user remains under sole control of her data. At the same time, the user also generates a re-encryption key based on a public key of the service provider and the user's private key.

3. The redacted identity data and the re-encryption key are sent to the identity provider in the cloud.

4. The identity provider verifies the authenticity and integrity of the identity data, i.e., the signature, and re-encrypts it for the service provider. Additionally, the identity data are structured accordingly for being transferred to the service provider.

5. The identity provider transfers the data to the service provider using appropriate existing identity protocols such as SAML or OpenID. To ensure authenticity and integrity, the identity provider signs the transferred data.

6. The service provider verifies the received data and decrypts the provided and asserted attributes. Based on the attribute values, the service provider either grants or denies access.

To securely and reliably support these functionality, we make some assumptions:

Assumptions: We assume that whenever we speak of public parameters or public keys, they are available in an authentic fashion, e.g., via a PKI. Furthermore, the channels between all parties provide confidentiality as well as authenticity, e.g., via the use of TLS.

4. APPLICATION TO THE AUSTRIAN EID SYSTEM

In this section we demonstrate the applicability of our model by applying it to an existing eID system, i.e., the Austrian eID system. Therefore, we briefly introduce the Austrian eID system and then illustrate the realization of the Austrian eID system when applying our proposed model.

4.1 The Austrian eID System

Unique citizen identification and secure authentication in Austria is based on the Austrian citizen card[6] [14], the official eID in Austria. Unique identification is based on a unique number, the so-called sourcePIN, which is wrapped in a special XML data structure, the so-called Identity Link (IDL), and stored on the citizen card. In more detail, the Identity Link includes the citizen's sourcePIN, first name, last name, date of birth, and a qualified certificate for creating digital signatures according to the EU Signature Directive [9] (the corresponding private key is also stored on the citizen card). To ensure authenticity and integrity of the Identity Link, it is digitally signed by the trusted SourcePIN Register Authority (SRA). We subsequently denote the Identity Link as $IDL = ((A_1, a_1), \ldots, (A_m, a_m))$ being a sequence of identity attribute name A_i and value a_i pairs.

To preserve citizens' privacy, it is prevented by law (according to the Austrian e-Government Act [21]) to directly use the sourcePIN for identification at online applications. Therefore, the Austrian eID system implements a sector-specific identification model using domain-specific pseudonyms. These so called sector-specific PINs (ssPINs) are uniquely derived from the sourcePIN and ensure citizen unlinkability across multiple sectors.

In the following we briefly describe the registration and authentication process in the Austrian eID System. Figure 2 illustrates the involved entities and their interactions.

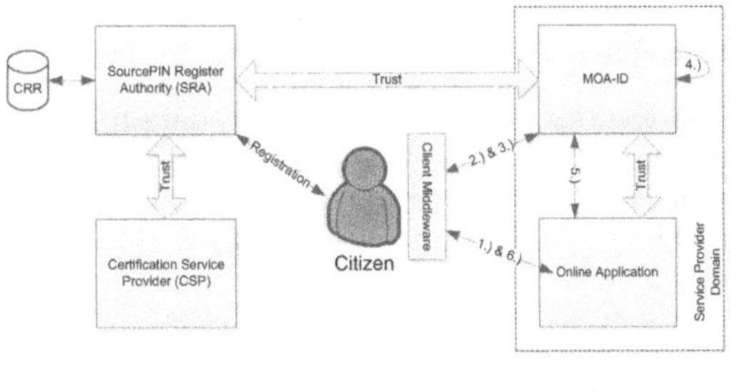

Figure 2: The Austrian eID system.

Registration Process: In order to activate an Austrian citizen card, citizens must prove their identity to the sourcePIN register authority (SRA). This can be done either in a registration office or via registered mail. The SRA finally creates the sourcePIN, the Identity Link, and the qualified certificate and issues the citizen card including these data to the citizen. More precisely, for this process the SRA relies on cryptographic key material provided by an certification service provider (CSP), which is accredited according to the EU Signature Directive.

---

[6]Currently, the Austrian citizen card is implemented as client-side approach using smart cards and as server-side approach involving the citizen's mobile phone.

Identification and Authentication Process: For facilitating the identification and authentication process using the Austrian citizen card at online applications, service providers usually rely on the open source module MOA-ID[7]. On the one side, this module manages the identification and authentication process with the citizen and, on the other side, provides citizen's identity data in a structured format to the online application. According to Figure 2, the identification and authentication process involves the following steps:

1. The citizen wants to access a protected resource, which requires citizen card authentication. The online application starts the authentication process and triggers MOA-ID.

2. First, MOA-ID reads the Identity Link from the citizen card through the client middleware and verifies it. This corresponds to the identification process.

3. Second, MOA-ID requests the citizen to create a qualified electronic signature[8] for authentication. The qualified electronic signature is verified by MOA-ID involving appropriate certificate revocation mechanisms (CRLs,OCSP) provided by the CSP.

4. MOA-ID derives the sourcePIN according to the domain the service provider is assigned to and thus creates a sector-specific PIN (ssPIN).

5. MOA-ID assembles a special data structure which includes the ssPIN and additional personal data of the citizen such as first name, last name, and date of birth. The assembled data structure, called *assertion*, follows the specification of SAML and is transmitted to the online application.

6. Based on the data received, the online application is able to provide the protected resource to the citizen.

4.2 Realization

The current deployment approach of the Austrian eID system foresees a local deployment of MOA-ID within each service provider's domain. Thereby, MOA-ID is fully trusted. While this approach has some clear benefits in terms of scalability and end-to-end security, a central approach may be still advantageous. However, a central approach probably lacks in terms of scalability. To overcome this issue, Zwattendorfer and Slamanig [25] proposed a move of MOA-ID into a public cloud, meaning into a semi-trusted environment. Nevertheless, the proposed approach has some clear disadvantages that our new model is able to overcome.

Subsequently, we present a use case of our user-centric and privacy-preserving Identity as a Service model for eIDs giving a concrete realization of the Austrian eID system. In our realization we make use of a proxy re-encryption scheme of Ateniese et al. [1], which omits the requirements of the service provider and MOA-ID to be registered at the SRA as in [25]. Additionally, we apply blank digital signatures [10] (used as a redactable signature scheme) for the Identity Link enabling the citizen to redact specific identity attributes out

---

[7]https://joinup.ec.europa.eu/software/moa-idspss
[8]Qualified electronic signature is a legal term for a digital signature which satisfies specific requirements according to the EU signature directive [9].

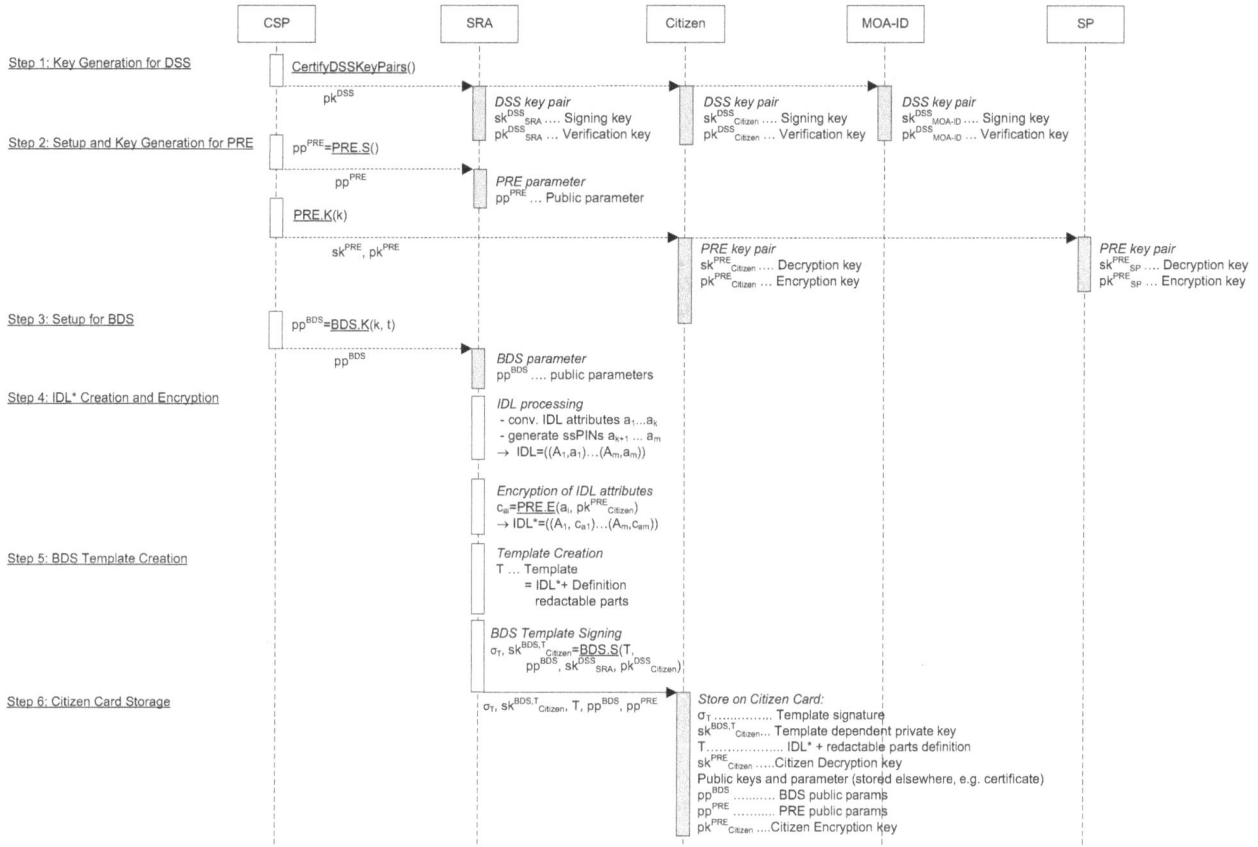

Figure 3: Sequence diagram of registration process.

of the Identity Link[9]. By using these technologies, our realization is easy integrable into the existing infrastructure and requires minimal changes on the service provider's side. In the following, we elaborate on the registration as well as on the identification and authentication process in detail.

Registration Process: From the user's and service provider's perspective the registration process does not change compared to the existing system. The required changes for applying our new model affect the creation of the data to be stored on the citizen card only and has to be done by the SRA as it is the case in the current approach. Figure 3 shows the sequence diagram of the registration process. In the following, we assume that the DSS secret keys are generated by the respective entities but for simplicity assume that the key pairs for the PRE scheme are generated by the SRA (in practice this can easily be done by every entity and only the public keys are certified by SRA or some CSP). The entire registration consists of the subsequent steps:

1. The CSP certifies the public signature verification key for the SRA (pk_{SRA}^{DSS}), the Citizen ($\mathsf{pk}_{Citizen}^{DSS}$), and MOA-ID ($\mathsf{pk}_{MOA-ID}^{DSS}$).

2. The CSP generates the public parameter pp^{PRE} for the PRE and publishes it. In addition, the CSP generates the PRE key pair for the Citizen ($\mathsf{sk}_{Citizen}^{PRE}, \mathsf{pk}_{Citizen}^{PRE}$), which will be stored on the Citizen's citizen card in

---

[9]The SRA represents the originator and the citizen the proxy in terms of BDS.

step 6. Finally, the PRE key pair for the service provider ($\mathsf{sk}_{SP}^{PRE}, \mathsf{pk}_{SP}^{PRE}$) is generated and given to the service provider.

3. The CSP generates the public parameter pp^{BDS} for the BDS scheme and publishes it.

4. The SRA creates a modified Identity Link IDL^* based upon the original IDL attributes. This IDL^* includes the attributes of IDL (e.g., name, date of birth, etc.) and *all* domain-specific pseudonyms (ssPINs) for all public sectors. Furthermore, the SRA encrypts these identity attributes for the Citizen using $\mathsf{pk}_{Citizen}^{PRE}$. Hence, $\mathsf{IDL}^* = ((A_1, c_{a_1}), \ldots, (A_k, c_{a_k}))$ is a sequence containing the encrypted attributes and additionally the encrypted ssPINs.

5. Based on this IDL^*, a BDS template T is generated, which defines the value pairs (A_i, c_{a_i}) to be redactable by the citizen. This template is then signed by the SRA using $BDS.S$. The BDS template signing process outputs the template signature σ_T and the template dependent private key $\mathsf{sk}_{Citizen}^{BDS,T}$ for the Citizen (i.e., only the citizen holding this key is able to redact data and to create signed message instances).

6. In the last registration step, the following data are stored on the corresponding citizen card: the BDS Template T representing the IDL^*, the Template signature σ_T, the Template dependent private key $\mathsf{sk}_{Citizen}^{BDS,T}$, and the PRE decryption key of the Citizen $\mathsf{sk}_{Citizen}^{PRE}$.

The PRE encryption key of the Citizen ($\mathsf{pk}_{\mathsf{Citizen}}^{\mathsf{PRE}}$), the public parameters for BDS ($\mathsf{pp}^{\mathsf{BDS}}$) and PRE ($\mathsf{pp}^{\mathsf{PRE}}$) are stored elsewhere, for instance in the appropriate certificates or public repositories.

Identification and Authentication Process: Similar to the registration, the identification and authentication process is designed to require minimal changes to the existing infrastructure. The main changes affect the (centrally deployed) identity provider MOA-ID and the client middleware. The slight changes on the service provider's side concerns the provisioning of its proxy re-encryption key and the decryption of the received identity attributes. Both issues can be realized quite straightforwardly. The sequence diagram of the identification and authentication process is illustrated in Figure 4. The entire procedure consists of the following steps:

1. The Citizen wants to access an application deployed and running at a service provider.

2. The service provider redirects the Citizen to MOA-ID to request authentication. The authentication request holds the information in which sector the service provider operates and the PRE encryption key $\mathsf{pk}_{\mathsf{SP}}^{\mathsf{PRE}}$ of the service provider.

3. MOA-ID sends a request to the Citizen to get the Citizen's identity data and signature.

4. The Citizen reads the BDS template, holding IDL*.

5. Due to data protection regulations, following redactions must be made: The sourcePIN and all pre-generated ssPINs not representing the given sector must be redacted out of IDL*; i.e., only the corresponding sector (in encrypted form) stays visible. In addition to these legally required redactions, the Citizen is able to redact more identity attributes out of IDL*, which the citizen does not want to be sent to the service provider. For instance, the Citizen may redact the name, but the date of birth is still available (as encrypted data).

6. The BDS instance (message) M is generated. This message includes the redacted IDL* and additional information:

   - Current date and time
   - Application data (e.g., application name, country in which the application is deployed, etc.)
   - Technical parameters (e.g., URL of the application, corresponding sector of the application, etc.)

   This message is instantiated and signed by the Citizen using the private key $\mathsf{sk}_{\mathsf{Citizen}}^{\mathsf{DSS}}$ and the template dependent private key $\mathsf{sk}_{\mathsf{Citizen}}^{\mathsf{BDS,T}}$. This outputs the message signature σ_{M}.

7. The Citizen generates a re-encryption key $\mathsf{rk}_{\mathsf{Citizen}\to\mathsf{SP}}^{\mathsf{PRE}}$ for MOA-ID based upon the PRE encryption key of the service provider $\mathsf{pk}_{\mathsf{SP}}^{\mathsf{PRE}}$ and the Citizen's PRE decryption key $\mathsf{sk}_{\mathsf{Citizen}}^{\mathsf{PRE}}$ by running $PRE.RK$.

8. The Citizen returns the identity data, consisting of the BDS message signature σ_{M} and the BDS message M, to MOA-ID. In addition, this response includes the re-encryption key $\mathsf{rk}_{\mathsf{Citizen}\to\mathsf{SP}}^{\mathsf{PRE}}$, the BDS public parameter $\mathsf{pp}^{\mathsf{BDS}}$, and the PRE public parameter $\mathsf{pp}^{\mathsf{PRE}}$ (the latter is optional, since the parameters are assumed to be public).

9. MOA-ID verifies the BDS message signature. In case this verification is positive, the message is authentic and a valid instance of the BDS template as defined by the SRA.

10. MOA-ID performs the re-encryption of the identity attributes in the BDS message M, thus creating a message M* representing the disclosed encrypted identity attributes $(\mathsf{rc}_{\mathsf{a}_i})_{i=1}^m$ re-encrypted for the service provider.

11. MOA-ID is obliged to delete the re-encryption key, due to security considerations[10].

12. MOA-ID creates an assertion Assert holding the available re-encrypted identity attributes and signs it using its private key $\mathsf{sk}_{\mathsf{MOA-ID}}^{\mathsf{DSS}}$.

13. MOA-ID transmits this signed assertion (Assert and σ_{A}) to the service provider.

14. The service provider verifies the assertion signature and proceeds if the assertion is valid.

15. The service provider decrypts the attributes in M* using its PRE decryption key $\mathsf{sk}_{\mathsf{SP}}^{\mathsf{PRE}}$. Thus, only these identity attributes are revealed for the service provider.

16. Depending on the available (decrypted) identity data of the Citizen and the corresponding access rights, the service provider is able to grant or deny access.

Use of Proxy Re-Encryption in Practice: In the above discussion, for the sake of simplicity of presentation, we have assumed that the attribute values are encrypted using the proxy re-encryption scheme directly. However, due to efficiency reasons, in a practical application it makes more sense to use a hybrid approach, i.e., to encrypt *each* attribute using a *distinct* random key of a secure symmetric encryption scheme and then encrypt the respective key using the proxy re-encryption key.

5. DISCUSSION AND CONCLUSIONS

In this section we discuss the different approaches for (selective) disclosure comparing it to our new model. Basis for our discussion are the following selected criteria (based upon the requirements given in Section 3.2):

Privacy and Selective Disclosure: How much (identity) data are revealed to the identity provider and service provider? Is the approach applicable as an Identity as a Service model?

---

[10]In case the service provider gets compromised and MOA-ID is still holding the re-encryption key, MOA-ID and the service provider might cooperate. This might enable MOA-ID being able to re-encrypt the attributes for the forged service provider.

CSP | SRA | Citizen | MOA-ID | SP

Step 1: Access Resoucre at SP

Step 2: Redirect to MOA-ID

sector, pk^{PRE}_{SP}

sector, pk^{PRE}_{SP}

Step 3: Identity Data Request to Citizen

sector .... Sector of the SP
pk^{PRE}_{SP} .... PRE Encryption key of SP

Step 4: Read BDS Template

Read BDS template T
T ... Template
= IDL*+ Definition
redactable parts

Step 5: Redaction

Message creation
M ... Message representing the redacted IDL*

Step 6: Instantation

BDS instantiation
$\sigma_M = \underline{BDS.I}(T, M, \sigma_T, pp^{BDS}, sk^{BDS,T}_{Citizen}, sk^{DSS}_{Citizen})$

Step 7: Re-Encryption Key Generation for PRE

$rk^{PRE}_{Citizen \rightarrow SP} = \underline{PRE.RK}(sk^{PRE}_{Citizen}, pk^{PRE}_{SP}, pp^{PRE})$

Step 8: Identity Data Response to MOA-ID

σ_M, M, pp^{BDS}, pp^{PRE}, $rk^{PRE}_{Citizen \rightarrow SP}$

Identity data response
σ_M .... Message signature
M .... Redacted IDL*
pp^{BDS} .... BDS public parameter
pp^{PRE} .... PRE public parameter
$rk^{PRE}_{Citizen \rightarrow SP}$ .. Re-encryption key

Step 9: Verify Message

$\underline{BDS.V_M}(M, \sigma_M, pp^{BDS}, pk^{DSS}_{Citizen}, pk^{DSS}_{SRA})$

{true/false}

Step 10: Re-Encryption

Re-Encryption of non-redacted attributes in M
$rc_{ai} = \underline{PRE.RE}(pp^{PRE}, c_{ai}, rk^{PRE}_{Citizen \rightarrow SP})$
$\rightarrow M^* = ((A_1, redacted), \dots(A_i, rc_{ai})\dots)$

Step 11: Delete Re-Encryption Key

Delete $rk^{PRE}_{Citizen \rightarrow SP}$

Step 12: Create Assertion

$\underline{CreateAssertion}(M, sk^{DSS}_{MOA-ID})$
$\rightarrow$ Assert, σ_A

Step 13: Return Assertion to SP

σ_A, Assert, pp^{PRE}

Assertion handling
Assert .. Assertion
σ_A .... Assertion signature

Step 14: Verify Assertion

$\underline{SP.VerifyAssertion}(\sigma_A, Assert, pk^{DSS}_{MOA-ID})$

{true/false}

Step 15: Decrypt Attributes

$a_i = \underline{PRE.D}(pp^{PRE}, rc_{ai}, sk^{PRE}_{SP})$

Step 16: Grant Access

$\underline{SP.GrantAccess}()$

{true/false}

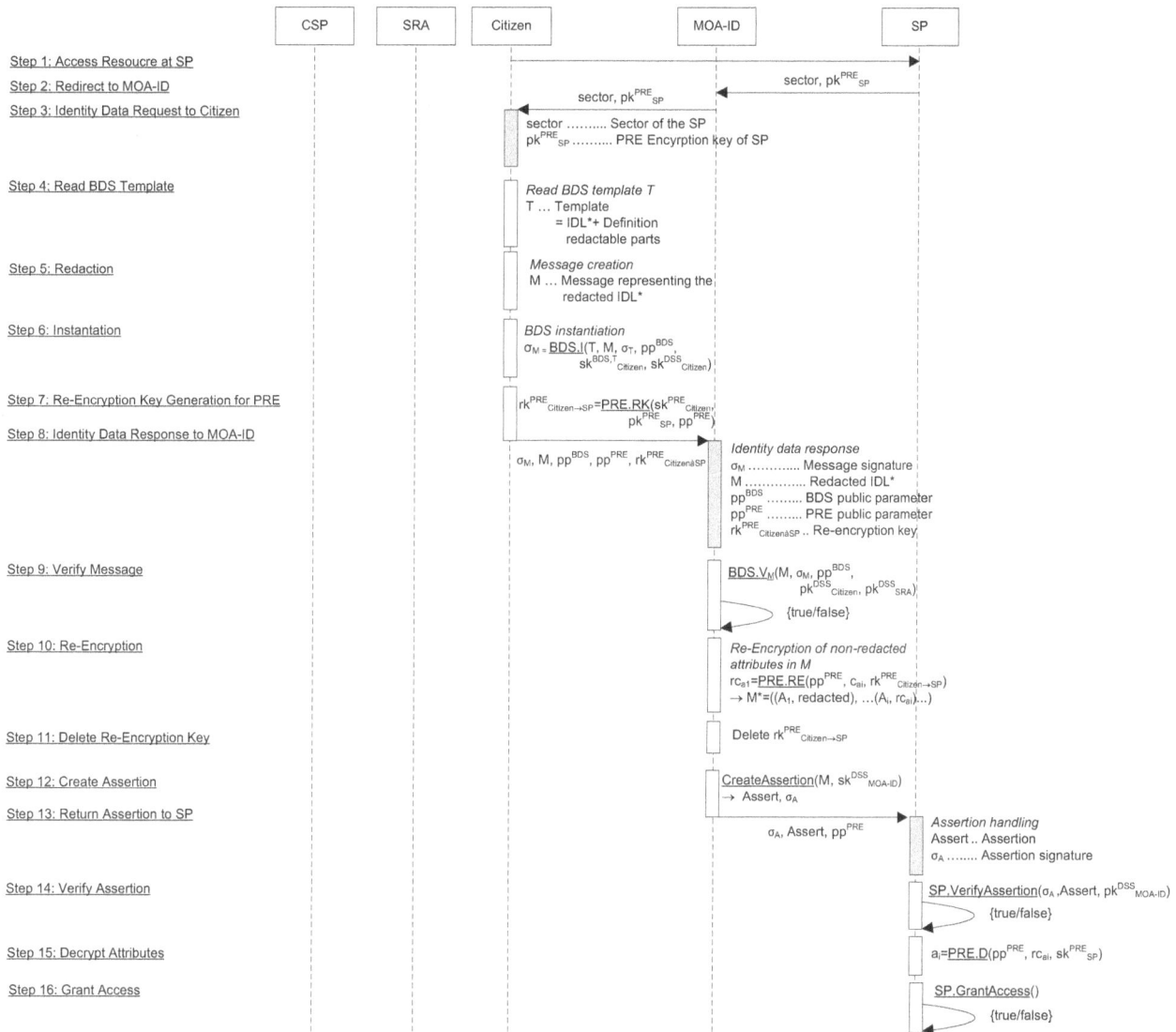

Figure 4: Sequence diagram of identification and authentication processes.

User-Centricity: Is the user herself able to disclose only parts of her identity data towards the service provider and the identity provider?

Integration effort and complexity: How much effort is required by adopting the approach? How complex is the integration of the approach, especially for the service provider?

Figure 5 gives a brief assessment of the different approaches discussed in Section 2 concerning these criteria. The trusted identity provider approaches represent the state-of-the-art and are already deployed in many cases. Thus, the integration effort and complexity are quite low. Due to requiring full trust on the identity provider, these approaches do not achieve a high grade on privacy, user-centricity, and selective disclosure. In contrast, anonymous credential systems allow a privacy-aware and user-centric (selective) disclosure of identity data. They achieve both anonymity and unlinkability with respect to the service provider and identity provider. Nevertheless, these systems require complex operations and

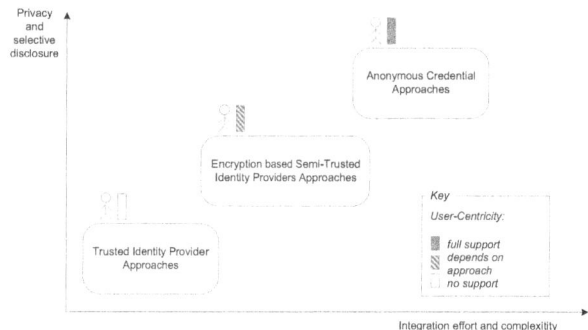

Figure 5: Overview assessment.

additional infrastructure and lack on deployment in practice. Semi-trusted identity provider approaches using proxy re-encryption steer a middle course. While they achieve anonymity of the citizen regarding the identity provider because of the encrypted attributes, they are not able to avoid linkability (identity providers, however, can only link actions to pseudonyms). Compared to the trusted identity providers approach, these approaches increase (slightly) the integration effort and complexity, but seem far more practical than anonymous credentials.

The approach of Nuñez et al. [19] uses proxy re-encryption and is therefore advantageous when the identity provider is not fully trusted in terms of privacy. Nevertheless, drawbacks are that this approach is server-side, and thus the user still needs to trust the identity provider that only the amount of data desired by the user is actually transferred to the service provider. Hence, the approach cannot be seen as user-centric in terms of selective disclosure. Moreover, the encrypted attributes stored on the OpenID provider may be self-asserted, hence no qualified and authentic attributes such as required when using eIDs can be provided to the service provider.

The second proxy re-encryption-based approach for semi-trusted identity providers of Zwattendorfer and Slamanig [25] allows a selective disclosure of identity data. Apart the fact that their approach is strongly tailored to the Austrian eID system, it is not fully user-centric as the user data are encrypted for a trusted third party and not the user herself. Additionally, the approach requires a pre-registration of identity providers and service providers at a registration authority, which issues the identity data. This strikingly decreases the practicability and extensibility of this approach.

In contrast, in our proposed model the user gets full control about her data. On the one hand, the identity data are encrypted for the user and the user herself generates the proxy re-encryption key (defining which service provider is able to decrypt the identity data). On the other hand, the user is able to define which data are disclosed before it is sent to the identity provider. Thus, the privacy and user-centric selective disclosure requirement is fulfilled. Furthermore, our approach does not need any pre-registration of the identity provider or the service provider. Finally, additional infrastructure components except additional decryption functionality at the service provider are not needed. Hence, our approach allows for a convenient integration into existing infrastructures and protocols.

Acknowledgements

We thank the anonymous reviewers for their valuable feedback. The first author has been partly supported by the European Commission through project FP7-FutureID, grant agreement number 318424.

6. REFERENCES

[1] G. Ateniese, K. Fu, M. Green, and S. Hohenberger. Improved proxy re-encryption schemes with applications to secure distributed storage. *ACM Trans. Inf. Syst. Secur.*, 9(1):1–30, 2006.

[2] M. Bauer, M. Meints, and M. Hansen. D3.1: Structured Overview on Prototypes and Concepts of Identity Management System. FIDIS, 2005.

[3] P. Bichsel, J. Camenisch, T. Groß, and V. Shoup. Anonymous credentials on a standard java card. In *ACM CCS*, pages 600–610. ACM, 2009.

[4] S. Brands. *Rethinking Public Key Infrastructures and Digital Certificates: Building in Privacy*. MIT Press, 2000.

[5] C. Brzuska, H. C. Pöhls, and K. Samelin. Non-Interactive Public Accountability for Sanitizable Signatures. In *EuroPKI*, volume 7868 of *LNCS*. Springer, 2012.

[6] J. Camenisch and A. Lysyanskaya. An Efficient System for Non-transferable Anonymous Credentials with Optional Anonymity Revocation. In *Advances in Cryptology - EUROCRYPT 2001*, volume 2045 of *LNCS*, pages 93–118. Springer, 2001.

[7] European Commission. IDABC. 2009. eID Interoperability for PEGS: Update of Country Profiles., 2009.

[8] European Parliament and the Council. Directive 95/46/EC of the European Parliament and of the Council of 24 October 1995 on the protection of individuals with regard to the processing of personal data and on the free movement of such data . http://eur-lex.europa.eu/LexUriServ/LexUriServ.do?uri=CELEX:31995L0046:en:HTML, 1995.

[9] European Union. Directive 1999/93/EC of the European Parliament and of the Council of 13. December 1999 on a community framework for electronic signatures.

[10] C. Hanser and D. Slamanig. Blank Digital Signatures. In *ACM ASIACCS '13*, pages 95–106. ACM, 2013. http://eprint.iacr.org/2013/130.

[11] R. Johnson, D. Molnar, D. X. Song, and D. Wagner. Homomorphic Signature Schemes. In *CT-RSA '02*, volume 2271 of *LNCS*, pages 244–262. Springer, 2002.

[12] A. Jøsang and S. Pope. User centric identity management. *AusCERT 2005*, 2005.

[13] A. Jøsang, M. A. Zomai, and S. Suriadi. Usability and privacy in identity management architectures. In *ACSW '07*, pages 143–152, 2007.

[14] H. Leitold, A. Hollosi, and R. Posch. Security Architecture of the Austrian Citizen Card Concept. In *ACSAC 2002*, pages 391–402, 2002.

[15] H. Leitold and B. Zwattendorfer. STORK: Architecture, Implementation and Pilots. In *ISSE 2010*, pages 131–142, 2010.

[16] M. Margraf. The new german id card. In *ISSE 2010 Securing Electronic Business Processes*, pages 367–373. Vieweg+Teubner, 2011.

[17] Modinis. The Status of Identity Management in European eGovernment initiatives. Deliverable D3.5, 2006.

[18] I. Naumann and G. Hogben. Privacy Features of European eID Card Specifications. Technical report, European Network and Information Security Agency (ENISA), 2009.

[19] D. Nuñez, I. Agudo, and J. Lopez. Integrating OpenID with Proxy Re-Encryption to enhance privacy in cloud-based identity services. In *IEEE CloudCom 2012*, pages 241 – 248, 2012.

[20] J. Palfrey and U. Gasser. CASE STUDY: Digital Identity Interoperability and eInnovation. Berkman Publication Series,, 2007.

[21] Republic of Austria. *Austrian Federal Act on Provisions facilitating electronic communications with public Bodies; part I, Nr. 10/2004.* Federal law Gazette, 2004.

[22] A. Sabouri, I. Krontiris, and K. Rannenberg. Attribute-Based Credentials for Trust (ABC4Trust). In *TrustBus 2012*, volume 7449 of *LNCS*, pages 218–219. Springer, 2012.

[23] A. Siddhartha. National e-id card schemes: A european overview. *Inf. Secur. Tech. Rep.*, 13(2):46–53, May 2008.

[24] R. Steinfeld, L. Bull, and Y. Zheng. Content Extraction Signatures. In *ICISC 2001*, volume 2288 of *LNCS*, pages 285–304. Springer, 2001.

[25] B. Zwattendorfer and D. Slamanig. On Privacy-Preserving Ways to Porting the Austrian eID System to the Public Cloud. In *SEC 2013*, AICT, pages 300–314. Springer, 2013.

[26] B. Zwattendorfer and D. Slamanig. Privacy-preserving realization of the stork framework in the public cloud. In *SECRYPT*, pages 419–426, 2013.

APPENDIX

A. CRYPTOGRAPHIC BUILDING BLOCKS

In the following we give a more formal description of the cryptographic primitives used in our model.

Proxy Re-Encryption.

A proxy re-encryption scheme (PRE) is a tuple (S, K, RK, E, RE, D) of polynomial-time algorithms. The algorithm $PRE.S$ represents the setup and produces system parameters $\mathsf{pp}^{\mathsf{PRE}}$. Every algorithm has access to these parameters. $PRE.K$ is a probabilistic key generation algorithm that takes a security parameter κ and outputs a private and public key pair $(\mathsf{sk}_A^{\mathsf{PRE}}, \mathsf{pk}_A^{\mathsf{PRE}})$ for party A. The re-encryption key generation algorithm $PRE.RK$ takes as input a private key $\mathsf{sk}_A^{\mathsf{PRE}}$ and a different public key $\mathsf{pk}_B^{\mathsf{PRE}}$, and outputs a re-encryption key $\mathsf{rk}_{A \to B}^{\mathsf{PRE}}$. The probabilistic encryption algorithm $PRE.E$ gets a public key $\mathsf{pk}_A^{\mathsf{PRE}}$ and a plaintext M and outputs $c_i = PRE.E(\mathsf{pk}_A^{\mathsf{PRE}}, M)$. The (probabilistic) re-encryption algorithm gets as input a ciphertext c_A under $\mathsf{pk}_A^{\mathsf{PRE}}$ and a re-encryption key $\mathsf{rk}_{A \to B}^{\mathsf{PRE}}$ and outputs a re-encrypted ciphertext $c_B = PRE.RE(\mathsf{rk}_{A \to B}^{\mathsf{PRE}}, c_A)$ under $\mathsf{pk}_B^{\mathsf{PRE}}$. The decryption algorithm $PRE.D$ takes the private key $\mathsf{sk}_B^{\mathsf{PRE}}$ and a ciphertext c_B and outputs $M = PRE.D(\mathsf{sk}_B^{\mathsf{PRE}}, c_B)$ or an error $\perp$.

Digital Signatures.

A digital signature scheme (DSS) is a triple (K, S, V) of poly-time algorithms, whereas $DSS.K$ is a probabilistic key generation algorithm that takes a security parameter κ and outputs a private and public key pair $(\mathsf{sk}^{\mathsf{DSS}}, \mathsf{pk}^{\mathsf{DSS}})$. The probabilistic signing algorithm $DSS.S$ takes as input a message $M \in \{0,1\}^*$ and a private key $\mathsf{sk}^{\mathsf{DSS}}$, and outputs a signature σ. The verification algorithm $DSS.V$ takes as input a signature σ, a message $M \in \{0,1\}^*$ and a public key $\mathsf{pk}^{\mathsf{DSS}}$, and outputs a single bit $b \in \{\texttt{true}, \texttt{false}\}$ indicating whether σ is a valid signature for M. We note that in practice one typically employs the hash-then-sign paradigm, i.e., instead of inputting M into $DSS.S$ and $DSS.V$, one inputs $H(M)$ where H is a suitable cryptographic hash function.

Redactable Signatures.

A redactable signature scheme (RS) is a tuple (K, S, V, R) of polynomial-time algorithms. The algorithm $RS.K$ gets a security parameter κ and generates a private and public key pair $(\mathsf{sk}^{\mathsf{RS}}, \mathsf{pk}^{\mathsf{RS}})$. The signing algorithm $RS.S$ gets as input the signing key $\mathsf{sk}^{\mathsf{RS}}$ and a message $m = (m[1], \ldots, m[\ell])$, $m[i] \in \{0,1\}^*$ and outputs a signature $\sigma = RS.S(\mathsf{sk}^{\mathsf{RS}}, m)$. The verification algorithm $RS.V$ gets as input a public key $\mathsf{pk}^{\mathsf{RS}}$, a message $m = (m[1], \ldots, m[\ell])$, $m[i] \in \{0,1\}^*$, a signature σ, and outputs a single bit $b = RS.V(pk^{RS}, m, \sigma)$, $b \in \{\texttt{true}, \texttt{false}\}$, indicating whether σ is a valid signature for m. The redaction algorithm $RS.R$ takes as input a message $m = (m[1], \ldots, m[\ell])$, $m[i] \in \{0,1\}^*$, a public key $\mathsf{pk}^{\mathsf{RS}}$, a signature σ, and a list MOD of indizes of blocks to be redacted. It returns a modified message with redacted blocks and a signature pair $(\hat{m}, \hat{\sigma}) = RS.R(m, pk^{RS}, \sigma, \mathsf{MOD})$ or an error $\perp$. In case that it should be publicly verifiable that the modified message $\hat{m}$ has been produced by some particular redactor (non-interactive public accountability [5]), the redactor is required to create a conventional digital signature on it.

Blank Digital Signatures.

A blank digital signature scheme (BDS) is defined as a tuple (K, S, V_T, I, V_M) of polynomial-time algorithms. Algorithm $BDS.K$ on input of a security parameter κ and an upper bound for the template size t generates public parameters $\mathsf{pp}^{\mathsf{BDS}}$. $BDS.S$ takes a template T, the public parameters $\mathsf{pp}^{\mathsf{BDS}}$, the private signing key of the originator $(\mathsf{sk}_O^{\mathsf{DSS}})$ and the public signing key of the proxy $(\mathsf{pk}_P^{\mathsf{DSS}})$, and outputs a template signature σ_{T} and a private template signing key for the proxy $\mathsf{sk}_P^{\mathsf{BDS},\mathsf{T}}$. Algorithm $BDS.V_T$ given the template T, the template signature σ_{T}, the public parameters $\mathsf{pp}^{\mathsf{BDS}}$, the public signing keys of originator and proxy $(\mathsf{pk}_O^{\mathsf{DSS}}, \mathsf{pk}_P^{\mathsf{DSS}})$, and the template signing key of the proxy $\mathsf{sk}_P^{\mathsf{BDS},\mathsf{T}}$, checks whether σ_{T} is a valid signature for T or not. $BDS.I$ on input of a template T, a corresponding instance M, a signature on the template σ_T, as well as the public parameters $\mathsf{pp}^{\mathsf{BDS}}$, the private template signing key $\mathsf{sk}_P^{\mathsf{BDS},\mathsf{T}}$, and the private signing key of the proxy $\mathsf{sk}_P^{\mathsf{DSS}}$ outputs a signature on the message σ_{M}. The algorithm $BDS.V_M$, when given an instance M of a template T, a signature on this instance σ_{M}, the public system parameters $\mathsf{pp}^{\mathsf{BDS}}$, and the public signing keys of proxy and originator $(\mathsf{pk}_O^{\mathsf{DSS}}, \mathsf{pk}_P^{\mathsf{DSS}})$, verifies whether σ_{M} is a valid signature on M and if M is a correct instantiation of T.

Towards Fine Grained RDF Access Control

Jyothsna Rachapalli, Vaibhav Khadilkar, Murat Kantarcioglu and
Bhavani Thuraisingham
The University of Texas at Dallas
{jxr061100, vvk072000, muratk, bxt043000}@utdallas.edu

ABSTRACT

The Semantic Web is envisioned as the future of the current web, where the information is enriched with machine understandable semantics. According to the World Wide Web Consortium (W3C), "The Semantic Web provides a common framework that allows data to be shared and reused across application, enterprise, and community boundaries". Among the various technologies that empower Semantic Web, the most significant ones are Resource Description Framework (RDF) and SPARQL, which facilitate data integration and a means to query respectively. Although Semantic Web is elegantly and effectively equipped for data sharing and integration via RDF, lack of efficient means to securely share data pose limitations in practice. In order to make data sharing and integration pragmatic for Semantic Web, we present a query language based secure data sharing mechanism. We extend SPARQL with a new query form called SANITIZE which comprises a set of sanitization operations that are used to sanitize or mask sensitive data within an RDF graph. The sanitization operations can be further leveraged towards RDF access control and anonymization, thus enabling secure sharing of RDF data.

Categories and Subject Descriptors

D.3.3 [**Programming Languages**]: Language Constructs and Features; D.4.6 [**Operating Systems**]: Security and Protection—*Access Control*

Keywords

RDF; SPARQL; Sanitization; Access Control; Security

1. INTRODUCTION

The Relational Database Management System (RDBMS) is one of the most popular paradigms to capture data and build applications in the IT domain. It is good for enterprise scale performance and reliability, however, it falls short on these metrics at the scale of the Internet. Semantic Web is

a popular emerging paradigm for capturing data based on requirements pertaining to Internet scale and has been perceived as the future of the web, comprising a global database.

There has been a significant amount of research in the database community in the area of data security, which can be broadly classified into access control research and data privacy research [1]. Relational databases have developed sound features for providing access control [2], [3], [4] and data privacy [5] (such as k-anonymity, l-diversity and t-closeness), which also includes differential privacy [6]. Although there have been attempts at developing access control techniques for RDF (see for example, [7], [8], [9], [10], and [11]), there is no agreed upon consensus for securing the underlying RDF data. Since security or privacy definitions and intent change by virtue of application requirements that span a vast number of domains, we need a general and fundamental mechanism for securing RDF graphs, which should essentially comprise RDF graph transformation operations. Towards this end, we present a language for sanitizing RDF graphs, which is an attempt at providing a formal foundational framework that will help in implementing various security and privacy features for RDF data.

We propose to secure RDF graphs through sanitization, which is a process of masking sensitive data within an RDF graph with an appropriate replacement value in order to reduce the risk of data exposure. There are two crucial requirements for performing sanitization of RDF graphs. Firstly, one needs to automate the generation of replacement values for any given sensitive data item. Secondly, one should be able to perform automatic synchronization, *i.e.,* a given sensitive data item is masked consistently not only within the given sensitive RDF subgraph but also everywhere else it occurs in the graph. Further, RDF sanitization can be useful under two use cases. In the case where an RDF dataset needs to be outsourced and shared with a third party, for *e.g.,* when a hospital wants to release patient data for research purposes. In this case sanitization can be performed on the entire RDF dataset before sharing. In an access control like scenario where data is present in original/unmasked form but needs to be hidden from those who are not authorized, sanitization can be performed dynamically, on a per query basis, on the relevant subgraph of the RDF dataset, which is being accessed by the user query.

Having described the process of RDF graph sanitization, we now describe why SPARQL based sanitization is crucial for fine grained RDF access control. Relational model pertaining to RDBMS is based on first-order predicate logic and set theory. The query language SQL, which is based on relational algebra or calculus, serves as a means to retrieve or operate upon data. On the other hand, in Semantic Web knowledge bases, the knowledge representation or ontology languages (OWL dialects) are based on description logics, which in turn are decidable fragments of first order logic with varying levels of expressivity. The data model used within Semantic Web is RDF, which is a graph data model. SPARQL [12] is an RDF query language that can be used to formulate queries ranging from simple graph pattern matching to complex queries, which may include operators such as union, optional, filters, path expressions *etc.* Since SPARQL is rich in expressivity (when compared to SQL), it can be used to formulate highly sophisticated queries to access or retrieve a wide variety of data items from RDF stores. Therefore, the mechanism to secure access to RDF data is required to commensurately match this expressivity.

In relational databases, views provide a very powerful security mechanism for controlling what information can be accessed. A view based approach essentially gleans data from various relations, which can be safely shared with an authorized user. A similar approach could be used to secure access to RDF data. However, unlike RDBMS where data is modeled as relations, in RDF data is captured as a graph comprising a set of triples. Creation of a view in the context of RDF would translate to creation of a view subgraph constructed by gleaning required data. However, since RDF is a graph data model, the problem of subgraph extraction may not always be feasible or it may be too tedious to create the desired subgraph by gleaning suitable data. Since this process may not lend the desired flexibility required for fine grained RDF access control, we take the process of securing RDF graphs a step further. Instead of creating secure view subgraphs from RDF datasets by gleaning data, we choose to dynamically and selectively mask the sensitive data within an RDF graph, which also preserves the correctness of ontological definitions of an RDF graph. We model the various graph transformation tasks in the form of query operations.

Since the existing SPARQL operations such as UPDATE or CONSTRUCT do not support RDF graph sanitization (details provided in Appendix 9.1), we propose a language for sanitizing RDF graphs in order to enable secure RDF data sharing. However, this language is not a replacement of a policy based RDF access control language. In fact, it is an essential tool that can be leveraged by a policy based language in order to effectively and efficiently provide fine grained RDF access control. Although we present a preliminary version of such a policy based access control language, we leave the extensive version of this language as a part of the future work and restrict the scope of this work to details of the RDF sanitization language.

In this paper we do not try to address the question: *"What Data to Sanitize?"*, we instead try to address *"How to sanitize RDF data?"*. In the following we explain the reason behind the same. The data captured in RDF, which is a graph data model, is semi-structured. Therefore, the flexibility of RDF can be used to capture a wide variety of data ranging from relational data (table) to social networks (graph) and provenance (directed acyclic graph). Since we provide a framework/language for sanitizing RDF data which is semi-structured, there is no formal general model (unlike RDBMS with relational model) upon which one can build general privacy definitions and formal adversarial model. Additional domain specific information, such as vocabulary or ontol-

ogy of the domain along with the ontology language used is required to build privacy definitions. Since the structure of the data that can be captured in RDF is variable and can change from one domain to another, privacy definition and utility requirements will change depending on the domain. Therefore, coming up with a general threat model or a formal adversarial model and privacy definitions is not feasible at RDF level. However, if such a definition exists, then using our framework and especially the masking function (*genUniq*), one can create their own custom masking functions, which are suitable for their data and application scenarios and override the original definition to meet the desired privacy requirements suitable for target application domain. The scope of this paper is to address the problem of RDF graph sanitization, which is general enough to be used with RDF data from any domain to build more sophisticated security features like fine grained access control and data privacy. *Our contributions are listed below:*

- We identify, formulate and delineate the requirements of RDF graph sanitization.

- We present a sanitization extension of SPARQL comprising a set of RDF graph sanitization operations along with their time complexity analysis.

- We present denotational/compositional semantics of this extension of SPARQL.

- We present a prototype system and its architecture based on a healthcare provenance scenario and illustrate how one can build a fine grained access control mechanism using our graph sanitization operations.

- We present empirical results showing the performance of the sanitization operations, which were evaluated on synthetic as well as real world datasets.

2. RDF GRAPH SANITIZATION

An RDF graph is made up of a set of triples which in turn are made up of a subject, predicate and an object [13]. A sensitive data item in an RDF graph can be (among many forms) a literal value or a resource node (IRI), a set or class of resource nodes or data values, an edge or a relationship between two nodes and a path or a subgraph containing multiple nodes connected by edges. We present a set of corresponding graph sanitization operations, namely Sanitize Node (SNode), Sanitize Edge (SEdge) and Sanitize Path (SPath). The paper first describes the sanitization operations in imperative (procedural) style, in the form of algorithms, which is technology agnostic, implementation friendly and facilitates complexity analysis and better comprehensibility. We then present the formal model using denotational semantics, which is declarative, *i.e.*, it unambiguously states what needs to be done without stating how it needs to be done. This offers flexibility of allowing others to come up with a more efficient algorithm for same semantics. In the following, we first describe a healthcare provenance scenario that will be used in the rest of the paper to better illustrate the functionality of the sanitization operations. We then describe some of the related formal notation, sanitization algorithms and formal semantics.

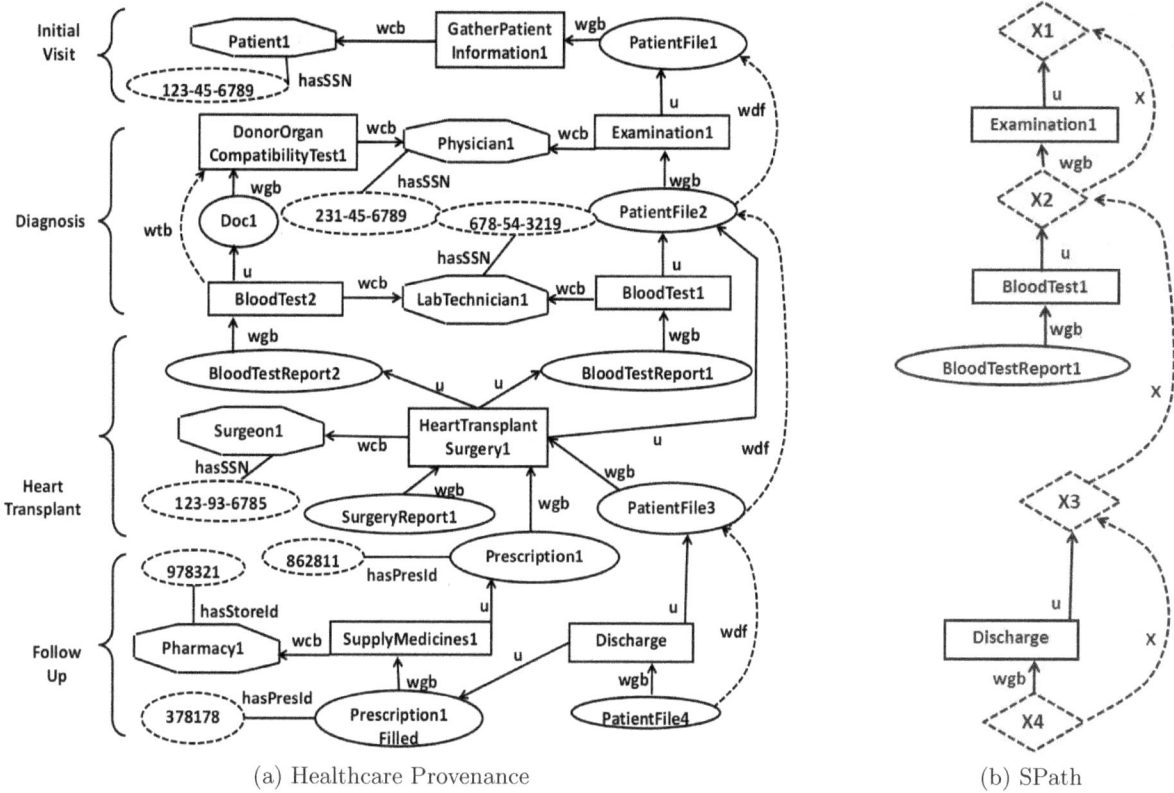

(a) Healthcare Provenance (b) SPath

Figure 1: Provenance Healthcare Scenario and SPath Sanitization Operation Illustration

2.1 Scenario: Healthcare Provenance

We built the healthcare provenance usecase based on the Open Provenance Model (OPM) [14], which is a general model of provenance. An OPM provenance graph comprises three types of nodes, namely Artifacts, Processes and Agents, which are represented by an oval, rectangle and hexagon respectively. It additionally defines five types of dependencies represented by edges connecting these nodes namely, used (u), wasGeneratedBy (wgb), wasControlledBy (wcb), wasTriggeredby (wtb) and wasDerivedFrom (wdf). We capture our usecase with an OWL ontology by extending Jun Zhao's Open Provenance Model Vocabulary (OPMV) [15], which is a lightweight vocabulary used to describe the core concepts of OPM.

Figure 1(a) depicts a sample provenance of a patient's electronic healthcare record (EHR). The provenance, or medical history of Patient1 is shown in various stages namely, **Initial Visit**, **Diagnosis**, **Heart Transplant** and **Follow Up**. During the initial visit, the patient filled out his information through the GatherPatientInformation1 process and an artifact PatientFile1 was generated by it. Physician1 conducted Examination1 (which generated document PatientFile2) and decided to perform a heart transplant surgery. Therefore, he carried out DonorOrganCompatibilityTest1, which triggered the BloodTest2 process (at donor side). This process was controlled by LabTechnician1, who also controlled process BloodTest1 for the recipient, Patient1. Subsequently, Surgeon1 controlled the HeartTransplantSurgery1 process, which used artifacts BloodTestReport1, BloodTestReport2, PatientFile2 and in turn gener-

ated SurgeryReport1, Prescription1 and PatientFile3. The process SupplyMedicines1 used document Prescription1, generated document Prescription1Filled and was controlled by Pharmacy1. Finally, the process Discharge used documents Prescription1Filled and PatientFile3 and generated PatientFile4. In the following, we will use this medical workflow to illustrate the various graph sanitization operations and will refer to it as G_q.

2.2 Related Formal Notation

RDF terms denoted by T, comprise disjoint infinite sets, I, B and L (IRI's, Blank nodes and Literals respectively). A triple $(s, p, o) \in (I \cup B) \times I \times (I \cup B \cup L)$, where s is a subject, p a predicate, and o is an object. A triple pattern, TP, is a triple of the form $(sp, pp, op) \in (I \cup V \cup L) \times (I \cup V) \times (I \cup V \cup L)$, where V is an infinite set of variables that is disjoint from the sets I, B, and L; and sp, pp, and op are a subject pattern, predicate pattern and object pattern respectively. A mapping μ is a partial function $\mu : V \to T$. Given a triple pattern t, $\mu(t)$ denotes the triple obtained by replacing the variables in t according to μ [16]. Domain of μ, $dom(\mu)$ is the subset of V where μ is defined and Ω is defined as a set of mappings μ. A property path is a possible route through a graph between two graph nodes [12]. A property path expression is similar to a string regular expression but over properties, not characters. The ends of the path may be RDF terms or variables. Variables cannot be used as part of the path itself, but only at the ends. A property path pattern is a triple pattern created by using a property path expression in place of a property or predicate. It is a member of the set $(T \cup V) \times PE \times (T \cup V)$, where PE is

167

the set of all property path expressions. In the following, we introduce some terms in addition to the standard ones provided in [12]: (1) *Predicate Triple Pattern* $TP' = \{tp|\ tp$ is a triple pattern where $sp \in V$, $pp \in I$ and $op \in V\}$. (2) *Type Triple Pattern* $TTP = \{tp|tp$ is a triple pattern where the predicate pattern, pp, is $rdf:type$, $sp \in V$ and $op \in I\}$. (3) *Type Graph Pattern* $GP' = \{gp|gp$ is a graph pattern of form tp_1 AND tp_2 where $tp_1 \in TTP \wedge tp_2 \in TP' \wedge (tp_1.sp = tp_2.sp \vee tp_1.sp = tp_2.op)\}$.

2.3 Node Sanitization (SNode)

The purpose of the Sanitize Node operation is to sanitize and protect a sensitive node/resource. This can be accomplished in two ways. Firstly, by masking or protecting the identifying attributes (object values) such as name, SSN's, health insurance id's (datatype predicates), *etc.* of a sensitive resource (subject of a triple). An example SPARQL query Q1 to perform such data sanitization is shown below. Query Q1 takes a triple as input and sanitizes the object part of the triple. When Q1 is run on G_q, only one triple is sanitized and the remaining graph stays the same, *i.e.*, the query transforms the SSN (U.S. Social Security Number) value from "123-45-6789" to "XXX" as shown in Figure 2(a). If one needs to conceal all SSN values in G_q, one may use the variation of SNode shown in Q2, where the sensitive data item is depicted by TP'. However, if one needs to conceal SSN values of a class of individuals in G_q, such as Physicians, then one may use the variation of SNode shown in Q3. Secondly, we consider an interesting case for masking or protecting a node/IRI, for *e.g.*, "Hide all the secret service agents who worked on top secret missions". Similarly, in Q4 as well, we try to hide the node identified in association with or dependent on a sensitive resource (surgery, top secret mission, *etc.*), which itself need not be hidden. Further, one may wish to perform synchronization, *i.e.*, "not only hide the surgeon (agent) in the given triple but also in the remaining triples of the graph". This step however, is optional depending on the application requirements.

```
Q1: SANITIZE Gq WHEREs {SNode (Surgeon1 hasSSN "123-45-6789")}

Q2: SANITIZE Gq WHEREs {SNode (?s hasSSN ?o)}

Q3: SANITIZE Gq WHEREs {SNode (?s rdf:type Physician . ?s hasSSN ?o)}

Q4: SANITIZE Gq WHEREs {SNode (?s rdf:type Surgery . ?s wcb ?o)} SYNC
```

The Sanitization query form comprises a sanitize clause, a where clause and optionally a synchronization clause. The sanitize clause uses keyword SANITIZE and specifies the sensitive graph that needs to be sanitized. The where clause uses keyword WHEREs and is used to specify the sanitization operation being used and the pattern used to access the sensitive resource. The letter "s" at the end of the keyword WHEREs is shown in lower case for better readability and used to indicate that a sanitization where clause is different from the SPARQL where clause keyword. Synchronization represented by the keyword SYNC is used only for consistently masking nodes or IRI's as synchronization of literal values is not meaningful. If keyword SYNC is not present then no synchronization is performed. In the case of SNode there is only one possible meaning or default meaning of Synchronization, *i.e.*, synchronization of the object node(s).

The SNode operation is essentially used to hide the object portion of sensitive triples, for *e.g.*, SSN values, Secret

---

Algorithm 1 SNODE()
Input: Graph G_q, *Pattern P*, Boolean *Sync*

1: $sensitiveTrpls = \emptyset$, $sanitizedTrpls = \emptyset$, $nodeSet = \emptyset$,
   $map = \emptyset$, $G_s = \emptyset$
2: **if** P *is a triple t* **then**
3:     **if** $t \in G_q$ **then** $G_s = t$ **end if**
4: **else**
5:     **if** P *is* TP' *or* GP' **then** $G_s = eval(G_q, P)$ **end if**
       {G_s *is the result triple set from evaluation of P on* G_q}
6: **end if**
7: $G_q = G_q - G_s$
8: **for** $t \in G_s$ **do**
9:     **if** $map.contains(t.o)$ **then** $o' = map.get(t.o)$
       else $o' = genUniq(t.o)$ **end if**
10:     **if** $t.o \in I$ **then** $map.put(t.o, o')$; $nodeSet.add(t.o)$ **end if**
11:     $newTriple = createTriple(t.s, t.p, o')$
12:     $sanitizedTrpls+ = newTriple$
13: **end for**
14: **if** $Sync$ **then**
15:     **for** $n \in nodeSet$ **do**
16:         $G_n = $ triples in G_q containing n
17:         **for** $t \in G_n$ **do** $sensitiveTrpls+ = t$;
           $sanitizedTrpls+ = synchronizeTrpl(t, map)$ **end for**
18:     **end for**
19: **end if**
20: $G_q = G_q - sensitiveTrpls$; $G_q = G_q \cup sanitizedTrpls$

---

service agents, *etc.* As depicted by Algorithm 1, it takes as input the graph G_q, which needs to be sanitized before being shared with a user. In addition, it takes as input a *Pattern* denoted by P, which specifies the sensitive data item that needs to be protected. The final argument *Sync* is used as a flag to guide synchronization decision. The sensitive data item can be contained in a triple, or a set of triples represented by a predicate triple pattern TP' or a type graph pattern GP'. When the input *Pattern* is a *triple*, the algorithm replaces the object portion of the triple with a sanitized value. If the object is a resource, then the sanitized value is also a resource and further, if the object is a data value/literal then the sanitized value is also a literal. When the input *Pattern* is a predicate triple pattern or a type graph pattern, it is evaluated upon the input graph and the resulting subgraph triples are sanitized to protect their object values. The complexity of evaluating TP'/GP' is polynomial, as stated in [16], since only AND operation is involved and moreover, the number of triple patterns can be at most two. The result of evaluating TP'/GP' is a mapping set which can be converted into triples by appropriately substituting the input triple patterns. Note that, in case of GP' we obtain the result triple set by substituting the triple pattern other than type triple pattern.

The masking function $genUniq$ takes a resource or literal value as input and returns a unique sanitized value. However, depending on the application/privacy requirements one can override $genUniq$ with a suitable custom masking function. Our current implementation, supports other custom masking functions, for *e.g.*, a more appropriate sanitized value for SSN "123-45-6789" could be "XXX-XX-6789". However, a comprehensive coverage of such masking functions and their use has been left as a part of future work and we will continue to use masking function $genUniq$ in the rest of the paper. Further, map is a data structure that stores pairs comprising a sensitive data item and its corresponding sanitized value. The operation $createTriple$ creates a triple using the three input arguments. If the object of the triple is a resource, then it may be a part of other triples

(a) SNode

(b) SEdge

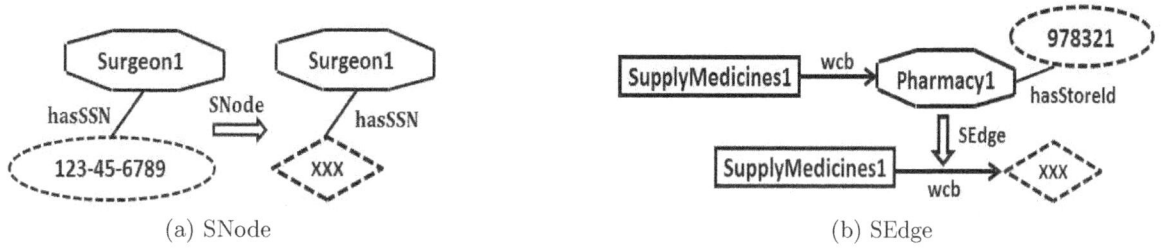

Figure 2: Sanitization Operations

as well. To sanitize such object resources (or perform synchronization), they are first collected in *nodeSet* (line 10) and then, all triples of G_q containing nodes from *nodeSet* are sanitized (lines 15 to 18). Synchronization is done when the boolean flag *Sync* is true (line 14) and it is performed using the function *synchronizeTrpl*, which takes a triple as input and updates the sensitive parts (only IRI's) of the triple with corresponding values from the *map* if any. Consequently, the overall complexity of the SNode algorithm is $O(n^2)$, where n is the number of triples in G_q. However, if the flag *Sync* is false then no synchronization is performed. Finally, a more sophisticated version of SNode, called Star, is presented in Appendix 9.2.

2.4 Edge Sanitization (SEdge)

This operation is designed to hide a relationship/link/edge between two nodes and alternatively to perform edge contraction, *i.e.*, to protect an edge along with its two nodes (where one of the nodes can be a data value). The example query Q5 using SEdge is illustrated with Figure 2(b).

```
Q5: SANITIZE Gq
    WHEREs {SEdge (Pharmacy1 hasStoreId 978321)} SYNC {Pharmacy1}

Q6: SANITIZE Gq
    WHEREs {SEdge (?s rdf:type Prescription . ?s hasPresId ?o)}
    SYNC{?s}
```

Algorithm 2 SEDGE()

Input: Graph G_q, *Pattern P*, Boolean *SyncSub*, *SyncObj*

1: $sensitiveTrpls = \emptyset, sanitizedTrpls = \emptyset, nodeSet = \emptyset,$
   $map = \emptyset, G_s = \emptyset$
2: **if** P *is a triple t* **then**
3:   **if** $t \in G_q$ **then** $G_s = t$ **end if**
4: **else**
5:   **if** P is TP' or GP' **then** $G_s = eval(G_q, P)$ **end if**
6: **end if**
7: $G_q = G_q - G_s$
8: **for** $t \in G_s$ **do**
9:   **if** $t.s \in I$ **then** $map.put(t.s, genUniq(t));$
      if $SyncSub$ **then** $nodeSet.add(t.s)$ **end if end if**
10:   **if** $t.o \in I$ **then** $map.put(t.o, genUniq(t));$
      if $SyncObj$ **then** $nodeSet.add(t.o)$ **end if end if**
11: **end for**
12: **if** $SyncSub \lor SyncObj$ **then**
13:   **for** $n \in nodeSet$ **do**
14:     G_n = triples in G_q containing n
15:     **for** $t \in G_n$ **do** $sensitiveTrpls+ = t;$
        $sanitizedTrpls+ = synchronizeTrpl(t, map)$ **end for**
16:   **end for**
17: **end if**
18: $G_q = G_q - sensitiveTrpls;$ $G_q = G_q \cup sanitizedTrpls$

Algorithm 2 takes as input G_q and pattern P containing the sensitive data item that needs to be protected, which can be

a triple or TP'/GP'. Additionally, it also takes boolean flags *SyncSub* and *SyncObj* which are used to determine the type of synchronization that needs to be performed. If one of the flags is true then only corresponding subject or object node of a sensitive edge are sanitized. However, if both the flags are true, then subject as well as the object node of a sensitive edge is sanitized. Since there are multiple ways in which synchronization can be performed in the case of SEdge, the appropriate arguments (variables) within the SYNC clause of the SANITIZE query form can be used to precisely state the type of synchronization desired. The default semantics of synchronization for SEdge operation is sanitization of both the nodes of the sensitive edge and is represented by keyword SYNC without any arguments. However, if synchronization clause is absent then no synchronization is performed.

When the input pattern P is TP' or GP', it is evaluated upon the input graph and the resulting subgraph triples need to be sanitized. This is the case in which one might want to sanitize a set of edges that connect subject or object resources belonging to some class. For example, Q6 tries to hide the edge or attribute hasPresId of the members of class Prescription and their respective values. The set G_s is computed in lines 2-6 in a similar manner as described in the SNode algorithm. Line number 7 accomplishes the task of hiding the link between the two nodes of a triple belonging to set G_s. Although the concrete triple is now deleted, the sensitive resources of the triple, its subject and object, may still be present as resources in other connected triples, *i.e.*, we may want to perform synchronization. For example, in Figure 2(b), there are two triples, SupplyMedicines1 wcb Pharmacy1 and Pharmacy1 hasStoreId 978321. The deletion of sensitive triple Pharmacy1 hasStoreId 978321, does not however, remove resource Pharmacy1 from the first triple: "SupplyMedicines1 wcb Pharmacy1". Now, it may be required by an application to sanitize all such connected triples (that contain the subject/object resource of t as their subject/object) by replacing the sensitive nodes with the corresponding sanitized value using the *map*, as shown in lines 13 to 16, which also leads to a $O(n^2)$ complexity of the algorithm (where $n = |G_q|$). The meaning of *genUniq* and *synchronizeTrpl* remains the same. Further, *map* stores the subject and object resources of a triple with their corresponding sanitized value (the hash value of the triple, which effectively results in edge contraction).

2.5 Path Sanitization (SPath)

The SPath operation is designed to protect a path containing multiple nodes connected by edges. Query Q7 using SPath hides the provenance of PatientFile4, which is expressed using the regular expression (PatientFile4 [wdf]+ ?o).

It is illustrated with Figure 1(b), which only shows the portion containing the sanitized subgraph as the remaining graph stays the same. The set of triples we get by evaluating the path pattern expression (PatientFile4 [wdf]+ ?o), on G_q, comprises three triples: PatientFile4 wdf Patient-File3, PatientFile3 wdf PatientFile2 and PatientFile2 wdf PatientFile1. Unlike SEdge, where we perform edge contraction, in SPath we simply replace each s, p and o value with it's corresponding sanitized value to preserve connectivity, provenance definition and directed acyclic graph property of the provenance RDF graph. Please note that the operations SNode, SEdge and SPath provide a variety of techniques for sanitizing a variety of sensitive data items and together they form a sanitization language with rich expressivity. The default semantics of synchronization for SPath is represented using keyword SYNC without any arguments and is performed by consistently sanitizing all the subject and object nodes of sensitive triples representing the path. Synchronization is not performed when the corresponding clause is absent. These are the only two possible synchronization semantics that have been provided for SPath.

Q7: SANITIZE Gq WHEREs { SPath (PatientFile4 [wdf]+ ?o)} SYNC

Algorithm 3 SPATH()

Input: Graph G_q, $PathPattern$ PP, Boolean $Sync$

1: $sensitiveTrpls=\emptyset$, $sanitizedTrpls=\emptyset$, $PathTrpls=\emptyset$, $nodeSet=\emptyset$, $map=\emptyset$, $setFoundTrpls=\emptyset$
2: $PathTrpls = eval(G_q, PP)$
3: **for** $t \in PathTrpls$ **do**
4:     **if** $map.contains(t.s)$ **then** $s' = map.get(t.s)$
        else $s' = genUniq(t.s)$ **end if**
5:     **if** $map.contains(t.p)$ **then** $p' = map.get(t.p)$
        else $p' = genUniq(t.p)$ **end if**
6:     **if** $map.contains(t.o)$ **then** $o' = map.get(t.o)$
        else $o' = genUniq(t.o)$ **end if**
7:     **if** $t.s \in I$ **then** $map.put(t.s, s')$; $nodeSet.add(t.s)$ **end if**
8:     **if** $t.o \in I$ **then** $map.put(t.o, o')$; $nodeSet.add(t.o)$ **end if**
9:     $sanitizedTrpls+ = createTriple(s', p', o')$
10:    $G_q = G_q - t$
11: **end for**
12: **if** $Sync$ **then**
13:     **for** $n \in nodeSet$ **do**
14:         $G_n = $ triples in G_q containing n
15:         **for** $t \in G_n$ **do** $sensitiveTrpls+ = t$;
            $sanitizedTrpls+ = synchronizeTrpl(t, map)$ **end for**
16:     **end for**
17: **end if**
18: $G_q = G_q - sensitiveTrpls$; $G_q = G_q \cup sanitizedTrpls$

The inputs to Algorithm 3 are graph G_q and a SPARQL $PathPattern$, PP and flag $Sync$. The aim of this algorithm is to firstly, identify the sensitive data item, which is a path or subgraph (in this case). The triples comprising the sensitive subgraph are evaluated in line 2, and deleted from the graph in line 10. Secondly, the algorithm stores pairs of original and corresponding sanitized resources in a map (lines 4, 5 and 6). The mapping helps one to perform consistent sanitization. A sanitized triple is constructed from the sanitized values of the original resources, s, p and o of the sensitive triple (line 9). Next, we perform synchronization in lines 13 to 16, which is again optional depending on whether the flag $Sync$ is true or not. Finally, we delete the sensitive triples from G_q and add the sanitized triples to it (line 18). The overall complexity of this algorithm depends on the evaluation of a path pattern (done by function $eval$), which is shown to be intractable [17].

3. DENOTATIONAL SEMANTICS FOR SANITIZATION OPERATIONS

Pérez *et al.* provided set-based denotational semantics for the core set of SPARQL operations in [16], which was later adapted by the W3C standard specification of SPARQL [12]. We further extend SPARQL by providing denotational semantics for the sanitization operations. Denotational semantics is compositional, *i.e.*, the meaning of an expression can be derived from the meaning of its subexpressions. It is given in terms of, abstract syntax definition of the language, semantic algebras and the valuation functions. In the following, we give a brief introduction to denotational semantics, a detailed exposition of which can be found in [18]. We assume the reader is familiar with the compositional semantics of SPARQL [16].

- **Abstract Syntax** is specified as BNF grammar. A Syntax domain denotes a collection of values with common syntactic structure.

- **Semantic Algebra** consists of a semantic domain accompanied by a set of operations. The operations are given in terms of the following parameters: (i) **Functionality** of a function $f : D_1 \times D_2 \times \cdots \times D_n \to A$, implies f needs an argument from each domain $D_1, D_2, \cdots, D_n$ to produce an answer belonging to domain A. (ii) **Description** is generally given as an equational definition.

- **Valuation Function** maps elements of syntax domain to elements of semantic domain.

Note: (1) In the following, we use compound domains known as disjoint union, tagged union or sum. It is a form of union construction on sets that keeps the members of the respective sets R and S separate: $R + S = \{(zero, x)|~x \in R\} \cup \{(one, y)|~y \in S\}$. (2) The cases operation for $m \in R+ S$ is defined as follows: cases (m) of $isR(x) \to ..x..|~isS(y) \to ..y..$, which should be read as "if m is an element whose tag component is R and value component is x, then the answer is $..x..$ else if the tag component is S and the value component is y then the answer is $..y..$".

We now describe the denotational semantics for SPARQL sanitization operations. The Abstract Syntax, shown in Figure 3(a), is given in terms of syntax domains and BNF rules. The phrase $SExpr \in SanitizeOpExp$ indicates that $SanitizeOpExp$ is a syntax domain and $SExpr$ is a nonterminal that represents an arbitrary member of the domain. The meaning of the other phrase can be inferred similarly. The first BNF rule states that a sanitization query expression ($SExpr$) can be one of the three possible kinds, namely, $SNode$, $SEdge$ or $SPath$. The second rule states that a $Pattern$ can be a $Triple$ or TP' or GP'. We then present semantic algebras for semantic domains $TRIPLE$, MAP and $GRAPH$ in Figure 3(b). *Assumptions:* We use set semantics instead of bag semantics. Further, we present denotational semantics assuming the default synchronization semantics for SNode, SEdge and SPath operations. These simplifications make the exposition more comprehensible without compromising the core complexity of the problem.

The operation $updateObj$ is defined over the semantic domain $TRIPLE$, which takes a triple and a resource/value as inputs and retains the first and second elements of the triple, represented by $t.s$ and $t.p$, as they are and replaces the triple's object with the resource/value. Note that, we will subsequently interpret the set union symbol $\cup$ of the semantic domain $TRIPLE$ as disjoint union.

3(a) Abstract Syntax	
Syntax Domain:	$SExpr \in SanitizeOpExp, Pattern \in PatternExp$
BNF Rules:	$SExpr ::= SNode\ Pattern \mid SEdge\ Pattern \mid SPath\ PP$
	$Pattern ::= Triple \mid TP' \mid TTP\ AND\ TP'$

3(b) Semantic Algebras for TRIPLE, MAP and GRAPH

$Semantic\ Domain:\ TRIPLE = (I \cup B) \times I \times (I \cup B \cup L)$

$Operations:\ updateObj : TRIPLE \times (I \cup L) \to TRIPLE$
$\textbf{updateObj}(t, r) = (t.s, t.p, r)$

$Semantic\ Domain:\ MAP = I \to I$

$Operations:\ newmap : MAP$ a newmap is an empty map, which maps all index arguments to null/error
$access : I \times MAP \to I\ \textbf{access}(i, m) = m(i)$
$genMap : (I + \mathcal{P}(I)) \to MAP$
$\textbf{genMap}(r) = cases(r)\ of$
$isI(i) \to \{(i, i') \mid i' = genUniq(i)\} \mid is(\mathcal{P}(I))(S) \to \{(i, i') \mid i \in S\ \wedge i' = genUniq(i)\}$

$Semantic\ Domain:\ GRAPH = \{x \mid x\ is\ TRIPLE\}$

$Operations:$

$union, diff : GRAPH \times GRAPH \to GRAPH$	$maskSPO : GRAPH \to GRAPH$
$\textbf{union}(g_1, g_2) = \{t \mid t \in g_1 \vee t \in g_2\}$	$\textbf{maskSPO}(g) = \{(s, p, o) \mid t \in g \wedge (s = genUniq(t.s)$
$\textbf{diff}(g_1, g_2) = \{t \mid t \in g_1 \wedge t \notin g_2\}$	$\wedge\ p = genUniq(t.p) \wedge o = genUniq(t.o))\}$

$getGraph : \Omega \times TP' \to GRAPH$	$genSO : GRAPH \to \mathcal{P}(I)$
$\textbf{getGraph}(\Omega_s, tp) = \{\mu(tp) \mid \mu \in \Omega_s\}$	$\textbf{genSO}(g) = \{n \mid t \in g \wedge n \in I \wedge (n = t.s \vee n = t.o)\}$

$sensitive : GRAPH \times (I + \mathcal{P}(I)) \to GRAPH$
$\textbf{sensitive}(g, r) = cases(r)\ of\ isI(i) \to \{t \mid t \in g \wedge (t.s = i \vee t.p = i \vee t.o = i)\}$
$\mid is(\mathcal{P}(I))(R) \to \{t \mid t \in g \wedge (t.s \in R \vee t.p \in R \vee t.o \in R)\}$

$sanitize : GRAPH \times (I + \mathcal{P}(I)) \times MAP \to GRAPH$
$\textbf{sanitize}(g, r, m) = cases(r)\ of$
$isI(i) \to \{(t.s, t.p, t.o) \mid t \in g \wedge (if\ t.s = i\ then\ t.s = m(t.s))$
$\wedge (if\ t.p = i\ then\ t.p = m(t.p)) \wedge (if\ t.o = i\ then\ t.o = m(t.o))\} \mid$
$is(\mathcal{P}(I))(R) \to \{(t.s, t.p, t.o) \mid t \in g \wedge (if\ t.s \in R\ then\ t.s = m(t.s))$
$\wedge (if\ t.p \in R\ then\ t.p = m(t.p)) \wedge (if\ t.o \in R\ then\ t.o = m(t.o))\}$

$sNode : GRAPH \times (TRIPLE + GRAPH) \to GRAPH$
$\textbf{sNode}(g, r) = cases(r)\ of$
$\textbf{isTRIPLE(t)} \to (cases(t.o)\ of$
$isL(o) \to Let\ t' = updateObj(t, genUniq(t.o))\ in\ union(diff(g, \{t\}), \{t'\}) \mid$
$isI(o) \to Let\ g_s = sensitive(g, t.o) \wedge m = genMap(t.o)\ in\ union(diff(g, g_s), sanitize(g_s, t.o, m)))$
$\mid \textbf{isGRAPH(gx)} \to Let\ t \in gx,\ gx' = diff(gx, \{t\}),\ g' = sNode(g, t)\ in\ sNode(g', gx')$

$sEdge : GRAPH \times (TRIPLE + GRAPH) \to GRAPH$
$\textbf{sEdge}(g, r) = cases(r)\ of$
$\textbf{isTRIPLE(t)} \to (cases(t.o)\ of$
$isL(o) \to (Let\ g' = diff(g, \{t\})$
$in\ (Let\ g_s = sensitive(g', t.s)\ and\ m = genMap(t.s)\ in\ union(diff(g', g_s), sanitize(g_s, t.s, m)))) \mid$
$isI(o) \to (Let\ g' = diff(g, \{t\})\ and\ nl = \{t.s, t.o\}$
$in\ (Let\ g_s = sensitive(g', nl)\ and\ m = genMap(nl)\ in\ union(diff(g', g_s), sanitize(g_s, nl, m)))))$
$\mid \textbf{isGRAPH(gx)} \to Let\ t \in gx,\ gx' = diff(gx, \{t\}),\ g' = sEdge(g, t)\ in\ sEdge(g', gx')$

$sPath : GRAPH \times GRAPH \to GRAPH$
$\textbf{sPath}(g, gx) = Let\ g' = diff(g, gx)\ and\ ml = genSO(gx)\ and\ gx' = maskSPO(gx)\ in$
$Let\ g_s = sensitive(g', ml)\ and\ m_1 = genMap(ml)\ in$
$union(diff(g', g_s), union(sanitize(g_s, ml, m_1), gx'))$

3(c) Valuation Functions	
S:	$SanitizeOpExp \times GRAPH \to (TRIPLE \cup GRAPH)$
	$\mathbf{S}[\![SNode\ Pattern]\!](G) = sNode(G, \mathbf{P}[\![Pattern]\!](G))$
	$\mathbf{S}[\![SEdge\ Pattern]\!](G) = sEdge(G, \mathbf{P}[\![Pattern]\!](G))$
	$\mathbf{S}[\![SPath\ PP]\!](G) = sPath(G, pathSubGraph([\![PP]\!]_G, PP))$
P:	$PatternExp \times GRAPH \to (TRIPLE \cup GRAPH)$
	$\mathbf{P}[\![Triple]\!](G) = Triple$
	$\mathbf{P}[\![TP']\!](G) = getGraph([\![TP']\!]_G, TP')$
	$\mathbf{P}[\![TTP\ AND\ TP']\!](G) = getGraph([\![TTP]\!]_G \bowtie [\![TP']\!]_G, TP')$

Figure 3: Denotational Semantics for Sanitization Operations

The semantic domain MAP uses elements of set I as an index to access its contents. It is a function that maps elements of I to unique elements of set I, where these elements are the sanitized versions of the original resources. The operation $access$ fetches the value stored in map m for element i and is denoted by $m(i)$. The operation $genMap$ takes as argument an element that is either from domain I or from power set of I denoted by $\mathcal{P}(I)$ and returns a corresponding MAP. If the input argument is a resource i, it returns a MAP in which i is paired with unique sanitized value i', which is generated by function $genUniq$. However, if the input argument is a subset of I, then the function returns a MAP comprising pairs of resources belonging to the subset along with their sanitized values generated by $genUniq$. The operation $sanitize$, sanitizes the triples in the input graph (g) by first checking whether any of its components (s, p, o) match with the sensitive input resource (r) and if it does match then it is updated using the corresponding sanitized value from the map (m). The function $maskSPO$ masks all the three components of a triple belonging to the input graph by replacing them with unique values generated by $genUniq$.

The operation SNode is defined based on two cases namely, base case and recursive case, which in turn are based on the input data item being sanitized. When the input data item to be sanitized is a triple then two sub cases follow from this base case, which depend on whether the object of the triple is a literal or an IRI. When the object is a literal the original triple is deleted from the graph and a sanitized version is added to the graph in replacement. However, when the object value is an IRI then the sensitive triples are computed, which are those that contain the IRI. These triples are deleted from the original graph and a sanitized version of them is added back to the remaining graph. The recursive case is defined for an input of type graph in contrast to the base case where the input was a triple. In the recursive case the triples belonging to gx need to be sanitized. A triple t is selected from set gx and sanitized within graph g to obtain g'. Then the triple is deleted from gx and gx' is obtained. Finally, a recursive call to $sNode$ is made using inputs gx' and g'. The semantics of operations $sNode$, $sEdge$ and $sPath$ are self-explanatory and similar to algorithms 1, 2 and 3 respectively.

Figure 3(c) gives a valuation function for each syntax domain along with a set of equations, one per option of the corresponding BNF rule for that domain. The domain of valuation function is the set of derivation trees of a language. The meaning of a derivation tree is determined by determining the meaning of the subtrees. For example, the functionality for S states that, S takes a member of the syntax domain $SanitizeOpExp$ and a graph (sensitive graph) as input and returns a graph (sanitized graph) as output. The semantics of $[\![TTP]\!]_G \bowtie [\![TP']\!]_G$ is the same as defined in [16], thus leveraging the compositional nature of denotational semantics. Similarly, the semantics for $[\![PP]\!]_G$ has been adapted from [12]. The function $pathSubGraph$, like function $getGraph$ renders the output of $[\![PP]\!]_G$ as a set of triples (graph).

4. PROTOTYPE ARCHITECTURE AND EXPERIMENTAL EVALUATION

In this section, we present a prototype system architecture, shown in Figure 5. A querying user submits a SPARQL

```
q)  SELECT ?n ?o ?e
    WHERE { ?s hasName ?n. ?s hasSSN ?o . ?s hasEmail ?e}

q') CONSTRUCT {?s hasName ?n. ?s hasSSN ?o . ?s hasEmail ?e}
    WHERE {?s hasName ?n. ?s hasSSN ?o . ?s hasEmail ?e}
```

Figure 4: User query and it's Construct query

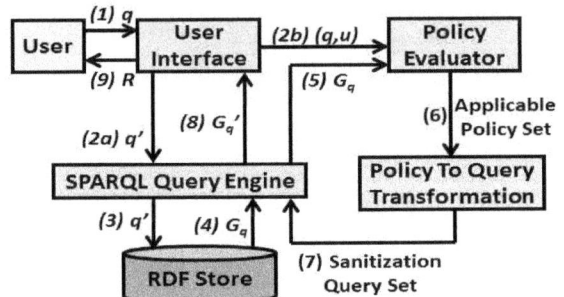

Figure 5: Prototype System Architecture

query to the user interface. The user interface first transforms the query into an appropriate construct query, q', and forwards it to the SPARQL query engine and also forwards the query q along with the user information to the policy evaluator as depicted by the arrow labeled (2b). The construct query q' is used in order to obtain the subgraph that is being accessed by the user, which we will refer to as Graph Of Interest (GOI). It is obtained using the construct query by instantiating the original query's triple patterns as illustrated in Figure 4. Once the SPARQL query engine receives the query q', it performs computation on the RDF store and returns the resulting subgraph G_q (the GOI) to the policy evaluator depicted by the arrow labeled (5). The policy evaluator now computes a set of applicable policies from the original policy set based on the three aforementioned inputs it receives (steps 2b and 5). Subsequently, the policies are parsed and transformed into corresponding SPARQL sanitization queries such as SNode, SEgde and SPath. Once the list of sanitization queries is obtained, we then apply them on to the RDF graph and return the sanitized graph to the user interface. We now apply the user query q to G_q' (sanitized GOI) and return the result (R) to the user.

In the case of healthcare provenance scenario, a querying user can be an insurance agent, researcher conducting epidemic studies or someone who may want to publish the data online. The policy author needs to carefully author policies to protect sensitive patient information. The policy language we use is a modification of the XML-based language proposed in [19]. A sample policy that uses this language to protect SSN values of all individuals is given in Figure 6, along with its translation to equivalent sanitization query. The tag $target$ is used to specify the set of users and data items (belonging to given datasets) to which the policy is applicable. The tag, $operationType$, specifies the type of sanitization operation that is needed to protect the sensitive data item. The tag, $sanitizationPatterns$, specifies the sensitive data item, expressed in the form of a triple pattern or graph pattern. The tag $effect$ specifies the intended consequence of a policy when it evaluates to true. We now

172

```
<policy id="1125">
 <target>
   <user>Insurance Agent</user>
   <dataSet>Gq</dataSet>
   <operationType>SNode</operationType>
   <sanitizationPatterns><pattern>
     <s>?s</s>
     <p>hasSSN</p>
     <o>?o</o>
   </pattern></sanitizationPatterns>
 </target>
 <effect>deny</effect>
</policy>


SANITIZE Gq WHEREs {SNode (?s hasSSN ?o)}
```

Figure 6: Example Policy and Equivalent Query

Dataset	Healthcare ($\approx$ 1K)	Twitter ($\approx$ 3M)	SEC ($\approx$ 1.8M)
Nodes	297	1705116	866627
Edges	979	2850579	1813175
Predicates	50	52	16

Figure 7: Experimental Datasets

present the results of an experiment that was conducted to validate the effectiveness of the sanitization algorithms.

Experimental Setup: We conducted the experiment using an Intel Core i7 3610QM Processor with a 750GB hard drive and 8GB main memory. Further, JRE v1.7.0_21 as the Java engine and Jena v2.10.0, ARQ v2.10.0 and Gleen v0.6.1 were used for development of the experimental code.

Experimental Datasets and Queries: The sanitization algorithms we described earlier are equally applicable to graphs generated by processing user queries and for those representing entire datasets that need to be published online. To demonstrate this notion, we performed the experiment using the following datasets: (i) **Healthcare Scenario**: We used six variants of the healthcare scenario presented earlier, each containing between $\approx$ 600-1000 triples. This dataset captures the applicability of the sanitization algorithms to query result graphs. (ii) **Twitter**: We used five variants of a Twitter subgraph containing between $\approx$ 3000-7500 users ($\approx$ 1M-3M triples). (iii) **U.S. Securities and Exchange Commission (SEC)**: We used five variants of the SEC RDF dataset[1] containing between $\approx$ 600K-1.8M triples. Datasets (ii) and (iii) capture the applicability of the sanitization algorithms to graphs representing entire datasets. Figure 7 shows the composition of each dataset, where the value in parentheses denotes the size of the largest variant of that dataset. Table 2 lists the queries that were executed on the corresponding datasets for evaluation. Note that, G_q denotes the particular dataset variant used for query evaluation, while "Affected Triples" denotes the number of triples that were sanitized or synchronized as a part of the given operation for the largest variant of the dataset. As one can observe, a larger number of affected triples entails a longer sanitization time (Figure 8).

Experiment with varying dataset sizes: The goal of this experiment was to measure the performance, in terms of overall sanitization time, of the different sanitization op-

---

[1]http://www.rdfabout.com/demo/sec/

Table 2: Queries used in Experimental Evaluation

Dataset	Queries	Affected Triples
Health care	SANITIZE G_q WHEREs { SNode(?s hasHealthcareId ?o) }	1
	SANITIZE G_q WHEREs { SEdge(?s type Patient . ?s hasSSN ?p) }	16
	SANITIZE G_q WHEREs { SPath(Prescription1Filled "[wgb]/[wcb]" ?o) }	20
Twitter	SANITIZE G_q WHEREs { SNode(?s Twitter_Id ?o) }	7286
	SANITIZE G_q WHEREs { SEdge(?s Tweet_Text ?o) }	37300
	SANITIZE G_q WHEREs { SPath(User63752681 "[Has_Tweet]/ [Reply_To_User]" ?o) }	92
SEC	SANITIZE G_q WHEREs { SNode(?s name ?o) }	144179
	SANITIZE G_q WHEREs { SEdge(?s Street ?p) }	529176
	SANITIZE G_q WHEREs { SPath(?s "[hasRelation]/[type]" TenPercentOwnerRelation) }	202283

erations when applied to increasing dataset sizes. As shown in Figure 8, the time to execute the operations increases as dataset size increases. An operation with limited scope, *viz.* SNode, requires a shorter execution time when compared with complex operations such as SEdge and SPath. The sanitization time depends on many factors such as dataset size, number of affected triples, triple store implementation, connectivity of a node, *etc.* In conclusion, the sanitization overhead is reasonable for it to be used in practice.

5. RELATED WORK

In [20], the authors address the problem of RDF data sanitization. This work essentially tries to address - what data needs to be sanitized? and proposes a solution based on the open world assumption. In contrast, our work addresses the problem of how to perform sanitization and thus complements the work done in [20]. A SPARQL update language is presented in [12] and [21], and further, [21] also provides operational semantics. In contrast, we present a language that not only allows updates but also consistent sanitization or synchronization. We also present denotational semantics, which blends well with the existing compositional semantics of SPARQL. In [22], authors presented a graph grammar based approach to secure RDF-based provenance data by performing redaction. However, the redaction mechanism was built at the application level and addressed only OPM-based provenance graphs. Additionally, the user is required to manually suggest a replacement resource and embedding connections. Since the number of resources in a provenance (or RDF) graph is exponential in the number of nodes [19], the manual embedding procedure is limited and not scalable. The approach presented in this paper overcomes this shortcoming by providing masking function *genUniq*, which

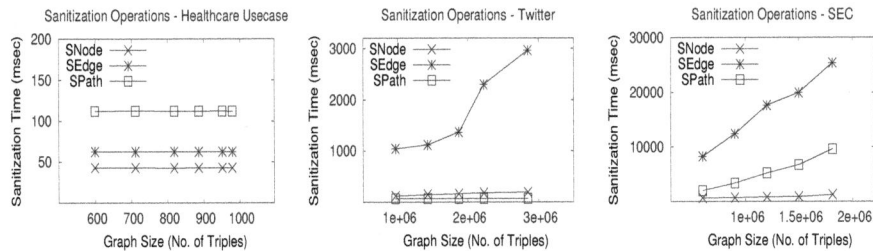

Figure 8: Performance of various types of sanitization operations on different datasets

enables automatic generation of a replacement, and a *map* data structure that enables consistent automatic embedding or synchronization of the replacement resource within the remaining graph. Additionally, our sanitization mechanism, which is built at the query language level, is general and applicable to any domain including OPM-based provenance data. More precisely, it is the first of its kind to address general purpose RDF sanitization, which primarily uses graph transformation to selectively mask sensitive data, thus enabling fine-grained RDF access control.

6. CONCLUSIONS

In this paper, we made an initial attempt to provide a fundamental, formal framework for securing RDF graphs through a set of sanitization operations. These graph transformation operations are built as an extension to the SPARQL query language as a new query form called SANITIZE. As a result, any system with RDF data, can build more sophisticated security, privacy and anonymization features using it. SPARQL Sanitize provides a valuable layer of security, which not only promotes integration of RDF datasets but also makes it practical and takes Semantic Web a step closer towards the vision of a global database. We illustrated the utility of our approach with a healthcare provenance scenario and showed how one can secure the data using the sanitization infrastructure provided by us. As a part of the future work, we would like to further fine tune the sanitization operations with pluggable masking routines to maintain a greater amount of control over data exposure and in turn meet a broad range of application requirements.

7. ACKNOWLEDGMENTS

This work was partially supported by National Institutes of Health Grants 1R0-1LM009989 and 1R01HG006844, National Science Foundation (NSF) Grants Career-CNS-0845803, CNS-0964350, CNS-1016343, CNS-1111529, CNS-1228198 and Army Research Office Grant W911NF-12-1-0558.

8. REFERENCES

[1] S. Chaudhuri, R. Kaushik, and R. Ramamurthy. Database Access Control and Privacy: Is there a common ground? In *CIDR*, 2011.

[2] R. S. Sandhu, E. J. Coyne, H. L. Feinstein, and C. E. Youman. Role-Based Access Control Models. *Computer*, 29(2):38–47, February 1996.

[3] S. Jajodia, P. Samarati, M. L. Sapino, and V. S. Subrahmanian. Flexible support for multiple access control policies. *ACM Trans. Database Syst.*, 26(2), 2001.

[4] M. Bishop. *Introduction to Computer Security*. Addison-Wesley Professional, 2004.

[5] L. Sweeney. *k*-anonymity: A model for protecting privacy. *International Journal of Uncertainty, Fuzziness and Knowledge-Based Systems*, 10(05):557–570, 2002.

[6] C. Dwork. Differential privacy. *Automata, languages and programming*, 2006.

[7] Oracle. Fine-Grained Access Control for RDF Data. http://goo.gl/WJSNB.

[8] L. Kagal, T. W. Finin, and A. Joshi. A Policy Based Approach to Security for the Semantic Web. In *ISWC*, 2003.

[9] T. W. Finin, A. Joshi, L. Kagal, J. Niu, R. S. Sandhu, W. H. Winsborough, and B. M. Thuraisingham. R*OWLBAC*: Representing Role Based Access Control in *OWL*. In *SACMAT*, 2008.

[10] J. Hollenbach, J. Presbrey, and T. Berners-Lee. Using RDF Metadata To Enable Access Control on the Social Semantic Web. In *CK2009*, volume 514, 2009.

[11] B. Carminati, E. Ferrari, R. Heatherly, M. Kantarcioglu, and B. Thuraisingham. A semantic web based framework for social network access control. In *SACMAT*, 2009.

[12] S. H. Garlik, A. Seaborne, and E. Prud'hommeaux. SPARQL 1.1 Query Language. http://www.w3.org/TR/sparql11-query/.

[13] O. Lassila, R. R. Swick, and World Wide Web Consortium. Resource Description Framework (RDF) Model and Syntax Specification, 1998.

[14] L. Moreau, B. Clifford, and J. Freire *et. al.* The Open Provenance Model core specification (v1.1). *Future Generation Computer Systems (FGCS)*, 27, 2011.

[15] O. Hartig and J. Zhao. Provenance Vocabulary Core Ontology Specification, 2010.

[16] J. Pérez, M. Arenas, and C. Gutierrez. Semantics and Complexity of SPARQL. In *ISWC*, 2006.

[17] M. Arenas, S. Conca, and J. Pérez. Counting beyond a Yottabyte, or how SPARQL 1.1 property paths will prevent adoption of the standard. In *WWW*, 2012.

[18] D. A. Schmidt. *Denotational semantics: A methodology for language development*. William C. Brown Publishers, Dubuque, IA, USA, 1986.

[19] T. Cadenhead, V. Khadilkar, M. Kantarcioglu, and B. Thuraisingham. A Language for Provenance Access Control. In *CODASPY*. ACM, 2011.

[20] M. Bishop, J. Cummins, S. Peisert, A. Singh, B. Bhumiratana, and D. A. Agarwal. Relationships and Data Sanitization: A Study in Scarlet. In *NSPW*, 2010.

[21] R. Horne, V. Sassone, and N. Gibbins. Operational Semantics for SPARQL Update. In *JIST*, 2011.

[22] T. Cadenhead, V. Khadilkar, M. Kantarcioglu, and B. Thuraisingham. Transforming Provenance using Redaction. In *SACMAT*, 2011.

9. APPENDIX

9.1 SPARQL UPDATE vs SANITIZE

The intent of the SPARQL UPDATE operation as its name suggests is to refresh the truth value, and is designed for that purpose by using Insertion and/or Deletion. It is possible to perform updates manually as the new value to update with is available. However, when one needs to conceal large amounts of sensitive data, the following questions arise - What should be the replacement value(s)? How to manage the magnitude (possibly millions) of replacements manually? How to preserve consistency or perform synchronization? How to perform updates securely with minimal manual intervention? As the number of replacements can be significant, the manual replacement strategy will neither scale nor be secure. Further, the semantics of the CONSTRUCT clause is to construct a new graph based on certain constraints, whereas the semantics of SANITIZE is to modify a given graph. Unlike CONSTRUCT operation, it does not return a graph. Since the intent of our sanitization operations is to secure and protect sensitive or identifying information in RDF graphs, it is designed accordingly with automatic masking and synchronization. None of the functionality offered by SPARQL shares the same intent, and is therefore not specifically designed or suitable for it. We do not want to extend or modify the existing operators/constructs as we do not want to alter their original semantics and overload them with this new functionality.

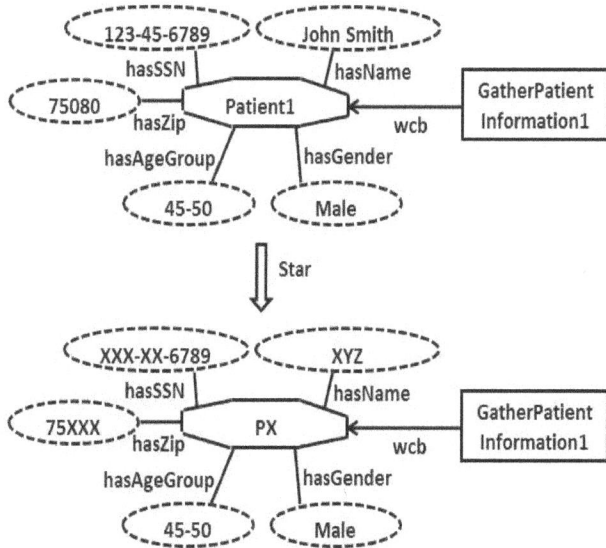

Figure 9: Star Sanitization Operation

9.2 Sanitize Node with identifying attributes

We now present a more sophisticated version of SNode operation and refer to it as the Star operation. The operation is named Star as the pictorial representation of a node and the set of identifying attributes represents a star shape. The intent of the Star operation is to mask a set of identifying attributes of a node or to mask a node along with its identifying attributes. For *e.g.*, one may want to hide identifying attributes such as SSN, Name, Employee ID (eid),

etc., of persons of type physician. Query Q8, describes the use of Star operation to perform sanitization. Unlike the previous sanitization operations, the Star operation takes two sets of arguments. The LHS set of arguments can be one among the following: *Null, TTP, TP', GP'*. The triple patterns used in the LHS enable one to identify the sensitive node/IRI that we need to access. The RHS of the Star operation comprises a list. The head of the list is either a node/IRI (for *e.g.* Patient1) or a variable (for *e.g.* ?s) representing a set of IRI's. The rest of the list is the set of attributes or datatype predicates whose value needs to be masked for the given node (head of RHS list). The example query Q8 sanitizes the attribute values SSN, Name and Id of all physicians.

```
Q8:  SANITIZE Gq
     WHEREs {(?s type Physician) Star (?s hasSSN hasName hasId)}

Q9:  SANITIZE Gq
     WHEREs {Star (Patient1 hasSSN hasName hasZip)} SYNC{Patient1}

Q10: SANITIZE Gq
     WHEREs {(?s hasSSN ?o) Star (?s hasSSN hasName)}

Q11: SANITIZE Gq
     WHEREs {(?s type Surgery . ?s wcb ?o) Star (?o hasSSN hasName)}
     SYNC  {?o}
```

Algorithm 4 STAR()

Input: Graph G_q, *Pattern lhs*, List *rhs*, Boolean *Sync*

1: $sensitiveTrpls = \emptyset, sanitizedTrpls = \emptyset, map = \emptyset, nodeSet = \emptyset$

2: $nodeSet = getNodeSet(Gq, lhs, rhs.head)$ {*sensitive node set computed using access pattern lhs and head of the list rhs*}

3: **for** $n \in nodeSet$ **do**
4:   $sensitiveTrpls =$ set of triples containing n from G_q
5:   $sensitiveTrpls1 = \emptyset; sensitiveTrpls2 = \emptyset$
6:   **for** $t \in sensitiveTrpls$ **do**
7:     **if** $t.s == n \wedge rhs.contains(t.p)$ **then**
8:       $sensitiveTrpls1 + = t$ {Triples containing n and a predicate from rhs}
9:     **else** $sensitiveTrpls2 + = t$ {Other triples containing n}
10:   **end for**
11:   $s' = genUniq(n); map.put(n, s')$
12:   **for** $t \in sensitiveTrpls1$ **do**
13:     $o' = genUniq(t.o)$
14:     **if** $Sync$ **then**
15:       $newTriple = createTriple(s', t.p, o')$
16:       $sanitizedTrpls + = newTriple$
17:     **else** $newTriple = createTriple(t.s, t.p, o')$
18:       $sanitizedTrpls + = newTriple$ **end if**
19:   **end for**
20:   **if** $Sync$ **then**
21:     **for** $t \in sensitiveTrpls2$ **do**
22:       $sanitizedTrpls + = synchronizeTrpl(t, map)$
23:     **end for**
24:   **end if**
25: **end for**
26: $G_q = G_q - sensitiveTrpls; G_q = G_q \cup sanitizedTrpls$

We now illustrate other ways of employing the Star operation. If we know a specific node/IRI whose attributes we want to sanitize then we do not need an access pattern on the LHS. Query Q9, shown in Figure 9, is used to sanitize Patient1 along with the identifying attributes such as SSN, Name and Zip. The node, Patient1, is consistently sanitized (or synchronized) using the synchronization clause. In Q10, we identify a set of nodes or IRI's using *TTP*. The set of sensitive nodes whose attributes need to be masked can easily be computed using *TTP* and the first element of RHS list. Once the set of sensitive nodes has been computed we then sanitize them along with their identifying attribute values (SSN, Name). Query Q11 is more expressive as it uses GP' as the access pattern on the LHS to identify the set of sensitive resources which need to be sanitized along with the attribute values. The query masks surgeons, who have performed surgeries, along with attributes SSN and Name. The semantics of synchronization for the Star operation is as follows: If the synchronization clause is absent then only identifying attributes of a node are hidden. However, if the synchronization clause is present then it must specify the Node/IRI/Variable as an argument to the keyword SYNC. In this case, the sensitive node is consistently sanitized along with the sensitive identifying attributes as shown in Figure 9.

Algorithm 4, takes as input, G_q, an access pattern lhs, a list rhs and boolean flag $Sync$. It first computes the set of sensitive nodes in line 2 and stores it in $nodeSet$. Next, we iterate over the nodes in $nodeSet$ and compute two sets of sensitive triples, namely $sensitiveTrpls1$ and $sensitiveTrpls2$, which contain triples containing node n and a predicate present in list rhs and triples containing n and a predicate not present in list rhs respectively (lines 8 and 9). The triples of set $sensitiveTrpls1$ are sanitized by masking the subject as well as object values (lines 15-16) if the $Sync$ flag is true, otherwise only the object values are sanitized (lines 17-18). If $Sync$ is true then synchronization is also performed on triples belonging to $sensitiveTrpls2$ (lines 20-24).

Redaction based RDF Access Control Language

Jyothsna Rachapalli, Vaibhav Khadilkar, Murat Kantarcioglu, Bhavani Thuraisingham
The University of Texas at Dallas
Richardson, Texas, USA
{jxr061100, vvk072000, muratk, bxt043000}@utdallas.edu

ABSTRACT

We propose an access control language for securing RDF graphs which essentially leverages an underlying query language based redaction mechanism to provide fine grained RDF access control. The access control language presented is equipped with critical features such as policy resolution and cascading policies that are essential for fine grained RDF access control. We present the architecture of our system which primarily features a flexible, scalable and general purpose RDF access control mechanism.

Categories and Subject Descriptors

D.3.3 [**Programming Languages**]: Language Constructs and Features; D.4.6 [**Operating Systems**]: Security and Protection—*Access Control*

Keywords

Access Control; RDF; SPARQL; Redaction

1. INTRODUCTION

Semantic Web builds on the Resource Description Framework (RDF), which provides a common framework that allows data to be shared and reused across application, enterprise, and community boundaries. Although RDF is specifically designed for data sharing and integration, there is no agreed upon standard for securely sharing data. The problem of data security is well researched in the database community, which can generally be classified into access control, data privacy, differential privacy *etc*. Although there has been work on securing RDF graphs using policy based access control mechanisms and view based security mechanisms [1], these techniques are not flexible enough to provide fine grained access control.

In the following, we describe the main challenges involved in the process of securing RDF data. RDF, which is a graph data model, is made up of triples of form (s,p,o). An RDF graph is a knowledge graph, which is an expressive encoding

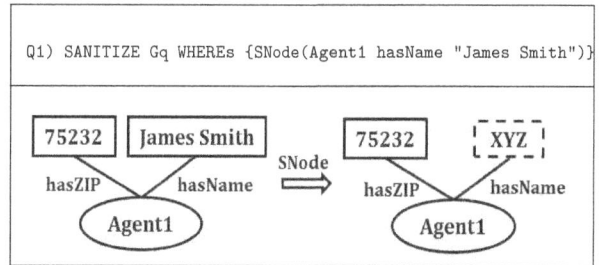

Figure 1: Sanitization Query Illustration

or conceptualization of the real world. Therefore, in comparison with RDBMS, which is based on relational model, it is not as straightforward to identify, isolate or mask sensitive information from the remaining information, *i.e.*, the process of subgraph (view) extraction is not viable. Moreover, a view based approach is not scalable when the number of users is large as this entails creation of larger number of views. The sensitive data item within an RDF graph can be in a variety of forms such as, an IRI, a link between two IRIs, a subgraph comprising sensitive triples, *etc.* SPARQL is an expressive query language and can be used to access a variety of data items. In order to secure access to RDF data, a critical requirement is to rewrite or transform the graph by removing or masking the sensitive data contained within it. We therefore presented a set of RDF graph sanitization operations which are built as an extension to the SPARQL query language in [2, 3]. We use the sanitization operations as a stepping stone towards fine grained RDF access control which provides the desired flexibility.

2. AN RDF ACCESS CONTROL LANGUAGE

In this section, we describe the details of the RDF access control policy language. However, since this language leverages underlying SPARQL based redaction mechanism (we use the terms redaction and sanitization interchangeably), we first provide a brief summary of the sanitization operations presented in [2, 3]. RDF is a graph data model and therefore, sensitive information can be contained as various components within the graph such as, literal values or nodes, edges or links, subgraph or paths, *etc.*, which can be protected, masked or sanitized using corresponding RDF graph sanitization operations namely, SNode, SEdge and SPath. An example SPARQL sanitization query Q1 and corresponding illustration is depicted in Figure 1. A sanitization SPARQL query comprises a SANITIZE clause, which

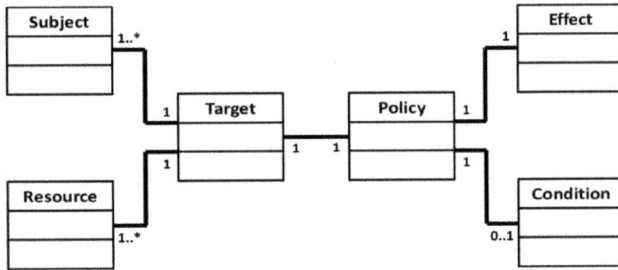

Figure 2: Policy Language

```
<policy id = "4523", graph = G1>
<target>
   <subject>?s rdf:type ex:Agent</subject>
   <resource>SNode(?x ex:hasName ?o)<resource>
</target>
<condition>?s ex:hasClearance ex:Secret</condition>
<effect>Deny<effect>
</policy>


ns:G1 pol:hasPolicySet ns:PS1 .
ns:PS1 pol:hasPolicy ns:P1 .
ns:P1 pol:hasId "4523" .
ns:P1 pol:hasTarget ns:P1T1 .
ns:P1T1 pol:hasSubject "?s rdf:type ex:Agent" .
ns:P1T1 pol:hasResource "SNode (?x ex:hasName ?o)" .
ns:P1 pol:hasCondition "?s ex:hasClearance ex:Secret" .
ns:P1 pol:hasEffect "Deny" .
```

Figure 3: XML Policy and Equivalent RDF Policy

specifies the dataset or RDF graph that needs to be sanitized, which is G_q, in case of Q1. The WHEREs clause contains a sanitization pattern which specifies a sanitization operation, such as SNode, SEdge *etc.*, along with the resource described in the form of a triple, triple pattern, graph pattern or path pattern. A SPARQL sanitization query when run on an RDF graph, transforms only the sensitive resource described in the WHEREs clause and the rest of the triples in the graph stay unchanged. The query Q1 sanitizes the name of Agent1 in RDF graph Gq as illustrated in Figure 1.

The RDF access control policy language is pictorially represented in Figure 2. The essential components of a policy are *target*, *effect* and *condition* (optional). We restrict the scope of this work to only one type of action that a user or subject can perform, namely query, as it is the the most predominant action that is performed on RDF stores. The *target* component is used to specify the set of subjects or resources to which the policy is applicable. The *subject* can be specified as a URI, triple pattern or graph pattern to identify an individual or a group/class of individuals to whom the policy is applicable, as illustrated in Figure 3. The element *resource* is used to describe the sensitive data item, which essentially comprises a sanitization pattern found in the WHEREs clause of a SPARQL sanitization query as shown in Figure 3. Further, *condition* is an optional element that can be used to describe additional restrictions in the form of a triple/graph pattern as described in Figure 3. Since query or read is the only type of action supported, we do not specify it as a part of the *target*.

3. SYSTEM ARCHITECTURE

In this section, we describe the architecture of the system that enables secure RDF information sharing as shown in Figure 4. There can be two usage scenarios arising in the case of secure RDF data sharing and management. Firstly, when data needs to be shared with an external organization, then the entire dataset(s) needs to be sanitized before sharing. We denote this as Inter-Organization Information Sharing, which is similar to assured information sharing presented in [4]. Secondly, when a user within an organization needs to access data within an RDF store, then they should be granted access to data that they are authorized to access after carefully redacting data that the user cannot access. We now provide a description of the various components of the architecture. This is followed by an outline of two demonstration scenarios of how users would interact with the system. The system was developed in the J2EE framework and comprises the following components:

Web Tier: This tier was developed using HTML5, CSS3 & Javascript, and serves as the point of entry for users to interact with the system. The Web tier provides a login mechanism to only allow authorized users to enter the system. This mechanism uses the Java simplified encryption (JASYPT[1]) library's salted hash technique to securely store usernames and passwords. The mechanism also incorporates a challenge-response authentication scheme to distinguish between automated attack bots and legitimate users.

Controllers: The two controllers, namely Query and Policy, were developed using Java Servlet technology. They serve as facilitators for passing user-initiated instructions (queries or administrative tasks) to the underlying Jena/Policy Engine and for relaying back sanitized query results to the Web Tier for consumption.

Jena: Since the underlying Redaction API[2] [2, 3] has been developed for Jena[3] (specifically as an extension to Jena's SPARQL query engine, ARQ), this framework serves as a major building block of the system. In particular, we use the RDF, SPARQL and Store API's of Jena. The RDF API allows one to create RDF graphs, store triples in them and find triples that match a given pattern using a high-level, user-friendly programming interface. The SPARQL API is Jena's implementation of the SPARQL W3C standards, and allows one to query/update RDF graphs using the SPARQL query language. The Store API converts user operations defined in the RDF API into low-level, implementation-specific operations on RDF graphs. Jena currently supports several ways to store RDF graphs including, an in-memory store, a SQL database or a custom disk-based tuple index. Jena also provides a point for users to plugin their custom storage solutions. In the future, we plan to extend the Redaction API, and consequently the current system, to other triple store implementations such as Sesame[4], through a connection factory that provides seamless access to the RDF graph creation and manipulation functionalities of underlying implementations.

Policy Engine: The policy engine was fully developed in Java and comprises several critical components that are essential for fine-grained RDF access control. Since this layer

---

[1]http://www.jasypt.org/
[2]http://goo.gl/u3jsXE
[3]https://jena.apache.org/
[4]http://www.openrdf.org/

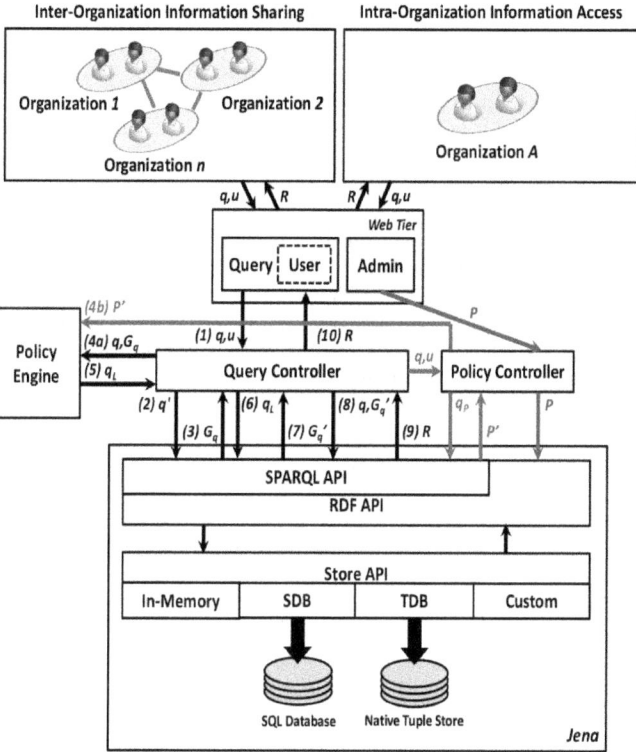

Figure 4: System Architecture

```
q) SELECT ?s ?n ?x ?z
   WHERE {?s ex:hasName ?n. ?s ex:hasID ?x. ?s ex:hasZip ?z}

q') CONSTRUCT {?s ex:hasName ?n. ?s ex:hasID ?x. ?s ex:hasZip ?z}
   WHERE {?s ex:hasName ?n. ?s ex:hasID ?x. ?s ex:hasZip ?z}
```

Figure 5: User query and CONSTRUCT query

is a crucial component of the system, the following section presents a detailed description of the various components and features of the policy engine.

Demonstration Scenarios: The are two usage scenarios in which a user interacts with the system. In the first case, a user interacts with the system to read or query data from the data store. Secondly, an administrator or domain expert interacts with the system to author, store or manage policies, that are used for implementing access control. In the following, we describe details of the two scenarios:

Policy Construction Scenario: An administrator or domain expert is assigned the task of authoring various policies (organizational, departmental, consent, privacy laws *etc.*) using the access control language presented in the previous section. These policies aim to protect sensitive resources within an RDF graph from unauthorized access and to facilitate fine grained access to those resources that have no access restrictions. This flexibility is attributed to the use of the underlying SPARQL based redaction mechanism. The user interface within the web tier offers an administrator with several options for authoring policies.

The most convenient option offers a policy web form, which has various fields corresponding to the elements of the policy language and further contains a drop down list that helps one select the desired value for a field wherever applicable. However, if an administrator is familiar with Semantic Web technologies such as RDF, then they can submit a list of policies authored in RDF based on our access control language (Figure 2) as shown in the second half of Figure 3. The policies thus authored are transformed into RDF policies for scalable storage, efficient management and

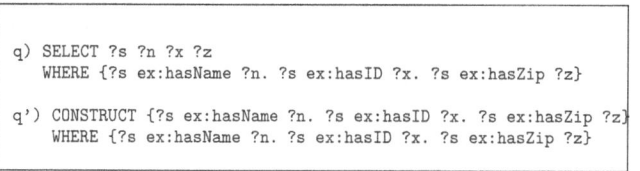

sophisticated retrieval using SPARQL. This transformation is performed by a separate module within the policy controller, which essentially performs a mapping between the respective elements of the policy language and facilitates storage and retrieval of policies from the RDF store.

Query Scenario: As stated earlier, users that query data within the data store can be of two types, namely an internal user who is a part of the organization, and an external user (belonging to an external agency) who tries to access publicly available datasets (or portions of datasets) of the organization. An internal user may typically access a subgraph of RDF graph(s), and an external user may typically access entire datasets, both of which can be expressed as SPARQL queries. For *e.g.*, an external user can request access to the entire RDF graph Gq using the following query:

Q2) SELECT ?s ?p ?o FROM NAMED Gq WHEREs {?s ?p ?o}

A user can request for data by writing a suitable SPARQL query q, and submitting it to the user interface, which is then forwarded to the query controller. The query controller now computes the relevant subgraph that the user is trying to access based on the input query. This is accomplished by transforming q into a CONSTRUCT query q' as shown above. The subgraph thus extracted may contain potentially sensitive information, which is protected by access control policies. Query q', as shown by arrow 2, is then forwarded to the SPARQL API which executes it on the RDF store and returns the relevant subgraph Gq to the query controller. The query controller now forwards q and Gq to the policy engine, while the policy controller forwards candidate policy subset P' (details provided in Section 4) to the policy engine. The policy engine processes the aforementioned inputs and returns sanitization query list q_L to policy controller. The policy controller now computes sanitized graph Gq' by applying sanitization queries from q_L on Gq using the SPARQL API. Once the query controller receives Gq', it forwards it along with q to SPARQL and RDF API (arrow 8). Then q is evaluated on sanitized graph Gq' and the result R is forwarded to the user via the query controller.

4. POLICY ENGINE

We now describe the details of the policy engine, which is shown in Figure 6. The policy engine receives as input q, Gq and candidate policy set P'. The candidate policy set P' is the relevant subset of the entire policy set P stored in the RDF store. It is computed by the policy controller using a SPARQL query, which finds all policies that are applicable to user u and the dataset (graph) specified in the FROM clause of query q (if specified). This step lends efficiency as we choose only a relevant policy subset for further processing and this was made possible by encoding polices as RDF triples and leveraging the query capabilities of SPARQL. The policy

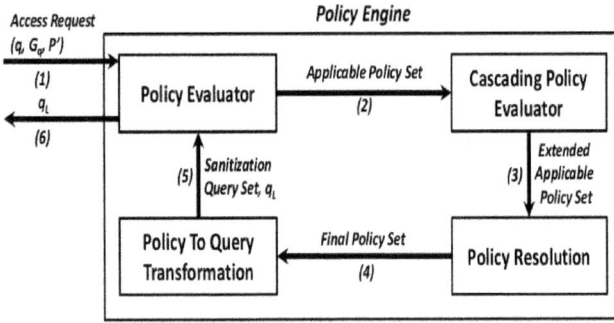

Figure 6: Policy Engine

evaluator now computes the applicable policy set from P' using inputs q and Gq. A policy is applicable if the data item protected by the element *resource* of the policy is either a part of q (computed using the pattern specified within its WHEREs clause) or Gq.

Once the applicable policies are thus computed, they are input to the cascading policy evaluator (optional component), which facilitates implementation of privacy definitions and anonymization for RDF graphs. Suppose a policy suppresses access to Zipcode value of a person's record and further if Zipcode is a subproperty of a property called Address (which also contains zipcode information) within the domain ontology, then Address value must also be suppressed. Therefore, the cascading policy evaluator will generate a new policy to accomplish the same. The cascading policy evaluator has access to the ontology which captures the security or privacy definitions, which will then be matched against the resources or predicates specified in the policy to check if it triggers generation of additional polices based on relationships among data attributes [5]. The goal is to enable integration of relationships among data attributes (which are modeled as a part of the domain ontology) into the process of data sanitization, thus facilitating the implementation of privacy definitions and anonymization of RDF graphs.

Algorithm 1 POLICY-RESOLUTION()

Input: Extended Applicable Policy Set S, G_q
Output: Final Policy Set S'
1: **for** $P_1 \in S$ **do**
2:    **for** $P_2 \neq P_1$ AND $P_2 \in S$ **do**
3:       $G_1 = eval(P_1.resource, G_q)$
4:       $G_2 = eval(P_2.resource, G_q)$
5:       **if** $G_1 \subseteq G_2$ **then** $S'.add(P_2)$
6:       **else if** $G_2 \subseteq G_1$ **then** $S'.add(P_1)$
7:       **else if** $G_1 \cap G_2 \neq \emptyset$ **then**
8:         **if** $greater(P_1.resource, P_2.resource)$
9:         **then** $S'.add(P_1)$ **else** $S'.add(P_2)$
10:    **end for**
11: **end for**
12: **return** S'

Once the extended policy set is thus generated the conflicts among the policies are resolved by the policy resolution module. It checks the list of applicable policies to see if there is any unintended policy duplication or overlap, which occurs when a resource protected by one policy is contained within the resource protected by another policy or when the resources protected by two policies are overlapping respectively. For the sake of simplicity assume that the effect of policies is always deny, *i.e.*, if a resource is not protected by a policy then it is accessible by default. Let G_1 and G_2 be two resources, graphs or sets of triples protected by policies P_1 and P_2 respectively. If $G_1 \subseteq G_2$ then only policy P_2 is added to the final policy list. The function *greater* (used in line 8) checks for the precedence of the sanitization operation of the resource and adds the polices to the output list according to the precedence. Similarly, further details regarding the policy resolution are precisely described in Algorithm 1.

The final policy set thus computed by the policy resolution module is then transformed into SPARQL sanitization queries by the policy to query transformation layer. This layer parses the policies and identifies the various elements of the policy and generates the equivalent sanitization query. For example, the equivalent sanitization query for the XML policy shown in Figure 3 is shown below (Q3). This layer outputs a list of sanitization SPARQL queries q_L that correspond to the input policies. The query list q_L is then forwarded to the policy controller via policy evaluator.

```
Q3) SANITIZE G1 WHEREs {?x ex:hasName ?o}
```

5. CONCLUSIONS

We presented a fine grained access control language for securing RDF graphs, which derives its flexibility by virtue of the underlying RDF graph redaction mechanism. We further presented critical features of the RDF policy engine, which contribute towards efficient, effective and scalable policy management. Finally, the system architecture describes how one can build access control and privacy features using the fundamental RDF graph redaction language.

6. ACKNOWLEDGMENTS

This work was partially supported by National Institutes of Health Grants 1R0-1LM009989 and 1R01HG006844, National Science Foundation (NSF) Grants Career-CNS-0845803, CNS-0964350, CNS-1016343, CNS-1111529, CNS-1228198 and Army Research Office Grant W911NF-12-1-0558.

7. REFERENCES

[1] P. Reddivari. Policy based access control for a RDF store. In *Proceedings of the Policy Management for the Web Workshop, WWW 2005*, 2005.

[2] J. Rachapalli, V. Khadilkar, M. Kantarcioglu, and B. Thuraisingham. REDACT: A Framework for Sanitizing RDF Data. WWW '13 Companion, 2013.

[3] J. Rachapalli, V. Khadilkar, M. Kantarcioglu, and B. Thuraisingham. Towards Fine Grained RDF Access Control. In *SACMAT*, 2014.

[4] T. Cadenhead, V. Khadilkar, M. Kantarcioglu, and B. M. Thuraisingham. A cloud-based RDF policy engine for assured information sharing. In *SACMAT*, 2012.

[5] M. Bishop, J. Cummins, S. Peisert, A. Singh, B. Bhumiratana, D. Agarwal, D. Frincke, and M. Hogarth. Relationships and Data Sanitization: A Study in Scarlet. In *Proceedings of the 2010 Workshop on New Security Paradigms*, NSPW '10, 2010.

A System for Risk Awareness During Role Mining

Sharmin Ahmed
University of Western Ontario
Department of Computer Science
London, Ontario, Canada, N6A 5B7
sahme47@csd.uwo.ca

Sylvia L. Osborn
University of Western Ontario
Department of Computer Science
London, Ontario, Canada, N6A 5B7
sylvia@csd.uwo.ca

ABSTRACT

This paper demonstrates a proof-of-concept prototype that is able to automatically and effectively detect and report different types of risk factors during the process of role mining. A role mining platform is embedded within the tool so that different role-mining algorithms can be used. Once roles are generated, a further analysis is done to detect risk presented by the roles output. To the best of our knowledge there is no such system that effectively detects risk factors and mines roles at the same time. The tool is easy to use, flexible and effective in automatically detecting risk. It can be useful for data analysts and role engineers.

Categories and Subject Descriptors

D4.6 [**Security and Protection**]: Access Controls, Verification

General Terms

Design, Security

Keywords

Mechanisms, systems, and tools, Risk, Usability

1. INTRODUCTION

The concept of Role Mining first emerged in 2003, when Kuhlmann et al. [6] proposed using data mining techniques to carry out bottom-up role engineering. There is little research that considers risk during the process of role mining, only, for example, [3], [4] and [2]. This paper demonstrates a proof-of-concept prototype that is automatically risk aware during role mining. Risk awareness in access control systems is a new but prominent issue as the need for enabling access in an agile and dynamic way has emerged. While this is true for an established access control system, being aware of risk even before the access control system is defined could mean identification of users, permissions and roles that represent what are likely the most dangerous and error-prone

situations from an administration point of view. Once a role is created, its lifecycle will follow the evolution of the company: new users or new permissions can be added and old ones can be removed or replaced, etc. This continuous modification of the access control system typically introduces noise within the data, namely permissions exceptionally or accidentally granted or denied, thus increasing the risk of making mistakes when managing the access control system. Having risk-based information available during the role engineering phase allows data analysts and role engineers to highlight users and permissions that are more prone to error and misuse when designed roles will be deployed.

We have implemented a proof-of-concept prototype that is able to automatically and effectively detect and report different types of risk factors during the process of role mining. A role mining platform is embedded within the tool so that different role-mining algorithms can be used. Once roles are generated, a further analysis is done for any post role mining risk. Finally, a role hierarchy is generated.

2. RISK METRICS

In this section we briefly describe the various risk factors that we take into consideration in the prototype, during the role mining process. We categorize the risk factors using four general risk metrics:

- **Similarity Index** The similarity index is the number of permissions that a given set of users share. We find this using the Jaccard Coefficient and then visualize the similarity index of each user with all the other users. The visualization of the similarity helps in the detection of outliers. We also add attribute information to this visualization to better identify the outlier users.

- **Compliance to policies** While policy is a very broad term, we restrict the policy risk factors for the tool to Separation of Duty constraints and the Principle of Least Privilege. The Separation of Duty constraints risk factors will be based on the separation of duty conficts' taxonomy as discussed in [7]. If the separation of duty constraints are available then these are crosschecked with the user-permission assignment table and any discrepancy is reported. The principle of least privilege is checked according to the method introduced in [5]. If a list of target privileges are available, then the user-role and role-permission assignments are checked as to whether the users have the minimum target privileges that they need to work

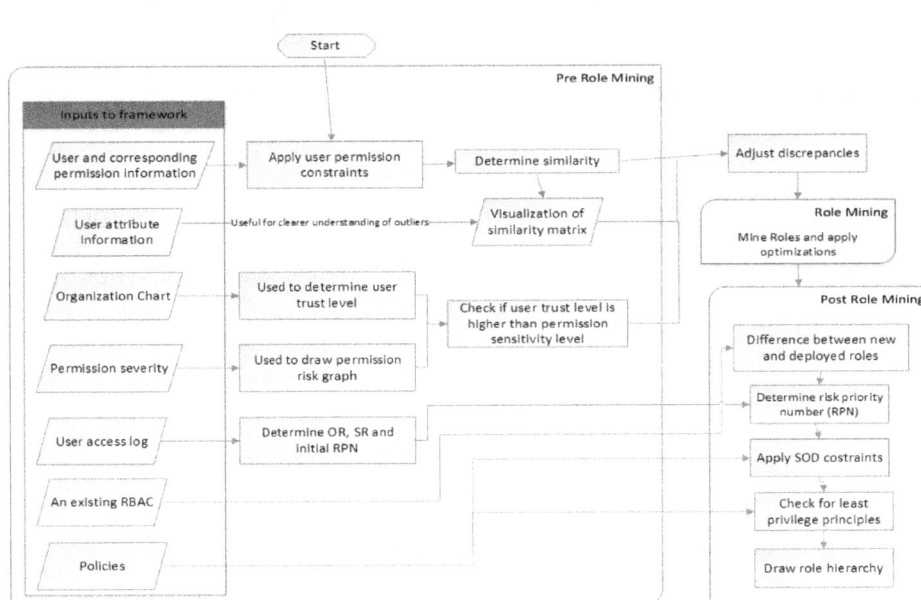

Figure 1: *An outline of the framework for the risk aware system*

properly. If target privileges have not been met in a role of a user, then this is also reported.

- **Trust and Sensitivity** We use an organization chart to determine user security level which we refer to as user trust level. We assume that the sensitivity of each permission is available. The permission sensitivity level is compared with the user trust level to see whether users are gaining access to permissions that are beyond their current level. If a user gets access to permissions that are beyond their current level (due to any kind of possible error in the data), then this is a risk factor.

- **Permission misuse and abuse** While a user may have legitimate access to a permission, if they misuse or abuse the use of that permission, then this is also an important risk factor. In [1], the authors incorporate a failure mode and effects analysis (FMEA) scheme for measuring user risks. They combine components as credentials, queries, role history logs and expected utility for a probabilistic formulation of risk. They use the risk priority number (RPN) that is defined as part of FMEA. The RPN is calculated as:

Risk Priority Number (RPN) = Occurrence Rating (OR) * Severity Rating (SR) * Detection Rating (DR)

We use this formula of RPN to determine permission misuse and abuse.

3. THE PROTOTYPE

In this section we discuss the different types of information that we use as input to the tool that are the risk factors. We also highlight the main features of the tool.

3.1 Inputs to the tool

Other than the user-permission assignment information, all the other different types of input information are optional since they may or may not be available in the organization. The presence of each of these kinds of information helps in the determination of risk. In the absence of any of this additional information, the tool will just mine the roles and show the role hierarchy. The different types of input information are as follows:

- User-Attribute information

- Permission usage data

- Organization Chart

- Existing RBAC information for optimization of deployed roles

- Set of Separation of Duty constraints and target privileges

The figure 1 shows the structure of our proposed framework for the tool. The entire process in the tool can be divided into steps before role mining. i.e Pre Role Mining, Role Mining and steps after Role Mining, i.e Post Role Mining.

3.2 Tool Features

The tool was implemented in Java with a MySQL database. The interface of the tool is designed in a software wizard style with each window providing the option to input each kind of additional information as shown in the framework in figure 1. Here we summarize the features of the tool.

- **Flexibility of input:** Other than the user permission assignment information, all other information is optional and the user has the option to either input the information in the step or skip the step. For example, in the first step, the user is asked to select any table that may contain any information regarding user-permission static constraints. If the user does not have

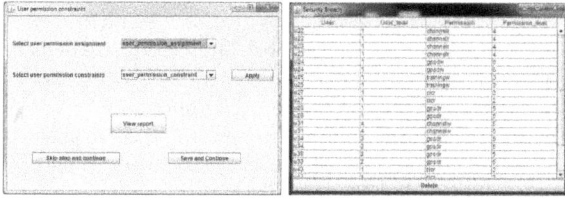

Figure 2: Sample Window showing selection of user permission constraint table and Sample Report Showing Security Breaches

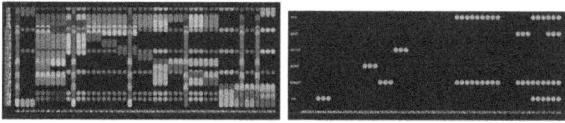

Figure 3: Sample Visualization of Similarity index of all the different users and the shared attributes

Figure 4: Overall Dashboard

this information, they may skip and proceed to the next step. If the user does have this information, they will select the table and the tool will check for any discrepancy.

- **Detailed Report in each step and an Overall Report:** In each step, any discrepancy in the data is found and recorded. There is a button that allows the user to view the discrepancy report in each step. The user may view this report or alternatively save the information and proceed to the next step. Once all the steps before role mining have been completed, the next window allows the user the option to view all the different reports in all the previous steps in an overall dashboard. This is useful for the user to make any form of cross checking.

- **Visualization of the Similarity index and attributes shared:** In the second step of the tool, the user has the option to visualize the similarity between the users as well as the attributes that they share. The user will also be able to view a report that prints any users that do not have a 100% permission match with any of the other users. Figure 3 shows examples of the similarity index and shared attributes.

- **Actions regarding discrepancy:** We propose two variations regarding actions. In our current tool, in

each step, if any discrepancy is found and if the user views it in a report, at the bottom of the report is a button for delete and flag. If the user feels that the discrepancy detected is correct and the user wishes to delete this particular user-permission assignment, then they may do so and this particular user-permission assignment will be deleted from the user-permission assignment table and the user may save the changes made and proceed to the next step. However, this may seem inappropriate as the user may be wrong and total deletion of the assignment would be too harsh. We thus also provide the option to 'flag' the particular user-permission assignment so that the flagged assignments can be dealt with later on. Based on necessity, any one of these may be activated in the tool.

- **Risk Priority Number Calculation:** We have already seen that the risk priority number is calculated as: OR*SR*DR. We consider the sensitivity level of each permission to be the Severity Rating. The occurrence rating is the percentage of usage of each permission. Thus, if a user u has used permission p_1 as 50% of their total usage of all permissions in a particular time, then their occurrence rating for permission p_1 is 50%. The initial detection rating (DR) before role mining is done based on the assumption that a set of users that have a 100% match of permissions could be considered as a set of users having the same set of roles. Thus, the detection rating is found for each permission of each user from this cluster. In the detection rating in [1], k-means clustering is used between the different users in each role. We use k-means clustering after role generation but before that we use the minimum difference between the usage of the user and the other users. For our particular study, we considered a minimum difference of 10 to be risky and accordingly these users were highlighted. After role mining, the k-means clustering is done and the values sorted with the highest value shown first. We look at an example to understand this. Three users, u_1, u_2 and u_3 all share the same set of permissions $\{p_1, p_2, p_3\}$. Thus, the set $\{u_1, u_2, u_3\}$ can be considered a cluster. Now suppose u_1, u_2 and u_3 have used permission p_1 5, 6 and 20 times respectively. The minimum difference between the usage of u_3 and the two other users is 14. Since we consider a minimum difference of 10 to be risky, this user can be considered to be misusing their privilege. We have also found through testing that this user u_3 does appear among the users with a high RPN value after role mining.

- **Policy Comparison:** We have taken into consideration static separation of duty constraints and the principle of least privilege. The tool checks for violation of separation of duty constraints both before and after role mining and also checks for conformation to the principle of least privilege. This is done by checking whether roles generated contain the target privileges.

- **Role Mining Platform:** A role mining platform is also embedded within the tool that is unbiased to the type of algorithm to be used.

4. CONCLUSIONS

We demonstrate a risk-aware role mining tool that is effectively able to detect and deal with risk factors before, during and after role mining. To the best of our knowledge there is no such system that effectively detects risk factors and mines roles at the same time. The tool is easy to use, flexible and effective in automatically detecting risk and can be useful for data analysts and role engineers.

5. ACKNOWLEDGMENTS

The financial support of the Natural Sciences and Engineering Research Council of Canada is gratefully acknowledged.

6. REFERENCES

[1] E. Celikel, M. Kantarcioglu, X. Li, and E. Bertino. A Risk Management Approach to RBAC. *Risk and Decision Analysis*, 1(2), November 2009.

[2] S. Chari, I. Molloy, Y. Park, and W. Teiken. Ensuring continuous compliance through reconciling policy with usage. In *Proceedings of the 18th ACM Symposium on Access Control Models and Technologies*, SACMAT '13, pages 49–60, New York, NY, USA, 2013. ACM.

[3] A. Colantonio, R. Di Pietro, A. Ocello, and N. V. Verde. Evaluating the risk of adopting rbac roles. In *Proceedings of the 24th Annual IFIP WG 11.3 Working Conference on Data and Applications Security and Privacy*, DBSec'10, pages 303–310, Berlin, Heidelberg, 2010. Springer-Verlag.

[4] A. Colantonio, R. Di Pietro, A. Ocello, and N. V. Verde. A new role mining framework to elicit business roles and to mitigate enterprise risk. *Decis. Support Syst.*, 50(4):715–731, Mar. 2011.

[5] H. Huang, F. Shang, and J. Zhang. Approximation algorithms for minimizing the number of roles and administrative assignments in rbac. In *Proceedings of the 2012 IEEE 36th Annual Computer Software and Applications Conference Workshops*, COMPSACW '12, pages 427–432, Washington, DC, USA, 2012. IEEE Computer Society.

[6] M. Kuhlmann, D. Shohat, and G. Schimpf. Role mining - revealing business roles for security administration using data mining technology. In *Proceedings of the eighth ACM symposium on Access control models and technologies*, SACMAT '03, pages 179–186, New York, NY, USA, 2003.

[7] M. Nyanchama and S. Osborn. The role graph model and conflict of interest. *ACM Trans. Inf. Syst. Secur.*, 2(1):3–33, Feb. 1999.

Re-thinking Networked Privacy, Security, Identity and Access Control in our Surveillance States

Andrew Clement
Faculty of Information
University of Toronto
140 St George Street, Toronto ON M5S 3G6
andrew.clement@utoronto.ca

Categories and Subject Descriptors: K.4.1

[**Computing Milieux**]: Computers and Society – *public policy issues*

Keywords: Surveillance, Privacy, Security.

1. INVITED KEYNOTE PRESENTATION

Mass surveillance activities by the security agencies of the Five Eyes countries (e.g. NSA, CSEC, etc) pose a significant challenge to those who care about the privacy, security and other democratic rights related to our burgeoning digitally mediated communications. The on-going media coverage of the Snowden documents has brought unprecedented attention to longstanding concerns about whether and how individuals can exercise effective control over their personal information as we increasingly lead our lives on-line. The revelations are also undermining comfortable assumptions about the institutions and infrastructures we depend on for the efficient and equitable functioning of a democratic society. We've seen agencies mandated to protect our networks compromise once trusted security standards, and secretly hoard vulnerabilities for later exploitation rather than fix them. We are witnesses to government and their corporate partners secretly accessing massive amounts of our data, and grudgingly acknowledge their activities only when forced to by whistleblowers. How can we restore trust in the organizations we interact with and hand our personal data to on a daily basis? How can we require them to be more open, transparent and accountable? What are the technically viable options that can help achieve the reliable protections that many regard as fundamental and wish they could take for granted?

Drawing on recent research, this talk will review some of the key surveillance challenges we face in the areas of internet routing and identity authentication. The IXmaps.ca project provides a mapping tool for visualizing the routes data packets take across the internet backbone, and in particular where one's own traffic may be subject to NSA interception at key internet routing choke points. It further documents patterns of 'boomerang routing', whereby domestic Canadian traffic is often routed via the US, exposing it to foreign surveillance, and compares the data privacy transparency of the various carriers which handle this traffic *en route*.

The Proportionate ID project similarly probes typically invisible personal information handling practices with the aim of helping users better understand these practices, their privacy implications and technical alternatives. To illustrate a minimally disclosing token approach to identity authentication, the project developed and makes publicly available plastic overlays that individuals can apply to their existing ID cards, such as driver licence and health card, that selectively provides only the information required for particular transactions. These ID card modifications protect both the individual and the organization from illegal excessive data collection, while opening up for discussion the topic of what are legitimate ID requirements. The project also developed the prototype Prop-ID digital wallet smartphone app, available on Google Play, that mimics certifiable anonymous identity authentication.

The presentation will conclude with proposed strategies for rendering surveillance practices publicly transparent and the responsible organizations more democratically accountable.

2. BIOGRAPHY

Andrew Clement is a Professor in the Faculty of Information at the University of Toronto, where he coordinates the Information Policy Research Program and is a co-founder of the Identity, Privacy and Security Institute. With a PhD in Computer Science, he has had longstanding research and teaching interests in the social implications of information/communication technologies and participatory design. Among his recent privacy/surveillance research projects, are IXmaps.ca, an internet mapping tool that helps make more visible NSA warrantless wiretapping activities and the routing of Canadian personal data through the U.S. even when the origin and destination are both in Canada; SurveillanceRights.ca, which documents (non-)compliance of video surveillance installations with privacy regulations and helps citizens understand their related privacy rights using the SurveillanceWatch app which enables users to locate surveillance cameras around them and contribute new sightings of their own; and Proportionate ID, which demonstrates through overlays for conventional ID cards and a smartphone app privacy protective alternatives to prevailing full disclosure norms. Clement is a co-investigator in The New Transparency: Surveillance and Social Sorting.

SACMAT'14, June 25–27, 2014, London, Ontario, Canada.
ACM 978-1-4503-2939-2/14/06.
http://dx.doi.org/10.1145/2613087.2613089

Path Conditions and Principal Matching: A New Approach to Access Control

Jason Crampton
Royal Holloway University of London
Egham, United Kingdom
jason.crampton@rhul.ac.uk

James Sellwood
Royal Holloway University of London
Egham, United Kingdom
james.sellwood.2010@live.rhul.ac.uk

ABSTRACT

Traditional authorization policies are user-centric, in the sense that authorization is defined, ultimately, in terms of user identities. We believe that this user-centric approach is inappropriate for many applications, and that what should determine authorization is the relationships that exist between entities in the system. While recent research has considered the possibility of specifying authorization policies based on the relationships that exist between peers in social networks, we are not aware of the application of these ideas to general computing systems. We develop a formal access control model that makes use of ideas from relationship-based access control and a two-stage method for evaluating policies. Our policies are defined using path conditions, which are similar to regular expressions. We define semantics for path conditions, which we use to develop a rigorous method for evaluating policies. We describe the algorithm required to evaluate policies and establish its complexity. Finally, we illustrate the advantages of our model using an example and describe a preliminary implementation of our algorithm.

Categories and Subject Descriptors

D.4.6 [**Operating Systems**]: Security and Protection—*Access controls*; H.2.0 [**Database Management**]: General—*Security, integrity and protection*

General Terms

Security, Design, Language, Theory

Keywords

access control; path condition; relationship; principal matching; authorization

1. INTRODUCTION

Access control is an essential security service in any multi-user computer system. It provides a mechanism by which different users are restricted in the actions they can perform within the system. An access control service typically comprises a policy decision point and a policy. An attempt by a user to interact with a system resource, usually known as an authorization request, is evaluated by the policy decision point and is only permitted if that interaction is authorized by the policy.

An access control model provides a syntax for authorization policies and a specification of the algorithm used by the policy decision point to evaluate requests. Many access control models focus on the user and authorizing the user to perform particular actions. As is customary in the literature, we will use the terms *subjects* and *objects* when referring to the parties who are to, respectively, perform and be the target of authorization (inter)actions.

Access control has been the subject of significant research and development in the last 40 years. As our use of technology and the connectivity of our devices has increased, the need for ever more robust and scalable access control models has also grown. New models attempt to improve on the failings of their predecessors, and often do so by redefining the policy foundations upon which authorization decisions are made. The protection matrix model, for example, simply enumerated all authorized actions. While this provides for precise specification of authorization policies, it does not scale well and is difficult to manage. In order to ease this administrative burden, various improvements have been employed by modern operating systems. The Unix operating system, for example, replaces the individual subjects with a mapping, performed at the time of request evaluation, to one of three security principals (owner, group and world) [6]. In this way, whilst each object must still be enumerated, the enumeration of subjects is limited to just these three security principals. With complex systems involving numerous users, this design dramatically reduces the space and administrative complexity of the underlying policy. However, it also greatly reduces the flexibility afforded when compared with defining authorization at the user level.

Role-based access control (RBAC), which is widely used and has been the subject of extensive research in recent years, assigns a user to one or more organizational roles. These roles are then authorized to perform certain actions on particular resources. These roles, which are defined on a per-system basis, thus reduce the administrative burden of the protection matrix (assuming the number of roles is significantly less than the number of users), and provide a level of flexibility not available within the Unix model. This increased flexibility also restores some of the clarity that was lost when users where abstracted behind Unix's three, very general, security principals.

A significant disadvantage with RBAC is that it takes no account of the specific relationship that might exist between a user and the resource for which access is requested. Thus every user assigned to a doctor role can access all electronic health records if the doctor role is authorized to do so. Clearly, it would more appropriate if the only users that are authorized to access a particular health record have a specific relationship with the subject of that record. In short, RBAC is not as "fine-grained" as its supporters claim. RBAC models that use private or parameterized roles have been introduce to tackle these kinds of problems [9, 10, 14]. However, this often leads to a proliferation of roles that undermines the advantages provided by the basic RBAC model (as the number of roles tends towards the number of users). Thus, we believe a new approach is required: an approach that combines the scalability of RBAC with the granularity of the protection matrix model and permits the specification of authorization rules on a per user-resource basis.

Recent research on access control in social networks has used the (social) relationship(s) that exist between users in such networks as the basis for specifying authorization rules [3, 4, 5, 7]. The relationship information available in social networks provides additional context from which access control decisions can be derived. We believe that relationship-based access control could be applied in many other scenarios. In particular, the coarse-grained decision-making in RBAC can be refined using such relationship information.

In this paper, therefore, we develop a novel access control model in which policies are specified in terms of path conditions. To a crude approximation our model takes inspiration from three sources: the overall design of the decision algorithm is similar to Unix; the path conditions are similar in spirit to some of the proposals for relationship-based access control; and the use of implementation-specific authorization principals bears some resemblance to RBAC. We believe our path conditions provide a more rigorous foundation for access control mechanisms than existing proposals for relationship-based access control. We also believe our use of authorization principals provides the desired scalability.

Our model introduces several novel contributions, the most significant being a generic model for access control systems using relationships that is not limited to social networks but can be used to describe access control within more traditional and more diverse environments. Our support for logical entities, as well as the more usual users and resources, allows for a fine grained definition of authorization capable of taking into consideration relevant contextual information encoded in the relationships a request's participants have with other entities. This is balanced with our abstraction of authorization policy to principals rather than subjects, allowing a scalable system which remains powerful and expressive.

In the next section, we describe our model for access control. This section includes the definitions of path conditions, principal-matching rules and authorization policies, and an explanation of how requests are evaluated. In Section 3, we consider the algorithm for matching principals in more detail, presenting a pseudo-code listing, an analysis of the algorithm's complexity and a description of a preliminary implementation in Python. We also describe the results of some simple experiments. We then compare our model to existing, related work and conclude the paper with a summary of our contributions and ideas for future work. The appendix includes an extended example, fragments of which are used throughout the paper. This extended example is used in our experiments.

2. THE AUTHORIZATION MODEL

Informally our model is based on the idea of a labelled graph, in which nodes represent entities within the system and edges represent relationships between entities. Nodes may represent concrete entities, such as users and resources, or logical entities, with which other entities are associated. The relationships' labels are used to define path conditions which can be matched by chains of edges within the graph. A path condition, essentially, identifies a set of authorization principals that is associated with a request. Those principals are authorized to perform actions, thus determining whether a request is authorized or not. Thus our model uses a two-stage decision process: we first identify the principals relevant to the request and then determine whether those principals are authorized.

As we allow entities of various types within our graph, we can make use of a variety of kinds of relationship when processing the authorization decision. If we were to solely include users within our graph, then it could mimic a social network and would be limited to inter-personal relationships for access control policy definition. By including group and resource entity types, we expand the possible subjects and objects, and also the possible relationships which can inform authorization decisions. In Section 2.5, we show that the RBAC model can be seen as an instance of our model. If, however, we include additional entity types and relationships then we can make more fine-grained decisions, as illustrated by the extended example in Appendix A.

2.1 The System Model

Formally, we assume the existence of a set of system entities, which includes the sets of subjects and objects. Each entity has a type and relationships may exist between certain types of entities. Some relationships, such as Sibling-of, are symmetric, while others, such as Brother-of, are not. A system model defines the types along with the entity relationships that are permitted.

DEFINITION 1. *A system model comprises a set of types T, a set of relationship labels R, a set of symmetric relationship labels $S \subseteq R$ and a permissible relationship graph $G_{PR} = (V_{PR}, E_{PR})$, where $V_{PR} = T$ and $E_{PR} \subseteq T \times T \times R$.*

The example in Appendix A defines a number of types, including Group, Project and User, and the relationship type Client-of. Part of the permissible relationship graph includes the edges (Group, Project) and (Group, User), both labelled with the Client-of relationship. Figure 6 (in the appendix) defines the entire permissible relationship graph.

DEFINITION 2. *Given a system model (T, R, S, G_{PR}), a system instance is defined by a system graph $G = (V, E)$ where V is the set of entities and $E \subseteq V \times V \times R$. We say*

G is well-formed *if for each entity v in V, $\tau(v) \in T$, and for every edge $(v, v', r) \in E$, $(\tau(v), \tau(v'), r) \in E_{PR}$.*

The system model constrains the 'shape' of the system graph by restricting the edges that can be specified. Note that we may have multiple edges between two entities in our system graph (because two or more relationships may exist between vertices). Such a graph is sometimes called a *multigraph*. We will depict an edge (v, v', s), when $s \in S$, without arrowheads, as can be seen in Figure 1 in the case of the Sibling-of relationship. (Due to the symmetry of s, the edge (v, v', s) implies an edge (v', v, s) and vice versa.) An edge (v, v', r), when $r \in R \setminus S$, is directed from v to v', depicted with an arrowhead pointing towards v' (see Figure 1a). The directed edges (v, v', r) and (v', v, r) represent two different relationships. Of course both may belong to E, in which case this will be depicted with arrowheads at both ends of the link between v and v' (see Figure 1b).

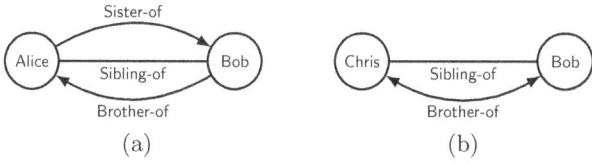

Figure 1: Illustrating different edges in the system graph

Figure 7 (in the appendix) depicts a system graph containing a substantial number of nodes of different types and the relationships that exist between those nodes. Figure 2 shows a simple example of a system graph for illustrative purposes, based on the one in the appendix. Users (such as U_1) are associated with projects (P_1); documents (D_1 and D_2) are grouped together in folders (F_1 and F_2) and allocated to one or more projects, either as part of a group or as a single resource. Relationships include Participant-of, Supervises, Resource-for, and Member-of.

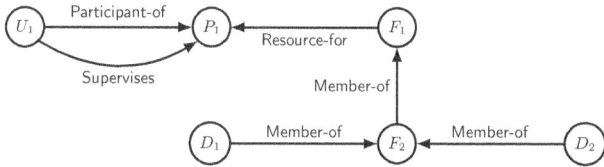

Figure 2: A fragment of a system graph

2.2 Path Conditions

We use path conditions to match requests to principals (described in Section 2.4). In this section, we define the syntax and semantics of path conditions, and establish some basic properties of path conditions, thereby allowing us to restrict our attention to simple path conditions.

DEFINITION 3. *Given a set of relationships R, we define a path condition recursively:*

- *$\diamond$ is a path condition;*

- *r is a path condition, for all $r \in R$;*

- *if π and π' are path conditions, then $\pi\,;\pi'$, π^+ and $\overline{\pi}$ are path conditions.*

A path condition of the form r or $\overline{r}$, where $r \in R$, is said to be an edge condition.

Informally, $\pi\,;\pi'$ represents the concatenation of two path conditions; π^+ represents one or more occurrences, in sequence, of π; and $\overline{\pi}$ represents π reversed. We define $\diamond$ for completeness. We note that individual edge conditions could be encoded using attribute-based access control (ABAC) but it is hard to see how ABAC could be easily employed to encode longer chains of relationships.

DEFINITION 4. *Given a system graph $G = (V, E)$ and $u, v \in V$, we write $G, u, v \models \pi$ to denote that G, u and v satisfy path condition π. Formally, for all G, u, v, π, π':*

- *$G, u, v \models \diamond$ iff $v = u$;*

- *$G, u, v \models r$ iff $(u, v, r) \in E$;*

- *$G, u, v \models \pi\,;\pi'$ iff there exists $w \in V$ such that $G, u, w \models \pi$ and $G, w, v \models \pi'$;*

- *$G, u, v \models \pi^+$ iff $G, u, v \models \pi$ or $G, u, v \models \pi\,;\pi^+$;*

- *$G, u, v \models \overline{\pi}$ iff $G, v, u \models \pi$.*

Note that an edge condition is satisfied by nodes that are adjacent in the system graph. We use $\diamond$ to identify an empty path condition, which is of particular use in our path-matching algorithm in Section 3.1.

In the context of the graph in Figure 2, for example, we have $G, U_1, F_1 \models$ Participant-of $;$ $\overline{\text{Resource-for}}$ since $G, U_1, P_1 \models$ Participant-of and $G, F_1, P_1 \models$ Resource-for.

DEFINITION 5. *Path conditions π and π' are said to be equivalent, denoted $\pi \equiv \pi'$, if, for all system graphs $G = (V, E)$ and all $u, v \in V$ we have*

$$G, u, v \models \pi \quad \text{if and only if} \quad G, u, v \models \pi'.$$

PROPOSITION 1. *For all path conditions π_1 and π_2: (i) $\overline{\overline{\pi_1}} \equiv \pi_1$; $\overline{\diamond} \equiv \diamond$; $\overline{\pi_1}\,;\pi_1$ (ii) $\overline{\diamond} \equiv \diamond$ (iii) $\overline{\pi_1\,;\pi_2} \equiv \overline{\pi_2}\,;\overline{\pi_1}$ (iv) $\overline{\pi_1^+} \equiv \overline{\pi_1}^+$.*

PROOF. All results follow immediately from Definitions 4 and 5. Consider (iii), for example. By definition, $G, u, v \models \overline{\pi_1\,;\pi_2}$ if and only if $G, v, u \models \pi_1\,;\pi_2$. And $G, v, u \models \pi_1\,;\pi_2$ if and only there exists w such that $G, v, w \models \pi_1$ and $G, w, u \models \pi_2$. Thus we have $G, u, v \models \overline{\pi_1\,;\pi_2}$ if and only if there exists w such that $G, w, v \models \overline{\pi_1}$ and $G, u, w \models \overline{\pi_2}$. That is $G, u, v \models \overline{\pi_2}\,;\overline{\pi_1}$. □

DEFINITION 6. *Given a set of relationships R, we define a simple path condition recursively:*

- *$\diamond$, r and $\overline{r}$, where $r \in R$, are simple path conditions;*

- *if $\pi \neq \diamond$ and $\pi' \neq \diamond$ are simple path conditions, then $\pi\,;\pi'$ and π^+ are simple path conditions.*

In other words, $\overline{\star}$ occurs in a simple path condition if and only if $\star$ is an element of R. It follows from Proposition 1 that every path condition may be reduced to a simple path condition. The path condition $\overline{r_1\,;r_2}\,;(r_1\,;r_3)^+$, for example, can be transformed into the equivalent path condition $(\overline{r_3}\,;\overline{r_1})^+\,;r_1\,;r_2$ using the equivalences in Proposition 1. Henceforth, we assume all path conditions are simple.

2.3 Policy Specification

Subjects within a system request authorization to perform actions on objects. The policies of a system define the authorized and unauthorized actions and the rules for determining the principals to which these actions are assigned. Principals are mapped to paths within the system graph, where these paths exist between the subject and object of an authorization request. The potential paths are described by path conditions, which are defined using relationships.

DEFINITION 7. *Let P be a set of authorization principals and let R be a set of relationship labels. A principal-matching rule has the form (π, p), where p is an authorization principal and π is either a path condition defined on R or the special symbol $\top$. The path condition π is called a principal-matching condition. A principal-matching policy ρ is a list of principal-matching rules.*

Informally, a principal-matching rule (π, p) is applicable to a request (s, o, a) if there is a path from s to o in the system graph that satisfies π.

In order to support scenarios where a default principal should apply, much like the concept of 'world' in the Unix access control system, we allow the definition of a special principal-matching rule with the principal-matching condition set to $\top$. This default principal-matching rule is, if present, always the last rule in the principal-matching policy and (whenever it is evaluated) is applicable to every request. This rule's associated principal, therefore, matches whenever the rule is evaluated.

DEFINITION 8. *An authorization rule has the form $(p, \star, a, b)$ or (p, o, a, b), where a is an action, p is a principal, o is an object and $b \in \{0, 1\}$. An authorization policy is a list of authorization rules.*

A rule of the form $(p, o, a, 0)$ asserts that p is explicitly *unauthorized* (or *prohibited*) to perform action a on object o, while the rule $(p, o, a, 1)$ explicitly authorizes p. Rules of this form allow us to specify on a per-object basis the actions for which a principal p is (un)authorized. A rule of the form $(p, \star, a, 0)$ asserts that the principal is unauthorized for all objects, while $(p, \star, a, 1)$ asserts that the principal is authorized for all objects. Rules of this form allow us to specify the actions for which a principal is (un)authorized, irrespective of the object to which access is requested. In this case, the authorization policy is concentrated in the principal-matching rule. Note also that we can combine rules $(p, \star, a, 0)$ and $(p, o, a, 1)$, for example, to specify that action a is generally unauthorized for principal p, but is, as an exception, authorized for object o.

Table 2 (in the appendix) lists the principal-matching rules for our example whilst Table 3 lists the authorization rules. A combination of authorization rules has been used in Table 3 to ensure that the Project Resource User is specifically unable to write to Func.Spec.#1 whilst other objects are writable by that principal.

A principal may be explicitly authorized or unauthorized for particular actions. The absence of any explicit authorization rules may itself be considered an implicit authorization depending on the default behaviour of the system. A default access control decision (allow or deny) needs to be specified in the event that no authorization rules apply to a request. Systems may need to support allow-by-default when the system enters an emergency state, such as the opening of fire exit doors when there is a fire. Other circumstances will commonly require fail-safe handling, where a deny-by-default strategy is implemented in order to ensure no unauthorised access is allowed. Some systems may be deemed so sensitive that there may be no conditions under which allow-by-default would be enabled. In Section 2.4.3 we discuss the specification of default strategies in our model.

2.4 Request Evaluation

Our model for request evaluation is inspired by the Unix access control model and relationship-based access control models and is summarized in Figure 3. From the Unix model, we take the idea of binding a request to a principal before computing an access control decision, which we combine with the idea of specifying authorization policies in terms of relationships. Firstly, we use the subject and object specified in the request to compute a set of applicable principals. Then we compute the actions for which those principals are authorized. Finally a decision is made to allow or deny the request based on those authorizations.

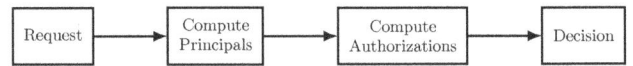

Figure 3: Processing overview

We now describe request evaluation, which has two main stages and is depicted schematically in Figure 4, in more detail. The first stage determines a list of matched principals for the request: in Figure 4 this stage is represented by the horizontal row of steps from 'START'. The second stage determines the authorizations explicitly defined for those matched principals identified in the first stage. This second stage is represented in Figure 4 by the vertical column of steps beginning at the 'MP list empty?' decision point. A conflict resolution process is employed to resolve any conflicting authorization rules and from this a decision is made.

2.4.1 Principal Matching

The list of matched principals is determined by the evaluation of principal-matching rules within the principal-matching policy. Thus, we first specify what it means for a principal-matching rule to be matched.

DEFINITION 9. *Let $q = (s, o, a)$ be a request and $G = (V, E)$ be a system graph. Then request q matches principal-matching rule (π, p) if $G, s, o \models \pi$. Given a principal-matching policy and a system graph, we write $G, q \xrightarrow{\pi} p$ if there exists a principal-matching rule (π, p) and request q matches (π, p).*

Informally, a principal-matching rule maps a (complex) relationship between entities in a graph to a principal; in other words, a principal-matching rule enables us, conceptually, to replace a path between two entities with a single edge labelled by a principal. Figure 5 illustrates such a matching, where request $q = (s, o, a)$ matches a principal-matching rule $(r_1; \overline{r_2}; r_3; r_4, p)$. It is worth noting that, based on the relationships shown in Figure 5, where r_4 is a symmetric label (identified by the lack of arrows on the edge), the principal-matching rule would also have been matched if the path condition had been $r_1 ; \overline{r_2} ; r_3 ; \overline{r_4}$.

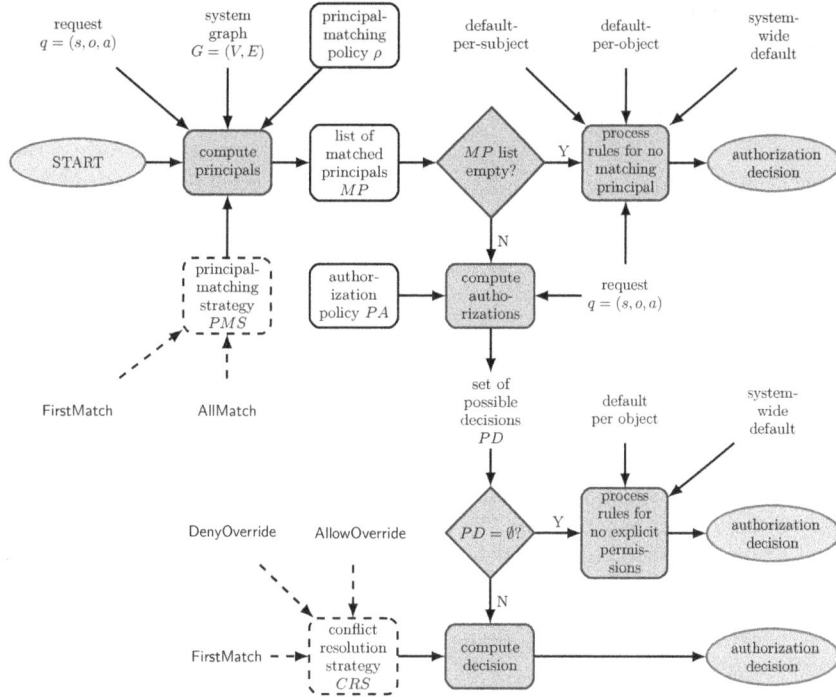

Figure 4: Detailed architecture

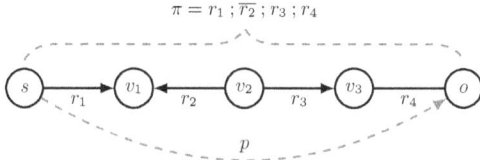

$$\pi = r_1 \, ; \, \overline{r_2} \, ; \, r_3 \, ; \, r_4$$

Figure 5: Principal-matching rule

A request may match more than one rule in the principal-matching policy. A *principal-matching strategy* (PMS) defines how the principals in matched rules should be combined (if at all). We consider two very natural PMSs: FirstMatch and AllMatch, but other options may be appropriate in some circumstances. The former evaluates the list of principal-matching rules in order and terminates when a path condition is matched, returning the corresponding principal. The latter evaluates the entire list of rules in the policy and returns a list of the principals in rules for which the request matches the path condition.

If used in conjunction with the FirstMatch PMS, the default principal rule $(\top, p)$, when present, would only be triggered, and so only apply, if no other rule matches. When used with AllMatch this rule would always apply, resulting in the default principal always being added to the list of matched principals.

An *authorization system* comprises a principal-matching policy ρ, a principal-matching strategy PMS, an authorization policy PA, and a conflict resolution strategy CRS (described in the next section). Given an authorization system, a system graph G and a request q, the list of *matched principals* MP includes those principals resulting from successful matches made in accordance with the specified principal-

matching strategy. We write $G, q \xrightarrow{\rho} MP$ to indicate that the list of matched principals for q (with respect to policy ρ and system graph G) is MP. If MP is empty then an authorization decision must be made based on pre-defined defaults. This process is described in Section 2.4.3.

2.4.2 Computing Authorizations and Decisions

The second stage of request authorization identifies whether the requested action (on the object) is explicitly authorized or unauthorized for one or more of the matched principals. Subsequently any conflicting assignments are resolved and we determine whether the requested action should, therefore, be allowed or denied.

DEFINITION 10. *Given a policy* ρ, *a request* $q = (s, o, a)$ *and a system graph* G *such that* $G, q \xrightarrow{\rho} MP$, *we define the set of* possible decisions, *denoted* PD, *to be* $\{b \in \{0, 1\} : (p, o, a, b) \in PA, p \in MP\}$.

PD can take one of four values: $\{0\}$, $\{1\}$, $\{0, 1\}$ and $\emptyset$.

- If $PD = \{b\}$, $b \in \{0, 1\}$, a decision can unambiguously be made (as a deny or allow, respectively).

- If $PD = \{0, 1\}$, we must employ a *conflict resolution strategy* (CRS) to determine the decision. We define three conflict resolution strategies: FirstMatch, Deny-Override and AllowOverride. The use of one of these strategies allows a single decision to be made from the conflicting assignments. In order to support the first of these, we require that the set of possible decisions be determined by considering each authorization, from the list PA, in turn.

The FirstMatch CRS takes the first element to be added to PD as the decision. In this way, if a positive authorization is identified first, then the request is

191

allowed. If a negative authorization is identified first, however, then the request is denied.

The DenyOverride and AllowOverride CRSs allow their respective elements, 0 and 1, to take precedence over the alternative, no matter which is identified first.

- The final case is $PD = \emptyset$. In this case, the authorization decision must once again be made using predefined defaults, as explained in Section 2.4.3 below.

2.4.3 Defaults

There are two circumstances when default decision making applies. The first is when no matched principals are identified, whilst the second is, as just described, when the set of possible decisions is empty.

To accommodate varying needs in these circumstances, we allow for default allow or deny of a request to be determined at one of the following levels: default-per-subject, default-per-object or system-wide default. We only support the default-per-subject when there are no matched principals, and not later, when there are no explicit authorizations. At the time when the set of possible decisions is determined, the subject is no longer directly relevant, having already been used to identify the appropriate matched principals. It is therefore unnecessary to reconsider the subject in order to evaluate the authorization decision.

The three defaults are evaluated in order, where specified, with the first applicable default determining the authorization decision. In this way, if there is a default specified for the subject s of the request $q = (s, o, a)$, the subject's default (allow or deny) applies. If no subject default is defined for s, then the default for the object o of the request shall apply, if specified. If there is no subject default for s and no object default for o, then the system-wide default shall apply. Whilst defaults for the subject and object are optional and may not be specified for the entities involved in the request, a system-wide default must be specified so as to ensure authorization decisions can be made in all circumstances.

2.5 Special Cases

The Unix access control mechanism employs a similar, albeit far simpler, mapping technique as that used above to identify principals from path conditions [6]. It can, therefore, be trivially represented using our model. In particular, the system model contains a set of three types: users, groups and objects, and a set of three relationships (none of which are symmetric): User-object, User-group and Group-object, which we will label uo, ug and go, respectively. The permissible relationship graph links the users to the objects and to the groups, as well as linking the groups to the objects (this is as our relationship naming suggests). There are three principal-matching rules: (uo, owner), (ug ; go, group) and, the default, ($\top$, world). Finally, we use the FirstMatch PMS and evaluate the rules in the above order.

Note also that we can configure our model to implement core RBAC [2]. We assume the set of entities is the disjoint union of users, roles, permissions and objects. Then there are two types of relationship, the User-role relationship, referred to as user assignment and abbreviated ua, along with the Role-permission relationship, referred to as permission assignment and abbreviated pa. At its simplest we then define a principal-matching policy where each rule has the form

(ua ; pa, p) where the principal p has the same name as the permission identified by the pa edge. The authorization policy contains elements $(p, ob, op, 1)$ which map the principals to objects, allowing them operations (as per the permission binary relation in RBAC).

Additionally, we can introduce the Role-role relationship (abbreviated rr) in order to extend this configuration to implement a role hierarchy. Finally, we could also introduce the User-permission relationship (abbreviated up), in order to articulate exceptions to the basic RBAC model by directly associating permissions with users.

Our model does not directly support the concept of sessions. However, if we were to introduce support for changing the system graph, we could employ a User-session-role relationship. The User-session-role relationship may only connect users and roles who are already joined by a User-role relationship. We then modify the original principal-matching rules to have the form (usr ; pa, p). Supporting (constrained) updates to the system graph in real time will be an important aspect of our future work.

3. PATH MATCHING

Principal matching, the first stage of request evaluation, described in Section 2.4.1, is the most complex part of request evaluation. (The second stage amounts to a sequence of simple lookups and comparisons.) Principal matching requires us to determine whether there exists a path in the graph from subject to object that matches a path condition. In this section, we describe the MatchPrincipal algorithm, which takes a path condition, two nodes (the subject and object of a request), the set of symmetric relationship labels and a system graph as inputs and returns a Boolean value indicating whether there exists a matching path in the graph.

The algorithm uses a (modified) breadth-first search to determine whether there exists a path in the system graph that begins at the subject and ends at the object such that concatenation of the relationship labels is equal to the path condition. It is employed iteratively to as many rules in the principal-matching policy as required, given the PMS in use: if FirstMatch is used then the algorithm is run on each principal-matching rule in turn, until a match is found; if the AllMatch PMS is used, the algorithm is run for every rule in the policy. In order to determine satisfaction of a simple path condition, we attempt to satisfy its component edge conditions one at a time. It is helpful to define the head and suffix of a path condition: the head is used to match edge labels in the graph, while the suffix determines the residual path condition.

DEFINITION 11. *Let $\pi \neq \diamond$ be a simple path condition. Then we define the* head *and* suffix *of π, denoted $H(\pi)$ and $S(\pi)$, respectively, as follows:*

- *$H(r) = r$ and $S(r) = \diamond$;*
- *$H(\bar{r}) = \bar{r}$ and $S(\bar{r}) = \diamond$;*
- *$H(\pi_1 ; \pi_2) = H(\pi_1)$ and $S(\pi_1 ; \pi_2) = S(\pi_1) ; \pi_2$;*
- *$H(\pi^+) = H(\pi)$ and $S(\pi^+) = S(\pi);\pi^*$, where π^* denotes 0 or more occurrences of π.*

PROPOSITION 2. *Let π be a simple path condition. Then $H(\pi)$ is equal to r or $\bar{r}$ for some $r \in R$. Moreover, $S(\pi)$ is a simple path condition.*

PROOF. The results follow immediately by a simple induction on the structure of simple path conditions. □

PROPOSITION 3. *Let π be a simple path condition. Then $\pi \equiv \mathsf{H}(\pi) ; \mathsf{S}(\pi)$.*

PROOF. The proof proceeds by induction on the structure of π. Consider the (base) case $\pi = r$. Then

$$G, u, v \models \mathsf{H}(r) ; \mathsf{S}(r) \Leftrightarrow G, u, v \models r ; \diamond$$
$$\Leftrightarrow G, u, v \models r$$

Thus $\mathsf{H}(r) ; \mathsf{S}(r) \equiv r$, as required. We prove the case $\pi = \bar{r}$ in a similar fashion. Now consider $\pi = \pi_1 ; \pi_2$ and assume the result holds for π_1 and π_2. Then

$$G, u, v \models \mathsf{H}(\pi_1 ; \pi_2) ; \mathsf{S}(\pi_1 ; \pi_2) \Leftrightarrow G, u, v \models \mathsf{H}(\pi_1) ; \mathsf{S}(\pi_1) ; \pi_2$$
$$\Leftrightarrow G, u, v \models \pi_1 ; \pi_2$$

Finally, consider π^+ and assume the result holds for π. Then

$$G, u, v \models \mathsf{H}(\pi^+) ; \mathsf{S}(\pi^+) \Leftrightarrow G, u, v \models \mathsf{H}(\pi) ; \mathsf{S}(\pi) ; \pi^*$$
$$\Leftrightarrow G, u, v \models \pi ; \pi^*$$
$$\Leftrightarrow G, u, v \models \pi^+$$

concluding the proof. □

We now develop the path-matching algorithm in more detail.

3.1 The Path-Matching Algorithm

The algorithm takes a start node (the subject), a target node (the object) and a path condition as part of its input. The current node is initialized to be the start node. The path-matching algorithm traverses the provided system graph 'consuming' the head of the path condition as it matches it against (one or more of) the relationship labels associated with incident edges of the current node. It then considers each of the adjacent edges in turn replacing the path condition with the relevant suffix. The algorithm terminates if it 'consumes' the entire path condition with the adjacent node equal to the target node or if no further matches can be made.

If we consider, for example, the graph in Figure 5, the request (s, o, a) and path condition $r_1 ; r_2$, then $\mathsf{H}(r_1 ; r_2) = r_1$, which is the label on edge (s, v_1, r_1). Hence, the edge is traversed and we next consider the node v_1 with path condition $\mathsf{S}(r_1 ; r_2) = r_2$. The algorithm terminates at this point (returning false) because there is no outgoing edge from v_1 labelled r_2.

The MatchPrincipal algorithm (listed in Algorithm 1) is, essentially, a modified breadth-first search algorithm. However, there are some awkward aspects to the design of the algorithm. First, we have to allow for nodes to be revisited. Second, we have to allow matching of edge conditions of the form r and $\bar{r}$. Finally, our algorithm has to be able to handle path conditions of the form π^+ without entering an endless loop, in order for the algorithm to terminate.

The algorithm uses a queue Q to track nodes that we have to visit. Unlike a conventional breadth-first search, we allow those nodes to be revisited because path conditions may be satisfied by a cycle in the system graph. However, if we revisit a node then we require a different non-empty path condition on each visit. In this way we avoid infinite loops whilst processing the path condition.

Algorithm 1 MatchPrincipal

Require: Graph $G = (V, E)$, set of symmetric relationship labels S, nodes u and v, and path condition π
Ensure: Returns true if $G, u, v \models \pi$ and false if it does not
1: Initialize empty queue Q
2: Initialize empty set of visited nodes $SEEN$
3: **add** (u, π) **to** Q
4: $SEEN = SEEN \cup \{(u, \pi)\}$
5: **while** Q is not empty **do**
6:     **dequeue** next entry (h, ϕ) from Q
7:     Initialize empty list of (node, suffix) tuples Θ
8:     // consider edges directed away from h
9:     **for** each edge $(h, w, r) \in E$ **do**
10:         **if** $\phi = \pi_1^* ; \pi_2$ **then**
11:             $\Theta = \Theta \sqcup [(h, \pi_2)]$
12:             $\phi = \pi_1^+ ; \pi_2$
13:         **end if**
14:         **if** $\mathsf{H}(\phi) = r$ **then**
15:             $\Theta = \Theta \sqcup [(w, \mathsf{S}(\phi))]$
16:         **end if**
17:         **if** $(r \in S$ and $(w, h, r) \notin E)$ **then**
18:             **if** $\mathsf{H}(\phi) = \bar{r}$ **then**
19:                 $\Theta = \Theta \sqcup [(w, \mathsf{S}(\phi))]$
20:             **end if**
21:         **end if**
22:     **end for**
23:     // consider edges directed towards h
24:     **for** each edge $(w, h, r) \in E$ **do**
25:         **if** $\phi = \pi_1^* ; \pi_2$ **then**
26:             $\Theta = \Theta \sqcup [(h, \pi_2)]$
27:             $\phi = \pi_1^+ ; \pi_2$
28:         **end if**
29:         **if** $\mathsf{H}(\phi) = \bar{r}$ **then**
30:             $\Theta = \Theta \sqcup [(w, \mathsf{S}(\phi))]$
31:         **end if**
32:         **if** $(r \in S$ and $(h, w, r) \notin E)$ **then**
33:             **if** $\mathsf{H}(\phi) = r$ **then**
34:                 $\Theta = \Theta \sqcup [(w, \mathsf{S}(\phi))]$
35:             **end if**
36:         **end if**
37:     **end for**
38:     // determine match or other nodes to visit
39:     **for** each $(n, \phi_s) \in \Theta$ **do**
40:         **if** $(n, \phi_s) \notin SEEN$ **then**
41:             **if** $\phi_s = \diamond$ **then**
42:                 **if** $n = v$ **then**
43:                     **return true** // match
44:                 **end if**
45:             **else**
46:                 **add** (n, ϕ_s) **to** Q
47:                 $SEEN = SEEN \cup \{(n, \phi_s)\}$
48:             **end if**
49:         **end if**
50:     **end for**
51: **end while**
52: **return false** // no match

Previously visited nodes, and the path condition at the time of the visit, are tracked using the set $SEEN$. At each node h we visit, we identify incident edges from our system graph $G = (V, E)$, it is these edges that we attempt to traverse by matching a label to the head of our path condition. Matched edges result in path condition suffixes relevant at specific adjacent nodes; we hold these in a list as node-suffix pairs. We use the notation $list_1 \sqcup list_2$ to indicate the concatenation of two lists, where the entries from $list_2$ are appended, in order, to the end of $list_1$.

The algorithm performs its edge condition matching in lines 8 to 22 and 23 to 37 for outgoing and incoming edges to the current node h respectively. However, the implementation is complicated by the handling of path conditions of the form π^+, whose suffix includes π^* (see Proposition 3), which may represent 0 occurrences of π or at least one occurrence of π. When processing path conditions, therefore, we first determine if it has the structure $\pi_1^* ; \pi_2$ (where π_2 may be $\diamond$) and, if so, we treat it as $\pi_1^+ ; \pi_2$; in addition we add π_2 (corresponding to 0 occurrences of π_1), along with the current node h, to our list of node-suffix pairs for consideration later (see Algorithm 1 lines 10 to 13 and 25 to 28).

After an edge condition is matched by the algorithm, each node-suffix pair is checked against *SEEN* and ignored if previously processed. The suffix ϕ_s of each unseen tuple is compared to $\diamond$, those matching indicate fully processed path conditions. If the node n associated with such a tuple is equal to the target node v then the path condition is considered to have been matched between u and v and the algorithm returns true. If the node isn't the target node, then the tuple is discarded as there is no remaining path condition to evaluate. Those unseen tuples, whose suffixes are not $\diamond$, are added to the queue of nodes to be visited (see Algorithm 1 lines 38 to 50).

Once all incident edges are considered for the current node, we move to the next node as indicated by the next entry in the queue Q. If the queue is empty and we have not already returned a value, then the path condition cannot be matched (because there are no further nodes to examine) and the algorithm returns false (see Algorithm 1 lines 5, 6 and 52).

Consider, for example, the system graph depicted in Figure 5 and the path condition $r_1^+ ; \overline{r_2} ; r_3 ; r_4$ with start node s and end node o. Then we are able to match edge condition r_1 and progress to node v_1 with path condition $r_1^* ; \overline{r_2} ; r_3 ; r_4$. We now attempt to match r_1 again, which fails. In addition, we add $(v_1, \overline{r_2} ; r_3 ; r_4)$ to the list of node-path condition pairs to consider. This will, eventually, lead to the node-suffix pair $(o, \diamond)$ being identified, at which point the algorithm will return a match (for path condition $r_1^+ ; \overline{r_2} ; r_3 ; r_4$ with start and end nodes s and o).

3.2 Correctness and Complexity

We first introduce the concept of the length of a simple path condition. Informally, it is equal to the number of edge conditions (r or $\overline{r}$) which it contains.

DEFINITION 12. *The length $\ell(\pi)$ of simple path condition π is defined as follows:*

- $\ell(r) = \ell(\overline{r}) = 1$;
- $\ell(\pi ; \pi') = \ell(\pi) + \ell(\pi')$;
- $\ell(\pi^+) = \ell(\pi)$.

The length $\ell(\rho)$ of a principal-matching policy ρ is equal to the length of the longest path condition of the principal-matching rules within ρ, $\ell(\rho) = \max_{\pi \in \rho} (\ell(\pi))$.

Our algorithm terminates because, with one exception discussed below, $\ell(\mathsf{S}(\pi)) = \ell(\pi) - 1$ because an edge is consumed in matching the head of the path condition. Thus, any node-suffix pair that is enqueued contains a shorter path condition. Eventually, the path condition will be reduced to $\diamond$ and we test whether the adjacent node is the target node. The exception arises when we consider a path condition of the form $\pi^* ; \pi'$. In this case, we enqueue a path condition of the form π' and also evaluate the path condition $\pi^+ ; \pi'$. Thus, we could, in the worst case visit every node in the system graph and evaluate the path condition $\pi^+ ; \pi'$. However, we do not enqueue a node-suffix pair if we have previously evaluated it (in the same way that a normal breadth-first search keeps track of visited nodes). Thus, for this exceptional case, we will eventually process the path condition π' (since $\pi^+ ; \pi'$ will either be discarded or fail to find a matching edge).

We can summarise our path-matching algorithm's processing as a breadth-first search through the graph, attempting to match edges to the remaining path condition. At each node the number of possible comparisons depends on the degree of that node. The path condition under consideration is re-written as each edge comparison is performed, with the head of the path condition removed if the edge satisfied the next element in the path condition. The path condition under consideration at adjacent nodes is, therefore, one element shorter than at the current one.

The time complexity of a standard breadth-first search is determined by the number of nodes and edges, since, in the worst case, each node and edge will be explored. For the PrincipalMatch algorithm, the number of "nodes" is determined by the number of nodes in the system graph and the length of the path condition. Specifically, the size of the queue is bounded by $|V| \cdot \ell(\phi)$. The number of edges in the system graph is $O(|V|^2 \cdot |R|)$. Thus, the total complexity of the algorithm is $O(|V| \cdot \ell(\phi) + |V|^2 \cdot |R|)$.

The MatchPrincipal algorithm determines whether a single path condition matches. In order to compute the list of matching principals in the worst case, every rule in the principal-matching policy ρ may need to be evaluated. The worst-case time complexity of principal matching is, therefore, determined by the complexity of matching one rule, the number of rules in the policy and $\ell(\rho)$.

3.3 Implementation

We have created a Python implementation of the Match-Principal algorithm which roughly follows the structure shown in Algorithm 1. We represent a path condition as a tree of nodes, where each node is a data structure containing (i) pointers to a left and a right node (ii) a relationship label if it is a leaf node (iii) a node type if the node is a non-leaf node (indicating the operation used to construct the path condition). Our implementation modifies the pseudo-code listed in Algorithm 1 in order to improve the processing of path conditions containing π^*. In particular, we process both possibilities for π^* when we meet it, rather than simply putting one aside for consideration later (as we do in lines 11 and 26 of Algorithm 1).

Using this implementation we evaluated the requests in our appendix example. The results are summarized in Table 1, which shows the number of nodes visited (n) and edges considered (e) during the evaluation of one specific principal-matching rule for each of these requests.

Path condition π	$\ell(\pi)$	Request	n	e	Found
$\mathsf{P};\overline{\mathsf{R}};\overline{\mathsf{M}}^{+}$	3	(Sales.#2, Func.Spec.#1, write)	5	19	Yes
$\mathsf{P};\overline{\mathsf{R}};\overline{\mathsf{M}}^{+}$	3	(Tech.#2, Test.Spec.#1, read)	7	24	Yes
$\mathsf{S};\overline{\mathsf{R}};\overline{\mathsf{M}}^{+}$	3	(Tech.#2, Func.Spec.#1, write)	4	15	Yes
$\mathsf{S}^{+};\overline{\mathsf{M}};\mathsf{S};\overline{\mathsf{D}};\overline{\mathsf{M}}^{+}$	5	(CTO, Proj.#1 Report#1, read)	17	58	Yes
$\mathsf{S}^{+};\overline{\mathsf{M}};\mathsf{S};\overline{\mathsf{D}};\overline{\mathsf{M}}^{+}$	5	(CEO, Proj.#1 Report#1, read)	7	24	No

Table 1: Running our implementation of MatchPrincipal using path conditions and requests from Tables 2 and 4

Notice that the algorithm may visit many more nodes than exist on the shortest path between the subject and object of the request. This is because we are using a breadth-first search. Notice also that two different subject nodes may be the same distance from the object node (as is the case for the subjects in the first and second rows) and yet one request is resolved with less computational effort. It would be interesting to see whether there is any advantage to be gained in using a depth-first search. This is certainly something we hope to investigate in future work.

4. RELATED WORK

We have already noted those aspects of the Unix access control model and role-based access control that have influenced the design of our model. Our work also takes inspiration from the formal model developed for Unix by Crampton [6], which suggested that the two-stage evaluation process used by Unix could provide inspiration for novel relationship-based access control models. We now compare our model with related work in the literature.

The widespread use of social networks and restricting the access to resources within such networks has inspired the development of research into relationship-based access control. The early work of Kruk *et al.* used friend and friend-of-a-friend relationships to determine access to resources [12], while the work of Ali *et al.* was based on the trust relationships between users [1]. Carminati *et al.* synthesized these elements to create an access control model for social networks based on relationships [3]. They represent a social network as a graph in which the edges are labelled by relationships (such as friend) and all nodes represent users. Each edge is also labelled with a trust value, indicating the "strength" of the relationship. An access condition has the form (u, r, d, t), where u is a user, r is a relationship label, d is the depth and t is the trust threshold. An access rule has the form (o, C), where o is an object and C is a set of access conditions. A user v is authorized to access the resource o if v satisfies the access conditions specified in C. More recent work has built on this model to provide additional features, such as joint management of access policies, but only in the context of social networks [11].

If we ignore the trust threshold, access conditions are a special case of path conditions. Specifically a relationship r of depth d can be represented by the path condition $r;\ldots;r$ (repeated d times). Moreover, we can specify relationships of unbounded depth using the path condition r^{+}. However, access conditions certainly cannot represent arbitrary path conditions. In other words, our approach significantly extends the possibilities for policy specification. (Trust thresholds may be useful in social networks, but we feel their use for our intended applications is inappropriate. Of course,

our framework may be easily adapted to accommodate trust thresholds by having a path condition built from pairs of the form (r, t), where r is a relationship label and t is a threshold.)

Fong's recent work on relationship-based access control also concentrates on access control in social networks and models the social network as a graph in which the edges are labelled by relationships and all nodes are users [7, 8]. Fong's work specifies a policy for each resource, where a policy is specified using a multi-modal logic.[1] Thus Fong's work provides a richer policy language than that of Carminati *et al.* The policy syntax is specified by the grammar

$$\phi, \psi ::= \top \mid \mathsf{a} \mid \neg\phi \mid \phi \vee \psi \mid \langle i \rangle \phi$$

where i is a relationship identifier. Informally, $\top$ serves the same purpose as our default path condition $\top$; a is analogous to $\diamond$; $\langle i \rangle$ is equivalent to our path condition r. Fong's language can encode alternatives (using $\vee$); we would simply specify alternative principal-matching rules. Fong's language does support negation, which we do not. Conversely, our language does support unbounded path conditions, which are useful when traversing a sub-graph comprising similar types of elements that might have arbitrary diameter (as in a directory tree, for example). A limitation of Fong's language is that a policy has to be specified for every resource and admits no relationships, other than ownership, between users and resources. In our approach, we simply identify the principals that apply to a request, given the subject and object of the request, thereby leveraging some of the advantages of a role-based approach. Moreover, we allow for arbitrary relationships between the nodes (subject to the constraints in the permissible relationship graph) in the system graph.

Cheng *et al.* also focused on the use of relationship-based access control within Online Social Networks [4, 5]. Their work allows for the specification of user-to-resource relationships (other than ownership). However, our model is more general still in its support for entities of any kind (including logical ones) and policies not focused on, but still applicable to, social networks. Cheng *et al.* employ a path checking algorithm which is comparable to our concept of path matching. However, their approach directly assigns permissions, whereas we introduce some of the benefits of RBAC and Unix access control by abstracting that assignment to matched principals. Their path expressions are directly based on regular expressions, including wildcards,

---

[1]The rationale for using a modal logic is that each relationship specifies an accessibility relation between users, which is used to provide semantics for policies. We do this more directly by working with path conditions and specifying their semantics in terms of a graph.

although they constrain rules containing wildcards so that such rules could, in fact, be enumerated as different alternatives. (Thus paths of arbitrary length are not properly supported.) In contrast, we only provide direct support for π^+ in path conditions, but do not limit the number of edges across which it can match, something that is crucial when dealing with variable depth data structures such as directory trees. Moreover, as we have seen, we can encode alternation in a rule's path condition as two (or more rules): the rule $(\pi_1 \mid \pi_2, p)$ is simply defined as two principal-matching rules (π_1, p) and (π_2, p). Similarly, we can handle (π^*, p) by defining the rules (π^+, p) and $(\diamond, p)$.

5. CONCLUSION

We have formally defined a new graph-based model for access control based on two concepts: path conditions and principal matching. We believe that path conditions are a novel contribution to the literature on relationship-based access control and that these conditions allow us to specify a wide range of policies that are relevant to access control in a wide range of applications, not just in the usual context of social networks. Principal matching enables us to leverage the advantages of both Unix and RBAC and extend the capabilities of both models. We also believe our model provides significant advantages over existing models for relationship-based access control, both in terms of the expressive power of path conditions and the relatively straightforward request evaluation process. Additionally, our model is generic, thus able to describe systems of various forms be they social networks, IT systems (singularly or as networks) or entire businesses. We have illustrated how the model can be implemented by describing an algorithm to support principal matching and, thereby, enable request evaluation within our model.

There are many opportunities for further work. In particular, we would like to investigate alternative path-matching algorithms and compare their efficiency with the one described in Section 3. SPARQL is an RDF query language that may well be an suitable alternative. We would also like to extend the policy language to include more expressive matching as a means of directly supporting access constraints such as separation of duty, binding of duty and Chinese Wall. We believe that such constraints can be supported simply by introducing conjunction within, and negation of, path conditions. Extending this further we plan to consider the matching of subgraphs, rather than paths, and to investigate the trade-offs in increased expressive power with the more expensive request evaluation algorithms that will be required. We also intend to develop an administrative model to manage components such as the system graph. In this way, we should be able to handle dynamic concepts, such as sessions in RBAC. RT is a family of role-based trust management languages [13] that combine features of RBAC with distributed access control models. Many of the rules of RT can, like the assignment relations in RBAC, be encoded as a single type of relationship within a system graph in our model. However, the RT delegation rule $A.r \leftarrow A'.r'.r''$ cannot be directly encoded within our model. We would like to be able to provide support for distributed access control, in which different parts of the subgraph form different administrative domains. Then RT-like rules would specify the edges that link different subgraphs. Finally, we would also like to enrich the model with stateful objects, such as work-

flow tasks, for which the set of authorized individuals may change over time. We expect that this will result in the system graph being updated as the state of an object changes (for example to support task-based separation of duty).

6. REFERENCES

[1] ALI, B., VILLEGAS, W., AND MAHESWARAN, M. A trust based approach for protecting user data in social networks. In *CASCON* (2007), K. A. Lyons and C. Couturier, Eds., IBM, pp. 288–293.

[2] ANSI. *American National Standard for Information Technology - Role Based Access Control (359-2004)*. ANSI INCITIS, 2004.

[3] CARMINATI, B., FERRARI, E., AND PEREGO, A. Enforcing access control in web-based social networks. *ACM Trans. Inf. Syst. Secur. 13*, 1 (2009).

[4] CHENG, Y., PARK, J., AND SANDHU, R. S. Relationship-based access control for online social networks: Beyond user-to-user relationships. In *SocialCom/PASSAT* (2012), IEEE, pp. 646–655.

[5] CHENG, Y., PARK, J., AND SANDHU, R. S. A user-to-user relationship-based access control model for online social networks. In *DBSec* (2012), N. Cuppens-Boulahia, F. Cuppens, and J. García-Alfaro, Eds., vol. 7371 of *Lecture Notes in Computer Science*, Springer, pp. 8–24.

[6] CRAMPTON, J. Why we should take a second look at access control in unix. In *13th Nordic Conference on Secure IT Systems* (2008), NORDSEC'08, ACM.

[7] FONG, P. W. L. Relationship-based access control: protection model and policy language. In *CODASPY* (2011), R. S. Sandhu and E. Bertino, Eds., ACM, pp. 191–202.

[8] FONG, P. W. L., ANWAR, M. M., AND ZHAO, Z. A privacy preservation model for facebook-style social network systems. In *ESORICS* (2009), M. Backes and P. Ning, Eds., vol. 5789 of *Lecture Notes in Computer Science*, Springer, pp. 303–320.

[9] GE, M., AND OSBORN, S. L. A design for parameterized roles. In *DBSec* (2004), C. Farkas and P. Samarati, Eds., Kluwer, pp. 251–264.

[10] GIURI, L., AND IGLIO, P. Role templates for content-based access control. In *ACM Workshop on Role-Based Access Control* (1997), pp. 153–159.

[11] HU, H., AHN, G.-J., AND JORGENSEN, J. Multiparty access control for online social networks: Model and mechanisms. *IEEE Trans. Knowl. Data Eng. 25*, 7 (2013), 1614–1627.

[12] KRUK, S. R., GRZONKOWSKI, S., GZELLA, A., WORONIECKI, T., AND CHOI, H.-C. D-FOAF: Distributed identity management with access rights delegation. In *ASWC* (2006), R. Mizoguchi, Z. Shi, and F. Giunchiglia, Eds., vol. 4185 of *Lecture Notes in Computer Science*, Springer, pp. 140–154.

[13] LI, N., MITCHELL, J. C., AND WINSBOROUGH, W. H. Design of a role-based trust-management framework. In *IEEE Symposium on Security and Privacy* (2002), IEEE Computer Society, pp. 114–130.

[14] SANDHU, R. S., COYNE, E. J., FEINSTEIN, H. L., AND YOUMAN, C. E. Role-based access control models. *IEEE Computer 29*, 2 (1996), 38–47.

APPENDIX

A. CORPORATE EXAMPLE

The following example applies our model to the project environment within a fictional company. To support this specific system, we initially define the underlying system model $(T, R, S, G_{\mathrm{PR}})$ where the set of types is

$$T = \{\mathsf{File}, \mathsf{Folder}, \mathsf{Group}, \mathsf{Printer}, \mathsf{Project}, \mathsf{User}\}$$

The set of relationship labels used in the system model is

$$R = \{\mathsf{Client\text{-}of}, \mathsf{Deliverable\text{-}for}, \mathsf{Member\text{-}of},$$
$$\mathsf{Participant\text{-}of}, \mathsf{Resource\text{-}for}, \mathsf{Supervises}\}$$

There are no symmetric relationship labels. Finally, the permissible relationship graph G_{PR}, defined using T and R, is shown in Figure 6.

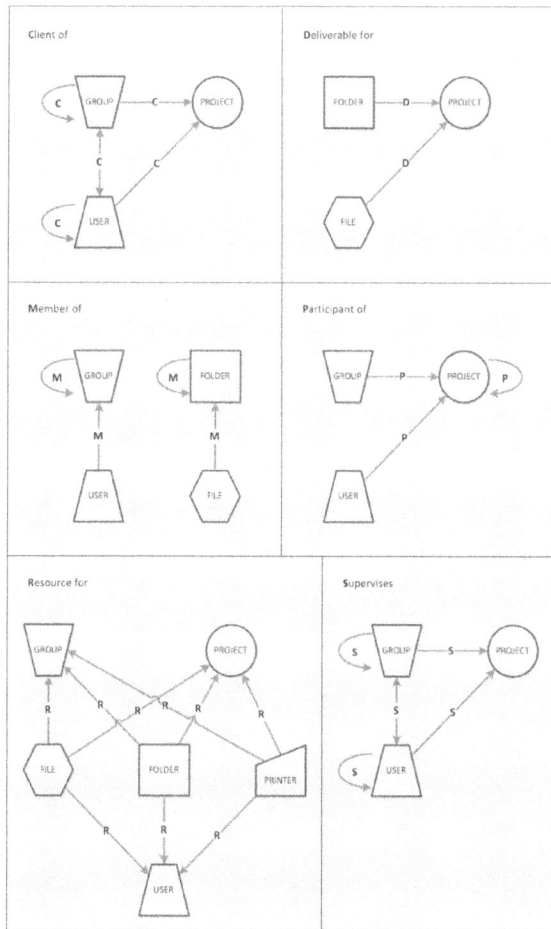

Figure 6: Permissible relationship graph

Using this system model we then describe the project environment using the system graph shown in Figure 7.

Within our authorization system we define the principal-matching rules shown in Table 2 and make use of the All-Match PMS.

Additionally, we define the authorization policy shown in Table 3 and whilst we define no per-subject or per-object defaults, we define the system-wide default as deny-by-default. We employ the FirstMatch conflict resolution strategy.

#	Principal-Matching Rule
1	$(\mathsf{C} ; \overline{\mathsf{D}} ; \overline{\mathsf{M}}^{+}, \text{Deliverable Client})$
2	$(\mathsf{S}^{+} ; \overline{\mathsf{M}} ; \mathsf{S} ; \overline{\mathsf{D}}, \text{Deliverable Reviewer})$
3	$(\mathsf{S}^{+} ; \overline{\mathsf{M}} ; \mathsf{S} ; \overline{\mathsf{D}} ; \overline{\mathsf{M}}^{+}, \text{Deliverable Reviewer})$
4	$(\mathsf{S} ; \overline{\mathsf{D}}, \text{Deliverable Supervisor})$
5	$(\mathsf{S} ; \overline{\mathsf{D}} ; \overline{\mathsf{M}}^{+}, \text{Deliverable Supervisor})$
6	$(\mathsf{P} ; \overline{\mathsf{D}}, \text{Deliverable User})$
7	$(\mathsf{P} ; \overline{\mathsf{D}} ; \overline{\mathsf{M}}^{+}, \text{Deliverable User})$
8	$(\mathsf{S} ; \overline{\mathsf{R}}, \text{Project Resource Supervisor})$
9	$(\mathsf{S} ; \overline{\mathsf{R}} ; \overline{\mathsf{M}}^{+}, \text{Project Resource Supervisor})$
10	$(\mathsf{P} ; \overline{\mathsf{R}}, \text{Project Resource User})$
11	$(\mathsf{P} ; \overline{\mathsf{R}} ; \overline{\mathsf{M}}^{+}, \text{Project Resource User})$
12	$(\mathsf{M} ; \overline{\mathsf{R}}, \text{Team Resource User})$

Table 2: Principal-matching policy

#	Authorization Rule
1	$(\text{Deliverable Client}, \star, \mathrm{read}, 1)$
2	$(\text{Deliverable Reviewer}, \star, \mathrm{read}, 1)$
3	$(\text{Deliverable Supervisor}, \star, \mathrm{read}, 1)$
4	$(\text{Deliverable Supervisor}, \star, \mathrm{write}, 1)$
5	$(\text{Deliverable User}, \star, \mathrm{read}, 1)$
6	$(\text{Project Resource Supervisor}, \star, \mathrm{read}, 1)$
7	$(\text{Project Resource Supervisor}, \star, \mathrm{write}, 1)$
8	$(\text{Project Resource User}, \star, \mathrm{read}, 1)$
9	$(\text{Project Resource User}, \mathrm{Func.Spec.}\#1, \mathrm{write}, 0)$
10	$(\text{Project Resource User}, \star, \mathrm{write}, 1)$
11	$(\text{Team Resource User}, \star, \mathrm{write}, 1)$

Table 3: Authorization policy

Table 4 lists some illustrative requests, together with the result of their evaluation. Requests 1 and 2 would result in the list of matched principals [Project Resource Supervisor, Project Resource User]. Requests 3 and 4 would result in the matched principal lists [Project Resource User] and [Deliverable reviewer], respectively, while the final request would match no principals.

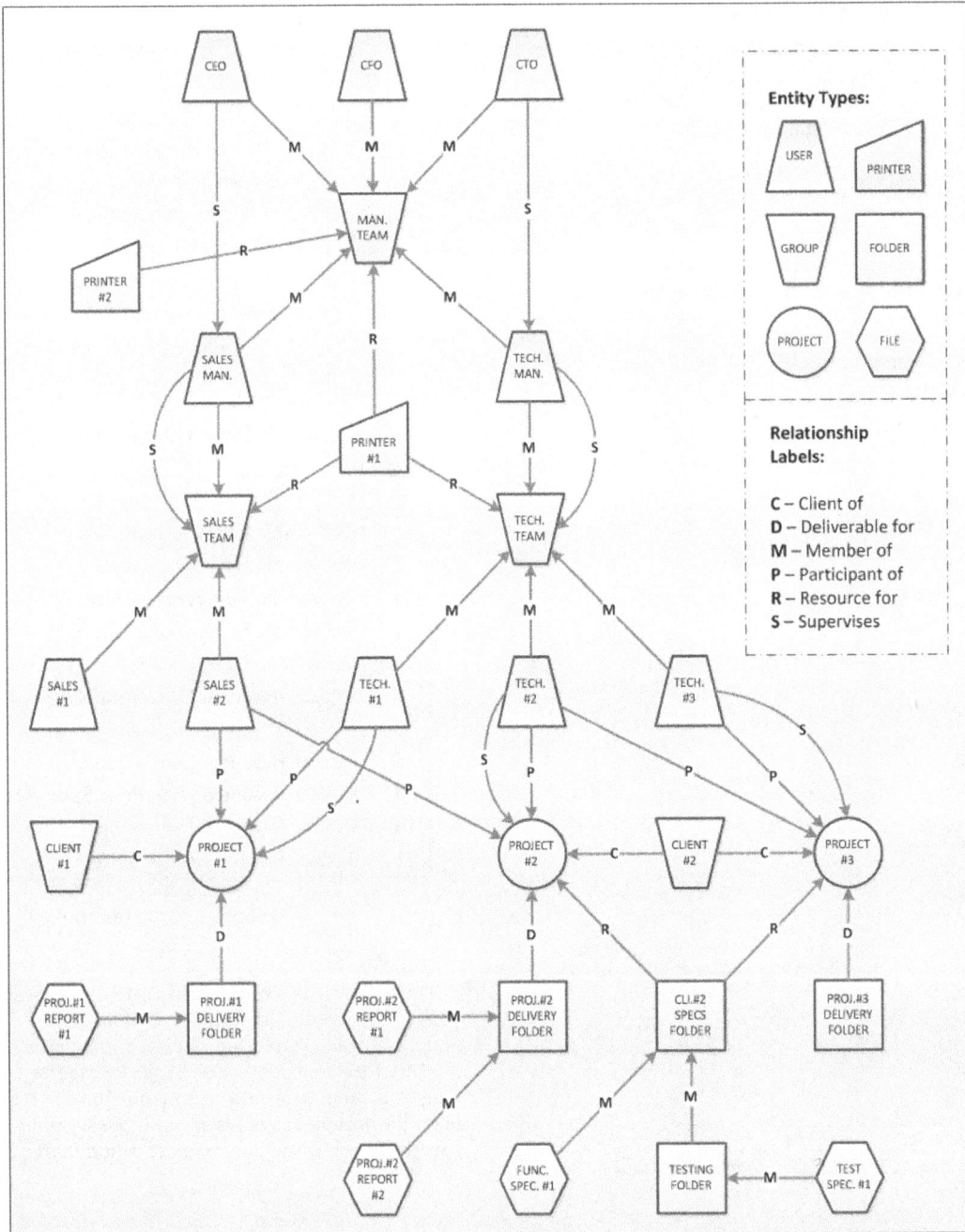

Figure 7: System graph

#	Request	Decision set	Outcome	Comment
1	(Tech.#2, Test.Spec.#1, read)	{1}	Allow	
2	(Tech.#2, Func.Spec.#1, write)	{1,0}	Allow	First match
3	(Sales.#2, Func.Spec.#1, write)	{0}	Deny	
4	(CTO, Proj.#1 Report#1, read)	{1}	Allow	
5	(CEO, Proj.#1 Report#1, read)	{}	Deny	System default

Table 4: Sample requests

An Actor-Based, Application-Aware Access Control Evaluation Framework

William C. Garrison III
Dept. of Computer Science
University of Pittsburgh
bill@cs.pitt.edu

Adam J. Lee
Dept. of Computer Science
University of Pittsburgh
adamlee@cs.pitt.edu

Timothy L. Hinrichs
VMware, Inc.
thinrichs@vmware.com

ABSTRACT

To date, most work regarding the formal analysis of access control schemes has focused on quantifying and comparing the expressive power of a set of schemes. Although expressive power is important, it is a property that exists in an *absolute* sense, detached from the application context within which an access control scheme will ultimately be deployed. By contrast, we formalize the access control *suitability analysis problem*, which seeks to evaluate the degree to which a set of candidate access control schemes can meet the needs of an application-specific workload. This process involves both reductions to assess whether a scheme is *capable* of implementing a workload (qualitative analysis), as well as cost analysis using ordered measures to quantify the *overheads* of using each candidate scheme to service the workload (quantitative analysis). We formalize the two-facet suitability analysis problem, which formally describes this task. We then develop a mathematical framework for this type of analysis, and evaluate this framework both formally, by quantifying its efficiency and accuracy properties, and practically, by exploring an academic program committee workload.

Categories and Subject Descriptors

D.4.6 [**Operating Systems**]: Security and Protection—*Access controls*; K.6.5 [**Management of Computing and Information Systems**]: Security and Protection

Keywords

Access control; Suitability analysis; Actor-based simulation

1. INTRODUCTION

Access control is one of the most fundamental aspects of computer security, and has been the subject of much formal study. However, existing work on the formal analysis of access control systems has focused largely on comparing the *relative expressive power* of two access control systems

(e.g., [1, 3, 10, 19, 21, 22, 24, 25]). Although expressive power is a meaningful basis for comparing access control systems, it exists only as a comparison made in absolute terms. That is, the knowledge that a system $\mathcal{Y}$ is more expressive than another system $\mathcal{Z}$ provides no assurance that $\mathcal{Y}$ is the best access control system for use within the context of a particular real-world application. It could be the case, for instance, that $\mathcal{Z}$ is *expressive enough* for a particular application and also has lower administrative overheads than $\mathcal{Y}$ would in the same situation. As was noted in a recent NIST report, access control is not an area with "one size fits all" solutions and, as such, systems should be evaluated and compared relative to application-specific metrics [13]. This position is supported by the recent introduction of application-specific access control analysis techniques [9, 11].

Considering the wide availability of many diverse access control systems and the relative difficulty of designing and building new secure systems from the ground up, an interesting topic for exploration is that of *suitability analysis*. Informally, this problem can be stated as follows: *Given a description of an application's access control needs and a collection of candidate access control systems, which system best meets the needs of the application?* Instances of this question can arise in many different scenarios, encompassing both the deployment of new applications and the reexamination of existing applications as assumptions and requirements evolve. A variant of this question was tackled by parameterized expressiveness [11], which evaluates an access control system's qualitative suitability to an application by assessing the strength of the security guarantees that it can satisfy while operating within that application. However, this type of suitability analysis provides no *quantitative* guidance in choosing the best access control solution for an applications.

In this paper, we identify and formalize the two-facet access control suitability problem, which considers both qualitative and quantitative metrics. We then propose techniques to facilitate this type of suitability analysis. As in parameterized expressiveness [11], we first formalize the notion of an access control workload to abstract the application's access control needs and the expected uses of these functionalities. Analysis then consists of two orthogonal tasks: (i) demonstrating that each candidate access control system can *safely* implement the workload, and (ii) quantifying the *costs* associated with using each candidate system. Toward carrying out such an evaluation, we develop techniques for representatively sampling from the workload's functionality, guidelines for formally specifying access control cost metrics, and a simulation framework for carrying out Monte Carlo-based cost analysis. In doing so, we make the following contributions:

- We formalize the *two-facet access control suitability analysis problem*, and articulate a set of requirements that should be satisfied by two-phase suitability analysis frameworks.

- We develop the first *two-phase suitability analysis framework*. We first establish whether candidate systems are expressive enough to safely implement the functionality of the workload via reduction. We then utilize a constrained, actor-based workload invocation structure to sample workload usage patterns and drive a simulation-based cost analysis that explores the expected costs of deployment.

- We evaluate our framework *formally* by proving that our simulation procedure is fixed-parameter tractable, and *practically* via a case study demonstrating how our framework can be effectively used to gain insight into a realistic scenario based on an academic conference management system.

Outline. In Section 2, we describe prior work in both access control expressiveness and simulation techniques, and summarize the tools that we use for the first phase of suitability analysis. In Section 3, we formalize the suitability analysis problem and articulate a set of requirements for suitability analysis frameworks. Sections 4 and 5 describe our approach to the second phase of suitability analysis, cost evaluation. We describe a case study investigating the use of our framework in Section 6. We then discuss the properties upheld by our framework and areas of future work (Section 7) and conclude (Section 8).

2. PRIOR WORK AND EXPRESSIVENESS

In this section, we describe related work in expressiveness analysis, including background details on the most relevant expressiveness framework, parameterized expressiveness [11]. We then discuss the shortcomings of even this expressiveness framework to motivate our approach. Finally, we discuss prior work on simulation techniques that have influenced our own cost analysis procedures.

2.1 Prior Work: Expressiveness

The formal study of access control systems began with a seminal paper by Harrison, Ruzzo, and Ullman [10]. This paper formalized a general access control model and proved that determining whether a particular access right could ever be granted to a specific subject—the so-called *safety problem*—was undecidable. Lipton and Snyder showed that in a more restricted system, safety was not only decidable, but decidable in linear time [19]. These two results introduced the notion that the most capable system is not always the right choice—that restricting our system can yield higher efficiency and greater ease in solving relevant security problems.

This, in turn, led to many results investigating the relative expressive power of various access control systems (e.g., [1, 3, 17, 21, 22, 24]). Relative expressiveness analysis frameworks typically provide analysts with the tools to prove statements of the form, "System $\mathcal{Y}$ is at least as expressive as system $\mathcal{Z}$." Informally, this means that $\mathcal{Y}$ can simulate the behavior of $\mathcal{Z}$, and assures us that we can use $\mathcal{Y}$ in any scenario in which $\mathcal{Z}$ can be used. However, without formal justification for their simulation requirements, many such frameworks proved to be too relaxed, allowing almost any two reasonable systems

to be shown to be equivalent: using such relaxed notions of simulation, systems in which safety is trivially decidable have been shown to simulate others in which it is undecidable [25]. Furthermore, due to various differences between notions of simulation, there have been conflicting relative expressiveness results that are difficult to reconcile [24, 25]. Thus, none of this prior work supports the comparison of access control systems with regards to their ability to perform *well* within a particular environment, a lack which was pointed out by a recent NIST technical report [13]. This has hindered the adoption of relative expressiveness analysis as a practical technique that enables analysts to choose the access control system that best meets their needs.

Parameterized expressiveness (PE) [11], by contrast, makes use of an access control *workload* to capture the requirements of the application. Expressiveness mappings (*implementations*) are then constructed between the workload and the access control systems that are candidates for accomplishing these requirements. An implementation is evaluated through the strength of the security requirements that it can preserve while satisfying the workload. In this way, systems can be compared by how well they can perform within the specific environment in which they are to be deployed.

2.2 Parameterized Expressiveness

Conducting expressiveness evaluation within PE begins by formalizing the requirements of the application and the access control systems that are candidates for accomplishing these requirements. Candidate systems are specified as state machines belonging to a particular access control *model*. Intuitively, an access control model is (i) a collection of data structures that store information pertinent to access control and (ii) a collection of procedures that expose only certain kinds of information about those data structures to an external observer. Each snapshot of the data structures in the model is an *access control state*. Each method that exposes information about the state is a *query*. An access control model differs from an arbitrary data structure because every state supports a special set of queries, the authorization queries, that define the access control policy to be enforced in that state. The access control policy for a state dictates which of all possible access control *requests* are granted. The authorization queries are denoted $auth(r)$, where r is one of the access control requests, e.g., a subject-object-right triple.

Definition 1 (Access Control Model) *An access control model $\mathcal{M}$ has fields $\langle \mathcal{S}, \mathcal{R}, \mathcal{Q}, \vdash \rangle$, where:*

- $\mathcal{S}$ *is a set of states*
- $\mathcal{R}$ *is a set of access control requests*
- $\mathcal{Q}$ *is a set of queries including $auth(r)$ for every $r \in \mathcal{R}$*
- $\vdash$ *is a subset of $\mathcal{S} \times \mathcal{Q}$ (the entailment relation)*

If $\mathcal{M} = \langle \mathcal{S}, \mathcal{R}, \mathcal{Q}, \vdash \rangle$, we use $States(\mathcal{M})$ to denote $\mathcal{S}$ and $Queries(\mathcal{M})$ to denote $\mathcal{Q}$. We use the term theory to denote a truth assignment for all the queries in $\mathcal{Q}$. For state $s \in \mathcal{S}$, we use $Th(s)$ (a subset of $\mathcal{Q}$) to denote the set of all $q \in \mathcal{Q}$ such that $s \vdash q$ (a convenient representation of the theory that holds at s). We use $Auth(s)$ (a subset of $Th(s)$) to denote the set of all $auth(r) \in \mathcal{Q}$ such that $s \vdash auth(r)$. ◇

Definition 2 (Access Control System) *An access control system $\mathcal{Y}$ has fields $\langle \mathcal{M}, \mathcal{L}, next \rangle$, where:*

- $\mathcal{M}$ *is an access control model*
- $\mathcal{L}$ *is a set of labels (also called commands)*
- $next : States(\mathcal{M}) \times \mathcal{L} \to States(\mathcal{M})$, *the transition function*

If $\mathcal{Y} = \langle \mathcal{M}, \mathcal{L}, next \rangle$, we use $Labels(\mathcal{Y})$ to denote $Labels(\mathcal{M})$, $States(\mathcal{Y})$ to denote $States(\mathcal{M})$, and $Queries(\mathcal{Y})$ to denote $Queries(\mathcal{M})$. The theories of $\mathcal{Y}$ are all the theories of $\mathcal{M}$. For a finite sequence of labels $l_1 \circ \cdots \circ l_n$, we use $terminal(s, l_1 \circ \cdots \circ l_n)$ to denote the final state produced by repeatedly applying $next$ to the labels $l_1, \cdots, l_n$ starting from state s. ◇

The access control demands of an application are captured in an *access control workload*. The workload includes a state machine similar to an access control system that formalizes the application's required protection state, commands and queries. In addition, the workload contains a specification of the valid utilization patterns of this functionality, encoded as a set of *traces* through the system. Each trace defines an initial state and a sequence of labels that are executed.

Definition 3 (Workload) *An* access control workload *is defined by* $\langle \mathcal{A}, \mathcal{T} \rangle$, *where:*

- $\mathcal{A} = \langle \mathcal{M}, \mathcal{L}, next \rangle$ *is the operational component: an abstract access control system*

- $\mathcal{T}$ *is the invocational component: a set of pairs* $\langle s_0, \tau \rangle$ *where* $s_0 \in States(\mathcal{A})$ *and* $\tau = l_1 \circ l_2 \circ \ldots$ *is a sequence where* $\forall i.l_i \in Labels(\mathcal{A})$. ◇

The representational similarity between the workload's operational description and access control systems enables us to construct *implementations* of the workload: mapping states, labels, and queries in the workload to states, (sequences of) labels, and (procedures over) queries in the systems.

Definition 4 (Implementation) *Given a workload* $\mathcal{W}$ *and a system* $\mathcal{Y}$, *an* implementation of $\mathcal{W}$ in $\mathcal{Y}$ *is defined by* $\langle \alpha, \sigma, \pi \rangle$, *where:*

- $\sigma : States(\mathcal{W}) \to States(\mathcal{Y})$ *is the state mapping*

- $\alpha : States(\mathcal{Y}) \times Labels(\mathcal{W}) \to Labels(\mathcal{Y})^*$, *the label mapping*

- $\pi = \{\pi_q | q \in Queries(\mathcal{W})\}$, *where* π_q *is a function from theories for* $\mathcal{Y}$ *to* $\{\text{TRUE}, \text{FALSE}\}$, *the query mapping* ◇

Security properties that an implementation must uphold can be expressed as constraints on these mappings, and proofs are manually constructed to ensure their preservation. While most prior works propose *fixed* sets of security properties defining their particular notion of expressive power, PE describes a set of properties that can be "mixed and matched," and implementations are evaluated qualitatively by which properties they satisfy. For example, implementations can be restricted to mapping each workload label to a single system label (label atomicity), or string manipulation can be restricted to prevent the implementation from packing arbitrary data into string constants such as usernames (homomorphism).

Unfortunately, although PE evaluates access control systems in a way that takes into account the specific application and *qualitatively* evaluates suitability to that application, it does not enable analysts to *quantitatively* evaluate suitability (i.e., by considering efficiency/costs). In this work we develop a cost analysis framework which complements PE to allow both qualitative and quantitative suitability analysis.

2.3 Prior Work: Simulation Techniques

Our cost analysis procedure will need to efficiently sample representative *traces* of actions from the full description of allowed behavior within an application. For inspiration in generating access control traces, we turn to trace generation work in other domains. In the field of disk benchmarking, Ganger [6] observed that interleaved workloads provided the

most accurate approximation of recorded traces. Thus, mechanisms for representing access control workloads must be capable of simulating the interleaved actions of multiple actors. This view is reinforced by the design of IBM's SWORD workload generator for stream processing systems [2]. This work also points out that synthetic workloads need to replicate both volumetric and contextual properties of an execution environment in order to provide an accurate indication of a system's performance within that environment. Thus, we conjecture that access control workloads as well may need to be capable of expressing not only volumetric statistics such as number of documents created, but also contextual statistics such as the type of content in created documents.

When formalizing the ways in which users of a system work together, it is important that one user does not execute an action which will render another user's work impossible to complete. Thus, during simulation, we must solve instances of the *workflow satisfiability problem* (WSP), a problem whose runtime complexity has been studied in the past and found to be NP-complete [26] but fixed-parameter tractable [4].

Our work is not the first to utilize Monte Carlo analysis when evaluating access control systems. For instance, Molloy et al. use Monte Carlo analysis to explore cost/benefit trade-offs in the context of risk-based access control systems [20]. Our framework, on the other hand, uses this analysis technique to explore an arbitrary array of analyst-specified costs associated with the use of particular access control systems in the context of a given workload.

3. SUITABILITY ANALYSIS

In this section, we identify the access control suitability analysis problem and develop a set of practical requirements that solutions to this problem must satisfy.

3.1 Problem Definition

Given an access control workload, i.e., a formalization of an application's access control requirements, we postulate that assessing the *suitability* of an access control system for that application will involve two classes of measures: **expressiveness** (*qualitative* measures of the system's ability to *securely* satisfy the requirements) and **cost** (*quantitative* measures of the system's ability to *efficiently* satisfy the requirements). As such, suitability analysis is done in two phases. In the first phase, the analyst must ensure that the candidate systems are expressive enough to safely meet the needs of their application. This phase includes formalizing the candidate access control systems and the capabilities required by the application (the workload), followed by constructing—and proving security properties of—implementations that describe how the systems can safely satisfy the workload. Upon completion of this phase, the analyst will have narrowed down the list of systems to those that are expressive enough to safely operate within the application and described each system's qualitative suitability to the application. One approach to this process is presented in [11].

The notion of costs, on the other hand, requires examining ordered measures of suitability such as administrative overheads, workflow throughput, and additional storage that result from the choice of a particular candidate access control system. In the cost analysis phase, the analyst formalizes the cost measures of interest, structures used for sampling from the expected usage of the access control system, and the expected costs of actions within each system. These are then

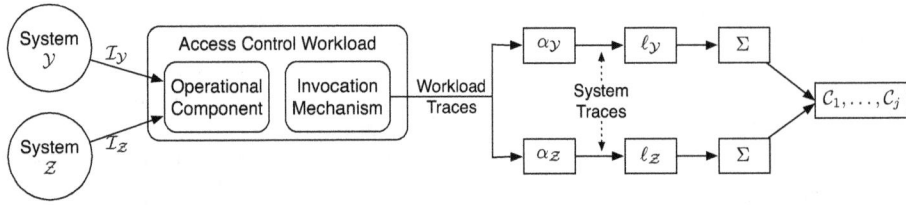

Figure 1: Overview of an application-aware analysis framework for access control

used to determine a partial order over the candidate systems describing their relative suitability to the application. More formally, these two phases describe the following problem:

Problem (Suitability Analysis) *Given an access control workload* $\mathcal{W}$*, a set of candidate access control systems* $\mathfrak{Y}$*, a set of security guarantees* $\mathcal{G}$*, and a set of ordered cost measures* $\mathfrak{C} = \{\mathcal{C}_1, \ldots, \mathcal{C}_m\}$*, determine:*

(i) the subset $\mathfrak{Y}' \subseteq \mathfrak{Y}$ *of systems that admit implementations of* $\mathcal{W}$ *satisfying maximal subsets of* $\mathcal{G}$

(ii) the subset $\mathfrak{Y}'' \subseteq \mathfrak{Y}'$ *of systems that admit cost-optimal implementations of* $\mathcal{W}$ *relative to the lattice* $\mathcal{C}_1 \times \cdots \times \mathcal{C}_m$

3.2 Solution Requirements

We now explore requirements for suitability analysis frameworks. First, we consider requirements in how representative traces through an access control workload ($\mathcal{W}$) are generated for exploration in cost analysis. Recall from Definition 3 that the workload specifies a (possibly infinite) set of traces. Exploring all possible traces during cost analysis will likely be impractical. Thus, in cost analysis, we must sample from this set in a way that selects traces that are representative of the expected behavior. Our first two requirements ensure that the framework can generate traces that accurately model the tasks carried out within an organization, and the interactions required to support and process these tasks.

Domain exploration Large applications are complex systems with subtle interactions, the emergent behaviors of which may not be captured during workload specification. It must be possible to efficiently explore many initial conditions (e.g., types of actors, operations supported, organization size, and operation distributions) to examine the effects of various levels of concurrency and resource limitation.

Cooperative interaction Tasks within large organizations typically require the interaction of many individuals. As such, suitability analysis frameworks should support operational workflows and constraints on their execution.

Next, we must ensure that the suitability analysis framework can be tuned to meet the specific needs of an application via choosing the metrics used to assess the suitability of an access control system for a given workload. This includes both the security guarantees used in expressiveness evaluation ($\mathcal{G}$) and the cost metrics used in cost evaluation ($\mathfrak{C}$).

Tunable safety There may be many different ways for some system to implement a given workload. Without enforcing structure on the implementation mapping, even the most under-expressive systems can appear to implement a workload [25]. It must be possible for an analyst to specify the security guarantees for implementations of their workload.

Tunable cost There is no single notion of cost that is sensible for use in every access control analysis [13]. A suitability analysis framework must be capable of representing many types of costs (e.g., computational, communication, and administrative), and examining multiple costs simultaneously.

Finally, we consider requirements that ensure that the suitability analysis framework remains practical to use, even for large-scale application workloads.

Tractability Steps of the analysis process that can be automated should be done so using tractable (e.g., polynomial time or fixed-parameter tractable) algorithms that remain feasible to use even for large systems.

Accuracy Since exploring all possible traces is impractical, it must be possible to approximate the expected error of costs obtained by exploring only a specific subset of traces.

These requirements guided the development of our suitability analysis framework; we will discuss our ability to achieve these requirements in Section 7.

3.3 Approach Overview

Figure 1 depicts an overview of our approach to solving the suitability analysis problem. First, we carry out expressiveness analysis as described in Section 2. This consists of constructing a workload, systems, and implementations, and then proving that the implementations satisfy the desired security guarantees. Then, we augment the operational component of the workload (the set of all valid traces) with a mechanism for generating *representative* traces that satisfy desired properties. We then formalize the *cost measures*, which represent the quantitative metrics our application is sensitive to, and label the actions within each system with their respective costs. Finally, we use Monte Carlo simulation to repeatedly generate workload traces, translate them into equivalent system traces using the mappings constructed during expressiveness analysis, and execute the system traces while recording the costs of each action.

Cost analysis imposes minimal requirements on the expressiveness components that precede it in the analysis pipeline. Although we utilize PE for its flexibility, if an analyst desires some particular fixed set of security properties, other formalisms for expressiveness mappings can easily be used within our cost analysis framework. Although such an analysis will not have the benefit of PE's ability to *qualitatively* evaluate access control suitability, our cost analysis techniques for *quantitative* evaluation will work with any notion of expressiveness that satisfies several general properties:

State equivalence The expressiveness mapping includes a function that determines, given any workload state w, the equivalent system state s.

Action construction The expressiveness mapping includes a function that determines, given any system state s and workload action (label l or query q), a procedure in system

(a) Actor machines

Constraints:
$\{\langle \neq, C, D\rangle\}$

(b) Workflow

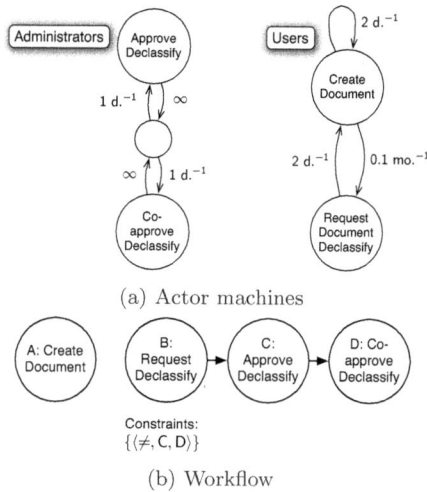

Figure 2: Example invocational structures

labels and/or queries for effecting results equivalent to those caused by l or q.

Determinism Regardless of what labels or queries will be executed in the future, each workload state w always maps to the same system state s, and each (system state, workload action) pair maps to the same procedure in system actions.

Parameterized expressiveness clearly satisfies these properties by definition. Many other notions of expressiveness in the literature can also be rephrased to meet these requirements (i.e., by using them to construct mappings between a workload and a system, rather than between two systems). Notable examples include the state matching reduction [25], as well as the simulations defined by Chander et al. [3] and Ammann et al. [1].

4. TRACE GENERATION

The invocation mechanism of an access control workload describes valid usage of the access control system within the application being described. This is represented as a set of traces through the system's actions (labels and queries). In cost analysis, we need to sample from this set of traces in a way that is representative of the *expected* usage. We also need to do so in a way that satisfies the requirements set forth in Section 3.2. For example, *Domain Exploration* requires that we are able to alter input parameters. Implicitly in this requirement is the assumption that the trace reacts to these initial state parameters (e.g., more users typically means more frequent execution of labels and queries).

To this end, we define an extension of the invocation mechanism that utilizes the concepts of *actors* carrying out *actions* within the system. Actors are human users, daemons, and other entities that act on the access control system in ways that are described by *actor machines*. We express the various ways in which actors cooperate to complete a task using *constrained workflows*. This structure specifies dependencies between related actions, and utilizes constraints to restrict which user can execute each action. Together, these structures enable the modeling and simulation of complex and concurrent behaviors of the entities in a workload.

We now formalize *actions*, the basic units of work executed by an actor in the system. An action is a parameterized

generalization of queries and labels. This allows us to specify the generic description of the action (e.g., check an access, assign a role) and separately assign the precise parameters (e.g., the specific users, documents, and roles involved). These can be assigned statically by the executing actor's behavior machine or dynamically during execution.

Definition 5 (Action) *Given an access control system, $\mathcal{Y}$, an access control action for $\mathcal{Y}$ is a function from a set of parameter spaces (derived from States($\mathcal{Y}$)) to the system's set of operations, and is defined as $\mathcal{A} : P_1 \times \cdots \times P_j \to Labels(\mathcal{Y}) \cup Queries(\mathcal{Y}) \cup \{\varnothing\}$, where:*

- $P = \langle P_1, \ldots, P_j \rangle$ *is the set of parameter spaces from which the actions's j parameters are drawn (e.g., the set of subjects, objects, roles).[1] We denote $P_1 \times \cdots \times P_j$ as P^*.*

- $\mathcal{A} : P_1 \times \cdots \times P_j \to Labels(\mathcal{Y}) \cup Queries(\mathcal{Y}) \cup \{\varnothing\}$ *maps each parameterization to a label or query in $\mathcal{Y}$, or to $\varnothing$, which designates no label or query is to be executed* ◇

To describe the behavior of actors, we employ state machines that we call *actor machines*. Each state is labeled with an action and a (possibly incomplete) parameterization. Transitions in this state machine are labeled with *rates* akin to those used in continuous-time Markov processes (e.g., [18]). We generate representative traces of actor behavior by probabilistically walking this machine, following transitions with probabilities proportional to their rates.

Definition 6 (Actor Machine) *Let $\mathcal{Y}$ be an access control system, A a set of actions from $\mathcal{Y}$, and $\mathfrak{V}$ a set of variable symbols. An actor machine for $\mathcal{Y}$ is the state machine $\langle S, \Phi, R \rangle$, where:*

- S *is the set of actor machine states*

- $\Phi : S \to A \times (P_1 \cup \mathfrak{V}) \times \ldots \times (P_j \cup \mathfrak{V})$ *labels each state with an action and a partial parameterization of that action (i.e., parameters can be assigned a static value or a variable to be assigned dynamically during execution)*

- $R : S \times S \to \mathbb{R}$ *is the set of transition rates* ◇

The semantics of the execution of an actor machine are as follows. R describes the rates of transitioning from one state to another. To achieve the Markov property, the time spent waiting to exit a state is exponentially distributed, with rate parameter proportional to the sum of the rates of all exiting transitions. An actor carries out a state's action upon entering the state (possibly after a pause, e.g., an action to submit a comment to a forum may pause for several minutes while the message is composed).

Example actor machines are demonstrated in Fig. 2a. In this example, we classify actors into administrators and users. Users generate documents and occasionally request a document be declassified for public consumption, while administrators approve declassification requests. Due to the labeled rates on this machine, an administrator is expected to approve a declassification request on average in one day, and roughly 10% of users request a declassification each month. Transitions labeled with ∞ occur immediately.

To describe dependencies between actions taken by one or more actors, we present the notion of a *constrained access control workflow*, which organizes the execution of actions. Formally, this structure specifies the partial order describing

---

[1]We typically use the first parameter of an action to represent the executing entity. For queries, this allows different responses for different queriers. For commands, this allows restrictions on the entities permitted to execute.

action dependence as well as constraints that restrict the set of users that can execute various actions.

Definition 7 (Constrained Workflow) *Let $\mathcal{Y}$ be an access control system and $\mathfrak{A}$ a set of access control actors within $\mathcal{Y}$. We say that $W = \langle A, \prec, C \rangle$ is an constrained access control workflow over the system $\mathcal{Y}$, where:*

- *A is the set of actions from $\mathcal{Y}$*
- *$\prec \subset A \times A$ is the partial order describing action dependencies. If $a_1 \prec a_2$, then a_2 depends on a_1, and a_2 cannot be executed until after an execution of a_1.*
- *C is the set of constraints, each of the form $\langle \rho, a_1, a_2 \rangle$ (with $a_1, a_2 \in A$). Here, ρ is a binary operator of the form $\mathfrak{A} \times \mathfrak{A} \to \{\text{TRUE, FALSE}\}$. For example, $\langle \neq, a_1, a_2 \rangle$ says that a_1 and a_2 must be executed by different actors.* $\diamond$

Figure 2b displays a constrained workflow with two *tasks* (disjoint subsets of the workflow): document creation and declassification. The former is a degenerate task containing a single unconstrained action. Declassifying a document, on the other hand, requires the approval of two different administrators. The workflow allows administrators to approve declassification only after the request, and the approvals must be executed by distinct administrators.

Our *actor-based invocation mechanism* combines these components; it refines the set of traces included in an access control workload (Definition 3) using a constrained workflow, a set of actor machines, and a method for extracting the active actor machines from an access control state.

Definition 8 (Actor-Based Invocation) *Let $\mathcal{Y}$ be an access control system. We say that $I^{\mathcal{Y}} = \langle W, \mathfrak{A}, M \rangle$ is an constrained, actor-based access control invocation mechanism over the system $\mathcal{Y}$, where:*

- *W is a constrained workflow over $\mathcal{Y}$*
- *$\mathfrak{A}$ is the set of all actor machines*
- *$M : States(\mathcal{Y}) \to \wp(\mathfrak{A})$ is the actor machine liveness function (i.e., a function that maps access control states to the sets of actor machines active in states)* $\diamond$

5. QUANTITATIVE COST ANALYSIS

5.1 Cost Measures

An important part of cost analysis is choosing relevant cost measures. These measures should be descriptive of what types of costs are important to the analysis, while also enabling the analyst to easily label actions with costs. For example, while "operational cost per day" may be representative of evaluation goals in industry, it is hard to assign costs in this measure to any access control action. A measure such as "average administrative personnel-hours," on the other hand, is more easily quantified and enables the same types of analyses. In this paper, we do not commit to a particular cost measure, but rather develop our framework to operate on any measure satisfying a number of simple properties.

Definition 9 (Cost Measure) *A cost measure is defined by the ordered abelian monoid $\mathcal{C} = \langle C, \bullet, \preceq \rangle$, where C is the set of costs, $\bullet$ is the closed, associative, commutative accrual operator over C with identity 0_C, and $\preceq$ is a partial order over C such that $\forall a, b \in C : a \preceq a \bullet b \wedge b \preceq a \bullet b$.* $\diamond$

Definition 9 can be used to encode a variety of interesting access control measures, including several of those noted in a recent NIST report on the assessment of access control systems [13]. Costs like "steps required for assigning and dis-assigning user capabilities" and "number of relationships required to create an access control policy" can be represented using the cost measure $\langle \mathbb{N}, +, \leq \rangle$. Our notion of measure is general enough to represent many other types of costs as well. Measures for human work such as "personnel-hours per operation" and "proportion of administrative work to data-entry work" can be represented using the cost measures $\langle \mathbb{Z}^+, +, \leq \rangle$ and $\langle \mathbb{Z}^+ \times \mathbb{Z}^+, +, \leq \rangle$, respectively. Maximum memory usage can be represented using $\langle \mathbb{N}, \max, \leq \rangle$.

In order to calculate the total cost of a particular implementation, costs of executing the various actions within the implementing systems must be determined. Sometimes, the cost of any execution of an action is constant (e.g., creating a document requires a constant amount of I/O). In other cases, the parameters affect the cost (e.g., adding a user is more expensive for classes of users with greater capabilities). In addition, some costs depend on the current state (e.g., granting access to all documents with a certain property may require inspecting each document, a procedure that grows in cost with the number of documents in the system). Thus, a cost function is required to map each (action, parameterization, state) to an element of the relevant cost measure.

Definition 10 (Cost Function) *Let $\mathcal{Y}$ be an access control system, A a set of actions from $\mathcal{Y}$, and $\mathcal{C} = \langle C, \bullet, \preceq \rangle$ a cost measure. A cost function for $\mathcal{C}$ in $\mathcal{Y}$ is a function $\ell_{\mathcal{C}}^{\mathcal{Y}} : A \times States(\mathcal{Y}) \to C$, which maps each action and state to the member of the cost measure that best represents the costs associated with executing that action in that state.* $\diamond$

In addition to the cost functions that are of specific interest to the analyst, our cost analysis simulation process also requires the specification of each system's *time function*. The time function is a cost function with measure $\langle \mathbb{R}, +, \leq \rangle$, describing the duration of time required to complete an access control action. This time corresponds to the duration that an actor pauses before completing an action when entering a state in the actor machine (e.g., the declassification example from Section 4).

5.2 Simulation Procedure

Once the analyst has defined the trace generation structures, a set of cost measures, and cost functions for each candidate system, she can conduct cost analysis via simulation. Our main simulation procedure, ACCostEvalSim (shown in Algorithm 1), conducts a single, randomized run of the system. First, each system's initial state is populated by sampling from a distribution provided by the analyst. An actor machine is then launched for each actor in these systems. At each time step, the clock is incremented and each actor machine is inspected for the next action, as per the execution semantics of the actor machine (Section 4). If the actor machine returns an action, an instance of the workflow satisfiability problem (WSP) [4, 26] is solved to ensure that the actor can execute the action without rendering the constrained workflow instance unsatisfiable. For independent actions (i.e., those in $\{a_1 \mid \nexists a_2.(a_2 \prec a_1)\}$), a new workflow instance is created and added to the pool of partially-executed workflows. Otherwise, the action is taken in the context of an existing workflow instance that is already in progress. After all actions for a time step are collected (and verified by WSat), their changes are effected in the state and their costs are accrued. Finally, the set of actors is adjusted according to changes in the state. Once the goal time is reached, the total costs are output.

Algorithm 1 Monte Carlo cost analysis simulation

Input: $\mathfrak{Y}$, set of candidate systems
Input: Σ, set of implementations $(\forall \mathcal{Y} \in \mathfrak{Y} : \sigma_{\mathcal{Y}} \in \Sigma)$
Input: $\mathfrak{C}$, set of cost measures $(\tau = \langle \mathbb{R}, +, \leq \rangle \in \mathfrak{C})$
Input: L, set of cost functions $(\forall \mathcal{Y} \in \mathfrak{Y}, \mathcal{C} \in \mathfrak{C} : \ell_{\mathcal{C}}^{\mathcal{Y}} \in L)$
Input: $I = \langle W, \mathfrak{A}, M \rangle$, invocation mechanism
Input: $s_0 \in States(\mathcal{W})$, start state
Input: T_f, goal time
Input: t, time step
Input: χ, number of Monte Carlo runs

procedure ACCostEvalSim$(\mathfrak{Y}, \Sigma, \mathfrak{C}, L, I, s_0, T_f, t)$
  $\mathbf{S} \leftarrow \{\}$ ▷ Initialize set of running AC systems
  $T \leftarrow 0$ ▷ Initialize master clock
  for all $\mathcal{Y} \in \mathfrak{Y}$ **do**   ▷ Initialize state
    $\mathbf{S} \leftarrow \mathbf{S} \cup \{\mathcal{Y}\}$
    $s_{\mathcal{Y}} \leftarrow \sigma_{\mathcal{Y}}(s_0)$ ▷ Current state of system $\mathcal{Y}$
    for all $\mathcal{C} \in \mathfrak{C}$ **do**
      $c_{\mathcal{C}}^{\mathcal{Y}} \leftarrow 0_{\mathcal{C}}$ ▷ Total cost of system $\mathcal{Y}$ in $\mathcal{C}$
    $\mathbf{A}_{\mathcal{Y}} \leftarrow M(s_{\mathcal{Y}})$ ▷ Set of running actor machines
    for all $\alpha \in \mathbf{A}_{\mathcal{Y}}$ **do**
      $T_{\alpha} \leftarrow 0$ ▷ Per-actor clocks
  while $T \leq T_f$ **do**   ▷ Main loop
    $T \leftarrow T + t$ ▷ Increment clock
    for all $\mathcal{Y} \in \mathbf{S}$ **do**   ▷ Each AC system
      $K = \{\}$ ▷ Clear action list
      for all $\alpha \in \mathbf{A}_{\mathcal{Y}}$ **do**   ▷ Choose next actions
        if $T_{\alpha} < T$ **then**   ▷ Check actor busy state
          $\langle k, P_k \rangle \leftarrow$ nextAction(α)
          if $k \neq \varnothing \land$ WSat$(k, \alpha, P_k) \neq \varnothing$ **then**
            $T_{\alpha} \leftarrow T + \ell_{\tau}^{\mathcal{Y}}(k)$ ▷ Busy state
            $K \leftarrow K \cup \{\langle k, \alpha, P_k \rangle\}$ ▷ Save action
      for all $\langle k, \alpha, P_k \rangle \in K$ **do**   ▷ Compile costs
        for all $\mathcal{C} \in \mathfrak{C}$ **do**
          $c_{\mathcal{C}}^{\mathcal{Y}} \leftarrow c_{\mathcal{C}}^{\mathcal{Y}} \bullet_{\mathcal{C}} \ell_{\mathcal{C}}^{\mathcal{Y}}(\sigma_{\mathcal{Y}}(\langle k, \alpha, P_k \rangle))$
        if k is a command **then**
          $s_{\mathcal{Y}} \leftarrow \sigma_{\mathcal{Y}}(next(s_{\mathcal{Y}}, k(P_k)))$ ▷ Update state
  for all $\mathcal{Y}' \in \mathfrak{Y}$ **do**
    Log $\left\langle \mathcal{Y}', c_{\mathcal{C}_1}^{\mathcal{Y}'}, \dots, c_{\mathcal{C}_m}^{\mathcal{Y}'} \right\rangle$

To address the requirement of *Tractability*, we present the following theorem (proved in Appendix A), which states that ACCostEvalSim is fixed-parameter tractable (i.e., has polynomial runtime if a particular parameter is bounded). For an overview of parameterized complexity, see, e.g., [26].

Theorem 1 *Assuming that workflow constraints are restricted to $\{=, \neq\}$ (i.e., binding and separation of duty), the simulation procedure* ACCostEvalSim *is* fixed-parameter tractable *with the number of actions in the largest task (i.e., the size of the largest disjoint subgraph of the workflow graph).*

We also define two drivers for using this simulation procedure (see Appendix B). The first, ACCostEvalMC, randomly samples start states from a given distribution and uses the Monte Carlo technique to generate large numbers of data points, allowing the analyst to detect trends across a variety of start states. An alternative driver, ACCostEvalCI, decides how many simulation runs to conduct based on a desired confidence and the assumption of a particular distribution of costs across runs. This allows the analyst to fix a start state and repeatedly execute ACCostEvalSim until she can be confident that the results are accurate.

6. CASE STUDY

In this section, we demonstrate the suitability analysis process using our framework. This case study explores a workload based on an online management system for an academic conference, including paper submissions, reviews, and discussion. The specification of the workload is done in a group-centric secure information sharing model [14, 15], and our candidate systems include two variants of role-based access control [5, 23] and traditional UNIX user-group-other

permissions [7]. The qualitative phase is conducted using parameterized expressiveness [11], and the quantitative phase is conducted using several cost measures that indicate how naturally the systems can implement the workload.

6.1 Workload and Candidate Systems

The workload's operational component (i.e., the abstract system that describes the application's requirements) is based on that used in [9] for a group-based program committee workload, as this system contains all the state, labels, and queries we need to *naturally* represent our conference workload. Users can join and leave groups, and objects can be added and removed from groups. The log of these events is used to decide whether a user can access an object. Users who perform a *strict join* to a group receive access only to objects added after they join, whereas a *liberal join* grants immediate access to all existing objects. A *strict leave* rescinds all of the user's accesses within the group; a *liberal leave* allows the user to retain access. All objects (i.e., papers, reviews, discussion messages) are added to groups via *liberal add*, and thus whether a user can access an object in a group is determined solely by the relative times the join and add took place and the variants of join/leave that was performed.

These capabilities naturally satisfy the requirements of the academic conference. When the program committee is formed, a *discussion group* is created, and each reviewer joins. Each paper is submitted to an *author group*, which holds the objects the author can see (initially, only the submitted paper). During the reviewing period, a *review group* is created for each paper, which the paper's reviewers join. Discussion about papers in contention takes place in the discussion group. When the group discusses a paper with which a reviewer has a conflict of interest, this reviewer will temporarily leave the discussion group (executing liberal leave to retain previous accesses and strict join to return without gaining access to the conflicted discussion).

We consider several role- and group-based candidate systems for implementing the conference workload. As such systems provide a level of indirection between subjects and objects, they are more likely to be effective at implementing the group-based conference workload than systems without this level of indirection (e.g., access control list systems). We choose widely-deployed candidate systems from both the industrial and consumer spaces, making them likely candidates for developing the type of system described by our conference workload. We evaluate the following candidate systems.

RBAC $RBAC_0$ is the most basic role-based access control system in the RBAC standard [23]. States contain the set of users U, set of roles R, and set of permissions P, as well as relations between them: $UR \subseteq U \times R$ describes users' membership in roles, and $PA \subseteq R \times P$ describes permissions' assignment to roles. A user u is authorized to permission p if $\exists r.(\langle u, r \rangle \in UR \land \langle r, p \rangle \in PA)$. Labels allow adding to and removing from all of U, R, P, UR, and PA.

Hierarchical RBAC While $RBAC_0$ grants a level of indirection between users and permissions, $RBAC_1$ includes a hierarchical structure over roles to further extend this abstraction. $RBAC_1$ includes all state elements of $RBAC_0$ as well as the role hierarchy $RH \subseteq R \times R$, a binary relation over R whose transitive closure is the *Senior* partial order (we sometimes designate the transitive, reflexive closure $\geq$). In hierarchical RBAC, a user inherits all permissions from roles junior to roles she is explicitly assigned. That is, a user u is authorized to permission p if $\exists r_1, r_2.(\langle u, r_1 \rangle \in UR \wedge \langle r_2, p \rangle \in PA \wedge r_1 \geq r_2)$. Labels allow full manipulation of all state elements.

UNIX Permissions Finally, the *ugo* system [7,9] is based on the *user, group, other* system of access control in UNIX. Thus, if $RBAC_0$ and $RBAC_1$ fill the need for a commonly-used industrial standard system, *ugo* fills the role of a common consumer system. In *ugo*, objects can be associated with an owner user and group, and permissions are then granted to the user, the group, or everyone else.

6.2 Qualitative Analysis

In this section, we summarize the qualitative analysis we conducted to ensure that each of our candidate systems is capable of satisfying the conference workload. For brevity, and given the availability of other case studies discussing in-depth qualitative suitability analysis (e.g., [9,11]), in this case study we omit full proofs of expressiveness theorems (to be presented in an accompanying technical report), and consider a fixed set of implementation guarantees. For example expressiveness proofs which are sufficiently similar to our proofs of the theorems below, see [9]; for formal definitions of the implementation properties, see [9,11].

Correctness Correctness is a bare minimum requirement for an implementation in parameterized expressiveness. Intuitively, correctness says the following: a workload state's image in a system answers mapped queries exactly as the original state answers the original queries; and the same system state is reached by executing a workload action and mapping the result into the system or by mapping the initial state and executing the action's image in the system.

Weak AC-Preservation AC-preservation says that $\pi_{auth(r)}$ must map authorization request r from workload state w to system state $\sigma(w)$ directly, checking whether $\sigma(w) \vdash auth(r)$. This forces the workload and system to have identical sets of requests, which is not always the case (e.g., access matrix systems typically use subject-object-right triples, while role-based systems often use user-permission pairs). Weak AC-preservation captures the spirit of AC-preservation (ensures the use of the authorization procedure of the system) but allows us to define a request transformation function to map workload requests to system requests.

Safety Safety ensures that the intermediate states through which a system travels while implementing a single workload label do not add or remove granted requests except as determined to be necessary by the start and end states.

We implement the conference workload in $RBAC_1$ (role-based access control with role hierarchy) using techniques presented in [9]. Members who strict join a group are granted a subset of the permissions of older members, a pattern we can mirror naturally using a role hierarchy. In a way, older members "inherit" access to all added objects; new members only receive access to objects added after they joined. We thus create a chain in the role hierarchy for each group. When a g-SIS group is created, the top of the chain is created in $RBAC_1$. We name the top role of the chain after the group, and use this to correlate chains to groups.

When an object is added to a group, it is available to all members, and thus the corresponding permission in $RBAC_1$ is added to the bottom of the chain, where access to it

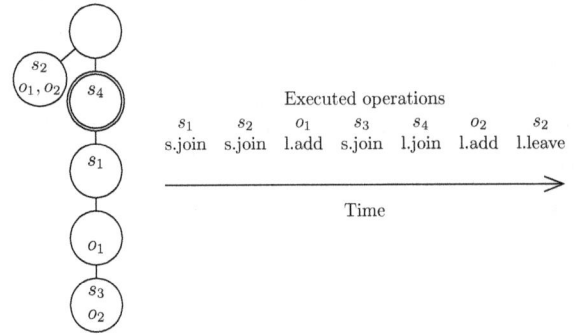

Figure 3: An example role hierarchy implementing the conference workload in $RBAC_1$

will be inherited upward (to older members). When a user *liberal* joins a group, they gain access to all existing objects, and thus we add this user in $RBAC_1$ to the top of the role chain, where she will inherit permission corresponding to each object. When a new user *strict* joins a group, they create a new "view" of the group, since they are not authorized to any existing objects. Thus, we create a new $RBAC_1$ role (named arbitrarily) and link it to the bottom of the group's chain.

When a user *strict* leaves a group, she is removed from any roles in the group's role chain, losing access to all objects in the group. When a user *liberal* leaves a group, on the other hand, she should retain access to the current set of objects. Thus, we create an *orphan role*, which does not inherit any permissions from other roles, and from which no users inherit permissions. Then, the leaving user is added to the orphan role, and the role is granted access to the group's objects to which the user currently has permission. Then, when the user is removed from the main role chain, she does not lose accesses. We give a demonstrative example of the role hierarchy structure in Fig. 3.

Using this technique, we can implement the conference workload in $RBAC_1$ while preserving correctness, weak AC-preservation, and safety.

Theorem 2 *There exists a correct, weak AC-preserving, and safe implementation of the conference workload in $RBAC_1$.*

To implement the workload in $RBAC_0$ (role-based access control without role hierarchy), we follow the same procedure, but store the role hierarchy encoded in role names. This expands the set of roles to include a role named for every path through the logical hierarchy in the downward direction. Thus, if in $RBAC_1$ we would store a hierarchy that says $A \geq B$, $B \geq C$, and $A \geq D$, we represent this in $RBAC_0$ with roles $\{A, B, C, D, AB, ABC, AD, BC\}$. For every role r a user would be assigned to in $RBAC_1$, she will be assigned to each role starting with r in $RBAC_0$. In the previous example, if $\langle u, A \rangle \in UR$ in $RBAC_1$, then in $RBAC_0$ this maps to $\{\langle u, A \rangle, \langle u, AB \rangle, \langle u, ABC \rangle, \langle u, AD \rangle\} \subset UR$ in $RBAC_0$. This allows us to implement the conference workload in $RBAC_0$ while preserving our chosen implementation guarantees.

Theorem 3 *There exists a correct, weak AC-preserving, and safe implementation of the conference workload in $RBAC_0$.*

Finally, although *ugo* has the inherent disadvantage that each object is owned by only a *single* user and group, it can implement the conference workload by mapping a workload object assigned to multiple groups to an object with a single group owner. This group then represents all groups with authorization and includes as members all users with access.

(a) Author's submit phase actor machine

(b) Conflict-of-interest workflow

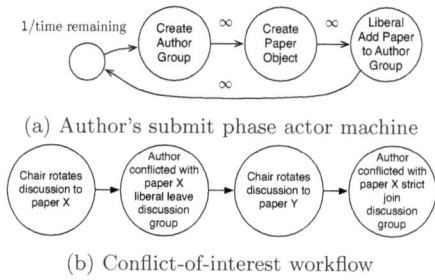

Figure 4: Case study invocational structures

Of course, this incurs a storage penalty; the magnitude of this overhead will be explored in quantitative analysis.

Theorem 4 *There exists a correct, weak AC-preserving, and safe implementation of the conference workload in ugo.*

6.3 Quantitative Analysis

To perform simulation-based cost analysis, we formalized actor machines for the conference program chair, authors, and reviewers, as well as workflows that describe how these actors interact. These instantiations of the structures defined in Section 4 allow us to describe the usage of the workload system (which, recall, is essentially the system of the program committee workload in [9] with a different expected usage).

The actors in our system are a program chair, a set of reviewers, and a set of authors. Each paper is assigned three reviewers, and each reviewer is assigned nine reviews, and thus we have three times as many authors as reviewers (without loss of generality, we assume that one author is registered to submit each paper). The program chair is responsible for administrative tasks such as creating groups (the discussion group and each paper's review group), assigning reviews to reviewers, copying the submitted papers into their respective review groups, and rotating through the submitted papers during discussion. The program chair also transitions between the phases of the simulation, which determines the actions that the other actors can execute at any particular time. The phases proceed in the following order:

1. *Create* Chair creates the discussion group

2. *Recruit* Chair adds the reviewers to the discussion group

3. *Submit* Authors create author groups and submit papers

4. *Review* Chair creates review groups and adds assigned reviewers; reviewers add reviews to the review groups

5. *Discuss* Chair rotates discussion between various papers; reviewers add comments in the discussion group; conflicted reviewers leave during discussion

6. *Notify* Chair adds review summaries to author groups; authors read their summaries

Formally, actor machines include the actions from all phases, and the chair uses workflows to ensure that only the current phase's actions are enabled. For simplicity, we often consider them as separate actor machines between which the actor transitions. Figure 4a demonstrates an example single-phase actor machine, and Fig. 4b demonstrates a particular workflow task, the conflict-of-interest workflow.

To conduct cost analysis, we built a Java implementation of ACCostEvalMC to simulate the conference workload. We repeated the simulation for 200 runs, randomly selecting the number of authors and reviewers (preserving the proportion of 3 times as many authors as reviewers).

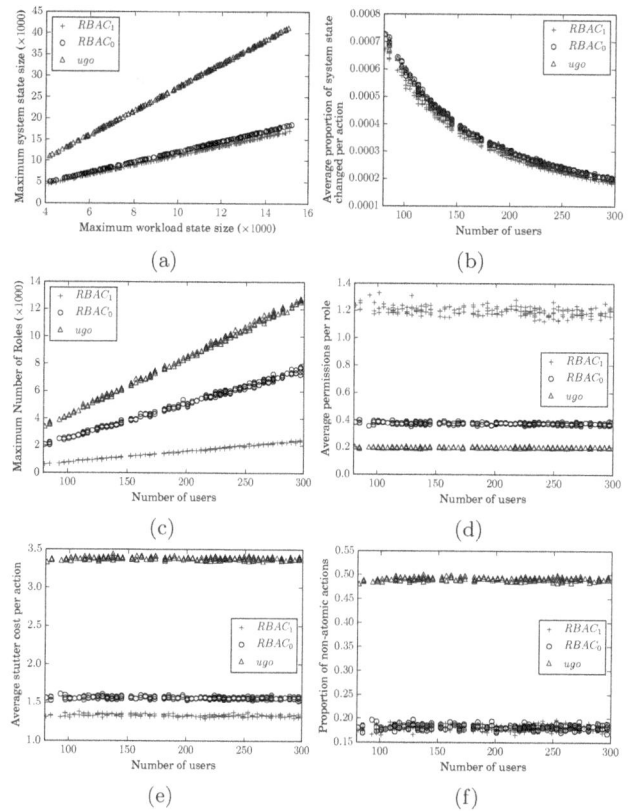

Figure 5: Conference workload cost analysis using ACCostEvalMC and 200 runs

In Fig. 5a, we compare the maximum system state size to the size of the equivalent workload state, demonstrating the storage overhead needed to utilize each system. While the role-based schemes use a small amount of additional state, *ugo* requires several times the storage of the workload. This is due to *ugo*'s restriction that each object is owned by a single group; an object that should be accessed by multiple groups must be owned by a combined group which contains all the members of the originals. Figure 5b shows that a similar *proportion* of each system's state changes on average for each action executed, but given the larger storage required by *ugo*, this system will require much greater I/O as well.

We compare the number of users to the number of roles (groups in *ugo*) created in each system in Fig. 5c. $RBAC_0$ uses many extra roles to simulate hierarchy information, and *ugo* creates even more since each object is owned by only a single group. However, even $RBAC_1$ uses several times as many roles as there are users in the system, potentially indicating a poor fit from all three systems, as the administrative value of using roles is reduced when the the number of roles exceeds the number of users [27]. As indicated in Fig. 5d, roles in all three systems are particularly permission-sparse, averaging 1.2, 0.4, and 0.2 permissions per role in $RBAC_1$, $RBAC_0$, and *ugo*, respectively. In particular, $RBAC_0$ and *ugo* utilize many additional roles to store simulated hierarchy information, and many of these roles are never assigned permissions.

In Fig. 5e, we investigate the average number of *stutter steps* per action, or the average number of system commands that must be executed to simulate each workload command. $RBAC_1$, $RBAC_0$, and *ugo* must execute, on average, 1.3,

1.6, and 3.4 actions (respectively) for each workload action simulated. Furthermore, as shown in Fig. 5f, 18% of workload actions incur some stuttering in the role-based systems, and 49% incur stuttering in *ugo*. In scenarios where multiple users will be interacting with the system, this loss of atomicity necessitates the incorporation of an additional locking layer to ensure the system is not accessed in an inconsistent state.

6.4 Summary of Findings

The preceding case study shows that, under the lens of several cost measures, $RBAC_1$ is a better choice than $RBAC_0$ or *ugo* for implementing the conference workload, due to its native support for role hierarchies, a structure that can mimic the pattern of authorized requests common in the workload. However, even $RBAC_1$ utilizes a large number of permission-sparse roles, indicating that even it may be a tenuous fit for the workload. More importantly, though, our case study demonstrates that the concepts of our two-facet suitability analysis framework can be applied to a realistic workload and evaluate access control systems that are common in practice with respect to that workload. Our simulation procedure allows us to easily determine the overheads of using each system, and with an average runtime of around eight minutes per five-month simulation run, does so efficiently. The simulation procedure is also trivially parallelizable (since each run is independent), further enforcing its feasibility.

7. DISCUSSION AND FUTURE WORK

Requirements, Redux In Section 3.2, we outlined requirements to guide the development of our suitability analysis framework. We now discuss the degree to which each requirement was met. The *Domain Exploration* requirement is addressed by our workload formalism and our Monte Carlo simulation procedure: the former allows the analyst to specify a broad range of workloads, while the latter enables cost analysis over many workload instances. *Cooperative Interaction* is met by combining our invocation formalism with the WSP solver leveraged by ACCostEvalSim: constrained workflows articulate the ways in which cooperation must be carried out, while the use of actor graphs and the WSP solver ensures the generation of compliant traces. Although this paper makes use of a fixed set of implementation guarantees to define implementation safety, this is not mandatory. Proofs of safety are carried out manually, allowing any notion of safety to be used and providing *Tunable Safety*. Section 5 demonstrated that our notion of cost measure is capable of representing a wide range of system- and human-centric costs and thus provides *Tunable Costs*. Supporting multi-user workflows is seemingly at odds with the *Tractability* requirement, as the workflow satisfiability problem has been shown to be NP-complete [26]. However, the proof of Theorem 1 makes use of recent results [4] to show that ACCostEvalSim is fixed-parameter tractable in maximum task length (typically a small constant). More concretely, simulating each 5-month period in our case study took, on average, around 8 minutes. The *Accuracy* requirement is addressed in Appendix B, where we discuss how to calculate confidence intervals for point estimates of cost. In conclusion, the analysis framework developed in this paper meets each of the desiderata outlined in Section 3.2, and provides a flexible, efficient, and precise mechanism for analyzing instances of the access control suitability analysis problem.

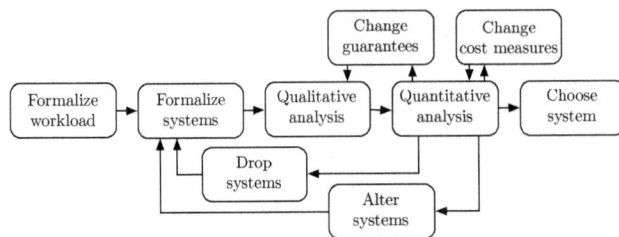

Figure 6: A possible two-facet, suitability analysis workflow supported by our framework

Unified Workflow This work explores a qualitative analysis in which we fix the security guarantees that implementations are required to preserve, and a single instance of quantitative analysis revolving around the implementations constructed during the fixed qualitative analysis. While this is an appropriate and demonstrative case study that supports the practical usefulness of our framework, in practice, analyses may be much more complex. For instance, qualitative analysis may yield very secure implementations (i.e., those that preserve very strict requirements), but quantitative analysis may reveal that all of these implementations are infeasibly inefficient. As a result, although a system may be *capable* of admitting an implementation satisfying stronger security guarantees, it may not necessarily be worth the additional cost to do so. The trade-off between strictness of security guarantees and efficiency became apparent in a more detailed case study that we conducted in prior work [9]. In this case, we chose to conduct cost analysis using the strongest expressiveness guarantees that allowed a feasible (i.e., quadratic or better) implementation using each candidate system. In general, this trade-off may inspire an analyst to revisit any number of the inputs to the analyses. For example, one may consider multiple implementations that preserve a range of weaker security guarantees and higher efficiencies. One might also consider introducing additional candidate systems. Thus, a practical analysis may be less linear than our case study and incorporate more backtracking, as in, e.g., Fig. 6. The techniques presented as part of our two-facet suitability analysis framework are general enough to naturally support such complex analysis workflows.

Future Work We have identified several important directions for future work in suitability analysis. Small changes in an access control system can be the difference between being able or unable to implement a workload safely [11] and/or efficiently [9]. To maximize reuse of existing, trusted systems, we are developing methods that allow an analyst to make small tweaks to a system that are *safe* (i.e., that preserve its desirable security properties and capabilities) while enabling greater expressiveness and/or efficiency. We have already shown that one particular method of tweaking systems is safe with respect to strong security guarantees, and have used this method to increase systems' expressiveness, allowing them to satisfy new workloads [8]. We are working to generalize this technique, formalize additional methods of tweaking, and prove safety for a range of security guarantees.

Encouraged by our success in using parameterized expressiveness, we are also working to extend the core concept of this expressiveness framework by defining granular sets of implementation guarantees that are more closely grounded in access control application. Rather than providing guarantees that prevent certain, somewhat arbitrary types of abuse, we aim to provide guarantees that reflect what an implementation mapping can do without violating the assumptions inherent in the application's usage of the chosen system.

Finally, this paper focuses on a form of the suitability analysis problem that is specific to access control. However, we believe that a more general formulation could enable better understanding of the trade-offs between the formal requirements and practical costs of solutions to a wider range of security problems.

8. CONCLUSION

Historically, most work regarding the formal analysis of access control systems has focused on expressive power, yielding a meaningful view of a system's capabilities but an incomplete view of its suitability for any particular application. In contrast, this work formalizes the *suitability analysis problem* to address both expressiveness and efficiency, and presents a methodology for application-specific evaluation of access control systems' suitability.

We show that this methodology satisfies a number of formal requirements for suitability analysis frameworks, covering flexibility, tractability, and accuracy. Furthermore, we present a case study that provides practical validation of the applicability of our methods to a realistic access control problem. Several access control systems (two role-based systems and traditional UNIX permission bits) are shown to be capable of implementing an academic conference workload with uniformly strong expressiveness guarantees but varying degrees of efficiency, enforcing the importance of measures aside from expressiveness and the significance of the suitability analysis problem.

Acknowledgements This work was supported in part by the National Science Foundation under awards CNS–0964295 and CNS–1228697.

9. REFERENCES

[1] P. Ammann, R. J. Lipton, and R. S. Sandhu. The expressive power of multi-parent creation in monotonic access control models. *JCS*, 4(2/3):149–166, 1996.

[2] Kay S. Anderson et al. Sword: scalable and flexible workload generator for distributed data processing systems. In *Winter Simulation Conference (WSC)*, pages 2109–2116, Dec 2006.

[3] A. Chander, J. C. Mitchell, and D. Dean. A state-transition model of trust management and access control. In *IEEE CSFW*, pages 27–43, 2001.

[4] J. Crampton, G. Gutin, and A. Yeo. On the parameterized complexity and kernelization of the workflow satisfiability problem. *ACM TISSEC*, 16(1), 2013.

[5] David F. Ferraiolo et al. Proposed nist standard for role-based access control. *ACM TISSEC*, 4(3):224–274, 2001.

[6] G. R. Ganger. Generating representative synthetic workloads: An unsolved problem. In *International CMG Conference*, pages 1263–1269, Dec 1995.

[7] S. Garfinkel, G. Spafford, and A. Schwartz. *Practical UNIX and Internet Security*. NIST special publication: Computer security. O'Reilly Media, 2003.

[8] W. C. Garrison III, A. J. Lee, and T. L. Hinrichs. The design and demonstration of an actor-based, application-aware access control evaluation framework. Technical Report arXiv:1302.1134, Feb 2013.

[9] W. C. Garrison III, Y. Qiao, and A. J. Lee. On the suitability of dissemination-centric access control systems for group-centric sharing. In *CODASPY*, 2014.

[10] M. A. Harrison, W. L. Ruzzo, and J. D. Ullman. Protection in operating systems. *CACM*, 19(8):461–471, Aug 1976.

[11] Timothy L. Hinrichs et al. Application-sensitive access control evaluation using parameterized expressiveness. In *IEEE CSF*, June 2013.

[12] J. Hromkovic. *Algorithms for Hard Problems: Introduction to Combinatorial Optimization, Randomization, Approximation, and Heuristics*. Springer-Verlag, Berlin, Heidelberg, 2010.

[13] V. C. Hu, D. F. Ferraiolo, and D. R. Kuhn. *Assessment of Access Control Systems*. National Institute of Standards and Technology, 2006.

[14] Ram Krishnan et al. Group-centric secure information-sharing models for isolated groups. *ACM TISSEC*, 14(3):23, 2011.

[15] Ram Krishnan et al. Foundations for group-centric secure information sharing models. In *ACM SACMAT*, pages 115–124, 2009.

[16] A. Law. *Simulation Modeling and Analysis*. McGraw-Hill, 2006.

[17] N. Li, J. C. Mitchell, and W. H. Winsborough. Beyond proof-of-compliance: security analysis in trust management. *J. ACM*, 52(3):474–514, May 2005.

[18] T. M. Liggett. *Continuous Time Markov Processes: An Introduction*. Graduate Studies in Mathematics Series. American Mathematical Society, 2010.

[19] R. J. Lipton and L. Snyder. A linear time algorithm for deciding subject security. *J. ACM*, 24(3):455–464, 1977.

[20] I. Molloy, P.-C. Cheng, and P. Rohatgi. Trading in risk: using markets to improve access control. In *NSPW*, 2008.

[21] S. Osborne, R. Sandhu, and Q. Munawer. Configuring role-based access control to enforce mandatory and discretionary access control policies. *ACM TISSEC*, 3(2):85–106, May 2000.

[22] R. Sandhu. Expressive power of the schematic protection model. *JCS*, 1(1):59–98, 1992.

[23] Ravi S. Sandhu et al. Role-based access control models. *IEEE Computer*, 29(2):38–47, 1996.

[24] R. S. Sandhu and S. Ganta. On testing for absence of rights in access control models. In *IEEE CSFW*, pages 109–118, 1993.

[25] M. V. Tripunitara and N. Li. A theory for comparing the expressive power of access control models. *JCS*, 15(2):231–272, 2007.

[26] Q. Wang and N. Li. Satisfiability and resiliency in workflow authorization systems. *ACM TISSEC*, 13(4), 2010.

[27] Dana Zhang et al. RoleVAT: Visual assessment of practical need for role based access control. In *ACSAC*, pages 13–22, Dec 2009.

APPENDIX

A. PROOF OF THEOREM 1

Theorem 1 *Assuming that workflow constraints are restricted to $\{=, \neq\}$ (i.e., binding and separation of duty), the simulation procedure* ACCostEvalSim *is* fixed-parameter tractable *with the number of actions in the largest task (i.e., the size of the largest disjoint subgraph of the workflow graph).*

PROOF Our proof is by observation of Algorithm 1. The first loop (**for all** $\mathcal{Y} \in \mathfrak{Y}$) handles assignments and initializations. The final loop (**for all** $\mathcal{Y}' \in \mathfrak{Y}$) outputs results. The main loop, then, contains all of the computationally intensive code.

The expensive section of the algorithm starts after several nested loops, adding multiplicative factors for number of time steps (T_f/t), number of systems ($|\mathfrak{Y}|$), and number of actors. The steps with computational overhead are nextAction, which polls an actor machine for the next action, and WSat, which calculates whether a particular action can be taken by an actor without causing any workflow instances to become unsatisfiable (i.e., WSat solves an instance of the WSP problem).

By previous work [26], WSP can be solved in $\mathcal{O}(C \cdot A^\alpha)$, where C is the number of constraints, A is the maximum number of actors, and α is the number of steps in the largest task (i.e., the size of the largest disjoint subgraph of the workflow graph). This greatly exceeds nextAction, which executes a single step in a continuous-time probabilistic machine (polynomial in actor machine size). Thus, the dominant factor in the complexity of Algorithm 1 is $\mathcal{O}(S \cdot C \cdot T \cdot A^{\alpha+1})$, where $S = |\mathfrak{Y}|$ is the number of systems and $T = T_f/t$ is the number of time steps to simulate. Since T is an input, this means the algorithm is pseudo-polynomial in T and FPT in α. Since FPT is considered to be a generalization of pseudo-polynomial time [12], we refer to the complexity of Algorithm 1 as FPT, thus meeting our definition of tractable. □

B. SIMULATION DRIVERS

Algorithm 2 Monte Carlo driver for ACCostEvalSim

Input: $\mathfrak{Y}$, set of candidate systems
Input: Σ, set of implementations ($\forall \mathcal{Y} \in \mathfrak{Y} : \sigma_{\mathcal{Y}} \in \Sigma$)
Input: $\mathfrak{C}$, set of cost measures ($\tau = \langle \mathbb{R}, +, \leq \rangle \in \mathfrak{C}$)
Input: L, set of cost functions ($\forall \mathcal{Y} \in \mathfrak{Y}, \mathcal{C} \in \mathfrak{C} : \ell_{\mathcal{C}}^{\mathcal{Y}} \in L$)
Input: $I = \langle W, \mathfrak{A}, M \rangle$, invocation mechanism
Input: $\Pr(s)$, probability distribution over start states
Input: χ, number of Monte Carlo runs
Input: T_f, goal time
Input: t, time step

    procedure ACCostEvalMC($\mathfrak{Y}, \Sigma, \mathfrak{C}, L, I, \Pr(s), \chi, T_f, t$)
        for all $[1, \chi]$ **do**   ▷ Monte Carlo loop
            $s_0 \leftarrow$ random sample from $\Pr(s)$
            ACCostEvalSim$(\mathfrak{Y}, \Sigma, \mathfrak{C}, L, I, s_0, T_f, t)$

Since ACCostEvalSim executes only a single run of the simulation, in this appendix we present two drivers for using this simulation procedure for different analysis goals.

Algorithm 2 presents ACCostEvalMC. This driver utilizes the Monte Carlo technique; it calls ACCostEvalMC repeatedly, each time randomly sampling a start state from the given distribution. This allows the analyst to generate a large number of data points across a predefined pattern of start states, which makes it particularly effective in detecting trends across various start states. For example, in Section 6, we randomly choose a number of users in the system for each

run, allowing us to see the effect this parameter has on the costs of using each system.

Because the repeated execution in ACCostEvalMC contributes to the complexity of the full analysis by only an additional pseudo-polynomial factor, ACCostEvalMC, like ACCostEvalSim is in FPT.

Corollary 5 *Under the same assumptions as Theorem 1, the simulation procedure* ACCostEvalMC *is in* FPT.

PROOF The driver ACCostEvalMC calls ACCostEvalSim χ times. Thus, the runtime complexity of ACCostEvalMC is a factor of χ greater than that of ACCostEvalSim. Since χ is an input, this contributes an additional pseudo-polynomial factor over the runtime complexity of ACCostEvalSim, and thus ACCostEvalMC is in FPT. □

Algorithm 3 Confidence-bounding driver for ACCostEvalSim

Input: $\mathfrak{Y}$, set of candidate systems
Input: Σ, set of implementations ($\forall \mathcal{Y} \in \mathfrak{Y} : \sigma_{\mathcal{Y}} \in \Sigma$)
Input: $\mathfrak{C}$, set of cost measures ($\tau = \langle \mathbb{R} \times \text{time}, +, \leq \rangle \in \mathfrak{C}$)
Input: L, set of cost functions ($\forall \mathcal{Y} \in \mathfrak{Y}, \mathcal{C} \in \mathfrak{C} : \ell_{\mathcal{C}}^{\mathcal{Y}} \in L$)
Input: $I = \langle W, \mathfrak{A}, M \rangle$, invocation mechanism
Input: s_0, start state
Input: T_f, goal time
Input: t, time step
Input: $u \in (0, 1)$, desired confidence level
Input: $v \in (0, 1)$, desired tolerance

    procedure ACCostEvalCI($\mathfrak{Y}, \Sigma, \mathfrak{C}, L, I, s_0, T_f, t, u, v$)
        $n \leftarrow \emptyset$
        while $t_{|n|-1, 1-u/2} \sqrt{\dfrac{S^2(n)}{|n|}} > v \cdot \bar{X}(n)$ **do**
            $n \leftarrow n \cup$ ACCostEvalSim$(\mathfrak{Y}, \Sigma, \mathfrak{C}, L, I, s_0, T_f, t)$

In the interest of satisfying the *Accuracy* requirement, we also present a second driver, which allows the analyst to achieve an intended confidence in the cost value generated for a particular start state. Using this approach, we can decide the number of simulation runs to conduct based on a desired confidence and the assumption of a particular distribution of costs across runs, terminating when a satisfactory confidence is reached. For example, assuming a normal distribution of costs across runs, we can use the fixed-sample-size procedure for point estimate of a mean [16], which says that the confidence interval for a mean is:

$$\bar{X}(n) \pm t_{|n|-1, 1-\frac{\alpha}{2}} \sqrt{\frac{S^2(n)}{|n|}}$$

where $\bar{X}(n)$ is the sample mean, $\frac{S^2(n)}{|n|}$ is the sample variance, and $t_{\nu, \gamma}$ is the critical point for the t-distribution with ν degrees of freedom. The resulting range is an approximate $100(1 - \alpha)$-percent confidence interval for the expected average cost of the system. During simulation, we repeatedly calculate the confidence interval for incrementing n, terminating when a satisfactory confidence is reached. For example, assuming we desire a 90-percent confidence interval of no more than 0.1 of the mean, we run the simulation repeatedly until:

$$t_{|n|-1, 0.95} \sqrt{\frac{S^2(n)}{|n|}} \leq 0.1 \bar{X}(n)$$

Algorithm 3 demonstrates ACCostEvalCI, which uses this approach to execute ACCostEvalSim until a desired confidence is reached, rather than executing for a fixed number of runs.

Policy Models to Protect Resource Retrieval

Hayawardh Vijayakumar, Xinyang Ge, and Trent Jaeger
Systems and Internet Infrastructure Security Laboratory
Department of Computer Science and Engineering
The Pennsylvania State University
hvijay@cse.psu.edu, xxg113@cse.psu.edu, tjaeger@cse.psu.edu

ABSTRACT

Processes need a variety of resources from their operating environment in order to run properly, but adversary may control the inputs to resource retrieval or the end resource itself, leading to a variety of vulnerabilities. Conventional access control methods are not suitable to prevent such vulnerabilities because they use one set of permissions for all system call invocations. In this paper, we define a novel policy model for describing when resource retrievals are unsafe, so they can be blocked. This model highlights two contributions: (1) the explicit definition of adversary models as *adversarial roles*, which list the permissions that dictate whether one subject is an adversary of another, and (2) the application of data-flow to determine the adversary control of the names used to retrieve resources. An evaluation using multiple adversary models shows that data-flow is necessary to authorize resource retrieval in over 90% of system calls. By making adversary models and the adversary accessibility of all aspects of resource retrieval explicit, we can block resource access attacks system-wide.

Categories and Subject Descriptors

D.4.6 [**Operating Systems**]: Security and Protection—*Access controls*

General Terms

Security

Keywords

Resource Access Attacks; Protection

1. INTRODUCTION

Processes need a variety of resources from their operating environment in order to run properly, such as files, IPCs, and sockets. When a process retrieves a resource from the system, it may select any resource to which it is authorized. However, the retrieval of some authorized resources may lead to vulnerabilities, depending on how those resources are to be used. Consider a web server that both serves content supplied by untrusted users and authenticates requests from remote parties. It is easy to see that vulnerabilities would result if the web server used its permissions to read the password file when serving HTML pages or used untrusted HTML pages when authenticating remote parties. In this paper, we explore methods to extend access control mechanisms to prevent the retrieval of resources that will lead to program vulnerabilities, which have been called *resource access attacks* [61].

In principle, such vulnerabilities may occur for a variety of reasons. First, a programmer may not expect that a particular system call invocation may retrieve a resource controlled by one of its adversaries, *expanding the attack surface* of the program [31]. In such cases, the integrity of the running program and/or the data it produces may be compromised by using adversary-controlled input. In the web server example, the use of untrusted content for authentication would compromise the integrity of the web server. Second, a programmer may not expect that a particular system call invocation may retrieve a resource that contains security-sensitive data that should not available to an adversary, leading to a *confused deputy attack* [28]. In such cases, the confidentiality and/or integrity of that sensitive data may be compromised. In the web server example, the serving of the secret password file would compromise the confidentiality of that file. Finally, an adversary may be able to control the inputs that guide the retrieval of resources to redirect a process to a resource of the adversary's choosing, leading to an *attack during name resolution* (e.g., time-of-check-to-time-of-use (TOCTTOU) attacks [40, 8]). By supplying malicious input for file names or controlling the namespace bindings (e.g., links and directories in a file system namespace), adversaries can compromise either the confidentiality or integrity of the process. In the web server example, either an adversary may be able to redirect the server to choose the web content file when the password file is expected or vice versa.

Conventional access control mechanisms are fundamentally unable to prevent such vulnerabilities because permissions are associated with the process at large. *Access control list* mechanisms [35] associate a set of subject identifiers with each resource (i.e., object), authorizing any process running under one of those subject identifiers to access the resource. Thus, any system call invocation by an authorized process will be allowed. Similarly, conventional operating systems that enforce *mandatory access control* [67, 2, 24, 64, 59] (MAC) associate labels with processes and resources, storing a mapping between the subject labels and the resource labels to which they are authorized. Again, any system call of any process running under a subject label that is authorized to access resources of the target resource's label will be allowed, regardless of how this mapping is stored. In the web server example, access control list mechanisms cannot prevent the password file from accessed by mistake when serving HTML pages, or vice versa, because the web server has access to both resources.

On the other hand, *capability systems* [36] permit processes to restrict the permissions available per system call, but such mechanisms are only available in limited ways in conventional systems. Capability systems permit programmers to select the permissions available per system call, by using specialized references to resources that include permissions, themselves called *capabilities*, and by managing the permissions available to the process flexibly [20]. Researchers have shown that capability systems may be used to prevent some of the vulnerabilities above, such as confused deputy vulnerabilities [28]. However, using a capability system presents a challenge to programmers because they must reason about both the functionality and security of their programs concurrently. As a result, capability systems principles have only been adopted in limited ways, such as sandboxing, that do not permit the flexible control of permissions envisioned for a general capability system [37]. The result is that a variety of ad hoc solutions have been proposed to block resource access attacks (see Related Work in Section 3), but these solutions have been found to be broken [10] or fundamentally flawed [12].

One recent insight is that a system mechanism whose sole purpose is to protect processes during resource retrieval can gather knowledge from both the program and the system to block vulnerabilities [61]. They highlight the fact that access control mechanisms perform two tasks simultaneously, both *protecting* benign processes from attack by limiting adversary access to its resources and *confining* malicious processes from attacking other processes. As a result, access control mechanisms cannot leverage program internal state for their decision-making because a malicious process may spoof the system and break confinement. By separating protection from confinement during resource retrieval in a separate layer of defense called the Process Firewall [61], a variety of resource access attack vulnerabilities can be blocked. As the Process Firewall cannot confine a malicious process, it only augments access control by blocking operations authorized by conventional access control that would only lead to vulnerabilities in the current program state, while still depending on access control for confinement. In the web server example, the Process Firewall examines program internal state to identify whether the system call should retrieve the adversary-accessible HTML file or the adversary-inaccessible password file, and allows only the appropriate resource.

While the Process Firewall mechanism can prevent resource access attacks, the current policy model was also shown to be limited. The Process Firewall allows using program-internal state to determine whether that particular system call should access adversary-accessible or adversary-inaccessible resources. The proposed policy model associates program *entrypoints*, the instructions that invoke the system call library with whether the expected resource retrieved should be adversary-accessible or not. However, the entrypoint may be invoked in multiple contexts, some of which may access different resources, or use name values derived from multiple data flows, only some of which may be under adversary control. As a result, the entrypoint alone is insufficient to express policies to prevent resource access attacks. In addition, the Process Firewall policy model implicitly depends on the definition of *adversary accessibility*. However, we find that there are different types of accessibility that matter depending on the context. In some cases, the adversary must have write permission to the relevant resource, but in other cases the adversary only needs read or execute permissions. The lack of precision and explicit models of adversary accessibility will likely to errors in preventing resource access attacks.

In this paper, we present a novel policy model for expressing rules to protect processes from resource access attacks, such as could be enforced by a Process Firewall mechanism. The policy model is described by a new authorization query rule, called the *resource retrieval query* (RRQ), that binds all of the relevant facets of resource retrieval into a single concise query. We show that the RRQ enables prevention of the resource access attacks listed above in a straightforward way. The main challenges in applying an RRQ policy model are to make adversary accessibility explicit and determine adversary control of names used in resource retrieval. First, we define a novel, role-based approach for describing *adversarial roles*, which list the permissions that dictate whether one subject is an adversary of another. Second, we show how existing work can be applied to compute the data flows impacting a name value used in resource retrieval. Using these methods, adversary control of names can be expressed using concise descriptions, even utilizing entrypoints in some cases, which we call *name control*.

In this paper, we make the following contributions:

- We define a policy model for preventing resource access attacks, whose schema is defined by the *resource retrieval query* (RRQ). In addition to the standard (subject, object, operation), the RRQ requires an explicit representation of the adversary model and program flow to protect the process.

- We define concepts for specifying adversary models and program flows, called *adversarial roles* and *name control*. The former associates subjects with the permissions that define their adversaries, analogously to a role. The latter specifies the control- or data-flow impact on the name used in resource retrieval.

- We evaluate the impact of different adversary models on whether data-flow analysis is necessary to determine adversary accessibility to names. We find that over 60% of the entrypoints in which system calls are invoked can be associated with either adversary-accessible or adversary-inaccessible resources, but over 90% of the system call invocations occur on entrypoints where such a judgement is not possible. Thus, data-flow is important to preventing resource access attacks.

The remainder of the paper is structured as follows. In Section 2, we define the problem of resource access attacks. In Section 3, we examine a variety of efforts to prevent resource access attacks to date and the reasons for their failures. In Section 4, we provide an overview for our approach. In Section 5, we design a policy model based on the *resource retrieval query* (RRQ) to block resource access attacks and address the challenges in deploying such a model. In Section 6, we evaluate the need for adversary models and dataflow tracking mandated by the RRQ design. In Section 7, we conclude the paper.

2. RESOURCE ACCESS ATTACKS

Once started, a process often needs additional system resources to execute correctly (e.g., libraries, configuration files, logs, etc.) and may need to retrieve task-specific resources to complete any task (e.g., web content files, web requests via sockets, IPCs to worker processes, etc.). We use the term *resource* for objects obtained from the operating system. For convenience, resources are often retrieved by name, using a method known as *namespace resolution* [45, 21]. In a namespace resolution, a client (the process) provides a *name* to a name server (the operating system), which retrieves a reference to the resource to which the name maps via *namespace bindings* managed by the name server.

Resource access attacks are possible because the names, namespace bindings, and resources themselves used by the resolution mechanism may be controlled by adversaries. We use the code snippet in Figure 1 to demonstrate the possible problems. First, many processes obtain resources using names supplied by potential adversaries, particularly server processes that process client requests. In Figure 1, the function `set_up_socket_dir` uses an environment variable `SOCKET_DIR` to name the directory to be created. If adversaries can assign `SOCKET_DIR`, then they could escalate adversary privilege (i.e., by creating a directory in a location they are not authorized for) or could control security-critical operations (i.e., by creating the directory in a location that is accessible to the adversary). These are examples of *untrusted search path* attacks [16], but other kinds of attacks such *directory traversal* and *untrusted library load* similarly occur because adversaries can manipulate the names used in name resolution.

Second, many namespaces allow untrusted parties to specify the namespace bindings used for resolution. Namespaces are often designed to enable sharing of resources among subjects to provide flexibility in application deployment, but such sharing may lead to vulnerabilities if used incorrectly. For example, the X11 script shown in Figure 1 also creates a directory of the name `SOCKET_DIR` in `/tmp/.X11-unix`, where `/tmp` is shared among all processes. Lines 6-8 check if a file already exists that is not a directory, and, if so, moves it to create a fresh directory. In Line 9, the programmer creates the directory, and assumes it will succeed because the previous code had just moved any file that might exist. However, because `/tmp` is a shared directory, an adversary scheduled in between the moving of the file and the `mkdir` might again create a file at `/tmp/.X11-unix`, thus breaking the programmer's expectation. If the file is a link pointing to, for example, `/etc/shadow`, the `chmod` on Line 11 will make it world-readable. In general, using adversary-controlled namespace bindings may lead to problems because adversaries may create bindings that refer to resources they cannot normally access (e.g., symbolic links to attempt *link traversal attacks* [17]). These problems are all difficult to prevent because adversaries may change namespace bindings at any time (e.g., to create race conditions in *TOCTTOU attacks* [40, 8], as in this case).

Third, adversaries may take advantage of the program's ignorance of the namespace and their adversaries' access to that namespace to launch attacks. For example, in the attack above, the adversary plants a link at a file name that the adversary knows that the program will use, `/tmp/.X11-unix`. However, an adversary may cause vulnerabilities simply by creating resources of predictable names in advance (e.g., *squatting attacks* [14]). Such resources are under the adversary, but the victim process may use them without this knowledge, enabling the adversary to control the victim process. In Figure 1, the file created right before the `mkdir` operation was simply a directory the adversary created, the adversary could change the content.

As a result, in order to detect attacks during resource retrieval, any comprehensive defense must authorize the combination of name, bindings, and resource accessed. Current defenses only authorize a subset of such items. Defenses for controlling adversary access to names is limited to ad hoc filtering, which may be error-prone [4]. Most efforts to block attacks during resource retrieval focus on preventing time-of-check-to-time-of-use (TOCTTOU) attacks. Some methods enforce invariants on the resources accessed [15, 54, 58, 50, 65, 57], some enforce use of namespace bindings [13, 49], and some aim for "safe" access methods [18, 56]. Interestingly, the methods are also distinguished by those that augment the program [15, 50, 18, 56] and those that extend the kernel [54, 65, 13, 49, 57, 58]. However, both program and system methods have been found to be fundamentally flawed [10, 12]. Program defenses cannot control how the system allows adversaries to update namespaces and system defenses lack information about programmer intent about which resources are expected in any system call. Our goal in this paper is to address these two limitations by extending access control to reason about program and system concepts.

3. RELATED WORK

In this section, we examine the reasons that current access control models fail to prevent attacks during resource retrieval. We first examine conventional access control and then investigate some proposed research access control models that enable the evolution of permissions as the process runs.

3.1 Limits of Conventional Access Control

A question is whether conventional access control mechanisms may be sufficient to prevent resource access attacks. Several commodity operating systems now enforce mandatory access control policies [67, 64, 2, 41], but these mechanisms cannot prevent such attacks because they grant the same permissions to all system calls for the same process. An important characteristic of resource access attacks is that a resource that is unsafe for a particular victim system call is safe for some other victim system call. For example, a webserver can access `/etc/passwd` legitimately when it wants to authenticate clients, but it should not do so when serving a user web page. As a result, other access control mechanisms that restrict permissions process-wide cannot prevent resource access attacks, such as sandboxes [25, 3, 26, 5].

Capability systems implement an alternative access control mechanism to those above [36], where the programmer chooses the capabilities to present to the operating system to confine access. It has been shown that capability systems can defeat *confused deputy* attacks [28], of which some

```
01 SOCKET_DIR=/tmp/.X11-unix
...
02 set_up_socket_dir () {
03   if [ "$VERBOSE" != no ]; then
04     log_begin_msg "Setting up X server socket directory"
05   fi
06   if [ -e $SOCKET_DIR ] && [ ! -d $SOCKET_DIR ]; then
07     mv $SOCKET_DIR $SOCKET_DIR.$$
08   fi
09   mkdir -p $SOCKET_DIR
10   chown root:root $SOCKET_DIR
11   chmod 1777 $SOCKET_DIR
12   do_restorecon $SOCKET_DIR
13   [ "$VERBOSE" != no ] && log_end_msg 0 || return 0
14 }
```

(a)

```
01 SOCKET_DIR=/tmp/.X11-unix
...
02 set_up_socket_dir () {
03   if [ "$VERBOSE" != no ]; then
04     log_begin_msg "Setting up X server socket directory"
05   fi
06   if [ -e $SOCKET_DIR ]; then
07     mv $SOCKET_DIR $SOCKET_DIR.$$
08   fi
09   mkdir $SOCKET_DIR
10   if [ $? -ne 0 ]; then
11     echo "Unable to create $SOCKET_DIR, possible race!"
12     exit 1
13   fi
14   chmod 1777 $SOCKET_DIR
15   do_restorecon $SOCKET_DIR
16   [ "$VERBOSE" != no ] && log_end_msg 0 || return 0
17 }
```

(b)

Figure 1: A code snippet that is vulnerable to resource access attacks that we found in an X11 startup Bash script in the Ubuntu 11.10 distribution (a), and a possible fix to the TOCTTOU vulnerability (b).

resource access attacks are instances. Some interesting research capability systems have been proposed recently, such as DIFC systems Flume and HiStar [34, 69], which enable flexible control of the permissions used by a process. The problem with capability systems in general is that they push the problem of access control back onto the programmers, presenting yet another API for them to solve the complex problems above. To reduce the complexity on programmers, other recent research on capability-like systems, such as Capsicum [63], relinquishes the flexibility necessary to control access per system call. While we may yet produce an API for programmers to manage capabilities effectively, we propose instead to protect programs from resource access attacks given the current system call API.

3.2   Limits of Research Models

Researchers have previously identified that some attacks may not be prevented unless the access control mechanism accounts for the context in which the program is run. For example, the Brewer-Nash model (aka Chinese Wall model) reduces the permissions a process based on its authorized accesses [11] (e.g., to prevent a conflict of interest). Alternatively, the low-water-mark policy (LOMAC) reduces the permissions of a subject when a lower integrity resource is retrieved [23] (e.g., to prevent unauthorized modification). A corresponding high-water-mark policy blocks raises the secrecy level of subjects when reading higher secrecy data to prevent leakage [66] and other policies protect both secrecy and integrity dynamically [39]. The main limitation of these approaches is that they still restrict the process as a single unit, restricting *all* future accesses.

Researchers have also explored methods for computing permissions based on temporal or contextual properties of the process. For example, traditional role-based access control (RBAC) models [1] were augmented with temporal constraints that alter the permissions available to their processes [6, 33]. In general, a user may be assigned a set of roles, but the roles that may be active at any time may depend on the temporal constraints that have been satisfied. A limitation is that temporal RBAC models apply to all processes simultaneously, whereas resource access attacks affect one process at a time. Alternatively, RBAC models have also been extended to integrate other contextual factors, such as trust, in models that are said to perform *usage control* [51,

52] (UCON). In this model, subjects and objects are associated with attributes, some of which may be mutable based on the subject's access to objects. Authorization requirements are checked prior to and throughout a transaction, which could address attacks that rely on the lack of atomicity, such as TOCTTOU attacks. However, as is typical of conventional access control, UCON (and temporal RBAC models as well) guess at the programmer intent using factors external to the program execution, such as time and system events. In addition, UCON does not reason about how the permissions of other subjects (one's adversaries) may impact whether a resource access should be authorized.

Researchers have also explored methods to reason about permissions by using the program's control or data flow. For example, stack introspection uses the principals responsible for each function on a call stack to deduce the permissions for an operation, such as a resource retrieval [27, 62]. Such methods reason about the security labels of code, but to prevent resource access attacks one must reason about other factors: the data (i.e., used to build names), namespace bindings, or system resources that may be under adversary-control. Alternatively, researchers have developed methods to control access using the program's data flow, enforcing information flow [19, 43]. These methods enable fine-grained reasoning about information flow, which is often difficult for programmers to get right [29], whereas our focus is only on the construction of names for retrieving resources. In addition, these methods do not reason about the implications of bindings on resource retrieval.

3.3   An Alternative: The Process Firewall

Recent work proposed that resource access attacks could be prevented by detecting whether the bindings used and resource accessed in name resolution are unsafe for the "program context" at the time of a name resolution system call, enforced by a kernel mechanism called the Process Firewall [61]. Unsafe accesses were detected using the "adversary accessibility" of the bindings used and resource retrieved in name resolution. For a program context that expected an adversary-accessible resource (e.g., HTML file), the Process Firewall prevents retrieval of resources that are not accessible to program adversaries blocking confused deputy attacks [28]. For a program context that expected an adversary-inaccessible resource (e.g., password file), the Process Firewall prevents retrieval of resources that are accessible to program adversaries limiting the program attack surface [31]. The Process Firewall could also prevent TOCTTOU attacks by restricting multiple program contexts to the same resource.

The Process Firewall is an extension to the SELinux Linux Security Module, which compares resource access system calls authorized by SELinux using a modified version of iptables [38]. The Process Firewall is capable of providing different protections for each system call invocation based on the rules that apply for the current process state (e.g., its call stack), the prior system calls that have been executed by the process, and the current state of the system resource namespace. Because the Process Firewall controls the system resources that individual system call invocations may access, the Process Firewall is analogous to a firewall for the system call interface. Even though the system call interface is much lower latency than the network interface, the Process Firewall incurs only a 2-4% overhead for a variety of macrobenchmarks while enforcing a rulebase of over 1000 rules.

While Process Firewall is capable of preventing resource access attacks efficiently, there is a significant challenge in policy modeling. First, the Process Firewall requires a precise definition of "process context," but this is not a concept in with a precise meaning in general. Cai *et al.* [12] state that a system defense must understand the "programmer intent" to correctly block resource access attacks, but that information is not available. The program "entrypoint"[1] for Process Firewall policies, where runtime analysis was used to classify the entrypoints that always accessed adversary-accessible and adversary-inaccessible resources. However, the Process Firewall experiments exhibited some false positives where entrypoints may be misclassified. Also, there may be many entrypoints that retrieve resources both accessible and inaccessible to adversaries. Second, the Process Firewall requires a precise definition of "adversary accessibility", but there is not a consensus for this concept's meaning. Researchers often apply some notion of a threat model, identifying those resources controlled (e.g., modifiable) by an adversary, but each experiment may propose its own threat model. Even where threat models are computed automatically, different methods are proposed. For example, researchers have proposed multiple automated approaches for computing the resources that are untrusted by each system subject from available discretionary and mandatory access control policies [53, 13, 32, 60].

4. SOLUTION OVERVIEW

To build a policy model for preventing resource access attacks, we want to identify the fundamental principles behind the enforcement policies of the Process Firewall, generalize those principles, and finally simplify the articulation of policy decisions over those principles. To do this, we examine the novel perspective of the Process Firewall design is shown in Figure 2. First, unlike information flow security models, such as Biba integrity [7], the Process Firewall allows processes to retrieve resources controlled by their adversaries, without impacting the permissions of the process overall, unlike LOMAC [23] and other dynamic models [39]. Second,

unlike capability systems [36] and recent work on decentralized information flow control [34, 69], the Process Firewall enables enforcement of different policies for individual system call invocations, but it does not require program modifications for such enforcement. Instead, the Process Firewall protects processes during resource retrieval by introspecting into both the system to determine "adversary accessibility" and the process to estimate the "program context" for enforcing rules that deny unsafe retrievals. The Process Firewall authors show that introspection can be used to *protect* the process because even if a malicious process tampers with such information to spoof the Process Firewall, conventional access control is still able to *confine* the process using the original permissions.

As a result, Process Firewall policies must articulate both the "process context" and "adversary accessibility" over each system call invocation. To reason about adversary accessibility and process context, the Process Firewall proposed extending the traditional authorization query to the rule format below:

$$\texttt{pf\_invariant}(\textbf{subject}, \textbf{entrypoint}, \textbf{resource\_ID},$$
$$\textbf{object}, \textbf{adversary\_access}, \texttt{operation}) \rightarrow \texttt{Y|N|log}$$

Note that the subject, object, and operation correspond to the normal inputs to an authorization query. In addition, `pf_invariant` extends this query with the following arguments: (1) the *entrypoint*, which is the program instruction that invokes the system call library for this system call invocation; (2) the *resource ID*, which restricts the resource to a specific ID to prevent TOCTTOU attacks [40, 8]; and (3) *adversary access*, which is whether the binding or resource is accessible to process adversaries or not[2]. The entrypoint and resource ID specify requirements on the process context and the adversary access specifies requirements on bindings and the retrieved resource for authorization or denial of the requested operation.

However, as noted in the previous section, while this language for Process Firewall policies enabled the prevention of a variety of resource access attacks, it is prone to both false positives and false negatives. The ad hoc nature of this policy language is the contributing factor to both problems. This languages lacks the generality to express either the program context or adversary accessibility sufficiently to block attacks. However, a concern is that once a general policy language is identified it may be far too complex for policy writers or, importantly in this case, automated tools to produce policies. Fortunately, we have identified some insights, which we highlight below, that motivate our design of policy model that enables prevention of resource access attacks broadly, where the policies may be simplified in many cases.

Expressing the process context requires identifying whether the particular name resolution is expected to retrieve an adversary-accessible resource or not. The Process Firewall paper used only the entrypoint to express the process context for each system call invocation. This limitation led to

---

[1] A program entrypoint was said to be an instruction that invoked the system call library.

[2] The input *syscall trace* has been removed from this discussion for simplicity, but was part of TOCTTOU defenses. We capture all the information necessary to prevent TOCTTOU attacks by logging resource IDs in the "check" operation and validating them in the "use" operation. We describe this in detail in Section 5.2.

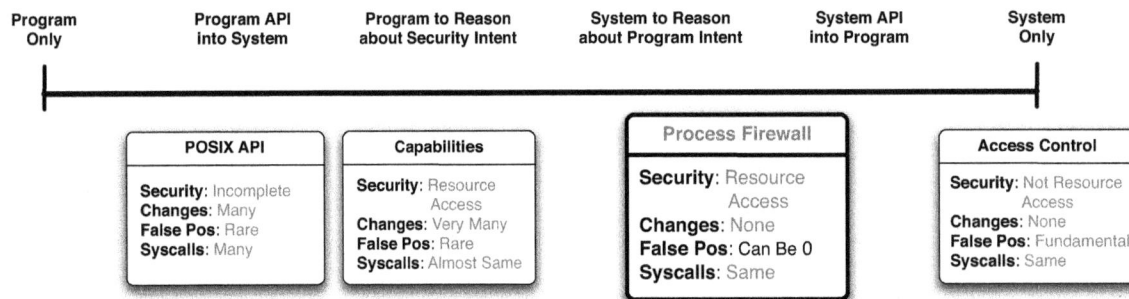

Figure 2: Resource access protection continuum. Until recently no system enforcement mechanisms introspected into the process to protect it from vulnerabilities.

two causes for false positives: different control flow and adversary control of data flow. In one case, a library (that performs system calls) is invoked from multiple callers, but only occasionally does a caller provide a name for an adversary-accessible file. In the other case, the dynamic analysis only tested cases where a particular program entrypoint retrieved files protected from adversaries, but in some rare cases that entrypoint uses adversary input to retrieve files accessible to adversaries. We suggest that the adversary-accessibility of the resource the program intends to retrieve in each system call invocation depends on whether the adversary controls the name of the resource. This is the "process context" that we need to determine to decide whether a retrieved resource is unsafe. In general, determining adversary control of a variable is a data flow problem [19]. However, we find that for many entrypoints, all the data flows leading to that entrypoint are either adversary controlled or not, meaning that we need not track the data flow at runtime in these cases. However we wish to detect whether a name is controlled by an adversary or not, the Process Firewall needs to reason about *adversary control of names*.

Expressing adversary accessibility is conceptually simpler in general, but harder to automate in practice. Conceptually, if an adversary is authorized to perform the requested operation on the resource retrieved, then the resource is adversary-accessible. However, it would be a tedious task to identify the individual resources that may be accessible to adversaries. Researchers have found that the resources accessible to adversaries can be computed from the set of adversaries and the access control policy [53, 13, 32, 60], so we focus on a policy model that expresses adversaries. However, as we mentioned in the last section, there is no agreed-upon method for selecting the adversaries of each process, and selecting them individually would also be tedious. Instead, leverage the notion that researchers had a high-level principle behind their choice of adversaries, so we aim for the Process Firewall to reason about the *the method for identifying adversaries* rather than the individual adversaries.

5. POLICY MODEL DESIGN

In this section, we generalize the authorization rule proposed originally for the Process Firewall [61] to enable more accurate control during resource retrieval with less likelihood of false positives. In Section 5.1, we propose a new authorization rule, called a *resource retrieval query* (RRQ),

and show how it can prevent the various types of resource access attacks in Section 5.2. In Section 5.4, we show how to express adversary control of names in terms of *flow statements*. Finally, in Section 5.3, we show how to express the adversaries of a process using *adversarial roles*.

5.1 Resource Retrieval Queries

The goal is to block processes from retrieving resources that can only lead to resource access attacks. We find that in general we need to know: (1) whether the name resolution process is under adversary control and (2) whether the retrieved resource is adversary accessible or not.

To understand exactly what we mean it is necessary to have precise definitions for adversary control and adversary accessibility. In general, adversaries may *control* the inputs to a name resolution, names and bindings, and *be authorized to access* the output of name resolution, the resource retrieved. For inputs, a name or binding is *adversary-controlled* if the adversary is authorized to modify the source of that input. For names, if an adversary can modify any of the resources from which the name is constructed, then the adversary is said to control that input. For bindings, if an adversary can modify the filesystem links (e.g., directories and symbolic links) used in a name resolution, then the adversary is said to control the binding. For outputs, a resource is *adversary-accessible* if the adversary is authorized to perform the requested operation on the retrieved resource. If an adversary is only authorized to read a resource, then a system call that retrieves a resource for writing would be considered inaccessible to that adversary.

On every system call that performs name resolution, we propose to query both conventional access control (for confinement and some protection) and perform a second query designed to prevent resource access attacks, called a *resource retrieval query* (RRQ). We define the format of the RRQ below.

RRQ(subject, **adversarial_role**, object, **name_control**, **object_control**, operation) → Y|N|log

Like `pf_invariant`, the RRQ specifies the conditions under which a resource retrieval is deemed unsafe, where the default assumption is that an operation is safe (i.e., after all it has been authorized by the traditional access control policy). Note that this semantics is analogous to that of a traditional network firewall, where the default is to allow the traffic.

Our definition of RRQ makes the following changes relative to `pf_invariant`. First, the RRQ associates each subject with its *adversarial role*, which explicitly identifies the threat model used for identifying this subject's adversaries. That is, the subject's adversarial role explicitly relates the system call's subject to the other system subjects who may threaten it by identifying the *permission sets accessible to non-adversaries*. The adversarial role is used to identify adversary control of names and bindings and adversary accessibility of resources. Second, we express adversary control of names using *name control*, which associates a control or data flow of the program with the authorized bindings and resources for that flow (via object control below). Note that the entrypoint is one instance of a name control value, as it implies a single node flow graph. Importantly, we show that in some cases complex data or control-flow relationships may be reduced to a simpler representation, even down to an entrypoint alone, without loss of information. Finally, we change the argument *adversary_accessibility* from `pf_invariant` into *object control*. Object control simply specifies a constraint on the authorized resources given a name control's flow. Normally, object control will either specify that adversary-accessible or adversary-inaccessible resources may be authorized given a name control flow. Note that the object being authorized is either a binding or a resource[3], where the operation being performed uniquely identifies whether the object is a binding or a resource. We note that the *resource ID* field of `pf_invariant` is folded into the object control by expressing further constraints on the objects that may be accessible given a flow and optionally prior resources retrieved (e.g., to prevent TOCTTOU attacks).

When an RRQ query is run, the enforcement mechanism (e.g., Process Firewall) uses the subject and adversarial role to determine whether the object (binding or resource) being authorized is unsafe and must be blocked. First, the enforcement mechanism will determine whether a name control rule matches the control (e.g., call stack) or data flow (e.g., variable taints) that the program used to retrieve the resource for that system call invocation. If so, then the enforcement mechanism will compare the object control value to the RRQ's object (i.e., bindings used or resource retrieved depending on the operation) to determine whether the object matches the object control requirement. If so, then the rule's action is taken (accept, deny, etc.).

5.2 Preventing Attacks with RRQs

In this section, we show that confused deputy, expanded attack surface, and TOCTTOU attacks can be blocked using RRQs.

For a confused deputy attack [28], the problem is that an adversary in control of a name and/or binding can redirect the victim to a resource that is not accessible to the adversary. First, consider the case where the name is controlled by an adversary. Using RRQs, we identify the name control flows where the name is controlled by an adversary. If such a flow matches, then an adversary-inaccessible resource would be unsafe, so the RRQ object control would specify "adversary accessible" for a "deny" rule. Note evaluating adversary control of bindings is not necessary for the decision.

Second, consider the case where the name is not controlled by an adversary, but the name resolution uses an adversary-controlled binding. Normally, we would expect to retrieve an adversary-inaccessible resource, but the the use of an adversary-controlled binding to retrieve such a resource may enable a victim to be redirected to an unexpected resource. Using RRQs, the object control would specify "adversary accessible" bindings for a "deny" rule. This defense was implemented as a library function called "safe-open" by Chari *et al.* [13].

For an expanding attack surface attack [31], the problem is that an adversary is in control of a resource, but not the name. Using RRQs, we identify the name control flows when the adversary does not control the name and associate those with the object control where the resource is "adversary accessible" for a "deny" rule. Such a rule would be in used in combination with the "safe-open" RRQ above to prevent multiple possible attacks in one system call invocation.

Finally, TOCTTOU attacks occur because an adversary can change the bindings used in name resolution to direct the victim to a different resource, even when the same name is used. Using RRQs, we identify a name control flow that uses a name that will reused. An RRQ can log the resource in an object control specification of the rule when the log directive is provided. Other RRQs define the name control flows when that object control will be enforced. In these RRQs, the object control will be the resource logged previously.

The power of the RRQ approach lies in the adversarial role and name control, which are not specified in the examples above. The adversarial role enables precise specification of the meaning of adversary controlled and adversary accessible relative to a role (i.e., set of permissions). As we can see above, knowledge about adversary control and adversary accessibility is fundamental to preventing resource access attacks. In addition, the name control enables precise specification of adversary control of names, which was missing in the Process Firewall's rule language. As we can see above, knowledge of the adversary's control of names is fundamental to reasoning about resource access attacks. We examine how to use both of these concepts in the following subsections.

5.3 Defining Adversaries

To compute adversary control and adversary accessibility, we first need to identify the subjects who are adversaries. Given a set of adversarial subjects and an access control policy, researchers have shown that they can compute the permissions (resources and operations) that enable adversary control and accessibility [53, 13, 32, 60].

To help guide our thinking, we first review how researchers have applied adversary accessibility in experiments previously. For example, researchers have long used user IDs in discretionary access control systems to distinguish friend from foe [53, 13]. In these experiments, all processes trust root processes and those running under the same user ID. If processes running under other user IDs (except root) may modify the input used to build names, the bindings used in name resolution, and/or the end resource retrieved, then caution must be observed during resource retrieval. Similarly, researchers have applied a variant of this idea to mandatory access control (MAC) policies, using the subject labels as the guide [32]. Since MAC policies aim to reduce the privileges of root processes, a problem is that it is more difficult

---

[3]An operating system will perform an authorization for each binding in the pathname and the final resource separately. Thus, each authorization will evaluate access to either a binding or a resource.

to identify which subject labels that run root code are trustworthy. Researchers have proposed a threat model whereby processes running under a particular subject label only trust processes that have permissions to modify their executable code or write to kernel memory [60] (applied transitively). Interestingly, this threat model was found to correspond well to reported vulnerabilities. That is, these relatively simple threat models have proven useful for experimentation.

A problem has been that researchers have not been convinced that these simple threat models used in experiments can be used in practice to prevent attacks without causing numerous false positives. The problem has been that just identifying where an adversary has access to a binding or a resource is insufficient to detect an unsafe access. Consider the confused deputy attack [28]. If the process uses adversary-inaccessible bindings to retrieve an adversary-inaccessible resource, it may still be unsafe if the adversary controls the name used. Thus, adversary accessibility of system objects (bindings and resources) must be combined with adversary accessibility of program objects (names) to reason about resource access attacks comprehensively. Thus, the combination of system and program is required to leverage adversary accessibility effectively.

A second problem is that administrators did not have any guidance for selecting adversaries for a program. However, as prior research has shown there are a few simple and effective ways of describing the adversaries of a program. In this paper, we highlight three such cases, which we will express below using adversarial roles. First, researchers have often employed the notion that processes running with your user ID and a root user ID are trusted, which we call the *root role*, such as used previously in DAC systems [53, 13]. This approach reflects some practical issues in trust. All processes must trust root processes, and any process with the same user ID can perform the same operations. Second, researchers recently proposed an approach for identifying trusted subjects in MAC policies, where one subject only trusts the MAC subjects that may write to kernel memory or their executable code [60], which we call the *local role*. The advantage of this approach is that it also considers the practical issues of trust. Any process that can modify kernel memory or your processes's executables must be trusted. Third, researchers have proposed adversaries directly as those processes with network access, which we call the *remote role*. Some conventional operating systems employ a policy where only network-facing daemons are untrusted [47, 48]. This approach differs from the ones above in that it focuses on adversaries rather than trusted processes, although the number of adversaries is smaller in practice.

In formulating an approach to express adversarial roles we highlight three facts. First, whether a subject is an adversary does depend on the permissions they hold. Second, some permissions may indicate that the subject is trusted whereas others identify the subject as an adversary. Third, some of these permissions are subject-specific, such as the permissions to modify the subject's executable code files. As a result, we define an *adversarial role* relative to a subject s as $AR(s) = (P, f(s, \mathcal{P}), \{\sqcup, \dashv\})$, where P is a set of permissions, $f(s, \mathcal{P})$ is a function that computes subject-specific permissions from the access control policy $\mathcal{P}$, and $\{t, a\}$ identifies whether possession or lack of those permissions makes one an adversary. For example, local role above includes a set of permissions to write to kernel objects in

P and subject-specific permissions to their executable code files $f(s, \mathcal{P})^4$, where the subjects with those permissions are the only trusted subjects $\{t\}$. As in role-based access control, administrators could predefine such roles. In practice, we expect that the number of adversarial roles in use will be modest, enabling such adversarial role definitions to be reused across deployments, as roles can be reused for multiple users.

5.4 Expressing Name Control

In general, whether a resource retrieval is unsafe or not requires knowledge about the adversary's control of the names used in resource retrieval. Our goal is to define a method for specifying whether a name is adversary-controlled or not using the program constructs. However, as described above, program entrypoint is too limited to express adversary control of names in all cases. Nonetheless, where an entrypoint is sufficient to express adversary accessibility, we would like our specification to "compile" into an entrypoint.

Whether a name may be modified by an adversary is fundamentally a data flow problem. For example, Denning defines an information flow model for programs [19] that is sufficient to identify whether the value of a name variable is controlled by an adversary of a program statically. This model has been applied to develop automated methods [43] to determine whether the security requirements of a "channel" in which a variable is used (e.g., a resource retrieval system call) complies with the security requirements of the variable itself (e.g., an adversary-controlled name).

In this context, we could apply static program information flow analysis [43] to determine whether all the data flows to a name variable at a system call entrypoint include data from an adversary controlled input (e.g., file). Conversely, we could use static program analysis to determine whether no data flow to a name variable at a system call entrypoint includes data from an adversary controlled input. In either case, then knowledge of the entrypoint alone is sufficient to identify whether the name is adversary-controlled or not, enabling enforcement using the Process Firewall rules in Section 4. Thus, where static analysis can prove the adversary control of an resource retrieval entrypoint in all cases, the entrypoint is sufficient for RRQ rules as well.

However, not all information flows may be derived statically, as some names may only be under adversary control some of the time. For example, some names may be derived from inputs that may sometimes originate from adversary-controlled files and sometimes not. In this case, program information flow analysis utilizes runtime labels [42]. Such analysis would log the runtime labels of files that may be used to provide name input and determine the label of the name variables at name resolution system calls. This approach has been leveraged to connect program information flow with system labels for SELinux [30]. Using this method, adversary control of names is determined at runtime, which the enforcement mechanism can then extract to enforce the RRQs. For the prior work, APIs were designed to enable information flow-aware programs (in the Jif language [44])

---

[4] In an SELinux policy [55], executable files have a special label that distinguishes them from regular files. The SELinux policy also specifies the subject labels that may execute those files. If this subject can execute a file of a particular object label, then permission to modify that file (label) is added to the adversarial role [60].

to retrieve the necessary labeling information from SELinux to authorize access (in the traditional manner). As shown in Figure 2, the Process Firewall works in the opposite direction by extracting program context (the label of the name variable) from the program memory. However, this can easily be done by creating a map in program memory between the name variable at the entrypoint and the label of the variable. Thus, the RRQ name controls associate the variable, entrypoint and adversary-control status expected to dictate the allowed adversary accessibility.

A practical problem is that very few programs are written in the Jif programming language. In practice, dynamic taint analysis [68, 22] would be used to determine whether an adversary-controlled a name variable. However, full dynamic taint analysis is very expensive. Fortunately, we are only interested in a few variables, but unfortunately, many complex data flows may impact their values. Dynamic taint analyses have been designed to distinguish between different (adversary-controlled and not) sources [9, 46, 68]. However, taint analysis does not handle certain kinds of information flow (implicit flows), meaning that it is currently less accurate than the information flow analysis above. Nonetheless, using dynamic taint analysis techniques, we can write the same RRQ rules.

Finally, note that programmers may want to use application-specific sanitization to untaint a flow that has a dependence on adversary input. Information flow analysis uses endorsers to remove adversary control from data, whereas taint analyses also support this in a somewhat more ad hoc way. Note that with above analyses, RRQs could be generated automatically, excepting for such sanitization operations.

6. EVALUATION

In this section, we evaluate the impact of different adversary models on the use of the entrypoint alone to describe name controls. This study was performed on a newly-installed Ubuntu 12.04 Desktop filesystem protected by the SELinux reference policy [55]. The analysis data was produced using a runtime analysis driven by Linux package test suites and normal use. As runtime analysis is inherently incomplete, this analysis provides an upper bound for the number of entrypoints that may be classified as accessing only one type of resource.

Under that limitation, we notice three interesting trends. First, as shown in Table 1, the adversary model has a significant impact on the ability to classify entrypoints. Second, in all models, a significant number of entrypoints are classified as either retrieving only adversary-accessible or adversary-inaccessible resources. In those cases, RRQs can use the entrypoint for name control. However, Table 2 shows that a vast majority of the individual system call invocations are made at entrypoints that retrieve both adversary-accessible and adversary-inaccessible resources. This shows that it is important that RRQs handle data flow in a more flexible way for the remaining entrypoints, as they are most often used.

Adversary Models. We evaluate three different adversary models: one based on the DAC policy, and two based on SELinux MAC policies. All of them assume both remote and local adversaries. In the DAC adversary model (**Root** from Section 5.3), a user ID has as adversaries all other user IDs, excepting the superuser `root`. This model holds for systems that use only DAC to control access. The first MAC

Adversary Model	Adv. Acc Resources	Adv. Inacc Resources	Both
Root	8334	360	2371
Local	5436	1675	3954
User	8652	880	1533

Table 1: Adversary accessibility for entrypoints.

Defense Rule Invoked	Syscalls	%
Only adv. inacc.	**Root** 439379	9.40%
	Local 29017	0.62%
	User 74716	1.6%
Only adv. acc.	**Root** 582	0.01%
	Local 2035	0.04%
	User 1073	0.02%
safe_open	**Root** 138825	3.0%
	Local 1019481	21.8%
	User 119560	2.5%
Total	4671037	–

Table 2: The number and percentage of system calls for which the entrypoint alone is sufficient to prevent resource access attacks.

adversary model [60] (**Local** from Section 5.3) assumes only a minimal system and application trusted computing base. This model is conservative; for example, network daemons are adversarial to the local system. This scenario holds when network daemons are broken into, and try to further escalate privileges. The second MAC adversary model (**User**) assumes only two subjects – `user_t` and `guest_t` (assigned to unprivileged users) – and all the resources modifiable by these two subjects, untrusted. This corresponds to adversarial local users who have a login to the system and are constrained by MAC policies.

Sufficiency of Entrypoint Context. In Table 1, we show the number of entrypoints that retrieve only adversary-accessible resources, only adversary-inaccessible resources, or both, for the three different adversary models.

This table shows that under the **Root**, **Local** and **User** models, we can classify 78.5%, 64.2% and 86.1% of entrypoints respectively as accessing either only adversary-accessible resources or only adversary-inaccessible resources. Thus, it appears likely that a significant portion of RRQs can use entrypoints to describe name controls.

System Call Frequency. We examine the distribution of system calls relative to those that can be protected using name controls specified by entrypoint. This tells us the number of system calls, regardless of entrypoint, for which the entrypoint alone is sufficient to describe the program data flow. Table 2 shows the number of times a system call associated with that classification was invoked. In this case, we also include *safe open* defenses which do not require knowledge of the adversary control of names for comparison.

Table 2 shows that only a small percentage of the system calls are run using entrypoints that only access adversary-accessible or adversary-inaccessible resources. On examining the cause for the low percentages, we found that many system calls are made through a few commonly invoked entrypoints, and most of these commonly invoked entrypoints

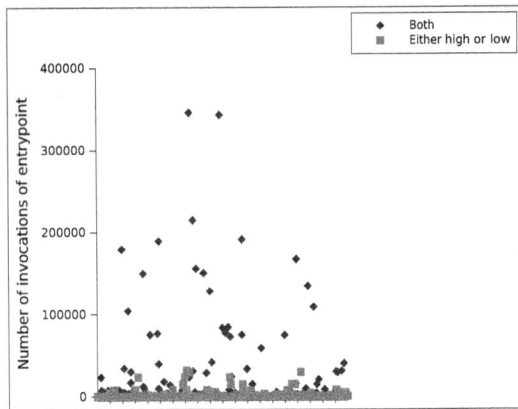

Figure 3: Number of Invocations per Entrypoint

use both adversary-accessible and adversary-inaccessible resources. This is shown in Figure 3. Many of these entrypoints belong to common programs; for example, the 50 most commonly invoked entrypoints belonged to either the Python or Bash interpreter. For these entrypoints, the RRQ's name controls should in addition be based on knowledge of program data flow.

7. CONCLUSIONS

In this paper, we presented a policy model to prevent resource access attacks. While a variety of methods have been proposed, this is the first method to make explicit all aspects of resource retrieval: adversaries, using *adversary roles*; adversary control of the names used in resource retrieval, using *name controls*; the adversary control of the bindings used in name resolution; and adversary access to the resource retrieved. In particular, we focus on the challenges of adversary roles and name control via program flows, defining simple models for expressing each that leverages a variety of prior work. Our evaluation shows both that the adversary models chosen make a significant difference how resource access attacks must be prevented and that data-flow tracking is fundamental to a comprehensive defined for resource access attacks. Often, well over 90% of the individual system calls require data-flow tracking to prevent resource access attacks accurately.

8. ACKNOWLEDGMENTS

This material is based upon work supported by the Air Force Office of Scientific Research (AFOSR) under grant AFOSR-FA9550-12-1-0166. The views and conclusions contained in this document are those of the authors and should not be interpreted as representing the official policies, either expressed or implied, of the Army Research Laboratory or the U.S. Government. The U.S. Government is authorized to reproduce and distribute reprints for Government purposes notwithstanding any copyright notation here on.

9. REFERENCES

[1] *RBAC '98: Proceedings of the Third ACM Workshop on Role-based Access Control*, New York, NY, USA, 1998. ACM. Chairman-Youman, Charles and Chairman-Jaeger, Trent.

[2] Solaris Trusted Extensions Developer's Guide. http://docs.sun.com/app/docs/doc/819-7312, 2008.

[3] A. Acharya and M. Raje. MAPbox: Using parameterized behavior classes to confine untrusted applications. In *Proceedings of the 9th USENIX Security Symposium*, August 2000.

[4] D. Balzarotti *et al.* Saner: Composing static and dynamic analysis to validate sanitization in web applications. In *Proceedings of the IEEE Symposium on Security and Privacy*, 2008.

[5] A. Berman *et al.* TRON: Process-specific file protection for the UNIX operating system. In *USENIX TC '95*, 1995.

[6] E. Bertino, P. A. Bonatti, and E. Ferrari. Trbac: A temporal role-based access control model. *ACM Transactions on Information and System Security (TISSEC)*, 4(3):191–233, 2001.

[7] K. J. Biba. Integrity considerations for secure computer systems. Technical Report MTR-3153, MITRE, April 1977.

[8] M. Bishop, M. Dilger, et al. Checking for race conditions in file accesses. *Computing systems*, 2(2):131–152, 1996.

[9] BitBlaze. BitBlaze binary analysis project. http://bitblaze.cs.berkeley.edu, 2014.

[10] N. Borisov *et al.* Fixing races for fun and profit: How to abuse atime. In *USENIX Security '06*, 2005.

[11] D. F. C. Brewer and M. J. Nash. The Chinese Wall security policy. In *Proceedings of the IEEE Symposium on Security and Privacy*, 1989.

[12] X. Cai *et al.* . Exploiting Unix File-System Races via Algorithmic Complexity Attacks. In *IEEE SSP '09*, 2009.

[13] S. Chari, S. Halevi, and W. Venema. Where do you want to go today? escalating privileges by pathname manipulation. In *NDSS*, 2010.

[14] E. Chin *et al.* Analyzing Inter-Application Communication in Android. In *MobiSys*, 2011.

[15] C. Cowan, S. Beattie, C. Wright, and G. Kroah-Hartman. Raceguard: Kernel protection from temporary file race vulnerabilities. In *USENIX Security Symposium*, pages 165–176, 2001.

[16] CWE. CWE-426: Untrusted Search Path. http://cwe.mitre.org/data/definitions/426.html.

[17] CWE. CWE-59: Improper Link Resolution Before File Access. http://cwe.mitre.org/data/definitions/59.html.

[18] D. Dean and A. J. Hu. Fixing races for fun and profit: How to use access (2). In *USENIX Security Symposium*, pages 195–206, 2004.

[19] D. Denning. A lattice model of secure information flow. *Communications of the ACM*, 19(5):236–242, 1976.

[20] J. B. Dennis and E. C. V. Horn. Programming semantics for multiprogrammed computations. *Communications of the ACM*, 9(3):143–155, 1966.

[21] Domain Names - Implementation and Specification. http://http://www.ietf.org/rfc/rfc1035.txt.

[22] W. Enck, P. Gilbert, B.-G. Chun, L. P. Cox, J. Jung, P. McDaniel, and A. Sheth. Taintdroid: An information-flow tracking system for realtime privacy

monitoring on smartphones. In *OSDI*, volume 10, pages 1–6, 2010.

[23] T. Fraser. LOMAC: Low water-mark integrity protection for COTS environments. In *Proceedings of the 2000 IEEE Symposium on Security and Privacy*, May 2000.

[24] Mandatory Access Control - FreeBSD. `http://www.freebsd.org/handbook/mac.html`.

[25] T. Garfinkel *et al.* Ostia: A delegating architecture for secure system call interposition. In *NDSS '04*, 2004.

[26] Goldberg *et al.* A secure environment for untrusted helper applications. In *USENIX Security '96*, 1996.

[27] L. Gong, R. Schemers, and S. Microsystems. Implementing protection domains in the java development kit 1.2, 1988.

[28] N. Hardy. The confused deputy:(or why capabilities might have been invented). *ACM SIGOPS Operating Systems Review*, 22(4):36–38, 1988.

[29] B. Hicks, K. Ahmadizadeh, and P. McDaniel. From Languages to Systems: Understanding Practical Application Development in Security-typed Languages. In *Proceedings of the 22nd Annual Computer Security Applications Conference (ACSAC)*, December 2006.

[30] B. Hicks, S. Rueda, T. Jaeger, and P. McDaniel. From trusted to secure: building and executing applications that enforce system security. In *USENIX Annual Technical Conference*, June 2007.

[31] M. Howard, J. Pincus, and J. Wing. Measuring Relative Attack Surfaces. In *Proceedings of Workshop on Advanced Developments in Software and Systems Security*, December 2003.

[32] T. Jaeger, R. Sailer, and X. Zhang. Analyzing integrity protection in the SELinux example policy. In *Proceedings of the 12th USENIX Security Symposium*, Aug. 2003.

[33] J. B. D. Joshi, E. Bertino, U. Latif, and A. Ghafoor. A generalized temporal role-based access control model. *IEEE Trans. on Knowl. and Data Eng.*, 17(1):4–23, Jan. 2005.

[34] M. N. Krohn, A. Yip, M. Brodsky, N. Cliffer, M. F. Kaashoek, E. Kohler, and R. Morris. Information flow control for standard OS abstractions. In *Proceedings of the 21st ACM Symposium on Operating Systems Principles (SOSP)*, October 2007.

[35] B. W. Lampson. Protection. *ACM SIGOPS Operating Systems Review*, 8(1):18–24, 1974.

[36] H. M. Levy. *Capability-based Computer Systems*. Digital Press, 1984. Available at `http://www.cs.washington.edu/homes/levy/capabook/`.

[37] T. A. Linden. Operating system structures to support security and reliable software. *ACM Computing Surveys*, 8(4):409–445, Dec. 1976.

[38] R. Marmorstein and P. Kearns. A Tool for Automated iptables Firewall Analysis. In *Proceedings of the USENIX Annual Technical Conference*, 2005.

[39] D. McIlroy and J. Reeds. Multilevel windows on a single-level terminal. In *Proceedings of the (First) USENIX Security Workshop*, Aug. 1988.

[40] W. S. McPhee. Operating system integrity in OS/VS2. *IBM Syst. J.*, 13:230–252, September 1974.

[41] MSDN. Mandatory Integrity Control (Windows). `http://msdn.microsoft.com/en-us/library/bb648648%28VS.85%29.aspx`.

[42] A. C. Myers. Jflow: Practical mostly-static information flow control. In *In Proc. 26th ACM Symp. on Principles of Programming Languages (POPL)*, pages 228–241, 1999.

[43] A. C. Myers and B. Liskov. A decentralized model for information flow control. In *Proceedings of the 16th ACM Symposium on Operating System Principles*, October 1997.

[44] A. C. Myers and B. Liskov. Protecting privacy using the decentralized label model. *ACM Trans. Softw. Eng. Methodol.*, 9:410–442, October 2000.

[45] R. Needham. *Chapter: Names. In S. Mullender (Ed): Distributed Systems*. Addison-Wesley, 1989.

[46] J. Newsome and D. X. Song. Dynamic taint analysis for automatic detection, analysis, and signatureregeneration of exploits on commodity software. In *Proceedings of the 2005 Network and Distributed System Security Symposium*, 2005.

[47] AppArmor Linux application security. `http://www.novell.com/linux/security/apparmor/`, 2008.

[48] Security-enhanced linux targeted policy. `http://www.centos.org/docs/5/html/Deployment_Guide-en-US/rhlcommon-chapter-0001.html`.

[49] OpenWall Project - Information security software for open environments. `http://www.openwall.com/`, 2008.

[50] J. Park, G. Lee, S. Lee, and D.-K. Kim. Rps: An extension of reference monitor to prevent race-attacks. In *PCM (1) 04*, 2004.

[51] J. Park and R. Sandhu. Towards usage control models: Beyond traditional access control. In *Proceedings of the Seventh ACM Symposium on Access Control Models and Technologies*, SACMAT '02, pages 57–64, New York, NY, USA, 2002. ACM.

[52] J. Park and R. Sandhu. The UCONABC usage control model. *ACM Trans. Inf. Syst. Secur.*, 7(1):128–174, Feb. 2004.

[53] C. Pu and J. Wei. A Methodical Defense against TOCTTOU Attacks: The EDGI Approach. In *ISSSE*, 2006.

[54] K. suk Lhee and S. J. Chapin. Detection of file-based race conditions. *Int. J. Inf. Sec.*, 2005.

[55] Reference Policy. `http://oss.tresys.com/projects/refpolicy`, 2008.

[56] D. Tsafrir, T. Hertz, D. Wagner, and D. Da Silva. Portably solving file tocttou races with hardness amplification. In *FAST*, volume 8, pages 1–18, 2008.

[57] E. Tsyrklevich and B. Yee. Dynamic detection and prevention of race conditions in file accesses. In *Proceedings of the 12th USENIX Security Symposium*, pages 243–255, 2003.

[58] P. Uppuluri, U. Joshi, and A. Ray. Preventing race condition attacks on file-systems. In *SAC-05*, 2005.

[59] C. Vance, T. Miller, R. Dekelbaum, and A. Reisse. Security-enhanced darwin: Porting selinux to mac os x. In *Proceedings of the Third Annual Security Enhanced Linux Symposium, Baltimore, MD, USA*, 2007.

[60] H. Vijayakumar, G. Jakka, S. Rueda, J. Schiffman, and T. Jaeger. Integrity walls: Finding attack surfaces from mandatory access control policies. In *Proceedings of the 7th ACM Symposium on Information, Computer, and Communications Security (ASIACCS 2012)*, May 2012.

[61] H. Vijayakumar, J. Schiffman, and T. Jaeger. Process firewalls: protecting processes during resource access. In *Proceedings of the 8th ACM European Conference on Computer Systems*, pages 57–70. ACM, 2013.

[62] D. S. Wallach, A. W. Appel, and E. W. Felten. Safkasi: A security mechanism for language-based systems. *ACM Trans. Softw. Eng. Methodol.*, 9(4):341–378, Oct. 2000.

[63] R. Watson, J. Anderson, and B. Laurie. Capsicum: practical capabilities for UNIX. In *Proceedings of the 19th USENIX Security Symposium*, 2010.

[64] R. N. M. Watson. TrustedBSD: Adding trusted operating system features to FreeBSD. In *Proceedings of the FREENIX Track: 2001 USENIX Annual Technical Conference*, pages 15–28, 2001.

[65] J. Wei *et al.* A methodical defense against TOCTTOU attacks: the EDGI approach. In *IEEE International Symp. on Secure Software Engineering (ISSSE)* , 2006.

[66] C. Weissman. Security controls in the adept-50 time-sharing system. In *Proceedings of the November 18-20, 1969, Fall Joint Computer Conference*, AFIPS '69 (Fall), pages 119–133, New York, NY, USA, 1969. ACM.

[67] C. Wright, C. Cowan, S. Smalley, J. Morris, and G. Kroah-Hartman. Linux Security Modules: General security support for the Linux kernel. In *Proceedings of the 11th USENIX Security Symposium*, pages 17–31, August 2002.

[68] H. Yin, D. Song, M. Egele, C. Kruegel, and E. Kirda. Panorama: Capturing system-wide information flow for malware detection and analysis. In *Proceedings of the 14th ACM Conference on Computer and Communications Security*, CCS '07, pages 116–127, New York, NY, USA, 2007. ACM.

[69] N. Zeldovich, S. Boyd-Wickizer, E. Kohler, and D. Mazières. Making information flow explicit in HiStar. In *Proceedings of the USENIX Symposium on Operating Systems Design and Implementation (OSDI)*, November 2006.

Author Index